MYTHOLOGY'S LAST GODS

MYTHOLOGY'S LAST GODS

Yahweh and Jesus

William Harwood

Prometheus Books

59 John Glenn Drive
Amherst, NewYork 14228-2197

02 01 00 99 98   5 4 3 2

Library of Congress Cataloging-in-Publication Data

Harwood, William R., 1935
    Mythology's last gods : Yahweh and Jesus / by William R. Harwood.
        p.   cm.
    Includes bibliographical references and index.
    ISBN 0–87975–742–6
    1. Myth in the Bible 2. Bible—Miscellanea. I. Title.
BS534.H33   1992
220.6'8—dc20   92–15252
                                                                      CIP

Printed in the United States of America on acid-free paper

To Ron and Harry, Abe and Linda, Elaine and Dorrie, and the Great Zubrick:

This is the big one, my friends. This is where we find out which is stronger—
the intelligence you were born with, or a lifetime of brainwashing.

You can make it. I did.

God is dead.
—Nietzsche

Nietzsche is dead.
—God

God and Nietzsche are dead.
—history

Acknowledgements

I express my appreciation to the following for their gracious permission to quote from copyrighted works:

Alfred A. Knopf, Inc., for the excerpt from E.H. Carr's *What Is History?*

A.P. Watt, Ltd., on behalf of the Trustees of the Robert Graves Copyright Trust, for the excerpt from Robert Graves's *The Nazarene Gospel Restored.*

Scott Meredith Literary Agency, Inc., for excerpts from Isaac Asimov's *In the Beginning; The Tragedy of the Moon; Quasar, Quasar, Burning Bright; Science, Numbers, and I; Asimov on Physics;* Carl Sagan's *Cosmos; The Cosmic Connection; Broca's Brain;* and Arthur C. Clarke's *Profiles of the Future.*

Richard Curtis Associates, Inc., for the excerpt from Barry B. Longyear's *The Tomorrow Testament.*

Spectrum Literary Agency, on behalf of Mrs Heinlein, for the excerpt from Robert A. Heinlein's *Time Enough for Love.*

Curtis Brown, Ltd. and Brian Herbert, for excerpts from Frank Herbert's *The Eyes of Heysenberg* and *The White Plague.*

I also wish to thank my editor at Prometheus, Ranjit Sandhu, without whose expertise an embarrassing number of imperfections would not have been eliminated.

Original painting, reproduced in monochrome on page 14, painted by Walter Wasmeier, designed by William Harwood after Botticelli, based on an idea by Lenny Bruce.

The conclusions reached in this book are my own, and are not necessarily shared by the authors, agencies or heirs listed above.

Table of Contents

Table of Charts

Preface

This work is based on the author's doctoral dissertation accepted by Columbia Pacific University. Most of the research for this book was completed while the author was in attendance at Cambridge University with the aid of a grant from the Canada Council. Parts of this book have previously appeared in slightly different form in *The American Rationalist, Cal-Amity, Free Inquiry, The Humanist, Humanist in Canada,* and MC².

Mythology's Last Gods was accepted for publication for the first time in 1980, but the publisher went out of business before it could be produced. It was accepted for the second time in 1985, but the publisher died before it could be produced. It was accepted for the third time in 1991, by which time considerable revisions were necessary to take into account recent publications. This is a completely new edition that confirms most of the conclusions of the dissertation but abandons or revises others.

This book utilises the methodology of history, in which, as in every scientific discipline, conclusions must conform to the evidence; not the methodology of theology, in which evidence must be made to conform to predetermined conclusions.

Introduction

In 1135 CE Geoffrey of Monmouth wrote *The Chronicle of the Kings of Britain*. Instead of acknowledging his authorship, Geoffrey claimed that his work was merely a Latin translation of a much older book written in Welsh. Since the art of documentary criticism, as practised by the modern historian, did not exist in the twelfth century, Geoffrey's imaginative fiction was for more than four hundred years accepted as historical fact. Then one day a scholar noticed something strange. In or about the year 500 CE King Arthur's father, Uther Pendragon, lusting after Arthur's mother, Igerna, chased her into Tintagel castle—600 years before it was built! Further examination revealed so many similar anachronisms, self-contradictions, and statements that had great propaganda value in 1135 but little connection to the history of the sixth century, that the pretence that the *Chronicle* was nonfiction could no longer be entertained. Since no powerful hierarchy existed that depended for its survival on the maintenance of the pretence that Geoffrey's imaginings were Revealed Truth, their exposure was sufficient to discredit the *Chronicle* permanently.

More than one hundred years ago historians began applying the same methods of documentary analysis that had enabled them to expose Geoffrey's *Chronicle* as fiction, to the Judaeo-Christian bible. To scholars who had hoped to prove the bible's authenticity, the results were traumatic. A prophet who claimed to be an eyewitness to the fall of Babylon and adviser to the King was shown to have been mistaken in his identification of the King and to have named as Babylon's conqueror a man who did not exist. A passage in *Genesis* stating that Noah was to take two of each kind of animal was followed a few sentences later by a declaration that he was to take seven of the same animals aboard the Ark. The author of *Apocalypse* (*Revelation*), after prophesying the death of Nero, then prophesied that the

Second Temple would never be destroyed. Yet the Second Temple outlived Nero by only two years. *Matthew*'s account of Jesus' birth was totally dependent for its credibility on the dating of that event to 4 BCE or earlier; whereas *Luke*'s account was equally dependent on dating that same event to 7 CE. Yahweh had promised King David that his dynasty would be kings in Jerusalem forever; yet in 586 BCE David's line of kings was deposed and has never been restored.

One by one the various books of the bible were discovered to contain errors of fact; inaccurate guesses; rationalisations; prophecies *ex post facto*, usually combined with prophecies of the future that proved inaccurate; and unmistakable, deliberate lies. Had this discovery been allowed to reach the general public, Judaeo-Christian mythology would have suffered a blow from which it could not have hoped to recover.

Facing elimination, the current Pope appointed his own historians to examine the secular historians' conclusions and find the flaw in their evidence that he believed *must* be there. The outcome was that the Papal historians confirmed that their bible really was falsifiable fantasy. They presented the Pope with their reports and, when he promptly suppressed them, they all ceased to be Catholics. So the Pope ordered his propaganda machine to invent an alternative methodology to combat that of the historians, a methodology created for the specific purpose of reaching the conclusion that the Judaeo-Christian bible is nonfiction, no matter how severely the evidence had to be distorted in order to achieve that objective. That methodology was 'theology,' as practised by divinity faculties to this day, but not used by earlier theologians who had no reason to simulate the methods of a scientific discipline that did not yet exist.[1]

And it worked. Having no competence to determine which methodology was valid, believers simply accepted the one that reached emotionally satisfying conclusions, unaware that theology can also be used to prove that *Alice in Wonderland* is nonfiction. No attempt was made to stop historians from publishing, but their books were effectively confined to university libraries where the public would never learn of their existence.

Such was the power of the world's theocracies that, despite the publication of thousands of scholarly books and articles refuting every part of the Judaeo-Christian bible, to this day the existence of unchallengeable proof that the bible is a work of fiction is unknown to ninety percent of the population of Christian-dominated societies. The minority who have encountered ancient history at a university know that, 3000 years before the Christian saviour-god Jesus rose from the dead, the Egyptian saviour-god Osiris rose from the dead, and thousands of years before Osiris the saviour-

---

1. See M. Baigent, *et al.*, *The Messianic Legacy*, Corgi ppb., 1988, pp. 15 ff.

goddess Easter rose from the dead. Between Osiris and Jesus there were Greek, Assyrian, Phoenician, Persian, Hittite, Chinese and a dozen other saviour-gods that rose from the dead.

Centuries before the interpolator of 1 John documented his three-person god, the ancients worshipped a three-person goddess. One thousand years before the volcano-god Yahweh dictated a lawcode to Moses, the Babylonian sun-god Shamash dictated an almost identical lawcode to Hammurabai. As for the ten commandments associated with Moses: not only were they borrowed from an earlier god; they were also composed four hundred years after Moses' death.

The concepts of the 'Chosen People' and the 'Promised Land' were invented retroactively by a Jewish mythologian at the court of King Rekhobowam c. 920 BCE, to give a theological legitimacy to the brutal conquests of Rekhobowam's grandfather, David, and the uncompromising genocide of the Jews' ancient sheikh, Yahuwshua.

For a century this information has been available only to students willing to wade through dozens of books that each dealt with only one aspect of Judaeo-Christian mythology. It is hoped that, by bringing together information on the origin and development of every part of the Yahweh- and Jesus-myths, this book will make the facts available to a large enough segment of the population to end the equation of god-mythology with history permanently.

Spelling of Proper Names

The names of the kings of Israel and Judah have been transcribed into as close an approximation of the original Hebrew as possible, for the purpose of demonstrating the frequency of the god-affixes, *yah* and *yahuw*. For this purpose, I have rendered *yod-heh-vaw* (YHW) as *yahuw* in all cases, ignoring vowel points that reflect the pronunciation of 500 CE rather than the manuscripts' original dates of composition. For prophets, I have chosen a compromise that is close enough to the spelling of the King James bible to allow for easy recognition, but I have retained all *yah* affixes. For the names of books, King James spelling has been retained. Thus an early prophetic book has been called *Isaiah*, even though the author is referred to as Isayah. For the Christian gospels, the names Mark, Matthew, Luke and John have been used for the anonymous authors of those books; while for the historical and mythical persons wrongly alleged to have been the authors, Greek forms have been used: Markos, Maththaios, Loukos, Ioannes.

A list of names likely to present recognition problems, and their King James equivalents, follows:

Abiyahuw	Abijam, Abijah	Yahuw	Jehu
Akhab	Ahab	Yahuwakhaz	Jehoahaz
Akhaz	Ahaz	Yahuwash	Joash
Akhazyahuw	Ahaziah	Yahuwdah	Judah
Amatsyahuw	Amaziah	Yahuwikhin	Jehoiachin
Athalyahuw	Athaliah	Yahuwikim	Jehoiakim
Azaryahuw	Azariah, Uzziah	Yahuwnathan	Jonathan
Isayah	Isaiah	Yahuwram	Jehoram, Joram
Jeremyah	Jeremiah	Yahuwshafat	Jehosaphat
Khezekyahuw	Hezekiah	Yahuwshua(kh)	Joshua
Khilkyahuw	Hilkiah	Yahweh	the LORD
Levit	Lot	Yakhonyah	Jeconiah
Pekhakh	Pekah	Yerobowam	Jeroboam
Pekhakhyah	Pekahiah	Yoshyahuw	Josiah
Rekhobowam	Rehoboam	Yowtham	Jotham
Tsedekhyahuw	Zedekiah	Zekharyah(uw)	Zechariah

Dates

Dates used throughout are the connotatively neutral BCE (Before the Common Era) and CE (Common Era). AD, whether interpreted as *Anno Domini* or *Anno Deceptitatis*, has no place in a work of scholarship.

Biblical Quotations

Although English bibles were consulted for comparison purposes, most of *Mythology's Last Gods* is based on the original-language bibles mentioned in the bibliography. Biblical quotations are from my *The Judaeo-Christian Bible Fully Translated*, of which a copy of the first volume can be found in the dissertation library of Columbia Pacific University, and also in the National Library of Canada. The reason this translation was necessary is that all existing translations contain so many deliberate falsifications, designed to perpetuate the pretence that biblical authors believed the same things as modern religions, as to be worthless. As an obvious example, *all* English language bibles render *ha-elohiym* as 'God,' when the correct translation is the generic plural, 'the gods.' Also, most falsify the proper name, Yahweh, into 'the LORD.' And where existing translations gloss over Yahweh's atrocities by couching them in the most positive euphemisms, I chose synonyms that drive home the true nature of Yahweh's actions. Thus, where the *New American Bible* has 'You will rout them utterly until they are annihilated,' my translation reads, 'You're going to exterminate them in a massive genocide until they're eliminated.' Since the four Samuel-Kings books are titled differently in different bibles, they are here cited as *1 Samuel*, *2 Samuel*, *3 Kings* and *4 Kings*.

MAP OF THE UNIVERSE,
ACCORDING TO THE JUDAEO-CHRISTIAN BIBLE

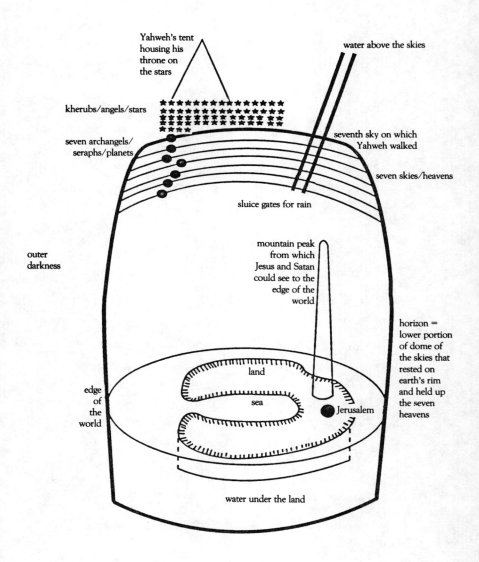

Yahweh's tent housing his throne on the stars

water above the skies

kherubs/angels/stars

seven archangels/ seraphs/planets

seventh sky on which Yahweh walked

seven skies/heavens

sluice gates for rain

outer darkness

mountain peak from which Jesus and Satan could see to the edge of the world

horizon = lower portion of dome of the skies that rested on earth's rim and held up the seven heavens

land

sea

Jerusalem

edge of the world

water under the land

One

And Woman Created Goddess:
The Origin of Religion

No document can tell us more than what the author of
the document thought—what he thought had happened,
what he thought ought to happen or would happen, or
perhaps only what he wanted others to think he thought,
or even only what he himself thought he thought.

E.H. Carr, *What is History?*

Very few people today believe that the universe was hatched from the egg
of a primeval goddess. Rather more believe, despite the discovery of seventy-
million-year-old dinosaur fossils and four-million-year-old hominid remains,
that Yahweh-Elohiym created the universe at 9 a.m. on October 23, 4004
BCE (or Tishri 1, 3760 BCE). The origin of both beliefs will be discussed
in later pages.[1] For the moment, mythology will be ignored and the evolution
of humankind and his world will be summarised, within the limits of present-
day knowledge, in more-or-less chronological order.

The most widely-held theory today is that the universe began with a
gigantic explosion that occurred between fifteen and twenty billion years
ago, the effects of which are still observable in an ever-expanding sky. The

---

1. For a rebuttal of creation mythology (which its proponents call *creation science*), see
Laurie Godfrey, ed., *Scientists Confront Creationism*, Buffalo, 1983.

Big Bang admittedly remains unproven, but it is a logical hypothesis based on the observation that the entire universe is retreating at a speed that is a function of each portion's distance from the initial point. What seems to have happened is that all matter in existence was drawn together by gravity with such force that it collided at the centre where a nuclear reaction was triggered that blasted the entire mass into an outward course that is still continuing. Such was the heat generated by the Big Bang that to this day empty space retains a temperature four degrees above the absolute zero that it continues to approach. Scholars are divided on the question of whether the expansion will continue forever, or whether the gravity that caused the Big Bang will eventually overcome inertia, cause the expanding universe to contract and ultimately trigger another Bang. If the latter hypothesis is correct (and it can only be correct if ninety percent of the mass of the universe is contained in undetected black holes), then the Big Bang of c. seventeen billion years ago may not have been the first.

As the universe rushed outwards after the Bang, lumps of whirling gas were drawn together by gravity and formed stars. Stars in turn generated gravitational fields that caused matter to be sucked into the star's equatorial plane where it coalesced into planets. Stars by the billions were born, burned out their hydrogen, expanded, collapsed, and finally became black dwarfs, neutron stars or black holes, pockets of matter so dense that their gravity will not allow even light to escape. Our own sun, at various times called Hyperion, Helios, Apollo, Phoebos, Ra, Aton, Mithra, and thousands of other names that all meant god-of-light-and-warmth, is a comparative newcomer. Old Sol is so new that it is still in its first, or hydrogen-burning, stage. Not for billions of years will it reach the point where the fusion of the last of its hydrogen into helium will cause it to expand beyond the orbit of planet earth, the sometime Aia, Gaia, Adamah, Khavah, Rhea, Dia (and various other goddess names that all meant Mother), and thereby destroy all life. With luck, before that happens *homo sapiens* will be in a position to migrate to a newer, more hospitable star.

On certain planets, including earth, an accidental combination of the appropriate elements, temperature and environmental conditions (e.g., an ocean capable of screening out ultraviolet light) caused the formation of relatively stable amino acids which in turn combined to form protein molecules, particles that in a sense constituted the bridge between life and nonlife. In a universe of 10^{11} galaxies, each containing 10^{11} stars, the number of distinct kinds of protein molecules that evolved can be estimated at several trillion. The number that evolved on planet earth was a few dozen.

Since the probability of any particular protein evolving at all is close to zero, the likelihood of any earth-type protein evolving elsewhere in the universe in less than twenty billion years is vanishingly small. Because of this we can be certain, not only that the interbreeding of terrestrial and extraterrestrial life is more impossible than the crossbreeding of a snapdragon and a snapper (which at least share common proteins), but also that the incompatibility of life forms based on different proteins will make it impossible for humans ever to eat any kind of organic matter that did not evolve on earth. A 'Mr Spock' there can never be—and a *homo sapiens* descended from one of Erich von Däniken's space-gods there can also never be.[2]

From the first protein to the first protozoan was a giant step, but a predictable and inevitable one, even though this second step in the generation of life has not yet been duplicated in the laboratory. Every possible permutation of protozoan formed, and those that accidentally possessed the traits that aided survival survived. Millions of years later so many accidents had proven beneficial to the myriad organisms that had evolved that we had a planet laden with two distinct forms of life, plant and animal, each thriving on the other's waste.[3]

Charles Darwin and Alfred Wallace described the process of evolution in the nineteenth century, Darwin coining the term *natural selection*, which Spencer promptly distorted into *survival of the fittest*. Darwin is often misrepresented as postulating that living organisms can somehow *adapt* to the imposition of a hostile environment, particularly by a recently developed pseudoscience called sociobiology,[4] but Darwin in fact specifically repudiated such an interpretation:

---

2. For a complete rebuttal of von Däniken, see the works of Thiering and Story listed in the bibliography.

3. For a discussion of the inevitability of life forming under favourable circumstances, see the following books by Isaac Asimov: *Twentieth Century Discovery*, chapter 2; *Of Matters Great and Small*, chapter 8; and *The Planet That Wasn't*, chapters 9 and 17. All are in nontechnical language that a nonscientist can easily follow.

4. A single example of the new discipline's thinking should suffice: Sociobiologists postulate that, in the days when humans were breastless and copulated by rear-mounting, men were sexually aroused by well-rounded buttocks. With the advent of face-to-face copulation, women were obliged to develop breasts as a substitute stimulant in place of the now out-of-view buttocks. In fact such a development could only have occurred if, at the time that a random mutation caused a few women to have a degree of hemispherical protrusion behind the nipples, men found the new look so arousing that they refused in significant numbers to copulate (and, as a side effect, breed) with women whose chests remained flat. Unless the statistically improbable mutation that led to the formation of breasts suddenly and inexplicably appeared in a near-majority of women at approximately the same time, such an effect upon men's orgasm-releasing behaviour would have been utterly impossible. For a much more plausible explanation of the development of breasts, that recognises that breasts could only have developed in an environment that made them a significant aid to survival and/or reproduction, see Elaine Morgan's *The Descent of Woman*, NY, 1972.

Some have even imagined that natural selection induces variability, whereas it implies only the preservation of such variations as arise and are beneficial to the being under its condition of life.[5]

To use the giraffe as a random example: Darwin did not suggest that, because giraffe food grew on tall trees, the giraffe was somehow able to develop a long neck in order to reach it. That kind of 'adapting to the environment' would have been absolutely impossible. What Darwin's theory did imply was that, because giraffe food grew on tall trees, only those giraffes that already had slightly longer necks than their fellows were able to survive and reproduce. Each generation produced a proportion of offspring with marginally longer necks than their parents, and in the competition for the limited supply of food even a few centimetres of neck could, and did, prove a decisive factor in determining which giraffes lived to breed. Similarly the evolution of the 210 cm Watusi and the 120 cm Pygmy from common ancestors can be attributed to tallness being a significant aid to survival in one part of Africa, and shortness in another.

Four million years ago evolved the most complex organism that has yet lived on earth, a mutant ape with a computer brain.[6] It would be misquoting Darwin to say that humans evolved from apes. Rather, humans and apes evolved from a single ancestor. However, if that ancestor were to be given a name, a more accurate name than ape would be hard to find. The physiology of human and ape is so similar, ninety-eight percent of humankind's structural genes being identical with those of the chimpanzee, that any theory of humankind's origin (including the nonsense of Erich von Däniken) that does not account for the similarity must be dismissed as unrealistic.

Ultimately, all animals including humans evolved from the first protozoa, since the sub-particles of human genes, four kinds of nucleotides that can be combined into trillions of permutations called nucleic acids, are identical with those of every life form on earth: plant, animal, bacterial and viral. Similarly, the protein that constitutes the exterior of all human cells is formed from the same nineteen amino acids that perform the identical function in all other life forms. A process analogous to evolution occurs in the nine months from conception to birth; at an early stage of its development the human foetus has gills and a tail just like its remote ancestors. That evolution occurred is an observable and fully-proven fact. That it occurred through natural selection is the most reasonable theory of how

    5. *Origin of Species*, Mentor edition, 1958, p. 88.
    6. For arguments as to whether humankind's four-million-BCE ancestor was *australopithecus afarensis* (Johanson) or *homo habilis* (Leakey), see D. Johanson and M. Edey, *Lucy: The Beginnings of Mankind*; and R. Leakey and R. Lewin, *Origins*.

and why.[7]

At a very early stage in humankind's evolution the mutation occurred that led to the human male's acceptance of the role of protector and provider of individual females and their young. Women were born who, unlike their mothers, were capable of orgasm and desirous of copulation at all times rather than only during or near ovulation. Previously, following copulation, a man had realised that a woman would not want him again for a whole month, whereas his own need was bound to recur in a matter of hours or days. He had consequently abandoned the out-of-season woman and sought another whose immediate need coincided with his own. The result was that a woman with more than one child to support had found the task insuperable, and the offspring had usually died.

With the birth of the mutants, men were no longer obliged to seek new partners every couple of days. A woman who was able and willing to mate as often as a particular man wanted found herself possessed of an incentive that could attach a man to herself permanently. In exchange for the certainty of sexual gratification on demand, a man was willing to devote a portion of his time to finding food for more children than the woman could have supported alone.[8]

The result was that the mutants were able to produce surviving offspring whose mating needs duplicated those of their mothers, while the children of women whose needs remained seasonal did not survive. Within a few generations all human females carried the mutant genes, and seasonal sexual

---

7. Upholders of creation mythology tend to misinterpret the acknowledgement of paleontologists that natural selection cannot be experimentally proven, and rationalise that evolution is likewise unproven. This is not so: *Evolution is a fact amply demonstrated by the fossil record and by contemporary molecular biology. Natural selection is a successful theory devised to explain the fact of evolution.* (Carl Sagan, *The Dragons of Eden*, Ballantine edition, p. 6). *There is so much similarity in the biochemical workings of all organisms, not only if we compare men and monkeys, but if we compare men and bacteria, that if it weren't for preconceived notions and species-centered conceit, the fact of evolution would be considered self-evident.* (Isaac Asimov, *Of Matters Great and Small*, Ace edition, NY, 1976, pp. 150-151). *Evolution is a law of nature as compelling as gravitation. The evidence for it is as plain as the falling apple. Nobody who knows the process of DNA can doubt the theory of evolution.* (Arthur Kornberg, Nobel laureate, *Discover*, April 1981, p. 62). *As new species evolved, nature didn't throw away old parts of the brain. Rather, new systems were added. Everyone has a fish brain deep inside. Outside the fish brain there is a reptile brain, depressingly similar to the way it would look in a lizard. Wrapped around the reptilian brain there is a mammalian brain, and then, finally, the cerebral cortex in such animals as monkeys and human beings.* (Donald Pfaff, Rockefeller University, ibid., p. 18). *Evolution on an ancient earth is as well-established as our planet's shape and position. Our continuing struggle to understand how evolution happens (the 'theory of evolution') does not cast our documentation of its occurrence—the 'fact of evolution'—into doubt.* (Stephen Jay Gould, *Skeptical Inquirer*, Winter 1987-1988, p. 186.)

8. For an elaboration of this point, see H.E. Fisher's *The Sex Contract* (NY, 1982), especially the chapter of the same name.

activity had ceased to be a human characteristic. A similar mutation occurred among gibbons. It is no coincidence that humans and gibbons, the only primates not subject to an oestrus cycle, are also the only primates that practise monogamy.[9]

Homo sapiens evolved as a single species and remains a single species. Any fertile human male is capable of impregnating any fertile human female and producing viable offspring. Distinct species exist only when this is not possible. Humankind did, however, evolve into races, for convenience designated as black, brown, red, yellow and white. Generally it has tended to be the yellow and white races that have appointed themselves lords of the earth and categorised other races as their inferiors.

For four million years humankind survived by mating with every and any partner who happened to be available. He did not reproduce intentionally, in full awareness that sexual recreation caused pregnancy. He satisfied an appetite, and in so doing reproduced as a side effect without ever associating cause with consequence. He mated freely and indiscriminately, with no awareness of such later concepts as adultery, incest, fornication or perversion. Man had no knowledge of his role as father, and therefore had no reason to institute taboos whose sole purpose was the prevention or encouragement of pregnancy. If any god, whether from a metaphysical heaven or a flying saucer, had instructed him to 'be fruitful and multiply,' he would have had no idea how to comply with such a demand. He viewed propagation as a spontaneous female prerogative, with males existing for no higher purpose than to provide sexual recreation for their female overlords.

With the evolution of intelligence, the human animal began to observe and speculate on the cosmography of his universe. Observation and common sense informed him that he lived on a piece of land that anybody could see was basically flat with a circular horizon and was therefore shaped like a dinner plate. That it floated on water was obvious, as the sea descended far enough below the land to allow the largest ship to sink without a trace. There was also a sea above the sky, a sea that poured onto the land as rain whenever the movement of one of the sky's transparent plates opened the sluice gates to let it through.

---

9. Although some higher monkeys and apes are receptive to sexual advances at any time, including during pregnancy, they are still subject to an oestrus cycle, as women and gibbons are not. Since gibbons are not humankind's closest relatives, the parallel cannot be attributed to a common ancestor, but must have occurred at a time when humans (and likewise gibbons) had emerged as distinct species. For the most plausible account of humankind's evolution from a hairy, breastless quadruped with a dorsal vagina and tiny penis, into a hairless biped with hemispherical breasts, ventral vagina and the proportionally largest penis of any higher animal, see Morgan, *op. cit.*, and also her follow-up book, *The Aquatic Ape*, Briarcliff Manor, NY, 1982.

The sky itself was observably high in the middle, perhaps so high that the Tower of Babylon, designed to reach it, might have taken generations to complete. And since the sky was blue, and the blue could be seen to reach the ground at the horizon, it logically followed that the sky was firmly planted on the earth's rim. The problem of keeping such a huge dome from collapsing in the middle was solved by assuming that there was a mountain, Mount Atlas (later the god Atlas), placed in the middle of the land to hold it up.

Obviously, the dome of the sky was solid. How else could it keep the upper waters from pouring down in a continual rainfall? Equally obviously, the sun, moon and stars were securely attached to the solid dome of the sky; otherwise they would have fallen to earth long before. And anybody could see that the sky rotated once a day, while the earth remained immobile at the centre of the universe. Such were the beliefs that existed for perhaps as much as 100,000 years. Such were the beliefs that were eventually promoted to the status of Revealed Truth in the Judaeo-Christian bible.

As new discoveries were made, they were incorporated into a purely oral cosmography that was as readily modified in pre-bible days as is all science today. As long as there was no kind of bible, new cosmography could replace old and within a generation all previous theories would be forgotten. Even after the invention of writing, inaccurate beliefs that had been permanently recorded could still be abandoned. For example, from the time of Aristotle, no educated person has been unaware that the earth is (almost) a sphere.

An instance of the total transition from one belief system to another in a single generation in the present century can be found among the Dogon tribe of the African republic of Mali. Early in the twentieth century the Dogon learned from European visitors that Jupiter has four satellites; that Saturn is ringed; that the planets, including Earth, orbit the sun; and that Sirius has a white dwarf companion that orbits it every fifty years. In the 1930s, an anthropologist visited the Dogon and learned, not only that they had such advanced astronomical knowledge, but also that they had no awareness of a time when they did not have such knowledge. The Dogon assumed that their knowledge of the heavens had been revealed to them by a god. More recently, the suggestion has been put forward that it was revealed to them by ancient astronauts. The truth is more mundane.[10]

---

10. Ian Ridpath, 'Investigating the Sirius "Mystery,"' *The Skeptical Inquirer*, vol. 3, no. 1, Fall 1978, pp. 56-62.

Perhaps as early as 30,000 BCE (burial customs suggest this date),[11] *homo sapiens* became sufficiently aware of such recurrent patterns as birth and death, the twenty-eight-day death-and-rebirth lunar cycle to which women's menstrual periods were inextricably tied, and the thirteen-lunation solar cycle that brought fertile and barren seasons, to ask himself: Why? Why do females alone reproduce? Why do a majority of women die in childbirth when, with rare exceptions, animals do not? Why do only humans and higher primates menstruate? Why do animals have a seasonal rather than continuous desire for sexual recreation? Why does human alone need to cover himself with the skins of other animals to keep warm? Why does human alone understand fire? make tools? anticipate rain and carry tents for shelter? Why do the stars not fall out of the sky? Why, among the myriad unmoving stars, are there five wanderers? Are the kherubs (stars) fixed, and the serafs (planets) free to move, because the serafs are higher-ranking gods? Why is there a barren season? Why do pink mushrooms cause waking dreams? Since the beings that orbit the sky live forever, why don't humans? Not until 3500 BCE did he finally ask himself: Why do men exude a white phlegm-like substance when they pleasure their mistresses?[12]

Then as now, human was sufficiently logical to recognise that all possible answers could be classified under two broad headings: accident and design. For four million years he had, albeit unconsciously, accepted the accident explanation. Now the alternative found favour. All things happened as they did because some form of ruling intelligence had so decreed. The planets wandered, the sun gave forth light and heat, the moon died and was reborn at monthly intervals, and the earth produced the food that sustained life, because they were living, thinking creatures with powers far beyond the capacity of mere humans. And whereas men lived perhaps forty-five years if they were fortunate, and women probably less, the sun, moon and stars

---

11. Cro-Magnon man buried his dead in a foetal position, and paleoanthropologists have not unreasonably interpreted this as good evidence for a belief in rebirth. *Homo neanderthalensis* buried his dead as long ago as 100,000 years. However, if burial *per se* were to be accepted as proof of an afterlife belief, we would be obliged to conclude that elephants and other animals that practise burial of the dead have metaphysical beliefs. (See R.K. Siegel, 'Life After Death,' in G. Abell and B. Singer, eds., *Science and the Paranormal*, NY, 1981, pp. 165-171).

12. Sociobiology, besides being based on a misinterpretation of evolution, is equally dependent on the pretence that animals below *homo sapiens* are aware of the biological relationship between sire and cub. They are not. The new mythologians also defend male supremacy as 'natural' by claiming that human societies have always been male-dominated. In fact men were second-class humans from the time of the invention of Goddess by Cro-Magnon man until the retaliatory invention of God almost thirty thousand years later. Male supremacy began with the Big Discovery of *c.* 3500 BCE (see pages 46-47).

lived forever. And since the moon-goddess could die and be reborn, was there some way she could be persuaded to bestow that power of resurrection on mortals? And so were born humankind's first gods, not at first objects of worship capable of aiding favoured followers, but simply immortals whose existence was noted as the existence of an equally immortal river might be noticed.

There is no way of gauging the elapsed time from the creation of the first god to the creation of the first religion; for mere belief in gods did not constitute a religion. (Even Eskimo tribes that have never had any religion, have included gods among the phenomena of the external world whose existence they have casually noted.) Not until the first true sun-worshipper turned his face toward the god in the sky and asked it to ripen his crop in exchange for a gift, or until the first ambitious junior executive asked a river-god to drown her rival, also in exchange for a designated gift, did nature deification evolve into religion.

Once the idea had evolved that a god could intervene in human affairs, it was just a matter of time before every event that affected humans was blamed upon a god. As more and more mundane accidents, ranging from a successful crop to annihilation by an erupting volcano, came to be attributed to divine intervention, words that had once meant nothing more than 'an immortal' came to have incompatible connotations among separated tribes. Nowhere is this development easier to document than among persons whose ancestors spoke the language generally termed Indo-European.

The Indo-European word for an immortal seems to have been *devas*, or something similar. In Latin *devas* became *divus*, from which English derived *divinity*; *divum*, which meant god-the-sky; *deus*, source of the English word *deity*; and *Jove*; all of which connoted a force for good. In Greek, *devas* at an early date became *devos*, from which evolved the diminutive *diabolos*, a little god. *Diabolos* later came to denote a slanderer, and is the source of the English words *devil* and *diabolic*.[13] *Devos*, retaining good connotations, became *theos*, from which *theology* is derived; and *Zeus*. In Persian, *devas* became *dervish*, at first a malicious demon, later an Islamic monk. *Devas* became *deva* in both Sanskrit and Zend, with the difference that it meant a god in the former and a devil in the latter. Since gods and devils have long been credited with identical capricious behaviour, the difference between them has ever been in the eye of the beholder.

Later earth-gods could intervene decisively in human affairs. Earlier sky-gods could not. They could, however, exert some influence. Even the fixed kherubs, while not as powerful as the wandering serafs, were possessed of

---

13. Whether *diabolos* or *diaballo* came first is a chicken-and-egg question. In my view, the ultimate derivation of both words from *devos* has not been refuted.

some authority over mortal humans. They were particularly influential when groups of kherubs acted in concert, and more so when the sun and moon, the most powerful of the sky-gods, wandered into their field of dominance. The theory that the stars in a particular segment of the sky were cooperating gods that ruled over that segment led to the formation of the religion known as astrology.[14]

To an observer on earth, the sun appears, in the course of a year, to travel a complete circumference of the sky along a fixed path that astronomers call the *ecliptic*. In so doing, it appears to pass through only a minute percentage of so-called constellations (groups of stars) that happen to lie in the same direction from earth as the ecliptic. In fact, not only does the sun not pass through any constellation, the nearest of which is hundreds of light years away; the constellations have no objective reality. They consist of stars that could be a galaxy apart, but which appear to be a single cluster solely because we happen to be viewing them from the direction of Sol 3.

To the ancients, who imagined that the sun, moon and stars were attached to the dome of the skies, the constellations were accepted as genuine groupings that were together in fact as well as perspective. The constellations straddling the ecliptic were arbitrarily divided into thirteen, corresponding to the number of lunar cycles per solar cycle, on the basis of a group's imagined resemblance to a crab, a scorpion, a lion, or some other object. Since most of the ecliptic's thirteen constellations were pictured, probably under the influence of hallucinogenic mushrooms, as animals, the complete circuit was named the *zodiac*, meaning 'circle of animals.' Persons born while the sun appeared to be in one of the thirteen zodiacal constellations were deemed to possess tendencies inflicted upon them by that constellation's kherubs.

Probably the zodiac's original inventors credited each of its constellations with a period of influence that corresponded to the apparent length, in degrees, of the constellation's east-west axis. Since the sun appeared to be in Leo for thirty-eight days each year, Virgo forty-seven days, Libra twenty-five days, Ophiuchus eighteen days, Scorpio six days, and the other eight constellations for various lengths of time, crediting Scorpio (for example) with more than six days' influence would have been illogical.

Sometime after 3500 BCE, however, for reasons best known to themselves, the ancient astrologer-priests decreed that each group of twinkling gods exerted its influence on the newborn for precisely twenty-eight days. This did not coincide with the observable twenty-nine and a half days of

---

14. For a detailed rebuttal of the absurdity of astrology, see L. Jerome, *Astrology Disproved*, Buffalo, 1978; and R. Culver and P. Ianna, *Astrology: True or False?*, Buffalo, 1988.

the synodic month, the period between new moons; but it was a nice round figure, an exact multiple of the number of serafs (sun, moon and five known planets), and a precise thirteenth of the 364-day ancient 'year.'

The most significant change in the zodiac occurred probably between 3000 and 2000 BCE. This was the millennium during which the serpent-goddess, whose reign as Goddess the Mother had lasted over twenty thousand years, was supplanted in most cultures by God the Father,[15] and mythology made not only such changes as were necessary to accommodate the new deity, but also unnecessary changes whose only function was to denigrate the deposed Mother still further. The constellations of the zodiac were reduced to twelve by the simple expedient of pretending that Ophiuchus, the serpent-bearer, did not exist, and reassigning the portion of the sky actually filled by Ophiuchus to neighbouring Scorpio.

It was at this time that the number thirteen, in view of its sacred position in goddess-religion, was deemed hateful to the conquering male gods,[16] and the thirteen-month year was redivided into twelve thirty-day months (with up to five additional intercalated days, depending on the accuracy of a particular tribe's astronomy). The number twelve was promoted to the sacred status previously enjoyed by the now-taboo thirteen, and in certain priest-ridden societies a base-twelve sacred mathematics was concocted to compete with the secular base-ten used by all cultures with ten fingers. Base-twelve ultimately failed (there has never been a society in which base-twelve was the primary math), and its only surviving remnants are the concepts *dozen* and *gross*, and the two-by-twelve-hour day. In Babylon, the secular and ecclesiastical forces eventually cooperated to produce a base-sixty math, the lowest common multiple of twelve and ten. Base-sixty remnants survive in the hours-minutes-seconds and degrees-minutes-seconds systems.

There may have been other zodiacal changes at the same time as the purging of Ophiuchus. All or most of the surviving constellations may have originally been female; but this is uncertain. Almost certainly Saggitarius the archer was originally a huntress, a personality that was later transferred to the Roman moon-goddess Diana. Probably Virgo remained as the only zodiacal female because virginity, a male concept imposed on women for reasons that will be explained later, was not deemed a threat to the new ruling classes.

With the exact science of hindsight, it is easy today to recognise that astrology is self-evidently absurd. We know, as the ancients did not, that

---

15. The name God is a contraction of *Godan*, 'Father Goth,' the Gothic *Odin*/*Woden*.
16. The combination of the moon-goddess's sacred number and the fertility goddess Frig's name day produced the double-feminine, 'Friday the Thirteenth,' held in superstitious dread by male-god worshippers to this day.

stars are not gods, that constellations are optical illusions, and that the sun is not actually in or close to any of the zodiacal constellations, ever. We also know, as the astrologers who permanently tied the twelve equalised signs of the zodiac to the existing solar calendar in 100 BCE did not, that the sun's apparent entrance into each constellation occurs twenty minutes later each year. Thus, although the sun indeed entered Aries on March 20, 100 BCE, and remained in Aries until April 11 (and in the artificially equalised 'sign' of Aries until April 19), today it does not enter Aries until April 18. Yet modern astrologers continue to inform their victims that persons born during the period that the sun was in the constellation Pisces, March 10 to April 17, are permanently imprinted with the personality and destiny officially credited to subjects of the constellation Aries, on the ground that the sun was in Aries on those dates in 100 BCE.

Astrology's role in surviving god-mythology has diminished considerably over the past few centuries, but the two have not totally separated. No Pope, Patriarch or Chief Rabbi has ever repudiated the biblical declaration: *The gods said, 'Let lights be attached to the dome of the skies to . . . serve for signs* (i.e., horoscopes) *and seasons and days and years'* (GEN. 1:14). Nor has the 'Revealed Truth' label been removed from the assertion that: *They fought from the skies; the stars in their orbits fought against Sisera* (JUDG. 5:20). Furthermore, Easter and Passover continue to be observed on dates calculated on the basis of the conjunction of solar and lunar calendars, as if the ancients' interpretation of such a conjunction as an agreement between the gods were objectively correct.

But whereas modern god-mythologies tend to speak in absolutes, modern star-mythology is content to speak in terms of tendencies. The stars influence but do not compel, just as the zodiacal gods, being invented at a time when a god was merely an immortal without the powers credited to later gods, could likewise influence but not compel. Fixed-star gods were never more than political eunuchs, and today the one mythology that credits them with 'influence' simultaneously denies their original status as living, thinking immortals.

The serafs, or planets, were not as impotent as the kherubs, and at the height of Hellenism, Ares, Hermes and Aphrodite were deities to be reckoned with indeed. But like their immobile compatriots, they were invented at a time when absolutism did not exist among mortals and could not be imagined among the gods. Consequently they were never credited with the unlimited power and authority granted to later gods. They were gods in the sense that an immortal is a god by definition, but they were never awe-inspiring, never demanded blind, unquestioning obedience, never demanded 'worship' in the modern sense of the word, and never acquired a priesthood that kept the masses in line by terrifying them with threats of the consequences of incurring the gods' anger. To this day, four of the surviving planetary gods—Gabriel (Mercury), Mikhael (Mars), Rafael (Jupiter) and Uwriel (Saturn)—are regarded as the comparatively harmless messengers of the terrifying earth-god Yahweh, while the fifth, the Satan (Venus), is thought to have no more power than Yahweh permits him.

The first gods in the modern sense, capricious beings that needed to be constantly appeased lest they unleash the malevolence that was their most universal feature, were not the sky-gods but the much more accessible earth-gods. The earth itself was generally hailed and adored as the Mother of all things. Her elder children, the birds that are not bound to the surface; the horse that can outrun any man; the sow that suckles a dozen infants to woman's one; the cow and goat without whose milk human was unlikely to survive; the fig tree, or tree of life, whose ripened fruit so resembled the vulva that was the source of all life; and a host of other plants, animals, rivers and like immortals, human recognised to possess capacities that were lacking in himself.

Not yet having the conceit that led to the creation of anthropomorphic gods, namely that Human is the universe's crowning achievement and master of all that breathes, primitive human worshipped the superior beings whose mortal counterparts were faster, stronger, nobler and more fecund than himself. Not until the second millennium BCE did the Greeks, the first people to limit their worship to gods created in their own image, manufacture men and women out of the bull Zeus; the cow Hera; the stallion Poseidon; the mare Demeter; the owl Athena; the multi-breasted pig Artemis; the goat Pan; the snake Apollo; the mushroom Hermes; the ram Ares; the volcano Hephaistos; the earth-mother Hestia; the sun and moon who also became Apollo and Artemis; the corn spirit who divided into the triple-goddess Demeter/Persephone/Hekate; the sea whose earlier personification had been Aphrodite, also a moon and fertility goddess, and which later became identified with Poseidon; the oak tree that became in turn Artemis, Hera and Zeus; the ant and honeybee that became lesser, non-Olympian gods; the personified vulva that became Easter/Ishtar/Astarte/Artemis/Ashtaroth/Aphrodite; and the phallus that became in turn Ouranos, Pan, Hermes and Priapos.

The earliest religions survive in barely recognisable form in the Christian junior god, Jesus, whose birth on the sun's rebirth day after its death at the winter solstice, and death on the full moon after the vernal equinox, show him to be simultaneously a sun-god and moon-goddess. But the most recognisable survival is in Hinduism, where the cow-mother continues to be revered in a manner not unlike that abandoned by the Greeks 3,500 years ago.

With the creation of gods, such cosmography as had previously existed needed to be modified to accommodate the immortals. Since there were seven wandering sky-gods, logically there must be seven skies, or 'heavens,' as *skies* came to mean once they were thought of as the abodes of gods, each rotating at a different speed. The existence of seven heavens remains Muslim doctrine to this day: *He created the seven heavens one above the other, placing in them the moon for a light and the sun for a lantern* (KORAN 71:15-16). Judaism acknowledges only one metaphysical heaven, even though all Jewish sacred writings refer to the demesnes of the gods as *ha-shemiym*, 'the skies,' and Hebrew does not have a singular word, 'sky.' Christianity likewise postulates a single heaven, carefully ignoring the reference to *the third sky* by Paul of Tarsus (2 COR. 12:2), and blissfully unaware that the Essene documents from which Jesus derived his sermons endorsed all seven. In much of the world, *seventh heaven* remains a metaphor for a state of euphoria or ecstasy.

In a male-dominated world, Popes, Caliphs, Ayatollahs, Prophets, Messiahs, priests and rabbis tend to be male; but this was not always so. Primeval religion was very much a woman's invention. Just as man/woman recognised that the cow was his superior because she sustained him with her milk, so he/she recognised that woman was man's superior because she produced the children who ensured the species's continued survival. Because the gods were conceived as the givers of life, and only females could give life, the first gods were not surprisingly goddesses. While men could accept a religion that legitimised and perpetuated their status as inferior beings in a goddess-ruled world, just as modern women have been conditioned to accept a similar status in a world of male gods, they could not have originated it. From the analogy of modern mythologies we can safely conclude that all mythologies, including the first, were invented by their immediate beneficiaries; and the beneficiaries of the first religion were women.

Religion took different forms in different parts of the world, for the obvious reason that the elements most necessary to life were different in different parts of the world. Peoples who depended on sheep, goats and grapes for their survival developed a belief in a goat-and-wine goddess who, following the male revolution of c. 3500 BCE, became the god Dionysos. Tribes that ate beef and drank mead formulated a milk-and-honey goddess, and after male liberation gave the job of King of Heaven to bull-Zeus, and the job of resurrected saviour, previously held by Persephone, to Dionysos's bovine equivalent, Zagreus. Equestrian tribes' first goddess, the mare Demeter, reigned for 25,000 years before being supplanted by her male counterpart, Poseidon.

Black people created black gods. Red people created red gods. Yellow people created yellow gods. White people created white gods. Centuries later, when Europe conquered and enslaved Africa, blacks were subjected to the ultimate degradation of being coerced into expelling their entire race from the heavens and worshipping gods created by the white conquerors in their own image. For black women, the European religion was doubly degrading, for the white gods were also male. To this day Christian missionaries preach the white male god Jesus to male and female blacks, as if the superiority of white over black and male over female, whether gods or mortals, were self-evident.

Since societies created their gods in their own moral as well as physical image, inevitably cultures that were perfectly sane and virtuous by the standards of five thousand, or four thousand, or two thousand, years ago, but insane and evil by the standards of today, created gods that were likewise insane and evil by the standards of today. That would not have presented a problem had the gods been allowed to evolve with their creators. Unfortunately, the invention of writing led to the depiction of capricious, temperamental, xenophobic, genocidal, morally retarded gods in sacred scrolls in which their every atrocity and irrationality was not merely acknowledged but unequivocally applauded by their equally vicious and irrational creators.

The consequence was that, while the god-worshippers who created them continued evolving, their gods' moral evolution ceased as soon as their concept of right and wrong was frozen in a 'bible,' in the case of the Jewish and Christian gods, two thousand years ago and more. By categorising fiction composed by a morally retarded culture as Revealed Truth, Judaism and Christianity are to this day saddled with gods that, to quote George Smith, *by any reasonable standard of human decency, must be judged as morally repugnant.*[17] John Wyndham reached a similar conclusion when he had one of his characters reject biblical injunctions on the ground that, *We've got to believe that God is sane.*[18]

Pastoral people created pastoral gods such as Pan, whom the agriculturist Jews absorbed into their pantheon in the third century BCE as the Satan. With the adoption of permanent settlements and the raising of crops came the worship of the barley mother, one of whose names was Easter. The invention of boats and the art of piracy led people whose welfare depended on the sea to worship a sea-goddess such as the Jewish Tehowm and the Greek Aphrodite. The domestication of pet animals led to the worship of a god who domesticated pet humans such as Abraham and Moses.

Tribes living on the slopes or in the fallout area of an active volcano promoted their smoking home to the status of tribal goddess and regularly threw captured enemies into her lava-filled vulva in the hope of dissuading her from erupting over them. One such volcano, in Anatolia, was Mount

17. *Atheism: The Case Against God*, Buffalo, 1979, p. 313.
18. *The Chrysalids*, 1955, Penguin edition, p. 78.

Yahuwah,[19] whose worshippers were the Jews. Others were (the original female names do not survive) Hephaistos, Vulcan and Prometheus. Later, when the Jews became patriarchal, Mount Yahuwah was renamed Mount Yahweh, dropping the feminine ending, and her/his worshippers took their volcano-god with them when the invading Babylonians drove them out of Anatolia and into Phoenicia around 2000 BCE.

Elsewhere, the fashioning of tools and weapons led man the manufacturer to envision a creator-god who had manufactured the universe. In the reign of King Rekhobowam, Yahweh, too, became a creator-god. That there was never a creator-goddess indicates the lateness of the deity-as-creator concept. No goddess ever created the cosmos; she gave birth to it.

Most modern god-mythologies centre on a creator-god. Unfortunately for such mythologies' credibility, they are irrevocably committed to bibles in which their gods created, not the universe that is now known to exist, but the universe described earlier that the ancients thought to exist: a flat, unmoving earth covered by a series of solid domes called *skies*. The Priestly author who composed the cosmography that believers have been trying to rationalise away for centuries wrote:

The gods made the skies and the land.   (GEN. 1:1)

The gods said, 'Let there be a solid dome to divide the waters from the waters.'   (GEN. 1:6)

The gods called the solid dome SKIES.   (GEN. 1:8)

In the 600th year of Noakh's life . . . all the waters of the subterranean ocean gushered up, and the sluice gates of the skies were opened.   (GEN. 7:11)

'You're not to make yourself a carved representation of any shape found in the skies above or on the land below, or in the water on which the land floats.'   (EXOD. 20:4)

The Judaeo-Christian bible, being composed at a time when cosmography was primitive, reflects the ignorance (by today's standards) of its

---

19. The ending *-ah* was feminine singular. For a long period the Jewish god was Yahuw, as is attested in documents from Egypt. When *Yahuwah* was masculinised to *Yahweh*, the consonants-only spelling, YHWH, remained unchanged, but the pronunciation no longer ended in *-ah*. It is inconceivable that a feminine ending would have later been added. I therefore deduce that the reappearance of YHWH represented a survival of the name's earlier form, and that therefore YHWH was female. To retain the traditional spelling while maintaining that the god was male, a change of pronunciation *must* have taken place. (Evidence for Yahuwah/Yahweh originally being a volcano will be given in chapter 13.)

authors. It expressly endorses a flat earth (DAN. 4:10; MAT. 4:8; APOC. 7:1); an earth that neither orbits the sun nor revolves on its axis (PS. 93:1; 96:10; 104:5); a solid sky (JOB 22:14; APOC. 6:14; ACTS 10:11); stars tiny enough to fall to earth (APOC. 6:13; 8:10; MAT. 2:9); and a moon that is not a reflector of light but a source of light (GEN. 1:16). Also, as most people are aware, it declares that the billions-of-years-old universe was created by 'the gods' less than ten thousand years ago.

Attempts to rationalise that biblical myths are somehow 'true' have ranged from an allegorical interpretation to the uncompromising fundamentalism of scientific illiterates, and from the rewriting of half a dozen sciences by desperate cranks such as Immanuel Velikovsky[20] to the *Chariots of the Gullible* contention that the myth of Adam depicts the injection of genes for intelligence into pre-*sapiens homo* by visiting spacemen. The simple truth is that, to the authors of the Judaeo-Christian bible, their fables were not intended to be read as metaphors but as literal truth. Biblical cosmography is totally inaccurate because the biblical authors wrote at a time when everybody, including Jewish gods, believed that the earth was flat, immobile, covered by a solid dome, and only a few generations old.

At different times, humankind's view of the birth process led to the invention of gods who emulated the status of their creators. Woman the mother created Goddess the Mother, who gave birth to woman in her own image. After 3500 BCE, man the father created God the Father, who created man in his own image. And following the female counterrevolution of the twentieth century CE, proponents of equal rights came up with God-the-Father-and-Mother, in a predictable attempt to retain the god-concept while simultaneously throwing out the misogyny that the god had been created to legitimise in the first place.

The development of political hierarchies headed by kings whose power was absolute and unlimited led to the promotion of a culture's most indispensible god to the monarchy of the heavens. In keeping with his new status as an autocrat, King Zeus (Shamash, Yahweh, Ra, Elohiym, Amen, Sin, Jupiter, Odin, Woden, Godan, Aton, Manitou) was granted the same rights enjoyed by his earthly prototypes. Any law attributed to the King of Heaven was to be obeyed without question, no matter how timeserving, partisan, unjust, sadomasochistic or illogical it happened to be. Like his mortal equivalent, God the King could do no wrong. To this day, God the King is credited with causing all deaths, so that without his consent, 'Not a sparrow can fall to the ground' (MAT. 10:29), nor can an earthquake, famine or disease kill millions. Yet believers in such a doctrine are incapable

---

20. For an excellent rebuttal of Velikovsky's fantasies, see D. Goldsmith, ed., *Scientists Confront Velikovsky*, NY, 1977.

of questioning their god's atrocities, because God the King has the absolute right to do anything he wishes.

Since God the King was created with the *right* to do anything he wished, it was inevitable that he would eventually be credited with the *power* to do anything he wished. Thus he evolved an omnipotence that, in surviving god-mythologies, he still has—even though omnipotence is by definition impossible. And since he would wish to be all-knowing, he likewise evolved omniscience, even though omnipotence and omniscience are mutually exclusive.

Absolute omnipotence involves the ability to do *anything*. Thus an omnipotent god could create a triangle with four sides; a number that is greater than ten but less than nine; a rock so heavy that he could not lift it; and an effect that preceded its cause. Since none of the foregoing can exist, it follows that omnipotence cannot exist, and therefore a creature possessed of such a trait cannot exist.

Most modern god-worshippers, shown that omnipotence cannot exist, would be willing to credit their paramount god with limited omnipotence: anything that a Disney animator could accomplish in a cartoon, their god could accomplish in reality. Thus a four-sided triangle would remain impossible, even to their god; but a mouse could give birth to a brontosaurus; a living human could be created out of clay, even though clay does not contain organic molecules; and a seventeen-billion-year-old universe could be created retroactively, six thousand years ago.

Unfortunately, even limited omnipotence is incompatible with omniscience. If a god *knows* what will happen in the future, and knows that it *will* happen and that he will not change it, then he in fact cannot change it and is therefore not omnipotent. And if he can, when the time comes, change the future from what he knows it must be to something else, then he did not in fact know what it would be and is therefore not omniscient. If he did know that he would change it, then he was incapable of not changing it, and is therefore not omnipotent. And if he . . . . Ultimately, a god cannot be simultaneously omnipotent and omniscient, and a god that is both cannot exist.

Furthermore, omniscience is itself definitively impossible, since the only way anyone could have perfect knowledge of the future would be for information to travel backwards in time, creating a situation in which an effect (knowledge of an event) preceded its cause (the event foreknown). A god could know the future only if every thought and action was an inevitable, predetermined consequence of the present, and there was no such thing as free will or probability. A god with limited omnipotence and limited omniscience (perfect knowledge of past and present) could also be omnibenevolent only in a universe in which such evils as natural disasters, accidents, diseases and malicious homicides did not exist. Yet omnibenevolence is a trait also claimed by modern god-worshippers for their paramount deities.

Sun-worship was the most universal religion. In every part of the world the quality of life depended to a greater or lesser degree on a regular supply of sunshine. In Egypt, where the sunshine factor was paramount, the sun-god Ra became the heavenly Pharaoh. When monotheism was first conceived by the mad Pharaoh Ikhenaton c. 1380 BCE, it was inevitable that his universal god would be Aton, the sun. In those places where sunshine was deemed less vital than regular and adequate rainfall, rain-goddesses such as Nuah (later transmogrified into Noah) ruled the sky. Zeus was such a rain-god.

Goddesses tended at first to be universal, as did the gods who succeeded them. Yet from a quite early date there were local deities. While no tribe could reasonably claim Mother Earth or the moon-goddess as its exclusive property, a goddess such as the Nile obviously had no interest in people not living in the vicinity of her river. Where a local phenomenon such as regular earthquakes or the omnipresence of an active volcano such as Yahweh outweighed universal factors, tribes in the area developed the habit of appeasing the destructive forces by worshipping the earthshaker or the lava-spewer as a jealous, easily-angered tyrant who would not tolerate the worship of any other god within the area of his hostile influence. Clearly, a jealous god could only have evolved in a culture in which the ruling king, sheikh or overlord was himself a jealous tyrant whose subjects were effectively prohibited from offering the obeisances that constituted the original meaning of *worship* to any of his rivals.

But authoritarian male gods were a late development. Until approximately 3500 BCE, perhaps a little earlier in some places, the world was ruled by goddesses. In all likelihood the first mythologies were monolatrous, with all worship centering on the single natural phenomenon (earth-mother, moon-mother, barley-mother, volcano-mother) most relevant to the tribe's welfare. As tribes with different goddesses communicated, each came to recognise that the other tribe's goddess was simply its own patroness under a different name—usually. The moon-goddess, for example, whether she was called Artemis, Astarte, Ashtaroth, Ishtar, Easter, Isis, Sin, Diana, Aphrodite, Helene, Selene, Eve, Lilith, Leda, Vesta, Hestia, Rakhel or Leah, was still the moon; and there was only one moon.

When, however, some aspect of a moon-goddess's personality conflicted sharply with a tribe's own conceptualisation, the foreign goddess was often accepted as a different person and added to an existing pantheon. The introduction of orgasm-loving Aphrodite to Greece at a time when Artemis had become a virgin led to her adoption as a different deity, even though each was originally the same moon-goddess, earth-mother and personified vulva. Ultimately the Greek Olympos housed six goddesses, of whom all six had been earth-mothers and at least three had been moon-personifications.

From the time of their creation by answer-seeking women, earth-goddesses were conceived as objects of worship. The Mother was credited with supplying all of humankind's needs, and it seemed highly desirable, if she was to be encouraged to continue her bounty, that she be given something in return.

At first the offerings were haphazard and consisted of whatever the worshipper needed least. A Greek myth told of how a sacrificed bull was divided into two portions, one containing the meat and the other containing the bones, offal, fat and hide. The two portions were covered, and Zeus was offered his choice for a sacrifice. Being greedy, he chose the larger portion. From that time, the meat of sacrifices was eaten by the worshippers, while the waste was given to Zeus.

No similar Hebrew myth survives, possibly because it was suppressed by a later author who would not permit Yahweh to be so easily deceived. But there must have been one. The Priestly author's ritual for sacrifices stipulated that the blood, fat and entrails were to be burnt on Yahweh's altar, while the meat was to be eaten by the priests (LEV. 7:1-7).

Gradually, by a process similar to the learning patterns of B.F. Skinner's pigeons, which automatically repeated any act that was followed by a reward, woman learned that the goddess preferred specific offerings at specific times of year. Offerings in March were quite likely to be followed by a good crop, but no amount of bribes in December could keep the Mother from imposing the inevitable winter.

It was probably as a desperation move following a long drought that the Mother was first sacrificed a living animal in the hope that, since life was the goddess's gift that she arbitrarily gave and took away, she just might be satisfied with the terminating of a dispensable life in exchange for those she might otherwise have taken. When she showed her acceptance by ending the drought, the pattern for future sacrifices was as firmly imprinted on humans as could be achieved with any pigeon. To this day, the behavioural similarities of the more fundamentalist god-worshippers and pigeons out-weigh the differences.

Sacrifices were the best offerings. Nonetheless, earlier offerings that had proven effective were not abandoned. One of the earliest fertility rituals, and one of the longest surviving, was the offering of sacred blood in the menstruation dance. Originally performed at any time of the year, it eventually came to be limited to those dates on which the Mother had tended to respond. Like any offering to a corn-goddess, it had been found to be most effective on the night of the full moon following the vernal equinox. That date was retained when, following the male revolution of 3500 BCE, the festival was rededicated to male gods. The same date was retained when, in the last years of the Davidic monarchy, the Jewish mythologian known as the Deuteronomist retroactively associated the unleavened bread festival borrowed from the Phoenicians with the Israelites' departure from Egypt by combining it with the lamb-sacrifice known as PASSOVER. Essentially the same date is retained in the festival that commemorates the annual death-and-rebirth of the Germanic fertility goddess Easter's current equivalent, Jesus.

The ritual dripping of menstrual blood into the womb of Mother Earth in the presence of the full moon acknowledged the equation of the earth, moon and fertility goddesses. Even where, as in Greece, the three had come to be worshipped as separate persons, the recognition of their original unity as One Goddess was not lost. Although three persons, they remained, in some inexplicable sense, One. Thus arose the concept of the immortal trinity, one goddess in three persons.

In time the trinity came to be worshipped as pre-pubertal virgin, mother, and post-menopausal hag, and also as moon, earth and underworld queens. Hera was worshipped in all three capacities at Stymphalos until the rite was suppressed by male-god worshippers (ostensibly by Herakles) in the early thirteenth century BCE; while at Lerna the triple-goddess was from an early date the long-lasting Demeter/Persephone/Hekate.[21]

Trinitarianism lasted well into the days of god-rule but, except among those women whose stubborn adherence to the old religion had earned them the designation of Amazons, it had disappeared in Europe by 800 BCE. It was not revived until the third century CE, when, in a male-dominated world, the mother and the daughter and the holy ancestress became the father and the son and the holy spirit.

The dance was necessarily performed naked, in order that the sacred blood of life would fall upon the Mother's womb and not upon whatever clothing was customarily worn to keep out the cold. In effect, the offering of blood was not inferior to the offering of a life, since the blood *was* the life. Long before the idea arose that it was the breath rather than the blood that constituted the abstraction called Life, two Jewish mythologians declared the equation of blood with life Revealed Truth when they wrote: *The life of every body is its blood* (LEV. 17:14); and *The blood is the life* (DEUT. 12:23).

To make the blood spill faster, the dancers leaped high into the air. As skill at the dance increased, branches of trees were introduced for the women to leap over. In its final form the dance was performed with the

---

21. Robert Graves, *The Greek Myths* 128:3; 124:4. The triple-goddess Diana Triformis was worshipped in Scotland as Saint Triduana until 1560 CE, when her shrine was torn down by followers of John Knox.

branch between the legs. So adept did some dancers become at leaping astride their broomsticks—as the branches came to be contemptuously called by later male-god cultists—that they were often depicted in rock drawings as leaping up level with the moon-goddess herself.

The development of sacred kingship—the custom of appointing a figurehead king who would be sacrificed to the Mother at the end of his short reign—saw the dance augmented by the mandatory sacrifice; but in its original form it managed to survive well into modern times. Indeed, among the fertility cultists in England who call themselves witches, there is some doubt that the dance has been abandoned at all.

As it was in the skies, so it was on earth. Goddesses ruled the metaphysical world; women ruled the physical. Priestesses reigned for life, often accepting homage as goddesses-on-earth. In an orderly world hatched from the egg of the goddess and run by her mirror-image, woman, men accepted that they had no rights and did as they were ordered, just as in the modern world there are women so conditioned to the belief that they are hereditary slaves, created by a male god as second-class humans, that they give speeches urging State Legislatures to refuse to ratify a constitutional amendment granting full human status as equals to women. There is, however, considerable doubt that men were ever exploited by women prior to the revolution of 3500 BCE, as women since that date have been oppressed and dehumanised by men. There was never, for example, a female-absolutist equivalent of the sixth-century-CE synod of Macon, at which Christian bishops earnestly debated whether women were human beings; or the seventh-century Council of Nantes that, in its third canon, resolved the question by restricting immortality to males and pronouncing women 'soulless beasts' whom the chief male god had given Man to use as he saw fit.

Men were never private property, owned by one woman and arbitrarily forbidden from providing sexual pleasure to any woman but herself. At least, they were not in the days of goddess-rule. Men accept such a designation today (or pretend to) as the price they must pay to impose similar private ownership on their breeding women; but this, too, is a consequence of the male revolution. When the idea began to evolve that monogamy was either right or wrong, and that there should not be different standards for men and women, the ruling males declared, in effect, 'We won't annul your sexual slavery—but we'll agree to share your captivity by submitting to the same exclusivity.' No such illogic existed in the Mother's reign.

From the sacrifice of living animals to the sacrifice of living humans was a short and predictable step. Probably the first sacrifices were captives. Not having developed a slave economy, primitive societies had little alternative to killing their enemies. Sacrificing them to the Mother was a logical means of eliminating waste. Gradually the idea evolved that such sacrifices were not really free offerings but were the Mother's just due, a tax or tribute of a designated number of expendables per year as compensation for her forgiving the capital insults of the rest of the tribe. By the fifth century BCE, the gods' absolute entitlement to human sacrifice caused a Jewish lawgiver to have Yahweh order Moses:

> No part of a man's property that he has formally vowed to sacrifice to Yahweh, whether a human or an animal or a hereditary field, is to be sold or redeemed. Anything formally vowed to Yahweh is sacrosanct. No human who has been solemnly vowed is to be redeemed. He's to be sacrificed without fail.
>
> (LEV. 27:28-29)

Even as late as Roman times, the execution of Jesus the Nazirite for rebellion was retroactively hailed by his followers as a sacrificial substitute for the deserved death of a multitude of 'sinners.'

In one sense men were exploited under priestess-rule: sacrificial victims were always men. Women were the propagators of the human race, formed in the Mother's image. As such, their lives were sacred and inviolable. Not until the age of male absolutism was any woman ever sacrificed, and even then the breach with ancient practice was viewed with horror by men and women alike. Agamemnon's high-handed action, for example, in sacrificing a priestess of Artemis for a fair wind to Troy, was so unacceptable to his later admirers that they transferred responsibility for the sacrifice to Apollo's priest. Further to whitewash Agamemnon, the sacrificed Iphigeneia was declared to have been his beloved daughter whom he tried vainly to save from Kalkhas's malice.[22]

With the discovery that human blood was the Mother's favourite food, an orthodoxy developed whereby the priestess-queen became the sole arbiter of when a sacrifice was necessary and who should be the victim. Even men of the priestess's own tribe became conditioned never to question her right to send them to the Mother, with or without advance warning. It is reasonable to assume that, prior to the Big Discovery that triggered the male revolution, the sexual recreation with the priestess-queen that later became the sacrificial victim's consolation prize was not part of the original ritual. Sacrifice was a fertility exercise, a life given to the Mother in exchange for a good crop of wheat and babies. As long as there was no known connection between sexual recreation and procreation, copulation at a fertility rite would have been deemed intrusive and irrelevant, although it might have been indulged in afterwards as part of the celebration of a successful sacrifice.

The twenty-five thousand years in which goddesses reigned and women

---

22. *Ibid.* 161:2.

ruled saw the development of fairly cohesive societies. The building of the world's oldest walled city, Jericho, has been dated to this period, and such an immense undertaking would not have been possible except by a well-ordered division of labour. Also, a city wall would not have been needed in the absence of an equally cohesive, well-organised enemy.

At some time before the male revolution there evolved the concept of private property, and with it the world's first taboo: stealing. We cannot be certain of the fate of thieves, but in a world ruled by a bloodthirsty goddess who could only be appeased by sacrifice, the obvious answer is likely the true one. To justify the execution of thieves, the priestess-queens would have put into the mouth of the Mother a commandment, 'You are not to steal.' King Hammurabai of Babylon put such a commandment into the mouth of his god Shamash at about the beginning of the second millennium BCE, and the author of the Holiness code attributed the same law to his god Yahweh-Elohiym in c. 800 BCE.[23] A ban on stealing was part of the lawcode of Sparta's legendary lawgiver, Lykurgos, ostensibly received from the god Apollo, while the lawcode attributed to Crete's King Minos was ultimately declared to have come from Zeus.[24] There is no reason to doubt that new taboos were legitimised by the same means under goddess-rule.

Stealing was the oldest taboo, much older than the ban on the capricious killing of a member of one's own tribe without the tribe's consent, that was the original meaning of *murder*. The stealing taboo came into existence because private property could not have existed without it. The attribution to a deity of a law that made sound common sense did not come about as a result of any belief that the Mother was just and rational and must therefore approve of a just and rational law. On the contrary, the Mother's persistence in killing two out of three women in childbirth, despite all the sacrifices that she had been offered to cease the practice, showed that she was far from just. She was arbitrary, capricious, vicious and vengeful (characteristics that her male successors have retained to this day), and it was this aspect of her character that made her such a useful source of all law. While people could not be persuaded that it was ultimately in their own interests to avoid stealing (and later killing), they could be intimidated into fearing the vengeance of a terrible goddess who demanded the death penalty for all who disobeyed.

---

23. Parts of the Holiness code duplicate J's Ten Commandments (EXOD. 34:17-26 *and* 20:23; 22:29-30; 23:12-19). However, if H had predated J, J would surely have borrowed from it much more extensively. More likely, H used J, or a pre-J Big Ten list, as *his* source, and H is therefore to be dated between J (920 BCE) and E (770 BCE). Since E included the complete Holiness code (EXOD. 20-23), it is attributed to E rather than H in the chart in chapter 6.

24. Josephus, *Against Apion* 2:161.

Not surprisingly, the effectiveness of attributing laws, particularly irrational laws, to a metaphysical lawgiver was recognised by the male-god worshippers who overthrew the Mother around 3500 BCE. Male gods, too, could demand absolute obedience, both to new taboos imposed for the benefit of the current ruling class, and to old taboos whose original purpose, being no longer applicable, had long been forgotten.[25] Male gods, too, could terrify worshippers by prescribing death or torture for all who broke the taboos. The Priestly author of *Leviticus* around 600 BCE accused Yahweh of demanding the death penalty for any act by a Jew that the author considered too Babylonian. But the most vicious portrayal of his god as a vengeful psychopath was painted by Jesus the Nazirite and is to be found in the Christian gospels. To this day, Christians are reminded to 'Fear God' and to beware of Jesus' eternal torture chamber where Yahweh condemns taboo-breakers to be slowly barbecued by flamethrowers and eaten by a worm that never dies. And this penalty is imposed, not only on hurters, persons who assault, kill and steal, but also on persons who, in an age of fully effective birth control, share joy, on the ground that the taboo on such recreation, imposed for the purpose of preventing pregnancy, is still valid long after its only justification has ceased to exist. According to the current Head Christian, Yahweh will permanently torture all persons who attempt to save the human race by practising population control; but the Head

---

25. Non-procreational recreation involving a married person and a non-spouse continues to be labelled 'adultery' and proscribed, even though the human race was never so insane as to invent a taboo on sheer recreation, and adultery originally meant the property-infringement of fraudulently impregnating another man's breeding woman and thereby saddling him with a bastard. So distorted has the adultery taboo become, that surrogate mothers who bear children from the sperm of men with infertile wives insist on artificial insemination, in the absurd belief that being impregnated by a non-spouse does not constitute adultery but recreating with him does. Recreation between siblings, even when non-procreational, continues to be proscribed as 'incest,' even though incest was also a breeding taboo, invented for reasons described in chapter four. Homosexual recreation continues to be a religious taboo in an overpopulated world, even though the taboo was invented to maximise procreation in an underpopulated culture. Premarital recreation continues to be deemed immoral in an age of reliable birth control, even though the taboo was invented at a time when a woman's first child was believed to have been jointly fathered by all of her previous lovers, and a non-virgin bride's first child was automatically sacrificed as a bastard. And Jews and Muslims continue to proscribe pork-eating, even though the sow-goddess once honoured by such feasting is now regarded as nonexistent.

The distortion of laws from another age into something they were never intended to mean can be seen in the USA Supreme Court's invention of laws that benefit *only* the guilty, in the pretence that they were merely clarifying eighteenth-century laws designed to prohibit torture and other 'unreasonable' procedures that could throw the legitimacy of evidence so obtained into doubt. Just as the inventors of 'adultery' never intended to restrict behaviour known to be non-procreative, so the authors of the Bill of Rights never intended to exclude relevant evidence that no reasonable person could deem to have been obtained unreasonably.

Christian himself, as a reward for attempting to murder the entire human species by forcing it to overpopulate itself into starvation and extinction, will be given the privilege of watching them burn. Although permanent torture in Hell was invented by a Jew, it belongs strictly to Christian mythology. It has never been part of the mythology of the Jews.

Of all private property, the most sought-after has always been a position at the top of the social and political hierarchy. When other positions became hereditary, the office of priestess-queen in many communities did likewise. Generally, under the prevailing system of ultimogeniture, the priestess-queen's youngest daughter succeeded to her mother's office, while the old queen's sons replaced her brothers as commanders of what might loosely be termed the community's militia. When a woman died daughterless, it is probable that there were tribes that allowed her property to pass to a son; but the more common procedure would have been for sons to be bypassed in favour of the mother's nearest collateral heiress. A similar situation existed in England's hereditary peerage, in which new titles could be inherited only by male heirs.

The Mother eventually became anthropomorphic. Statues of her in human form dating from as early as 6000 BCE have been found in all parts of the Greek world and elsewhere. Given woman's role as mother, it was inevitable that she would come to picture the Mother-of-All in her own image. But for at least ten thousand years, and in some places well into Roman times, the more common conception was that of a planet-sized vulva/womb. The Mother had no husband for the obvious reason that the concept *husband* did not exist, and no lovers because she was no more credited with the human desire for sexual recreation than she was credited with the need to eat or defecate. It is ironic that, even though the act of sexual recreation played the pivotal role in the revolution that replaced Goddess the Mother with God the Father, the Mother's dysfunctional recreational equipment was eventually transferred to the male gods who replaced her. The oldest surviving deities, the planetary gods Mercury/Gabriel and Mars/Mikhael, are to this day credited by three mythologies with possessing phalluses that are totally nonfunctional.

Some versions of the Mother were never given husbands, and for that reason eventually entered bisexual pantheons as eternal virgins. In most communities, however, following the male revolution triggered by the Big Discovery of 3500 BCE, the Mother was given an impregnator in the person of her eldest son who, although virgin-born himself (there being no preexisting male to sire him), became the father of all future life.

The Big Discovery did not occur everywhere at the same time. Among the Aborigines of Melville Island to the north of Australia it was not made until the nineteenth century CE. In some places it may well have taken place much earlier than 3500 BCE, which is the best available estimate of the approximate date at which it became widespread. To persons who have grown up in a society in which such knowledge is taken for granted, it is difficult to convey the tremendous significance for future history of the first discovery by men that the organ with which they pleasured their mistresses *also made babies*.[26] The Big Discovery meant that women were no longer the sole purveyors of life—and neither were goddesses! From being the reproducers of life, women found themselves demoted to the level of incubators, of no more relevance to the birth process than the dirt in which an ear of corn grew into an adult plant.

Men were physically stronger than women. This had long been known and rationalised to fit a female-dominant theology, and only men's acceptance of their insignificance in the divine order kept them from taking over the world much sooner. Following the Big Discovery, nothing could stop them and nothing did stop them. However, the takeover did not occur right away. Compared with the male revolution, the industrial revolution was accomplished overnight. Before the mind could conceive of any change in the social structure of human society, it had first to postulate a similar change in the heavens. Thus before there could be any king reigning on earth, there had to be created a King of Heaven, a God the Father, who was the Mother's superior and by whose impregnation she produced her children.[27]

Just as the first paramount goddess had been an earthly vulva, so the first King of gods and men was a heavenly phallus. Statues of him in that form have been found, among other places, on the Aegaean seabed in the sunken remains of the island of Thira-Santorini, destroyed by the volcanic

---

26. A small number of phalluses appear in paleolithic art, but so few compared to mother-images that it is feasible to interpret them as simply representations of male humans and animals. The sudden proliferation of phallic images and ithyphallic gods c. 3500 BCE supports the conclusion that the Big Discovery was made at that time and triggered a radical revision of religion and social mores. In Chinese mythology, the man credited with making the Big Discovery was the patriarch Fu Hi (Pao Hsi).

27. While sociobiologists are the main opponents of the Big Discovery theory, some legitimate scholars are also troubled by it, arguing that the vulva's tripartite involvement in intercourse, menstruation and birth would have led the ancients to infer a relationship among the three. While that argument is not without validity, it seems less compelling than the observation that goddesses and priestesses were suddenly supplanted by male gods and kings, a transition that is surely best explained by the sudden upsurge in male self-respect brought on by the discovery that not mothers but fathers were the true and only (as they then thought) biological begetters of future generations. Male scholars who feel threatened by the theory of an age of matriarchy have argued that such a theory goes beyond the evidence. That is true, but it is a logical extrapolation of the evidence. Goddesses and priestesses could not reasonably have had a higher status than male counterparts in a culture in which their whole sex did not enjoy a similar supremacy.

eruption of c. 1500 BCE, and in the ruins of Pompeii and Herculaneum.[28] The Jews pictured Yahweh as a phallus from the time of Abraham (GEN. 24:2-3) until the reign of King David (2 SAM. 6:14; see also p. 179) and beyond (4 KGS. 17:9-12). Babylon's original phallus-god, Shamash, evolved into a sun-god, even though the Semitic word *shamash* has retained the meaning of phallus to this day. And in Greece the planetary god Hermes likewise began his heavenly career as a personified phallus.

Greece had several phallus-gods, including Hermes and Priapos. The earliest, however, was Ouranos, Father Sky. He was the son of Mother Earth, and the rain was his sperm with which he quickened her womb and caused all things to grow. Ouranos's role as his mother's husband was never suppressed even after mother-son copulation had become a Greek taboo. Ouranos was, however, the god of the pre-Greeks, and it may be that that was why the Greeks did not see his impregnation of his mother as an embarrassment that needed to be expurgated. The Greeks did suppress Zeus's impregnation of his mother Hera, by turning her into his sister.

In other cultures, new creation stories were composed that did not require the gods to breach what had by then become their own taboos. In Babylon, for example, instead of impregnating his mother Tiamat, Marduk simply sliced her in two and created the universe out of her remains. The story was borrowed by the Aaronic Jew known as the Priestly author who, in the opening chapter of *Genesis*, had the goddess's creator-son Elohiym ('the gods') deal similarly with his mother Tehowm:

> At commencement the gods created the skies and the land. The land was shapeless Tehowm, and on Tehowm's face was darkness. The breath of the gods moved on the waters' (*Tehowm's*) face. . . . The gods said, 'Let there be a solid dome in the middle of the waters, and let it divide the waters from the waters.' So the gods made the dome, and divided the waters under the dome from the waters above the dome (*bisected Tehowm*). . . . The gods called the solid dome SKIES.   (GEN. 1:1-2, 6-8)

It was the concept of god-as-phallus that gave rise to the earliest of the son-of-god cults. Just as the concept of goddess-the-vulva had led to the reverence of the vulva-shaped fig, almond and pomegranate as the fruit of the tree of life, made in the Mother's image, so now edible phallic images acquired a similar status. There were many plants that resembled the human phallus, including the mandrake (GEN. 30:14-16, 22-23), and the Big Discovery made them all sacred. But among them was one that, unlike other plants, did not grow from any kind of seed. This was the hallucinogenic

---

28. A. Mondadori, ed., *Eros in Antiquity*, pp. 24, 71, 91, 109, 113, 122, 124-128.

mushroom, *amanita muscaria*, that sprang up spontaneously after rain. A truer offspring of the Sky Father and the Earth Mother, moulded in the Father's image, could not be conceived. The digestion of any sacred object constituted a mystical union between human and god; but the consumption of the sacred mushroom, the very Son of God, produced visions that as never before made communion with the god a unique reality.[29]

Later, when gods had been redesigned into human form, a mushroom could no longer be accepted as the Incarnation of an anthropomorphic god. At that time the sacred mushroom was replaced by a food that conformed more closely to the god's new image. The flesh and blood of a sacred king who was the annually-resurrected corn-god's surrogate were consumed instead. Later still, when human sacrifice was abandoned as wasteful, and cannibalism, like all formerly-sacred customs, became a taboo, god-eating degenerated into a symbolic act in which the flesh and blood of the corn-god were transubstantially consumed in the form of the corn products of bread and alcohol.

The choice of bread and barley ale/mead/wine as visible representations of the body and blood of a fertility god was not difficult to explain. Bread, made from the grain that was the corn-god's body, could easily be identified as the flesh of the god. Similarly, water that had been transformed into an intoxicant by contact with the god's flesh, in the absence of any understanding of the chemical process of fermentation, was logically interpreted as the god's blood. The discovery that grapes (among other things) also mysteriously transformed water into an intoxicant, led to the advent in the second millennium BCE of the wine god Dionysos/Bacchus. It was in the form of bread and wine that the god Ilion (Allah) was eaten by the priest-king Molokhiy-Tsedek in c. 1800 BCE (GEN. 14:18).[30] It was in the form of bread and barley wine that the Egyptian *Book of the Dead* at about the same time instructed worshippers of the resurrected-saviour-god Osiris to eat his flesh and drink his blood. It is in the form of bread and wine that the transsexual resurrected-saviour-goddess Easter is eaten to this day.

Human has been eating his gods and goddesses for thirty thousand

---

29. John Allegro, in *The Sacred Mushroom and the Cross*, postulates that Christianity began as a mushroom cult and that Jesus the Nazirite was not a person from history. In fact the original Jesus sect, the Ebionites, bore no resemblance to the mushroom cults. The god-incarnate and sacramental-cannibalism elements that indeed paralleled the rites of the mushroom-eaters were grafted onto the Jesus legend only after Christianity had become gentile.

30. A translation of this passage appears in Appendix B. Bread and alcohol as the body and blood of Osiris were prescribed as sacramental food in the Egyptian *Book of the Dead*, and the custom survived three thousand years later when the author of *Mark* attributed such a meal to Jesus. Since J wrote a good thousand years after the oldest extant manuscript of *Book of the Dead*, it is a reasonable assumption that a priest offering bread and wine was being sacramental.

years, ever since he/she first made the terrifying discovery of the inevitability of death.[31] It was that dreadful certainty that led him to create in his mind an annulment of death, in the form of either an eternal existence in a metaphysical afterlife, or the reincarnation of one's essential being in a new body. Only the former alternative gave rise to god-eating. Warriors ate their conquered enemies in order to absorb their strength. By eating an immortal, human too could gain immortality. However, since immortality was a new concept, before humankind could gain eternal life by ingestion it had first to create the immortal gods.

Gods live forever. The sun, moon, earth and planets, which had been old when the tribe's oldest member's grandmother had been alive, observably lived for ever. Logically they must be gods. But knowing that there were immortal gods was not enough. Some way had to be found for the gods momentarily to surrender a portion of their immortality in order to confer it on their worshippers. Two observable phenomena gave the clue as to how this might be accomplished. The more obvious was the monthly death of the old moon and rebirth of the new moon. The second was the annual cycle of summer and winter.

Clearly, the Mother provided the corn. Just as clearly, winter had to be the time when she could not give life to her soil because she was dead herself. Since, therefore, death as the price of life had already been paid by the Mother, it followed that when she rose from the dead with the greening of spring she would likewise raise from the dead the immortal shades of all who had ingested her immortality by eating her flesh and drinking her blood. Thus was born the concept of the divine 'saviour,' the everliving, eternal, indestructible, immortal, undying goddess who died, and who by that absurd self-contradiction granted eternal life to mortal humans.

The existence of the seasons led directly to the concept of a fertility goddess who died in winter and was resurrected in spring. But it could not have done so if the idea of rebirth had not already been triggered by the observation of the monthly reborn moon. The moon was the second-brightest goddess in the skies, and every twenty-nine and a half days she could be seen to wane from a circular disk to a diminishing crescent that finally disappeared into the sun's furnace. But no sooner had the old moon died than the *new moon* miraculously reemerged and, by waxing steadily until she was again her complete self, demonstrated that, at least for a goddess,

---

31. To this day, an estimated one-sixth of the human race lack the moral courage to cope with the finality of death, and without the mind-deadening opiate of religion to delude themselves that they are going to live forever they would probably have to be institutionalised. This book cannot harm such persons, as they are incapable of believing it.

death was no more than a temporary inconvenience. If a goddess could die and be reborn, then it must not be impossible for humans to do likewise. It is small wonder that the monthly new moon was an occasion for rejoicing, and remains the basis of the Jewish and Muslim calendars to this day.

If the moon had not been seen to undergo death and rebirth at regular intervals, it is unlikely that the possibility of the sun's doing so would ever have been considered. But, given the lunar precedent, astrologer-priests did turn their eyes sunwards and did discover that Sol, too, reached his highest point in the skies on June 22 and spent the next six months dying. On December 22, the northern winter solstice, Sol reached his lowest point and, although still visible, by analogy with the moon was assumed to have died.

For three days, during which time no departure from Sol's minimum trajectory could be detected, he remained dead. But on the third day, December 25, the sun's path through the heavens was at last measurably higher than it had been during the three days of his death. December 25 was recognised as the birthday of the invincible sun. Since death and rebirth were the hallmarks of the divine saviour, the birthday of every saviour-god from Osiris and Dionysos to Mithra and Jesus was celebrated on December 25. But male saviour-gods who were also sun-personifications were a late invention. The earliest saviours were moon-deities, and female.

Persephone was the first saviour-goddess. At least, that was her name in Greece. To the Babylonians she was Ishtar, and by the time that name reached western Europe it had been modified into *Easter*. Persephone was part of the moon-trinity whose tripartite existence explained the recurrence of summer and winter. Demeter, the corn-goddess who was Mother of all that grew on earth, gave birth to Persephone. Since Demeter *was* Persephone, the Mother ceased to exist at the moment of the Daughter's birth. The virgin Persephone reigned for a season, then entered the underworld as Hekate, personified death. While she was underground the upper earth lacked a fertility goddess, and nothing grew. In the spring Hekate returned to earth as Mother Demeter. Demeter gave birth to Persephone, and the yearly cycle started over again.

Persephone's story was changed many times before it reached the form that modern readers have probably heard. The first significant change was the abolition of transformations. Demeter and Persephone became separate persons, with the consequence that Persephone alone died, descended into Tartaros where she reigned under her own name instead of becoming Hekate, and rose from the dead at the end of winter. Her mother Demeter, pining for her daughter, refused to allow anything to grow during the months that Persephone was in the underworld.

With Persephone's annual defeat of death, the permanence of death was conquered for all humanity. By taking upon herself the burden of dying, Persephone thus became the saviour of all who would accept her gift of eternal life by eating the fig or pomegranate that was her very flesh. Since the goddess was basically a vulva, and the fig and pomegranate, when allowed to ripen fully and split open on one side, bore a remarkable resemblance to the human vulva, the choice of such fruit as the Mother's sacramental body, the fruit of the tree of life, was a logical one.

It was in that form that Persephone's death, resurrection, and bestowing of immortality on her worshippers were reenacted annually when salvation mythology was first instituted at the Greek city of Eleusis. Later, when the male role in breeding became known, the sacramental pomegranate was discarded and the goddess's voluntary death was emulated by a sacred king, whose corpse was then boiled and eaten in its place, not as a mortal body but as the transubstantiated Body of Goddess.

The ritual changed again c. 800 BCE, at which time the sacred king was replaced by a doll made of living corn. After a ritual execution, the doll was buried for three days. When it was dug up and found to have sprouted shoots, the joyful news was proclaimed of the saviour's resurrection. All future saviours were likewise resurrected on the third day.

Outside of Eleusis, Persephone's role was degraded to one more acceptable to a male-dominated world at a much earlier date. Instead of dying that humankind might live, she was carried off and raped by the god Hades, who alone was lord of the underworld. By sharing with her ravisher six pomegranate seeds, sexual symbols that represented her acknowledgement that recreation with a male was indispensable to her, she committed herself to spend six months of every year with him in his underground demesne. The permanence of the summer/winter cycle was thereby guaranteed.

The salvation aspect of Persephone's death and resurrection was taken from her and given to male gods, of whom the earliest was the Egyptian Osiris c. 3000 BCE and the most recent was the posthumously-deified Jesus. Thus men, who had already decreed that the supreme ruler of the heavens must be male, now declared that the resurrected saviour without whose sacrifice the crops would not grow and humans would not attain immortality, must also be male. Apart from Jesus, whose worship will outlast the publication of this book by 150-200 years (see the differential equation on page 371), saviour-gods' resurrection festivals were popular from the days of the sacred kings until the victory of totalitarian Christianity. An annual procession celebrating the third-day resurrection of the Syrian virgin-born resurrected-saviour-god Adonis was held at Antioch until its suppression by a Christian Emperor in the late fourth century CE.[32]

---

32. A.P. Davies, *The First Christian*, p. 184.

The final step in the degradation of women was not taken until perhaps two thousand years after their reduction to slave status as men's 'wives' following the Big Discovery. Not content with denying women their ancient role in Creation and Salvation, the phallusocracy now came up with the myth that male gods had created a perfect world which women had subsequently rendered imperfect by their culpable inadequacy. In Greek godmythology the first woman was Pandora, whom Zeus gave to Prometheus to be his wife as a punishment (???) for giving man fire. Pandora was endowed with a sealed box and warned never to open it.[33] She disobeyed Zeus's admonition, and out of her box leaped disease, famine and all of the other evils with which Man has since been punished for Woman's crime.

In the Semitic version of the same myth, the humanised goddess Eve first yielded to a serpent-goddess's invitation to worship her, in defiance of the ruling male god's instruction to worship him alone, then corrupted the man she had been created to serve.[34] That only a chronic misogynist could have composed such a fable is obvious enough. That only a misogynic culture could believe it should be no less obvious.

Salvation mythology (with a female saviour) existed for millennia before the Big Discovery, and even after Persephone's supersedure by male saviours it did not immediately acquire the status of the mind-crippling tyranny that it was later to become. What made that development possible was the invention of a concept that, like adultery and bastardy, was a logical consequence of the male revolution: SIN. *Sin* was the Babylonian moon-goddess. Following the invention of male gods, everything that the male-liberationists wished to abolish as female-oriented was categorised as sacred to Sin and therefore hateful to Shamash, or Zeus, or Yahweh.[35] How long it took the primitive god-pushers to realise the tremendous value of *sin* as a means of securing their grip on the minds of entire populations is uncertain; but within a few centuries a priestly caste had arisen that recognised the enormous degree to which its power depended on convincing the masses that they were all congenital sinners. Since only a small percentage of the population

---

33. The sexual symbolism here should need no explanation.

34. The transformation of the serpent-goddess into the male Satan will be detailed in chapter 13.

35. The English word *sin* and the Babylonian concept, 'sacred to Sin,' are not etymologically connected. They are, however, identical in meaning, and that is the point of the paragraph.

The contention that Sin was ever female is disputed by many scholars, and the sources that agree with my conclusion, such as Robert Graves's *The White Goddess* (Vintage ppb., NY, p. 398) are at best questionable. However, since the moon was deified millennia before there were ever male gods, at a time when the correlation between the monthly lunar cycle and menstruation was central to theological speculations, the absence of any myth about Sin taking over the moon by conquering a female predecessor strongly implies that his predecessor was in fact himself as a female.

would ever commit such genuine immorality as killing or stealing, it was to the priesthood's advantage to invent new sins so self-evidently *not* immoral that the masses *would* commit them—and then seek out a priest to perform a rite of propitiation.[36] The solution was to impose such severe and absurd restrictions on who could engage in sexual recreation, and on where, when, how and with whom such recreation could be shared, that all but the most chronic masochists (Buddhist monks, Christian nuns) would refuse to comply. Those who did comply were even more effectively enslaved than those who disobeyed and then sought forgiveness, for the compliers then needed constant reinforcement of the belief that their unnatural joy-rejection was pleasing to the tribal god; and that reinforcement could only come from a priest.

The result was a population conditioned to believe that *sin* was inevitable for all but the most masochistic 'saints,' and that participation in a priest-led ritual was the sinner's only means of buying salvation. The more guilty a believer could be made to feel for his moments of rationality when he broke irrational taboos, the more absolute and tyrannical became the power of the priest. There is some suspicion that the current Head Christian's affirmation of taboos calculated to overpopulate the human race to the point of starvation/extinction, taboos that he knows will not be observed by the sane majority, is simply a continuation of the priestly practice of keeping the masses guilt-ridden in order to maintain personal power.

One further factor has often been suggested as contributing to human-kind's creation of gods, although one would need to take an extremely pessimistic view of the human race in order to take it seriously. More than one apologist for god-mythology has argued that, 'If God did not exist, Man would have to invent him' (as of course he did). That argument tacitly acknowledges that the god-addict subjugates himself to a superior life form in the sky in order to be too incompetent to accept the responsibility for his own situation. Perhaps worshippers do have such an inadequacy—now. But the argument also presupposes that the inadequacy is innate, and that God-the-slavemaster was created by persons already possessed of a slave mentality.

Such reasoning is not merely abhorrent; it is unnecessary. To an optimist, it seems more likely that, just as Uncle Toms only developed slave men-talities as a consequence of being slaves, so compulsive god-slaves could

---

36. To this day, the overwhelming majority of god-worshippers participate in the victim-less joysharing they have been conditioned to think of as 'adultery,' 'fornication' and 'perversion.' Yet those same persons would never commit the truly immoral acts of killing or stealing, as they would surely do if they were 'weak' and unable to 'resist the temptation.' The explanation is that, in the rational part of their minds that religious hypnosis cannot reach, they are still aware that an action that does not hurt somebody is *not* a sin.

only have become what they are in a world in which Ol' Massa in the sky was already a part of their conditioned thought processes. Humans did not create gods because they needed the degradation of mental enslavement; they developed the slave mentality as a consequence of their earlier creation of omnipotent gods.[37]

Nonetheless, a slave mentality once acquired is not easily repudiated. Modern believers in such contrary-to-fact nonsense as astrology, spiritualism, Bermuda Triangles, magical burial shrouds, past-life fantasies, near-death dreams, water witching, psychics, prophecy, palmistry and ancient astronauts, differ very little from god-addicts in their need to subjugate themselves to some 'higher power' to which their own intellectual impotence can be attributed. Typical of the new nonsense is the religion-without-gods of UFOlogy.

Since 1947 CE the need to believe in higher life forms has led many tens of thousands of persons all over the world to misidentify weather balloons, airplanes, clouds, the planet Venus, helicopters, and a dozen other mundane objects that cannot immediately be identified with certainty, as spacecraft manned by superior beings from Alpha Centauri and beyond. Just as god-worshippers are able to believe simultaneously that the earth is four billion years old but that the chief Christian god nonetheless created it six thousand years ago, so UFO addicts are able to believe that the speed of light is an insurmountable absolute, but that nonetheless flying sorcerers from fifty light-years away are able to flit back and forth between earth and their home planet as easily as an airline pilot flits back and forth between London and New York. It is no coincidence that believers in metaphysical superior beings that intervene in human affairs are more likely also to believe in physical superior beings that are secretly visiting earth.[38]

God-mythology has never stopped evolving. In the nineteenth century CE the mentally-disturbed Mary Baker Eddy based her 'Christian Science' on the dogma that the human body does not physically exist and can therefore never be afflicted with illness. Christian Science (the name is a self-contradiction) became a problem in a Japanese prison camp near Singapore during World War II, when its missionaries persuaded many prisoners to refuse

---

37. A similar effect was visible in the worst years of communist rule in eastern Europe, when the oppressed masses dared not even *think* that Big Brother was ungood, lest word of that thoughtcrime got back to the secret police and the result was permanent transition to unperson status. In 1949 George Orwell used the analogy of communism to describe the horrors of contemporary England under totalitarian Christianity, and the slave mentality of the Anglican masses, in a novel that he wanted to call *1949* but which his publisher forced him to rename *1984* to disguise it as a prophecy of the future.

38. For a rebuttal of the allegation that misidentified aerial objects are extraterrestrial artifacts, see Philip J. Klass, *UFOs Explained*, NY, 1975; and Robert Sheaffer, *The UFO Verdict: Examining the Evidence*, Buffalo, 1986. For more on the connection between religion and the paranormal, see Paul Kurtz, *The Transcendental Temptation*, Buffalo, 1986.

medical treatment. However, when the last convert died of a curable ailment, the problem died with him.[39] And whereas the Christian Science church has for more than a century been hailing Mary Baker Eddy as a mere mortal, it recently accepted a $90 million bribe to publish and promote a book by Bliss Knapp acclaiming Mrs Eddy a goddess.

Ellen White,[40] the equally irrational humbug who founded the Seventh Day Adventist sect, published a Revelation from the god created in her own image, to the effect that masturbation causes its practitioners to become cripples and imbeciles. Medical practitioners tend to disagree. More recently, George Baker, 'Father Divine,' founded a mythology that banned all sexual intercourse, and declared that he, Baker, was the universe's One God. He has since died.

New combinations of mythological elements can, obviously, still produce creeds that are not identical with any earlier cult. A century ago a semiliterate peasant boy named Joseph Smith, finding the manuscript of an unpublished historical novel, was able to pretend that it was nonfiction and had been dictated to him by an 'angel' named Moroni, and founded a new mythology that survives to this day.[41] The elements of even the newest mythology, however, invariably date back to the religions of the ancients. With the development of the son-of-god cults of the mushroom-eaters and the saviour-god cults of the dozen or more male Persephones, every aspect of modern god-mythology was in existence except one. Although the original Persephone myth implied an afterlife, and the Egyptians added a Judgement that allowed only taboo-observers to live forever, and the Persian Zarathustra concocted a Purgatory in which sinners were cleansed by fire, not until it was invented by King Jesus two thousand years ago did any mythology come up with the everlasting torture of the Christian Hell.

---

39. Peter Reveen, *The Superconscious World*, Montreal, 1987, pp. 38-41.

40. For several years, the Seventh Day Adventist church tried to conceal and cover up the discovery that Ellen White, like Joseph Smith, was a plagiarist whose pretended divine revelations were in fact plagiarised from earlier writers. See W.T. Rea, *The White Lie*, NY, 1982.

41. The novel was written by Solomon Spaulding, who died in 1816. In 1977 handwriting experts established that twelve pages of Smith's manuscript were in Spaulding's handwriting. Smith also wrote an imaginative fiction called *The Book of Abraham*, which he claimed to be a translation of Egyptian papyri in his possession. In fact the discovery of the Rosetta Stone and the consequent true decipherment of hieroglyphics showed that the pages of papyrus (some of them upside-down) were funerary scrolls unrelated to Smith's pretended translation. And he took the bait, publishing a pretended translation, when his opponents forged pseudo-hieroglyphs on the 'Kinderhook plates' for the purpose of discrediting him. This information has been known to the Mormon hierarchy for a century, but even into the 1980s, they were still actively plotting to cover it up. See Persuitte's *Joseph Smith and the Origins of the Book of Mormon*.

Two

Creation and Sin:
The God Who Invented Death

The atoms of clay are not at all the kind that are common in living tissue. If the description had been of a man being formed of coal dust and water, it would have been more impressive.

Isaac Asimov, *In the Beginning*.

In the beginning there was Chaos (*Tiamat, Tehowm, Khaos*). Chaos, a disorderly goddess, encompassed a mixed-up universe of sea and sky hopelessly intermingled. Chaos gave birth to the first god, who promptly cut her in two and placed the skies above and the sea below. Only then, with a male god in charge, could there be any order or progress.

That, more or less, was the archetypal creation story triggered by the Big Discovery. It is found in the mythology of the Greeks, the Sumerians, the Akkadians, the Phoenicians and the Jews.

Chaos's name in Old Babylonian (Akkadian) was Tiamat. The Hebrew name of the same goddess was Tehowm. Tiamat's son Marduk was from the start pictured as being humanoid. Tiamat, however, continued to be pictured in the common sea-goddess form of a snake. Marduk's victory when he sliced Tiamat in two and assumed the rule of a now orderly world was described in the Babylonian creation epic.

The Jewish retelling of the Marduk creation myth was, in the fifth century BCE, inserted at the front of what is now the book called *Genesis*. As the

Priestly author told it: In the beginning the land was Tehowm. The gods divided the waters above the dome of the skies (Tehowm's upper body) from the waters under the dome (her lower body), just as Marduk had done in the Babylonian version that was the biblical author's source.

The Priestly author who wrote the *Genesis* creation myth, more than a thousand years after the Babylonian version, was a Jewish priest of the educated Levite caste who was thoroughly familiar with the myths of his tribe's neighbors. That he consciously adapted Babylonian tales for his own purpose is not in doubt, since his six-day creation paralleled the six-stage creation invented by Zarathustra, while the order of his creation followed exactly the order in which Marduk created everything in the Jewish author's Babylonian source.[1]

Marduk outranked his mother Tiamat, and Elohiym outranked his mother Tehowm. The comparative status of god and goddess does not, however, constitute proof that when the myths were composed any serious upheaval in the female-supremicist society had already occurred. Such a system could be envisioned by men long before it was imposed on women. The emergence, however, of a story that a goddess was forcibly deposed by a god who then took her place, is much more significant. Just as the morality and ethics of a god constitute an accurate measure of the morality and ethics of the worshippers who created him, so tales of wars and revolutions among the immortals convey to the historian a reasonably precise picture of the social upheavals on which the myths would have been based.

The paramount god overthrew the paramount goddess: Men overthrew women. The Queen of the heavens gave way to the King of the heavens: Queens on earth gave way to kings. The male revolution, although accomplished over a long period with a minimum of violence, was indeed a revolution.

Men gained political power. But power that was not hereditary was meaningless. Just as mothers had always been able to identify their daughters, now fathers wanted to be able to identify their sons. It was for this reason that men imposed upon women a logical extension of the private property concept, the chattel-slavery known as marriage. And with marriage came the first sexual taboo: You're not to commit adultery.

Adultery was a crime against property. A woman, owned by one man, who allowed herself to be impregnated by another, thereby robbed her husband's natural heir of the inheritance that could conceivably have been usurped by her lover's 'bastard'[2] (another new concept). Had the discovery

---

1. See the Babylonian 'Creation Epic' in J.B. Pritchard's *Ancient Near Eastern Texts Relating to the Old Testament.*

2. The original *bastard* concept seems to have been 'child of many fathers.' Thus the child of a married woman who had ever taken another lover was automatically a bastard; whereas the child of a young girl still living in her father's house, provided she had only ever had one lover, was not.

that sexual recreation causes pregnancy been coupled with the realisation that births can be positively traced to those couplings that occurred roughly nine months earlier, the adultery taboo would never have been so severe. As it was, the taboo was based on the assumption that a woman's child had been jointly fathered by all of her previous lovers, regardless of whether she had coupled with them five months before the birth or twenty years.[3]

Since adultery was a crime against the adulteress's husband, an attempt to rob him of his right to pass on his property to his lawfully conceived sons, it followed that an act of recreation involving an unmarried woman did not constitute adultery. Even a sacred king, whose priestess wife far outranked him, was free to recreate with whom he would, while demanding semi-fidelity (the adultery taboo was suspended during fertility festivals) from his queen. The generalisation of adultery to include recreation between married men and unmarried women did not occur until after Siddhartha Gautama's invention of the myth that abstinence from recreation could somehow be virtuous in itself.

Later sexual taboos, such as incest, homosexuality and priestess-tupping, came about for reasons that will be explained in later chapters. Taboos came into existence at approximately the following times:

stealing (i.e., from one's own tribe) . . . . .c. 10,000 BCE
murder (i.e., killing within the tribe) . . . . .after 10,000 BCE
adultery (i.e., generating a bastard) . . . . .3500 BCE
cannibalism (in Egypt; much later elsewhere) . . . . .2500 BCE
premarital recreation for women
   (in Babylon; later elsewhere) . . . . .2500 BCE
incest (in Greece; much later elsewhere) . . . . .2000 BCE
human sacrifice (in Greece; much later elsewhere) . . . . .1300 BCE
male homosexuality (by Zarathustra; Judah 600 BCE) . . . . . .650 BCE

---

3. While the 'critical mass' explanation of pregnancy was the most widespread, there were others: (a) Societies that instinctively recognised that children have a single father nonetheless accepted 'critical mass' and believed that a baby could only grow from considerably more sperm than could be intromitted in a single sexual encounter. That belief led to the myth that Zeus needed to pour his sperm into Alkmene for thirty-six hours to produce Herakles. (b) Some sperm was incompatible, and, instead of combining, remained separate to produce twins. This was particularly true when a god seduced a married woman, causing her to produce one mortal and one immortal twin. Until quite recently, some cultures viewed the birth of twins as proof of adultery. (c) Just as a field in which nothing but corn had been planted for twenty years could still produce weeds grown from seed that had lain dormant for a generation, so could a non-virgin bride's first child have been fathered by any lover she had taken since infancy.

Not until the discovery of the ovum in the nineteenth century was the analogy between plant seed (Greek: *spermos*) and human seed recognised as less than perfect, and children acknowledged to have as close a biological relationship to their mothers as to their fathers.

masturbation (by Zarathustra) . . . . .650 BCE
celibacy (by Zarathustra, to encourage breeding) . . . . .650 BCE
zoophilia (*Deuteronomy*) . . . . .621 BCE
infant sacrifice (*Deuteronomy*) . . . . .621 BCE
intra-tribal slavery (*Leviticus*) . . . . .600 BCE
all sexual recreation (by Gautama) . . . . .550 BCE
private property (by Gautama) . . . . .550 BCE
nakedness . . . . .434 BCE
fornication (i.e., tupping a goddess's nun) . . . . .434 BCE
blasphemy (i.e., pronouncing Yahweh's name) . . . .*c.* 250 BCE
killing a foreigner (by Essene Righteous Rabbi) . . . . .140 BCE
extramarital sexual recreation for men . . . . .Roman times
homosexuality for women . . . . .Christian times
profanity (god-related expletive) . . . . .Christian times
premarital sexual recreation for men . . . . .Christian times
killing of non-Christians . . . . .late Christian times
abortion (USA 1830; RC church 1869) . . . . .late Christian times
slavery (England 1791; USA 1865) . . . . .late Christian times
birth control . . . . .late Christian times

Perhaps the strangest and least explainable of the above taboos, the only sexual taboo invented neither to prevent nor encourage pregnancy, was the social ban on recreating in public. No such ban existed in *c.* 920 BCE when the Yahwist had Isaac tup his wife Rebekah in full view of King Abiymolokh of Gerar (GEN. 26:8). Then in the fifth century BCE Herodotos reported that all of the tribes of India still followed the ancient practice of copulating openly *like cattle* (HIST. 3:101). Clearly Herodotos's own society had adopted a behind-closed-doors policy toward sexual recreation, or he would not have deemed the behaviour of the Indians worth recording. And in 1492 CE, Columbus was startled to discover that the Caribs of Hispaniola likewise did not regard sexual recreation as an activity of questionable legitimacy that must only be performed out of view of casual observers.[4]

The origin of the taboo can only be guessed. Clearly it was not an extension of a nakedness taboo, for no nakedness taboo reached Greece until long after Herodotos's time. Since the masses tend to follow the prac-

---

4. A Greek myth told of how Zeus transformed himself into the likeness of Amphitryon to seduce Herakles's mother. Geoffrey of Monmouth had Merlin transform Uther Pendragon into the likeness of her husband in order to seduce Arthur's mother. And the *Toldot Yeshu* told of how Jesus' mother was seduced when Pandera climbed into her bed and posed as her husband. All three stories appear to reflect cultures in which sexual recreation could only be performed, not merely behind closed doors, but also 'in bed with the lights out.'

tices of their leaders, it may be that aging autocrats spread the word that they preferred to recreate in private rather than acknowledge that they were impotent.

It was the abolition of infant sacrifice that led to the imposition of cradle-to-marriage joy-deprivation on half of the human race. Previously women had grown up copulating freely throughout childhood with brothers and cousins and neighbours. At the age of eleven or twelve those that had not been sold to husbands would take adult lovers, most commonly their fathers, and recreate diligently until such time as they could demonstrate their fertility by becoming pregnant. Women who, although nubile, had never produced a live infant and were therefore bad breeding risks, were stigmatised by the pejorative label, *virgin*.

Once a woman had given birth, an event that often did not occur until the age of fifteen or sixteen, her chances of being purchased as a wife increased significantly. Men wanted good breeders, and a woman who had demonstrated not only fertility but also the ability to survive childbirth could expect a wide range of suitors, all of whom would share her favours until such time as her father accepted the highest bid.[5] The first child of the marriage, regardless of how many years might have elapsed before its birth, being of multiple paternity would be sacrificed to Molokh, or Baal, or Yahweh, or Allah, or whichever other god had the local baby-burning concession. Following the birth and sacrifice, the wife would observe an adultery taboo. All future children could then be attributed with absolute certainty to her legal owner.[6]

Once a woman was sold to a husband, her status as a privately-owned breeder was stamped or sealed onto her body. Sometimes a coloured spot was tattooed in the middle of her forehead. More commonly, though, she was mutilated by having a hole pierced through her ear or nose, and a ring inserted into the hole. Among the Jews, ear-piercing was used to identify all persons, not merely wives, who had volunteered for permanent slave status (EXOD. 21:6; DEUT. 15:17). With the invention of divorce, the need for a previously-owned woman to display her new availability led to the transfer of the marriage ring from the ear, which needed to be pierced, to the finger, which did not.

In modern times, a woman's status as property was incorporated into her name, which changed with every change of ownership. Thus, when John Jones sold his daughter, Jill Jones, to be the wife of Jim Smith, she became Jill Smith. If she divorced Smith and married Bill Briggs, she became Jill Briggs. Similarly, when Ol' Massa Kernel sold his slave, Kissy Kernel, to

---

5. J.J. Bachofen, *Myth, Religion and Mother Right*, pp. 94-95.
6. The reference to King David's first child by Bathsheba dying (2 SAM. 12:15-18) almost certainly disguises the child's sacrifice as a dually-fathered bastard.

Ol' Massa Sanders, she became Kissy Sanders. Most American blacks bear the names of their ancestors' owners, and for this reason some have abandoned the slave-names and adopted African names.

Eventually all societies recognised that, with women dying in childbirth as a matter of course, live births were too rare to be wasted and infant sacrifice must be abolished. That meant that some new method had to be found whereby a man could be certain that the first child born to his new bride was of his own begetting. The solution was to deny unmarried girls the opportunity to bring to the marriage bed a womb that might already be carrying years-old seed that could produce a cuckoo's chick. Women were informed that henceforth they were to practise total premarital joy-rejection, and that any woman who failed to spill hymeneal blood onto the marriage blanket could expect to be promptly executed (DEUT. 22:13-21). Thus from sheer ignorance concerning the duration of pregnancy and the durability of sperm, men stole from women the basic human right to sexual fulfilment, a right that only the recent perfection of dependable contraception techniques has enabled them to reclaim. And the word *virgin*, formerly pejorative, now came to mean a woman capable of producing a legitimate heir, since no man had ever ejaculated into her womb sperm that would eventually mix with her husband's to produce a bastard.

The Greek creation myth did not end with the deposition of the Mother by her son the creator. Ouranos (Sky) wed his mother Gaia (Earth) and sired upon her the seven Titans and seven Titanesses that represented the sun, moon and five known planets. So important were the seven observable sky-gods, that societies so culturally and geographically separated as to make interdependence minimal all managed to invent a seven-day week, with each day being named after one of the sky-gods:

Germanic	Roman	Greek	Babylonian	Hebrew
Sun	Sol (Apollo)	Apollo	Shamash	Galgaliy-El
Moon	Luna (Diana)	Artemis	Sin	Ofaniy-El
Tiw	Mars	Ares	Nergal	Mikha-El
Woden	Mercury	Hermes	Nabu	Gabriy-El
Thor	Jupiter (Jove)	Zeus	Marduk	Rafa-El
Frig	Venus (Lucifer)	Aphrodite	Ishtar (Easter)	Khazaz-El (Satan)
Saturn	Saturn	Kronos	Ninib	Uwriy-El

Centuries later, when Jewish monolatry was evolving into monotheism, a *menorah*, a seven-stemmed candlestick, was introduced into Jewish ritual to illustrate that the seven planetary gods were simply aspects, or branches, of the paramount god Yahweh.[7] The Deuteronomist drove home the same point in 621 BCE when he had Yahweh explain that the reason for certain new taboos was, '*so that you might realise that I, Yahweh, am your gods*' (DEUT. 29:6).

Gaia also bore to Ouranos the Kyklopes, one-eyed volcano-gods that the earliest known inhabitants of Greece must have brought with them from an earlier volcanic homeland; the hundred-handed monster Briarias, god of the Kentaurs; and the giants, also featured in Jewish mythology (GEN. 6:4; 1 ENOCH 7). The youngest Titan, Kronos, originally a crow but later, by confusion with *khronos*, identified as Father Time, married his sister Rhea (Mother Nature), rebelled against Ouranos whom he overthrew and castrated, and established himself as the new King of gods and men, with Rhea as his queen. His reason for needing to castrate his father was that, under the prevailing system of ultimogeniture, his position as Ouranos's heir depended on Ouranos's never having another son.

Kronos and Rhea had three sons: Poseidon, Hades and Zeus; and three daughters: Hestia, Demeter and Hera. Fearful of suffering the same fate as his father, Kronos swallowed all of his children at birth. Only Zeus escaped, by a trick, was raised secretly in a cave in Crete, and eventually succeeded in freeing his siblings and leading them in a successful revolt against their Titan father. By mutual agreement, Zeus became King of sky and earth, Poseidon King of the seas, and Hades King of the underworld. There was an assumption by later Greeks that Zeus's paramountcy as King of gods and men dated from that time, but in all likelihood it did not. The earliest form of the myth would have made Zeus, Poseidon and Hades equals, in recognition of the equal partnership of their original worshippers, the Aiolians, Ionians and Akhaians. Only when the Indo-European invaders of Greece came to recognise their dependence on rain would they have granted the rain-god Zeus his absolute supremacy.

Having no written history of pre-Mycenaean Greece that we would recognise as such, we are obliged to deduce what happened by analysing the myths. This is not as difficult as it might sound, although of course we end up with the barest outline of the social and religious history of several centuries. The essential point is that the gods represent the worshippers who created them. The Titan-worshippers invaded Greece and subjugated the earlier phallus-worshippers. The logical rationale for their victory was that their god Kronos had overthrown the aborigines' god Ouranos. The same kind of rationale can be found in the Jewish bible, where every Jewish military victory was hailed as evidence of the invincibility of Yahweh. The only difference between the Greek myths and the surviving

---

7. Josephus, *Jewish War* 5:5:5; *Zechariah* 4:10 (see Appendix B).

Jewish myths is that, by the time the Jewish bible reached its present form, all references to Yahweh personally subduing other gods had been expunged.

The Olympians, Zeus and his siblings, aided by Briarias and the second-generation Titan Prometheus, conquered and replaced the Titans. The Olympians were the Hellenes, or Greeks. There is ample archaeological evidence that the first Greeks to enter Greece were the Ionians, whose god was Poseidon. So many northern-Greek myths involved Zeus that it seems certain that he was originally the god of the Aiolians. That would seem to indicate that Hades was the god of the Akhaians, the pre-Dorian conquerors of the Peloponnesos. The clue to the success of the Greek conquest can be found in the references to Zeus's elder-god allies. Briarias was the god of the Kentaurs, a tribe of mountain men who acquired their name from their practice of organising themselves into combat units of one hundred men. The Kentaurs allied themselves with the horse-riding Ionians, and helped the invaders steal the lands of the Kentaurs' ancient rivals, the Lapiths.

So thoroughly did the Kentaurs adapt to the Ionian practice of horse-riding (as did the native Americans after the horse was introduced by Cortez), that the myth arose of the *hippokentauros* (centaur), a creature half man, half horse.

That Prometheus also aided the Olympians shows that tribes of Titan-worshippers, recognising that invaders with bronze weapons and horses must inevitably triumph over stone-age pedestrians (as the iron-age Dorians later annihilated the bronze-age Akhaians), chose to be on the winning side.

Ouranos was accepted as the deposed father of his conqueror Kronos, and Kronos was accepted as the deposed father of his conqueror Zeus. No such concession to a defeated enemy is to be found in Jewish mythology. Like his Babylonian equivalent, Marduk, the Jewish Elohiym ('the gods') began his reign by dividing his mother Tehowm, the personified sea, in two. Just as the Olympians Artemis and Apollo *became* the sun and the moon following the defeat of the sun and moon Titans, so, to the author of a hymn to Elohiym, Elohiym's defeat of the sea-goddess made him the sea-god: O Elohiym. . . . *Deep calls to deep at the noise of your waterspouts. All your waves and billows are gone over me* (PS. 42:7).

Apart from his assimilation of his defeated mother, the Jewish-Israelite hybrid god Yahweh-Elohiym remained a one-god family with no other ancestors and no descendants. Yet Yahweh, like Zeus, conquered and took possession of lands that had once worshipped other gods. Why did Yahweh not accept the gods that he had defeated as his deposed forebears? The answer is not very flattering to Yahweh or to his worshippers.

Zeus conquered Kronos. That is to say, the Greeks conquered the Pelasgians. They defeated them. They subjugated them. They imposed the Greek religion on them. *But they did not exterminate them.* Even a cursory glance through the books of *Joshua* and *Judges* reveals why Yahweh did not need to reach any accommodation with the gods of Phoenicia. Whereas the Greeks had enslaved some defeated enemies, reduced others to serfdom, accepted the majority as not-quite-equal partners, and stressed the continuity of religion by making the victor the son of the vanquished, Yahuwshua and his successors eliminated the need for any kind of compromise by systematically massacring every man, woman and child unfortunate enough to be residing in any city the Jews wished to steal.

Four centuries after Yahuwshua's death, in a transparent attempt to justify the ancient sheikh's policy of genocide (the first instance of genocide in recorded history, although *homo sapiens*'s extermination of the Neanderthals must be similarly described), Yahweh's first official biographer concocted the pretence that Yahuwshua's victims unlawfully occupied *Lebensraum* Yahweh had long before promised to Yahuwshua's ancestor Abraham. That Yahuwshua's massacres did occur, despite the archaeological evidence that Jericho and other Phoenician cities were not subjected to destruction or change of ownership in the thirteenth century BCE (when Moses lived), becomes an acceptable conclusion once it is realised that Yahuwshua lived and fought in the early fourteenth century BCE, and was not (as claimed in the Towrah) the successor of the much-later hero, Moses, whose tribe, the Israelites, did not form an alliance with the Jews until a century after Yahuwshua's death.[8]

Zeus reigned supreme. But in time he, too, faced rebellion from as unlikely a source as his wife Hera. The rebellion was suppressed, and Zeus stretched Hera across the sky tied down with golden chains. He intended to leave her there forever, but was prevailed upon to restore her to her queenly position on condition that she took an unbreakable oath never again to challenge his supremacy.

A superficially different tale, but in fact based on near-identical events, told of the birth of Athena. Prior to wedding Hera, Zeus mated with the Titaness Metis ('Wisdom'). When she became pregnant, Zeus had second thoughts about propagating a new generation of Titans, and swallowed her whole. Later, having developed an unbearable headache, he had Hephaistos split his head open, and out leaped Metis's daughter, Athena, fully grown and fully armed. Athena never married, but remained a virgin like her sister Artemis.

The tale of Hera's abortive revolt did not, as might be supposed, mythologise a counterrevolution by women against the men who had staged the great takeover. As in all myths, the gods represented their worshippers, and Hera's worshippers were whole tribes, not just the women. Just as there

---

8. Evidence in support of this conclusion will be found in chapters 5 and 6.

were Confederate slaves who fought against Mr Lincoln's attempt to over-throw the only social structure they had ever known, so there were men to whom goddess-worship was the only true religion and who gladly joined the Mother's army against the usurping Zeus. Prior to the goddess-worshippers' rebellion, Hera would have been Zeus's mother. To appease the rebels following their defeat, she was allowed to remain Queen of the heavens—but only as Zeus's obedient consort. Since the idea of mother-son marriage had become unacceptable, she was transformed into Zeus's sister.

Similarly, the swallowing of Metis mythologised the Greeks' brutal suppression of a Titaness cult, only to find that it could not be kept down. To end a continuous state of rebellion by the adherents of the old religion, a watered-down Titaness was allowed to spring forth fully formed. As the daughter of Metis she was acceptable to the original inhabitants; but as the daughter of King Zeus she was clearly his subordinate and could only be worshipped as such.

In fact Athena's virginal state shows that she was much older than Zeus, and simply another form of the primeval Mother. The absence of a husband indicates that she had been worshipped since the days before the Big Discovery, when the concept *husband* did not exist. While most versions of the Mother (Rhea, Hera, Demeter, Aphrodite, Pandora, Eve) were subjected to husbands in the early days of patriarchy, in those places where the local Mother managed to retain her dominion long past the publication of Hesiod's *Theogony*, the opportunity to mate her was permanently lost and she became a perpetual spinster. However, by the time that had happened the ban on extramarital and premarital recreation for women had led to the belief that gods, too, obeyed human taboos. Consequently the eldest goddesses, who had not married because marriage did not exist, were transformed from eternal mothers into eternal virgins, as befitted their unmarried state.

The emergence of virgin goddesses, not surprisingly, led to the rationalisation that the masochism of perpetual virginity must be a good thing. The emergence of immortal virgin-mothers led to the belief that the definitively impossible was a good thing. Ancient goddesses who were both virgin and mother included Isis, mother of the saviour Horus; Semele, mother of the saviour Dionysos, magically sired by the King of Heaven; and Danaë, magically impregnated by Zeus in the form of a ray of light. The Christian earth-goddess Mary, a Queen of Heaven virtually identical with Isis, is worshipped as virgin and mother to this day.

While Zeus's subjugation of earlier patriarchal gods is not paralleled in the Judaeo-Christian bible, his constant struggle for supremacy with the earth-goddess is. Throughout the Hebrew testament the most vehement polemic was directed against the Phoenician fertility goddess Ashtaroth and against those Jews who showed any degree of toleration toward her worship. The pattern was set by what was originally the first myth in the Towrah (before the Redactor inserted P's six-day creation five hundred years later), the tale of the terrible fate that overtook the first man when he turned from Yahweh and put his faith in the goddess.

Tehowm was a gigantic sea serpent. She was not created by Yahweh because, as his mother, she had existed before him—as even the later prophets were well aware. Second Isayah,[9] for example, writing shortly after the fall of Babylon in the late sixth century BCE, referred to Yahweh's bisecting of the goddess in the words: *Wasn't it you who sliced Rahab, wounded the dragon?* (ISA. 51:9). He followed that up with a prophecy that Yahweh would eventually win final victory over the serpentine sea-mother, promising that *Yahweh is going to punish Leviathan, that twisted serpent. He's going to kill the dragon that's in the sea* (ISA. 27:1).[10]

That view of Leviathan's inevitable fate was not shared by the psalmist who saw the serpent-goddess, not as Yahweh's evil mother but as his created concubine: *There is the sea. There go the ships. There you made Leviathan to recreate with* (PS. 104:26).

To persons conditioned to believe that the authors of the Judaeo-Christian bible adhered to modern doctrines that in many cases originated centuries later, it may not be obvious from the *Isaiah* passages that pseudo-Isayah saw the serpent-goddess as Yahweh's predecessor rather than his creation. But as late as the seventh century BCE when the Priestly author wrote

---

9. Although *Isaiah* contains many interpolations, not all of which can be identified (e.g., 26:19 dates from the second century BCE, while the monotheistic passage, 45:21b, 21d, 22b, is equally late), it is mainly the work of four authors or groups of authors. Genuine Isayah wrote only chapters 1 to 12, around 700 BCE. Second Isayah can be precisely dated to 538/537 BCE, since only during the few months between King Kyros's order to rebuild Yahweh's Temple and his annulment of that order would any Jew have hailed him as Yahweh's Anointed. Second Isayah wrote chapters 13-14, 24-27, 34-35, and 40-55. Third Isayah wrote chapters 15-23, 28-33, and 36-39, in which he 'prophesied' most of the events of the sixth century BCE, shortly after that century's end. Since chapters 56-66 were composed toward the end of the fifth century BCE, their authors can perhaps be called Fourth Isayah, even though they appear to be a mishmash of interpolations by many individuals. This chapter breakdown is endorsed by the *New American Bible*, the *Jerusalem Bible*, and *James Moffat's Bible*, although naturally those documents date the prophecies to a time *before* they had come to pass.

10. Theologians maintain that *Leviathan*, *Rahab* and *Tehow(m)* are not simply interchangeable names for the same sea serpent who was Yahweh's mother. That was not the view held by Second Isayah. His reference to Yahweh slicing Rahab clearly identified Rahab as the primeval sea-goddess out of whose body Yahweh fashioned the land and the skies, the goddess called Tehow(m) by the Priestly author. Elsewhere he described Leviathan in such terms as to indicate that he was referring to the same Yahweh-versus-serpent battle of the Rahab scene. And he went on to talk of Leviathan using feminine forms (27:2-3). The beliefs of bible authors were very different from those of modern-day theologians.

the opening chapter of *Genesis*, the serpent still represented the primeval goddess whom Yahweh had overthrown, not the later underworld god with whom it was equated by the first-century-CE Jesus the Nazirite. As for Yahweh indulging in sexual recreation with a goddess: although goddess-hating prophets would have denied the possibility at a much earlier date, the idea would not have been unthinkable to the average Jew until Seleukid times. Yahweh made Leviathan to *recreate* with, and Isaac revealed that Rebekah was his wife by *recreating* with her. The same Hebrew verb described both relationships.

The first appearance of the serpent-goddess in Jewish mythology occurred in the fable of the temptation of Eve (*Khavah*), herself another manifestation of the primeval Mother. The author of that fable was a learned man, either a prophet or an officer of the king's civil service, perhaps both, who lived and wrote in Jerusalem at the court of David's grandson Rekhobowam. Because of his practice of referring to his god as YAHWEH from the beginning of his work (whereas another writer used the name ELOHIYM in all myths prior to the advent of Moses), he is generally referred to by biblical scholars as the Yahwist (German: *Jahwist*), usually abbreviated to J. The Yahwist wrote all of the pre-patriarchal myths of *Genesis* that now constitute chapters two to eleven, utilising and retelling tales that had originated in Sumer, Akkad, Syria, Phoenicia and Egypt. His serpent-in-Eden tale, while essentially Babylonian, contained elements that were recognisably Egyptian.

The *asherah*, or moon tree, or tree of life, or tree of knowledge, or pomegranate tree,[11] sometimes fig tree, was sacred to the fertility goddess. It acquired its name, *asherah*, 'source of life,' from the resemblance of its ripe fruit, noted earlier, to the ultimate Source of All Life, the Mother's sacred *asherah*, called in Latin *vulva* and *vagina*, and in Old and Middle English *cunt*.[12] Yahweh's great enemy, the goddess Ashtaroth, sometimes called Lilith,[13] was often depicted as the tree, with a tree-trunk, branches and crescent-moon head.[14] The juice of the *asherah* was variously called SOMA, NECTAR, and several lesser-known names. It was believed to be the drink of the gods and to confer immortality upon all who drank it. The fruit was regarded in Egypt and elsewhere as the flesh of the Mother,

---

11. 'Pomegranate' was used as a euphemism for vulva in *Song of Songs* 8:2.

12. Cunti, wife of Siva, was the Hindu equivalent of Ashtaroth or Easter, the personified vulva. A similar example of a goddess's name acquiring a purely mundane (and some would say vulgar) meaning in a world that no longer worshipped her, is the Germanic fertility goddess Frig. Another is Nuah/Nuwkhah/Anuket (Nukie).

13. Various myths identify Lilith as the first wife of Adam; as the wife of Cain; and as the wife of Jesus. Her name meant *night*.

14. Islam's *asherah*-worshipping origins can be seen in its retention of the crescent moon as the symbol of its now-masculine deity, and also in its continued veneration of the *Kaaba* at Mecca, a stone vulva-image once sacred to the Mother of the Gods, Kubela/Kybele.

so that to eat the fruit of knowledge from the tree of life was to consume the very *asherah* of the *Asherah*, and to become one with the goddess and share in her resurrection.

The Yahwist wrote his Adam-and-Eve fable around 920 BCE. There was no risk of the symbolism that he used being misunderstood. Solomon's policy of religious toleration, so hateful to Yahweh's self-styled spokesmen ('prophets'), had led to the establishment of *asherahs*, vulva-shaped shrines to the Mother,[15] throughout Israel and Judah (3 KGS. 11:4-8). As the fanatically partisan chronicler bemoaned: *They've built themselves phalluses and vulvas on every high mountain and under every evergreen tree, and there burned incense and slaved for godlets* (4 KGS. 17:10-12). The Yahwist's purpose in using the tree of knowledge imagery would have been clear even without the personal appearance of the goddess in her traditional serpent form.

Adam and Eve, according to the Yahwist, were the direct creations of Yahweh. They had never known any other god. The goddess tempted them to eat the vulva image that was her sacramental flesh, or in other words to worship her, and they did so. Instead of the eternal life that such salvation mythology was believed to bestow (the Jews of the period had no afterlife belief, and therefore no salvation concept), Yahweh's rebels found only death, discomfort, painful childbirth,[16] physical labour, and expulsion from Eden.[17] Not only were the primeval goddess-worshippers condemned to death for their backsliding in a male god's world; so were all of their descendants.

It is in the penalty inflicted by Yahweh for reviving the old religion that the function of the forbidden-fruit myth can be clearly detected. Like his spiritual predecessors of thirty thousand years earlier, and like scientists today, the Yahwist was a seeker of answers. Death existed. It was a fact of life. The Yahwist could understand why his creator-god would inflict death upon the gentiles who denied him his due worship; but he could

---

15. A stone vulva, inscribed, 'Daphne dedicates this to Zeus,' is pictured in A. Mondadori, ed., *Eros in Antiquity*, p. 27.

16. By an odd coincidence, the Yahwist's linking of the pain and dangers of childbirth to the acquisition of knowledge has a factual basis. Anthropologists agree that the development of the cerebral cortex, requiring an enlarged skull to enclose it, without adequate compensating enlargement of the pelvic opening, turned woman into the first animal likely to die in childbirth.

17. Carl Sagan, expanding on some ideas of Sigmund Freud and Stanislav Grof, suggests that the derivation of humankind's expulsion-from-paradise myth is a dim, distorted recollection of the universal traumatic experience of being born. (*Broca's Brain*, Ballantine edition 1980, pp. 354-365). Sagan's reasoning is not incompatible with the interpretation given here, since he is dealing with the unconscious thought processes of the human race, while this reconstruction deals with the conscious thought processes of one individual, the Yahwist. Birth memories certainly appear to contribute to near-death (flatline) hallucinations, although cultural religious conditioning is a more important factor.

not understand why Yahweh would kill his own tribe. The only conceivable answer was that in the far distant past some remote ancestor of Jew and gentile alike must have offended Yahweh beyond measure. To an intolerant, god-centred, chauvinistic sexist bigot like the Yahwist, there was no doubt as to what that offence must have been.

The most monstrous, unspeakable abomination imaginable was goddess-worship. Just as Solomon had been led by his wives into establishing the Mother's worship in his kingdom, so the first man must have been seduced by his wife into doing likewise. For such a heinous offence he had been sentenced to the only conceivable punishment: the permanent extinction of death.

The Yahwist's fable was written to explain death, and nothing but death. The belief that a tendency to 'sin' is a human trait inherited from Adam was invented centuries later, and not by Jews but by Christians. Nor did Yahweh's action in executing billions of innocents for their remote ancestors' crime, an action utterly incompatible with any modern concept of morality and justice, present any problems to a mythologian of the tenth century BCE. A felon's children were routinely executed to prevent one of them from becoming his father's avenger of blood. Executing children for the crimes of the parents, and vice versa, was at that time standard procedure and did not strike anybody as morally wrong. The Yahwist can hardly be blamed for crediting his god with the unevolved morality of his own age, or for failing to realise that three thousand years later the execution of a criminal's children would be viewed with abject horror.

Similarly, the Yahwist cannot be expected to have known that a later age would regard Yahweh's mother the goddess as nonexistent, and that the presence of her *asherah* in Eden would consequently have to be attributed to Yahweh's caprice. No doubt even in 920 BCE a parent who deliberately left the cookie jar open to tempt his children would not be deemed guiltless. But in the original myth Yahweh did no such thing. It is worth comparing the Yahwist's original myth with its Sumerian source and its modern Christian interpretation:

Sumerian original	The Yahwist's intended meaning	Christian interpretation
The first human, Adamuw, could have achieved immortality just by eating the fruit of the tree of life. But the gods were jealous and, for the purpose of reserving immortality to themselves, they informed Adamuw that eating the forbidden fruit would kill him. Adamuw believed their lie, refrained from eating the fruit, and so died.	Yahweh created a man to worship him, and a paradise in which the man was to live. But there was a problem. Yahweh's mother, the goddess, wanted Adam to worship her instead. Since the goddess had existed before him, Yahweh could not solve his problem by the simple expedient of refraining from creating her. She was a fact of life, and Yahweh had to allow for her existence. So he ordered Adam not to worship her. When Adam disobeyed, by eating the fruit that was the goddess's sacramental body, Yahweh inflicted upon him the standard tenth-century punishment for heinous crimes: death to the evildoer and all of his kin.	Yahweh created a paradise. Sin was impossible because nothing was forbidden. So that he could have something to ban, Yahweh unnecessarily forbade the acquisition of knowledge by forbidding the fruit of the tree that offered it, even though the forbidden tree seemed to be identical to the Tree of Life, whose fruit it would seem necessary to eat. Adam ate the fruit. For Adam's disobedience, Yahweh inflicted the cruel and unusual punishment now abolished by every civilised government in the world: death, not only for the lawbreaker, but also for all of his offspring. Yahweh also decreed that Adam's tendencies to evil were to be inherited by all future generations.

Having deduced an explanation for death that satisfied him, the Yahwist wrote it as fact; and future generations have accepted as literal truth that, although the human race has been living and dying for four million years and evolved from lower species that also lived and died, it was deprived of immortality because the first man and woman ate a pomegranate less than six thousand years ago. And modern religion teaches that a kind, loving, omnibenevolent father figure in the sky, to fulfil a death sentence he passed on the entire human race at that time in punishment for their ancestors' crime, is currently executing his beloved creations at the rate of two hundred thousand men, women, and children a day. What would he do to us if he did *not* love us? believers in such a doctrine must surely wonder.

Three

Cain and Abel:
The Sacrifice of the Sacred King

The slow death of the Moon's crescent as it merged with the rising sun, and the birth of a *new* Moon from the solar fires of sunset, may have given mankind the first push toward the notion of death and rebirth, which is central to so many religions.

Isaac Asimov, *The Tragedy of the Moon.*

With the Big Discovery of c. 3500 BCE came the male revolution. Men rebelled against the inferior social status that could no longer be theologically justified. In a few places they made significant gains quickly, but generally progress was slow. Women resisted change, and conceded only as much at any given moment as was necessary to avoid violent confrontation. It was because women were wise enough not to resist the compromises that gave men nominal equality while retaining real power in their own hands, that women were able to delay for two thousand years the complete reversal of roles that eventually saw men as absolute despots and women as chattels with no rights whatsoever.

From the time of the Big Discovery, women accepted the institution of marriage and its corollary, the adultery taboo. In so doing they gave up a certain amount of pleasure; but they also blunted the revolution, and that was adequate compensation. Even priestess-queens acquired designated husbands who took the title of *king*. Those kings were not, however, rulers, but merely expendable consorts who paid dearly for their single year (later great year)[1] as titular heads of state. These were the sacred kings.

Women retained the priesthood. The queen, not the king, was the Mother's representative on earth. The Mother now had a husband, King Zeus or some equivalent, to whom she was theoretically subject and to whom live-animal sacrifices were offered. But the Mother retained her dominion over fertility. The Easter sacrifice (to use the Mother's Germanic name) was still to the Queen of Heaven, not the King. Every spring the sacred king of the old year was ritually slaughtered by the man who would take his place in the priestess's bed.[2] His edible parts were consumed under the name of ambrosia—sacramentally, since by his sacrifice his body and blood were transubstantiated into those of the fertility-god (saviour) who was the Mother's son and lover—while his bones and other remains were ploughed into the cornfield to be resurrected in the next year's crop.

Sacred kings were volunteers, not conscripts. This can be deduced from the myth of Akhilleus (Achilles), who was forced to choose between a short and glorious life (as a sacred king) and a long and insignificant one (if he refused the role). Akhilleus's decision to kill the old king (Hektor in the *Iliad*, but no doubt Peleus in the original myth), knowing that his own death from the designated poisoned arrow must inevitably follow, would have been typical of ten thousand sacred kings who likewise preferred glory to long life.

That was the custom, already abandoned by the Jews long before the story was written down by the Yahwist, that was commemorated in the myth of Cain (*Kayin*) and Abel (*Habel*). Like the tale of Eve's *asherah*-eating, the first murder fable did not originate in the Yahwist's own mind, but was merely adapted by him from a tale told in Egypt two thousand years earlier. For the sake of continuity the Yahwist made his protagonists the sons of Adam and Eve, but they in fact represented the unknown sacred king (later emulated by Tydeus, Herakles, Priamos and Odysseus) who first chose not to die at the end of his designated reign, and the unknown captive who paid the price for that decision.

Cain killed the childless Abel, and then Eve bore a third son, Set, *to replace Habel whom Kayin killed* (GEN. 4:25). In the older Egyptian version

---

1. A great year was the time taken for the sun and moon to complete coinciding cycles. Originally set at eight lunar years, it was later recalculated to nineteen solar years. For more details on lunar years, solar years, and lunar-solar calendars, see chapter 1 of Isaac Asimov's *Of Time, Space, and Other Things*.

2. A comprehensible and highly readable account of sacred-king sacrifice, which gives the reader a clear understanding of why most sacred kings accepted their fates but a certain percentage did not, can be found in Mary Renault's excellent novel, *The King Must Die*.

it was Set who was the murderer. That Cain and Set were originally the same person (just as Aphrodite, Artemis and Athena were the same person) can be seen when we compare the Yahwist's genealogy of the descendants of Cain (GEN. 4) with the Priestly genealogies of the descendants of Set (GEN. 5, 10):

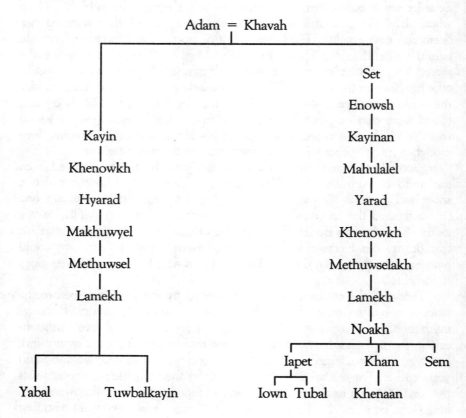

Except that a later copyist has transposed the names of Khenowkh and Makhuwyel/Mahulalel (variant spellings represent dates of composition 500 years apart), the six generations from Cain (Kayin/Kayinan) to Lamekh in the two genealogies were identical. But the Yahwist's Cainite pedigree listed as sons of Lamekh men who, in the Priestly genealogy, were Lamekh's great-grandsons. Clearly a genealogy once existed that showed Adam's eldest son to be Set, and Cain to be Set's grandson. Since, following the Egyptian pattern, the murderer and his victim had to be brothers, it follows that in the earliest Hebrew version, as in the Egyptian, the murderer was Set.

A tradition that the murderer was Cain and that Set was his younger brother must have existed in the Yahwist's day; otherwise J's removal of Cain from his place in the Set genealogy would be inexplicable. Just where J placed Noah (*Noakh*), we can only guess. He may have made Noah a descendant of Cain (but not a *Cainite*).[3] For while the Yahwist's genealogy from Adam and Cain to Tuwbalkayin survives, his version of the descendants of Set ends with Enowsh. The final Redactor's (R) expurgation of the Yahwist's Set genealogy, and his substitution of the same names that J had declared to be descendants of Cain, can probably be attributed to his desire to establish that Noah, the ancestor of Sem and Abraham, was not descended from a goddess-worshipper who practised human sacrifice.

It need hardly be stressed that neither J's nor R's genealogy has any validity. J's was composed to add continuity where none existed, while R's was nationalistic propaganda composed to turn tribal demigods into ancestors of the whole Jewish nation. The first character named in *Genesis* who was a real person from history was Abraham. Therefore the question of whether the nonexistent Cain was the nonexistent Set's brother or grandson has no reality. To the Yahwist the killer and his victim were Cain and Abel. To an earlier Jewish mythologian they were Set and Abel. And to the original Egyptian storyteller they were Set and Osiris. Set was the sacred king who first conceived the idea of saving his own life by sacrificing a substitute.

We have no valid account of the historical event behind the Cain-and-Abel myth. We can only attempt to reconstruct it from the fourth-hand retelling in *Genesis*; the Egyptian Osiris myth; a Druidic epic adapted into a nursery rhyme ('Who Killed Cock Robin?') by English-speaking Celts in late medieval times; and the odd relevant clue that can be gleaned from the mythology of ancient Greece. Of course, the reconstruction is likely to bear more resemblance to the last such sacrifice than the first, and will almost certainly contain elements from separate cultures that never appeared together in the same sacrifice anywhere in the world.

Set (Cain) became sacred king by killing his predecessor and marrying the dead man's widow, the moon-priestess Isis. He expected to service her for a year and be sacrificed in his turn. He was, as *Genesis* stated, a farmer. Only a culture dependent on planted crops ever saw the need to plough

---

3. The evidence here is conflicting. The Elohist, whose narrative contained neither a flood nor the Tower of Babylon, clearly equated Sumerians with Cainites (NUM. 24:21-22), and it seems unlikely that that equation arose only after J's time, or that J was not aware of it. Therefore J's avoidance of the term *Cainites* in connection with the builders of the Tower must have been deliberate, to avoid having Cainites alive when they should have all been drowned. So he obviously did not view Noah as a Cainite. Yet Noah appears as a descendant of *Kayinan*, who is identical with Cain, in the genealogy that R transferred from Cain to Set, implying that J had made Noah Cain's descendant. While a degree of doublethink would have been involved in making Noah Cain's descendant but not a Cainite, J does appear to have done just that.

a sacrificial victim into the earth to repay the Mother for the expected fruitful yield.

At some time prior to the spring festival at which he was doomed to die, Set captured a wandering shepherd and had him ritually adopted by the Mother (Eve), as Set himself had been adopted at the beginning of his term. That the chosen victim was a pastoralist indicates that Set belonged to a settled community that was sufficiently populous and organised to prey upon itinerant herdsmen without fear of reprisal.

The sacrificial victim had to be the sacred king. There had been spring sacrifices before there had been sacred kings, but by now the custom was too firmly entrenched to change. The sacred king was both the Mother's son and, through his marriage to the priestess who was her earthly incarnation, her lover. If he was not given to her in perpetuity at the end of his year of office, her wrath would know no bounds. Only by elaborate preparations could Set hope to fool the moon-goddess into believing that she had been sacrificed the sacred king.

On the full moon following the vernal equinox (Passover), Set resigned his throne and had his pastoralist captive, Osiris (Abel), crowned king. The new king was formally married to the priestess-queen. He was persuaded to consummate the union in the cornfield that would become his burying place, in full view of the orbiting goddess and the population of the village. By this means Set guaranteed that the goddess whom he feared, and the mob whom he feared even more, would accept that the victim was indeed the legitimate king. Osiris spent his last night in the sacred king's tent, wearing the sacred king's robes, tupping the sacred king's wife, and surrounded by the sacred king's bodyguard whose job it was to prevent his escape.

The following day Osiris was taken back to the cornfield dressed in the feathered robes of the sacred king's totem bird, the cock robin. Set was dressed in the sparrow-feathered headdress of Isis's priest. The various priestesses and villagers wore the costumes of the totem birds (formerly tribal gods) of the village's several clans. Perhaps the priestess recited a hymn of praise to the cock robin god, similar to the psalmist's hymn of praise to hawk-Yahweh: *He will cover you with his feathers, and keep you safe under his wings* (PS. 91:4).

Set (Cain) shot Osiris (Abel) with a bow and arrow. His blood spilled into the cornfield, feeding the goddess who had only yesterday received the offering of his sperm. Further to convince the Mother that a beloved king had been taken from them, the priestesses, still costumed as the birds of the air, fell to sighing and sobbing at the death of the cock robin.

Osiris's body, except for the inedible parts that were buried where he had fallen, was gathered into the waiting stewpots. The sacred body, now called ambrosia, was fed to the incoming king of the new year (Set), the priestess-queen (Isis), and perhaps as many as fifty lesser priestesses. By consuming the ambrosia, the body of the saviour, the communicants ensured that the goddess would resurrect them in the afterlife.

As soon as Osiris was dead, Set descended into a shallow grave that he had previously prepared. He would remain underground until the third day, the day on which the new king would be officially proclaimed, that there be no king above ground during the interregnum to reveal to the Mother that she had been duped.

Later sacred kings who followed Set's example and refused to die, most notably Eurystheus of Tiryns, used as their three-day graves man-sized clay pots that were buried up to the neck. Set, or Cain, or whatever the innovator's real name was, would have spent his forty hours in bare earth. And whereas Eurystheus, as a reigning king in a man-ruled world, conducted official business from his hole in the ground, Set, as the figurehead consort of a reigning priestess, would have had no such responsibilities.

While still underground Set shaved his head so that Osiris's shade would not recognise him and take vengeance. He also marked his forehead with the coloured spot that fertility nuns, priestesses who copulated with temple patrons as an act of worship, used to proclaim their holiness. Henceforth anybody who saw the 'mark of Cain' on his forehead would know at a glance that his life was sacred to the Mother and must not be taken out of season.[4] On the third day Set emerged from the grave to resume the throne that he had vacated to his pastoralist 'brother.' He would repeat the procedure with another captive in a year's time.

The next events had been so distorted by the Egyptians that the Yahwist rejected them as baseless mythology and excluded them from his Cain-and-Abel fable. However, the probable sequence can be postulated with reasonable plausibility.

In rising from the grave on the third day, Set assumed the name HORUS rather than retain a name that Osiris's shade might recognise. Since Horus had risen from the womb of Mother Earth, whose human incarnation was Isis, Horus came to be accepted as the son of Isis. Further, since Horus (under his previous name) had been Isis's husband, and Osiris had been Isis's husband, Horus became identified with Osiris. Since Isis's husband had died and Isis's husband had risen from the grave, the belief arose that Horus was Osiris risen from the dead. And since Horus had entered the Mother's womb only after the death of her husband Osiris, Horus came to be regarded as the son of a virgin mother. The myth of the female saviour who died in winter and rose again in the spring was well on the way to

---

4. The world's most unchanged mythology, Hinduism, continues to daub the king-killing castes the same way, even though the original meaning of the caste-marks has been forgotten.

being replaced by the myth of the male saviour who was sacrificed as an atonement for sin and rose again on the third day. Osiris was so regarded in Egypt as early as 3000 BCE.

Only in Egypt did the sacred-king myth retain the primitive form in which the sacrificed Osiris did not rise from the dead in his original form but was reborn as his virgin-wife's son Horus. In the Hebrew version, resurrection was dismissed as a foreign superstition. Instead, the sacred king killed his substitute and was cursed by Yahweh for so doing. In Greece, Horus's dual role as Isis's son and husband, as well as the slayer of her previous husband, evolved into the myth of Oidipous (Oedipus), the Theban sacred king, who killed his father and married his mother.

The Thrakian poet Orpheus, raised to divine status by Pythagoras but later reduced to a mere demigod by Apollonius, may have been responsible for the version that later became most popular. Thinking that the dead Osiris rather than the living Set had risen from the grave, Orpheus seems to have composed an epic poem in which Dionysos ('The god of Nysos'), the divine son of King Zeus and the virgin moon-goddess Semele, suffered death for the sins of the world and rose again to everlasting life, and a seat in Olympos, on the third day.

There were other variations of Orpheus's tale. In a compromise that was an amalgam of a Babylonian myth of the saviour-goddess's descent to the underworld and return to the upper earth, and the Egyptian equivalent with its male resurrected saviour, Dionysos died for the sins of the world and would have remained in Tartaros forever had his mother Semele not gone down to fetch him out. By classical times, it was Semele, demoted to mortal status, who died, and her divine son who braved Tartaros to rescue her.

Orpheus himself became the hero of another version. His beloved Euridike died, and he descended into Tartaros, charmed Hades into letting Euridike go on certain conditions, and ultimately failed to live up to those conditions.

From Thrakia, Orpheus's misinterpretation of a sacrifice to the Mother spread to Syria, where the risen Set was called Adonis. It was from the Adonis myth, which, except for the method of execution, was basically identical with the later Jesus myth (as an acknowledged fertility god, Adonis died by emasculation), that Christianity derived its core dogma. The same tale, with only the names changed, reached Babylonia, where the risen saviour was called Tammuz. Around 590 BCE, the Jewish prophet Ezekiel upbraided Jewish women guilty of *weeping for Tammuz* (EZEK. 8:14). Like the much-later Jesus, Tammuz was described as the only begotten son of the King and Queen of the Heavens, Ea and Davkina. He was, like other saviours, a sun-god (his name was a dialectal form of Shamash), and he wed his sister Ishtar, the moon. Jesus was eventually credited with the characteristics of both, being born on Tammuz-day, December 25, and resurrected on Ishtar/Easter day.

In Anatolia, the resurrected saviour was called Atthis. In Persia he was called Mithra, and the forces of evil that he overcame were portrayed as a bull. Believers absorbed Mithra's immortality and accepted his salvation by standing under a grid above which a bull was slaughtered, so that they were washed in the blood of the bull. Later a lamb was substituted for the bull. In China the risen saviour was Deng, and his virgin-mother was called Shinga-moo. And in Palestine the entire Adonis myth was posthumously attached to the executed rebel, Jesus the Nazirite.

Of the various heroes whose names survive in saviour-god myths, only Jesus was almost certainly a person from history; Osiris may well have been historical; and Tammuz (without his heavenly parents) could conceivably have been historical. Cain and Abel were not persons from history.

Four

Incest:
The Abolition of Endogenous Marriage

> The assertion that 'God created man in his own image,'
> is ticking away like a time bomb at the foundations of
> Christianity. As the hierarchy of the universe is slowly
> disclosed to us, we will have to face this chilling fact: If
> there are any gods whose chief concern is man, they cannot
> be very important gods.
>
> Arthur C. Clarke, *Profiles of the Future*

Sacred kingship gave way to royal kingship as sacrificial consorts became ruling monarchs. As kings became more secure, even the sacrifice of surrogates ceased. When this happened, the abolition was usually sanctified by being backdated to the time of a tribal demigod in the distant past. Among the Greeks, for example, the tale was invented that the sacrifice of Athamas had been prevented by Herakles on the ground that, 'Father Zeus detests human sacrifice.' Yet the much older myth of Herakles's madness reveals that Herakles was a typical sacred king who sacrificed child surrogates in order to extend his life and reign.

The Redactor pretended that the sacrifice of first-born males had been ended by sheikh Abraham who had lived more than one thousand years earlier (GEN. 22:11-16a). In fact, despite the Redactor's citing of such an authority as Abraham for the abolition of the practice, Jews were still sacrificing their babies to the Phoenician god Molokh at the time of the fall of Jerusalem in 586 BCE (JER. 32:35). And among the Israelites whose territories King David had annexed to his Jewish kingdom by promoting a mythical genealogy that gave Jews and Israelites common ancestors, infant sacrifice had been ordained by their dictator Moses (*Mosheh*) as one of his original ten commandments: *Yahweh ordered Mosheh, 'Sanctify* (i.e., sacrifice) *to me all of the firstborn, the first issue of every belly. It belongs to me'* (EXOD. 13:1-2).

In Egypt, sacred kingship and its sacrifices were dead by the onset of the dynastic age, centuries earlier than in Europe and western Asia.[1] Old kingdom Pharaohs were monarchs who ruled as well as reigned. Nonetheless, they were kings as husbands of the hereditary queen, not as sons of a hereditary king. It was the willingness of Egyptian men to recognise the legitimacy of female descent and accommodate themselves to it, and to make as few changes as possible in the social system that had existed under goddess-rule, that enabled them to usurp all real power within the space of three or four centuries. In those parts of the world where male-liberationists tried to stand the orderly practices of twenty-five thousand years on their heads in a single generation, the revolution was violently resisted and societies remained matriarchal much longer.

The first Pharaoh died and was succeeded by his son. Yet the rightful heir was not the king's son but the queen's daughter. The logically practical Egyptians solved the problem of instituting *de facto* patrilineal succession while maintaining *de jure* female inheritance, by the simple expedient of marrying the incoming Pharaoh to his heiress sister.

It is not certain at what point Pharaoh became the son-of-the-sun and god-on-earth. Since such titles were part of the sacred-king hoax, it may be that with the evolution of regnant kingship the old titles began to be taken seriously. Nobody could have believed that a randomly-chosen king-for-a-season was 'really' descended from the gods; but such a claim was rather more plausible from a ruling dynasty. In his biography of Alexander of Macedon, Arrian reported that, on the occasion of Alexander's visit to the Egyptian temple of Zeus/Amen, the god informed the Macedonian that he was indeed his begotten son, *or so Alexandros said when he came out.* Clearly Arrian had some reservations about the veracity of Alexander's claim—but it did not occur to him that such a claim was absurd. Gods did sire offspring on mortal women, and it was perfectly logical that such offspring should be kings. The claim made by the interpolator of *Matthew,* seventy years after the death of King Jesus, that his dead leader had been

---

1. Greek myths of thirteenth-century demigods reveal that Akhilleus, Agamemnon and Idomeneus were sacred kings who died at their appointed times; Odysseus was a sacred king who escaped the sacrifice once but later succumbed; and Herakles and Priamos were sacred kings who avoided their designated fate.

sired upon a mortal woman by the King of Heaven, could only have been taken seriously by a culture such as the Greek that did not regard god-mortal couplings as unprecedented.

The moment Pharaohs were recognised as descendants of the sun-god, brother-sister marriage would have had to be made compulsory even if Pharaoh had not needed an heiress-wife to justify his title. The idea of a god-on-earth marrying below his station was repugnant. Certainly some kinds of god-mortal couplings were necessary. Temple nuns, as brides of the god Osiris, were obliged to copulate with any man who paid the appropriate fee, accepting the worshipper as a surrogate for the invisible bridegroom. And Pharaoh's dignity demanded that he own the largest harem in Egypt, a virtual impossibility if he excluded women of less than royal descent. However, while Pharaoh was allowed a wide choice of concubines, for the role of Great Royal Wife and consort of a god, his sister, herself god-descended, was the only possible choice. Pharaohs married their sisters for three thousand years, with no noticeable reinforcement of recessive genes, until the Egyptian monarchy was abolished by Augustus Caesar in 30 BCE. If the last Egyptian monarch, Kleopatra VII, had any genetic imperfections, her lovers, Julius Caesar and Marcus Antonius, failed to notice them. She produced healthy children by both, and was herself the product of several generations of the kind of line breeding that, in horse racing, is used to produce the thoroughbred (see facing page).

Among the Jews, the only one of King David's alleged ancestors to marry his sister (apart from the mythical sons of Adam) was the nineteenth-century BCE demigod Abraham. Since the Israelite author whom historians call the Elohist took great pains to point out that Sarah was merely Abraham's half-sister, being the offspring of a different mother, we can be fairly certain that by the time the passage was written, c. 770 BCE, full brother-sister marriages had become taboo. Half-blood unions were not banned until the composition of *Deuteronomy* in 621 BCE.

In the early tenth century BCE, David's eldest son Amnown raped his half-sister Tamar, and was murdered by the girl's full-brother Abshalowm in consequence (2 SAM. 13). However, the crime for which Abshalowm took vengeance appears to have been, not the rape, but Amnown's refusal to atone for destroying the girl's market value by accepting her as his wife. It is of course possible that the treacherous Abshalowm seized upon the rape as a plausible excuse for eliminating a man who stood between himself and the crown, but nonetheless Abshalowm's action was pardoned by his father as justifiable in the circumstances. According to the chronicler, Tamar attempted to dissuade Amnown from his violent intent with the words, '*Ask the King, and he won't refuse to give* (marry) *me to you.*' Since the chronicler was not an eyewitness to the rape (which occurred long before his birth),

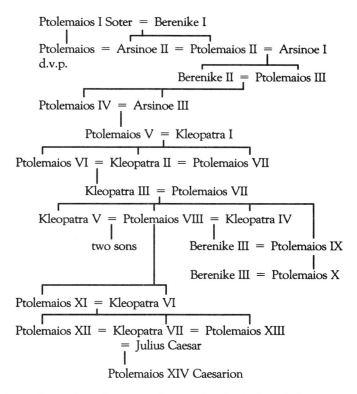

the quoted words can be taken to indicate what he believed that a virtuous woman must have said. If the author of *Samuel* could imagine David marrying his daughter to her half-brother, then we must conclude that the concept of incest did not yet include such a relationship.

Brother-sister marriages remained the norm for Aiolian Greeks long after they had become taboo among Akhaians and Ionians. The Aiolians seem to have abandoned the practice a little before 1400 BCE, not from any practical consideration but under pressure from neighbouring adherents of the new orthodoxy. To the Greeks, marrying sisters was the prerogative of the gods, a custom too *sacred* (i.e., taboo) to be imitated by mortals. Zeus's many wives had included his sisters, Demeter and Hera. The Titans had all married sisters. Deukalion (the Greek Noah) and his wife were children of the same goddess, Pandora, by brother Titans. Aphrodite never fully developed into a daughter of Zeus, but she was in a propinquitous sense the sister of her bed-fellows, Hephaistos, Hermes and Ares.

The more common marriage, both for Greeks and the Jewish patriarchs, was between uncle and niece or first cousins. The former was still popular among Jews in early Roman times, as is evidenced by three of King Herod's sons marrying nieces. The latter remained popular among European royalty until the present century. Uncle-niece marriages are currently banned by many mythologies, while first-cousin marriages are forbidden only for Roman Catholics.

So many Greeks from the Heroic period married close relatives that there is little point listing more than four or five. History set the pattern for mythology when Hades emulated his worshippers and married his niece Persephone. Closer to ground, the original concocted parents of Perseus, founder of Mycenae, were an uncle and niece, Proitos and Danaë. Since Perseus was in fact almost certainly a conquering foreigner, and the pedigree added posthumously to legitimise his usurpation by making him a descendant of Danaos, the evidence that uncle-niece marriages were prevalent and respectable is particularly strong. The inventors of Perseus's retroactive parentage would not have made him the product of a union anathematised by the gods. Perseus was later made the son of Zeus, who impregnated Danaë without compromising her virginity; but that amendment was made at a time when all Greek heroes had to be sons of gods. Once Paul of Tarsus had taken Jesus the Nazirite from the Jews and given him to the Greeks, it was inevitable that a Greek would eventually turn him into the son of a god.

Herakles's parents were first cousins, the parents of each being a son of Perseus and a daughter of Pelops. Agamemnon and his brother Menelaos married sisters, and Agamemnon's son then married Menelaos's daughter. Agamemnon's daughter married his sister Anaxibeia's son. Two of Atreus's three wives were his nieces. The story of Atreus was simply the fate of a sacred king rewritten to conform to the ideals of a later patristic age; but again this strengthens the view that, at the time the myth was reconstructed, Atreus was credited with the kind of marriages expected of an ancestor and demigod.

Atalanta was an Arkadian, a member of a tribe that after several centuries of continuous subjugation had not become integrated with the conquering Akhaians. She married her cousin Melanion (not Hippomenes, who was a northerner). Among the Aiolians of the north, Salmoneus's daughter married two of her uncles. Nestor of Pylos, a northerner by birth, married his niece. The sons of Aiolos, by which we can understand the earliest generations of Aiolians, married their sisters. That these genealogies were no more historical than those of the Judaeo-Christian bible is irrelevant. Mythmakers did not attribute to their heroes behaviour that was both unflattering and unhistorical, although it was bound to be one or the other. The marriage of so many heroes to their nieces and cousins can be taken as an accurate reflection of the social mores, if not of the fifteenth and fourteenth centuries BCE when the heroes lived, then certainly of the later age when the genealogies were composed.

The same absence of any concept of incest other than relations between parent and child can be found in the oldest parts of the Judaeo-Christian bible:

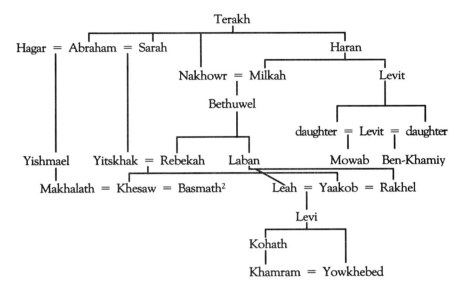

It will be noticed that Abraham married a half-sister; Nakhowr married a niece; Khamram married an aunt; Jacob (*Yaakob*) and Esau (*Khesaw*) married first cousins; and Isaac (*Yitskhak*) married a second cousin. The above genealogy includes only relationships specified in the Jewish bible, and does not include relationships that first materialised in the Talmud.

For example, the Talmud declared that Jacob's junior wives, Bilhah and Zilpah, despite being his senior wives' slaves, were also their sisters, daughters of Laban's concubines. To the Jews of the Talmudic period (200-500 CE), the possibility of a tribal patriarch having a gentile mother was unacceptable, so Bilhah and Zilpah were retroactively made descendants of Abraham's father to preserve the purity of the race. Such thinking today would be called *racism*.

For a similar reason, the patriarch Joseph's Egyptian wife Asnath (GEN. 41:45) was turned into his niece, the daughter of his sister Diynah. Since Joseph (*Yowsef*) was alleged to have married at the age of thirty (GEN.

---

2. *Genesis* 36:2-3 (P) named Basmath as Ishmael's daughter, and Esau's wife Khadah as the daughter of Eylown the Hittite. But in R's genealogies, it was Basmath who was identified as Eylon's daughter (GEN. 26:34), and Esau's wife Makhalath who was the daughter of Ishmael (GEN. 28:9).

41:46), and (the nonexistent) Diynah was his nearest sibling, the Talmud author explained Asnath's nubility by declaring that *Diynah was six years old when she gave birth to Asnath, whom she bore to Shekhem* (SOPHRIM ch. 21).

Levit sired Mowab and Ben-Khamiy, the eponymous ancestors of King David's enemies, the Mowabites and Ammonites (*Khamowniym*), on his own daughters. This story falls into a rather different category from the Towrah's other close-relative matings. David was a warrior king. His annexation of Mowab and Ammon can appropriately be compared with Mussolini's annexation of Ethiopia. His absorption of Israel, although begun as a military venture, had ultimately been accomplished by negotiation and sealed by a marriage between David and the Israelite King Saul's daughter. Consequently the genealogy that was composed in order to mollify the Israelites into accepting a Jewish king made the Jewish demigod Yahuwdah and the Israelite demigod Joseph brothers.

No such equality could be offered Mowab and Ammon. They had been brutally subjugated, and the kind of genealogy needed was one that would justify that subjugation. The Mowabites and Ammonites were therefore declared to have sprung from an unchaste relationship between Abraham's nephew and his own daughters. That the Yahwist, who composed the fable, viewed such a union as taboo is evident from the circumstance that the daughters needed to get their father drunk in order to accomplish their purpose. Anything that David did to the descendants of such a wicked mating could not be unjust. The Hasmonean priest-kings used the Yahwist's vicious fantasy as their justification when they completed the genocide of the Mowabites in the second century BCE.

Many societies escaped the incest taboo entirely, while others limited the concept, or at least limited enforcement, to the lower classes. Diogenes in the fourth century BCE praised the Persians for having no more incest laws than fowls, dogs or asses; while seven hundred years later the Emperor Julian could still ask: *What Hellene, for instance, ever tells us that a man ought to marry his sister or his daughter or his mother? Yet in Persia this is accounted virtuous.*[3]

Zarathustra favoured parent-child and brother-sister marriages, and did not question the propriety of his paramount god Ahura Mazda's mating with his daughter Vohu Manah. In the Emperor Commodus's time (180-192 CE), two out of three marriages in the Egyptian town of Arsino were between brother and sister.[4] Indeed, in Egyptian poetry the words for brother and sister also meant lover and beloved. And in Hebrew poetry it cannot

---

3. Julian, *Against the Galilaeans* 138 B.
4. O. Rank, *Das Inzest-Motiv in Dichtung und Sage*, Leipzig, 1912.

be insignificant that the author of the most widely-acclaimed paean to physical love ever written, the Sadducaic *Song of Songs*, chose *my sister, my love*, to whom to sing:

My beloved is to lie all night between my breasts.   (1:13)

My beloved put his hand into my cavern, and my entrails throbbed for him.   (5:4)

The joining-place of your thighs is like jewelry.   (7:1)

How beauteous and accommodating you are, beloved, for pleasuring.   (7:6)

I'll have you drink from the wine spiced with the nectar of my pomegranate (*i.e., vulva*).   (8:2)

His left hand is under my head, while his right hand titillates me.   (8:3)

In more recent times, Peruvian men prior to the Spanish conquest married their mothers, sisters and daughters with no sense of impropriety.[5] Late nineteenth century researchers found that brother-sister marriages were popular in Cambodia, Bali, Polynesia, Malaya, Burma and Siberia; mother-son marriage was especially favoured by the Kalangs of Java and by the Bantu; father-daughter unions were common in the Solomon Islands; grandparents wed their grandchildren among the Baigas; and the Kodiak Eskimos and the Dyaks of Borneo had no incest concept whatsoever. A primitive tribe in Sarawak still does not.

In Christianised society, the best-known example of a taboo-maker deeming himself above the taboos (just as a traffic policeman is not obliged to refrain from speeding) was that of Pope Alexander VI (1492-1503). When his daughter, Lucretia Borgia, bore his child, Alexander at first acknowledged his paternity in a papal bull; but when hostile reaction exceeded his expectations, Alexander issued a second bull, this time attributing Lucretia's pregnancy to her other lover, her brother Cesare. So passionately did Cesare love his sister that he personally strangled her husband rather than tolerate competition.[6]

Incest has always meant different things to different people. Sharing joy with a nun, although the original nuns were mortal surrogates through

---

5. N. Schiller-Lietz, *Folgen, Bedeutung und Wesen der Blutverwandschaft im Tier- und Pflazenleben*, Berlin, 1892.

6. H. Maisch, *Incest*, pp. 29, 35.

whom worshippers could join their bodies with the Mother in the sacrament of Holy Fornication, came to be viewed as incest by medieval Christians on the ground that nuns were 'sisters' of the entire human race. England's Henry VIII, quoting *Leviticus* 20:21, declared his marriage to his brother's widow incestuous. Later, when his second wife became a nuisance to him, that marriage to a woman whose sister had borne his child was similarly categorised on the basis of *Leviticus* 18:18.

To some Melanesian tribes, marriage between the children of sisters was incestuous but marriage between the children of brothers was not. A man could marry his brother's daughter, but marriage to a sister's daughter fell under the restrictions of the local incest taboo. Children of the same mother could not marry, but children of the same father faced no such restriction.[7]

Persia's King Kambyses, on adding Egypt to his empire in the sixth century BCE, asked the magi (Zoroastrian astrologer-priests) if, in order to live up to his new subjects' concept of pharaonic dignity, he might marry his sister. He was informed that the only law relevant to such a situation was that the King of Persia could do anything he wished.[8]

Mother-son intercourse was probably the oldest incest taboo. Since all incest taboos were directly related to the pregnancy factor, there could not have been such a ban before the Big Discovery; but it probably dated from soon afterwards. Certainly when the first Pharaohs inherited their fathers' harems the new ruler's mother was removed from her son's service. Probably protocol demanded that a former Great Royal Wife not be degraded to a position of equality with the new Pharaoh's concubines and, as usually happened, custom hardened into taboo. Certainly by the time of the Emperor Nero, mother-tupping had fallen into such disrepute that Nero's interludes with his mother, Agrippina the younger, were viewed with universal revulsion, not least by Agrippina's reluctant lover, Nero himself.

Not all Pharaohs excluded their mothers from their harems, however. Ikhenaton, perhaps as a consequence of spending his formative years in Persia, sired children upon his mother and his daughter, as well as on his best-known wife, his cousin Nefertiti. And the daughter, after being mated to her father, was then married to her brother and finally to her grandfather:

---

7. In Jennie Gunn's memoir of the Australian outback, *The Little Black Princess*, five-year-old Bet Bet was obliged to 'shutim eye quickfella' in the presence of her uncle Goggle-eye because, 'Him little bit father belong me.' What Mrs Gunn and most of her readers failed to realise was that 'little bit father' was not merely an uncle, but rather any of her father's male relatives who were entitled to sexual access to Bet Bet's mother.

8. Although Herodotos's statement that Kambyses married two of his sisters was correct, his declaration that *it had never before been a Persian custom for brothers and sisters to marry*, was so inaccurate as to raise doubts about the veracity of the whole magi incident (HISTORIES 3:32).

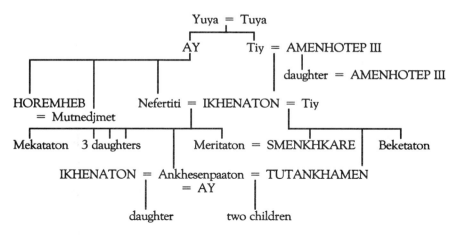

Ay, who appears to have been the real power in Egypt throughout the reigns of Smenkhkare and Tutankhamen, at Tutankhamen's death finally felt sufficiently secure to usurp the kingdom and make himself Pharaoh. However, in accordance with the long-standing tradition (breached by Amenhotep III) that the Pharaoh must legitimise his reign by marrying the true heiress, he promptly married his granddaughter Ankhesenpaaton, his predecessor's sister-wife. Ankhesenpaaton's three known children predeceased her, and when she died without bearing a child to her grandfather, the eighteenth dynasty came to an end. Horemheb, founder of the nineteenth dynasty, no doubt appropriated Ay's harem, but he did not make any of Ikhenaton's women the Great Royal Wife. That role went to his sister Mutnedjmet, Ay's daughter.

The son's inheritance of his father's wives was also the custom among the Jewish patriarchs and among the kings who succeeded them. The Yahwist reported that during Jacob's lifetime his eldest son Reuwben *tupped Bilhah, his father's concubine* (GEN. 35:22). At Jacob's death that incident was made the basis for Jacob's alleged bypassing of his three eldest sons (the other two for a different reason) and naming David's ancestor Yahuwdah as his heir (GEN. 49:4). What the line actually recorded was an attempt by Jacob's heir-apparent to guarantee his succession by usurping the sheikhdom while his father was still alive.

Taking possession of the sheikhly harem legitimised a new sheikh as effectively as being crowned at Reims legitimised a new king of France. Reuwben did not lust after his father's woman; he lusted after his father's job. David's eldest surviving son, Adonyahuw, used the same tactic of securing the harem in an effort to thwart David's bequest of his kingdom to his seventh son, Solomon. Adonyahuw failed, and paid the price, as had

Abshalowm, whose usurpation began with his publicly tupping David's harem (2 SAM. 16:22). Reuwben, since he was not executed, probably succeeded. With David's dynasty safely established but still needing to be justified, it was an easy matter for the Yahwist to pretend that Reuwben had never been Sheikh, and that Jacob had named Yahuwdah as the tribe from which the royal line would emerge. The attitude that recreation with a father's concubine constituted incest provided the justification for Reuwben's retroactive deposition.

Incest in the Yahwist's day was limited to relations between mother and son, father and daughter, probably grandparent and grandchild, and perhaps full brother and sister. The Elohist, writing 150 years later, did not expand the concept. The book of *Deuteronomy*, which can be dated to precisely 621 BCE, extended the ban to include siblings of the half-blood. It also forbade marriages to a previous wife's mother or daughter, as well as spelling out the criminal nature of the form of seduction attributed to Reuwben (DEUT 27:20-23). It was only in the Priestly author's seventh century BCE book of *Leviticus* that aunts and various in-laws (so useful to Henry VIII) were added to the you-shall-nots (LEV. 18:6-18). The Priestly author did not get around to banning marriages between uncle and niece (perhaps because *he* was married to his niece). Christianity borrowed that taboo from the puritanical Romans. Nor did he ban father-daughter copulation, since a father *owned* his children and could not be deprived of his unlimited right to do with them as he pleased.

So widespread has the incest taboo become in the four thousand years since its invention that today the reluctance of persons raised together to intermarry is often seen as a kind of artificial incest concept. Persons raised in an Israeli kibbutz, for example, almost never marry members of the same kibbutz. Not surprisingly, this situation is regularly cited as evidence of the 'naturalness' of the incest taboo, in the mistaken belief that persons growing up in the same household reject their familiars as prospective mates through some kind of instinct. In fact the explanation is much simpler, and has nothing to do with any 'instinctive' preference to mate with outsiders.

The nuclear family forms the basis of most modern societies. Almost without exception, those societies are conditioned to the metaphysical belief that sexual recreation is intrinsically immoral and can only be justified by a marriage certificate or a 'meaningful relationship.' Sex-play by children is totally forbidden. Consequently, when children reach the age of sexual curiosity and wish to satisfy that curiosity with the nearest available play-mate, who is bound to be a sibling, they are informed that such behaviour is 'wrong.' The warden means, of course, that all child-sex is 'wrong'; but the child assimilates the teaching that sex with the most convenient partner is wrong, and fifteen years of being kept away from that partner hardens

Incest: The Abolition of Endogenous Marriage   91

into an unbreakable taboo. When the age of sexual freedom is reached, a generation of regarding a particular individual as out-of-bounds causes the new adult to turn to potential partners who have not been so categorised.

The identical situation occurs in a kibbutz. A three-year-old boy, showering with a girl, notices that her anatomy differs from his own and, curious, reaches between her legs. The adults present intervene, just as happens when siblings behave in a similar manner in a nuclear family. The children are immediately conditioned to the belief that one does not touch the sexual apparatus *of the other children in the kibbutz*. Naturally, kibbutz graduates continue to regard each other as taboo long after the restrictions of childhood have been withdrawn. They could hardly do otherwise.

Incest is an artificial concept, no more a part of 'natural law' than the long-enforced meatless Friday. That incest meant different things in different places and at different times adequately proves this. But the significant question is: How did such a concept as incest come to be invented in the first place? Although genetic factors are often cited by persons who wish to provide a rational basis for biblical taboos where none exists, anthropologists are agreed that such a consideration played no part in the taboo's formation. Indeed, the entire pretence that incest causes psycho-biological harm has been fully disproven by genetic research.[9] All taboos were instituted to solve an immediate, usually temporary, problem, and by sheer inertia hardened into the immutable will of the tribal god. Incest is no exception.

Human beings of both sexes evolved with a regular and recurring need for orgasm; a decided preference for satisfying that need in the company of a partner of a particular sex; and a desire for sexual security analogous to a pastoralist's desire to settle in the vicinity of fertile ground. For that reason, we can be fairly certain that monogamous matings, although without an adultery taboo, were widely favoured before the Big Discovery. Marriage, however, did not exist, and neither (obviously) did the compulsion to prove one's virility by securing and impregnating a good breeder as soon as possible.

The Big Discovery, and the consequent desire of men to sire children whose parentage they could not doubt, led to the imposition upon women of the institution of marriage, an institution created by men for the benefit of men. But by that same institution men deprived themselves of the opportunity to recreate with the ninety-five percent of women who were already somebody else's private property. The chattel-slavery of marriage solved one problem for men whose vanity demanded that they propagate their genes; but, as Nietzsche pointed out in the nineteenth century, it created another:

---

9. Maisch, *op. cit.*, pp. 75 ff.

All good things were originally bad things; every original sin has turned into an original virtue. Marriage, for example, seemed for a long time a transgression against the rights of the community; one had to make reparation for being so immodest as to claim a woman for oneself (hence, for example, the *jus primae noctis*, which in Cambodia is still the prerogative of the priests . . .).[10]

The price of imposing private ownership on women was high, in terms of lost pleasure, but men paid it. But that created the problem of finding a breeding woman ('wife') for oneself. With men not managing to kill themselves in war as fast as women were dying in childbirth, the demand for wives greatly exceeded the supply. Consequently potential mothers were snapped up as soon as they were physically able to mate. In a competitive market, the first man to learn of a girl's availability would have become her owner ('husband'). In very few cases would that have been anyone but her brother. In time a situation developed where nobody was marrying anybody but a sibling, and this led to a problem far more recognisable than a hypothetical proliferation of defective genes.[11]

A father with six daughters and no sons may have sold some of them to an outsider. But where there was a surplus of only two or three, spare daughters would have been reserved for sons not yet mature or not yet born. Consequently an unacceptable proportion of the population would not have married at all, or not married until they were no longer breedable. This in turn would have caused a serious drop in population, raising the fear that under the existing system one's family was likely to become extinct.[12] The solution was to mate all of one's children as soon as they reached puberty, and this could only be done by marrying them to outsiders.[13]

It was one thing to formulate a solution, and quite another to implement it. If a society accustomed to seeking mates within the immediate family were to be persuaded to look elsewhere, the alternative of following the old way would have to be removed: *Because of strong tendencies to mate within the family, the familial incest taboos were necessary to insure exogamy.*[14] Thus

---

10. F. Nietzsche, *On the Genealogy of Morals*, 3rd essay, sec. 9.

11. Adonis was born from the mating of Myrrha with her father, Kinyras. Since Adonis was the most beautiful of the demigods, the Greeks who composed the myth could not have heard of the degeneration-of-species theory.

12. A similar fear led the patriarchal Jews to compose a law that, when a man died childless, his closest surviving relative was obliged to impregnate the dead man's widow. The offspring of such a mating would be deemed the dead man's legitimate son and heir.

13. No anthropologist to my knowledge has attributed the incest taboo to precisely the situation described above; but all agree that its causes were socio-economic. (See Maisch, *op. cit.*, pp. 47 ff.)

14. D.F. Aberle, *et al.*, 'The Incest Taboo and the Mating Patterns of Animals,' in P. Bohannan and J. Middleton, eds., *Marriage, Family and Residence*, p. 6.

the traditional mating practice of four million years was declared sacred to the gods (taboo); and a new word was coined for a breach of that taboo: *unchastity* (incest).

Like all taboos, the incest concept was eventually attributed to the gods. The Greeks attributed it to Zeus; Hammurabai to Shamash; and the Priestly author to Yahweh-Elohiym. To this day societies that regard the anti-Babylonian propaganda called *Leviticus* as god-authored, including societies whose constitutions prohibit the making of laws *pertaining to the establishment of a religion*, maintain laws that legitimise the purely religious concept of incest and criminalise the taboo's nonobservance.

Five

Jews, Israelites and History

Testimony that is invalidated in part is invalidated entirely.
Talmud, *Bava Kama* 73a.

The institution of regnant kingship was closely followed by the invention of writing. Obviously the one was not a consequence of the other. It merely happened that, at about the time that kings and gods were reconstructing history into their own patriarchal image, they found themselves presented with a weapon that enabled them to do so with a hitherto uncontemplated efficiency. If it was true that a lie spoken often enough became truth, it was trebly true that a lie immortalised on stone or parchment became the irrefutable Word of the tribal god. Hammurabai four thousand years ago wrote the retributive law code of his god Shamash (plagiarised by the Deuteronomist's god Yahweh in 621 BCE) on a great stone stele for all to see, and from that moment a concept of justice written at a particular time and place to accord with a particular author's frame of reference became the immutable word of the King of Heaven that always had existed and always would exist.

From the first 'Word of God,' in the form of a written lawcode, to the first bible, or collection of infallible revelations, was a predictable but long-delayed step. Among the earliest bibles were the Hindu *Vedas* in India, and the *Odyssey*, *Iliad* and *Theogony* in Greece. Each was regarded as the infallible word of the gods. Such authority did they have, that the reason Herakles never became a full-fledged Olympian, despite the efforts of later

Greeks to deify him, was that Homer in the *Odyssey* had placed him in Tartaros, from which place he could never be extricated without repudiating the authority of Homer's bible.

Of the three works that passed for sacred scripture in Hellenic religion, the most authoritative was the *Iliad*, to which the Greeks granted a status identical with that attached by modern Jews to the Towrah, Christians to the gospels, and Muslims to the Koran. Yet the *Iliad*, like all bibles past and present, contained inconsistencies incompatible with its claim to be Revealed Truth, for it sometimes killed off the same warrior two or three times in different books. Unwilling to accept their bible as a work of the imagination, the Greeks explained away its inconsistencies with the words, 'Homer nodded,' an explanation that had the virtue of being rather more realistic than the incredible rationalisations with which the veracity of modern bibles has been defended.

But bibles were a comparatively late invention, the earliest not appearing for several centuries after the invention of writing. Among the oldest written documents so far discovered are some clay tablets dating from 2400 BCE that were found in what seems to have been a royal archive in the city of Ebla in what is now northern Syria. The abundance of tablets containing the proper names Abraham, David, Jacob and Yahweh leaves little doubt that the Jews who conquered southern Phoenicia (Judah) in the early fourteenth century BCE were descendants of refugees from this northern area, driven south by the ravages of their original homeland by the conquering forces of the king of Babylon.

Ebla fell to Babylon before 2000 BCE. Jericho fell to the Jews a little after 1400 BCE. For the six hundred intervening years the Jews were nomadic herdsmen and traders, plying the caravan routes between Syria and Egypt. Some scholars are of the opinion that the word *Khibriy* (Hebrew), first applied to the Jews and related tribes invading southern Phoenicia between 1380 and 1362 BCE, at which time it meant Easterner (i.e., from east of the Jordan river), was ultimately derived from a word that meant camel-driver.

Whether the Jews had kings prior to their expulsion from the territory between Mount Yahweh and Ebla is uncertain; the palace at Ebla was surely the property of a hereditary dynasty. But from the time of their expulsion or shortly afterwards, until three centuries after the conquest of Judah, they were led by autocratic sheikhs or judges, of whom the earliest recorded who can be accepted as historical was *Avrum the Easterner* (GEN. 14:13). To the Yahwist, writing eight hundred years after Abraham's death, the ancient sheikh was more than a mere demigod; he was an ancestor. And there can be no doubt that the Jews of the nomadic period were ancestor-worshippers.

It is part of Greek folklore that Nestor was the first to swear an oath by *Herakles*. That oath was viewed as the earliest declaration of Herakles' divinity, for only immortals who were objects of worship were ever invoked in solemn oaths. Jacob, in making an agreement with his father-in-law Laban, *invoked the curse of his ancestor Yitskhak* (GEN. 31:53). The survival into the tenth century BCE of folk tales about sheikhs of a much earlier age who were all touted as ancestors of the entire Jewish people is further evidence that ancestor-worship was standard Jewish practice.

The patriarchal Jews were also phallus-worshippers. In extracting an oath from a slave, Abraham ordered the man to *put your hand under my crotch while I have you invoke a curse before Yahweh* (GEN. 24:2-3). Jacob likewise worshipped Yahweh as a phallus: *Yaakob erected a stone phallus on which he poured an offering of wine and oil* (GEN. 35:14). Yahuwshua worshipped a stone phallus as Yahweh in the fourteenth century (JOSH. 24:26), while Solomon did likewise four hundred years later (3 KGS. 3:4). And David, celebrating the recovery from the Philistines of the chest housing Yahweh's treaty, danced before Yahweh wearing only the wooden dildo that was the god's image (2 SAM. 6:14). The practice of depicting Yahweh as a phallus was still going on in the late eighth century BCE, but by that time prophets and chroniclers were denouncing it as *against Yahweh their gods* (4 KGS. 17:9-12).

It has already been mentioned that, despite the pretence of the Yahwist and all later writers to the contrary, the Jews and Israelites were two separate peoples. The Jews came from an area that reached as far south as Ebla and as far north and west as Mount Yahweh in Anatolia, somewhere in the vicinity of modern Adana. In the fourteenth century BCE they conquered and settled the area south of Jerusalem.

The Israelites can be traced no further back than the fourteenth century BCE. At that time they were driven out of their Midian homeland by the conquering Easterners, of whom the most powerful were Yahuwshua's Jews. Because an Israelite named Yanhuma was Pharaoh Ikhenaton's viceroy of Phoenicia, the displaced Israelites were invited by Ikhenaton to settle on the eastern shore of the Nile delta, in Goshen, on the condition that they help defend Egypt's northern border in the event that the Easterners attempted to invade Egypt proper.[1] Roughly one hundred years later they were expelled from Egypt during the reign of Pharaoh Ramoses II, and shortly thereafter, on returning to Midian only to find their reception less than hospitable, settled more or less peacefully in the section of Phoenicia north of Jerusalem, and formed an alliance with the Jews that lasted until

---

1. Ikhenaton's reason for inviting the Israelites to settle in Goshen is, of course, my own speculation. But it is a matter of record that Roman Emperors regularly settled tribes of foreigners on their borders for just such a purpose.

the death of Solomon.

The Towrah, the first six books of the Jewish bible, contains roughly equal amounts of Jewish and Israelite history, broken down as follows:

Jewish history	Israelite history	lawcodes and propaganda	mythology
GENESIS 12-29	GENESIS 37 to	EXODUS 25-31	GENESIS 1-11
NUMBERS 32	EXODUS 24	EXODUS 35 to	GENESIS 30-36
JOSHUA	EXODUS 32-34	NUMBERS 9	
JUDGES	NUMBERS 10-25	NUMBERS 26-31	
		NUMBERS 33-36	
		DEUTERONOMY	

Abraham, Isaac, Jacob, Reuwben, Shimeown, Levi and Yahuwdah were Jewish demigods. Leah was a Jewish goddess. Israel, Joseph, Menasheh and Efrayim were Israelite demigods. Rakhel was an Israelite goddess. Other patriarchs named as sons of the hybrid Jacob/Israel were demigods of tribes with whom the Jews and Israelites formed a confederacy in the twelfth century BCE. The Benjaminites (or Benoniy) were a tribe that had already allied with the Israelites in Midian. The coincidence that simplified the task of giving the Jews and Israelites common ancestors (although such a loophole was not really necessary) was that each tribe numbered among its ancestor-demigods a warrior-sheikh named God's Penis.

Yaakob meant Yahweh's Phallus.[2] *Yisrael* meant Allah's Erection. In order for the Yahwist to pretend that Yahweh's stud and Allah's stud, both apparently historical, were the same man, it was first necessary to pretend that the volcano-god Yahweh of the Jews, and the sky-god Allah of the Israelites, were the same god. Ultimately the task proved insuperable, and from the death of Solomon in the tenth century BCE until the disappearance of the Israelites from the face of the earth in 721 BCE, the Israelites rejected the Jewish Davidic dynasty as foreign kings, and the Jewish Yahweh as a foreign god. Yet, as the Elohist (E) narrative written almost two hundred years after the death of Solomon reveals, they did accept the imposed genealogy that made Jacob and Israel the same man. The improbability of such an equation is easily demonstrated.

In a passage deleted because it contradicted E, and ultimately replaced by a Priestly version (GEN. 35:10), the Yahwist must have offered some explanation as to why the same man was known as Jacob to the Jews and as Israel to the Israelites. It would be pointless to try to guess what that

---

2. I am assuming that *Yaakob* was once *Yahkob*.

explanation might have been; but it would not have involved a change of name. To the Yahwist, a change from a name honouring Yahweh to a name honouring another god would have been unthinkable. It was the Elohist, an Israelite who knew that *El*, not *Yahweh*, was the god of Israel's true name, who first concocted the tale that Jacob changed his name (GEN. 32:28). The J/E Redactor, confronted by incompatible accounts of why a man had two names, preferred the Elohist's version and omitted the Yahwist's alternative. In accordance with his own mythology, the Priestly author (P) added that the change was directly ordered by the gods (*elohiym*). What P failed to realise was that a change of name implied a change of gods.

Amenhotep IV in 1380 BCE changed his name to Ikhenaton. The change indicated his abandonment of the god Amen and acceptance of the god Aton. Later his son Tutankhaton reversed the process, forsaking his father's god for the god of the majority in order to retain his throne, and called himself thereafter Tutankhamen. Aton-moses, a prince of Egypt, dropped the first part of his name when he wisely decided against imposing the name of Aton on his grandfather's Israelite slaves, whom he calculated would accept monolatry more readily if the name of the god was not identified in their minds with Egypt. In each case the change from a name honouring one god to a name honouring another indicated an unequivocal change of religion. For Yaakob to change his name to Yisrael would have been equivalent to the Pope changing his name to Mohammed.

Abraham, Isaac and Jacob were historical sheikhs. They were not, however, successive generations of the same dynasty. The Yahwist made them so for the sake of continuity. The Yahwist's history contained very few anecdotes concerning the adult Isaac, all of them identical with tales E later told of Abraham (GEN. 26:26-33 and 21:22-32; GEN. 12:11-20 and 26:6-11). This suggests that J used Isaac solely as a transitional device, making him simultaneously the son of Abraham and the father of Jacob in order to tie the two together. While an Isaac may have filled both roles, almost certainly the demigod Isaac was neither.

Critical history is a modern art. Until recently chroniclers tended to attribute to an earlier age the customs and mores of their own age. Geoffrey of Monmouth, for example, turned the sixth-century CE guerilla leader Arthur of Britain into a twelfth-century English feudal lord. Homer, editing and revamping a collection of related and unrelated poems into a single epic in the eighth century BCE, attributed to thirteenth-century Greeks and Trojans the practices of contemporary Ionia. It therefore comes as something of a surprise that details of Abraham's life as described by the Yahwist were consistent with the social and economic practices of the eighteenth century when Abraham lived, but not with those of the Yahwist's own tenth century.

For example, in *Genesis* 15:2-3 it is indicated that the childless Abraham's heir-presumptive was his chief steward. In the event that Abraham had a natural son, the steward would be displaced. There are ample documents from Mesopotamia and Ugarit to indicate that, in the eighteenth century BCE, it was common practice for a moneylender to demand as collateral that he be adopted as the borrower's conditional heir. In the event that the borrower died leaving a natural son, that son would succeed to his wealth. But in the absence of a natural son, the adopted heir's position was unassailable. The accuracy of this minor detail has been optimistically cited by mythologians as evidence of the Judaeo-Christian bible's veracity; but the simpler explanation is that the story of the long-awaited birth was a recurrent theme in Jewish mythology, and because of its significance the Abraham legend was preserved orally with little change.

Parts of the Yahwist's patriarchal tales were accurate, as parts of modern-day historical novels are accurate. The majority of the stories were fabulous. For example, the Yahwist described how Abraham, fearing that he would be killed by someone who lusted after Sarah, passed her off as his sister. As a result Sarah was made the concubine of Pharaoh. Yahweh punished Pharaoh's unintentional adultery with plagues, and Sarah was consequently returned to her husband. Nowhere did the Yahwist suggest that Abraham's behaviour was reprehensible (or that Yahweh's punishment of the innocent was reprehensible); nor did he dispute that Pharaoh had engaged in sexual recreation with his new harem girl (GEN. 12:11-20).

A few paragraphs on, the Yahwist repeated the tale; but this time the patriarch who became his wife's pimp was Isaac, who allowed King Abiymolokh of the Philistine city of Gerar to believe that Rebekah was his unmarried sister. In the Abiymolokh version there was no adulterous consummation, and Rebekah was able to remain Isaac's private property even while he maintained that she was not (GEN. 26:6-11).

The mere repetition of a single anecdote with different heroes (if that is the right word) stretches the reader's credulity. But sandwiched between the Yahwist's tales in the edited Towrah is an alternative version by the Elohist in which the pimp was Abraham, the wife-introduced-as-sister was Sarah—and the unwitting cuckolder was Abiymolokh, King of Gerar! (GEN. 20:2-18). That the Philistines did not enter Phoenicia in significant numbers until the twelfth century BCE is further evidence that the story was pure fantasy. There could not have been a Philistine city as early as the time of Abraham or Isaac.

Such fables, although historically unfounded, are nonetheless not useless as a source of social history. The first version of the tale of the pandered wife was the oldest, containing as it did an acknowledgement of consummated adultery that was expunged from the later versions as unacceptable in a tribal matriarch. It was clearly composed to convey the message that in gentile lands it was better to forfeit one's wife than one's life. While it reveals something of Jewish mores during the period that they were nomads, there is no reason to suppose that it reflected an attitude that still existed in the Yahwist's day. Whether E's tale of the sacrifice of Isaac (in E, Isaac *was* sacrificed) was related to Isaac's status as a possible cuckoo's chick, we can only guess (GEN. 22:1-10, 16b-19).

With the introduction of Jacob/Israel into his narrative, the Yahwist proceeded from purely Jewish mythistory to a blending of Jewish and Israelite. That he could knit the two into a unified whole is remarkable. As was said of the dog that walked on its hind legs, the wonder was not that he could do it so well but that he could do it at all. Not surprisingly, not even the smoothest stitching job could hide the seams. The Yahwist's biography of the hybrid Jacob/Israel was such an amalgam of incompatible cultural backgrounds that the hero's origin as two different persons from completely different societies cannot reasonably be denied.

Jacob stole his brother Esau's birthright, and later his paternal blessing. Such a story could only have come from a patriarchal society such as the Jewish. Sons of matriarchs did not have birthrights to surrender. The protagonist of that story was the Jew, Jacob.

But the alleged same man then spent twenty years in his wives' land working for his wives' father, strange behaviour indeed for the heir of a patriarchal sheikh. Israel, not Jacob, married the heiress of Laban the Aramaean and thereby became his heir-apparent. Later Israel secretly departed from Kharan, in the process stealing his father-in-law's flocks. Although consistent with the character of a man who became his father's heir by cheating his brother, the story was accompanied by the detail that Israel's wife stole her father's *terafiym*, household gods. That incident confirms that the story was originally told of the Israelite Israel, not the Jew Jacob.

Household gods were standard furnishings in the homes of Jews and Israelites alike. Even in later monolatrous times a cautious thief would have hesitated to leave them behind in case they informed their owner of the thief's whereabouts. But terafiym were more than mere gods. The carved godlets were the symbols of a sheikh's rank, and their possession was comparable with possession of the harem. By stealing her father's gods, Rakhel was guaranteeing Israel's position as Laban's heir.

In Jewish society, as in Aiolian, sons succeeded fathers. In Israelite society, as in Akhaian, sons-in-law succeeded fathers-in-law. The Jew David legitimised his annexation of Israel by marrying the Israelite King Saul's heiress. In the absence of such specific cross-cultural circumstances, in no ancient society could a man have been simultaneously his father's heir and the heir of a father-in-law who had sons.

Abraham or Isaac, or perhaps both, pandered his wife for material gain.

Jacob was a swindler. Reuwben was a usurper who deposed (or tried to depose) his still-living father. Yahuwdah was a lawbreaker who withheld from his widowed daughter-in-law his youngest son, whom Jewish custom demanded that she wed (GEN. 38). Shimeown and Levi set the pattern for von Ribbentrop by making a treaty of alliance as a prelude to massacring their unsuspecting allies (GEN. 34). Abraham was prepared to regain his vicious wife's favours by acceding to her demand that he send his concubine and son to their deaths (GEN. 21:14-16). The common element in such tales was that the patriarchs were revealed as something less than admirable. They may have been no worse than other autocrats of their time, but they were not the kind of saintly ancestors that a mythologian would have invented. No single story of a patriarch's reprehensible behaviour can be accepted as historically accurate; but collectively the fables strongly affirm that we are dealing with historical sheikhs, not demythologised gods.

From Jacob/Israel, demigods who can probably be dated to the seventeenth century BCE or thereabouts, the Yahwist proceeded to the story of Joseph, an Israelite whose real name was Yanhuma and who rose to prominence in the reign of Pharaoh Ikhenaton (1380-1362 BCE).

Ikhenaton's predecessors had detested Semites, for a good reason. Around 1730 BCE Egypt had been conquered by a Semitic tribe known as the Hyksos. The Hyksos constituted Egypt's fifteenth to seventeenth dynasties, ruling the Egyptians for 160 years until they were expelled by Amenhotep I, founder of the eighteenth dynasty. Who the Hyksos were and what became of them is uncertain. The story of Abraham's stay in Egypt suggests a connection; but it seems unlikely that, if Jews had once ruled Egypt, the Yahwist would have failed to be aware of that fact and report it.

Following the expulsion of the sheep-herding Hyksos around 1570 BCE, the Egyptians became anti-Semitic and anti-sheep-herders. Even though the patron god of the eighteenth dynasty was the ram Amen, not for a century were sheep-herders tolerated within Egypt's borders. As for the possibility of a Semite, or indeed any non-Egyptian, obtaining even the lowliest position in Pharaoh's administration, such a denigration of Egyptian superiority would have been unthinkable. Then came Ikhenaton.

Ikhenaton succeeded his father Amenhotep III in 1380 BCE. Originally styled Amenhotep (IV), he changed his name when he changed his god. So radical was Ikhenaton's new mythology, and so hateful to the priestly caste whom Ikhenaton suppressed, that after his death Ikhenaton was relegated to the status of permanent unperson. Just as Ikhenaton had removed the name of the opposition god Amen from all public buildings, so did the priests of Amen remove from the city of No-amen (which Herodotos called Thebes) all evidence that the heretic Pharaoh Ikhenaton had ever lived. Not until Ikhenaton's short-lived capital of Akhet-aton (Tell Amarna) was excavated in the late nineteenth century CE was his name again restored to the pages of history.

Ikhenaton's new mythology, unlike anything seen before anywhere in the world or anything that would be seen again until the Jews reinvented it more than a thousand years later, was monotheism. Not only did Ikhenaton stubbornly refuse to worship any god but the sun, Aton; he vehemently denied that any other god existed. And whereas under Amen the god's own people were intrinsically superior to non-Egyptians (just as, to Aristotle, Greeks were superior to non-Greeks, who were only fit to be slaves; and to Jews, gowyim were similarly inferior), under Ikhenaton's universal god all of Aton's people, literally everybody under the sun, whether Egyptian, Phoenician or Ethiopian, were equal. Egypt was not ready for such a god and, except for the select priesthood that Ikhenaton established, which survived long enough to produce Moses, the world's first One God died with its creator.

Ikhenaton appointed a Semite, apparently an Israelite from Midian, his viceroy of Phoenicia. This was Yanhuma, whom the biblical authors called Joseph (Yowsef). Yanhuma, like Churchill, found himself in the unenviable position of presiding as the king's first minister over the disintegration of a mighty empire. For at the same time that Ikhenaton's religious reforms were tearing Egypt apart internally, Egypt's Phoenician province was being invaded by hordes of Hapiru, of whom the best organised and most murderous were Yahuwshua's Jews. Beset by internal strife and regarded by his own commanders as a damnable heretic, Ikhenaton was in no position to answer the desperate m'aidez messages that were pouring into Yanhuma's office from city after city in his Phoenician satrapy, demanding reinforcements to fight off the invaders.

The fate of those cities that, denied Ikhenaton's help, nonetheless tried to resist the Hapiru, is starkly revealed in two passages by P: The inhabitants of Jericho and ha-Khay were utterly exterminated, both man and woman, young and old, with the blade of the sword . . . in compliance with the orders that Yahweh had given Yahuwshuakh (JOSH. 6:21; 8:27). Most of the besieged cities, however, as surviving letters from the kings of Jerusalem, Bethelehem and vicinity make clear, chose to reach some kind of accommodation with the Easterners, often an alliance against those kings who continued to hold out.[3]

There is no direct testimony, either in Joshua or in the Amarna letters, that any Phoenicians surrendered their cities to the Easterners in exchange for nothing more than the right to emigrate in safety; but that is what the Israelites must have done. It is known that Yanhuma was a native of the

---

3. J.B. Pritchard, Ancient Near Eastern Texts, Amarna letters.

province over which he was Viceroy, and it is by no means implausible that, when his own tribe was threatened by the advancing Jews, Yanhuma was permitted by Ikhenaton to settle them in Goshen on the condition that they help defend the border.

Yanhuma's influence in Egypt died with Ikhenaton. The nineteenth-dynasty Pharaohs who restored Egypt's glory would not have failed to regard the Semites in their midst as an unpleasant reminder of the collapse of their empire—and also as a security risk: '*We have to deal with them prudently, in case they expand so much that, if war breaks out, they'll abandon our country and join our enemies and fight against us*' (EXOD. 1:10). Probably Ramoses I (Horemheb) was the Pharaoh who *knew nothing of Yowsef* (EXOD. 1:8), who turned the great heretic's allies into slaves. We may well believe that the long-reigning Ramoses II forced the Israelites to build the storage towns of Pithom and Raamses. Less believable is the tale that Pharaoh came to depend upon slave labour (in the midst of mass unemployment), and that the Israelites escaped from Egypt against his will. Far more likely is it that the Israelites were expelled at the demand of starving Egyptians who wanted their jobs.

An Egyptian version of the Exodus told a much different story from that of the Yahwist and the Elohist. The Israelites (according to the Egyptian source) were an undisciplined people whose unsanitary habits poisoned the Nile and caused so many plagues, that Ramoses eventually sent his war chariots to drive them out of Goshen and into the Arabian desert.[4] While more believable than the fantasy of an extinct volcano's repetitious demands to '*Let my nation go*,' the Egyptian tale was composed at such a late date, eight hundred years after the Yahwist's version, that no historical authenticity can be attached to it at all. Like the *Toldot Yeshu*, it was a myth composed to rebut a myth. The Jewish historian Flavius Josephus suggested that the expulsion of the Hyksos was the historical event behind the Exodus fable, but the reasonable equation of the historical Yanhuma with 'Joseph' points to a much later date.

The facts behind the Exodus myth become a little easier to unravel once the identity has been determined of the Israelites' great dictator, Moses. H.G. Wells, among others, postulated that Moses did not exist, citing in support of such a conclusion the complete absence of Moses' name in surviving Egyptian records.

The first objection to such reasoning is that the expurgation of Ikhenaton's name from Egyptian records reveals what could easily have happened to Moses and a dozen other individuals whose names the Egyptians deemed best forgotten. But the more obvious explanation is that, from the Egyptian viewpoint, Moses never did anything worth recording. Had Moses even once, let alone ten times, threatened Pharaoh with a plague and then fulfilled

---

4. Josephus, *Against Apion* 1:305-311.

his threat, such an event would certainly have been recorded by the Egyptian scribes. Just as the historical Dick Wittington had no talking cat, so the historical Moses had no mandate from an extinct volcano to work miracles.

Moses promised to lead the Israelites to a land rich in milk and honey, and died with that promise unfulfilled. That failure is the evidence of Moses' existence. Invented heroes do not fail. A fictitious Moses would have entered and conquered the 'promised land.' He would not have left the task to an unidentified successor whom the Yahwist turned into the long-dead Jew Yahuwshua.

Moses was an Egyptian.[5] He spoke no Hebrew, and for that reason needed the bilingual Aaron as his interpreter: *'What about your kinsman Aharon the Levite? I know he can translate'* (EXOD. 4:14). To win acceptance by the Israelites as their leader, he may well have had himself adopted by Aaron's father. He was in fact the son of Pharaoh's daughter, his maternal grand-mother being a (possibly Israelite) concubine of Ramoses II.

Moses was a priest of Aton, one of a small priestly school that had managed to survive since the death of Ikhenaton over one hundred years earlier. His full name would likely have been Aton-moses, 'Son of the Sun.' Such a name would have been perfectly acceptable to his grandfather Ra-moses, whose name also meant 'Son of the Sun.' When Aton-moses decided to make himself leader of the Israelites, whose god was Allah (*El*), or perhaps already *elohiym*, 'the gods,' he apparently dropped the Egyptian god from his name and became simply *Moses*. *Moses* became *Mosheh* in Hebrew and, when the Towrah was translated into Greek and Latin, *Moyses* in the former and back to *Moses* in the latter. Since *Mosheh* happened to be the Hebrew word for 'drawn out of water,' the Yahwist borrowed an Assyrian myth of how Sargon I had been set adrift as a babe and rescued to become king, and grafted the same tale onto Moses.

Moses probably spent his early years trying to convert his fellow Egyptians to his spiritual father Ikhenaton's monotheism. He was likely not yet thirty when he recognised the hopelessness of such a task, and conceived the idea of transferring his attentions to his grandfather's Israelite slaves. Ramoses was probably already convinced that the disadvantages of having

---

5. Moses' Egyptian identity was first recognised by Sigmund Freud (*Moses and Monotheism*). Freud's failure to realise that the Yahweh-worshipping Yahuwshua preceded the Aton/Allah-worshipping Moses, led him to suppose that the Moses who was Pharaoh's grandson and the Moses who was Reuwel/Yithrow's son-in-law were two different persons. The awareness that the Jewish god Yahweh was imposed (unsuccessfully) on the Israelites only long after Moses' death makes such a postulation unnecessary. The probability of Moses' assassination was also first recognised by Freud.

There currently exists a popular school of thought that maintains that Israelite monolatry arose independently of Atonic monotheism. However, this argument would assume that Moses, who came from Ikhenaton's land, taught Ikhenaton's basic religious philosophy by pure coincidence. Though possible, such a postulation is surely a violation of Occam's razor.

a foreign slave population on his doorstep outweighed the advantages, particularly if landless Egyptians were objecting to good farmland being wasted on foreigners. When his grandson offered to lead the slaves east and reconquer the oases of Midian that the Israelites had a century earlier surrendered to the *Hapiru*, Ramoses would not have hesitated to agree. He accordingly gave the Israelites the order to get out of Egypt by sundown. Faced with expulsion into an inhospitable desert, the Israelites gladly accepted the leadership of an Egyptian prince who offered them a new homeland more fertile than the one they were being forced to flee—on his terms.

Moses' terms were not harsh. Absolute obedience to a tyrant's every whim had long been a normal condition of life in every part of the known world. Acceptance of a leader's god was also customary. Only one aspect of Moses' rule was innovative. Moses insisted that his god was afflicted with the human psychosis of jealousy, and would tolerate worship of no other god in its land. That was a hard condition for people accustomed to honouring a number of gods, but the Israelites offered acceptance. So long as the god of Moses was able to protect them and keep its promises, they would worship it alone.

The identity of Moses' god presents a problem. Moses grew up as a devotee of Aton; but by the time Moses had been dead one hundred years the Israelites worshipped *elohiym*. It is possible that the Israelites worshipped Aton during Moses' lifetime and that, after his death, recognition of the failure of a single god to benefit them caused them to switch their allegiance to 'the gods.' But in view of the way Moses was rehabilitated a generation after his assassination, being credited with feats on *elohiym*'s behalf unparalleled in hero-mythology, this seems far from likely.

According to the Yahwist, Moses travelled to Midian alone prior to the Exodus, and there married the daughter of a priest of El, called Reuw-El by J (EXOD. 2:18), although E named him Yithrow (EXOD. 3:1). It may be that Moses learned the name of El in Midian and, equating one sky-god with another, decided to impose upon the Israelites a god with a Semitic name rather than an Egyptian one. It is equally possible that the Israelites already worshipped El, and that Moses wisely refrained from changing their god's name. One thing is certain: The Priestly narrative that had the Israelite god introduce himself to Moses as *Yahweh* was anachronistic. Yahweh was the god of the Jews, with whom the Israelites were not yet allied. He was not the god of the Israelites, and he was not the god of Moses (EXOD. 6:2-3).

For forty years the Israelites put up with Moses' tyrannical leadership, and for forty years they remained a stateless people. Whether the decision to abandon hope of regaining Midian and move north was made in Moses' lifetime or after his death is uncertain. Possibly the Israelites recognised the necessity of such a move, and Moses vetoed it on the ground that it would necessitate making compromises with other gods. Certainly Moses' policies were strongly opposed. The Yahwist and the Priestly author each recorded rebellions against his leadership that Moses succeeded in putting down. Finally, whether as an act of simple tyrannicide or as the only means of implementing an alliance secretly negotiated behind his back with the Jews, he was assassinated.[6] With Moses dead, the Israelites concluded the aforesaid alliance, and with Jewish help carved out a permanent homeland in that part of Phoenicia north of Judah that became Israel.

The clue to the Israelite settlement is to be found in the book of *Joshua*. Adhering to the pretence originated by the Yahwist that the earlier Jewish leader Yahuwshua had been the successor of the later leader of the Israelites, Moses, a Redactor attributed to Yahuwshua what was in fact the Israelites' only military victory, a victory that occurred more than a century after Yahuwshua's death.

Of all the massacres and city-sackings credited to the Jewish sheikh, the only one not in Judah was at the northern city of Khatsowr in Israel. Khatsowr was the capital city of a Phoenician confederacy that was almost certainty hostile to the southern confederacy of tribes under the hegemony of the Jews. The Israelites, who could not have numbered more than one thousand fighting men,[7] united with the Jews to sack Khatsowr. The other northern cities, accepting the fate of Khatsowr as a warning, permitted the Israelites to settle in their midst and no doubt offered marriage alliances to cement the agreement (JOSH. 11:10-13; JUDG. 1:27-29).

The Exodus, although the only surviving account of it is so totally fantastic as to be worthless as a source of accurate information, was indeed an event from Israelite (not Jewish) history. It ended with the razing of Khatsowr and the settlement in Israel. While it can easily enough be dated to the late thirteenth century BCE once it is recognised that it had no connection whatsoever with the Jewish conquest of Judah, confusion on that point, and refusal to believe that the biblical account is fraudulent, have been presenting historiographical problems for 2,500 years.

For example, somewhere around 600 BCE a chronicler wrote that the Exodus took place 480 years before the building of Solomon's Temple.

---

6. Nowhere in the Judaeo-Christian bible is this directly stated; but it is implicitly acknowledged in such passages as DEUT. 34:6; 3 KGS. 19:14; NEH. 9: 26; ISA. 1:4-5; JER. 2:30; and HOS. 12:13-14.

7. It has been calculated that the largest number of nomads capable of living off the Sinai desert is about 3000. That the Israelites indeed numbered between 2000 and 3000 is evident from Exodus 1:15, which indicated that they had, and therefore needed, only two midwives. The Priestly author's figure of 603,550 fighting men, plus women, children, teenagers and Levites, was so absurd that many historians have dismissed the whole 'exodus' tale as fantasy.

That would put the departure from Egypt in approximately 1447 BCE, and the death of Moses in 1407 BCE, a date that accords closely with Yahuwshua's accession as sheikh of the Jews. Since the chronicler was well aware of when Yahuwshua had lived, dating the Exodus forty years earlier was a logical move (3 KGS. 6:1).

However, at about the same time, the Priestly author was so reckless as to state that the Israelites' sojourn in Egypt had lasted 430 years (EXOD. 12:40). When the two dates are harmonised, we find that the Israelites must have entered Egypt in 1877 BCE, 150 years before the Hyksos, and remained there for a further 120 years after the Hyksos were expelled by Semite-hating Egyptians! That simply did not happen. The Jews, who had never been to Egypt, conquered the territory around Jericho in the early fourteenth century BCE; and the Israelites, who had come from Egypt, settled the territory around Khatsowr more than a century later.

The influx of three tribes of Israelites, and the destruction of the Khatsowr hegemony, led to the formation of a new confederation that stretched from the Sinai desert to the Lebanon. The Israelite tribes of Menasheh, Efrayim and Benoniy joined the original Jewish tribes of Reuwben, Shimeown, Levi and Yahuwdah, and six client tribes located mainly north of Israel, to form a Judaeo-Israelite amphictyony of thirteen tribes, the sacred number that corresponded to the number of new moons in a lunar year. Later, when anything that honoured the moon-goddess had become unacceptable to the patriarchal Jews, and the number thirteen was declared taboo, the tribes were reduced to twelve by the simple expedient of pretending that the Menashehites and Efrayimites were half-tribes, branches of a nonexistent Yowsef tribe. That it was the Israelites who suffered this indignity leaves little doubt that the Jews were the confederacy's senior partners.

The Jewish-Israelite confederacy also included the remnants of a fully-matrilineal Diynah tribe. The Diynahites do not appear, however, to have been granted recognition as a tribe. To bind the new confederacy together more tightly, and to prevent a repetition of the war between the Jews and the Benoniy that seems to have occurred in the late twelfth century BCE (JUDG. 20), the genealogy was composed that made the eponymous ancestors of the twelve tribes (except Menasheh and Efrayim, who became sons of 'Joseph') sons of the hybrid Jewish/Israelite demigod Jacob/Israel.

Thus was born the equation of Yahweh with Allah; Jew with Israelite; and Yahuwshua with the unknown successor of Moses; that is accepted as historical fact by the adherents of three major mythologies to this day. The tragic irony of the current intra-Phoenician cold war is that the Jews, who call their state Israel but do not worship the Israelite god, Allah, are at war with the Arabs, who do worship the god of Israel but mistakenly imagine themselves to be descended from a Jew.

Six

The Yahwist

> The critical issue is the quality of the purported evidence, rigorously and skeptically scrutinized—not what sounds plausible, not the unsubstantiated testimony of one or two self-professed eyewitnesses.
>
> Carl Sagan, *Cosmos*.

For the two hundred years from the mid-thirteenth to mid-eleventh centuries BCE Judah and Israel were ruled by nonhereditary sheikhs or judges. It is unlikely that the judges, of whom the best known was Samson, exercised more than regional authority. No Jew would ever have judged Israelites, and no Israelite would ever have judged Jews. Then sometime around 1020 BCE the Israelites persuaded Allah's spokesman (usually translated 'prophet') Samuel to depose his sons, whom he had appointed judges, and choose for them a hereditary king.

Samuel was the first of Israel's major spokesmen. To some extent a spokesman (*nabiya*) was credited with the fortune-telling capacity usually associated with the word *prophet*, since he usually carried a kind of die that enabled him to ascertain whether the tribal god would or would not follow a designated course of action in a given circumstance (heads for 'yes'; tails for 'no'). But basically a spokesman was a self-appointed priest, usually a student of Yahwistic or Elohistic literature but occasionally an illiterate carpenter, who spent his time exhorting the masses to abandon the policy of religious toleration that life in a multi-theistic society had made necessary, and resume the brutal suppression of all worship not dedicated to the spokesman's particular god. Perhaps the closest modern-day equivalent to an ancient spokesman was Iran's Ayatollah Khomeini.

The king chosen by Samuel was Saul (*Shauwl*). Samuel's chronicler wrote that Saul was a random choice; that Samuel, after consulting Yahweh, resolved to anoint the first stranger to ask him for directions after the morning sacrifice (1 SAM. 9:12-18). While it is possible that Samuel went through the motions of doing just that, or announced afterwards that he had done so, the choice of Saul was in fact carefully calculated. Saul was centimetres taller than his fellow Israelites, a significant qualification in a king. He was also the son of a rich warlord, described by the chronicler as *a powerful strong-man* (9:1). Saul allegedly made himself king of Judah as well as Israel, and since a Jewish general named David was one of his commanders this is likely accurate.

The Jews did not long tolerate an Israelite king. While Saul was still king of Israel, David was elected king of Judah (by his army, the same electorate that chose Emperors of Rome). To legitimise his reign David had himself anointed by Samuel, whom he imported from Israel for the purpose. Much later the story was invented that David had been anointed by Samuel while still a boy. Later still, the story was invented that the boy David had killed the Palestinian warrior, Goliath, actually killed by Elkhanan after David's election to the dual crown (2 SAM. 21:19).

David promptly waged war on Israel, with considerable success. The death of Saul in battle did not immediately lead to a united monarchy, but the death of Saul's son did. Seven years after becoming king of Judah, David was also accepted as king of Israel. As one of the conditions of that acceptance, David was obliged to marry (or resume an earlier marriage) with Saul's daughter Mikhal. Since Israel had hitherto been matrilineal, it may be that the Israelites regarded Saul's son-in-law as the true heir and Saul's son as the usurper. It may also be that Saul's intent to bypass custom and be succeeded by his son, rather than his designated heir, David, was what led David to rebel in the first place.

David was a warrior, chosen king for his prowess in battle: '*Shauwl has slaughtered his thousands, and David his ten thousands*' (1 SAM. 18:7). Not only did he consolidate his hold on the two lands of Judah and Israel; he also conquered the Mowabites, Ammonites, Edomites, Philistines, and the various smaller communities in Phoenicia that Yahuwshua had failed to exterminate, and established an empire that encompassed all effectively-occupied territory between Egypt, Ugarit, Assyria and Babylonia. Despite constant civil wars started by his sons, two of whom proclaimed themselves King in David's lifetime, David succeeded in retaining his kingdom and passing it intact to his designated heir, his 'sacred seventh' (or youngest) son Solomon (*Shlomoh*).[1]

Solomon further enlarged the empire, not so much by wars as his father had done but by marriage alliances. Solomon is credited with acquiring a harem that Pharaoh would have envied, consisting of seven hundred royal wives, each the daughter of a subject king, and three hundred lower-ranking wives, most of whom would also have been goodwill offerings or hostages from subjugated or tributory states.

Non-Jews had no difficulty recognising that the Jewish empire was far too large, and the proportion of Jews far too small, for it to have any hope of surviving. An imaginative Jew, however, had a different explanation for David's improbable success: The Jewish god Yahweh was the mightiest god in the world, *the most awesome of all the gods* (PS. 96:4). He was invincible, and as long as he was given his daily quota of psalms and sacrifices he would make the Jews invincible. It was at this point that the books that eventually were expanded into *Genesis* (*Bereshiyth*), *Exodus* (*Veleh Shmowth*) and *Numbers* (*Bemidbah*) were born.

The Towrah was primarily the work of four authors (plus two Redactors, one of whom greatly expanded *Leviticus*). The first of the four was inspired to write by King David's phenomenal success in establishing a Jewish empire. However, almost from the time the Towrah was completed in 434 BCE until the present, the pretence has been maintained that the author was Moses. Before discussing the work's actual authorship, perhaps it would be well to consider those lines in the Towrah that self-evidently were not written during or near the lifetime of Moses:

To this day no one has ever found his (*Moses'*) grave.   (DEUT. 34:6)

Since then there hasn't been a spokesman in Yisrael comparable with Mosheh, whom Yahweh knew face to face.   (DEUT. 34:10)

At that time there were still Phoenicians in the land.   (GEN. 12:6)

These were the kings who reigned in the land of Edowm before there was any king reigning over the descendants of Yisrael.   (GEN. 36:31)

When Avrum heard that his kinsman was a captive, he . . . chased them as far as (*the city of*) Dan.   (GEN. 14:14)

---

1. As a seventh son himself, David would have named his own 'sacred seventh' as his heir, making Solomon the doubly-sacred 'seventh son of a seventh son.' (1 CHR. 2:15; 3:1-5; 2 SAM. 12:15-24).

It is not feasible that the line, 'No one has ever found his grave *to this day*,' could have been written until long after Moses' death. The line implied extensive attempts to locate Moses' grave, carried out over a long enough period for the writer to be despaired of ever succeeding.

It is equally inconceivable that the lack of a subsequent spokesman comparable with Moses would have been deemed remarkable until at least a century had gone by. An American of the 1990s might conceivably observe that, 'There hasn't been a President of comparable stature since Lincoln,' but he would hardly make such a remark of Kennedy, a mere thirty-odd years after his death. Also, Moses would not have been described as a *spokesman* any earlier than the sheikhdom of Samuel, since it was in Samuel's time that the word was coined (1 SAM. 9:9). The same is true of *Miriam the spokeswoman* (EXOD. 15:20).

That there were Phoenicians in the land *at that time*, could only have been written at a time when there were no longer Phoenicians in the land; and the Phoenicians survived Moses by many generations.

There was no king in Israel or Judah until Saul. Clearly no writer who lived earlier than Saul could have referred to a time *before there was any king reigning over the descendants of Yisrael*.

The city of Laish was not renamed Dan until long after the death of Moses.[2]

The six men who actually created the Towrah cannot be positively identified, although speculations have been made concerning the identity of three of them. For convenience they have therefore come to be known by descriptive titles, often abbreviated to initials. In chronological order, they were the Yahwist (J), a Jew who served King David and wrote after the death of Solomon; the Elohist (E), an Israelite who wrote during the period of relative tranquility after Israel's victory over the Aramaeans in the early eighth century, but before there was yet cause to fear the Assyrians who ended Israel's existence in 721 BCE; the Deuteronomist (D), whose book was written a few days before its discovery behind a loose brick in Yahweh's Temple in 621 BCE; the Priestly author (P), who wrote as much as the three previous authors combined *c.* 600 BCE; and the two Redactors (R), the first of whom combined J and E and composed new passages to harmonise them; and the final Redactor of 434 BCE, who composed passages to harmonise J/E with P or to make J/E conform to the theology of his time, and who incorporated other, older documents into the finished Towrah.

Allowing for possible errors, particularly in passages from incidents

---

2. All of the material in the preceding paragraphs is taken from A.P. Davies, 'Fact and Fable: A Problem for Scholars,' in W. Ohlsen's *Perspectives on Old Testament Literature*, pp. 14-20.

described by more than one author, the best estimate of the most probable author of each passage is as follows:

Genesis

P. 1:01-2:03	P. 8:13a	J. 14:03a	J. 24:01-25:06
R. 2:04a	J. 8:13b	R. 14:03b	P. 25:07-25:11a
J. 2:04b-2:24	P. 8:14-8:19	J. 14:04-14:07a	J. 25:11b
R. 2:25	J. 8:20-8:22	R. 14:07b	R. 25:12
J. 3:01-3:07a	P. 9:01-9:17	J. 14:07c-14:08a	P. 25:13-25:18
R. 3:07b	J. 9:18a	R. 14:08b	R. 25:19
J. 3:08-3:10a	R. 9:18b	J. 14:08c-14:17a	P. 25:20
R. 3:10b	J. 9:18c	R. 14:17b	J. 25:21-25:26a
J. 3:10c-3:11a	R. 9:18d	J. 14:18-14:20a	R. 25:26b
R. 3:11b	J. 9:18e-9:22a	R. 14:20b	J. 25:27-26:14
J. 3:11c-4:26	R. 9:22b	J. 14:21-15:02a	R. 26:15
R. 5:01-5:28	J. 9:23-9:27	R. 15:02b	J. 26:16-26:17
J. 5:29	R. 9:28-10:01	J. 15:03-15:06	R. 26:18
R. 5:30-5:32	P. 10:02-10:07	R. 15:07	J. 26:19-26:33
J. 6:01-6:04a	J. 10:08-10:12a	J. 15:08-15:12	R. 26:34-26:35
R. 6:04b	R. 10:12b	R. 15:13-15:16	J. 27:01-27:40a
J. 6:04c-6:08	J. 10:13-10:19	J. 15:17-16:02	R. 27:40b
R. 6:09a	P. 10:20	P. 16:03	J. 27:41-27:45
P. 6:09b-6:22	J. 10:21	J. 16:04-16:15	R. 27:46
J. 7:01-7:05	P. 10:22-10:23	R. 16:16	P. 28:01-28:08
R. 7:06	J. 10:24-10:30	P. 17:01-17:27	R. 28:09
J. 7:07-7:08	P. 10:31-10:32	J. 18:01-19:28	J. 28:10-28:11a
P. 7:09	J. 11:01-11:09	P. 19:29	E. 28:11b-28:12
J. 7:10	R. 11:10-11:27a	J. 19:30-19:38	J. 28:13-28:16
P. 7:11	P. 11:27b-11:28	R. 20:01	E. 28:17-28:18
J. 7:12	J. 11:29-11:30	E. 20:02-20:17	J. 28:19a
P. 7:13-7:16a	P. 11:31	R. 20:18	R. 28:19b
J. 7:16b	R. 11:32	J. 21:01-21:02a	E. 28:20-28:21a
P. 7:17a	J. 12:01-12:04a	P. 21:02b-21:04	R. 28:21b-28:22
J. 7:17b	P. 12:04b-12:05	R. 21:05	J. 29:01-29:14a
P. 7:17c	J. 12:06a	P. 21:06	R. 29:14b
J. 7:17d	R. 12:06b	J. 21:07	J. 29:15-29:23
P. 7:18-7:21	J. 12:07-13:05	E. 21:08-21:32	R. 29:24
J. 7:22-7:23	P. 13:06	J. 21:33	J. 29:25-29:28
P. 7:24-8:02a	J. 13:07a	E. 21:34-22:10	R. 29:29
J. 8:02b-8:03a	R. 13:07b	R. 22:11-22:16a	J. 29:30-29:35
P. 8:03b-8:05	J. 13:08-13:11a	E. 22:16b-22:19	E. 30:01-30:08
J. 8:06-8:07a	P. 13:11b-13:12a	J. 22:20-22:24	J. 30:09-30:16
P. 8:07b	J. 13:12b-14:02a	R. 23:01	E. 30:17-30:20
J. 8:08-8:12	R. 14:02b	P. 23:02-23:20	J. 30:21

E.	30:22-30:24a	R.	33:18b	J.	37:23	J.	45:10
J.	30:24b-31:01	E.	33:18c-33:20	E.	37:24	E.	45:11-45:18
E.	31:02	P.	34:01-34:02a	J.	37:25-37:27	J.	45:19
J.	31:03	J.	34:02b	E.	37:28a	E.	45:20
E.	31:04-31:16	P.	34:03-34:04	J.	37:28b	J.	45:21-45:28
J.	31:17	J.	34:05	E.	37:29-37:30	E.	46:01a
P.	31:18	P.	34:06	J.	37:31-37:35	R.	46:01b
E.	31:19-31:20	J.	34:07	E.	37:36	E.	46:01c-46:05a
J.	31:21a	P.	34:08-34:10	J.	38:01-39:23	J.	46:05b
E.	31:21b-31:23a	J.	34:11-34:13	E.	40:01-41:44	P.	46:06-46:07
J.	31:23b	P.	34:14-34:17	P.	41:45-41:46a	R.	46:08-46:25
E.	31:23c-31:24	J.	34:18	E.	41:46b-41:54	P.	46:26-46:27
J.	31:25a	P.	34:19-34:24	J.	41:55-42:04	J.	46:28-47:06
E.	31:25b-31:43	J.	34:25a	E.	42:05-42:07	E.	47:07
J.	31:44	R.	34:25b	J.	42:08-42:14	P.	47:08-47:10
E.	31:45	J.	34:25c-34:27	E.	42:15-42:16	E.	47:11-47:12
J.	31:46	P.	34:28-34:29	J.	42:17-42:18a	J.	47:13-47:27a
R.	31:47	J.	34:30-34:31	E.	42:18b-42:19	P.	47:27b-47:28
J.	31:48-31:49	E.	35:01-35:08	J.	42:20	J.	47:29-47:31
E.	31:50	P.	35:09-35:15	E.	42:21-42:24	E.	48:01-48:02
J.	31:51a	E.	35:16-35:20	J.	42:25-42:28a	P.	48:03-48:06
E.	31:51b	J.	35:21-35:22a	E.	42:28b-42:29	R.	48:07
J.	31:52a	P.	35:22b-35:29	J.	42:30-42:35	E.	48:08-48:15a
E.	31:52b	R.	36:01	E.	42:36-42:37	R.	48:15b
J.	31:52c	P.	36:02-36:30	J.	42:38-43:13	E.	48:15c-48:16a
R.	31:52d	R.	36:31-36:43	R.	43:14a	R.	48:16b
J.	31:52e-31:53a	P.	37:01	J.	43:14b-43:22	E.	48:16c-48:22
E.	31:53b	R.	37:02a	E.	43:23a	J.	49:01-49:24a
R.	31:53c	J.	37:02b-37:03a	R.	43:23b	P.	49:24b-49:26
E.	31:53d	R.	37:03b	E.	43:23c	J.	49:27
J.	31:54a	J.	37:03c-37:17	J.	43:24-43:28	R.	49:28
E.	31:54b-32:02	E.	37:18	E.	43:29-43:31a	P.	49:29-49:33
J.	32:03-32:21	J.	37:19-37:20a	J.	43:31b-45:01	J.	50:01-50:11
E.	32:22-32:32	E.	37:20b	E.	45:02-45:04a	P.	50:12-50:13
J.	33:01-33:17	J.	37:20c	J.	45:04b-45:05a	J.	50:14
E.	33:18a	E.	37:21-37:22	E.	45:05b-45:09	E.	50:15-50:26

Exodus

R.	1:01-1:05	E.	1:15-1:21	J.	3:02-3:04a	J.	3:07-3:08
P.	1:06-1:07	J.	1:22-2:23a	E.	3:04b	E.	3:09-3:15
J.	1:08-1:12	P.	2:23b-2:25	J.	3:05	J.	3:16-3:20
P.	1:13-1:14	E.	3:01	E.	3:06	E.	3:21-3:22

J.	4:01-4:16	J.	9:25b-9:26	P.	14:08	E.	19:16b-19:17
E.	4:17-4:18	P.	9:27	J.	14:09a	J.	19:18
J.	4:19-4:20a	J.	9:28-9:34	P.	14:09b	E.	19:19
E.	4:20b-4:21a	R.	9:35	J.	14:10	J.	19:20a
R.	4:21b	J.	10:01a	E.	14:11-14:12	P.	19:20b
E.	4:22-4:23	P.	10:01b-10:03a	J.	14:13-14:14	J.	19:21
J.	4:24-4:26	J.	10:03b-10:08a	P.	14:15-14:18	P.	19:22a
E.	4:27-4:28	R.	10:08b	E.	14:19a	J.	19:22b
J.	4:29-4:31	J.	10:08c	J.	14:19b-14:20	P.	19:23-19:24a
E.	5:01-5:02	R.	10:08d	P.	14:21a	J.	19:24b
J.	5:03	J.	10:08e-10:10a	J.	14:21b	P.	19:25
E.	5:04	R.	10:10b	P.	14:21c-14:23	E.	20:01-20:10[3]
J.	5:05-5:20a	J.	10:10c-10:11a	J.	14:24-14:25	P.	20:11
R.	5:20b	R.	10:11b	P.	14:26-14:27a	E.	20:12-20:16
J.	5:20c-5:23	J.	10:11c-10:13	J.	14:27b	P.	20:17
E.	6:01	P.	10:14a	P.	14:28-14:29	E.	20:18-24:15a
P.	6:02-6:12	J.	10:14b	J.	14:30-15:18	P.	24:15b-24:18a
R.	6:13-6:30	P.	10:15-10:17	R.	15:19	E.	24:18b
P.	7:01-7:13	J.	10:18-10:19	E.	15:20-15:21	P.	25:01-29:26
J.	7:14-7:18	R.	10:20	R.	15:22a	R.	29:27-29:30
P.	7:19-7:20a	J.	10:21-10:26	J.	15:22b-15:25	P.	29:31-29:37
J.	7:20b-7:21a	R.	10:27	P.	15:26	R.	29:38-29:42
P.	7:21b-7:22	J.	10:28-10:29	R.	15:27-16:01	P.	29:43-31:17
J.	7:23-8:04	E.	11:01-11:03	E.	16:02-16:04a	R.	31:18a
P.	8:05-8:08	J.	11:04-11:08	P.	16:04b-16:30	E.	31:18b-32:13a
J.	8:09-8:11	R.	11:09-11:10	E.	16:31a	R.	32:13b
P.	8:12	P.	12:01-12:28	P.	16:31b	E.	32:13c-32:24
J.	8:13-8:14	J.	12:29-12:30	R.	16:32-16:34	J.	32:25-32:29
P.	8:15-8:19	E.	12:31-12:36	P.	16:35a	E.	32:30-32:35
J.	8:20-8:25a	R.	12:37	E.	16:35b	J.	33:01
R.	8:25b	E.	12:38-12:39	P.	16:36	E.	33:02a
J.	8:25c-9:07	P.	12:40-12:42	R.	17:01a	J.	33:02b-33:03a
P.	9:08-9:12	R.	12:43-13:10	E.	17:01b-18:02a	E.	33:03b-33:08
J.	9:13-9:14	P.	13:11-13:15	R.	18:02b	R.	33:09-33:10
P.	9:15-9:16	E.	13:16-13:18a	E.	18:03-18:27	E.	33:11
J.	9:17-9:18	J.	13:18b	P.	19:01	J.	33:12-33:17
P.	9:19-9:21	E.	13:19	R.	19:02a	E.	33:18-33:23
J.	9:22-9:23	R.	13:20	E.	19:02b-19:09	J.	34:01a
P.	9:24a	J.	13:21-13:22	P.	19:10-19:13a	R.	34:01b
J.	9:24b	P.	14:01-14:04	E.	19:13b	J.	34:02-34:04a
P.	9:25a	J.	14:05-14:07	P.	19:14-19:16a	R.	34:04b

---

3. The basic content of *Exodus* 20:1-17 was part of the Holiness code included in E, and was copied by P with only a few word changes. However, the precise wording of *Exodus* 20:1-17 is that of P, whereas E's wording is preserved in *Deuteronomy* 5:6-21.

J. 34:04c-34:05a R. 34:20a   R. 35:02-35:04   P. 39:01-40:38
E. 34:05b-34:09   J. 34:20b-34:28 P. 35:05-38:20
J. 34:10-34:19   P. 34:29-35:01   R. 38:21-38:31

Leviticus

P. 1:01-2:16a	R. 7:37b	P. 18:01-19:04	R. 23:39-23:43
R. 2:16b	P. 7:37c-9:23	R. 19:05-19:08	P. 23:44-24:11a
P. 2:16c-4:27	R. 9:24a	P. 19:09-19:37	R. 24:11b
R. 4:28a	P. 9:24b-10:03	R. 20:01-20:27	P. 24:12-24:15a
P. 4:28b-5:06a	R. 10:04-10:11	P. 21:01-21:10a	R. 24:15b-24:16a
R. 5:06b	R. 10:12-10:15	R. 21:10b	P. 24:16b
P. 5:06c-5:16	R. 10:16-10:20	P. 21:10c-21:12a	R. 24:17-24:21
R. 5:17-5:19	P. 11:01-11:23	R. 21:12b	P. 24:22-25:25
P. 6:01-6:09a	R. 11:24-11:40	P. 21:12c-21:17a	R. 25:26-25:34
R. 6:09b	P. 11:41-13:46	R. 21:17b	P. 25:35-25:40a
P. 6:10-6:15a	R. 13:47-13:59	P. 21:17c-21:22a	R. 25:40b-25:42
R. 6:15b	P. 14:01-14:08a	R. 21:22b-21:23a	P. 25:43
P. 6:15c-6:18a	R. 14:08b-14:32	P. 21:23b-22:02a	R. 25:44-25:46
R. 6:18b	P. 14:33-14:55a	R. 22:02b	P. 25:47
P. 6:19-6:20a	R. 14:55b	P. 22:02c-23:02a	R. 25:48-25:52
R. 6:20b	P. 14:55c-16:03	R. 23:02b-23:03	P. 25:53
P. 6:20c-6:29	R. 16:04	P. 23:04-23:18a	R. 25:54
R. 6:30	P. 16:05-17:05	R. 23:18b-23:19a	P. 25:55-26:38
P. 7:01-7:21	R. 17:06	P. 23:19b-23:20	R. 26:39-26:45
R. 7:22-7:27	P. 17:07-17:14	R. 23:21-23:22	P. 26:46
P. 7:28-7:37a	R. 17:15-17:16	P. 23:23-23:38	R. 27:01-27:34

Numbers

P. 1:01-2:03a	P. 2:14a	P. 2:27a	P. 5:18c-6:21a
R. 2:03b-2:04	R. 2:14b-2:16a	R. 2:27b-2:28	R. 6:21b
P. 2:05a	P. 2:16b-2:18a	P. 2:29a	P. 6:21c-9:06a
R. 2:05b-2:06	R. 2:18b-2:19	R. 2:29b-2:31a	R. 9:06b
P. 2:07a	P. 2:20a	P. 2:31b	P. 9:06c-9:14
R. 2:07b-2:09a	R. 2:20b-2:21	R. 2:31c-2:33	R. 9:15-9:23
P. 2:09b-2:10a	P. 2:22a	P. 2:34	P. 10:01-10:12
R. 2:10b-2:11	R. 2:22b-2:24a	R. 3:01	R. 10:13
P. 2:12a	P. 2:24b-2:25a	P. 3:02-5:18a	P. 10:14-10:21a
R. 2:12b-2:13	R. 2:25b-2:26	R. 5:18b	R. 10:21b

P. 10:22-10:27
R. 10:28
J. 10:29-10:32
R. 10:33-10:34
J. 10:35-10:36
E. 11:01-11:10
P. 11:11-11:12
E. 11:13
P. 11:14-11:17
E. 11:18-11:21a
R. 11:21b
E. 11:21c-11:23
P. 11:24-11:25
R. 11:26-11:29
P. 11:30
E. 11:31-11:34
R. 11:35
E. 12:01-12:04
R. 12:05
E. 12:06-12:15
R. 12:16
P. 13:01-13:16
J. 13:17-13:20
P. 13:21
J. 13:22a
R. 13:22b
J. 13:23-13:24
P. 13:25-13:26a
J. 13:26b-13:31

P. 13:32a
J. 13:32b
P. 13:33a
J. 13:33b-14:01
P. 14:02-14:03
J. 14:04
P. 14:05-14:10
J. 14:11-14:16
E. 14:17-14:18
J. 14:19-14:25
P. 14:26-14:35
R. 14:36-14:38
J. 14:39-14:45
R. 15:01-15:31
P. 15:32-16:01a
J. 16:01b-16:02a
P. 16:02b-16:11
J. 16:12-16:15
P. 16:16-16:24a
R. 16:24b
J. 16:25-16:26
P. 16:27a
R. 16:27b
P. 16:27c
J. 16:27d-16:32a
R. 16:32b
J. 16:32c-16:34
P. 16:35-19:22
R. 20:01a

E. 20:01b
P. 20:02-20:13
J. 20:14-20:21
R. 20:22
P. 20:23-20:29
J. 21:01-21:03
R. 21:04a
E. 21:04b-21:09
R. 21:10-21:20
J. 21:21-21:35
R. 22:01
J. 22:02-22:03a
E. 22:03b-22:06
J. 22:07a
R. 22:07b
J. 22:07c
E. 22:08-22:20
J. 22:21a
R. 22:21b
J. 22:22-22:35a
E. 22:35b-24:01
J. 24:02-24:09
E. 24:10-24:14
J. 24:15-24:19
E. 24:20-24:25
J. 25:01-25:05
P. 25:06-25:13
R. 25:14-25:18
P. 26:01-26:04a

R. 26:04b
P. 26:05-26:08
R. 26:09-26:11
P. 26:12-26:62
R. 26:63-26:65
P. 27:01-27:14a
R. 27:14b
P. 27:15-27:23
R. 28:01-29:40
P. 30:01-30:08
R. 30:09
P. 30:10-31:14a
R. 31:14b
P. 31:14c-31:16a
R. 31:16b
P. 31:17-31:48a
R. 31:48b
P. 31:48c-31:52a
R. 31:52b
P. 31:53-31:54a
R. 31:54b
P. 31:54c-32:33a
R. 32:33b
P. 32:33c-32:38a
R. 32:38b
P. 32:38c
R. 32:39-33:49
P. 33:50-36:13

Deuteronomy

D. 1:01a
R. 1:01b-1:02
D. 1:03-1:23a
R. 1:23b
D. 1:24-1:36
R. 1:37-1:39
D. 1:40-2:09
R. 2:10-2:12
D. 2:13-2:19
R. 2:20-2:23
D. 2:24-2:28

R. 2:29a
D. 2:29b-3:08
R. 3:09
D. 3:10
R. 3:11
D. 3:12-3:13a
R. 3:13b-3:17
D. 3:18-3:19a
R. 3:19b
D. 3:19c-4:02
R. 4:03-4:04

D. 4:05-4:31
R. 4:32-4:39
D. 4:40-4:48a
R. 4:48b
D. 4:49-5:04
R. 5:05a
D. 5:05b-6:19
R. 6:20-6:25
D. 7:01-7:08
R. 7:09-7:10
D. 7:11-10:01a

R. 10:01b
D. 10:02a
R. 10:02b-10:03a
D. 10:03b-10:04
R. 10:05-10:09
D. 10:10-10:21
R. 10:22
D. 11:01-11:12
R. 11:13
D. 11:14-11:17
R. 11:18-11:21

D. 11:22-11:28
R. 11:29-11:30
D. 11:31-12:12a
R. 12:12b
D. 12:13-12:14
R. 12:15-12:16
D. 12:17-12:18
R. 12:19
D. 12:20-14:29a
R. 14:29b

D. 14:29c-19:04
R. 19:05a
D. 19:05b-24:03a
R. 24:03b
D. 24:04-26:02
R. 26:03-26:04
D. 26:05-27:04
R. 27:05-27:07
D. 27:08-28:40
R. 28:41

D. 28:42-28:67
R. 28:68a
D. 28:68b-29:11a
R. 29:11b
D. 29:12-29:15
R. 29:16-29:17
D. 29:18-31:13
E. 31:14
R. 31:15
D. 31:16-31:22

E. 31:23
R. 31:24-31:30
D. 32:01-32:47
R. 32:48-33:29
E. 34:01-34:03
D. 34:04
E. 34:05-34:07
P. 34:08-34:09
D. 34:10-34:12

Joshua

D. 1:01-1:18
E. 2:01-2:09
R. 2:10
E. 2:11-3:01
P. 3:02-3:08
E. 3:09-3:10
P. 3:11-3:13a
E. 3:13b
P. 3:14-3:15
E. 3:16
P. 3:17
E. 4:01
P. 4:02
E. 4:03a
P. 4:03b
E. 4:03c
P. 4:04-4:07
E. 4:08
P. 4:09-4:13
E. 4:14
P. 4:15-4:19a
E. 4:19b-4:23a
R. 4:23b
E. 4:24-5:01
P. 5:02-5:12
E. 5:13-6:03
P. 6:04
E. 6:05-6:06a
P. 6:06b
E. 6:07a

P. 6:07b
E. 6:08a
P. 6:08b-6:09
E. 6:10
P. 6:11-6:13
E. 6:14a
R. 6:14b
E. 6:14c-6:16a
R. 6:16b
E. 6:16c
P. 6:17a
R. 6:17b
P. 6:18-6:19
E. 6:20
P. 6:21
E. 6:22-6:23
P. 6:24
E. 6:25a
R. 6:25b
E. 6:25c-6:27
P. 7:01
E. 7:02-7:05
P. 7:06
E. 7:07-7:09
P. 7:10-7:26
E. 8:01-8:03a
P. 8:03b
E. 8:04-8:09
P. 8:10-8:13
E. 8:14a

P. 8:14b
E. 8:14c
P. 8:15-8:16
E. 8:17
P. 8:18-8:19a
E. 8:19b-8:20
P. 8:21a
E. 8:21b
P. 8:21c
E. 8:22-8:23
P. 8:24-8:28
E. 8:29
D. 8:30-8:31a
R. 8:31b
D. 8:32-8:35
E. 9:01-9:09
R. 9:10
E. 9:11-9:16
R. 9:17-9:21
E. 9:22-10:11
R. 10:12-10:14
E. 10:15-10:27
R. 10:28
E. 10:29a
R. 10:29b-10:31a
E. 10:31b-10:32a
R. 10:32b-10:33
E. 10:34-10:35a
R. 10:35b
E. 10:36

R. 10:37-10:42
E. 10:43-11:09
R. 11:10-11:13
E. 11:14
D. 11:15
P. 11:16-13:03a
R. 13:03b-13:04a
P. 13:04b-13:14
R. 13:15-13:33
P. 14:01-14:10a
R. 14:10b
P. 14:10c-15:04a
R. 15:04b
P. 15:05-15:08a
R. 15:08b
P. 15:08c-15:12
J. 15:13-15:15a
R. 15:15b
J. 15:16-15:19
P. 15:20
R. 15:21-15:62
J. 15:63
P. 16:01-16:09
J. 16:10
P. 17:01-17:09a
R. 17:09b
P. 17:09c-17:11a
R. 17:11b
J. 17:12-17:18
E. 18:01-18:06

R. 18:07	R. 19:23b	P. 19:47-19:48a	P. 24:02-24:09
E. 18:08-18:10	P. 19:24-19:25a	R. 19:48b	R. 24:10a
P. 18:11-18:20	R. 19:25b-19:26a	E. 19:49-19:50	P. 24:10b-24:12a
R. 18:21-18:28	P. 19:26b-19:27	R. 19:51	R. 24:12b
P. 19:01	R. 19:28	P. 20:01-20:03	P. 24:12c-24:13
R. 19:02-19:09a	P. 19:29	R. 20:04-20:06a	E. 24:14-24:19
P. 19:09b-19:14	R. 19:30	P. 20:06b	R. 24:20
R. 19:15	P. 19:31a	R. 20:06c	E. 24:21-24:25
P. 19:16a	R. 19:31b	P. 20:07-21:08	R. 24:26a
R. 19:16b	P. 19:32-19:34	R. 21:09-21:42	E. 24:26b-24:28
P. 19:17	R. 19:35-19:38	P. 21:43-21:45	P. 24:29-24:31
R. 19:18-19:21	P. 19:39a	D. 22:01-22:08	R. 24:32
P. 19:22a	R. 19:39b	P. 22:09-22:34	P. 24:33
R. 19:22b	P. 19:40	D. 23:01-23:16	
P. 19:23a	R. 19:41-19:46	E. 24:01	

Judges

J. 1:03	J. 1:10-1:15	J. 1:20-1:21	J. 1:27-1:29

The Yahwist was the author of the second-oldest writings in the Judaeo-Christian bible, only the Song of Deborah (JUDG. 5) being older. He was also the third mythologian whose peculiar innovations eventually coalesced into a nationalistic deistic conceit known as Judaism.

Ikhenaton was the man who first conceived the idea of a single, universal god who needed to make no compromise with other gods because they did not exist. This was true monotheism, a creed that, after Ikhenaton's death, was not seen again for more than a thousand years. However, given the fanatic intensity of the monolatry that the Jews derived from the Israelites, who derived it from Moses, who derived it from Ikhenaton, it was inevitable that monotheism would eventually reappear.

Moses succeeded where Ikhenaton had failed. He made no attempt to impose monotheism on polytheists, otherwise he would have had no more success than Ikhenaton. But he did succeed in imposing the nearest thing, monolatry, belief in many gods but worship of only one. Moses persuaded a whole nation to accept the concept of a jealous god who demanded exclusive worship and would inflict vicious, sadistic punishments on the entire tribe if a single one of its worshippers dared honour any of its rivals.

The Yahwist added the final touch that gave Judaism the xenophobic bigotry without which it would not have survived long enough ever to reinvent monotheism: he invented covenant mythology.

The Yahwist was King David's man. The best guess is that he was either a scribe in David's civil service or a spokesman for Yahweh, or perhaps both. The suggestion has been made that he was the spokesman Nathan; but while the philosophy of Nathan was consistent with that of the Yahwist, the identification is based solely on the absence from the record of the names of any of Nathan's like-minded contemporaries. The only other spokesman of the period whose name survives was Gad; and J was certainly not Gad.[4]

The Yahwist (like Nathan) believed that Yahweh, far from being a mere tribal god with no interests outside his territorial borders, was King of gods and men, Ruler of the universe, creator of the land and the skies, and manufacturer of the first humans (but not in the god's own likeness; that conceit was Priestly); and that David was Yahweh's chosen King. He set out to write a history of the world that would begin with the first man, trace the origins of the nations that David had subjugated and show the past event that justified that subjugation, and end with the final working out of Yahweh's plan in the establishment of the Jewish empire and the Davidic monarchy, each of which was guaranteed to last forever. He probably formed his conceit during David's lifetime, but not until he had seen his belief in a perpetual monarchy confirmed by the accession of David's son and grandson did he actually sit down to write.

In trying to reconstruct the workings of the Yahwist's mind, we are not completely groping in the dark. We have no earlier examples of the kind of thought processes that he must have used, but there is no shortage of comparable circumstances from later days.

Two hundred years after the writing of the Yahwist's covenant-view of history, a Greek editor-poet known as Homer combined perhaps as many as twenty-four different poems, at least two or three of which had been composed earlier than the time of the Trojan war, into an epic that contained ninety percent of the present-day *Iliad*. Homer's amalgam, although designed to entertain, was also intended as interpretive history. He told his hearers not only what had happened at Troy, but also why it had happened. And

---

4. Richard Friedman, in *Who Wrote the Bible?*, raised the possibility that J might have been female, and Harold Bloom made that theory the basis of *The Book of J*. However, the conclusion that J's forbidden-fruit myth stemmed from a pathological hatred of goddess-worship is incompatible with such a possibility. Friedman attributed to J passages that could not have been written earlier than the 840s BCE. I attribute those passages to R. The combination of Friedman's evidence that J wrote no earlier than the accession of Rekhobowam, and Peter Ellis's evidence (*The Yahwist*) that J's hero-worship of David indicated a working relationship, convinces me that J wrote during Rekhobowam's lifetime.

that *why* was supplied from Homer's own frame of reference.

Homer believed in gods. He believed in Zeus, King of all gods, who was necessarily neutral in a conflict between mortals; he believed in the European gods, Poseidon and Athena, who favoured the Greeks; and he believed in his own Asian gods, Apollo and Aphrodite, who favoured Troy. He knew the details of what had happened at Troy, and he (or the poems' original composers) explained it all in terms of the gods.

For example, he knew that Menelaos had fought a duel with Paris; he knew that Menelaos had overcome his opponent; and he knew that Paris had fortuitously escaped before Menelaos could kill him. To Homer, the explanation was self-evident: Paris had escaped for the clear and obvious reason that his patron-goddess had rescued him. Similarly the death of mighty Hektor, and the plague that led to the breach between Agamemnon and Akhilleus, were given the only explanation that Homer could accept as logical: the intervention of a god.

The Yahwist thought likewise. He saw Jewish victories as Yahweh's reward for worshipping him. Jewish defeats were attributed to Yahweh's wrath when his tribe abandoned him for the fertility goddesses whose nuns and monks (*kedeshowth* and *kedeshiym*) offered sexual services not provided by the spokesmen for Yahweh.

The Israelites had left Egypt (fact) because Yahweh had decided to end their slavery (Yahwist's mythology). Moses failed to reach the Israelites' final homeland (fact) because he had somehow angered Yahweh (interpretation). Yahuwdah's sons had died childless because the first *did things that Yahweh viewed angrily, so Yahweh wasted him* (GEN. 38:7), while the second also *was viewed angrily by Yahweh, so he wasted him too* (38:10).

Humans died (fact) because the first man disobeyed Yahweh's ban on worshipping the Mother (Yahwist's mythology). David and Solomon reduced the Edomites to serfdom (fact) because Isaac had blessed Jacob and made Esau his slave (rationalisation). The latter fable not only explained David's imperialism; it justified it.

The Yahwist committed to writing the fabulous genealogy that made the eponymous ancestors of the tribes of the Jewish-Israelite confederacy sons and grandsons of a single demigod who was both Jew and Israelite. The pretence that Jews and Israelites were the same tribe was too artificial to succeed, and the shaky alliance was permanently terminated at the death of Solomon. Nonetheless, the genealogy, once written down, became established fact for Jew and Israelite alike. It is ironic that, when the Jews reconquered a portion of David's empire in 1948 CE, they named it, not after their own eponym, Yahuwdah, whose name the land had borne for two thousand years, but after the eponym of a non-Jewish tribe that had been extinct for 2700 years.

Composing a fictitious genealogy for the sake of political expedience was simple enough. To the modern reader it might seem that the real problem would have lain in persuading anybody to accept it. In fact, as a well-documented parallel from Greece demonstrates, the improbable creation of artificial ancestors was far from unique, and was successfully accomplished as recently as 500 BCE.

Prior to 500 BCE the Greek *polis* of Attika was divided into four tribes, equivalent to the four Jewish-Israelite matriarchies of Leah, Rakhel, Bilhah and Zilpah. The four tribes were subdivided into a total of twelve fraternities, the sacred zodiacal number so important to the ancients. Each fraternity was further broken down into a number of clans, each named after an eponymous ancestor. The problem with the system as it then existed was that the tribes and subtribes were regional, so that, for example, a dispute between adjacent suburbs over grazing rights would automatically be expanded into an inter-tribal issue. In such a situation, armed altercation that pitted one part of the *polis* against another was not uncommon.

Kleisthenes, founder of the Athenian democracy, formulated a scheme to end regional hostilities. He abolished all existing tribes, fraternities and clans, and founded ten new tribes that were multi-regional. He assigned to each tribe a segment of Attica containing roughly one-tenth of the population of Athens; one-tenth of the rural inland; and one-tenth of the shore. He declared that any person residing in a designated area on the day that the new tribes were instituted, regardless of where he might move at a later date, was a member of the tribe to which the area had been assigned and a descendant of the tribe's designated ancestor. Kleisthenes's invention of ancestors was absurd, impractical—and successful. The political necessity of such a scheme was understood, and the Athenians were intelligent and cooperative enough to make the fiction work.

In the same way, Jews who were well aware that their demigod Yahuwdah had never had an ancestor named Yisrael, and Israelites who knew their demigod had never heard of any Abraham, Yitskhak or Yaakob, pretended that they had. The Yahwist committed the new folklore to writing, and fiction became fact.

The Yahwist's explanation of how King David, leader of a tribe as small and insignificant as the Jews, had made himself the equal of the kings of Babylonia and Egypt, was a logical extension of his conceit that Yahweh was the most powerful god on earth: the Jews were Yahweh's Chosen Nation. Yahweh, so the Yahwist reasoned, had arbitrarily chosen a minor Phoenician tribe and set them up as rulers of a monolatrist empire. To show that such had been Yahweh's plan from the beginning, the Yahwist made the Choosing retroactive, and assigned to Abraham, Isaac and Jacob beliefs and practices that in fact had come into existence since their deaths.

As part of the same mythology inspired by David's observable success, the Yahwist also originated the (retroactive) concept of the Promised Land. Since Yahweh must have long previously ordained that his Chosen Nation would conquer Judah, it logically followed that he would not have withheld that information from his favoured demigods. Consequently the Yahwist composed dialogues in which Yahweh 'promised' Abraham, Isaac and Jacob that the lands then occupied by various tribes of Phoenicians would be 'given' to their descendants. That the 'promised land' was the only Middle East real estate with no oil under it, Yahweh was apparently unaware. That land peacefully occupied for a thousand years by other tribes was not Yahweh's to give, was no more comprehensible to the Yahwist than it is to the terrorists-turned-politicians who constitute an influential force in modern-day Israel.

To explain why Yahweh should have chosen Abraham as the beneficiary of his partisanship, the Yahwist had Yahweh initially make Abraham the offer, 'If you will leave your land and your kinsmen and your father's family and go to a land I'll show you, then I'll make you (ancestor of) a large tribe' (GEN. 12:1-2). To show that Abraham had been tested and found worthy of such an offer, J fabricated a tale of his pious hospitality to strangers (GEN. 18). Yahweh demanded blind, unquestioning obedience to capricious laws, the same kind of unquestioning obedience demanded by Yahweh-the-King's prototype, David. When Abraham showed his willingness to grant such obedience, Yahweh made him founding ancestor of the Chosen Nation. Since the promise of continued obedience constituted a complete expla-nation of the treaty (usually translated 'covenant') between Yahweh and Abraham, the Yahwist saw no reason to have Abraham slice off his fore-skin as a further sign of his special relationship with the god. The Egyptian custom of circumcising slaves as a mark of identification, which the Priestly author later backdated to Abraham (GEN. 17:10), the Yahwist acknowl-edged to have been introduced into Phoenicia from Egypt by Moses (EXOD. 4:24-26).[5]

In order to sell Yahweh to the fanatically exclusivist Israelites, J had to convince them that Yahweh was identical with the gods they already worshipped. Moses had conditioned them to the monolatrous worship of Aton or Allah, a god whose most distinguishing characteristic was jealousy of his peers. The switch to the worship of elohiym, 'the gods,' that probably occurred after Moses' death, was little more than a semantic quibble, since the plural Elohiym remained every bit as jealous as the singular Allah.

---

5. The Encyclopedia of Religions (Mircea Eliade, ed., New York, 1987) lists ten theories for the origin of circumcision, including 'marked captives,' and then blandly states, 'None of these theories is accepted today.' The author of the entry does not, however, offer a better explanation, and of all the theories I have encountered, slave identification makes the most sense.

The Jews, despite the central position that Yahweh occupied in their mythology, were not at that time monolatrous, any more than the central role of Artemis in the religious orientation of Hippolytos made him monolatrous. To make a single mythology acceptable to both Jews and Israelites, what J had to do was turn the Jews into monolatrists, and turn the Israelites into worshippers of a god whose worship 'the gods' had expressly forbidden. The result was *Yahweh elohiym*, 'Yahweh the gods,' a Jewish/ Israelite hybrid who was somehow possessed of the singularity of Yahweh and the exclusivity and uncompromising jealousy of Elohiym. The Jews eventually fully accepted the reality of 'Yahweh the gods'; but the Israelites never did.

Equating unrelated gods by combining their names was easy. The Yahwist's real problem in composing a chronicle that would be accepted as history by Jew and Israelite alike, was the necessity of blending the Israelite remembrance of an Egyptian captivity into a Jewish tradition that knew nothing of any such event. Clearly he could not deprive the Jews' greatest hero, the mass-murderer Yahuwshua, of the permanence of his conquest by having the hybrid Jews/Israelites enter Egypt after Yahuwshua's victories. Nor could he tamper with the tradition that Moses had died with his promise to win the Israelites a new homeland unfulfilled.

J's solution to what should have been an insurmountable problem was a slight juxtaposition of events. He placed everything else in correct chronological order, but dated the conquest of Judah by Yahuwshua to the period following the death of Moses, 150 years later than it actually occurred, and named the fourteenth-century BCE Yahuwshua as the successor to the thirteenth-century BCE Moses. As insurance against detection, he omitted such details as the name of Joseph's Pharaoh (Ikhenaton), the name of the Pharaoh in Yahuwshua's day (also Ikhenaton), and the name of Moses' Pharaoh (Ramoses II), that might have drawn attention to the impossible chronology.

The Yahwist began his narrative: *On the day that Yahweh the gods made the land and the skies, there was as yet no . . . man to till the soil. . . . Yahweh the gods formed the human* (adam) *from the soil* (adamah) *of the land, and breathed into his nostrils the breath that is life* (GEN. 2:4-7). He did not attempt to date humankind's creation. The genealogies that put that event precisely 1,656 years before Noah's flood were added by the Redactor five hundred years later (GEN. 5). He chronicled humankind's steady deterioration from the goddess-worshipping Adam ('human'), through the murderer Cain, to the savage, vengeful Lamekh (GEN. 4:24). He then jumped to the righteous Noah, whom the Redactor made a descendant of Set. Following the castration of Noah by his youngest son Khenaan, which the Redactor expurgated, and the Tower of Babylon myth, he jumped again, to the patriarch Abraham, in the process switching from pure mythology to what might loosely be termed history. Again the Redactor later 'rectified' the Yahwist's omission of a satisfactory transition by inserting a genealogy that showed Abraham's descent from Noah's son Sem (GEN. 11:10-27).

The Yahwist chronicled the lives of Abraham and Jacob, joining them together through the person of Isaac. He used a similar means to make the transition to Israelite history. Knowing that the Israelites had entered Egypt through the intercession of Yanhuma, whom he called Joseph, he made Joseph simultaneously the son of the Jewish demigod Jacob and the father of the Israelites' earlier-age eponyms, Menasheh and Efrayim.

From Joseph he jumped to Moses, again leaving it to the Redactor to provide the Egyptian with a Levite pedigree. He described the fairy tale Israelite version of the departure from Egypt under Moses in about 1250 BCE. Since later prophets knew about it (although the Elohist did not), it seems a reasonable assumption that he described the assassination of Moses. The deletion of that event from the finished Towrah may have been the work of R's busy scissors; but it is not unlikely that it was expurgated before R's time.

As a probable spokesman himself, with a vested interest in maximising the status and prestige of spokesmen, J credited Moses with performing miracles. He composed the anecdotes, later borrowed by the Priestly author, in which Moses brought down ten plagues on Egypt, and dried up the Sea of Reeds. However, knowing that he could not himself accomplish marvels of such immensity, J also had Moses perform two conjuring illusions that he could perform himself: the leprosy trick[6] and the cane-to-snake trick.[7] In P's later version, however, to emphasise the superiority of priest over spokesman, P had the cane-to-snake trick performed by Aaron. And since P dared not dispute that Egyptian astrologer-magicians could also do the cane-to-snake trick, he one-upped the Egyptians by having Aaron's snake eat the Egyptians' snake.

J's account of the origin of circumcision remains perplexing, for it offered no rational explanation for the institution of the ritual:

> Mosheh took his wife and his sons and loaded them onto a donkey and set out for the land of Egypt. On the journey, at a campsite, Yahweh ambushed him with the intention of killing him. But Tsiporah took a flint knife and

---

6. By placing a rubber ball under the armpit and squeezing it with the arm, it is possible to cut off the flow of blood, thereby giving the arm a white, leprous appearance. Releasing the pressure restores the arm to normal.

7. By slightly twisting a snake's head, a handler can induce a state of catalepsy so that the snake can be passed off as a cane. Dropping the snake onto the floor will then give the impression that a cane has come to life.

hacked off her son's foreskin and dedicated his phallus. 'You're a bloody bridegroom to me indeed,' she said. So he spared him. (EXOD. 4:20a, 24-26)

Since Moses was returning to Egypt at Yahweh's specific order (EXOD. 4:19), why did Yahweh suddenly get it into his head to kill him? And why did he change his mind when Moses' Midianite wife, for no apparent reason, circumcised her son? The Yahwist's failure to answer those questions suggests that perhaps he saw Yahweh's actions as too capricious for mere mortals to comprehend. Yet elsewhere J did offer rationalisations for some of Yahweh's irrational behaviour. Why not here? A rationalisation was available: Hitherto, an Israelite's circumcision had been a visible sign of his status as Pharaoh's slave. Henceforth, it was to symbolise his new status as the Chosen slave of his new god. That J did not offer such an explanation is strong evidence that in J's time circumcision was not yet regarded as having any connection with the treaty between the Jewish/Israelite confederacy and its hybrid god. P would not make that connection until three hundred years later.

From the assassination of Moses around 1200 BCE, the Yahwist took a great leap backwards, to c. 1370 BCE, and described Yahuwshua's conquest of Judah. In all likelihood he did not write a detailed account, and what he did write has not survived. R mentioned a *Book of the Wars of Yahweh* that was E's probable source for chapters two through ten of *Joshua* (NUM. 21:14), and it seems likely that *Wars of Yahweh* would have been composed, mainly in the form of victory songs, soon after the events described. With a history of the conquest already existing, the Yahwist would have seen no necessity for duplicating its contents. Probably he wrote a summary. Certainly he wrote something. His narrative continually foreshadowed the conquest and the establishment of the Davidic monarchy, and any conclusion that did not show Yahweh's fulfilment of his promises to Abraham, Isaac and Jacob would have been anticlimactic.

The Yahwist was a historian. Today no person claiming such a title would dare use the literary techniques employed by the Yahwist. In 920 BCE what would today be rejected as blatant falsification was as much an integral part of storytelling as Thoukydides's practice six hundred years later of composing speeches that may or may not have resembled speeches actually made. Like Thoukydides, the Yahwist invented speeches. He composed speeches for the historical Abraham, the mythical Adam, and the god Yahweh. He wrote speeches that were purely expository, such as Yahweh's instructions to Noah concerning the purpose of the ark (GEN. 7:1-4), and he wrote speeches that had the purpose of foreshadowing, or 'prophesying,' events that were to occur later in his story.

The Yahwist's prophecies of events that had already happened were written for the legitimate purpose of enhancing his readers' expectations and adding a unifying motif of promise-and-fulfilment to an otherwise purely episodic cataloguing of unrelated events. Yahweh's repeated promises to the patriarchs that he would give the land of Phoenicia to their descendants foreshadowed the victories of Yahuwshua and David, and gave a new dimension to Judah itself by retroactively turning it into the Promised Land. The blessings and curses put into the mouths of the patriarchs fulfilled the same function.

For example, in his myth of the castration of Noah, the Yahwist had Noah curse his youngest son:

> Cursed be Khenaan.
> He is to be the slave
> Of his brothers' slaves.
> Blessed by Yahweh the gods is Sem.
> Khenaan is to be his slave.
> The gods are to expand Iapet.
> He is to live in Sem's tents,
> And Khenaan is to be his slave.
> (GEN. 9:25-27)

Noah's sons, Sem, Iapet and Khenaan, represented the Jews, Philistines and Phoenicians.[8] The Yahwist devised Noah's curse to foreshadow that part of his narrative in which the three sons' putative descendants would enact the roles assigned to them by their righteous ancestor.

The Yahwist was neither the first nor the last mythologian to justify an inequitable *status quo* by making it the unalterable will of a tribal god. Little more than a century ago white Americans justified slavery by pointing to its endorsement by the Judaeo-Christian bible. And a thousand years before J's time the white Brahmanas conquered India and imposed on the aborigines a god-ordained caste system that rated themselves as far above the black Sudras in the theological hierarchy as J's Chosen Nation was above the subject Edomites and Mowabites. Like the Jews, the Brahmanas discouraged intermarriage with the unchosen. In a fable composed by the viciously xenophobic Priestly author, an Israelite married a Midianite woman and thereby caused Yahweh to send a plague that killed twenty-four thousand. But when the future High Priest murdered the offending couple, Yahweh's wrath was stilled (NUM. 25:6-9). The Brahmanas declared that the offspring of a Brahmana who married a member of a lower-ranking ruling caste would be Sudras; while the offspring of Brahmana-Sudra matings would have no

---

8. The Priestly author later made Sem, *Kham* and Iapet the sons of Noah, and Khenaan the son of Kham.

caste at all and be classified as Untouchables.

To keep the lower castes from rebelling, the Brahmanas promoted a bible, *Veda*, that decreed death or torture for even the mildest attempt to claim equality with a member of a higher caste, but offered the certainty of eventual reincarnation as a Brahmana to unquestioning Uncle Toms.[9] Since in the Yahwist's day the Jews had been a ruling caste for less than two generations, and no problems had arisen that could not be solved militarily, the Yahwist's retroactive justification of unequal status for Jews and gentiles was designed to flatter the masters, not to reconcile the slaves.

The Yahwist's central 'prophecy,' the fulfilment of which was his climax and purpose in writing, was the deathbed speech attributed to the demigod Jacob:

> Yahuwdah, it's to be you whom your kinsmen glorify,
> Your hand on your enemies' neck.
> Your father's descendants are to prostrate themselves before you.
>
> .   .   .   .   .
>
> The royal staff is not to pass from Yahuwdah,
> Nor the royal power from between his legs,
> Until the one comes to whom it belongs,
> To whom the nation is to grant obedience.

(GEN. 49:8-10)

With the fulfilment of that 'prophecy' in the person of King David, the Yahwist's saga was complete.

---

9. M. Larson, *The Story of Christian Origins*, pt. 1, ch. 8. To this day the *status quo* is strongly defended by many Hindu fundamentalists. The *Manchester Guardian* (4 April 1991) reported that in Mehrana village in northern India, after a 15-year-old upper caste girl, with the assistance of a lower caste friend, eloped with her lower caste boyfriend, a vigilante mob sentenced the offenders to be hanged by their own fathers, who had to be kicked and beaten to perform this task. The two lovers survived the lynching, but were then put onto a funeral pyre, along with their dead friend, where they were burned to death.

Seven

The Yahwist's Tales

If you follow the evidence you *must* change as additional evidence arrives and invalidates earlier conclusions. It is those who support ideas for emotional reasons only who can't change. Additional evidence has no effect on emotion.
Isaac Asimov, *Quasar, Quasar, Burning Bright.*

Of the sixty-two stories in *Genesis*, more than fifty were written by the Yahwist. At the centre of the Yahwist's narrative, as at the centre of the *Iliad*, lay a hard core of historical fact; but basically he was as much a collector and weaver of fanciful fables as Jacob Grimm. He borrowed myths and legends from many sources and adapted them to his Jewish/Israelite history wherever they could be tailored to fit. He occasionally told the same story twice. The conflict between twins in the womb, for example, found in the Greek tale of Proitos and Akrisios and the Roman legend of Romulus and Remus, appeared twice in the Yahwist's work, the first time involving Jacob and Esau (GEN. 25:22), and later in connection with Parets and Zarakh (GEN. 38:28-29).

For his primeval or pre-patriarchal history, the Yahwist drew upon opposing mythologies that were in many cases incompatible. According to the flood myth, the descendants of Cain were all destroyed. Yet the Yahwist utilised the tradition that the Cainites, Sumerians, had built the Tower of Babylon. So that the confusion of languages would not be reversed by the extermination of all but one Hebrew-speaking family, J placed the Tower's construction after the flood. Then, in order not to show Cainites alive at a time when they should have been drowned, J avoided calling the builders Cainites, even though he had earlier identified Cain as the first man to journey eastward into Sumeria. He did identify Sumeria as the fable's location, but gave the site in Sumeria its later Akkadian name of Bab-El (Babylon) rather than its original Sumerian name of Kadingira.

The Yahwist took care to disguise the incompatibility of the Tower of Babylon fable and the flood myth by having the Tower built by descendants of Noah. The Towrah's final Redactor was less careful. By including both J's flood, in which all Cainites drowned, and E's tale in which Cainites were still flourishing in Moses' day (NUM. 24:21-22), he created the very incompatibility J had so skillfully avoided.

The Redactor's clumsiness in allowing Cainites to survive even though none was on the ark led to the invention (by whites) of the slur that the 'mark' by which Cain was permanently branded as a murderer was blackness. In post-Columbian days the mark-of-Cain myth was used as a justification for slavery; while in the nineteenth century CE the neo-Christian mythologian Joseph Smith stated explicitly in his *Pearl of Great Price* that the black races descended from Cain.

Smith furthered his concept of dark skin as a punishment for sin in his *Book of Mormon* (plagiarised from a historical novel written some years earlier), in which he declared that the formerly-white American natives were stained red for such a cause. Smith added, however, that an American who abandoned his red gods in favour of Smith's white gods could eventually turn white. If any such transformation has ever taken place the news media must have missed it.

A few centuries earlier, the absence of a black man from Noah's ark led the Priestly author to remove Khenaan, ancestor of the white Phoenicians, from his original role of Noah's son, and substitute Kham, whose name was the Egyptian word for 'black.' In the Priestly genealogy, Kham's descendants included, besides Khenaan, Khuwsh, Sheba and Kheth, eponyms of the Sudanese, Ethiopians and Hittites.

The Yahwist's first myth, the creation of Adam from clay, was borrowed from the Greek tale that Prometheus fashioned the first human from clay. J also followed the Greeks in making Eve a later, subsidiary creation. To Adam and Eve he attached a fantasy, partly Sumerian and partly original, that purported to explain and justify death.

Following his Adam-and-Eve and Cain-and-Abel myths, the Yahwist told of how the sons of the gods (*beney ha-elohiym*) intermarried with the daughters of the human (*benowth ha-adam*). Embarrassed mythologians of a monotheistic culture have rationalised that the sons of the gods were the sons of Set, while the daughters of the human were the daughters of Cain.

In fact, by *beney ha-elohiym*, the Yahwist meant the minor gods of the Jewish pantheon, once literally sons of the King of gods but later demoted to the status of his created messengers, the angels.

The full story of the sons of the gods and the daughters of the human was eventually written down in the *Book of Enoch*, a second-century BCE Essene composition regarded as sacred for three centuries by the Jewish followers of King Jesus. The highest order of angels, the serafs (planets), having no females of their own since Jewish sexist bigotry had decreed that only males could be immortal, lusted after mortal women in defiance of Yahweh's long-standing prohibition of matings that would produce undesirable offspring. While this was the first instance in Jewish mythology of the concept, so common to the Greeks, of gods seducing women, it was anticipated that it would not be the last. Paul of Tarsus in the first century CE ordered that women at prayer were to cover their heads lest their naked tresses arouse the lust of the angels (1 COR. 11:10).

The offspring of the serafs' illegitimate matings were the giants, humanoid creatures 137 metres tall possessed of perishable protoplasmic bodies inherited from their mortal mothers, and imperishable astral bodies inherited from their immortal fathers. The giants' mortal bodies were destroyed by Noah's flood; but because, unlike humans, they had immortal parts, 'souls,' they could not be totally destroyed, and their astral bodies survived as the evil spirits (1 ENOCH 7; JUBILEES 5). Since the evil spirits had grown accustomed to occupying human bodies, they attempted to replace their drowned carcasses by taking over the bodies of others. Exorcists such as Jesus were able to make a good living capitalising on this belief, curing victims of religious hysteria by deluding them (and themselves) that they were expelling evil spirits.

The remainder of *Enoch*'s fable originated long after the death of the Yahwist: For their disobedience the serafs were expelled from the skies and sentenced to spend eternity in darkness. Their leader Khazazel (the planet Venus) became known thereafter as The Enemy (*ha-satan*), occupying a position in Jewish mythology analogous to the Zoroastrian Prince of Darkness, Ahriman. But that was a development the Yahwist could not have anticipated. To him, Yahweh's great Enemy was the goddess. As for the serafs' illegitimate offspring, the giants: even though J had them flourishing before the flood and, since none was on the ark, disappearing at that time, they nonetheless reappeared alive and well at Khebrown in the days of Moses (NUM. 13:33). But it was the Redactor's inclusion of both J's pre-flood giants and P's post-flood giants that caused that inconsistency. J, as previously noted, was not so clumsy.

The Yahwist's philosophy of metahistory was not startlingly different from that of the inventors of Christianity. He, too, saw humankind's progress as a steady deterioration from the culpable naivete of Adam to the vindictive savagery of Lamekh, necessitating a new beginning under a born-again second Adam. The Yahwist's second Adam, the perfect man whom all future generations could proudly claim as their ultimate ancestor, reborn from a water-borne symbolic womb in which he was confined for three months, was the mythical Noah.

There are two versions of Noah's flood in *Genesis*, one by the Yahwist and one by the Priestly author. So thoroughly has R intertwined P's flood myth with J's that contradictory statements can be found in successive sentences:

J	P
(7:2-3) Of every clean animal, you are to take seven of each kind, a male and his females; and of unclean animals you are to take two, a male and his female; and of birds of the air, seven of each kind, male and female.	(6:19-20) Of every living thing . . . you are to bring two of each kind . . . male and female. Of every kind of bird, every kind of livestock . . . two of each.
(7:12) The rain fell upon the land for forty days and forty nights.	(7:11) In the 600th year . . . on the 17th day of the 2nd month . . . the subterranean ocean gushed up and the sluice gates of the skies were opened.
(8:2b-3a) The rain from the skies was stopped, and the waters gradually ebbed from the land.	
(8:6-7a, 8-9) At the end of forty days Noakh . . . sent out a raven. . . . Then he sent out a dove (which,) finding no perch for its feet, returned to him on the ark.	
(8:10) He then waited seven days and again sent the dove.	
(8:12) He waited a further seven days and released another dove, which did not return.	
(8:13b) The surface of the land was dry (on the 94th day).	(8:13a, 14) In the 601st year . . . on the 27th of the 2nd the land was dry (*on the 364th day.*)[1]
(9:18) The sons of Noakh who went out of the ark were Sem and Iapet and Khenaan.	(9:18) The sons of Noakh who went out of the ark were Sem *and Kham and* Iapet. And *Kham is the father of* Khenaan.

Among the more obvious disagreements between the two versions is that, in the Yahwist's flood story, the ground was dry fifty-four days after

---

1. Twelve lunar months at 29½ days is 354 days. So from 2.17.600 until 2.27.601 is 12 months plus ten days, 364.

the cessation of the rain, whereas the Priestly version kept Noah afloat for several more months. Also, not knowing that the distinction would one day be attributed to the yet-unborn Moses, J's Noah differentiated between clean and unclean animals. P, familiar with *Deuteronomy* 14:4-20 (written 300 years after J's death), assumed that J's backdating to Noah of a taboo instituted by Moses was anachronistic, and deleted twelve of the birds and cattle. In fact the exclusion from Jewish menus of sacred animals dated back to the earliest days of god-worship. The pig, the main unclean animal, had been worshipped as Ashtaroth, and for that reason the eating of her body, once sacramental, had become taboo as soon as Yahweh replaced the Mother as the author of all life. The pig's equation with the fertility goddess survives in the Greek custom of calling the vulva a sow.

Flood myths had been around for over one thousand years before the Yahwist's day.[2] In the most primitive version known, that of the Hindus, the rain-goddess's attempt to destroy all life was thwarted when the generative principles, the primeval phallus and vulva, conjoined to form an enclosed ark with erect mast that floated on the hostile waters. Prior to the formation of the mythology that only Yahweh could cause natural disasters, the Jews likewise attributed the flood to the rain-goddess, as the flood hero's name, a masculinisation of the goddess Nuah/Nuwkhah/Nukie, indicates.

The Sumerians, while attributing the decision to send the flood to male gods, blamed that decision on the advice of a goddess: *Then Ishtar the sweet-voiced Queen of Heaven cried out . . . 'Why did I command this evil in the council of all the gods?'*[3] The Persians viewed the flood as a dastardly deed perpetrated by the Prince of Darkness, Ahriman, and identified the god who warned the righteous man to build an ark as Mithra, the Persian Jesus. The Armenian flood myth contributed the detail that the ark's landing place was Mount Ararat in Armenia.

The Yahwist's immediate source, however, was an Akkadian or Assyrian translation of the *Epic of Gilgamesh*, composed in Sumerian around 2000 BCE.[4] *Gilgamesh* told of how the god Enlil, unable to sleep on account of human-kind's cacophonous chatter, decided to wipe out the human race in a world-

---

2. Isaac Asimov writes, 'Noah's flood *did* happen. There was a vast and disastrous flood in the Tigris-Euphrates some six thousand years ago.' (*Asimov on Astronomy*, Anchor edition, p. 26.) That all flood myths represent a tribal memory of a historical flood of titanic proportions is not in dispute. Asimov may be correct in attributing the flood at Ur, which left an enormous layer of sediment c. 3200 BCE, to a meteor hitting the Persian Gulf rather than a river flooding. But he is inaccurate in assuming that any flood ever covered the entire Tigris-Euphrates valley. Floods comparable with that at Ur occurred also at Babylon and Erikh— but not within centuries of each other. No flood in history has covered as much as 10,000 square kilometres.

3. *The Epic of Gilgamesh*, Penguin edition, p. 107.

4. There are extant versions in all three languages.

covering flood. But Ziusudra (Utnapishtim in the Akkadian translation) was virtuous and was warned by Ea to build an ark, that he might survive:

GILGAMESH	GENESIS
Tear down your house, I say, and build a boat. These are the measurements of the barque as you shall build her: let her beam equal her length . . . then take up into the boat the seed of all living creatures. . . . Each side of the deck measured one hundred and twenty cubits. . . . The boat grounded; on the mountain of Nisir the boat held fast. . . .	Make yourself an ark . . . the length . . . is to be 300 cubits; the width is to be 50 cubits. . . . They went into the ark . . . pairs of every life form. . . . The ark came to rest on the mountains of Ararat.
When the seventh day dawned I loosed a dove . . . but finding no resting place she returned. I loosed a raven . . . and she did not come back. . . . I made a sacrifice. . . . When the gods smelled the sweet savour, they gathered like flies over the sacrifice. . . . Then Ea opened his mouth and spoke to warrior Enlil, 'Wisest of gods, hero Enlil,	. . . sent out a raven. . . . He then waited seven days and again sent the dove . . . which did not return. . . . Noakh . . . offered burnt offerings upon the altar. Yahweh smelled the sweet savour.
how could you so senselessly bring down the flood?' [5]	. . . 'Never again will I curse the soil.'

The Greek flood myth showed points of comparison with the Yahwist's version that indicate a borrowing from the older version. Iapet(os) was one of the fourteen Titans worshipped in Greece before the coming of the Greeks. Iapetos's grandson, Deukalion, was the Greek Noah. The Yahwist made Iapet Noah's second son. Deukalion's father was Prometheus, the Greek Yahweh who created humankind. His mother was Pandora, the Greek Eve. His son was Hellen, eponymous ancestor of the Greeks, just as Noah's first son was Sem, eponym of the Semites. The Yahwist's giants were destroyed in a flood that saw a new beginning under the second Adam. The Greek giants were eliminated in a war that saw a new beginning under King Zeus.

The rebellious angels whose progeny were destroyed in Noah's flood were in the Hellenistic age confined to outer darkness, and in later Christian mythology became occupiers of the underworld. The Titans who fought against Zeus were confined underground. Prometheus was a volcano-god whose worshippers took him to Greece. Yahweh was a volcano-god whose worshippers took him to Judah. In the surviving myth, Deukalion was chosen for his virtue by Zeus; but it is a safe assumption that in the pre-Greek

---

5. *Op. cit.*, pp. 105-109.

version of the story he was rescued by Prometheus. Noah was chosen for survival by Yahweh, a combination of King-of-Heaven Zeus and creator-of-humankind Prometheus.

From theological necessity the Yahwist restored to his flood myth an original feature not found in his immediate sources. In neither the Gilgamesh epic nor the Deukalion tale were the persons and animals on the ark earth's only survivors. Noah's crew were. To the Yahwist, a god who set out to destroy the human race and overlooked a few mountain dwellers above the floodline was less than thorough. And when it came to the systematic genocide of the unchosen, Yahweh was nothing if not thorough.

Noah became in the Yahwist's tale the Hebrew Ziusudra. He also became the Yahwist's Ouranos. Just as Ouranos was castrated by his youngest son, Kronos, so was Noah castrated by his youngest son, Khenaan.

The Yahwist wrote: *Noakh . . . drank wine until he was drunk, and he lay uncovered in his tent. Khenaan saw his father's helplessness, and told his two brothers* (GEN. 9:21-22). In a passage later expurgated by the Redactor, the Yahwist then described Noah's castration by Khenaan. Khenaan, like Kronos, sought his brothers' support; but as part of his justification of the later enslavement of the Phoenicians, the Yahwist had Sem and Iapet refuse to participate. The story concluded:

> Sem and Iapet took a cloak and . . . covered their father's ruin. They kept their faces backward, so that they did not see their father's disgrace. Then Noakh awakened from his drunken stupor and saw what his youngest son had done to him, and he cried out, 'Cursed be Khenaan.'   (GEN. 9:23-25)

That something has been deleted between verses 22 and 23 is beyond dispute. The words, *saw what his youngest son had done to him*, are meaningless in their present context. The expurgated version of the son's crime, looking at his father's nakedness, would make sense only to someone familiar with the nakedness taboos of *Genesis* 3:10; but those taboos, the Redactor's invention, did not exist in the Yahwist's day. Despite R's attempt to suppress it, the story of Noah's castration survived long enough to find its way into the Talmud: *He castrated him. By emasculating him, he deprived Noakh of the possibility of a fourth son* (who would have replaced Khenaan as Noakh's heir under the prevailing ultimogeniture) (SANHEDRIN 70a).

Besides censoring the nature of the crime, the Redactor was also responsible for transferring to Kham a myth that originally involved Khenaan. The Yahwist had Khenaan specifically cursed by Noah to be his brothers' slaves, and the following verses left no doubt that those brothers (or 'kinsmen') were Sem and Iapet (GEN. 9:25-27). The curse was inflicted on account of *what his youngest son had done to him*. The Redactor, familiar with the Priestly version in which Noah's sons were Sem, *Kham* and Iapet, and in any case needing a berth on the ark for an ancestor of the black races, 'rectified' what he saw as the Yahwist's error. In thus making Kham the criminal while leaving the consequent curse on Khenaan, long after the Deuteronomist had abolished the practice of punishing children for their parents' crimes (DEUT. 24:16), R transformed a story that was brutal but, by the standards of the Yahwist's day, strictly moral, into one that was pointless and immoral and further evidence that a god who would enforce such a curse must be morally retarded.

The original Tower of Babylon fable must have acquired its setting during the period when the Jews were nomadic traders whose only permanent residence was the hump of a camel. Never having seen a building more than two or three stories high, their first encounter with the ruins of a huge, unfinished ziggurat at Babylon would have overwhelmed them. Unable to conceive of any other reason for the building of such a mammoth structure, they concluded that the Cainites (Sumerians) must have tried to build a Tower that would reach the solid dome of the skies, which they understood to be just above the clouds, so that they could invade and occupy the demesne of the gods and gain immortality by eating the food of the gods from the tree of life.

To the Yahwist, who likewise believed that the solid skies were little higher than the clouds, the possibility of reaching them was entirely feasible, and he therefore credited his god with similarly regarding such a project as feasible. Yahweh, terrified that *'Now nothing they decide to do will be impossible for them'* (GEN. 11:6), was forced to take desperate measures to stop the project. He consequently deprived the builders of their common language. A modern god, knowing the distance even to the nearest star, would laugh at such an enterprise; but the Yahweh of 920 BCE can hardly be blamed for being as ignorant as his biographer.

In the older Akkadian version of the myth it was Bel who, angry at the Sumerians' *hubris*, sent Anu (Nabu, Hermes, Gabriel) to confound the builders' language so that they could never again cooperate for a similar purpose. The surfeit of languages in southern Mesopotamia probably contributed to the identification of Babylon (*Bab-El*) as the source of a primeval confusion of languages.

There were Greek parallels to the Babylonian tale of the attempt to climb to the demesne of the gods. Hesiod told of how the giants and Titans assaulted Olympos, only to be struck down by the thunderbolts of Zeus. Homer's *Odyssey* (11:316) detailed the giants' plot to pile three mountains one upon the other, *so that the skies might be climbed*. Bellerophontes, following the taming of the winged horse Pegasos, tried to fly to Olympos. The outraged Zeus sent a gadfly to sting Pegasos, causing it to throw its rider to the ground. Bellerophontes spent his last years as an outcast and a cripple, a not uncommon fate for Greek Heroes who succumbed to *hubris*. The main theme of the Sumerian *Epic of Gilgamesh* was the Hero's attempt to gain immortality, only to fail.

The Yahwist took his fable directly from the Akkadian version, making no change other than the theologically necessary substitution of Yahweh for Bel and Anu. As in several other borrowed tales, he attempted to strengthen his interpretation by adding a spurious etymology. He declared that *Babel* derived its name from the Hebrew verb *balbel*, to confound. In fact *Bab-El* was a direct translation into Akkadian of Babylon's original Sumerian name, *Kadingira*, 'God's Gate.' J was also wrong in stating that *they stopped building the town* (GEN. 11:8). Four centuries after J's death the ziggurat that inspired the myth was finally completed by King Nabu-akh-adon-assur and became known as the Hanging Gardens of Babylon.

A common legend in many cultures was that of the potentate denied an heir. Only after years of waiting, and usually following some exceptional circumstance that fulfilled a prophecy, was he granted the son destined for greatness. A Greek example was the myth of Aigeos's begetting of Theseus as a result of Pittheus's understanding of the meaning of a Delphic oracle. The Yahwist used the story four times.

Abraham's wife Sarah was barren. Only in Abraham's old age when Sarah had reached the comparatively old age of late-thirtyish did she produce the demigod Isaac (GEN. 18:11).[6] Following Abraham's long wait, Yahweh's plan for his Chosen Nation was again frustrated by the barrenness of Isaac's wife Rebekah (GEN. 25:21). Then Jacob's wife Rakhel remained childless while her rivals bore him six sons (GEN. 29:31).

In the Yahwist's fourth delayed-pregnancy legend, Yahuwdah's first two sons died childless and only his seduction by his widowed daughter-in-law in the guise of Ashtaroth's nun brought about the birth of Parets, the ancestor of King David (GEN. 38). A later writer put further obstacles in the way of the birth of the Yahwist's ultimate hero when he had Tamar's long wait for a dead husband's kinsman reenacted by David's great-grandmother in the *Book of Ruth*. The story also turned up in *Judges* and again in *Samuel*.

The Yahwist's tale of the fate of Sodom and Khomorah, like the gospel accounts of the life of Jesus, appears to have been a blending of a historical event with mythology that was much older. Essentially the tale was simply one more version of the destruction-of-humankind myth. Yahweh destroyed the world with his thunderbolts; but Levit was righteous and, along with his family, was allowed to escape. That Levit, like Noah, was originally

---

6. The Yahwist's Sarah was old by childbearing standards, but no specific age was suggested. It was the Priestly author who assigned to her the absurd age of 90 years.

humankind's only survivor, was revealed in the line spoken by his daughter before seducing him: '*Our old father is the only man left on earth to get into us, as is the custom throughout the land*' (GEN. 19:31).

That, despite the myth that became attached to their destruction, Sodom and Khomorah were historical cities destroyed by a volcanic eruption in the third (*not* the second) millennium BCE, becomes a reasonable conclusion when we compare the Yahwist's description with the known facts of the annihilation of Pompeii and Herculaneum:

> Yahweh brought down burning sulphur (lava) on Sodom and Khomorah . . . from the skies. . . . He turned those towns upside down, and the whole plain, including all the people of the towns . . . . Abraham . . . looked toward Sodom and Khomorah and across the plain, and he saw smoke rising from the land like smoke from a furnace.   (GEN. 19:24-28)

The Yahwist located Sodom and Khomorah in the Valley of Demons at the south end of the Dead Sea (GEN. 14:3). Archaeologists, satisfied that there are no ruins near or under the Dead Sea that could possibly be the remains of the destroyed cities, have concluded that Sodom and Khomorah did not exist. It may be, however, that the Dead Sea location represented the Yahwist's guess as to where he believed the buried cities must be, and that the search should be redirected far to the north.[7]

One of the kings who waged war against Sodom was the king of Sumer (GEN. 14:1). Sumer still existed in the third millennium BCE, but not in the second. If the Sodom stories that the Yahwist associated with the demigod Abraham, who flourished c. 1800 BCE, were originally connected to a much earlier Abraham (the name was in use in Ebla in 2400 BCE), they could well date from the time when the Jews occupied the volcanic area of south-central Anatolia and northern Syria. A war between Sumer and southern Anatolia, at opposite ends of fertile land that both wanted, was much more feasible than a war between Sumer and Phoenicia, located on opposite sides of a hostile desert. Perhaps the search for Sodom and Khomorah should be directed to the area of Turkey between Adana, Maras and Antakya. If the buried cities are located, it would then be reasonable to identify the volcano that buried them as the original Yahweh, the god of the Jews.

There is a revealing parallel between the Yahwist's Sodom tale and the *Epic of Gilgamesh*:

---

7. The Yahwist may have found Sodom's true location in his source, and changed it because he could not believe that the source was accurate. Plato seems to have done the same thing in locating Atlantis west of the Pillars of Herakles, refusing to believe Solon's declaration that it was a tiny island, now called Thira, not far south of Greece.

GILGAMESH	YAHWIST
Enlil said to the gods in council, 'The uproar of mankind is intolerable, and sleep is no longer possible on account of the babble.' So the gods in their hearts were moved to release the deluge. [8]	We are going to destroy this place, because a great outcry against them has come to Yahweh's attention and Yahweh has sent us to destroy it. (GEN. 19:13)

Given the advanced ethics of 920 BCE compared with one thousand years earlier when *Gilgamesh* was written, the Yahwist could not accept a *great outcry* that was keeping Yahweh awake as a sufficient reason for Noah's flood, so he therefore justified the flood by saying that *the disobedience of humankind was great in the land* (GEN. 6:5). However, as it did seem an adequate reason for wiping out a couple of cities, he transferred the god's cure for insomnia to Sodom and Khomorah. Being neither (in J's opinion) an unjust god who would annihilate Sodom and Khomorah just to silence their detractors, regardless of the merits of the accusations, nor an omniscient god who could evaluate the accusations on the basis of his own perfect knowledge, Yahweh needed actually to transport himself to Sodom, *'to find out for myself whether the accusations that have reached me reflect what they have really done; for if they were lies I want to know that'* (GEN. 18:21). Yahweh learned that the Sodomites were indeed blatant offenders against the universally-practised hospitality code, and as such deserved to die.

There are many instances of the inviolability of the hospitality code in Greek mythology. When Bellerophontes was (falsely) accused of raping Proitos's wife, Proitos was helpless to take vengeance because Bellerophontes had been his houseguest and as such was under his protection. So he sent Bellerophontes to a fellow king, along with a sealed letter outlining the guest's crime and instructing the recipient to kill him. But by the time the letter was read that king, too, had granted Bellerophontes his hospitality and was therefore unable to do him any hurt. The Jews observed a similar code, and even a gentile was entitled to the full protection of his host while under the roof of a Jew. (GEN. 19:8b).

Yahweh's messengers were Levit's houseguests. That they were male had no relevance to the Sodomites' crime. In a similar tale in *Judges*, the inviolable houseguest raped by a mob was female (JUDG. 19-20). Jewish sexism limited immortality to males; otherwise J might have made the messengers female and the Sodomites' crime would have been the same. There was no homosexuality taboo anywhere in the world in 920 BCE, and the later designation of homosexual recreation as *sodomy* was anach-

---

8. *Op. cit.*, p. 105.

ronistic. By demanding that Levit surrender guests under his protection for the amusement of a mob, the Sodomites showed their contempt for the sacred rules of hospitality, and for this Yahweh destroyed them. In the *Judges* version, instead of having to chastise the offenders himself, Yahweh was able to call upon a Jewish army.

The Yahwist composed the myth of Ownan. Ownan, Yahuwdah's second son, was required under Jewish law to impregnate his dead brother's widow, Tamar. The son thereby produced would keep the dead man's name alive by ancestor-worship, not Ownan's. Ownan performed the recreational element of his obligation willingly enough, but made a point of withdrawing before ejaculation. The Yahwist implied that Ownan resented fathering a child obligated to worship his dead brother. It apparently did not occur to him that Ownan might have been enjoying his new duties, and was consequently in no hurry to terminate his obligation by achieving its objective. Yahweh disapproved of Ownan's timely withdrawals and struck him dead (GEN. 38:8-10).

The Ownan myth has been cited by adherents of modern mythologies as evidence of Yahweh's opposition to sperm-wasting, whether by masturbation or contraception. The word *onanism* has even been anachronously coined as a synonym for masturbation. In fact Ownan's crime had nothing to do with masturbation or sperm-wasting. It was for Ownan's refusal to fulfil a duty to a dead brother that Yahweh killed him. Had Ownan found Tamar repulsive and refused to recreate with her at all his crime would have been the same. Sperm-wasting, along with homosexuality and celibacy, first became taboo in Persia around 650 BCE when Zarathustra (or his priests) introduced new taboos that were intended to lead to the breeding of more Zoroastrians.[9]

Joseph had a coat with long sleeves. The inaccuracy of the 'many colours' translation has been known for decades, and no longer appears in RC bibles or in Protestant bibles not based on the *Authorized Version*. Nonetheless, there are still more people who believe that the Yahwist credited Joseph with a multicoloured coat than are familiar with the fable as actually written (GEN. 37:3).

Joseph was propositioned by Powtiyfar's wife and, when he virtuously resisted her advances out of regard for her husband, was falsely accused by her of rape and condemned to prison (GEN. 39:7-20).

Bellerophontes was propositioned by Proitos's wife and, when he vir-

---

9. Zarathustra taught that pregnancy-inducing recreation was such a sacred act that prayers uttered while copulating were ten thousand times as effective as at any other time. All non-procreative behaviour, including celibacy, he classified as heinous sins. (F. Müller, ed., *Zend Avesta*, Vendidad, Fargard 4:47:130; 8:27:77; 8:32:102; 15:8:25; 15:9:30).

tuously resisted her advances out of regard for her husband, was falsely accused by her of rape and sentenced to punishment.

Hippolytos was propositioned by Theseus's wife and, when he virtuously resisted her advances out of regard for her husband, was falsely accused by her of rape and hunted to his death.

The Yahwist needed such a legend to explain Joseph's transition from Powtiyfar's slave to deputy warden of Ikhenaton's prison. In fact Powtiyfar seems to have been Ikhenaton's chief jailer, and it is a plausible assumption that the Semitic Yanhuma (Joseph) began his civil service career as Powtiyfar's deputy. That Yanhuma won Ikhenaton's attention by offering the sycophant-hating mad Pharaoh a neutral interpretation of a dream, in contrast to the blatantly flattering interpretation that an Egyptian astrologer was bound to offer, is not impossible. But accepting such a tale as factually-based in the absence of corroboration would be ill-advised.

The parts of the Joseph story that may be historically accurate are that Yanhuma was a minor prison official, of slave status but never a prisoner in the commonly-understood sense (only J made him a prisoner; E did not), who rose to become Viceroy of Phoenicia under the only Pharaoh other than the Hyksos who would have given such an office to a non-Egyptian. When his tribe, the Israelites, were driven out of their Midian homeland by the advancing Easterners, Yanhuma persuaded Ikhenaton to allow them to settle in Egypt. After the death of Ikhenaton and his sons, the first two Ramoseses would have had little cause to regard a Semitic tribe installed by the great heretic as an ally. In the less favourable conditions that followed, the Israelites were bound to look back on the viceroyalty of 'Joseph' as the stuff of which legends are made.

Moses was threatened with death at birth. He escaped Ramoses's massacre of all Israelite children by being set adrift in an ark. He was raised as an Egyptian prince, but on reaching adulthood learned that he was really an Israelite commoner. He thereupon assumed his rightful position as leader of his father's tribe (EXOD. 1:22; 2:3; 2:10-11).

Perseus was threatened with death at birth to prevent him from fulfilling his prophesied destiny. He was saved by being set adrift in an ark. He was raised as a commoner of Seriphos, but on reaching adulthood learned that he was a prince of Danaopolis. He returned to Danaopolis (Mycenae) and claimed his kingdom.

Kyros was threatened with death at birth to prevent him from fulfilling his prophesied destiny. He was raised as a commoner, but fulfilled the prophecy by becoming king of the Medes.

Oidipous was threatened with death at birth to prevent him from fulfilling his prophesied destiny. He was rescued and raised as a Corinthian. On reaching adulthood he assumed his rightful position as king of Thebes.

He fulfilled the prophecy and learned his true identity as the son of Thebes' previous king.

Paris was threatened with death at birth to prevent him from fulfilling his prophesied destiny. He was raised as a commoner, but on reaching adulthood learned his true identity as a prince of Troy. He ultimately fulfilled the prophecy.

Abraham was threatened with death at birth to prevent him from fulfilling a prophecy. He escaped Nimrod's massacre of infants, and lived to become the founding ancestor of the Chosen Nation.

Krishna was threatened with death at birth to prevent him from fulfilling his prophesied destiny. He escaped Kansa's massacre of infants, and grew up as the eighth incarnation of Vishnu, the second person of the Hindu Trinity.

John the Immerser was threatened with death at birth. He escaped Herod's massacre of the children of Bethlehem, and grew up to reveal his identity as Messiah (*mashyah*), Yahweh's anointed king of the Jews.

Jesus the Nazirite was threatened with death at birth to prevent him from fulfilling his prophesied destiny. He escaped Herod's massacre of the children of Bethlehem by travelling to a foreign land. He was raised as a Galilean commoner, but grew up to claim his rightful position as king of the Jews.

Sargon I was threatened with death at birth. He was saved by being set adrift in an ark. On reaching adulthood he learned his true identity and assumed his rightful position as king of Assyria.

Theseus was raised in ignorance of his princely identity as heir of Athens. He was threatened with death to prevent him from fulfilling his destiny. He learned his true identity and succeeded to his father's throne.

Arthur, being of uncertain paternity, was given to the Druid priest Merlin to be sacrificed, but was saved when Merlin instead gave him to Sir Ector. He was raised as a commoner, but on reaching adulthood learned that he was really the son of the king. He assumed his rightful position as king of Britain.

In each of the foregoing myths of the birth of the dangerous child, attempts to thwart the gods' will by killing the child failed. In Moses' case no specific prophecy of such a one's birth survives; but his birth was implied in Yahweh's prophecy to pseudo-Israel concerning the Promised Land. To the Yahwist, an attempt to defeat Yahweh's purpose by killing the child destined to be Yahweh's instrument was theologically necessary.

As with several other of the Yahwist's myths, the story of Moses' setting adrift served the function of 'rectifying' history. It was necessary to turn an Egyptian prince who could speak no Hebrew into an Israelite. The Yahwist interpreted Moses' Egyptian name as if it had been Hebrew, and this gave him the idea of borrowing the ancient fable of how Sargon had been found floating in an ark, just as the Iranian god Apam Napat had even earlier been found floating in an ark. Since the Yahwist had omitted the massacre-of-infants myth from his life of Abraham, he added it to the life of Moses. And whereas other heroes had been raised as commoners only to learn that they were royal, the Yahwist gave an old story a new twist by having Moses raised as a prince only to learn that he was a commoner.

The Yahwist's last surviving fanciful tale was the fable of Balaam's ass. Balaam, a spokesman for Bel, was hired by the king of Mowab to curse the Israelites. Travelling to Mowab by donkey to comply with the request, Balaam's way was obstructed by a heavenly messenger sent by Yahweh to kill him. Yahweh, sharing his biographer's beliefs, feared Bel's curse and had no option but to prevent Balaam from uttering it. A monotheist biographer's Yahweh, aware of Bel's nonexistence, would have allowed Balaam to do his worst.

Balaam's ass, having better perception than her master, saw the invisible messenger. Three times she turned aside to save Balaam's life. Balaam thrashed the donkey, which then spoke to him in Hebrew and told him what was in his path (NUM. 22:21-35).

Nowhere else in the Yahwist's saga, or anywhere in the Judaeo-Christian bible, is there anything comparable with a talking ass. The serpent spoke in Eden, but she was not an ordinary serpent. The conversation between Balaam and his ass indicated that she was a common or garden talking ass. There is a parallel in the *Iliad* where Akhilleus spoke to and was answered by his horses, but as sòns of stallion Poseidon they, also, were not ordinary beasts. It is difficult to understand why the Yahwist introduced into his narrative an incident that even in 920 BCE must have created a credibility gap; but there is no reason to doubt that he intended his talking-ass tale to be taken as literal truth.

Balaam's ass was a nonsensical fable; but like most of the Yahwist's flights of fancy it served a functional purpose. It explained why the spokesman for a hostile god was persuaded to bless the Israelites, a blessing from Bel apparently being regarded as more potent than one from Yahweh. The blessing, quoted in full by the Yahwist, provided him with another opportunity to return to the central purpose of his work. In fact the tale of Balaam's blessing was as spurious as the tale of Balaam's ass. The tradition that a spokesman named Balaam laid a curse on the Israelites and was appropriately punished was recorded in the verse: *Among those killed was Balaam ben Beowr the conjurer, whom the Yisraelites killed with the sword* (JOSH. 13:22). It is most unlikely that the Israelites would have executed a man who prophesied:

The oracle of Balaam benow Beor,
The oracle of the man with farseeing eyes,
The oracle of him who hears Allah's voice.

.   .   .   .   .

I see him—but not in the present.
I behold him—but not nearby.
A star from Yaakob takes charge.
A sceptre arises out of Yisrael.
It crushes the brows of Mowab,
And the skulls of Set's progeny.
Edowm is annexed and occupied.
Seiyr is occupied by its enemies.
Yisrael acts with valour.
Out of Yaakob comes the one who is to rule,
And destroy the exiles of Khiyr.

(NUM. 24:15-19)

The subjects of David's grandson were well aware who was the star from Jacob and king from Israel who had crushed the Mowabites and annexed Edom. Those victories were a living memory. Even in the tale of a talking ass, the Yahwist managed to glorify King David. If he was not David's Prime Minister, he should have been.

Eight

The Elohist

How ignorant a man can become on a diet of managed history.

Frank Herbert, The Eyes of Heysenberg

There's nothing wrong with being ignorant. Guilt should attach only to anyone who remains ignorant in the presence of an opportunity to learn.

Frank Herbert, The White Plague.

Ignorance is self-inflicted stupidity.

Barry B. Longyear, The Tomorrow Testament.

Whereas J was a Jew, E was an Israelite. He has been plausibly identified as a Shiloh priest of the Moshite clan that claimed descent from Moses,[1] a claim disputed by the allegedly Aaronic Jerusalem priesthood that traced the Moshites to Moses' distant cousin Mowshiy. He probably wrote his chronicle during or shortly after the long reign of Yerobowam II (781-753 BCE), fourth king of Israel's seventh dynasty. His portion of *Genesis* can easily be separated from the Yahwist's because, prior to the advent

---

[1]. I owe this identification to Richard Friedman's *Who Wrote the Bible?* Most of the differences between this book and my 1983 dissertation can be attributed to Friedman's influence.

of Moses, he invariably called his deity Elohiym. Elohiym was the plural form of El (Allah), the chief sky-god of an area stretching from El's Town (Ilion, known to the Greeks as Troy) on the Hellespont, to Ur on the Persian Gulf. In *Exodus* and *Numbers* the Elohist's frequent use of the name *Yahweh* makes separation difficult, and in areas where the narratives coincided passages attributed to J may in fact preserve the wording of E.

The surviving portion of the Elohist's work began with Abraham. Over one hundred years had passed since the writing of the Yahwist's saga, and in that time, despite the failure of Solomon's son to hold the artificially-united kingdoms of Judah and Israel together, educated Israelites (but not the illiterate masses) had come to accept Jewish demigods as their own. Both J and E called the Israelite Joseph the son of the Jew Jacob; but whereas there is good reason to doubt that the Yahwist believed his own genealogy, no such suspicion can be levelled against the Elohist. The Elohist began his patriarchal history with Abraham because he did not doubt that Abraham was his ancestor.

The Elohist's concept of his adopted ancestors differed markedly from that of the Yahwist. He told many of the same stories; but wherever the Yahwist reported a circumstance that showed a patriarch in an unfavourable light, the Elohist's treatment of his honourable ancestors was somewhat more complimentary. For example:

J	E
Saray told Avrum . . . 'I gave you my slave-girl for your phallus, and when she saw that she was pregnant she regarded me with contempt. . . .' Avrum answered, . . . 'Do as you please with her.' So Saray treated her so badly that she ran away. . . . Yahweh's messenger told her, 'You are going to bear a son . . . a wild ass of a man. . . .' (GEN. 16:5-12).	Sarah noticed the son of Hagar . . . being impudent. So she demanded . . . 'Throw this slavegirl and her son out. . . .' This greatly distressed Abraham on account of his son. But the gods assured Abraham . . . 'Grant Sarah all that she asks. . . . I am going to make the slave-girl's son into a tribe' (GEN. 21:9-13).

J had simply reported observable facts. E gave Sarah a reason for her cruelty to Hagar, and credited Abraham with human emotions. And whereas J made no attempt to soften Abraham's callousness toward his pregnant concubine, E saw to it that Abraham already knew that Ishmael would not die before he turned the boy and his mother out.

J	E
(Laban promised to give Jacob all goats that were patterned and all sheep that were black.) *Yaakob took branches and peeled them into white stripes. . . . The flocks tupped in front of the striped branches and gave birth to striped, speckled and spotted offspring. . . . And whenever sturdy animals tupped, Yaakob placed the striped branches in front of their eyes.* (GEN. 30:37-41)	A messenger of the gods said . . . 'Watch and see that all the rams that tup the ewes are striped or spotted or piebald. For I've seen how Laban treats you.' (GEN. 31:11-12).

The Yahwist's belief that animals which mate in front of striped branches will produce striped young is seldom mentioned in modern pulpits. The Elohist, rejecting such superstition, limited Israel's duplicity to such action as a swindling son-in-law might have taken in the circumstances. However, while both authors accused Jacob of cheating Laban, E exonerated the demigod of all guilt by having the gods order him to act as he did in response to Laban's stinginess. And whereas J acknowledged that all cheating had been done by Jacob, E offered the justification that Laban had cheated first: 'Your father has cheated me and changed my wages ten times. . . . That's why the gods took your father's livestock and gave them to me' (GEN. 31:7-9).

E told some of the same stories as J, with the slight modification that, whereas J's hero had been Isaac, E's version involved Abraham:

J	E
Abiymolokh looked out and saw Yitskhak recreating (sexually) with his wife Rebekah. Abiymolokh demanded, 'I saw sure evidence that she's your wife. So how come you said, "She's my sister"?' Yitskhak answered, 'Because I thought I would be killed for her.' Abiymolokh asked, 'Just what have you done to us? One of my men might casually have tupped your wife, and you would have been the cause of our guilt.' (GEN. 26:8-10)	Abiymolokh called Abraham. . . . 'What possessed you to do such a thing?' Abraham answered, 'Because I thought, "Surely there is no reverence for the gods in this place, and they'll kill me to get my wife." Besides, she *is* my sister, the daughter of my father but not my mother.' (GEN. 20:10-12)

The tradition that a patriarch had pandered his wife to the Philistine King Abiymolokh to save his life is difficult to explain, since the patriarchs lived several centuries before the existence of any Philistine cities in Phoenicia. Even less comprehensible is the inclusion, in addition to the Elohist's version, of a second account of the incident by J, involving Sarah and Pharaoh (GEN.

12:10-20). E's original contribution was that he absolved the patriarch of the crime of lying, and thereby also relieved him of the responsibility for the consequences of his lie. In E's account, Sarah really was Abraham's sister, even though in the Yahwist's older narrative she was not (GEN. 11:29) and in P she was not (GEN. 11:31).

J	E
Abiymolokh came to see (Yitskhak), bringing the general of his militia, Piykhol. . . . They exchanged oaths. . . . The well they had dug . . . he named . . . Beer-Shebakh. (GEN. 26:26-33)	(Abraham) named the place *Beer-Shebakh,* because at the well (*beer*) they both swore an oath (*shebakhuw*). After they had made a treaty, Abiymolokh departed with Piykhol, the general of his militia. (GEN. 21:31-32)

J had attributed the digging of the wells at Beer-Shebakh to Isaac (GEN. 26:19-22). Since E's Isaac had been sacrificed as a baby (GEN. 22:1-10, 16b-19), E credited the same wells to Abraham (GEN. 21:25). To harmonise the two versions, the Redactor had the Philistines fill in Abraham's wells (GEN. 26:15) so that Isaac could redig them (GEN. 26:18)

Besides those tales in which the Elohist invented details unknown to the Yahwist for purely apologetic purposes, and legends in which only the name of the hero differed, there were also stories told by both J and E that differed in detail simply as a consequence of their oral transmission in different lands. Examples of a similar effect can be found in the medieval chronicles of England. A comparison of the references to England's last Yorkist king in the York *Municipal Records* with Thomas More's fiction makes one wonder if they were referring to the same Richard III. Red and White accounts of the events at Little Big Horn differ not only in perspective but also in details that have no propaganda value whatsoever.

For example, J named Moses' father-in-law Reuwel (EXOD. 2:18), whereas E identified him as Yithrow (EXOD. 4:18). J's sacred mountain was Sinai (EXOD. 34:2), whereas E's was Khoreb (EXOD. 33:6). J's river between Jacob and Esau was the Jordan (GEN. 32:10), whereas E's was the Yabbock (GEN. 32:22). And whereas J's Rakhel was alive years later (GEN. 37:10), E's Rakhel died giving birth to Benjamin (GEN. 35:16-19).

The Elohist's account of Joseph's sale into slavery differed totally from the Yahwist's:

J: GENESIS	E: GENESIS
(37:19-20a) They said to one another, 'Look! The dreamer's coming. How about we kill him?	(37:18) Yowsef's brothers saw him in the distance, and before he reached them they plotted to kill him
(37:20c) We can say that a wild animal ate him. Then we'll see what becomes of his dreams.'	(37:20b) and throw him into a well.
	(37:21-22) But Reuwben overheard, and rescued him from their clutches by suggesting, 'We don't have to kill him.' And Reuwben advised them, 'Instead of shedding blood, throw him into this well in the desert unharmed.' His intention was to rescue him from their clutches and return him to his father.
(37:23) When Yowsef reached his brothers, they stripped off Yowsef's coat, the coat with the full sleeves that he was wearing.	
(37:25-27) They saw a caravan of Yishmaelites coming from Gilead, with their camels loaded with gum that they were taking to Egypt. Yahuwdah asked his brothers, 'Where's the profit in killing our brother? Instead, how about we sell him to the Yishmaelites? It should not be our hands that harm him, since he is our brother.' His brothers agreed,	(37:24) So they seized him and threw him into an empty well containing no water.
	(37:28a) Some Midyanite merchants passed by. They reached down and lifted Yowsef out of the well.
(37:28b) and sold Yowsef to the Yishmaelites for twenty silver coins. They took Yowsef to Egypt.	(37:29) So when Reuwben returned to the well, he saw that Yowsef was not in the well.
(39:1-2) When Yowsef was taken to Egypt, Powtiyfar, one of Pharaoh's officials, commander of his bodyguard, bought him from the possession of the Yishmaelites who had taken him there. He prospered in (his) house.	(37:36) Meanwhile the Midyanites sold him in Egypt to Powtiyfar, one of Pharaoh's officials, commander of his bodyguard.

J's and E's version each survives complete and self-contained. In the Yahwist's account the brother who saved Joseph's life was, not surprisingly, David's ancestor Yahuwdah. The Elohist's hero was Reuwben. The Yahwist had the conspirators sell Joseph to some Ishmaelite merchants. The Elohist had them abandon him in a well from which, before Reuwben could return to rescue him, some Midianite merchants extracted him and carried him off. The Redactor's amalgam reads as if the Midianites sold Joseph to the Ishmaelites. R's editing was skilful, his only error being his inclusion of two endings that had Joseph sold to Powtiyfar twice, once by Midianites and once by Ishmaelites.

Whether the Elohist made the brothers' treatment of Joseph more or less reprehensible than in the Yahwist's version is debatable. While E acquitted the brothers of selling Joseph into slavery, he did accuse them of abandoning him to die in a well. Such an action was consistent with ancient practice. Placing a victim in a situation where he was bound either to starve or die of other causes was a common method of killing, used whenever the killers wished to avoid appearing guilty in the eyes of the gods. Kleon of Thebes, not daring to offend the Furies by killing Antigone, entombed her alive; while in Rome Vestal Virgins who took lovers suffered the same fate. E followed a tradition that Joseph had been thrown down a well, but weakened the story's credibility by declaring that it contained no water. Probably he hoped to exonerate his honourable ancestors of dishonourable conduct by implying that they really did not want Joseph to die. It may be that an Israelite demigod was indeed murdered by such a method.

Evolved Judaism credited Moses with a brother named Aaron (*Aharon*) and a sister named Miriam (1 CHR. 6:3). Neither J nor E, however, endorsed that identification. J gave Moses an unnamed sister (EXOD. 2:4) whom he never mentioned again, and nowhere mentioned any Miriam. E described how Miriam joined Aaron in castigating Moses for marrying a Kushite woman (NUM. 12:1), and later recorded Miriam's death (NUM. 20:1b). But while E called Miriam Aaron's sister (EXOD. 15:20), he did not call her Moses' sister. And that omission seems significant.

The section of the Elohist's chronicle that identified the ancestry of Aaron and the origin of Moses has not survived. Probably the Redactor expunged it because it contradicted the Yahwist's claim that they were Levites (EXOD. 2:1-10; 4:14). E may have had Moses, whom he probably correctly identified as an Egyptian (whereas J had made Moses an Israelite), adopted by Aaron's father. And since E as an Israelite would have known that Levites were Jews, not Israelites, he would also have identified Aaron as an Israelite of the tribe of Efrayim or Menasheh.

E's description of Miriam as Aaron's sister rather than Moses' sister strongly suggests that he had not made Moses and Aaron natural brothers. No chronicler would ever identify Richard III as the Duke of Clarence's brother, rather than Edward IV's brother; and it seems unlikely that Moses would have been similarly slighted. But even if E had emulated his predecessor in calling Moses and Aaron Levites and brothers, they were, nonetheless, neither.

The Elohist followed the Yahwist's precedent of offering fanciful explanations of proper names based on folk etymology. For example, he declared that Jacob acquired the name Israel as the result of a wrestling match with

Allah. His assumption that the name *Yisra-El* ('He/it stands up: Allah') meant 'He stands up *to* Allah,' was nonsense (GEN. 32:24-28). In fact the name referred to the bearer's prowess as a metaphysical stud, generating worshippers for his phallus-god by his military might, and is best translated 'Allah's Erection.'

The Elohist also incorporated elements from Mesopotamian mythology into his narrative, but his handling of the myths contrasted sharply with J's. The Yahwist had uncritically reported that at God's Gate (*Bab-El*) men had built a Tower that, but for Yahweh's intervention, would have enabled them to climb up to the star-studded skies. The Elohist turned the same myth into a dream:

> He had a dream, in which he saw a ziggurat standing on the land with its top reaching the skies. And he saw the messengers of the gods going up and down on it. He was afraid and said, 'How awe-inspiring this place is. This is nothing less than the house of the gods and the gateway to the skies.'
>
> (GEN. 28:12, 17)

E's Yahweh shared the same anthropomorphic limitations as J's. Just as J's god had needed personally to transport himself to Sodom to learn what was happening there (GEN. 18:21), so when E's Yahweh offered the Israelites a treaty, Yahweh's inability to be in two places simultaneously necessitated that, *Mosheh returned to Yahweh and gave him the nation's answer* (EXOD. 19:8).

Just as J's narrative was political propaganda written to glorify and justify the Davidic monarchy, E's was Moshite propaganda intended to denigrate the Jerusalem priesthood and its alleged ancestor, Aaron, and give the Moshites' alleged ancestor, Moses, a superior status that he did not enjoy in the southern kingdom.[2] For example, in the Priestly document which, although written more than a century after E, reflected a long-standing southern tradition, Moses rarely made a move without being accompanied by Aaron, who alone could perform priestly functions. In E, however, Moses' recognised deputy on significant occasions was Yahuwshua, a person not mentioned by J until after Moses' death. And since Yahuwshua was a purely secular leader, his presence on occasions calling for a priest, in the absence of any third person, clearly affirmed that Moses needed no other priest because Moses was a priest (EXOD. 33:11). Also, the subjugation of the secular leader, Yahuwshua, to the ecclesiastical leader, Moses, subtly contradicted J's philosophy that Yahweh's highest-ranking leaders were the Davidic kings.

---

2. Much of what follows is taken from Friedman, *op. cit.*

From the time of Solomon, the Aaronic priesthood had wielded power in Jerusalem while the Moshite priesthood at Shiloh had lived off the crumbs that metaphorically fell from the Aaronids' table. E composed a fable that had no purpose but to show Aaron, and by implication the Jerusalem priesthood, in an unfavourable light by having Aaron act in a manner that aroused the righteous ire of the true priest, Moses. That fable was the 'golden calf' (EXOD. 32:1-24).

E's choice of a golden bull ('calf' is a pejorative translation) as an object of illicit worship is readily explained. Golden bulls were worshipped at the religious centres of Dan and Beth-El in Israel, administered by priests whose legitimacy was repudiated by Moshites and Aaronids alike, as the visible representation of the Israelite god El. In having Aaron build such a godlet, E was putting down every priesthood but his own.

J had put into the mouth of Yahweh a commandment, *You're not to make yourselves any gods of metal* (EXOD. 34:17). At the time J wrote, that commandment was observably being violated by the golden bulls of the Dan and Beth-El shrines, but not by the gold-veneer kherubs in Solomon's Temple. E's equivalent commandment was, *You're not to make yourselves any carved . . . gods of silver or gold to stand beside me* (EXOD. 20:4, 23). E's wording was intended to illegitimise the Jerusalem kherubs. But it also illegitimised the golden bulls of Dan, Beth-El—and Aaron.

Moses, E's paramount hero as David was J's, was less angry with Aaron for his backsliding than was Yahweh. And Moses' status with Yahweh was clearly spelled out in the scene's denouement:

> Then Yahweh told Mosheh, 'I can see what pizzlenecks these people are. Leave me alone now so my temper can grow into a tantrum and I can waste them. But you I'll make into a large tribe.' Mosheh appealed to Yahweh his gods, 'Yahweh, why does your temper flare into a tantrum against your nation whom you led out of Egypt with great force and a powerful fist? Why enable the Egyptians to say, "He led them out treacherously, to kill them in the mountains and exterminate them from the surface of the land"? Control your savage temper and cancel this atrocity against your nation.' . . .So Yahweh cancelled the atrocity that he had been planning to perpetrate against his nation.   (EXOD. 32:9-14)

E was familiar with the tradition, recorded in J, that Moses had carved ten commandments onto two stone tablets (EXOD. 34:1a, 2-4a). He also knew, however, that no such tablets existed. So he wrote a tale in which Moses indeed received the two tablets, carved not by Moses, as in J, but by the gods (EXOD. 32:16). However:

As soon as he was near enough to the camp to see the bull and the balling, Mosheh lost his temper. He threw the tablets down and smashed them at the bottom of the mountain.   (EXOD. 32:19)

In the final edited Towrah, and also in J/E, E's scene in which the two tablets were smashed was placed ahead of J's scene in which they were first carved. The Redactor therefore had to compose a passage to harmonise the two versions:

J: EXODUS	R: EXODUS
(34:1a) Yahweh told Mosheh, 'Cut two tablets of stone.'	(34:1b) *just like the first.*
(34:4a) So he cut two tablets out of stone.	(34:4b) *similar to the first.*

To drive home the superiority of Moses over Aaron, and therefore of the Moshite priesthood over the Aaronic priesthood, E included in the golden bull scene a passage in which Aaron addressed Moses as 'Your Lordship' or 'my Master,' *adownay* (EXOD. 32:22). That same demonstration of the two men's comparative status was repeated in the scene of Miriam's leprosy (NUM. 12:11).

The Yahwist several times referred to the Chest of Yahweh's Treaty (translated as 'Ark of the Covenant' in the A.V.), an object that, despite a goddess-oriented origin (see p. 179), by E's time contained phallic stones placed in it by David. The Elohist, coming from a culture with a long matriarchal/vulva-veneration tradition, nowhere in his narrative mentioned the Chest, located at the time in the Temple in Jerusalem. Instead he highlighted the Tent of Meeting ('Tabernacle' in the A.V.), an item never mentioned by J even though it, also, was currently located in Solomon's Temple. To the later Priestly author, and presumably to the Jerusalem priesthood of E's time, the Tent of Meeting was intimately associated with Aaron (EXOD. 29:10). The Elohist identified it as Moses' tent (EXOD. 33:7-8), and declared that, when Moses was not in attendance, the Tent's resident guardian was not Aaron but Yahuwshua, a man who, under the Priestly author's retroactive rules, would not have been permitted to enter the Tent under pain of execution.

E also differed from J in his identification of the phenomenon that led and guided the Israelites throughout their years of wandering. Whereas J portrayed Yahweh as adopting the form of a phallus of cloud by day and a phallus of fire by night and personally leading his Chosen Nation to their Promised Land (EXOD. 13:21-22), E had Yahweh declare that he would not accompany them because, 'You're such a nation of pizzlenecks that I might waste you on the way' (EXOD. 33:3b). Instead, Yahweh sent his messenger, a minor god in E's time but later demoted to the status of 'angel' (EXOD. 33:2a). Because only J ever mentioned a phallus of cloud or the Chest of the Treaty, whereas only E mentioned the Tent of Meeting, it is possible to identify harmonising passages that combine J and E elements, such as Exodus 33:9-10 and Numbers 12:5, as the Redactor's interpolations into stories that were otherwise by E.

There is some suspicion that the Yahwist's equation of the Jewish paramount god Yahweh with the Israelite gods Elohiym was not working. J had offered no explanation of why the same god was known to two different peoples by different names. He had commenced his narrative, 'On the day that Yahweh Elohiym . . .' and let it go at that. More than a century later, possibly to gain credibility with Israelites who continued to regard Yahweh as a foreign god, E felt obliged to explain the disparate names. J had referred to his god as Yahweh from the beginning of his narrative. E, writing for Israelites, used only the Israelite name, Elohiym, up to the point where Moses entered his story. He then had Yahweh reveal his true name to Moses, and declare that he was to be known by that name thereafter (EXOD. 3:13-15). About the end of the seventh century BCE the Priestly author, utilising J/E as a source in order to write an alternative, also composed a scene in which the god of the patriarchs first revealed his true name to Moses (EXOD. 6:2-3).

A Greek myth told of how Zeus was tricked into promising one of his loves that he would appear before her in his full glory. Zeus knew that such a sight could not be borne by a mere mortal, but he was obliged to fulfil his oath sworn by the Styx, and Semele was vapourised. The Elohist's god was similarly too magnificent for mortal eyes to look upon, but being more resourceful than Zeus he was able partly to grant Moses a similar request:

> He asked, 'I beg you, show me your magnificence. . . .' But he added, 'You can't see my face, for no human is able to see me and survive. . . . While my magnificence is passing by I'll . . . cover you with my hand until I'm past. Then I'll remove my hand and you'll see my backside. But my face is not to be seen.'   (EXOD. 33:18-23)

Nobody since Moses has seen Yahweh's backside, and that is perhaps a pity.

Nine

The Deuteronomist

Of all the strange 'crimes' that human beings have legislated out of nothing, 'blasphemy' is the most amazing—with 'obscenity' and 'indecent exposure' fighting it out for second and third place.

Robert Heinlein, *Time Enough For Love.*

The Deuteronomist added a new dimension to literary deception. Whereas the Yahwist and the Elohist had not put any signature to their works, the Deuteronomist pretended that his scroll emanated from the quill of a man who had been dead for six hundred years. He supported that contention by writing his collection of taboos, ritual and propaganda in the first person. Among the later writers who followed D's precedent were the authors of *Enoch* and *Daniel*; Joseph Smith; and the two fourth-century CE Greeks, 'Dares' and 'Dictys,' who claimed to be survivors of the Trojan War. The Deuteronomist claimed to be Moses!

Deuteronomy was composed in the eighteenth year of the reign of King Yoshyahuw of Judah (640-609 BCE). Yoshyahuw was a pious king who won Yahweh's favour by suppressing competing mythologies, smashing their altars, slaughtering their priests, and burning the bones of their saints (4 KGS. 23:20; 2 CHR. 34:4-5). Yoshyahuw's fanatical persecution and extermination of heresy within his kingdom was accomplished in six years.

In 622 BCE Yoshyahuw levied a special tax. The 300-year-old Temple built by Solomon was in a state of decay, so Yoshyahuw raised funds for its repair. *And when they fetched out the money that had been brought into Yahweh's Temple, Khilkyahuw the priest found a book of the Towrah of Yahweh written by Mosheh* (2 CHR. 34:14). Yoshyahuw asked a spokeswoman how he could appease Yahweh, '*for Yahweh's temper is boiling because our ancestors have not performed the terms of this scroll and done everything that is written concerning us*' (4 KGS. 22:13).

In response to the spokeswoman's advice, Yoshyahuw made an agreement with Yahweh *to carry out the terms of the treaty that are written in this scroll* (2 CHR. 34:31). The description of Yoshyahuw's actions in obedience to the newly-discovered book reveals that the book was *Deuteronomy*.

Yoshyahuw ordered that the Passover be celebrated:

> as written in the scroll of this treaty. Surely such a *Pesakh* had not been held since the days of the sheikhs who judged Yisrael, not as long as there had been kings of Yahuwdah. But in the eighteenth year of King Yoshyahuw this *Pesakh* was held to Yahweh in Yeruwsalem.   (4 KGS. 23:21-23)

The description of Yoshyahuw's observance of the new Passover procedures was identical with the ritual prescribed in *Deuteronomy* 16:1-8.

The Deuteronomist was intimately acquainted with J/E, an amalgam of the two older documents intertwined and harmonised by a Redactor sometime during the hundred-odd years between E and D. He was not, however, familiar with the Priestly narrative, and this is the strongest reason for dating P after rather than before 621 BCE. However, in order to reach that conclusion it is necessary to attribute *Deuteronomy* 1:37-39, which quoted P, to the final Redactor of the fifth century. There is justification for so doing.

For example, J (and J/E) declared that, of all the Israelite adults who left Egypt, only Kaleb would live to enter the new homeland (NUM. 14:24). D quoted that passage (DEUT. 1:36). P, however, coupled Kaleb with Yahuwshua in an otherwise identical prophecy (NUM. 14:30). When the final Redactor placed the J and P passages side by side in his finished Towrah, he also inserted three extra verses into the appropriate section of *Deuteronomy* to harmonise it with J/E/P.

D referred to Moses' inability to govern unassisted, and his appointment of officers over thousands, hundreds, fifties and tens (EXOD. 18:21; DEUT. 1:15), a story found only in E (and J/E). But he showed no awareness of the Priestly alternative in which Moses gave the same authority to a Council of Seventy (NUM. 11:14-17). D knew of J's account of the ground swallowing Dathan and Abiyram (NUM. 16:1b-2a, 12-15, 25-26, 27d-32a, 32c-34), but knew nothing of the revolt of Korakh (NUM. 16:1a, 2b-11, 16-24a, 27a, 27c, 35-50) told by P. And D invented his own reason for Moses' failure to enter the promised homeland (DEUT. 1:37), which differed considerably from the reason that would one day be concocted by P.

D had never heard any of the stories invented by P, who was his contemporary but wrote slightly later. D therefore declared that Moses was
deprived of the privilege of entering the promised homeland on account of
the Israelites' stubbornness (DEUT. 1:37), unaware that P would one day
declare that punishment to have been imposed for Moses' reluctance to
believe that he could produce water out of a rock (NUM. 20:12).

D continued his predecessors' practice of justifying genocide. The Yahwist had set the pattern by making the savage conquest of Judah a consequence of patriarchal curses inflicted upon the conquered peoples' ancestors.
The Elohist had further absolved his ancestors of guilt by having Yahweh personally order the exterminations which the volcano-god's Chosen Nation
had piously carried out (JOSH. 8:2). The Deuteronomist confirmed Yahweh's
culpability, but put into the mouth of Moses the explanation that Yahweh's
no-survivors policy was designed to prevent the worshippers of an opposition
god from passing on their heresies to true believers (DEUT. 20 16-18).

The Deuteronomist's philosophy, that killing the adherents of every
mythology but one's own in order to protect believers from competing
doctrines was a godly and laudable act, was in medieval times carried to
its logical conclusion by the Christians who, over the course of several
centuries, dutifully massacred between thirty and fifty million enemies of
the various Christian gods in such events as the Crusades, the Inquisition,
the Thirty Years War, and various minor atrocities. Among the latter was
the extermination of possibly as many as seventy thousand Huguenots on
St. Bartholomew's Day 1572, a purging of heretics that caused the jubilant
Pope Gregory XIII to proclaim a year of celebration.

The Deuteronomist's god ordered the rampaging Jews to behave in a
manner that is best evaluated by comparing it with the behaviour of a
modern-day Yahweh:

DEUTERONOMY	ADOLF HITLER (paraphrased)
(7:1) When Yahweh your gods has set-tled you in the land you're about to occupy, and driven out many infidels before you . . . you're to cut them down and exterminate them. You're to make no compromise with them or show them any mercy.	When your Führer has settled you in the land you're about to occupy, and driven out many inferior races before you, you're to gas them down and extermi-nate them. You're to make no compro-mise with them or show them any mercy.
(7:5) Instead, this is how you're to deal with them: You're to destroy their altars, smash their stone phalluses, chop down their wooden vulvas, and burn their sacred icons. For you are a nation consecrated to Yahweh your gods.	Instead, this is how you're to deal with them: You're to destroy their synagogues, smash their mosques, chop down their wooden crosses, and burn their phylac-teries. For you are a nation of Supermen,

Yahweh your gods has chosen you to be his special nation, ahead of all nations on the surface of the land.
(7:23) You're going to exterminate them in a massive genocide until they're eliminated.

a Master Race chosen by nature to rule over every inferior race on the surface of the land. You're going to exterminate them in a massive genocide until they're eliminated.

In the adjacent area that the Jews did not intend to occupy themselves, close cities that surrendered were to be enslaved while in those that refused to surrender the men and boys were to be killed and the women and girls enslaved (DEUT. 20:11-14).

At the same time that D was justifying the atrocities of Yahuwshua and King David by having their brutality retroactively ordered by Yahweh, he also ordered, 'Be compassionate to foreigners, for you were foreigners in the land of Egypt' (10:19). How the Deuteronomist could preach universal compassion (love) while simultaneously applauding and justifying genocide and enslavement is difficult to understand. Perhaps, like a growing number of modern-day god-worshippers, he was genuinely horrified by the atrocities of the past, but was able to hypnotise himself into the belief that the tribal god's orders, no matter how monstrous, could only be incomprehensible, never unjust.[1] That the atrocities were of purely human origin, and that the god accused of ordering them perhaps did not exist, did not cross his mind. It certainly did not occur to him that Yahweh *could not* exist, because if he ever had existed he would long before have tortured himself to death from the sheer joy that he derived from hurting living things.

Despite this inconsistency, the Deuteronomist's sense of morality and justice was more evolved than that of his predecessors. He banned executions based on the testimony of a single witness (17:6), and banned convictions of any kind based on uncorroborated testimony (19:15). For perjurers he decreed a penalty equal to that which would have been meted out to the persons they accused (19:19). This was consistent with his overall scheme of retributive justice, 'Life for life, eye for eye, tooth for tooth, hand for hand, foot for foot' (19:21), borrowed almost verbatim from the Code of Hammurabai: 'If a seignior has destroyed the eye . . . they shall destroy his eye. If a seignior has knocked out a tooth . . . they shall knock out his tooth.'[2]

He retained the concept of inherited guilt, declaring that a *mamzer*, a

---

1. To this day, god-worshippers credit their gods with saving their lives when fortuitous circumstances caused them to miss an airplane that crashed, without ever considering that a god who could save one life could as easily have saved all who were killed. But the definitive example of godworshipthink was displayed by the Muslim theologian, Mahmud al-Qazwini (d. 1283), who declared that the greatness of Allah could be deduced from his only allowing rain to fall on fertile ground, and not on the desert where nothing would grow anyway.

2. J.B. Pritchard, *op. cit*, p. 175.

word that probably meant the offspring of a marriage between a Jew and a gentile, *is not to be admitted into Yahweh's community. Not even his tenth-generation descendant's to be admitted into Yahweh's community* (23:2). He did, however, remove the concept's most repulsive aspect by decreeing that henceforth the children and parents of felons were not to be executed for their kinsmen's crimes (24:16). A more repulsive inherited-guilt concept than had ever existed in Judaism was manufactured by the early Christians as the myth of Original Sin. But that antithesis of justice and sanity was essentially an extension of the two-thousand-year-old practice of enhancing priestly power by keeping the masses guilt-ridden; it was in no sense a return to pre-Deuteronomic Judaism.

D introduced a code of ethics for the treatment of captured women. A Jew who made a captured concubine his wife was deprived of the right ever to sell her.[3] In the event that his lust cooled and he was unwilling to continue the marriage, he was obliged to divorce her on the same terms as if she were a Jew, and renounce all claim to her thereafter. Marriage to a non-Jew was to be regarded as nothing less than a remission of her slavery (21:11-14). However, before D is acclaimed as a champion of human rights, it should be kept in mind that his new law was almost certainly designed to *prevent* Jewish men from marrying their gentile slavegirls.

The Deuteronomist repeated some ancient sexual taboos and introduced a few of his own. Adultery, for example, had been a crime for three thousand years and a *sin* from the time that injuries to the male ruling class had been classified as injuries to a god. E had banned it (EXOD. 20:14), but had not capitalised it. D did so: *If a man's caught tupping a (married) woman, then the both of them are to be killed, the man who tupped the woman, and also the woman* (22:22). No mention was made of consensual recreation between a married man and an unmarried woman. In a sense such a relationship constituted an injury against the woman's father, since he could not expect to obtain top price for a non-virgin, but it was not covered by a specific taboo, and it did not fall within the definition of adultery.

Rape, the favourite pastime of Zeus, Apollo and various other non-Jewish gods, was made subject to penalties. A man who raped someone else's privately-owned breeding woman was subjected to the same penalty as any other adulterer. A man who raped a virgin and was caught was obliged to pay her father an indemnity and marry her. He also forfeited his right ever to divorce her (22:25-29). D's code was somewhat milder

---

3. The original difference between a wife and a concubine seems to have been that a concubine was a widow or other non-virgin who had not given birth since her acquisition, and whose first or next child was destined for sacrifice as being of multiple paternity; whereas a wife was a virgin-bride, or a former concubine who had given birth and thereafter observed an adultery taboo, so that her first or next child would be legitimate.

than Hammurabai's, which for virgin-raping had prescribed death. D made no law restricting the rape of unmarried non-virgins, since their wombs already carried bastard-seed, and one more deposit could make no difference.

Some new incest laws were invented by the Deuteronomist. Relations with step-mothers and mothers-in-law were declared taboo, as was recreation with half-siblings on either side (27:20, 22, 23). Bestiality was proscribed (27:21). Jews were forbidden to be *kedeshowth* or *kedeshiym*, nuns and monks of the Mother who offered their respective orifices to male worshippers as sacramental surrogates for the invisible deity (23:17). Jewish men were not, however, forbidden from seeking sexual relief with male and female gentile practitioners of sacramental copulation. The ban on *zenuwth* ('fornication'), engaging in purchased recreation with a fertility nun, was not equated with worship of the nun's goddess until the Redactor categorised it as such two centuries later (LEV. 20:5).

D's denigration of *kedeshowth* and *kedeshiym* caused King Yoshyahuw to end the copulatory worship that may have been part of Yahweh-religion since the reign of Solomon, and fire Yahweh's nuns and monks. Yoshyahuw *stood beside the stone phallus and made a deal with Yahweh* (4 KGS. 23:3). He *removed the wooden vulva from Yahweh's Temple* (23:6), and *smashed down the temples of the kedeshiym beside Yahweh's Temple, where the women wove drapes for the vulva* (23:7). If D was resentful of the nuns and monks, the abolition of forms of worship in which he was not involved may have been his whole purpose.

The Deuteronomist's main claim to fame, however, is that he was the sole preserver of the original Elohistic version of the 'Ten Commandments.'

The concept of the Ten Words originated with the Yahwist. J wrote that Moses climbed Mount Sinai and engraved the Ten Words on two stone tablets (EXOD. 34:28). E also included Ten Commandments (EXOD. 20:1-10, 12-16), very different from J's, at the beginning of his three-chapter Holiness code. When P wrote his alternative to J/E, he preferred E's Big Ten to J's, but made two changes (EXOD. 20:11, 17). R preserved P's amended version. E's list consequently survived unchanged only in *Deuteronomy* (5:6-21).

The original Ten Commandments as formulated by the Yahwist in 920 BCE (EXOD. 34:14-26) were:

1. You're to offer worship to no other god, for Yahweh is most possessive about his name: Jealous Allah.
2. You're not to make yourself any gods of metal.
3. You're to celebrate the Feast of Unleavened Bread.
4. All that first issues from the belly belongs to me (*meaning: You're to sacrifice all firstborn males, human and animal, to Yahweh*).

5. You're to work six days, and on the seventh day you're to rest.
6. You're to celebrate the Feast of Weeks and the Feast of Ingathering.
7. Three times a year all of your men-children are to appear before his lordship Yahweh, the gods of Yisrael (*at the Temple in Jerusalem*).
8. You're not to offer the blood from my sacrifices with leavened bread.
9. You're to bring the best of the first-fruits of your land to the dwelling (*Temple*) of Yahweh your gods.
10. You're not to boil a kid in its mother's milk.

Seven of the Yahwist's commandments were anachronistic. They referred to customs that originated in Phoenicia and could not possibly have been taught by Moses. For example, the ritual of cooking a kid in its mother's milk as a sacrifice to Molokh could not have been encountered by the Israelites until after Moses' death. Also, festivals related to crop-raising would have been meaningless to people who as yet had no land to cultivate. And the eating of unleavened bread was a Phoenician custom of which Moses would have known nothing.

Commandments 1, 2 and 4 could have been instituted by Moses. Apart from the change of name to Yahweh, the instruction to worship only the prescribed god almost certainly originated with Moses. That rule was the core of the Atonic priesthood to which Aton-moses belonged.

The ban on metal gods was inconsistent with Moses' manufacture of a bronze snake for the Israelites to worship (NUM. 21:9). But it may be that Moses initially gave the Israelites a visible god to whom they could petition directly, saw that in so doing he had undermined his own position as the only spokesman and intermediary for an invisible god, and only later banned metal gods to prevent a recurrence of such a consequence. That would explain his chagrin at Aaron's reverting to ancient practice and depicting Allah (or Aton) as a golden bull (EXOD. 32:2-6),[4] just as he had been depicted as a bull in the original Daniel myth in which Baal prayed: 'Wilt thou not bless him (Daniel), O Bull El, my father. . . . So shall there be a son in his house,'[5] and as Zeus, Poseidon, Apis, Zagreus and other gods had been depicted as bulls.

The institution of infant sacrifice must be attributed to Moses. Evidence that Moses indeed ordered a mass sacrifice of firstborn children survives in the gruesome account of Yahweh's butchery of firstborn offspring prior

---

4. As indicated in the previous chapter, it is more likely that the golden bull incident occurred only in E's imagination. And since J, although not a fan of the Jewish priests, may nonetheless have resented the Israelite priests of Beth-El and their golden bulls, it is at least as likely that J composed the commandment retroactively proscribing such godlets, as that Moses did so.

5. J.B. Pritchard, *op. cit.*, p. 150.

to the Israelites' departure from Egypt (EXOD. 12:29-30). In the Yahwist's expurgated version of the slaughter, the dead infants became Egyptian. But it would have been the Israelites who sacrificed their children to El in preparation for their long journey. Since baby-eating gods tended to be insatiable, Moses would have ordered the practice to continue in perpetuity.

The Redactor, finding Moses' original order repulsive, added the loophole that firstborn humans were to be redeemed by sacrificing animals in their place. This was consistent with his implausible attempt (GEN. 22:11-16a) to attribute the abolition of such sacrifices to Abraham (who probably did sacrifice his firstborn son to Yahweh). The substitution clauses reflected a change that had begun under the Judges, but R backdated them to Moses on the logical ground that Moses could not have instituted a practice already abolished by Abraham (EXOD. 34:20a).

In fact it is self-evident that a law declaring that (a) the firstborn belongs to Yahweh, and that (b) it must be purchased back by offering an alternative sacrifice, could only have come into existence in two stages. The ancient custom of initially sacrificing sacred kings to the Mother, and later redeeming the sacred king by sacrificing a substitute, illustrates how surrogate-substitution laws came into existence. Moses ordered infant sacrifice; some later leader authorised the substitution of animals. The original law, with no substitution clause, was recorded by R: *Yahweh ordered Mosheh, 'Sacrifice to me all of the firstborn, the first issue of every belly. It belongs to me'* (EXOD. 13:1-2).

The Yahwist's narrative was so constructed as to leave no doubt that his decalogue was that of *Exodus 34*, recorded above. Immediately following the injunction against cooking a kid in its mother's milk (EXOD. 34:26) he wrote, *Yahweh ordered Mosheh, 'Put these commandments down in writing'* (EXOD. 34:27). *And he wrote the terms of the treaty, the TEN COMMAND-MENTS, on the tablets* (34:28).

The Deuteronomist ignored the Yahwist's decalogue and instead used E's, following it with: *Yahweh spoke those words from the middle of the flames and the steam and the volcanic ash. . . . Then he engraved them on two tablets and gave them to me* (DEUT. 5:22). The decalogue that preceded those words (5:7-21) was as follows:

1. You are to admit no foreign gods into where I gaze (*i.e., into Judaea*).
2. You're not to make yourself carved representations of any shape found in the skies above or on the land below or in the water on which the land floats, and kowtow in homage before them and honour them.
3. You're not to swear in Yahweh your gods' name that which is false.

4. You're to slave for six days, completing all of your chores. But the seventh day is Yahweh your gods' Seventh. You're not to do any chores.

5. Worship your father and your mother so that you'll live a long time (*without your deified ancestors killing you for neglecting them*) and prosper.

6. You're not to retsakh (*kill a fellow Jew*).

7. You're not to naf (*ejaculate sperm into the wife of a fellow Jew*).

8. You're not to goniv (*rob a fellow Jew*).

9. You're not to give perjured testimony against your compatriot (*fellow Jew*).

10. You're not to lust after your compatriot's wife. Nor are you to lust after your compatriot's dwelling, his farmland, his slave or his slavegirl, his ox or his ass, or anything else that your compatriot owns.

The meaning of most of E's Ten Commandments has been distorted by churches trying desperately to maintain that E and his god believed the same things they do. Number 1, for example, was neither an affirmation that Yahweh was the only god in existence, nor even a ban on worshipping other gods in their own lands. What it meant was that, while a Jew was not expected to refrain from honouring Babylonian gods when his business took him to Babylon, he was not to tolerate the worship of any god but Yahweh in Judah.

Number 6 was a ban on *retsakh*, defined as the killing of a fellow Jew without the consent of the tribe's authorised representative (judge, priest). Even centuries later when the Talmud was compiled, the concept *retsakh*, murder, did not include the killing of a gentile: *One who, intending to kill a gentile, kills a Yisraelite, is to be deemed guiltless* (SANHEDRIN 78b). A similar situation existed until the nineteenth century CE in America where, under most circumstances, the killing of a black did not constitute any kind of crime.[6]

The injunction against stealing also, under the provisions of the ancient hospitality code, protected a Jew's gentile houseguests; but once a departing guest had travelled a short distance from his host's tent he was again fair game with no more rights in Yahweh's world than a blowfly. The prohibition of adultery would also have covered the wives of gentile houseguests, but no other gentiles' wives: *Any man who commits adultery with another man's woman, provided that his adultery is with a compatriot's woman, is to be executed*

---

6. This is equally true of Australia. See Robert Hughes's *The Fatal Shore*, NY, 1987, pp. 277-280.

(LEV. 20:10). And the true meaning of adultery, as an impregnation taboo, not a recreational taboo, was spelled out by the Priestly author: *You're not to engage your compatriot's woman in carnal copulation in which semen is intromitted, for that would pollute her* (LEV. 18:20) Similarly, protection against perjury and lusting were limited to a Jew's compatriot (*reak*), a word never applied to gentiles.

E's tenth Commandment was a ban on lusting after the property of a fellow Jew. That the first kind of property mentioned was wives was coincidental. When P borrowed E's decalogue (EXOD. 20:1-17), he listed *your compatriot's dwelling* first, then *your compatriot's wife or his slave or his slavegirl*, followed by other kinds of property. The Roman Catholic numbering system, which added the ban on the manufacture of engraved godlets to the compulsory intolerance of foreign gods in Judah as part of an enlarged first Commandment, in order to divide number ten into two parts, cannot be justified. In the Priestly version such a division is not even possible, unless lusting after a compatriot's dwelling is counted as number nine, and lusting after wives and oxen and asses is counted as number ten. But even ignoring the Priestly version and looking only at E's in which the RC division is physically possible, such a division presupposes that E saw wives as qualitatively different from other forms of property. He did not.

Apart from the possibility of dividing it into two, E's tenth Commandment raises other questions. Since he was limited to *ten* Commandments, why did he waste one of them by merely reiterating the ban on stealing? Was there no alternative tenth Commandment that he could have instituted? Did he consider stealing so monstrous that he needed to ban it twice? The answer seems to be that E's tenth Commandment was not so much a repetition of numbers seven and eight as an affirmation of the validity of private property.

Siddhartha Gautama invented communism—the abolition of private property—three centuries after the composition of the Elohist's Ten Commandments. E was therefore not rebutting Gautama. But was Gautama really as radical a thinker as his teachings imply? Historians have often observed that the great 'movers' of history were in fact inevitable products of their environment. Hitler could not have existed (come to power) without a Treaty of Versailles to spawn him, and the Treaty of Versailles could not have failed to produce a Hitler. Similarly, Gautama could not plausibly have become a fanatic preacher against private property in a world in which the 'wrongness' of private property had never before been considered. Almost certainly communist philosophy was being debated, in Judah as well as in India, and E considered it such a potential threat to the ruling classes that he found it necessary to uphold a Jew's right to own property as one of his Ten Commandments.

E's second Commandment banned the carving of any shape found in *the skies above or the land below or the water on which the land floats* (DEUT. 5:8). A modern god so ignorant of physical geography as to believe that the inhabited world floated on a water foundation, as the ancients believed, would have little chance of being taken seriously. The point cannot be overemphasised that, at any given moment, the Judaeo-Christian bible's paramount god knew as much about science as his current speechwriter and no more.

The Deuteronomist's position on non-Jewish gods was as enigmatic as his attitude toward the treatment of gentiles. On the one hand he ridiculed *gods made by men's hands out of wood and stone, that neither see nor hear nor eat nor smell* (DEUT. 4:28). On the other hand he declared that, when Yahweh chose the Jews to be his nation, he gave the gentiles the sun, moon and stars to be their gods (DEUT. 4:19). The author of the Holiness code incorporated into E was similarly ambivalent: *You're not to revile the gods* (EXOD. 22:28). That he was referring to non-Jewish gods was confirmed by Josephus, who, although he did not accept the Towrah as literally accurate, was nonetheless a practising Yahweh-worshipper.[7]

For the six hundred years since they had formed their alliance with the Israelites, the Jews had been monolatrists, believers in many gods but worshippers of one. But the Zoroastrian belief that there would be an eventual showdown between Yahweh and all other gods, from which only Yahweh would emerge alive, was beginning to influence Judaism by D's time. The certainty of Yahweh's victory, and the claim that Yahweh was a Jewish Zeus, King of gods in a world of lesser gods, was spelled out by the psalmists who wrote:

Before the gods I will sing praise to you.   (PS. 138:1)

Yahweh is a great god, and a great King above all gods.   (PS. 95:3)

Yahweh is great, and greatly to be praised. He is to be reverenced above all gods.   (PS. 96:4)

Worship him, all gods! You, Yahweh . . . are exalted far above all gods.
                                                                (PS. 97:7, 9)

Elohiym has taken his place in the divine council. In the midst of the gods he holds judgement. I say you are gods, sons of gods, all of you. But you're going to die like men.   (PS. 82:1, 6-7)

---

7. *Against Apion* 1:237.

The Deuteronomist, with his reference to *gods made by men's hands*, advanced the concept of the destructability of Yahweh's rivals, and in so doing set the pattern for a series of fanatic spokesmen who, within about three centuries, converted the orthodox from monolatry to monotheism. By the time Judaism came into contact with Hellenism after the conquest of Alexander of Macedon, Yahweh had ceased to be the Jews' paramount god and had become their only god.[8]

D's contribution to the evolution of monotheism was morally neutral. Ethically, monotheism was neither a step forward nor a step backward. D can, however, be praised for his positive steps toward making religion ethical. He was as intolerant as his predecessors of foreign gods in Yahweh's land. But he also recognised the rights of gentile gods in their own territory. He put limits on the acceptance of gentiles: *You're not to intermarry with them* (DEUT. 7:3). But he urged that, excluding those whom Yahweh had ordered exterminated for occupying land that the Jews coveted, they were to be treated with compassionate consideration (10:19). Many whites have yet to make such a concession to blacks.

Overall, D must be judged favourably. However, in order to view his record in the right perspective, it must be remembered that he labelled as intolerable abominations the superstitious but intrinsically harmless rituals of priestesses of *mekashef* (18:10-12). It is perhaps not D's fault that *mekashefah* has consistently been translated in English bibles as 'witch'; but there is no question that he was confirming the Holiness code's institution of capital punishment for heresy (EXOD. 22:18) and must be held morally culpable for the hundreds of thousands of women burned to death by the Christian Inquisition.

The Christian concept of 'witch' changed considerably over the centuries. Originally it meant a card-carrying Satan-worshipper, and as such was roughly consistent with D's *mekashefah*. But by Cotton Mather's day it was applied to practically any woman who had outlived her teeth.[9] While D would not have endorsed the farcical witch trials carried out in Salem, Massachusetts, very few of the European witch-burnings would have failed to win his approval.[10] And he surely revealed something of his own character

---

8. The Jews, like the later Christians and Muslims, continued to believe in minor gods such as Gabriel, Mikhael and Satan, but rationalised that, as Yahweh's creations, they were not really 'gods' even though they met every definition of a god.

9. Isaac Asimov, 'The Wicked Witch is Dead,' *The Planet That Wasn't*, NY, 1976.

10. In 1485 two Dominicans, appointed inquisitors by Pope Innocent VIII, published *The Hammer of Witches* as a guide to witch-torturers. The document, endorsed by the University of Cologne, ordered, among other things, that women suspected of engaging in sexual recreation with demons were to be shaved from head to toe, and long needles were to be thrust into their breasts and genitals. The torture was to be carried out dispassionately in the presence of a priest. If the suspect refused to confess, she was to be further tortured until she did

when he became the first biblical author to credit Yahweh with the unmistakable mark of the sadist, the capacity to derive sensual pleasure from inflicting pain: *He'll derive pleasure from exterminating you and reducing you to ruin* (DEUT. 28:63).[11]

With the advantage of hindsight the Deuteronomist was able retroactively to curse the defunct kingdom of Israel, extinct since 721 BCE, out of existence for not keeping laws that, at the time of Israel's fall, had not yet existed:

> Yahweh will send an infidel against you from far away, from the end of the land, flying like an eagle, an infidel whose language you won't understand. . . . He'll besiege all of your towns until your high walls on which you depended throughout your land are levelled . . . if you fail to observe and obey all of the orders of this Towrah written in this scroll.
>
> (DEUT. 28:49, 52, 58)

As the Deuteronomist well knew, his new taboos had not been observed in the days before they were invented, and the king of Assyria, Sargon II, had indeed conquered Israel a century earlier and carried off the Israelite king and his subjects to Ninevah. D's obvious implication was that, unless the Jews now adopted the 'lost' laws of 'Moses,' they would suffer the same fate as the Israelites. What D did not know was that, although his literary swindle would succeed, Jewish independence would survive for only a further thirty-five years. In 586 BCE Nabu-akh-adon-assur (Nebuchadnezzar) of Babylon would raze Jerusalem as Sargon of Assyria had razed Samaria. There would, however, be one difference. The Jews would not become extinct.

The most plausible identification of the Deuteronomist is that, as postulated by Richard Friedman in *Who Wrote the Bible?*, he was the spokesman Jeremyah. There are several supporting arguments for such an equation.

Deuteronomy was allegedly found in the Temple by Khilkyahuw. Jeremyah's father had the same name and *may* have been the same man. D was

---

confess. After confessing, she was to be burned to death. That slow, painful method of execution was deliberately chosen because it enabled the dying victim to compare her present fate with the eternal fires awaiting her in Hell, and to save her soul by accepting the love of King Jesus in whose fevered imagination the eternal fires first materialised.

11. In the 1990s an American doctor was more than once charged with murder, despite prohibitions of any *law pertaining to the establishment of a religion*, when he made a 'suicide machine' available to terminal patients who consciously chose to end their intolerable agony. To incurable god-addicts, a sadist in the sky has the inalienable right to get its orgasm-substitute savouring the suffering of the afflicted, and suicide is viewed as a denial of that right. That a majority of Americans endorse a dying person's right to choose a dignified death is irrelevant to fanatics who equate masochism with virtue.

a Levite priest, and Jeremyah was a Levite priest. Jeremyah was hostile to P, saying of it, 'How can you say, "We are wise, for Yahweh's Towrah is with us"? For it is a sheer falsehood, fashioned by the lying pens of scribes' (JER. 8:8). *Deuteronomy* likewise repudiated *Leviticus* laws on many occasions, laws that may well have kept Jeremyah from serving in the Temple on a technicality. The phraseology of *Deuteronomy* and *Jeremiah* is identical throughout. But most important is that D put into the mouth of Moses a prophecy that there would someday be another spokesman who was Moses' equal (18:15-19). To conclude that that spokesman was intended to be anyone but D himself would be naive. In 621 BCE the only spokesman of note who could have claimed to be the fulfilment of such a prophecy was Jeremyah. The evidence that D was Jeremyah is not definitive, but it is strong. That would mean that the Priestly author wrote after the composition of *Deuteronomy*, but prior to the composition of *Jeremiah*.

Ten

The Priestly Author

We can understand why priests might make myths about
superior beings who inhabit the skies and give directions
to human beings on how to order their affairs. Among
other 'advantages,' such legends permit the priests to control
the people.

Carl Sagan, *The Cosmic Connection.*

The Yahwist wrote a history of the world that showed the culmination
of Yahweh's plan to be, not the establishment of the Jerusalem Temple
controlled by the Aaronic priesthood, but the establishment of the Davidic
monarchy. The Elohist wrote a history that glorified Moses at the expense
of Aaron. After J and E were combined into J/E, the Deuteronomist wrote
a sequel that, although partly based on a lawcode also utilised by P,[1] denigrated
the Aaronids by recognising all Levites as priests. Not surprisingly, J/E/D
was deemed extremely offensive by the Temple hierarchy. It was for the
purpose of repudiating J/E/D that the Priestly author wrote an alternative
intended to supersede it.

Just as the Deuteronomist had written with an open copy of J/E in
front of him, so the Priestly author wrote with an open copy of J/E/D
in front of him. He followed the sequence of his source quite closely, but
did not hesitate to delete anything he deemed trivial or heretical, rewrite

---

1. *Cf.* DEUT. 12:23-27 and LEV. 17:10-14; DEUT. 14:3-20 and LEV. 11:1-23, 41-43.

anything that could be made to convey a more acceptable message, and add priestly propaganda not found in J/E.

For example, J had begun his narrative: *On the day that Yahweh the gods made the land and the skies . . . .* (GEN. 2:4b); but he had not included any account of the making of the aforesaid land and skies. P remedied the deficiency, utilising the creation myths with which he was most familiar, the Babylonian and Persian. Just as Marduk had sliced his mother Tiamat in half and created the land and skies out of her remains, so P had Elohiym do to his mother Tehowm (GEN. 1:2, 7). And where Ahura Mazda had created the cosmos in six stages, followed by an aeon of rest, so P had Elohiym create all-that-is in six days and rest on the seventh.

For the sequence of creation, P simply followed his source and had Elohiym create everything in the same order delineated in the Babylonian creation epic of 1500 years earlier. In so doing, he had the earth created before its sun, and had trees bearing fruit before there was any sunlight to trigger the necessary photosynthesis. He even declared that *the nighttime and the daytime constituted the first . . . second . . . third day,* BEFORE *the gods made two powerful lights . . . to divide the light from the darkness* (GEN. 1:5, 8, 13, 18).

In naming the sun and moon as *two powerful lights,* P revealed his unawareness that the moon is not a source of light but a reflector of light. In locating the sun, moon and stars *attached to the dome of the skies,* he continued an ancient cosmography that modern astronomers tend to dispute.[2] And in declaring that *the gods made . . . also the stars,* he gave no hint of any suspicion that stars are distant suns.

P believed the same things all ancients believed. He believed that the earth was a flat disk covered by a solid dome called the skies, on which Elohiym walked. Earlier and later biblical authors had the same belief: *Since the land was founded, he has been sitting on the domed roof of the land, whose inhabitants are like grasshoppers. He stretched out the skies like a curtain and spread them like a tent to live in* (ISA. 40:21-22); *He walks on the dome of the skies* (JOB 22:14): *I saw a tree of great height in the middle of the land. It reached to the skies, and could be seen from the farthest boundaries of the land* (DAN. 4:10); *The slanderer* (diabolos) *took him to an extremely high mountain and showed him all the kingdoms of the cosmos* (MAT. 4:8); *I saw four messengers standing at Earth's four corners* (APOC. 7:1).

In all of the quoted passages a flat earth is expressly understood. Yahweh could hardly sit on earth's roof and look down at the inhabitants, seeing

---

2. 'The biblical term "firmament" attests to the primitive belief of the sky as a "firm" object, a solid substance.' (Isaac Asimov, *The Universe: Flat Earth to Quasar,* Avon ppb., p. 15.)

them as ant-sized, if the earth were a sphere that hid half of its population from any given point on the said roof. A flat earth could be pictured as having four corners, or ultimate extremities; a sphere could not. A tall tree could conceivably be seen from all points on a flat earth, but not from all points on a sphere. The *diabolos* could in theory show Jesus all kingdoms on earth from a high enough mountain—if and only if the earth were flat.

P also believed that the earth was an immobile structure at the centre of the universe. He did not say so, but there is no reason to suppose that he was better informed than the psalmist who placed the earth, not in solar orbit, spinning on its axis, but in a fixed spot from which it would *never be moved* (PS. 104:5); the two psalmists who wrote: *The world is fixed so that it cannot be moved* (PS. 93:1; 96:10); or the chronicler who declared: *The world is fixed in place, never to be moved* (1 CHR. 16:30).

P further believed that, when Elohiym built a solid dome called the skies to divide the waters above the dome from the waters on which the land floated, the dome contained shutters that could be opened to allow the upper waters to fall through as rain: *In the 600th year of Noakh's life, all the waters of the subterranean ocean gushered up, and the sluice gates of the skies were opened* (GEN. 7:11).

In view of the limited knowledge of astronomy that existed in 600 BCE, P can be excused for believing the same things that his contemporaries believed. But the claim that he received accurate information from a god is incompatible with his errors of fact. Nor is the claim tenable that the Judaeo-Christian bible's inaccurate cosmography was metaphorical. P's first readers accepted his cosmography as literally true because P himself (and the other quoted authors) believed it to be literally true. The bible's chief god was ignorant simply because his only sources of information, his speech-writers, were equally ignorant. For the same reason, he believed that bats are birds (LEV. 11:19), a belief comparable with *Jonah*'s delusion that whales are fish.

The Priestly author gave Yahweh a greater and more supernatural role in human affairs than had J. For example, J's explanation of Pharaoh's continued refusal to allow the Israelites to emigrate was that *Pharaoh's heart remained stubborn* (EXOD. 8:32). To P, Pharaoh's holding out against Yahweh's mounting atrocities was so inconceivable that it damaged the credibility of the whole 'plagues' myth. P therefore explained that Pharaoh remained stubborn only because *Yahweh hardened Pharaoh's heart* (EXOD. 9:12).

In order for the Israelites to cross the Sea of Reeds and escape Pharaoh's pursuing army, J had Yahweh work within the laws of nature by sending a wind that dried up the entire sea bed. Just as the Egyptians were emulating the Israelites by crossing the waterless sea bed, the wind changed and, in effect, the tide came in and swamped them (EXOD. 14:21b, 27b). P, on the other hand, had Yahweh foreshadow De Mille by magically carving a dry channel through deep water (EXOD. 14:22). And while both authors declared that the great majority of exiles from Egypt would not live to enter the new homeland, J declared that the only exception would be Kaleb (NUM. 14:23-24), whereas P made two exceptions: Kaleb and Yahuwshua (NUM. 14:30).

Like the Yahwist, P was not averse to telling the same story twice. He utilised both J's fantasy of how Moses had dried up the Sea of Reeds in order to escape the pursuing Egyptians (EXOD. 14), and E's myth that had Yahuwshua similarly divide the Jordan river (JOSH. 3:17). The tale of a Hero crossing a body of water without wetting his feet captured the Jewish imagination, for the same feat was eventually attributed to Eliyah (4 KGS. 2:8); while a watered-down version was told of Jesus the Nazirite (MARK 6:48).

J had included in his Ten Commandments an instruction to celebrate the Feast of Ingathering (EXOD. 34:22), a harvest festival borrowed from the surrounding Phoenicians. D had tried to make it peculiarly Jewish by converting it into the Feast of Booths (DEUT. 16:13). P dared not attempt to abolish a carnival that was undoubtedly as much an occasion for casual copulation among Jews as among gentiles. Instead, he preceded it with a neo-Sumerian festival of a quite different nature. Five days before the onset of Booths he introduced *Youm Kippur*, a day on which Jews were to *take no pleasure in breathing*, and *pay reparations for yourselves in the presence of Yahweh your gods* (LEV. 23:27-28). The contrast between the solemn observance of the Day of Atonement and the unrestrained joy of the concurrent Babylonian Feast of Thanksgiving[3] could hardly fail to underline for both cultures that Jews and Babylonians were very different. To a nationalist consciously striving to avoid being absorbed by a foreign culture, that of course was his whole purpose.

The term *Passover (pesakh)* appears to have been coined by the Yahwist from an Egyptian word for 'strike.' He incorporated it into his decalogue as a commemorative meal celebrating the massacre of Israelite infants prior to the departure from Egypt (EXOD. 34:25). It may even be that J ordered the annual sacrifice and consumption of a lamb as a means of weaning his northern neighbours away from the human sacrifice instituted by Moses. D incorporated Passover into the Feast of Unleavened Bread that the Jews had appropriated from the Phoenicians (DEUT. 16:1-8). P backdated the festival to the event that it commemorated, and invented a spurious etymology that made *pesakh* a Hebrew word for 'pass by' (EXOD. 12:27), the rationale being that the Messenger of Death had 'passed by' the Israelite houses and

---

3. Revived in North America in the 17th century, and celebrated to this day.

killed only Egyptians. Perhaps for political motives, he declared that: *If any foreigner wishes to observe the Pesakh . . . he may do so* (NUM. 9:14). Later, when Judaism had become more xenophobic, a priest whose document was incorporated into his Towrah by R reversed P and restricted it to Jews and circumcised slaves: *A foreigner or a hired hand is not to eat it* (EXOD. 12:43).

Perhaps to encourage *Yowm Kippur* observance by sandwiching it between less solemn festivals, P also instituted the festival now known as *Rosh ha-Shanah*, a day of rest on what was to the Babylonians and modern Jews New Year's Day, but to P was the first day of the seventh month (LEV. 23:24-25).

To bolster up the fading practice of sabbath-observance, and to create the impression that the Jewish custom of resting on the seventh day (Saturday) differed qualitatively from the Persian custom of resting on the god Mithra's name-day (Sunday), P added passages to the Elohist's chronicle that stressed the practice's antiquity. P declared that Moses had observed sabbaths in the desert, and had Yahweh show his retroactive approval of such suicidal behaviour by supplying a double issue of manna ('where-from?') on Fridays (EXOD. 16:22-30). In fact a nomadic tribe that refused to gather perishable food on the seventh day would not have survived.

P introduced into Judaism the theory, first formulated by Zarathustra (or his priests) a generation earlier, that homosexual recreation, as practised by Zeus with Ganymede, Poseidon with Pelops, and Apollo with Hyakinthos, was less commendable than the heterosexual kind.[4] He declared that: *You're not to tup a man the way you tup a woman* (LEV. 18:22). R added a death penalty (LEV. 20:13). P no doubt believed that, if a man whose natural inclination was toward other men were deprived of his preferred outlet, his need for orgasm would divert him toward behaviour that would help increase the dwindling Jewish population. Few modern behavioural analysts would subscribe to that expectation.

P made no mention of lesbianism, and probably viewed it as a safe alternative to adultery for unsatisfied women. Since relationships between women did not keep such women from breeding, in a culture in which it was not economically feasible for a woman to live without a man, P's failure to ban it supports the view that, like Zarathustra, his prime concern was to maximise procreation. Nonetheless, at least part of his reason for his ban on pederasty was that gentile culture (other than the Zoroastrians) did not deem it reprehensible. The Babylonians practised sexual recreation between men; therefore, to be observably different, Jews could not.

---

4. Since laws preventing consensual homosexual behaviour are demonstrably *law pertaining to the establishment of a religion*, the U.S.A. Supreme Court's upholding of such a law in 1986 clearly violated the Constitution that Court was formed to defend.

The Deuteronomist had banned zoophilia, declaring it cursed (DEUT. 27:21). P clarified the taboo, leaving no doubt that it applied to both men and women, and confirmed the Holiness code's death penalty (EXOD. 22:19; LEV. 18:23). R concurred (LEV. 20:15). That he made no reference to the offspring of such unions (whereas Greek imaginings on the subject had included a minotaur and centaurs) perhaps indicates that animal contacts occurred with sufficient prevalence for him to realise that they were always non-procreational.

After 2600 years, P's taboo on the utilisation by men of animals' recreational orifices continues to be viewed as god-authored by Jews and Christians; but the position of Shi'ite Muslims, as spelled out by the sect's late Imam, is quite different: *A man may have sexual relations with animals only if the animal is female. . . . What is recommended . . . is coitus with . . . dogs, cats, pigeons, donkeys and lambs.*[5]

P outlawed the practice of burning babies as a sacrifice to Molokh.[6] Had he been writing only for residents of Judah, such a prohibition would have added nothing to his first Commandment that Molokh was *persona non grata* throughout Yahweh's land. But elsewhere Jews were permitted to pay due honour to the local gods, and custom dictated that this included sacrificing children (LEV. 18:21).

There is little to criticise in the prohibition of baby-burning. But it would be unrealistic to credit P with humane or altruistic motives. He banned infant sacrifice for Jews partly because Babylonians practised it, partly because the wrong god was being fed, and partly because the orthodox Jewish population was dwindling too fast already to allow it to be depleted further by avoidable deaths.

P can, however, be given a certain amount of credit for being the first mythologian of a god cult to grant women associate membership of the human race. He did not free them of their slave status as the private property of husbands and fathers, and even declared that any vow made by a woman without her owner's consent was invalid (NUM. 30:3-8). But he did decree that, if a man died with no sons, his property was henceforth to pass to his daughters (NUM. 27:8). However, he added the stipulation that such heiresses were obliged to marry within their own tribes, that property of one tribe not pass to another (NUM. 36:3-9). To create the illusion that the new inheritance law originated with Moses, P invented a tale in which Moses was confronted by such a situation and married the heiresses to

---

5. Ayatollah Khomeini, quoted in *Playboy*, March 1980, p. 47.

6. Infant sacrifice, indefensible in any circumstances, should not be confused with the non-ritualistic infanticide of deformed or imperfect babies, a practice that at one time, by permitting only the strongest to breed, contributed to humankind's survival and continued evolution.

their first cousins on their father's side, who under the old law would have inherited the land in any case (NUM. 36:10-12). In practical terms, P's new law guaranteed the brotherless daughter a husband, since it forced the heir male to marry her in order to inherit her property.

P furthered the concept of the brotherhood of all Jews, begun by J with his Chosen Nation conceit. The Deuteronomist had delineated different codes of acceptable behaviour toward Jews and gentiles. He had, for example, in addition to quoting E's Ten Commandments to govern Jewish treatment of other Jews, declared that no Jew could lend money to another Jew and charge interest (DEUT. 23:19). The Priestly author repeated the usury restriction (LEV. 25:37), and placed a similar limitation upon slavery. Henceforth no Jew could fully enslave another Jew: *The descendants of Yisrael are MY slaves* (LEV. 25:55); *You're to treat him the same as a hired hand or a guest* (LEV. 25:37). The Redactor, justifying gentile enslavement, later clarified: *Both your men-slaves and your slavegirls are to come from the infidels who surround you* (LEV. 25:44).

R's declaration that only nonbelievers could be enslaved was taken more seriously by Christians than by Jews. In bar Kokhba's time (132-135 CE) Jews were still enslaving other Jews; while in the nineteenth century CE pious Christians quoted *Leviticus* as proof that their unevolved god endorsed the enslavement of blacks.

To reassure Jews that failure to worship the Mother would not deprive them of her bounty, P had Yahweh promise: *If you obey my laws and observe my customs, then I'll give you rain in the appropriate season and the soil will surrender her produce and the trees of the field will bear their fruit . . . and you'll eat your bread to the full* (LEV. 26:3-5).

He also listed a few consequences in case his (new) laws were not (retroactively) obeyed, including: *I'll scatter you among the infidels and I'll draw out a sword after you* (LEV. 26:33). It will be noticed that, throughout the Judaeo-Christian bible, Yahweh's most specific threats were always those that, at the time of writing, had already been carried out.

As a last resort in case more subtle measures failed, P wrote: *You're not to follow the customs of the land of Egypt where you used to live, nor the customs of the land of Phoenicia to which I'm taking you; neither are you to obey their laws. You're to accept my decisions and obey my laws and follow them. . . . I, Yahweh, am your gods* (LEV. 18:3-6).

Utilising an older source quoted extensively by D (DEUT. 14:3-20), P distinguished between clean and unclean animals (LEV. 11:1-23, 41-43). He also declared that anything an unclean organism touched was likewise unclean. Since Babylonians ate taboo foods, most notably the Mother's sacred pig, P's ordinances in effect declared Babylonians unclean. P's delineation of 'us' as clean and 'them' as unclean outlasted its author's original purpose to become the core dogma of almost every god-mythology on earth. Some centuries later a Talmud author prayed: *Yahweh, I thank you who have not made me a woman, an idiot or an infidel.* In medieval times, Christian bishops officially categorised sexual recreation with a Jew as bestiality. And in the twentieth century CE the leader of Islam's Shi'ite sect, the Ayatollah Khomeini, wrote: *Eleven things are impure: urine, excrement, sperm . . . non-Moslem men and women . . . and the sweat of an excrement-eating camel.*[7]

P found a story in J/E of how Reuwbenites led by Dathan and Abiyram had rebelled against Moses. He wrote a substitute in which the rebellion was against Moses *and* Aaron. And to make the point that the Levites were not all priests and equals of the Aaronids, he made the rebels Levites:

J (NUMBERS)	P (NUMBERS)
(16:1b-2a) Dathan ben Eliyab, Abiyram ben Eliyab, and Own ben Feleth, all Reuwbenites, rebelled against Mosheh.	(16:1a) Korakh, the son of Yitshar, the son of Kohath ben Levi,
(16:12-15) So Mosheh summoned Dathan and Abiyram, who answered, 'We refuse to come. Is it not enough that you've shanghaied us from a land rich in milk and honey, to kill us in the desert? Must you also make yourself our sheikh? You haven't led us to any land rich in milk and honey, nor have you given us any fields or vineyards to inherit. How blind do you think these men are? We won't come!' Mosheh threw a tantrum, and importuned Yahweh, 'Ignore their offerings. I haven't appropriated the ass of one of them, nor have I injured a single one of them.'	(16:2b-7) with 250 leaders of the Yisraelite community, conspired together against Mosheh and Aharon and told them, 'You presume too much. This whole community is consecrated. . . . So why should you set yourselves above Yahweh's community?' Mosheh informed Korakh, 'Tomorrow Yahweh'll show you who are consecrated. . . . Take your incense burners, Korakh and all his followers. Tomorrow, put incense in them and fire them in front of Yahweh. The man whom Yahweh accepts will be considered consecrated.'
(16:25-26) Mosheh went to Dathan and Abiyram. The seniors of Yisrael followed him. He told the community, 'Stand away from these perverse men . . . in case you too are destroyed for their offenses.'	(16:16-24a) Mosheh ordered Korakh, 'You and all your followers appear before Yahweh tomorrow, you and they and Aharon. Every man is to bring his incense burner . . . 250 incense burners . . . and Aharon with his incense burner. . . .' Korakh assembled the entire community to confront them at the entrance to the Tent of Meeting. . . . Yahweh instructed Mosheh and Aharon . . . 'Tell the community to get away from the dwelling of Korakh.'
(16:27d-32a) Dathan and Abiyram stood at the entrance of their tents. Mosheh said . . . 'If these men die a natural death . . . then Yahweh hasn't sent me. But if the soil opens her mouth and swallows them, and they go down to the underworld alive, then you'll know that these men have antagonised Yahweh.' The soil opened her mouth and swallowed them.	(16:27a) So they moved away from the dwelling of Korakh.

7. *The Little Green Book. Sayings of Ayatollah Khomeini,* Bantam Books, NY, 1980.

(16:34) . . . The Yisraelites fled, declaring, 'The soil must not swallow us.'

(16:35) Yahweh unleashed a flame that wasted the 250 men who offered incense. (16:41) But the next day the community blamed Mosheh and Aharon, declaring, 'You're murdering Yahweh's nation.'

In neither the Yahwist's nor the Priestly account of the mutiny do the rebels' grievances seem unreasonable, and in both versions the modern reader must recognise Yahweh's treatment of the shop stewards as worthy of Attila the Hun or Joseph Stalin. The Priestly author denigrated the non-Aaronic Levites' status by convicting Korakh and his followers of *hubris*, in that they dared to offer incense to Yahweh as if they were Aaronic priests. A comparable conceit would be for a Catholic layman to talk to a piece of bread and declare that he had turned it into the body of a dead Jew, a feat restricted to ordained priests. But just in case anyone missed the point, P spelled it out in the plainest words: *No outsider who is not descended from Aharon is to approach Yahweh to offer incense or he will suffer the fate of Korakh and his followers in accordance with the order Yahweh gave through the medium of Mosheh* (NUM. 16:40). Since the main target of P's propaganda was the Moshite clan, P strengthened his message by citing Moses rather than Aaron as the person responsible for putting the Levites in their place.

But P was not finished yet. J/E contained a story that explained how the Levites had acquired their status as priests. P composed an alternative that not only denied the Levites equality with the Aaronids, but even denied that they were legitimate priests, and elsewhere showed the Aaronids alone being appointed priests:

J	P
Mosheh yelled, 'Who's on Yahweh's side? To me!' All of the Levites ran to join him. He told them . . . 'Every man gird on his sword and rampage through the camp. Everyone kill his kinsman, his companion, his compatriot.' The Levites did as Mosheh instructed. The number wasted amounted to about 3000 men. 'Today,' Mosheh told them, 'you have been ordained priests for Yahweh, for winning his blessing by sacrificing, each of you, his son or his brother.' (EXOD. 32:26-29)	'You take too much upon yourselves, Levites,' Mosheh told Korakh. 'Isn't it enough that the gods separated you to conduct the worship in Yahweh's Dwelling? Do you demand the priesthood as well? . . . For who is Aharon that you blame him?' (NUM. 16:7b-11) Fiynkhas the priest, the son of Eleazar ben Aharon, and his descendants are granted perpetual priesthood, because he was fanatic about his gods. (NUM. 25:10-13)

If Moses indeed ordered such a massacre of his own followers as J described, then it is likely that his assassination occurred soon thereafter. Such behaviour would not have been atypical for a man with Moses' absolute power. Lord Acton once observed that absolute power corrupts absolutely, and the mass executions of Stalin, Hitler, Trujillo, Castro, Amin and Khomeini would seem to support such a thesis. If the massacre in fact occurred only in J's imagination, then one must wonder whether his purpose was to defame Moses (a non-Jew) or to praise him. As for the Levite caste's obtaining their priestly rank by committing an appalling atrocity, it may be that J, a spokesman, saw unquestioning obedience to a spokesman's every order as the highest virtue. Until quite recently, RC priests tended to expect no less; and the current Head Christian, in defying majority opinion on issues not mentioned in *Leviticus*, has made very clear that Sin is whatever he says it is.

In the Yahwist's creation myth in J/E, Yahweh had created Eve from Adam's rib as an afterthought (just as the Sumerian goddess Ninti had given women the power to make babies out of their ribs prior to the Big Discovery), when he realised that among the birds and animals of the land, *there was among them no suitable mate for the human* (GEN. 2:20). In P's version Adam and Eve were created simultaneously: *The gods said, 'Let us make human in our own shape, like one of us. . . .' The gods created human in his own shape, prong and tunnel* (GEN. 1:26-27), on the sixth day. By retaining both, R created a Towrah/bible in which Eve was created twice.[8] Some mythologians have rationalised that the first human was a hermaphrodite, created in chapter one and divided in chapter two; but no such possibility ever crossed R's mind. The two stories of Eve's creation were incompatible as a consequence of poor editing, not deliberate intent.

P borrowed E's Ten Commandments, making one minor and one major change. The former was in E's tenth Commandment. While both E and P listed the kinds of property of a fellow Jew that one was not to lust after in descending order of value, they had different opinions as to what was the most valuable:

---

8. The pitfalls of editing separate, self-contained accounts of the same events into a single narrative can be seen in other works compiled by the same method. Sir Thomas Malory wrote several stories about King Arthur and his knights, which William Caxton edited into a continuous story which he titled *Le Morte D'Arthur*. The result was that persons killed in one 'chapter' (actually story) sometimes turned up alive in a later chapter. The same effect can be seen in Homer's *Iliad*.

E	P
You're not to lust after your compatriot's wife. Nor are you to lust after your compatriot's dwelling, his farmland, his slave or his slavegirl. . . . *(DEUT. 5:21)*	You're not to lust after your compatriot's dwelling. You're not to lust after your compatriot's wife or his slave or his slavegirl. . . . (EXOD. 20:17)

The major change was that, whereas J had ordered the Jews to rest on the seventh day without giving any reason (EXOD. 34:21), and E had repeated the order with the explanation that the rest-day commemorated their release from slavery in Egypt (DEUT. 5:13-15),[9] P justified sabbath-observance as an emulation of Elohiym's action in resting on the seventh day (EXOD. 20:11).

Abraham's circumcision and its covenant connection were P's inventions (GEN. 17), added to J's covenant-mythology for the purpose of making the slave-identification system, which the Babylonians found repugnant, impossible to abandon. Also, Abraham's acquisition of the tomb of the patriarchs at Khebrown (GEN. 23), and the burial there of Abraham, Isaac, Jacob, Sarah, Rebekah and Leah (GEN. 25:10; 49:31; 50:13), came from the quill of P.

For reasons that may have been related to a tradition derived from the long-extinct Israelites, whose demigods had not worshipped Yahweh, P had Yahweh inform Moses that Abraham, Isaac and Jacob had known him only as *El Shaday* ('Allah the demon,' a demon being a minor god, not necessarily evil), not as Yahweh (EXOD. 6:3). In fact P was in error. It was the Israelites who did not learn the name *Yahweh* until after the death of Moses. Abraham, Isaac and Jacob had all called their tribal god Yahweh.

The Priestly author described in considerable detail the making of the Chest of the Treaty, and dated its origin to Moses' conversation with Yahweh at the top of Mount Sinai (EXOD. 25-30; 35-40). He declared that the Chest's purpose had been from the beginning to contain the scroll of the Towrah (EXOD. 25:16). While that assertion need not be taken seriously, it does seem likely that the Chest indeed originated with Moses. While references to the Chest in *Joshua* are Priestly and therefore of no value as evidence of the Chest's antiquity (JOSH. 3-6), there is no reason to doubt the chronicler who recorded that the Chest of the Treaty already played a large role in Israelite mythology during the sheikhdom of Samuel, c. 1030 BCE (1 SAM. 4:1-3).

---

9. The Jews had, of course, never been slaves in Egypt. The Israelites, who became extinct in 721 BCE, had been slaves in Egypt.

The Chest was not built to house something as abstract as a lawcode. Chests (arks) as symbols of the womb of the Mother were in common usage from Greece to India, and invariably contained stone representations of the generative principles, the deified phallus and vulva. Certainly that was what it contained when King David, after recovering the Chest from the Philistines:

> danced before Yahweh . . . clad in an *efowd bad*. . . . Shauwl's daughter saw David leaping and dancing before Yahweh and she despised him. . . . And she said, 'How glorious was the king of Yisrael today who uncovered himself in front of his servants' slavegirls, as one of those conceited boasters vainly displays himself.'   (2 SAM. 6:14, 16, 20)

P described the making of the *efowd* or *efod* (the spellings were interchangeable) in *Exodus* (28:6-32). It was a gold-plated embroidered wooden phallus, so constructed that the High Priest could wear it in erect or detumescent positions. It was hollow, so that black and white pebbles representing testicles could be inserted at the base and rolled out through the glans for the purpose of asking Yahweh questions. If the white pebble (*uwriym*) emerged first, Yahweh's answer was 'Yes.' When the black pebble (*thumiym*) emerged, then the answer was 'No.' The word *bad* meant a rod or digit. Used as an adjective, it would have meant 'rod-like,' i.e., rigid. The *efowd bad* that was David's only attire is best translated as 'erect dildo.' David honoured Yahweh by dancing naked but for a sacred phallus that was the god's image, in front of the Chest that contained a similar representation in stone. Probably David's dance was a transubstantiation ritual that turned the stone into the very substance and being of Yahweh. Mikhal scorned David because, while her husband was a phallus-worshipping Jew, she as a matriarchal Israelite viewed phallus-veneration in the same light that Jewish spokesmen viewed *asherah*-eating.

David himself would have placed the phallic stones in the Chest. Under Saul (*Shauwl*) it would have continued to house its original inhabitant, the Mother's sacred snake, placed there by Moses.

Moses may well have accepted the phallus-shaped snake as a symbol of his male sky-god, just as the Apollo-worshipping Greeks who overthrew Hera's oracle at Delphi accepted and retained her python with the proviso that it henceforth represented Apollo; but that Moses needed a snake at all indicates that he was forced to make concessions (ultimately insufficient to save his dictatorship) to the Israelites' goddess-orientation. Evidence that the Chest originally contained a snake can be found in a passage written by the Elohist:

Mosheh constructed the pole-mounted snake, and thereafter if a snake bit anyone he had only to look at the bronze snake and he lived.   (NUM. 21:9)

The Israelites worshipped the primeval Mother in her traditional snake manifestation, with Moses' consent, just as they allegedly worshipped El/Allah/Elohiym as a bull with Aaron's consent. Moses manufactured a bronze caduceus which he attached to a Chest containing a live snake. Three centuries later the caduceus was placed in Yahweh's Temple, where it remained and was offered incense until it was thrown out by the reformer King Khezekyahuw around 700 BCE (4 KGS. 18:4).

It was probably also Khezekyahuw who removed the stone phallus and vulva from the Chest of the Treaty, deeming them incompatible with Yahweh's current image, and replaced them with the Yahwist's document. Certainly the Priestly author's contention that Moses placed the scroll of the Towrah in the Chest (EXOD. 40:20) can be accepted as evidence that, at the time that P wrote, the Chest contained precisely that—his own Towrah, not J/E/D.

Possibly because, when Ninevah fell in 612 BCE, he had learned that the captive Israelites carried off to Assyria in 721 BCE had been integrated out of existence, and feared that the same thing could happen to the Jews, P instituted a policy of planned incompatibility with the surrounding gentiles. He hinted that, since they ate unclean food, they were themselves unclean (LEV. 11:43-44). He instituted a theological year that commenced in the middle of the secular year (EXOD. 12:2). He recognised that Jewish festivals such as the Feast of Unleavened Bread were observably Phoenician, so he invented alleged origins for the festivals that were peculiarly Jewish. To provide a contrast to the surrounding religious festivals at which worshippers honoured the gods' gifts of wine and sex by sacramentally enjoying both, he instituted *Yowm Kippur*, actually an adaptation of the less-solemn Sumerian festival of Kupparu. And he invented a host of laws designed to keep the priesthood observably busy performing an endless succession of daily, weekly, monthly and seasonal sacrifices that would give them the appearance of being hard workers, in contrast to the observable parasite status of gentile priests. Modern Christian priests perform 6 a.m. masses for essentially the same reason.

The Priestly author attributed to Moses a victory over the Midianites that, although spurious (otherwise the Israelites would have been able to remain in Midian, their original homeland, instead of continuing their wandering as far as Israel), was probably based to some extent on a victory in Midian won by the Jewish sheikh Gideown in the twelfth century BCE (JUDG. 7). The tale is valueless as history, for certainly Gideown did not commit the atrocity attributed to Moses; but it reveals a good deal about its author.

The Israelite army, according to P, returned victorious from battle with captured women and children, having already slaughtered every last Midianite man. Moses expressed his anger that the women had been kept alive: '*You saw them cause the Yisraelites, through the recommendation of Balaam, to insult Yahweh, causing an epidemic among Yahweh's community*' (NUM. 31:14-16). That scene was reminiscent of the opening of Homer's *Iliad*, in which Agamemnon's insult to Apollo brought a plague upon the Akhaians.

As punishment for the Midianites' alleged crime, Moses ordered that all male children and all women in whom Jewish fingers could not detect an intact hymen be massacred. The female children he ordered distributed for the recreation of the victorious warriors of Yahweh's army (NUM. 31:17).

By P's reckoning the spared virgins numbered 32,000 (NUM. 31:35). If we assume that all women below the marrying age of about thirteen years were virgins (any other assumption would necessitate a larger estimate), and that unmarried girls constituted as much as a quarter of the Midianite population, we can calculate that the number of women and boys executed was not less than 60,000, in addition to the 30,000 men slaughtered on the battlefield. P clearly endorsed Moses' genocide, for he boasted that Yahweh's share of the *shiksa* concubines amounted to thirty-two (NUM. 31:40). Since P did not credit Yahweh with the Greek and Christian gods' capacity to lust after mortal women, he had the god's bedslaves initiated into their recreational duties by the High Priest, Eleazar (NUM. 31:41).

P's estimate of 32,000 virgin slavegirls captured in a single campaign was as frivolous as the other statistics with which his Towrah abounded. P was, for example, the creator of the census figures that numbered the Israelites who survived forty years in the desert at 603,550 fighting men over the age of twenty years; and that figure excluded Levites, whom he deemed noncombatants (NUM. 1:46-7). The lowest number that can reasonably be projected from such a figure for the total population would be 2,500,000. P's figures for the Israelites alone, the tribes of Menasheh and Efrayim that really were in Egypt, numbered them at 72,700 adult men. Yet it has been calculated that the largest number of nomads capable of living off the Sinai desert is about 3,000. That the Israelites indeed numbered between 2,000 and 3,000 is evident from *Exodus* 1:15, which indicated that the Israelites had, and therefore needed, only two midwives. P's plentiful statistics were about as reliable as Herodotos's estimate that Xerxes's army which invaded Greece in 480 BCE numbered 1,700,000 fighting men (HIST. 7:60), plus a like number of prostitutes and other camp followers, an army that, marching four abreast to squeeze through Greece's narrow mountain passes, would have stretched all the way from Athens to the Hellespont.

It was in the Israelites' battle against the Midianites that P killed off Balaam, to whom Yahweh talked through his ass (NUM. 31:8). An alternative source quoted by R said the same thing (JOSH. 13:22).

P knew of a battle in Gideown's time in which the Jews (not the Israelites, who lived far from Midian) had inflicted a punishing defeat upon the Midianites. On that foundation he fabricated an atrocity that made J's account of Moses' massacre of one-quarter of his own followers pale by comparison. It may be not without significance that atrocities attributed to the Israelites' leader, Moses, were reported only by J and P, both Jews, whereas the atrocities of the Jewish sheikh Yahuwshua were first described by E, an Israelite; but it is more plausible to see Moses as the Hero into whose mouth P's own views on morality and piety were put, and Moses' murder of 60,000 women and children guilty of worshipping the wrong god as P's concept of ideal Jewish behaviour. Such an interpretation is consistent with P's other xenophobic horror story in which he reiterated that only Aaronids, not all Levites, were true priests:

> A Yisraelite man was seen bringing a Midyanite woman to meet his family, in full view of Mosheh and the Yisraelite community as they wailed at the entrance to the Tent of Meeting. Fiynkhas the priest, the son of Eleazar ben Aharon, saw them and followed the Yisraelite man to his tent and there speared them both through, the Yisraelite man and the woman, through her genital orifice. Thus the pestilence that had struck the Yisraelites was halted. Those who died in the epidemic numbered 24,000. Yahweh told Mosheh, 'Fiynkhas has redirected my tantrum away from the Yisraelites. He alone of them was as fanatically intolerant as I am, and because of him I didn't exterminate the Yisraelites in my jealousy. He and his descendants are granted perpetual priesthood, because he was fanatic about his gods and paid compensation for the Yisraelites.'   (NUM. 25:6-13)

Yahweh's execution of 24,000 innocent bystanders in reprisal for one man's alleged offence has never been equalled, even by Adolf Hitler. That P could accuse (credit) his god of inflicting such a penalty for the heinous crime of race pollution, marrying a gentile, suggests that he would have made a good Nazi.[10] While it is true that, in justifying the genocidal policies of a capricious and unstable god, and in categorising non-Jews as infidels (gowyim) who could be massacred with impunity, P was merely emulating his predecessors, it is equally true that he did so with a zeal and fanaticism that had not been seen since Yahuwshua and would not be seen again until the advent of the Christians. The conclusion would seem to be warranted that the Priestly author, the founder of modern Judaism, was a man

---

10. To the best of my knowledge, no one has ever tried to justify Adolf Hitler's treatment of the religion that invented genocide as 'poetic justice,' and it would be reprehensible to do so. It is equally reprehensible that certain Jewish organizations continue to impute guilt for Hitler's actions to persons not yet born when Hitler died.

not unlike Islam's Ayatollah Khomeini or Christianity's Grand Inquisitor Torquemada.[11]

Nonetheless, P's most pernicious long-term effect upon the human race was not his intolerance of dissent or opposition, today emulated only by the fanatics commonly called fundamentalists, but his entirely reasonable failure to foresee the conditions of a far distant future. Writing at a time when the possibility of an overpopulated earth was inconceivable, P had Elohiym command Adam and Eve, *'Be fertile and increase in numbers and fill the land and pacify it'* (GEN. 1:28). Since P was writing only for Jews, whom he wanted to breed prolifically and swamp the surrounding gentiles, he cannot be held accountable for the anthropocidal enforcement of over-breeding by Popes who cannot comprehend that, 2600 years after P's death, responsible birth control is as necessary for human survival today as intensive breeding was in P's day. As with so many other taboos and customs, a logical solution to a temporary problem has evolved into a greater problem than the one it was intended to alleviate, as even a majority of Catholics are well aware.

But P cannot be blamed for that.

---

11. The attitude that infidels and heretics do not have the same rights as human beings is far from extinct. A bounty that Ruhollah Khomeini placed on the head of a novelist for allegedly blaspheming Mohammed has been neither denounced nor rescinded by the late Imam's allegedly moderate successors. Israeli politicians denounce the United Nations' demands that they cease annexing lands outside of Israel's legally recognised borders as interference in their internal affairs. And Irish Catholic terrorists continue to murder those who resist their attempts to deny Northern Ireland's Protestant majority the right of self-determination, while the Catholic Pope, who has the power to excommunicate the murderers, remains conspicuously silent. Admittedly, the current Pope (1978-   ) has the valid excuse that no jury in the world would reject a plea of diminished responsibility, and few would deny that he is the most feeble-minded Head of State since the Emperor Caligula appointed his horse Incitatus a Consul of Rome. But Orthodox Christians and Catholics killing each other in what was Yugoslavia, Christians and Muslims killing each other in Azerbaijan, Jews and Muslims killing each other in Israel and Palestine, Sikhs and Hindus killing each other in the Punjab, Shi'ite Muslims and Sunni Muslims killing each other in Iraq, Shi'ite Muslims and Bahai Muslims killing each other in Iran, and quantity-of-life Christians terrorising quality-of-life Christians and others in North America, have no such excuse.

Eleven

The Redactor

> Any piece of evidence tending to support a 'Security Belief,'
> however frail and nonsensical it might be, is grabbed and
> hugged close to the bosom. Every piece of evidence tending
> to break down a Security Belief, however strong and logical
> that evidence might be, is pushed away. (Indeed, if the
> evidence against a security belief is strong enough, those
> presenting the evidence might well be in danger of violence.)
> Isaac Asimov, *Science, Numbers, and I.*

As with the Yahwist, the Redactor who was the Towrah's final editor can only be evaluated within the context of the age and circumstances in which he wrote. The Yahwist's purpose had been to create a sense of national unity among Jews and Israelites that would cause them to see the Davidic monarchy as the culmination of Yahweh's plan for his Chosen Nation. The Redactor's purpose was also nationalistic, but his nationalism was directed toward the urgent and immediate goal of survival.

Jerusalem had fallen. The Temple built by Solomon had been levelled. The Jewish people had been carried into captivity in Babylon. Following Babylon's fall to Persia forty-eight years later, only a minority of Jews had accepted King Kyros's offer and returned to Judah. The majority, including R himself, were by 434 BCE fourth-generation Babylonians. R, a Levite priest, saw his nation becoming steadily integrated into Babylonian culture: adopting Babylonian behaviour patterns and dress; abandoning circumcision; worshipping Babylonian gods and goddesses to the exclusion of the Jewish god Yahweh, particularly those Babylonian gods whose nuns and monks provided sexual recreation not available in Yahweh-worship since the reign of Yoshyahuw; marrying Babylonian women; marrying their daughters to Babylonian men; and even adopting the Babylonian language in their own homes. In short, he saw the Jews behaving at Babylon exactly as the Israelites had behaved at Ninevah. And he knew that the assimilation of the Israelites into Assyrian society had been so complete that, when Ninevah fell in 612 BCE, there had been no Israelites left, only Assyrians of Israelite ancestry.[1]

The Israelites had disappeared, permanently transformed by one hundred years of integration into Assyrians. Later Jews, unwilling to accept that fact, would invent the myth of the 'Lost Tribes of Israel.'[2] R was more realistic. He recognised that the Jews were following a pattern that could only lead to extinction, and he set out to prevent that from happening. P had already created new rituals, new taboos and new customs that, if observed, would force Jews to draw continual attention to their Jewishness and thus create a barrier between Jews and Babylonians that would make intermarriage or any other form of integration distasteful to both. The problem was that the existence of contradictory Towrahs, J/E/D and P, created a credibility gap. R needed the Priestly Towrah in particular. But he could not simply repudiate J/E/D, as P tried to do. It had too long a tradition behind it, and was too popular with the masses. So, in a move that would have had P turning in his grave in horror, the Redactor took J/E/D and P and riffled them together into a single chronicle. And since R was in possession of several documents, mainly lawcodes, genealogies and an exodus itinerary, not found in either of his source Towrahs, he inserted them at appropriate points in what would thereafter be the Jews' only Towrah.

The Towrah, in approximately its present form, first appeared in the hands of High Priest Ezra *(Khezraa)*, with no explanation of its origin, in 434 BCE, and for that reason the Redactor is thought by many scholars to have been Ezra. Evidence for that dating and that identification can be found in the books called *Ezra* and *Nehemiah*, composed around 300 BCE as continuations of *2 Chronicles*.

Both Ezra and Nehemyah were persons from history. Ezra was a

---

1. A parallel occurred in Scotland in medieval times, when integration with the conquering Scots caused the extinction as a separate people of the painted Picts.

2. In the 19th century CE, Solomon Spaulding wrote a historical novel in which the 'lost tribes' migrated to America and became the American Indians. The unpublished manuscript fell into the hands of a boy named Joseph Smith, who rewrote it into the semblance of nonfiction and called it *The Book of Mormon*. Two Mormon scholars who unearthed the original novel had completed its authentication and were on the verge of publication when they suddenly abandoned the whole project, for reasons that can only be guessed. (See the books by Persuitte and Taves listed in the bibliography.)

lawteacher and priest, later High Priest, born and raised in Babylon (EZRA 7:6). In 459 BCE, with the backing of Artaxerxes, he migrated to Jerusalem for the declared purpose of refurnishing Yahweh's Temple that had been rebuilt sixty years earlier (7:7). Nehemyah was an officer in Artaxerxes's civil service, resident at the royal palace in Susa (NEH. 1:1; 2:1). In 446 BCE the Great King appointed him Satrap (*pekhah*) of Judah (5:14), and gave him permission (or perhaps retroactively approved, since Nehemyah was recalled in 433 BCE but not executed) to rebuild the Jerusalem walls, which he completed in 434 BCE (6:15).

In what seems to have been the October of the same year that the walls were completed, Ezra read to the inhabitants of Jerusalem an excerpt from *the scroll of the Towrah of Mosheh that Yahweh imposed on Yisrael* (NEH. 8:1-3). What Ezra read was a description of the procedure to be followed in celebrating the upcoming Feast of Booths.

Conflicting formulas for the Feast of Booths are to be found in *Deuteronomy* 16:13-15 and *Leviticus* 23:39-43. The detailed account of the procedures followed in compliance with Ezra's reading leaves no doubt that the reading was from *Leviticus*. The chronicler added that the ceremony had not been conducted in such a manner *since the days of Yeshuakh ben Nuwn* (NEH. 8:14-18). Since the Feast of Booths was celebrated according to the Deuteronomic formula in 441 BCE and the Levitical formula in 434 BCE, Ezra must have acquired the finished Towrah between those dates. And since *Leviticus* 23:39-43 was originally a separate document, interpolated into the Priestly lawcode by R, the passage's presence in the *Towrah of Mosheh* indicates that the Towrah in question was the combined version, not P. Ezra's failure to draw attention to its newness, or explain its origin, strongly supports the theory that he compiled it himself. And the late-first-century-CE *4 Ezra* made the claim that, after the original Towrah was destroyed in the burning of the Temple in 586 BCE, Ezra rewrote it from a revelation.

In combining incompatible documents, R inevitably created self-contradictions. Sometimes R spotted the problem and solved it with a gloss. For example, when a J story showed Isaac digging the same wells E had earlier credited to Abraham, R (or the earlier J/E Redactor) added verses showing the Philistines filling in Abraham's wells so that Isaac had to redig them (GEN. 26:15, 18). And where J told several tales of the adult Isaac, even though E had had Isaac sacrificed as a child, R added verses to E's sacrifice tale in which Yahweh intervened to save Isaac's life (GEN. 22:11-16a).

Not surprisingly, R did not recognise and rectify every avoidable inconsistency. For example, he could, without harming the continuity of the Yahwist's primeval mythology, have deleted from the prelude to Noah's flood Yahweh's declaration that the lives of humans were *to be limited to 120 years* (GEN. 6:3). Just by moving the line to a later position, R could have avoided having Abraham live to the age of 175 several generations after Yahweh had limited all humans to less (GEN. 25:7). Similarly, he included passages showing giants and Cainites alive after Noah's flood, even though J had drowned both.

R's careless editing has been demonstrated before, in connection with the contradictory flood myths and the two creations of Eve. A further example is to be found in his inclusion, at widely-spaced time intervals, of two accounts of the fable of the waters of Meriybah:

E	P
(R: The Yisraelites moved from the desert of Siyn. . . .) There was no water. . . . Yahweh answered Mosheh . . . 'You'll see me on the rock at Khoreb. You're to strike the rock, and water will gush out of it'. . . . Mosheh did so in full view of the seniors of Yisrael. He named the place Masah ('testing') and Meriybah ('quarreling') because of the quarreling of the Yisraelites and because they tested Yahweh. (EXOD. 17:1-7)	(R: The Yisraelite community entered the desert of Tsin. . . .) There was no water. . . . Yahweh instructed Mosheh . . . 'Order the rock to start gushing water'. . . . 'Do we have to fetch you water out of this rock?' Mosheh raised his arm and struck the rock twice with his staff, and water gushed out in abundance. . . . These are the waters of Meriybah. (NUM. 20:1-13)

The myth of a Hero striking a rock to produce water was first told of Mithra. E or one of his oral sources may have seen a bas-relief of the Persian god and assumed that the central figure was Moses. The recurrence of the name *Meriybah* refutes any rationalisation that the two versions referred to separate incidents. Like Homer, R nodded. A more alert editor would have omitted E's account (P utilised his version to justify Moses' exclusion from the promised homeland) altogether.[3]

It was R who inserted priest-composed genealogies that traced Moses to Levi (EXOD. 6:16-20), Abraham to Sem (GEN. 11:10-26), and Noah to Adam (GEN. 5:1-32). He was also responsible for the 969 year lifespan of Methuwselakh, the 950 years of Noah, the 930 years of Adam, and the equally fatuous long lives of other pre-patriarchal demigods. Why he chose such conservative figures is difficult to estimate, considering that early Sumerian king lists credited their first dynasty with reigns of several thousand years each.

It was also R who, by his statement that Adam was 130 years old when he sired Set, who was 105 years old when he sired Enowsh, and

---

3. Compare Moses/Mithra's method of solving a water shortage with the solution of Pecos Bill, who, according to a Walt Disney lyricist, used a wooden stick to dig the Rio Grande.

so on, dated the creation of the four-million-year-old human race to 4004 BCE (as Bishop Ussher calculated) or 3760 BCE (according to the Jewish calendar).

R's predilection for chronology led to further incompatibilities:

E	R
On the day that Yitskhak was weaned Sarah noticed the son of Hagar being impudent. So she demanded, 'Throw this slavegirl and her son out'. . . . Abraham put the infant on her shoulder and sent her away. (GEN. 21:8-14)	Avrum was 86 years old when Hagar bore Yishmael to Avrum. . . . Abraham was 100 years old when his son Yitskhak was born to him. (GEN. 16:16; 21:5)

By R's reckoning, Ishmael could not have been less than fifteen years old when Abraham expelled the boy and his mother from his house. Yet R interwove that chronology with a passage by E in which Ishmael was pictured as an infant whom Hagar needed to carry.

It was the first (J/E) Redactor's editing that deprived Joseph of his status as Jacob's 'sacred seventh' son and relegated him to eleventh position in the patriarchal hierarchy. J (GEN. 29:30-35; 30:9-16), E (GEN. 30:1-8, 17-20, 22-24), and P (NUM. 26:5-8, 12-57) had all made Joseph the seventh son, or seventh in seniority:

J	E	P	R
Reuwben	Yahuwdah(?)	Reuwben	Reuwben
Shimeown	Levi(?)	Shimeown	Shimeown
Levi	Dan	Gad	Levi
Yahuwdah	Naftoliy	Yahuwdah	Yahuwdah
Gad	Yisaskhar	Yisaskhar	Dan
Asher	Zebuluwn	Zebuwlun	Naftoliy
YOWSEF	YOWSEF	YOWSEF	Gad
?	?	Benyamin	Asher
?	?	Dan	Yisaskhar
?	?	Asher	Zebuluwn
?	?	Naftoliy	YOWSEF
Benyamiyn	Benyamiyn	Levi	Benyamiyn

How J or E ordered the missing four names can only be guessed, but there is no doubt that they gave the twelfth position to Benjamin. R's scissors-and-paste editing, placing every patriarch named as being older than Joseph by either J or E ahead of him in the edited version, resulted in Joseph being demoted to number eleven son, while his sacred seventh spot was filled by the insignificant Gad. R failed to notice that, although E had specifically identified Yisaskhar and Zebuluwn as Jacob's fifth and sixth sons (GEN. 30:17-20), they became numbers nine and ten in R's edited version.

In addition to the two versions of the waters of Meriybah, R also included both the E and P accounts of the glut of quails (NUM. 11:31; EXOD. 16:13), and both accounts of *man huwa* ('where is it from?,' transcribed as *manna* in the A.V.), (NUM. 11:7-9; EXOD. 16:15), again at such widely spaced intervals as to indicate that each incident occurred twice. And whereas E's *wherefrom?* could be ground down into flour and preserved (NUM. 11:7-9), P's needed to be eaten fresh on the day it was gathered or it would melt in the sun, turn rancid, and become maggot-ridden (EXOD. 16:19-21). P, recognising that his absurdly inflated Israelite population could not otherwise have fed itself in a desert capable of supporting perhaps 3000, wrote that the wanderers lived on *wherefrom?* for forty years (EXOD. 16:35), and that it magically disappeared as soon as they reached their ultimate destination (JOSH. 5:12). Amazingly, the god capable of feeding 603,550 families with bread from the sky for forty years is nowhere to be found at a time when millions of Ethiopians, Somalians and other Africans (and others) are starving to death.

Only R could have written that a jar of the nonexistant *wherefrom?* had been preserved in Solomon's Temple, since he alone wrote at a time when the first Temple no longer stood and such a claim could not be falsified (EXOD. 16:33).

It was R who first introduced into the Towrah a stipulation that henceforth Jews were not to couple with Molokh's nuns, since such behaviour violated the Jews' meta-marriage with Yahweh and therefore constituted adultery with the foreign god (LEV. 20:5).[4] That his prohibition of fornication, meaning nun-tupping, echoed by Paul of Tarsus, has been misinterpreted by Christians as meaning something neither R nor Paul ever intended, should not be held against him.

R's ultimate absurdity was his invention of the world's first nakedness taboo. While accepting the Yahwist's assertion that Yahweh had created Adam and Eve naked, he added passages which implied that Yahweh's creation was already indecent but that Adam and Eve had to 'sin' in order to discover this:

---

4. Unawareness of the original meaning of adultery causes some modern scholars to imagine that the 'courtly love' of the Petrarchian age was unconsummated adoration, and others to imagine that it was simple adultery. It was neither. Consummation occurred, but without the sperm intromission that would have transformed chaste love into adultery. Courtly lovers (allegedly) practised *coitus interruptus*.

J	R
He answered, 'I heard your noise in the garden, and I was afraid and I hid.' He asked, 'Have you eaten from the tree from which I forbade you to eat?' (GEN. 3:10-11)	He answered, 'I heard your noise in the garden, and I was afraid *because I was naked* and I hid.' He asked, *'Who told you that you were naked?* Have you eaten from the tree from which I forbade you to eat?' (GEN. 3:10-11)

R added two additional lines: *Both of them were naked, the husband and his wife, but they were not embarrassed* (GEN. 2:25), prior to the *asherah*-eating; and: *They realised that they were naked, and they sewed figleaves together to make themselves loincloths* (GEN. 3:7b) afterwards; and the antiquity of humankind's newest and silliest taboo was established.

R's choice of figleaves as humankind's first clothing was predictable, coming as it did from an author who had grown up in the Persian empire's cosmopolitan metropolis. The Persian sungod Mithra, being born in a cold climate, had clothed himself in figleaves to keep warm.

As illogical as R's nakedness taboo was, like most of his innovations it had a practical purpose related to his ultimate goal. While Babylonians wore clothing as a protection against the Mesopotamian sun, they doffed such encumbrances when engaged in competitive sport. Jews competed in such events; and many, finding their circumcisions an object of ridicule, were submitting to operations to restore the 'natural' look to their mutilated phalluses.[5] By making nakedness a *sin*, R removed the main obstacle to the continued practice of circumcision.

And that was his whole point.

---

5. *1 Maccabees* 1:15. The Sadducee author declared that this practice was common under Antiokhos Epiphanes (d. 164 BCE), but there is no reason to doubt that it began in the earliest generations of Persian domination.

Twelve

Judges, Kings and Prophets

If the play of the world is produced and directed by an omnipotent God, does it not follow that every evil that is perpetrated is God's doing? I know this idea is an embarrassment in the West, and attempts to avoid it include the contention that what seems to be evil is really part of the Divine Plan, too complex for us to fathom.

Carl Sagan, *Broca's Brain.*

Most scholars accept that the *Book of Joshua* was an integral part of the Towrah as it first appeared in the hands of the High Priest Ezra in 434 BCE. However, there is no doubt that it became separated within a century. In the middle of the fourth century BCE the pentateuch was adopted by the Samaritans but *Joshua* was not.

The best-known tall tale in *Joshua* told of the Jewish sheikh's campaign at Gibeown:

> Yahuwshuakh appealed to Yahweh,
> And said in the presence of Yisrael,
> 'Sun, stand still over Gibeown,
> And you too, Moon, in the vale of Ayalown.'
> And the sun stood still, / And the moon halted,
> Until the nation had wreaked vengeance
> Upon their enemies.

Or so it says in the Book of Yasher, does it not?
The sun hung motionless . . . for about a whole day.
(JOSH. 10:12-13)

The Redactor's reference to his source, the lost book of the spokesman Yasher, was more typical of the later chroniclers than of the Towrah authors. The desperate appeal to the authority of Yasher was R's way of absolving himself from responsibility for an unbelievable story by pointing out that he had obtained it from a 'usually reliable source.' Note R's belief that, for the sun to appear motionless in the sky, the sun would have to stop orbiting the earth, rather than the earth stop revolving on its axis. As always, biblical cosmography reflects the scientific illiteracy of a pre-Copernican age, not the perfect knowledge of an omniscient god.

Yahuwshua was not the first person to make the sun stand still. Zeus ordered the sun-god Apollo not to rise, and Morpheus ('Dream') to work overtime, while he spent a thirty-six-hour night pumping into Alkmene the superabundance of sperm needed to generate his last and greatest son, Herakles. Since the day of Yahuwshua's long fight and the night of Zeus's long phallus each allegedly occurred around 1380 BCE, without the Egyptians, normally compulsive sky-watchers, recording anything unusual, perhaps Zeus and Yahweh made an agreement to accomplish their purposes simultaneously.

Following the death of Yahuwshua around 1350 BCE the Jews continued the practice of electing nonhereditary sheikhs or judges, usually chosen for their military skill. One notable exception was Deborah, described as a spokeswoman (JUDG. 4:4). Deborah was elected Judge, but she was no prototype Jeanne d'Arc. She sent her men into battle; she never led them. Her main claim to fame, in fact, was that she was a poet. The Song of Deborah (JUDG. 5) is generally reckoned the oldest part of the Judaeo-Christian bible.

The story of the barren wife who became the mother of a Hero, so familiar from *Genesis*, reappeared in *Judges*. The Hero was Samson (*Shamashoun*), greatest of the judges of Judah and, like Jesus the Nazirite, a person whose historicity has been obscured by posthumously-added hero-myths.

Much mythology was based upon a misinterpretation of ancient drawings whose real meaning had been forgotten. For example, Bellerophontes's abolition of the goddess-oriented lunar calendar with its lion, goat and snake seasons, was commemorated by depicting the reformer killing a monster that was a hybrid of the summer, winter and spring totems. A later generation took the drawing literally, and invented the tale that Bellerophontes had killed a *khimaira* (chimera).

The Samson myth was similarly deduced from an icon that showed the exploits of the sun-god, whose plentiful beams were mistaken for un-cut hair. The Hebrew mythologian accordingly created a demigod whose downfall was brought about by a breach of the nazirite vow never to cut his hair.

Samson originated as a sun-god. His name was a variant form of *Shamash*, the Babylonian sun-god and the Hebrew name for the sun. Samson's birth-place, Tsorah, was a short walk from Beth-Shamash, 'House of the Sun,' an ancient centre of sun-worship. Samson was shorn of his long hair before being blinded as a consequence of settling into the lap of his victorious playmate, *Delilah*, just as the sun was daily shorn of its long beams before settling, blinded, into the lap of victorious Night (*Lilah*). And, just as the sun's loss of the plentiful beams that were its strength was temporary, lasting only for the duration of the reign of Night, so Samson's shorn locks that were his strength regrew, enabling him to perform one final superhuman feat that resulted in his own death. That final modification was necessary since, while the sun never died, the historical Samson obvi-ously did.[1]

A messenger from the skies appeared to Samson's mother and told her that she would conceive a son who would be highly favoured by Yahweh (JUDG. 13:5). Such a story had been told by the Yahwist concerning Abraham and Sarah (GEN. 18:3-10). Much later it would be borrowed again and applied to Mary. Samson killed a lion with his bare hands. Herakles killed a lion with his bare hands. A riddle played a significant role at the beginning of Samson's career. A riddle played a significant role at the beginning of Oidipous's career. Samson killed one thousand men with a makeshift club. The Greek lion killer's main weapon was a club.

Samson died in a Philistine temple. Blind but with his strength returned, he pushed on the two pillars that were the temple's main supports. He brought the building down, killing three thousand men and women (JUDG. 16:26-30).

Only one Philistine temple has been excavated, but there is no reason to doubt that it was typical. The supporting pillars were 2½ metres apart. A Goliath could possibly have touched both pillars at the same time, with his fingertips. The arms of even the tallest Jew would have fallen short by several centimetres. The temple was large enough to have accommodated perhaps thirty people. Even if a larger temple remains to be discovered, any temple small enough to be destroyed by the collapse of two pillars could not have contained more than a tenth of the persons who allegedly died with Samson.

---

1. For additional information on Samson and other sun-gods, see 'The Flaming God' in Isaac Asimov's *Life and Time* (NY, 1978).

Samson's independent forays against the Philistines during a period of truce brought reprisals. To buy peace, the Jews made the Philistines a present of their great enemy.

That part of the Samson story sounds historical. A story that reflected unfavourably upon the Jews was unlikely to have been invented by a Jew. Probably the legends of a solar deity beguiled by Night were grafted onto the life of a historical judge of Judah who was handed over to the Philistines for execution.

Another Yahwistic tale reappeared in *Judges*. Two of Yahweh's messengers had entered Levit's house at Sodom. When the townsmen demanded that the visitors sexually gratify the multitude, Levit showed his understanding of the requisites of hospitality by offering his virgin daughters in his guests' place (GEN. 19:1-8).

In *Judges'* version of the story, the houseguest whom the townsmen wished to bugger was a mere mortal; but the host similarly offered the crowd his virgin daughter in place of the guest whom he was obliged to protect. Ultimately the mob was given the guest's concubine and gang-raped her to death. Her husband's reaction was to carve his concubine into twelve pieces and send the pieces into the twelve subdivisions of Israel (JUDG. 19:22-29).

The purpose of the foregoing fiction was revealed in the following chapters. The wronged husband was a Jew of the tribe of Levi. The communal rapists were Israelites·of the tribe of Benjamin. The incident led to a war that the author viewed as fratricidal, but in all likelihood the war to which the tale was attached occurred before the genealogy was composed that made Jews and Israelites kinsmen. In view of the immense slaughter of the war, it is feasible that the genealogy was composed to prevent a similar mutual massacre from ever happening again. The author's explanation of the cause of the war can be taken about as seriously as Aristophanes's claim that Perikles started the Peloponnesian War because a group of Spartans left Aspasia's whorehouse without paying.

That monolatry was fighting a losing battle in the period of the judges can be deduced from some of the judges' names. One of the earliest was Shamgar, identified as the son (follower) of the goddess Khanath (JUDG. 3:31). Gideown, who led the Jews for many years, was also named Yerubaal in honour of Allah's son and rival, Baal (7:1). Gideown made a golden phallus which he displayed in the town of Ofrah, *and all Yisrael went there nun-tupping in front of it* (8:27). And Gideown was succeeded by his son Abiymolokh, named after the Phoenician god Molokh (9:1).

The next judge to acquire significant authority was Yefthah, whose mother was a temple nun in the service of Ashtaroth (11:1). Yefthah was the man who rashly vowed to sacrifice to Yahweh the first living thing to greet him after a successful battle, and was obliged to sacrifice his daughter (11:30-40). Modern Jews and Christians who would not hesitate to condemn any person who fulfilled such a monstrous vow today, for some reason continue to regard Yefthah favourably.

And then there was Samson, who either *was* Shamash or bore a name that honoured Shamash.

By the middle of the eleventh century BCE the Israelites had tired of elective sheikhs and wanted a hereditary king. Saul was chosen. David, a Jew from Bethlehem, became one of his generals. David married Saul's daughter. He also fell in love with Saul's son.

David was not homosexually inclined. He had at least seven wives who bore him children, besides Saul's daughter who did not. Once he had acquired a harem there is no evidence that he ever again loved a boy. But that his relationship with Yahuwnathan was sexual is the only possible interpretation of the chronicler's words:

> The breath of Yahuwnathan was dependent on the breath of David, for Yahuwnathan loved him as his own breath. (1 SAM. 18:1)

> Yahuwnathan and David contracted together, for he loved him as his own breath. (18:3)

> Yahuwnathan, Shauwl's son, was utterly enraptured by David. (19:2)

> David said, 'Your father knows I am the delight of your eyes.' (20:3)

> Shauwl said . . . 'You have coupled with the son of Yishay to your own confusion and the confusion of your mother's vulva.' (20:30)

> They kissed each other and wept with each other until David orgasmed. (20:41)

> 'My brother Yahuwnathan, you have been very satisfying to me. Your love for me was wondrous, surpassing the lovemaking of women.' (2 SAM. 1:26)

David and Yahuwnathan were lovers. Yahweh did not disapprove, because his retroactive disapproval would not be invented by the Priestly author for a further three hundred years. David was an equal-opportunity lover, as were every man and woman on earth prior to about 650 BCE. A sizeable minority never engaged in any homosexual recreation; but they were observing a preference, not a taboo.

The spokesman who anointed Saul king of Israel and, fifteen years later,

David King of Judah, was Samuel. Samuel's mother was old and barren and despaired of ever having a son. She prayed to Yahweh for a manchild and . . . . Does this sound familiar? Like Samson's mother, Samuel's mother vowed that, if she were granted a son, the boy would be dedicated to Yahweh and his hair would never be cut (1 SAM. 1:5-11). Samuel became the first spokesman, since *a spokesman was previously called a far-seer* (1 SAM. 9:9), and the last judge.

Saul died and was succeeded by his son as king of Israel only. David was already king of Judah. At the death of Saul's son, David became king of Israel also, partly by right of conquest and partly as Saul's son-in-law and heir. He lusted after the wife of Uwriyah, a Yahweh-worshipping Hittite, ordered her to his bed, murdered her husband when he learned of her pregnancy, and married her (2 SAM. 11:2-27). She bore him Solomon, who succeeded to the dual crown.

Apart from the aforesaid murder and adultery, which the chronicler used to explain the constant state of rebellion in David's reign (2 SAM. 12:10-11), little to David's detriment was recorded by his biographers. Admittedly he bought peace with the Gibeonites by handing over seven of Saul's sons for the Gibeonites to hang; but as the hangings constituted a sacrifice to Yahweh, it did not occur to the chronicler that Yahweh might not have approved. It was in any case Yahweh's dice-tossing High Priest, having rolled 'heads'/white/*uwriym*, who told David that the Gibeonites must be appeased (2 SAM. 21:1-9).

That David was tyrannical and arbitrary may be inferred from his son Abshalowm's being able to capitalise on widespread discontent and mount a rebellion that forced David to flee Jerusalem (2 SAM. 15:13-14). The chronicler, not surprisingly, put all the blame for the unrest on Abshalowm. He did, however, accuse David of treating prisoners of war in a manner that modern readers may well view with horror:

> He brought forth the (Ammonite prisoners) and put them under saws, and under harrows of iron, and under axes of iron, and made them pass through the brickkiln.   (2 SAM. 12:31)

> He brought out the people and cut them with saws and with harrows of iron and with axes. In this manner David dealt with all the cities of the Khamownites.   (1 CHR. 20:3)

Normally, when a man is accused of monstrous crimes by persons whose discernible purpose is to praise him, the accusations can be believed. There is, however, considerable doubt that the authors of the quoted passages saw the torture of Ammonites as anything but meritorious. The passages were composed during the course of a long, indecisive war between the Jews and the Ammonites in the late fifth century BCE, and are more indicative of the chroniclers' beliefs about what David *should* have done to the Ammonites when he had the chance, than of David's actual behaviour. The same chronicler recorded a little later that David's descendant Amatsyahuw, a king who *did what Yahweh saw as right*, took ten thousand Edomite prisoners and *threw them down from the top of the rock so that they were all smashed to pieces* (2 CHR. 25:2, 12). Such reports were propaganda, not history.

At the death of Solomon in 930 BCE, his son Rekhobowam succeeded peacefully to the throne of Judah, but ran into problems when he tried to retain his father's grip on Israel. The Israelites, long disgruntled by Solomon's oppressive taxation, asked Rekhobowam to ease their burden. Rekhobowam's reply, we are told, was, '*My father punished you with whips, but I'm going to punish you with scorpions*' (3 KGS. 12:11). Not surprisingly, the Israelites threw off the Jewish yoke and elected their own king, Yerobowam.

Yerobowam's dynasty lasted two generations. It was followed by a fourth dynasty that lasted a similar two generations, and a fifth that lasted seven days. The founder of the sixth dynasty, Khomriy, a military leader (naturally), built the city of Samaria and made it his capital. Khomriy was succeeded by his son Akhab, who married the Tsiydonite princess, Jezebel (*Iyzebel*). Jezebel's main crime was that she worshipped Bel/Baal, a Jesus-type saviour-god, instead of Father El/Allah. However, she was as intolerant as any spokesman for Yahweh, and ordered the murder of an untold number of Yahweh's spokesmen (3 KGS. 18:13). It was during Akhab's reign that the spokesman Eliyah rose to fame.

Eli-Yahuw repaid *Iyze-Bel* in her own coin. To prove that 'My god can lick your god,' Eliyah staged a contest between himself and 450 spokesmen for Baal, to see whose god could set fire to a burnt offering without matches. As the chronicler told the story, Baal failed to answer his priests' incantations, causing Eliyah to inquire if he was perhaps engaged in a seduction or in relieving himself. Yahweh, on the other hand, demonstrated his superiority by hurling down the traditional storm-god's thunderbolt that consumed his offering in an instant (3 KGS. 18:27, 38).

It is not impossible that Eliyah did what the chronicler said he did. Such a feat could be duplicated today by a magician familiar with the properties of magnesium and phosphorus. But it is only necessary to look at the accounts of miracles performed by modern-day faith healers and messiahs as described in the healers' own publications, and compare those accounts with reports in more critical newspapers and magazines, to realise that a story written by a believer is unlikely to make any distinction between that which verifiably happened and that which the miracle-worker said had happened.[2] In recent times the mentally-disturbed Mary Baker Eddy had no difficulty persuading her credulous followers that she had several times resurrected the dead; but no newspaper or news magazine saw fit to report her claims as fact. The chronicler who reported as fact that Eliyah departed this planet in a flaming chariot must be deemed uncritical, to say the least.

In fact the contest staged by Eliyah appears to have been nothing more than a cold-blooded ambush. The El people surrounded the Baal people and murdered the 450 foreign spokesmen. A modern parallel would be for a Pope (or Ayatollah) to invite 450 rabbis (or bishops) to Rome (or Iran) to debate their conflicting mythologies, to declare himself the winner, and to execute the 450 losers for the greater glory of Jesus (or Mohammed). While Eliyah may have worked a chemical trick, it was more likely that he ignited the sacrifice by the usual method after the massacre, and had his stooges spread the word that Yahweh did it with a thunderbolt.

Akhab was succeeded by his son Akhazyahuw, who had a fatal accident in the first year of his reign. From his deathbed Akhazyahuw sent messengers *'to find out from Baal-Zebuwb Allah of Khekrown whether I'm going to recover from this injury'* (4 KGS. 1:2). Eliyah, in hiding from the wrath of the Khomriy dynasty, sent his adjutant to ask Akhazyahuw, *'Weren't there any gods in Yisrael whom you could have asked?'* In asking such a question, Eliyah revealed that, while he was a fanatic monolatrist who resented Akhazyahuw's going over Yahweh's head, like every Jew of his time he was not a monotheist, for he did not question that the Khekronite god existed. The only logical conclusion for such an incident was for Eliyah to prophesy Akhazyahuw's death, and for Akhazyahuw obligingly to die. The chronicler was nothing if not logical (4 KGS. 1:2-17).

The chronicler's reference to the Allah of Khekrown as *Baal-Zebuwb* tells a good deal about the ancient Jews' narrow-minded intolerance of every mythology but their own, an intolerance later emulated by Christianity and

---

2. The utter credulity of persons emotionally committed to a contrary-to-fact belief, and the ease with which such persons can be gulled, was spelled out in a hoax perpetrated by magician James Randi and assistants against the parapsychology department of George Washington University in St Louis. Two of Randi's associates, posing as possessors of psychic abilities (there is no such thing as psychic ability), fooled the pathetically unscientific investigators at G.W.U. into believing that they had seen absolute proof, impossible to fake, of ESP, psychokinesis and psychic photography; and publishing their allegedly scientific findings in *Research in Paranormal Psychology*. An account of the hoax was reported in *Discover*, March 1983, along with the explanation that, when parapsychologists persistently refused to be told that they were being deceived by conjurors, Randi saw little alternative but to prove his point by deceiving them himself. To this day, some of the incompetent researchers exposed by Randi's sting maintain that Randi's confederates really were psychics who are now falsely claiming to be magicians. For a complete rebuttal of all alleged evidence for the reality of ESP, see C.E.M. Hansel, *The Search for Psychic Power: ESP and Parapsychology Revisited*, Buffalo, 1989; and K. Frazier, ed., *Science Confronts the Paranormal*, Buffalo, 1986.

Islam. Nowhere in the world was there ever worshipped a god named 'Lord of the Flies.' The derogatory name *Baal-Zebuwb*, Lord of the Flies, was a Hebrew slur designed to ridicule *Baal-Zuwb*, Lord of the Phallus, for being too powerless to keep the flies away from his unattended meat offering. One wonders whether, in the absence of priests with swatters, Yahweh could have done any better.

Eliyah was the first of the Israelite miracle-workers. Fantastic tales first told of Eliyah were later borrowed by the authors of the fictional biographies of Jesus the Nazirite and applied to their hero.

For example, Eliyah raised the dead: A widow fed the spokesman when he was hungry, and in return he revived her dead son (3 KGS. 17:17-22; cf. MARK 5:22-24, 35-42). The widow had only *a handful of cereal in a barrel, and a little oil in a jar* (17:12), but Eliyah worked his magic so that the small amount fed three people for many days (17:16; cf. MARK 8:5-9). Eliyah journeyed into the desert where he was tended by a heavenly messenger. As a consequence he had no difficulty surviving forty days without food (19:4-8; cf. MARK 1:12-13). While the chronicler did not associate Eliyah's sojourn in the desert with the belief, recorded by Plinius, that a forty-day fast would enable a man to sire boys, he did have the messenger instruct Eliyah to anoint Eliyshakh as his successor (19:16), implying that Yahweh had given the spokesman a spiritual rather than a biological son.

While in hiding from Akhab, Eliyah was brought bread and meat twice a day by ravens (17:6). He emulated Yahuwshua's parting of the Jordan river (4 KGS. 2:8). Even Jesus' biographers dared not credit their hero with a feat of that magnitude. Instead they contented themselves with the claim that Jesus had crossed a lake dry-shod by walking on the water (MARK 6:48).

Eliyah did not die. Like his carbon-copy, Jesus, he was transported bodily to the skies. But whereas Jesus merely rose in a cloud (ACTS 1:9), Eliyah departed in a chariot of fire pulled by equally fiery horses in the middle of a whirlwind (4 KGS. 2:11). No doubt the chronicler or his ultimate source for the story saw a bas-relief of the Persian god Mithra ascending to the skies by identical means. The Greeks depicted Apollo in a similar manner. Only Eliyshakh, it seems, was permitted to see the chariot and horses. The *sons of the spokesmen* who were also present all thought they saw Eliyah swept away in a tornado, and spent three days searching for his body (2:16-17).

Eliyshakh, the second of Israel's miracle mongers and the source of more of Jesus' miracles, proclaimed his version of Yahweh's Word during the last reign of the sixth dynasty and the first three reigns of the seventh dynasty (852-781 BCE). He began his career by multiplying a widow's oil so that a single potful filled as many pots as she could borrow (4 KGS. 4:2-6). He followed this by feeding one hundred men with twenty bagels of barley bread and some ears of corn, having some left over (4:42-44;

cf. JOHN 6:9-13). He cured a leper by having him bathe seven times in the Jordan river (5:6-14; *cf.* LUKE 17:12-14). He turned a bitter spring into drinking water (2:21-22; *cf.* JOHN 2:7-9). He afflicted a man with leprosy as a punishment for greed (5:27; *cf.* ACTS 5:3). He made an iron axe float on water (6:6). Even after he was dead, a corpse that touched his bones was restored to life (13:21; *cf.* MAT. 27:52).

Eliyshakh successfully prophesied to a woman who was barren that she would bear a son (4:14-17). When the son died, Eliyshakh restored him to life (4:32-35). The description of Eliyshakh's miracle reads like mouth-to-mouth resuscitation, but it would be unduly credulous to interpret it as such. Spokesmen were expected to be wonder-workers, and were posthumously credited with whatever came into a biographer's mind. It is highly unlikely that any of the miracles attributed to Eliyah and Eliyshakh, and later appropriated to Jesus, were based on any historical event.

Israel's seventh dynasty lasted a record eighty-nine years, forty years of which constituted the twelve-year co-regency and twenty-eight-year sole reign of Yerobowam II. The eighth dynasty lasted one month, the ninth two generations, and the last two one generation each. In 721 BCE Howsheakh, Israel's last king, was defeated by Sargon II of Assyria. The Israelites were carried off to Ninevah and its tributaries, *Kalakh and Khabowr on the river Gowzan, and the towns of the Medes* (4 KGS. 17:6), never to return. A large minority escaped to Judah where by intermarriage and cultural absorption their descendants became Jews. The majority, by the same process, became Assyrians. And so Israelite history, which had begun in the reign of Pharaoh Ikhenaton in the fourteenth century BCE (or perhaps in Egypt four centuries earlier, if the Israelites had been part of the Hyksos) came to an abrupt and permanent end.

In Judah David's dynasty survived. His descendant Akhaz was king of Judah when Samaria fell to Sargon. It was during the reign of Akhaz's son Khezekyahuw (715-686 BCE) that the genuine Isayah (*Yeshayahuw*) wrote his twelve-chapter prophecy that a remnant of the captive Israelites would one day return from Assyria, led by a descendant of David's father Yishay (ISA. 11:10-11). He was wrong. The Israelites never returned.

Isayah, like all good spokesmen, was a miracle-worker. Mindful of how Yahuwshua had made the sun stand still over Gibeown, a chronicler had Isayah cause the shadow on Khezekyahuw's sundial to move backwards ten degrees (4 KGS. 20:11). Isayah was also credited with telling Khezekyahuw that his descendants would one day be eunuchs in the palace of the king of Babylon (4 KGS. 20:18). No such prophecy appeared in Isayah's own writing for the very good reason that in Isayah's lifetime the fall of Jerusalem to Babylon could not have been foreseen. By the time *Kings* was written, the Babylonian Captivity had already occurred.

Yoshyahuw was Khezekyahuw's great-grandson. In his reign *Deuteronomy* was written. Yoshyahuw was king of Judah when Ninevah was levelled by Nabu-apal-assur of Babylon and Kyaxares of Media in 612 BCE. The Assyrian empire followed the Israelites into permanent extinction, ridding the world of a regime whose brutality only Hitler managed to surpass. Jeremyah in about 580 BCE (or an interpolator before 538 BCE) prophesied an Assyrian comeback (JER. 50:3), but he was fortunately wrong.

In 588 BCE King Nabu-akh-adon-assur, whose father had conquered Assyria, besieged Jerusalem. For the two years that the siege lasted, the Jews were subjected to the rantings of a spokesman who had been making a nuisance of himself since the middle of the reign of Yoshyahuw. Jeremyah (*Yiremyahuw*), a Jewish Lord Haw Haw, urged the besieged King Tsedekyahuw to surrender Jerusalem to the Babylonians:

I also spoke these words to Tsedekyahuw: 'Bring your necks under the yoke of the king of Babylon and serve him and his nation and live. Why're you determined to die, you and your nation, by the sword, by the famine, and by the pestilence? For Yahweh has warned against the nation that refuses to slave for the king of Babylon.'　　　　　　　　　　(JER. 27:12-13)

For Yahweh says this, that after seventy years . . . causing you to return to this place.　　　　　　　　　　(29:10)

. . . whom I've sent out of this place into the land of the Kasidites for their own good.　　　　　　　　　　(24:5)

I'm going to raise out of David a righteous twig, a king who'll reign and prosper. . . . In his time Yahuwdah is going to be rescued. . . . His name: Yahweh's Righteousness.　　　　　　　　　　(23:5-6)

Despite Jeremyah's promise that, if the Jews submitted to Nabu-akh-adon-assur, Yahweh would bring them home after seventy years and re-establish the Davidic monarchy, the collaborator narrowly escaped lynching (26:8). Instead, Tsedekyahuw put him in prison where he remained until the city fell. Nabu-akh-adon-assur, appreciative of Jeremyah's efforts on his behalf, ordered his release (39:11-14). Tsedekyahuw was blinded and his children slaughtered. The king and the *remnant of the nation that had remained in the town* were transported to Babylon (39:6-9), where they were to remain as captives for forty-eight years. Jeremyah was released, went to Egypt, and probably died there.

Slavery is slavery. The Jewish experience in Babylon may not have been as severe as the African experience in America (although this is far from certain), but there is no reason to doubt that the poet expressed the feelings of all when he wrote:

> By the rivers of Babylon we sat down and wept,
> When we remembered Tsiyown.
> We hung our harps on the willows, in their midst.
> For our captors who had kidnapped us demanded that we sing.
> Those who were destroying us demanded gaiety:
> 'Sing to us from the songs of Tsiyown.'
> How can we sing Yahweh's song in a foreign country?
> O daughter of Babylon, who is going to be destroyed,
> How fortunate he will be, who repays you
> What you've done to us.
> How fortunate he will be, who takes your children
> And smashes them against the rocks.[3]
>
> (PS. 137)

The concluding demand for retribution may sound brutal in retrospect, but one wonders how many victims of the Nazi occupation expressed their resentment more mildly.

Jeremyah's prophecies did not cease with his apparent vindication. In Egypt he, or the interpolator who may have written chapters 50 and 51, turned his far-seeing against the conquerors:

> The words spoken by Yahweh against Babylon: . . . . Babylon is taken; Baal is confounded; Marduk is broken . . . for out of the north will come an infidel against her who'll make her land desolate.   (JER. 50:1-3)

Like all prophets before and since, Jeremyah pushed his luck too far when he stopped prophesying events in the process of happening and started prophesying the future. Jeremyah's prophecy was a declaration that Babylon would fall to a revived Assyria. Assyria never revived. Babylon was in fact taken in 538 BCE, ending the Jewish captivity after forty-eight rather than seventy years, by a conqueror from the opposite direction from the one Jeremyah had forecast, King Kyros of Persia. Jeremyah's prophecy that the Jews would be slaves for Nabu-akh-adon-assur *and his son and his son's son* (27:7) also failed. Nabu-akh-adon-assur's son's son was never king.

The Babylonian Captivity produced a second spokesman whose writing has survived. Like Jeremyah, Ezekiel (*Yekhezkiel*) wrote in the days immediately following the sack of Jerusalem. And like Jeremyah, he also claimed

---

3. In an ancestor-worshipping culture with no afterlife concept, killing an enemy's children was the ultimate punishment, since it deprived the enemy of the descendants who would have kept his only immortal part, his name, alive by their worship.

to have been forewarned by Yahweh that Nabu-akh-adon-assur's plans would succeed (EZEK. 12:10-16).

Ezekiel claimed, in chapter after chapter (2:1; 3:1; 4:1), that Yahweh habitually addressed him as *Ben Adam*. This salutation, usually translated 'son of man,' is more accurately rendered 'descendant of Adam,' or simply 'human.' Because the title *Ben Adam* carried the implication that the person so styled was the Second Adam, it came to be viewed as a title for the messiah, once the concept of a messiah was invented in post-exilic days. Both the *Book of Daniel* (7:13) and the *Book of Enoch* (46) referred to *Ben Adam* in terms that persons with a messiah-belief were bound to view as messianic. The first-century CE aspirant to messiahship, Jesus the Nazirite, who saw himself as the Second Adam sent to usher in the Last Days, learned the title from *Enoch* and liked it so much that he invariably referred to himself as Ben Adam, well aware that he was thereby designating himself Messiah.

Ezekiel referred to three men in a context that identified them as the most righteous figures in Jewish mythology. They were Noah, Daniel and Job. Noah was the anthropomorphised rain-goddess. Job (*Yowb*) was the equally-mythical 'patient man.' Daniel was the hero of a poem written one thousand years earlier, an upright king who sat by the town gate *judging the cause of the widow, adjudicating the case of the fatherless.*[4] Such was Ezekiel's ultimate influence that some centuries later books were written and credited to all three of his Heroes.

The *Book of Noah* was a retelling of *Genesis*. It was recognised as a late composition when the Jewish canon was compiled in the second century CE, and rejected. The *Book of Job* was a moral fable that promoted acceptance of the unacceptable as the surest way to Yahweh's favour. Its theme, that a man who stoically accepts undeserved misfortune without questioning his god's justice will eventually be rewarded, paralleled the Sumerian 'Lamentation to a Man's God,' written a millennium earlier.[5] The Sadducee author of *Job*, typical of his age, was a believer in palmistry, for he wrote: *Allah implanted signs and marks in the hands of all humans, that all may know their deeds* (JOB 37:7), thereby setting the stage for another Sadducee who elaborated: *Length of days in her right hand, and wealth and status in her left hand* (PROV. 3:16). Those lines are often quoted by palmists as evidence of the validity of their superstition, but they are better viewed as evidence of the invalidity of *Job* and *Proverbs*.[6]

---

4. J.B. Pritchard, *op. cit.*, p. 151.

5. *Ibid.*, pp. 589-591.

6. For evidence that there is no correlation between markings on the hand and future events unrelated to genetic disorders, see M.A. Park, 'Palmistry: Science or Hand-Jive?,' *Skeptical Inquirer*, Winter 1982-83, pp. 21-23.

Job's portrayal of the Satan as a male clearly indicates a date of composition later than *Ezekiel*, for not until the Jews had been under Babylonian and Persian domination long enough to assimilate the Zoroastrian Prince of Darkness, Ahriman, did Yahweh's prime antagonist cease to be the goddess Ashtaroth. Despite *Job*'s inclusion in the Judaeo-Christian bible, few mythologians categorise it as nonfiction. Yahweh's capricious murder of Job's children is much more acceptable to Yahweh-worshippers who can console themselves that the story is a mere parable.

Job was written as acknowledged fiction. Nonetheless it contributed significantly to Judaism's transformation from a monistic to a dualistic mythology. In the monism that had existed since the Yahwist's day, the creative force (Yahweh) had been seen as a unity, fully responsible for both good and evil. It has already been mentioned that it was ultimately Yahweh himself who caused Job's torments, since it was Yahweh who gave the Satan permission to carry them out. That was the essential weakness of monism in a culture that in post-captivity times had begun to develop a concept of morality that veered toward the objective. In the days when there had been no such concept as objective evil, and even the destruction of a whole city by an erupting volcano-god could be seen as a just punishment for crimes known only to the god, monism, the crediting of everything that happened to a single creative force, had presented no problems. But with the recognition that there were injustices in Yahweh's world, continued monism would have involved the recognition that Yahweh must be unjust.

Dualism, first conceived by Zarathustra, offered a solution. Zarathustra had divided the creative force into two beings, a good god responsible for all justice, and a bad god responsible for all injustice. However, in relieving the good god, Ahura Mazda, of any guilt for destructive 'acts of god,' Zarathustra had also relieved him of his omnipotence; for clearly if the god of light possessed the capacity to destroy the god of darkness and thereby end his evil influence, he would have already done so.

Continued monism was unacceptable to a nation with an evolving sense of morality. But dualism was equally unacceptable to a nation whose tribal monolatry was evolving into pseudomonotheism (many immortals, but only one designated 'God'). *Job* offered a compromise: The Satan was responsible for all evil and injustice; but he could do nothing without Yahweh's consent, and Yahweh only granted that consent to test his worshippers' faith. To this day Judaism and Christianity retain the rationalised dualism of *Job*; whereas Islam represents a reversion to the monism of the pre-captivity Jews.

The first author of the *Book of Daniel* presumably claimed to be the Daniel referred to by Ezekiel (later authors claimed to be the first author). The story of the original Daniel was told by one of the Ras Shamra tablets found in Ugarit and dated to the fourteenth century BCE. Daniel, a righteous king, prayed to the bull-god Allah to give him a son, and as a consequence his barren wife bore him Aqhat, a Hero not unlike Osiris.[7] Even if this was not the Daniel Ezekiel had in mind, there can be no doubt that Daniel was already a figure of popular mythology more than twenty years before Bel-ish-assur's feast; yet *Daniel*'s first redactor made that feast the significant event in his mythical hero's alleged life.

Daniel's earliest author wrote chapter four, in which his hero interpreted a dream for Nabu-akh-adon-assur; and chapter three, in which the heroes were Shadrakh, Meshakh and Abednego, and Daniel was not mentioned. It may be that, to give his 'Daniel' character credibility, he attached the Daniel tale to an already-existing fiery-furnace fable.

Second Daniel wrote chapters five and six, featuring Bel-ish-assur's feast, Daniel in the lions' den and the writing on the wall. It was Second Daniel who made the factual errors that later interpolators were obliged to maintain. For example, he named Bel-ish-assur as king of Babylon and son of Nabu-akh-adon-assur. Bel-ish-assur was neither king of Babylon nor the son of Nabu-akh-adon-assur. He was Prince Regent, the son of King Nabu-on-idos, a usurper who had overthrown Nabu-akh-adon-assur's grandson (his *daughter's* son).

Second Daniel had his hero interpret the writing on the wall to mean that Bel-ish-assur's kingdom would be divided between the Persians and the Medes. He then had Bel-ish-assur killed by an invading army led by Darius the Mede, who succeeded him as king. To uphold his claim of an alleged division of the kingdom, he finished his narrative with the declaration that *Daniel prospered in the kingdom of Darius, and in the kingdom of Kyros the Persian.*

The division of Babylonia between the Medes and the Persians simply did not happen. The Medes had shared with Babylon the distinction of conquering Assyria and dividing its empire in 612 BCE; but Media had been conquered by Kyros the Persian in 549 BCE. When Babylon fell in 538 BCE, its conqueror was Kyros and nobody else. Darius the Mede did not exist. And while it is true that Bel-ish-assur died in the decisive battle, the king of Babylon did not. Nabu-on-idos lived a further three months.

Third Daniel wrote the apocalypse that even mythologians acknowledge to be a retroactive prophecy of the rise and fall of Antiokhos IV and the establishment of the Hasmonean dictatorship that evolved into a monarchy. Accepting his predecessor's erroneous claim that the Jewish world (as part of the Babylonian empire) had once been ruled by the Medes, he 'prophesied' that Nabu-akh-adon-assur's monarchy would be succeeded by four world empires. Mythologians continue to interpret Third Daniel's retroactive proph-

7. S. Hooke, *Middle Eastern Mythology*, chap. 3.

ecy as referring to Imperial Rome, Islam, the Papacy, and various other post-Maccabean organisations. Since the fourth empire can be identified beyond any doubt as the Macedonian, founded by Alexander and continued by the Seleukids, the first three can only have been the Babylonian empire of Nabu-on-idos (which did exist); the Median empire of Darius (which did not exist); and the Persian empire of Kyros and his successors. Following the collapse of the fourth empire (at the death of Antiokhos IV), the Jews were to establish a kingdom of saints, independent of foreign overlordship, that would last forever. Such a kingdom was indeed established, by the Maccabees, but it lasted only a century, until 63 BCE, at which time Jewish independence was terminated by the world's new superpower, Rome. Third Daniel's portion of modern bibles consists of the whole of chapter seven, plus the portion of chapter two from 2:4b to 2:49.

The first three authors of *Daniel* wrote in Aramaic. Fourth Daniel wrote in Hebrew. His portion consisted of the segments from 1:1 to 2:4a, and from 8:1 to 12:13. Like his immediate predecessor, he was an apocalyptist. He did not, however, content himself with prophesying the past, but was sufficiently reckless to attempt to prophesy the future. Although his prophecies unquestionably failed, they were couched in such vague terminology that any attempt to date such items as the *seventy weeks* until the coming of the messiah would take up more space than it is worth.

Fourth Daniel introduced into Jewish thought the entirely new concept of an afterlife. That, and his naming of the newly-adapted minor gods, borrowed from Zoroastrianism, Mikhael and Gabriel, identifies him as a Pharisee. Like Third Daniel, he retroactively prophesied the rise and fall of Antiochus IV, and showed no awareness of any event after 164 BCE. Many scholars consequently maintain that Third Daniel wrote all of the passages attributed here to Fourth Daniel, even though the two segments were composed in different languages.

Fourth Daniel wrote: *Many of those who sleep in the dust of the land are going to awaken, some to everlasting life and some to shame and everlasting contempt* (12:2). In 164 BCE, such a passage could only have been written by a Pharisee, since there were as yet no Essenes. Earlier, around 200 BCE, the Sadducee author of *Ecclesiastes* had written: *The living are aware that they are going to die; but the dead neither know anything nor have any further reward, for their awareness has ceased* (9:5). Since both *Daniel* and *Ecclesiastes* found their way into the Judaeo-Christian bible, it is worth noting that that allegedly inerrant tome now affirms that there both is and is not a life after death.

Fourth Daniel was sufficiently familiar with Jewish history to declare that his hero had been carried off from Jerusalem at the time that Nabu-akh-adon-assur had captured King Yahuwikhin and taken hostages (597 BCE), an event that actually happened. He was also aware that the Persian empire had been overthrown by Alexander of Macedon, for he had Mikhael/Ares/ Mars prophesy that event, which occurred in 330 BCE, in a conversation with Daniel in 536 BCE. He made his only serious error when he dated a conversation between Daniel and Gabriel/Hermes/Mercury to the first year of the reign of Darius, son of Xerxes. There was never a Darius, son of Xerxes; and the only Darius, son of Artaxerxes, commenced his reign at a time when 'Daniel' would have been at least 173 years old, 425 BCE.[8]

Fifth Daniel wrote in Greek in the first century BCE, although his material, chapters thirteen and fourteen of RC bibles, may have been much older and actually predated the rest of *Daniel*. He credited Daniel with Solomon-like wisdom that saved a woman named Susanna who had been falsely accused of adultery. Such a story is entirely consistent with the original Daniel, the father of the resurrected saviour Aqhat. He also had Daniel thrown into a lions' den and miraculously spared when the lions refused to eat him. Since it is incredible that such a tale could have been specifically composed as an addition to a book that already contained it, the logical conclusion is that a written (but not Hebrew) version of Daniel-in-the-lions'-den already existed when Second Daniel added his version to the Shadrakh-Meshakh-and-Abednego tale of First Daniel. Since RC bibles incorporate the Greek chapters, whereas Protestant and Jewish bibles do not, Catholics are expected to believe that Daniel was thrown into a lions' den on two separate occasions.

That most of *Daniel* was composed in the second century BCE by authors who claimed to have lived 400 years earlier is acknowledged even by publishers of bibles. Its errors of fact refute any pretence that it was written during or near the time of the events depicted. The compilers of the Jewish canon recognised its lateness when they included it in the *Writings* rather than the *Prophets* where, if it were genuine, it surely belonged. Modern mythologians defend it as a moral allegory, blissfully ignoring the inescapable conclusion that every one of its authors was a liar who pretended to be writing nonfiction. While its tale of the three men in the furnace could perhaps be interpreted allegorically, although the author of the fantasy intended it to be accepted as literal truth, even that defence disintegrates when it is realised that the story was plagiarised from the myth of how Abraham had been thrown into a blazing furnace by King Nimrod of Babylon (Talmud, PESAHIM 118a).

Daniel was nothing less than unmitigated forgery. But it must be acknowledged that the appearance of such books as *Daniel*, *Noah* and *Enoch*, attributed to persons believed to have lived centuries earlier, was the inevitable consequence of Third Zekharyah's action in banning all future prophecy

---

8. Fourth Daniel may have been aware that Xerxes II reigned for a year between Artaxerxes I and Darius II (king lists from Babylon omit him as a pretender). But Xerxes II was Darius II's brother, not his father.

(ZEC. 13:2-3). Unable to sign their own names for fear of execution, later writers were forced either to use the name of a Hero of mythology, or to insert their work into the books of earlier spokesmen. The author of an interpolation into *Amos*, for example, tacked his prophecy of a return from the Babylonian Captivity (9:14) onto a book written two hundred years before that captivity had begun. Similarly, references to the rise of Persia can now be found in books whose original authors lived in Assyrian times, while books originally written under Persian overlordship contain interpolated passages that acknowledged the Jews' chief enemies to be the Greeks. A breakdown of the Judaeo-Christian bible's prophetic books, listing the main authors and undatable interpolations, appears at the end of this chapter, along with a chronology of the Jewish and nearby kings.

The defeat of Babylon by Kyros, and the subsequent return to Jerusalem of as many exiles as wished to do so, led to a reappraisal of the hated Jeremyah. He had prophesied the exile; he had prophesied the fall of Babylon, albeit not to the right conqueror; and he had prophesied the return to Jerusalem. By pretending that the exile had not officially ended until the completion of the second Temple in the reign of Darius I, it was even possible to rationalise that his prophecy of a seventy-year exile had been accurate. His theology was sound: the exile was Yahweh's punishment for disobedience. That the innocent had been enslaved along with the guilty did not strike the adherents of a morally retarded concept of justice as questionable. Jeremyah won from later generations of Jews a reputation quite different from that which he earned during his lifetime. Such is the irony of fate.

In his first weeks as ruler of Babylon, Kyros promised the Jews that he would rebuild Yahweh's Temple at Jerusalem. This led one jubilant writer, the anonymous Second Isayah, to acclaim him Messiah, 'Yahweh's Anointed' (ISA. 45:1). When Kyros learned that the Temple had been the focus of a vicious, xenophobic religion that regarded non-Jews as infidels and refused to tolerate the worship of Babylonian gods in Jerusalem (whereas Kyros was quite willing to tolerate the worship of Yahweh in Susa), he ordered work on the Temple to cease before the builders had finished laying the foundations. By that time, however, Second Isayah's hasty appraisal had become a permanent addition to the work of his eighth-century predecessor.

Second Isayah also included a retroactive prophecy of the fall of Babylon (ISA. 47:1-15). In gloating over the defeat of Nabu-on-idos, Second Isayah mockingly called him *Heylel*, 'Morning Star' (14:12). Translators of some bibles, attributing to ancient Jews the beliefs of a much later age, rendered *Heylel* as 'Lucifer,' the Morning Star's (Venus) Roman name.

Not a large proportion of Jews returned to Jerusalem in 538 BCE. According to *Ezra* (2:64-65), the number who accepted Kyros's invitation was 49,697. Since the High Priest Ezra lived more than a century after the fall of Babylon, and *Ezra* was composed more than a century after its hero's death, by an author sufficiently ignorant of his overlords' history to believe that Xerxes and Artaxerxes had reigned before Darius I (EZRA 4:5-7, 23-24), his figures cannot be considered authoritative. But it is not unlikely that the number of returning exiles was indeed below 50,000.

The number of Jews who chose to remain in Babylon was somewhat higher. Babylon was a cosmopolitan city, whereas Jerusalem was bound to be viewed by persons not born there as a frontier. Those who did return obtained Darius I's consent to resume work on the Temple, and it was completed in 516 BCE (EZRA 6:15). So confident were the Yahweh-worshippers that they had regained their god's favour, that four years before the completion of the Temple two spokesmen, Hagay (HAG. 2:2-9) and Zekharyah (ZEC. 4:6-14) prophesied that Zerubbabel, current head of the Davidic family, would refound the monarchy. They were wrong. The Davidic monarchy was never restored.

Judah remained a Persian dependency from 538 BCE until 330 BCE, when Darius III was defeated by the Macedonian Alexander and it became a Greek dependency. Then Alexander died in 323 BCE naming as his successor 'the strongest,' and his massive empire shattered. The Egyptian portion was seized by Alexander's general Ptolemaios, who also annexed Judah. Another general, Seleukos, acquired Persia.

The Seleukids wrested Judah from the Ptolemies in the war between Antiokhos I and Ptolemaios II, and for the next hundred years Jewish brides found themselves subjected to the *jus primae noctis* (1 MACC. 1:26; Talmud, KETH. 3b; SHAB. 23a). The Seleukids maintained their grip on the Jewish lands so long as they interfered only minimally with Yahweh-worship. But when Antiokhos IV (175-164 BCE) attempted to impose the Hellenic religion on all parts of his kingdom for the purpose of creating a homogeneous empire that could compete with Rome, a revolution broke out in Judah under the leadership of the men known as the Maccabees ('Hammers'), the five sons of the High Priest Mattathyah bar Hasmon.

Antiokhos was initially successful in occupying Jerusalem. He entered the inner sanctuary of the Temple, removed the sculpture of a male and female kherub copulating, and replaced it with the 'desolation-inducing sacrilege,' a statue of Olympian Zeus. The copulating kherubs he paraded through the streets of Jerusalem in a cage, sneering, '*You used to say that this nation was not serving idols. Now see what we found and what they were worshipping.*'[9]

Four of Mattathyah's sons died in the twenty-five-year war of independence that followed the Maccabees' revolt. Then in 143 BCE, despaired of ever defeating the fanatic rebels, Antiokhos VII signed a peace treaty

---

9. Quoted from a Midrash by R. Patai, *The Hebrew Goddess*, p. 84.

with Mattathyah's surviving son, Shimeown, that recognised Judah as an independent state. Officially, Shimeown was only High Priest and military governor, but as he was founder of the Hasmonean dynasty he is usually regarded as its first king.

Shimeown was a shrewd ruler. He recognised that the Seleukids and Ptolemies were merely awaiting a suitable opportunity to regain their lost province, and he signed a mutual defence treaty with Rome to prevent that from happening. He also recognised David's mistake in creating an empire that was too large and too gentile, and as a consequence deliberately reduced the Jewish state's borders. Following a victory in Galilee, the northern half of the former kingdom of Israel, in 163 BCE, he led all Galilean Jews south and abandoned Galilee to its totally gentile remaining population. Between gentile Galilee and Jewish Judah, he left unhindered the buffer state of Samaria, an area inhabited by a tribe whose adherence to the Towrah did not make them any less gentile in the eyes of orthodox Judaeans. Samaritans differed from Jews the way Methodists differ from Baptists, and the Jews hated them the way Shi'ite Muslims hate Bahai Muslims.

Shimeown's son Hyrkanos and his grandson Aristoboulos were less pragmatic. Early in Hyrkanos's reign he annexed the lands of the pagan Galileans in the north and Idumaeans in the south to his Jewish kingdom. Not content with that, he ordered the forcible circumcision of the entire population of the new territories, and the execution of all who refused to convert. Among the pagan Syrians and Arabs whose descendants thereby came to be raised as Jews were the ancestors of the Idumaean Herod and the ancestors of the Galilean Jesus the Nazirite, whose biographers would one day claim that he was descended from King David.

The descendants of Shimeown bar Mattathyah bar Hasmon reigned in Jerusalem until 63 BCE, in which year Judaea, as Judah was thereafter called, was conquered by Pompeius Magnus, who made it his private fiefdom until his defeat by Julius Caesar at Pharsala in 48 BCE. Caesar officially annexed Judaea to Rome, as Pompeius had not, and appointed an Idumaean (Edomite) named Antipatros as its procurator.

At Antipatros's death in 43 BCE his son Herod, who had married a Hasmonean princess, was named king of Judaea, Samaria and Galilee by the Triumvir Octavian (Augustus). There was, however, a surviving Hasmonean pretender, Antigonos bar Aristoboulos. Antigonos, with Parthian aid, rebelled against Herod and the Romans, and from 40 to 37 BCE ruled in Jerusalem as his dynasty's last king.

The might of Rome inevitably proved more formidable than the Jews' previous enemies (although the Jewish explanation was again that Yahweh was displeased with them), and in 37 BCE the Idumaean puppet King Herod was successfully imposed on the conquered province. Antigonos and forty-five members of his Sanhedrin were crucified by Herod and Judaea's current real ruler, Marcus Antonius.[10]

Thereafter Judaea alternated between Roman overlordship, under Herod and his sons and grandson, and direct Roman rule under procurators, of whom the most vicious and anti-Semitic was Lucius Pontius Pilatus. It remained Roman, or Byzantine after the division of the empire, until the seventh century CE when it fell to the Caliphs of Islam. It was thereafter Islamic, except for a brief Christian period following the First Crusade, bearing the name of the Jews' ancient enemies, the Philistines (Palestine), until 1948 CE when it again became Jewish under the misnomer, *Israel*.

Interpolation in the Prophets

Amos

A = Khamows   c. 760 BCE
B = 2nd Khamows, after 586 BCE
I = undatable interpolation

A.	1:01-1:08	A.	2:06-5:13	A.	6:03-6:08	A.	8:09-9:04
I.	1:09-1:12	I.	5:14-5:15	I.	6:09-6:10	I.	9:05-9:06
A.	1:13-2:03	A.	5:16-6:01	A.	6:11-8:07	A.	9:07-9:08a
I.	2:04-2:05	I.	6:02	I.	8:08	B.	9:08b-9:15

Hosea

A = Howsheakh   c. 700 BCE
I = undatable interpolation

A.	1:01-1:06	I.	7:16b	A.	8:08b-8:13a	I.	12:13
I.	1:07	A.	8:01-8:05a	I.	8:13b-8:14	A.	12:14-14:08
A.	1:08-7:09	I.	8:05b-8:06a	A.	9:01-12:04	I.	14:09
I.	7:10	A.	8:06b-8:07	I.	12:05		
A.	7:11-7:16a	I.	8:08a	A.	12:06-12:12		

---

10. Dio Cassius 69.

Micah

A = Miykhah   c. 700 BCE
B = 2nd Miykhah,   after 586 BCE
C = 3rd Miykhah   c. 400 BCE
D = 4th Miykhah   c. 300 BCE
I = undatable interpolation

A. 1:01-1:13a	I. 4:05	I. 5:03-5:04	D. 7:08-7:17a
I. 1:13b	B. 4:06-4:09	B. 5:05-5:14	I. 7:17b
A. 1:14-3:08a	I. 4:10	I. 5:15	D. 7:17c-7:20
I. 3:08b	B. 4:11-5:02a	C. 6:01-6:09a	
A. 3:08c-3:12	I. 5:02b	I. 6:09b	
B. 4:01-4:04	B. 5:02c	C. 6:09c-7:07	

Isaiah

A = Yeshayahuw   c. 700 BCE
B = 2nd Yeshayahuw   538 BCE
C = 3rd Yeshayahuw   c. 500 BCE
D = various interpolators   c. 440 BCE
I = undatable interpolation

A. 1:01-3:17	A. 7:20c-8:07a	C. 19:01-19:15	I. 28:05-28:06
I. 3:18-3-23	I. 8:07b	I. 19:16-19:24	C. 28:07-29:04
A. 3:24	A. 8:07c-9:14	C. 20:01-20:04a	I. 29:05a
I. 3:25-3:26	I. 9:15-9:16	I. 20:04b	C. 29:05b-29:06
A. 4:01-5:14	A. 9:17-10:09	C. 20:05-21:15	I. 29:07-29:08
I. 5:15-5:16	I. 10:10-10:13a	I. 21:16-21:17	C. 29:09-29:10a
A. 5:17-6:13a	A. 10:13b-11:02	C. 22:01-22:09a	I. 29:10b
I. 6:13b	I. 11:03a	I. 22:09b-22:11a	C. 29:10c
A. 7:01-7:04a	A. 11:03b-12:06	C. 22:11b-23:04	I. 29:10d
I. 7:04b	B. 13:01-13:22	I. 23:05	C. 29:11a
A. 7:05a	I. 14:01-14:04a	C. 23:06-23:12	I. 29:11b-29:12
I. 7:05b	B. 14:04b-14:32	I. 23:13	C. 29:13-30:05
A. 7:05c-7:08a	C. 15:01-15:05a	C. 23:14	I. 30:06a
I. 7:08b	I. 15:05b	I. 23:15-23:18	C. 30:06b-30:07a
A. 7:09-7:14	C. 15:05c-16:05a	B. 24:01-26:18	I. 30:07b
I. 7:15	I. 16:05b	I. 26:19	C. 30:08-30:28a
A. 7:16-7:17a	C. 16:05c-17:12	B. 26:20-27:05	I. 30:28b
I. 7:17b	I. 17:13a	I. 27:06	C. 30:29-33:24
A. 7:18-7:20a	C. 17:13b-18:06	B. 27:07-27:13	B. 34:01-35:10
I. 7:20b	I. 18:07	C. 28:01-28:04	C. 36:01-37:09a

I. 37:09b-37:21	I. 44:09-44:20	B. 48:08a	I. 51:20b
I. 37:22-37:32	B. 44:21-45:05a	I. 48:08b-48:10	B. 51:20c-52:02
I. 37:33-37:36	I. 45:05b	B. 48:11a	I. 52:03-52:06
C. 37:37-38:19	B. 45:05c-45:09	I. 48:11b	B. 52:07-53:02a
I. 38:20	I. 45:10	B. 48:11c-48:12a	I. 53:02b
C. 38:21-39:08	B. 45:11-45:14a	I. 48:12b	B. 53:02c-53:09
B. 40:01-40:07a	I. 45:14b	B. 48:13-48:21	I. 53:10a
I. 40:07b	B. 45:15-45:21a	I. 48:22	B. 53:10b-55:06
B. 40:08-42:18	I. 45:21b	B. 49:01-49:03a	I. 55:07
I. 42:19	B. 45:21c	I. 49:03b	B. 55:08-55:13
B. 42:20	I. 45:21d	B. 49:03c-49:08a	D. 56:01-57:06a
I. 42:21	B. 45:22a	I. 49:08b	I. 57:06b
B. 42:22-43:10a	I. 45:22b	B. 49:08c-49:21a	D. 57:07-59:20
I. 43:10b	B. 45:23-46:05	I. 49:21b	I. 59:21
B. 43:11-43:20a	I. 46:06-46:08	B. 49:21c-50:09	D. 60:01-60:11
I. 43:20b-43:21	B. 46:09-48:01a	I. 50:10-50:11	I. 60:12
B. 43:22-43:24	I. 48:01b-48:02	B. 51:01-51:05a	D. 60:13-65:25a
I. 43:25-43:26	B. 48:03	I. 51:05b	I. 65:25b
B. 43:27-44:06a	I. 48:04	B. 51:05c-51:15	D. 65:25c-66:13a
I. 44:06b	B. 48:05a	I. 51:16	I. 66:13b
B. 44:07-44:08a	I. 48:05b	B. 51:17	D. 66:14-66:22
I. 44:08b	B. 48:06-48:07a	I. 51:18	I. 66:23-66:24
B. 44:08c	I. 48:07b	B. 51:19-51:20a	

Nahum

A = Nakhuwm   *c.* 650 BCE

A. 1:01-3:19

Zephaniah

A = Tsefanyah   *c.* 620 BCE
I = undatable interpolation

A. 1:01-1:03a	A. 1:17c-2:02a	I. 2:06a	I. 2:11
I. 1:03b	I. 2:02b	A. 2:06b	A. 2:12-3:08
A. 1:03c-1:13a	I. 2:03	I. 2:07a	I. 3:09-3:10
I. 1:13b	A. 2:04-2:05a	A. 2:07b	A. 3:11-3:15
A. 1:14 1:17a	I. 2:05b	I. 2:07c	I. 3:16
I. 1:17b	A. 2:05c	I. 2:08-2:10	A. 3:17 3:20

Habukkuk

A = Khabakuwk   c. 600 BCE
B = various interpolators   after 434 BCE
C = psalmist 1   after 65 BCE
D = psalmist 2   after 65 BCE
I = undatable interpolation

A. 1:01 2:03   B. 2:06c-2:19a   C. 3:01-3:14a   D. 3:17-3:19a
B. 2:04-2:06a   I. 2:19b   I. 3:14b   C. 3:19b
I. 2:06b   B. 2:19c-2:20   C. 3:15-3:16

Jeremiah

A = Yiremyahuw   c. 580 BCE
B = interpolator?   before 538 BCE
C = editor   before 538 BCE
I = undatable interpolation

A. 1:01-1:02	A. 9:17 9:24	I. 17:12-17:13	I. 27:01
I. 1:03	I. 9:25 9:26	A. 17:14-18:06	A. 27:02-27:06
A. 1:04-3:05	A. 10:01-10:05	I. 18:07-18:12	I. 27:07
I. 3:06-3:13	I. ' 10:06-10:07	A. 18:13-18:20a	A. 27:08-27:12
I. 3:14-3:18	A. 10:08-10:10	I. 18:20b	I. 27:13
A. 3:19-3:24a	I. 10:11	A. 18:20c-21:13	A. 27:14-27:16a
I. 3:24b	A. 10:12-10:17	I. 21:14a	I. 27:16b
A. 3:25a	I. 10:18	A. 21:14b-23:10a	A. 27:16c
I. 3:25b	A. 10:19-10:22	I. 23:10b	I. 27:17
I. 4:01-4:02	I. 10:23-10:25	A. 23:10c-23:17	A. 27:18-27:19a
A. 4:03-4:04a	A. 11:01-11:16	I. 23:18	I. 27:19b
I. 4:04b	I. 11:17	A. 23:19-25:01a	A. 27:19c-27:20a
A. 4:04c-4:08	A. 11:18-12:03	I. 25:01b	I. 27:20b
I. 4:09-4:12	I. 12:04	A. 25:02	A. 27:20c
A. 4:13-5:17	A. 12:05-12:12a	I. 25:03-25:08	I. 27:20d
I. 5:18-5:19	I. 12:12b	A. 25:09a	A. 27:21a
A. 5:20-7:04	A. 12:12c	I. 25:09b	I. 27:21b
I. 7:05-7:07	I. 12:13	A. 25:09c	A. 27:22a
A. 7:08-7:26	A. 12:14a	I. 25:09d	I. 27:22b
I. 7:27	I. 12:14b	A. 25:09e-25:11a	A. 27:22c
A. 7:28-8:19a	A. 12:15-17:01a	I. 25:11b-25:14	I. 27:22d
I. 8:19b	I. 17:01b-17:03a	A. 25:15-25:16	A. 28:01a
A. 8:20 9:11	A. 17:03b-17:10	I. 25:17-25:26	I. 28:01b
I. 9:12 9:16	I. 17:11	A. 25:27-26:24	A. 28:01c-28:14a

I. 28:14b	I. 30:14b	I. 39:04-39:13	A. 49:07-49:24a
A. 28:15-28:16a	A. 30:15-30:22	A. 39:14-44:15a	I. 49:24b
I. 28:16b	I. 30:23-30:24	I. 44:15b	A. 49:25-49:30a
A. 28:17-29:14a	A. 31:01-31:05	A. 44:15c-44:19	I. 49:30b
I. 29:14b	I. 31:06	I. 44:20-44:23	A. 49:30c-49:35
A. 29:15	A. 31:07-31:25	A. 44:24-48:09	I. 49:36
I. 29:16-29:20	I. 31:26	I. 48:10	A. 49:37-49:38
A. 29:21-29:25a	A. 31:27-31:31a	A. 48:11-48:20	I. 49:39
I. 29:25b	I. 31:31b	I. 48:21-48:24	B. 50:01-51:11a
A. 29:25c	A. 31:31c-32:05a	A. 48:25-48:34	I. 51:11b
I. 29:25d	I. 32:05b	I. 48:35	B. 51:12-51:33
A. 29:25e-29:32a	A. 32:06-32:16	A. 48:36-48:40a	I. 51:34a
I. 29:32b	I. 32:17-32:23	I. 48:40b	B. 51:34b-51:56a
A. 30:01-30:03a	A. 32:24-32:28a	A. 48:41a	I. 51:56b
I. 30:03b	I. 32:28b-32:41	I. 48:41b	B. 51:56c-51:64a
A. 30:03c-30:04a	A. 32:42-33:01	A. 48:42-48:46	I. 51:64b
I. 30:04b	I. 33:02-33:03	I. 48:47a	C. 52:01-52:27
A. 30:05-30:09	A. 33:04-38:28	I. 48:47b	I. 52:28-52:30
I. 30:10-30:11	I. 39:01-39:02	A. 49:01-49:05	C. 52:31-52:34
A. 30:12-30:14a	A. 39:03	I. 49:06	

Ezekiel

A = Yekhezkiel   c. 550 BCE
I = undatable interpolation

A. 1:01	A. 3:06c-3:24	A. 9:01-9:04a	A. 16:56-17:09a
I. 1:02-1:03a	I. 3:25	I. 9:04b	I. 17:09b
A. 1:03b-1:04a	A. 3:26-4:01a	A. 9:04c-9:06a	A. 17:10-19:09a
I. 1:04b	I. 4:01b	I. 9:06b	I. 19:09b
A. 1:04c	A. 4:02-5:02	A. 9:06c-10:07	A. 19:09c-20:28a
I. 1:04d	I. 5:03-5:04a	I. 10:08	I. 20:28b
A. 1:05-1:09a	A. 5:04b-6:03a	A. 10:09-12:13a	A. 20:28c-22:18a
I. 1:09b	I. 6:03b	I. 12:13b	I. 22:18b
A. 1:10 1:11	A. 6:03c-6:06	A. 12:14-14:22a	A. 22:18c-22:24a
I. 1:12	I. 6:07	I. 14:22b	I. 22:24b
A. 1:13-1:23a	A. 6:08-6:09a	A. 14:23-16:26	A. 22:24c-23:04a
I. 1:23b	I. 6:09b	I. 16:27	I. 23:04b
A. 1:24a	A. 6:09c-7:04	A. 16:28-16:31	A. 23:05-23:07a
I. 1:24b	I. 7:05-7:09	I. 16:32	I. 23:07b
A. 1:25-2:06	A. 7:10-8:10a	A. 16:33-16:53a	A. 23:07c-23:37
I. 2:07	I. 8:10b	I. 16:53b	I. 23:38-23:39
A. 2:08-3:06a	A. 8:10c-8:18a	A. 16:54-16:55a	A. 23:40-24:06
I. 3:06b	I. 8:18b	I. 16:55b	I. 24:07-24:08

A. 24:09-24:21
I. 24:22-24:23
A. 24:24-27:07a
I. 27:07b
A. 27:07c-27:27a
I. 27:27b
A. 27:27c-28:13a
I. 28:13b
A. 28:13c-29:20
I. 29:21
A. 30:01-30:04
I. 30:05
A. 30:06-30:24
I. 30:25a
A. 30:25b
I. 30:26a
A. 30:26b-32:03a
I. 32:03b
A. 32:03c-33:12a
I. 33:12b

A. 33:13-34:02a
I. 34:02b
A. 34:02c-34:13a
I. 34:13b
A. 34:14-34:30
I. 34:31
A. 35:01-36:02
I. 36:03a
A. 36:03b-36:04a
I. 36:04b-36:05a
A. 36:05b
I. 36:05c
A. 36:05d
I. 36:06a
A. 36:06b-36:11
I. 36:12
A. 36:13-36:18a
I. 36:18b
A. 36:19-36:20a
I. 36:20b

A. 36:20c-37:16a
I. 37:16b
A. 37:16c-37:19a
I. 37:19b-37:21a
A. 37:21b-38:02a
I. 38:02b
A. 38:02c-38:05a
I. 38:05b
A. 38:06-38:07
I. 38:08a
A. 38:08b-39:09a
I. 39:09b
A. 39:09c-39:11a
I. 39:11b
A. 39:11c-39:15
I. 39:16a
A. 39:16b-39:18a
I. 39:18b
A. 39:19-40:04
I. 40:05

A. 40:06-40:16a
I. 40:16b
A. 40:16c-41:25a
I. 41:25b
A. 41:25c-41:26a
I. 41:26b
A. 41:26c-43:10
I. 43:11a
A. 43:11b-45:14a
I. 45:14b
A. 45:15-45:16a
I. 45:16b
A. 45:17-46:19a
I. 46:19b
A. 46:19c-47:13a
I. 47:13b
A. 47:14-48:35

Haggai

A = Hagay 520 BCE
I = undatable interpolation

A. 1:01-1:02
I. 1:03
A. 1:04-1:12

I. 1:13
A. 1:14-2:04

I. 2:05a
A. 2:05b-2:17

I. 2:18
A. 2:19-2:23

Zechariah

A = Zekharyah   520 BCE
B = 2nd Zekharyah   after 200 BCE
C = 3rd Zekharyah   after 150 BCE
I = undatable interpolation

A. 1:01a
I. 1:01b
A. 1:01c-1:07a

I. 1:07b
A. 1:07c
I. 1:07d

A. 1:07e-1:08a
I. 1:08b
A. 1:08c-1:09a

I. 1:09b
A. 1:10-1:19a
I. 1:19b

A. 1:19c-1:21a
I. 1:21b
A. 1:21c
I. 1:21d
A. 2:01-2:06a
I. 2:06b
A. 2:07-2:08a
I. 2:08b
A. 2:08c
I. 2:08d
A. 2:09a
I. 2:09b
A. 2:10-2:11a
I. 2:11b
A. 2:12-4:09a
I. 4:09b
A. 4:10-4:11
I. 4:12
A. 4:13-6:03a
I. 6:03b
A. 6:04-6:11a
I. 6:11b
A. 6:12a
I. 6:12b
A. 6:13-6:15a
I. 6:15b

A. 7:01a
I. 7:01b
A. 7:01c
I. 7:01d
A. 7:02-7:07
I. 7:08-7:09a
A. 7:09b-7:13a
I. 7:13b
A. 7:14-8:06a
I. 8:06b
A. 8:06c-8:09a
I. 8:09b
A. 8:10-8:13a
I. 8:13b
A. 8:13c-8:23
B. 9:01a
I. 9:01b
B. 9:02a
I. 9:02b
B. 9:02c-9:11a
I. 9:11b
B. 9:12-9:13a
I. 9:13b
B. 9:13c-9:14a
I. 9:14b
B. 9:14c-9:15a

I. 9:15b
B. 9:15c-9:16a
I. 9:16b
B. 9:16c-9:17a
I. 9:17b
B. 10:01-10:03a
I. 10:03b
B. 10:03c
I. 10:03d-10:04
B. 10:05a
I. 10:05b
B. 10:05c
I. 10:06
B. 10:07-10:08a
I. 10:08b
B. 10:08c-10:09a
I. 10:09b
B. 10:10-10:11a
I. 10:11b
B. 10:11c
I. 10:12
B. 11:01
I. 11:02a
B. 11:02b-11:05
I. 11:06
B. 11:07

I. 11:08a
B. 11:08b-11:17
C. 12:01-12:02a
I. 12:02b
C. 12:03a
I. 12:03b
C. 12:04a
I. 12:04b
C. 12:04c-12:08a
I. 12:08b
C. 12:08c-13:02a
I. 13:02b
C. 13:02c-13:08a
I. 13:08b
C. 13:08c-14:05a
I. 14:05b
C. 14:05c-14:07a
I. 14:07b
C. 14:07c-14:10a
I. 14:10b
C. 14:10c-14:13
I. 14:14a
C. 14:14b-14:21

Obadiah

A = Khowbadyah and others   *c.* 450 BCE
I = undatable interpolation

A. 1:01a   I. 1:01b   A. 1:01c-1:21

Joel

A = Yowel   *c.* 400 BCE
I = undatable interpolation

A. 1:01-1:14   A. 1:16-2:01a   A. 2:02b-2:11a   A. 2:12-2:20a
I. 1:15   I. 2:01b-2:02a   I. 2:11b   I. 2:20b

A. 2:21-2:26a   A. 2:27-3:11a   I.   3:11b   A. 3:12-3:21
I.   2:26b

Jonah

A = 1st author   c. 350 BCE
B = psalmist   c. 250 BCE

A. 1:01 1:17   B. 2:01-2:09   A. 2:10-4:11

Malachi

A = 'my messenger' (*Malakhiy*)   c. 250 BCE
I = undatable interpolation

A. 1:01-1:09a   I.   2:11-2:13a   A. 3:02-3:03a   I.   4:07
I.   1:09b   A. 2:13b-3:01a   I.   3:03b
A. 1:09c-2:10   I.   3:01b   A. 3:03c-4:06

Daniel

A = Aramaic author   c. 245 BCE
B = Aramaic author   c. 230 BCE
C = Aramaic author   164 BCE
D = Hebrew author Pharisee c. 164 BCE
E = Greek   after 100 BCE
I = undatable interpolation

D. 1:01-2:04a   B. 5:01-6:28   I.   12:11   E. 13:01-14:42
C. 2:04b-2:49   C. 7:01-7:28   I.   12:12
A. 3:01-4:37   D. 8:01-12:10   D. 12:13

GENEALOGY OF PATRIARCHS

Jewish chronology	R's genealogy	Ussher's chronology
3760-2830 BCE	Adam	4004-3074 BCE
3630-2718	Set	3874-2962
3525-2620	Enowsh	3769-2864
3435-2525	Kayinan	3679-2769
3365-2470	Mahulalel	3609-2714
3300-2338	Yarad	3544-2582
3138-2773	Khenowkh	3382-3017
3073-2104	Methuwselakh	3317-2348
		(drowned in Noakh's flood)
2885-2111	Lamekh	3130-2355
2704-1754	Noakh	2948-1998
2204-1602	Sem	2448-1846
2102-1664	Arpakhshad	2346-1908
2037-1573	Kheber	2281-1817
2003-1764	Peleg	2247-2008
1973-1734	Reuw	2217-1978
1941-1711	Seruwg	2185-1955
1911-1763	Nakhowr	2155-2007
1882-1677	Terakh	2126-1921
1812-1637	Abraham	2056-1881
1712-1532	Yitskhak	1956-1776
1652-1522	Yaakob	1896-1749

Yahuwdah		Levi
Parets		Kohath
Khetsron		Khamram
•		Aharon
7 generations		Eleazar
•		Fiynkhas
David 1040-970		

GENEALOGY OF LEVITES[11]

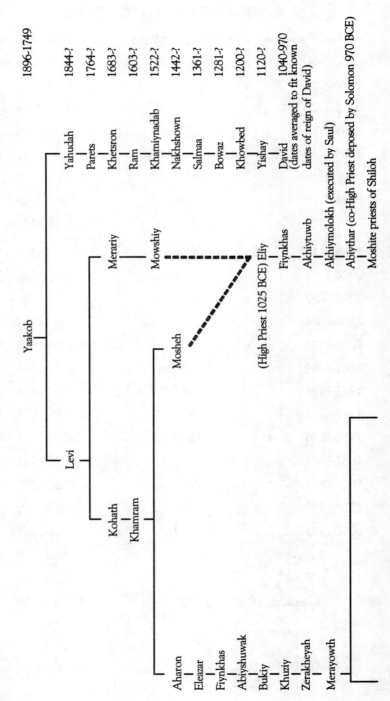

Ussher's chronology

1896-1749

Yaakob

Levi

Yahudah   1844-?
Parets   1764-?
Khetsron   1683-?
Ram   1603-?
Khamiynadab 1522-?
Nakhshown   1442-?
Salmaa   1361-?
Bowaz   1281-?
Khowbed   1200-?
Yishay   1120-?
David   1040-970
(dates averaged to fit known dates of reign of David)

Merariy

Mowshiy

(High Priest 1025 BCE) Eliy
Fiynkhas
Akhiytuwb
Akhiymolokh (executed by Saul)
Abiythar (co-High Priest deposed by Solomon 970 BCE)
Moshite priests of Shiloh

Kohath
Khamram

Mosheh

Aharon
Eleazar
Fiynkhas
Abiyshuwak
Bukiy
Khuziy
Zerakheyah
Merayowth

1 CHR. 6:1-14		EZRA 7:1-5	1 CHR. 9:11
Amaryah			
Tsadowk	(High Priest 970 BCE)		
Akhiymaats			
Khazaryah	(High Priest 960 BCE)		
Yowkhanan			
Khazaryah	(High Priest 910 BCE)	Khazaryah	Akhiytuwb
Amaryah	(High Priest 860 BCE)	Amaryah	Merayowth
Akhiytuwb		Akhiytuwb	Tsadowk
Tsadowk		Tsadowk	Meshalom
Shalowm		Shalowm	Khilkyah
Khilkyahuw	(High Priest 621 BCE)	Khilkyahuw	Khazaryah (Priest 586 BCE)
Khazaryah	(in Jerusalem after 586)	Khazaryah	(1 CHR. 9:11)
Serayah	(High Priest executed by Nabu-akh-adon-assur in 586 BCE)	Serayah	
Yahuwtsadok (1 CHR. 6:1-14)	(taken to Babylon 586 BCE)	Khezraa (High Priest 434 BCE) (EZRA 7:1-5)	

11. Bishop Ussher apparently believed that there were a thousand years between Abraham and David, and it did not bother him that the biblical genealogies could be nonfiction only if ten generations of David's ancestors all reached the age of eighty before fathering an heir. King Saul executed the Moshite High Priest Akhiymolokh and replaced him with Tsadowk. The genealogy that traced Tsadowk to Aaron would have been composed to justify that action. Since the Moshites continued to claim precedence over the Aaronids, the latter inserted 'Mowshiy' into the Levite genealogies to falsify the Moshites' claim to be descended from Moses. Note that two genealogies show Tsadowk as the son of Akhiytuwb, but a third inserts Merayowth between the two. And the author of *Ezra*, writing more than a century after Ezra's death, made his hero the son of a man who had flourished 152 years earlier. He also omitted the five generations between Merayowth and Khazaryah.

KINGS OF THE MIDDLE EAST

ISRAEL	ASSYRIA	BABYLON	JUDAH	PERSIA
Saul c. 1023-1005	Shamash-adad IV 1054-1050	Nabu-mukin-apal 1054-1050	Saul c. 1023-1010	
Ishbosheth 1005-1003	Assur-nasirpal I 1050-1031	Ninurta-kudur-assur 1050-1031	David 1010-970	
David 1003-970	Shalman-assur II 1031-1019	Mar-biti-akh-adon 1031-1019	Solomon 970-930	
Solomon 970-930	Assur-nirari IV 1019-1013	Shamash-mudamik 1019-1013	Rekhobowam 930-913	
Yerobowam I 930-909	Assur-rabi II 1013-972	Nabu-shum-ukin 1013-972	Abiyahuw 913-910	
	Assur-reshishi II 972-967		Asa 910-869	
Nadab 909-908	Tiglath-pil-assur II 967-935			
Baasha 908-885	Assur-dan II 935-912	Nabu-apal-adon 935-912 / -851		
Elah 885-884	Adad-nirari II 912-891	Marduk-bel-usate 851-850		
Zimriy 884	Tiglath-ninurta 891-884	Marduk-zakir-shum 850-838		
Khomriy 884-873	Assur-nasirpal II 884-859	Marduk-bel-atsuk-ab 838-811		
Akhab 873-853		name lost	Yahuwshafat 869-848	
Akhazyahuw 853-852		name lost		
Yahuwram 852-841	Shalman-assur III 859-824	Adad-shum-ibni 859-824	Yahuwram 848-841	
Yahuw 841-813	Shamash-adad 824-811	name lost 824-811	Akhazyahuw 841	
		name lost	Queen Athalyahuw 841-835	
Yahuwakhaz 813-798	Adad-nirari III 811-783	Marduk-bel-zeri 811-783	Yahuwash 835-796	
Yahuwash 798-781	Shalman-assur IV 783-773	Marduk-apal-assur 783-773	Amatsyahuw 796-767	
Yerobowam II 781-753	Assur-dan 773-755	Eriba-marduk 773-755	Azaryahuw 767-739	
Zekharyahuw 753-752	Assur-nirari V 755-745	Nabu-shum-ukin 755-745 / -747		
Shalum 752		Nabu-on-assur 747-734		
Menakhem 752-741		Nabu-on-adon-zir 734-732		
Pekakhyah 741-739	Tiglath-pil-assur 745-727	Ukin-zir 745-727 / 732-727	Yowtham 739-731	
Pekakh 739-731		Ululay 727-722	Akhaz 731-715	
Howsheakh 731-721	Shalman-assur V 727-722	Marduk-bel-adon 722-710		
as Assyria	Sargon II 722-705	as Assyria 710-705		
		interregnum 705-702		

(thereafter called GALILEE)

Khezekyahuw	715-686
Menasheh	686-642
Amown	642-640
Yoshyahuw	640-609
Yahuwakhaz	609
Yahuwikim	609-598
Yahuwikhin	598-597
Tsedekyahuw	597-586
as Babylon	
as Persia	

Assyria

Sin-akh-kherub	705-681
Assur-akh-adon I	681-669
Assur-nasirpal III	669-628
Assur-etil-ilani	628-626
Assur-akh-adon II	626-616
Sin-sharra-ishkun	616-612
as Babylon	
as Persia	

Babylon

Bel-ibni	702-700
Assur-on-adon-shum	699-693
Mushezib-marduk	693-689
interregnum	689-680
Shamash-akh-adon (as Assyria)	680-669
	669-648
Kandalanu	648-626
Nabu-apal-assur	626-604
Nabu-akh-adon-assur	604-561
Emil-marduk	561-560
Nirgil-assur	560-556
Labasi-kudar	556
Nabu-on-idos	556-538
as Persia	

Media

Kyaxares of Media	612-587
Astyages of Media	587-549
as Babylon	
as Persia	

Persia / Greece / Seleucids

Kyros	549-529
Kambyses	529-522
Darius I	521-485
Xerxes	485-465
Artaxerxes I	465-425
Darius II	425-405
Artaxerxes II	404-358
Artaxerxes III	358-338
Darius III	336-330
Alexander	330-323
Philip	323-317
Antigonos	317-311
Seleukos I	311-280
Antiokhos I	280-260
Antiokhos II	260-246
Seleukos II	246-226
Seleukos III	226-223
Antiokhos III	223-187
as Egypt	
as Persia	

EGYPT

as Persia	528-332
Alexander	332-323
Ptolemaios I	323-283
Ptolemaios II	283-246
Ptolemaios III	246-221
Ptolemaios IV	221-203

Egypt (Ptolemaioi)		Judah / Judaea		Seleukid (Syria)	
Ptolemaios V	203-180			Seleukos IV	187-175
Ptolemaios VI	180-145			Antiokhos IV	175-164
as Judah				Antiokhos V	164-162
				Demetrius I	162-150
		Judas Maccabaeus	166-160	Antiokhos VI	150
Ptolemaios VII	145-116	Yahuwnathan	160-142	Antiokhos VII	150-128
		Shimeown	142-135	Demetrius II	128-124
***************		Hyrkanos I	135-104	Seleukos V	124
***************				Antiokhos VIII	124-96
Ptolemaios VIII	116-107	Aristoboulos I	104-103	Antiokhos IX	115-95
Ptolemaios IX	107-88	Alexander Yanay	103-78	Seleukos VI	96-95
Ptolemaios VIII	88-80			Antiokhos X	95-83
Ptolemaios X	80			Demetrius III	95-88
Ptolemaios XI	80-51			Antiokhos XI	92
		Queen Alexandra	78-69	Philippos I	92-83
		Hyrkanos II	69-67	Antiokhos XII	87-84
		Aristoboulos II	67-63	Tigranes	83-69
		Pompeius Magnus	63-48	Antiokhos XIII	69-64
ROME				Philippos II	65-64
Republic	48	Antipatros	48-44	as Rome	
Julius Caesar		Antigonos Hasmon	43-37		
Kleopatra VII	51-30	Herod bar Antipatros	37-4		
Triumvirate	44-31	Arkhelaos bar Herod	BCE 4-6 CE		
as Rome		Coponius	6-9		
Augustus	BCE 31-14 CE	Ambibulus	9-12		
Tiberius	14-37 CE	Annius Rufus	12-15		
Gaius Caligula	37-41	Valerius Gratus	15-26		
Claudius	41-54	Pontius Pilatus	26-36		
Nero	54-68	Marcellus	36-37		
Galba	68-69	Marullus	37-41		
Otho	69	Herod Agrippa I	41-44		
Vitellius	69	Tiberius Alexander	44-48		
Vespasian	69-79	Ventidius Cumanus	48-52		
Titus	79-81	Felix	52-60		
Domitian	81-96	Porcius Festus	60-62		
Nerva	96-98				
Trajan	98-117				
Hadrian	117-138				

Herod 37-4

Herod Antipas BCE 4-39 CE

Herod Agrippa 39-44

as Judah

Antoninus Pius	138-161
Marcus Aurelius	161-180
Commodus	180-192
Pertinax	193
Septimius Severus	193-211
Antoninus Caracalla	211-217
Macrinus	217-218
Antoninus Elagabalus	218-222
Severus Alexander	222-235
Maximinus Thrax	235-238
Gordian III	238-244
Philip the Arab	244-249
Decius	249-251
Trebonianus Gallus	251-253
Valerian	253-260
Gallienus	260-268
Claudius II	268-270
Aurelian	270-275
Tacitus	275-276
Probus	276-282
Carus	282-283
Carinus	283-284
Diocletian	284-305
Maximian	286-305
Galerius	305-311
Constantinius	311-337
Constantius	337-361
Julian	361-363
Jovian	363-364
Valentinian I	364-375
Gratian	375-378
Theodosius	378-395

Albinus	62-64
Gessius Florus	64-66
Hanan bar Hanan	66-68
Zealots	68-69
Shimeown bar Goria	69-70
Legates	70-132
Shimeown bar Kokhba	132-135
as Rome	

Thirteen

From David to Jesus: The Age of the Messiah

> The great man-centered drama of sin-and-redemption, constructed in earlier times, looked puny against the new universe.
>
> Isaac Asimov, *Asimov on Physics*.

The Yahwist wrote:

> The royal staff is not to pass from Yahuwdah, nor the royal power from between his legs, until the one comes to whom . . . the nation is to grant obedience. (GEN. 49:10)

He also wrote:

> A star from Yaakob takes charge. A sceptre arises out of Yisrael.
> (NUM. 24:17)

Three centuries later, utilising a biography of David written by the spokesman Nathan (1 CHR. 29:29), the earliest of the chroniclers wrote:

> The word of Yahweh came to Nathan, saying: 'Go and tell my slave David . . . "I'm going to set up your descendant after you, begotten of your body . . . and I'm going to establish the throne of his kingdom forever."' (2 SAM. 7:4-13)

A little later still, probably within a decade either side of 600 BCE, another chronicler made that promise conditional:

> Yahweh appeared to Shlomoh . . . and said to him . . . 'If you obey my laws and my whims, then I'll establish the throne of your kingdom forever, as I promised to your father David when I said, "You'll never lack a man on the throne of Yisrael."' 		(3 KGS. 9:2-5; see also PS. 89:28-37; 132:11-18)

Yahweh's promise that a descendant of Yahuwdah, a star from Yaakob, would become king of the Jews, was fulfilled in the person of King David. Since David's grandson was already king at the time of writing, the Yahwist's powers of prophecy were not severely taxed in making such a prediction. On the other hand, Yahweh's promise that the descendants of David would rule Israel *forever* was broken in about 930 BCE. If the promise is viewed as applying to Judah rather than Israel, then it was broken in 586 BCE. No descendant of David has been king anywhere since that date. Now that the Davidic line is extinct, none ever can be.

Ignoring the Yahwist's promises, which did not specifically state that the Davidic monarchy was to be permanent, and the promise to Solomon that was dependent on conditions that Solomon failed to fulfil, there remains Nathan's promise to David. There are three, and only three, explanations for Yahweh's broken promise:

1. Yahweh lied.

2. Nathan lied. He pretended to David that his own wild guess was a revelation from Yahweh.

3. The chronicler lied. He put into the mouth of Nathan a promise that the spokesman never made.

It does not matter which of these alternative explanations one chooses to accept. In all three situations the claim of the Judaeo-Christian bible to be anything but the fallible beliefs of fallible men stands refuted. But the examination of *Daniel* established that point already.

To the Jews of the Babylonian Captivity, all three possible explanations were unacceptable. Yahweh had promised that a descendant of Yahuwdah would establish a Jewish monarchy that was to last forever; therefore it must be so. He had promised David that David's son/descendant (the same Hebrew word meant both) would usher in the permanent, uninterrupted kingdom; therefore it must be so. That son had not been Solomon, whose line had been deposed in 586 BCE; therefore he had to be a distant son, a descendant of David as yet unborn. Thus was born the concept of Yahweh's Anointed, *Mashyah* (Messiah), the Christened (anointed with chrism) King of the Jews.

The messiah, once conceived, was promptly backdated. Old foreshadowing passages that had retroactively prophesied the coming of King David were now seen as messianic. Miykhah, for example, had written about the time of the fall of Samaria: *Efrathah* (Bethlehem) . . . *out of you will he come forth to be ruler of Yisrael* (MIC. 5:2). David had indeed come out of Bethlehem to be ruler of Israel. Isayah's never-fulfilled (and unfulfillable) prophecy that *a shoot will emerge from the stem of Yishay, and a sprig* (netser)[1] *out of his roots* (ISA. 11:1), who would bring back a remnant of the conquered Israelites from Assyria, Egypt, Persia, Uganda, Arabia, Babylonia, Nimrod and Cyprus (11:10-11), was reinterpreted to apply to the king who would refound David's dynasty.

The first writer so to interpret the older prophecies and repeat them in the light of the new mythology was Jeremyah. Jeremyah quoted 3 *Kings* 9:5: *For Yahweh said this: David will never lack a man to sit upon the throne of Yisrael* (JER. 33:17). Even though the prophecy quoted was the conditional one to Solomon, Jeremyah ignored the conditions and treated the prophecy as utterly binding. He added his own reinforcement:

> You see the days approaching, says Yahweh, when I'm going to perform that good thing that I've promised. . . . I'm going to cause a righteous sprout (*tsemakh*) to grow up unto David.   (JER. 33:14-15)

Jeremyah wrote in about 580 BCE. Sixty years later another messianic prophecy issued from the quill of Zekharyah:

> Yahweh, commander of armies, says, 'Gaze on the man whose name is the Sprout. He's going to rebuild Yahweh's Temple, and sit down and rule as a priest upon his throne.'   (ZEC. 6:12-13)

Zekharyah's book was written after Darius I had ordered work resumed on the second Temple, halted since the first year of the reign of Kyros. To Zekharyah, the messiah's main task, since there was no longer a Captivity for him to end, was the completion of the Temple. Once that was done, Zekharyah expected him to be crowned and *rule as a priest upon his throne*, in other words to become a new kind of king, a theocrat, analogous to the medieval Popes and Muslim Caliphs. And since Zekharyah was writing

---

1. The significance of *netser*, particularly since Jeremyah and Zekharyah used the word *tsemakh*, similar in meaning but phonetically different, will be explained in the following chapter.

about events in the process of happening, he had no difficulty identifying who that theocrat would be: *The hands of Zerubbabel laid the foundations of this Temple. His hands will finish it* (ZEC. 4:9a).

Zerubbabel did complete the second Temple; but the Jews did not *take the silver and gold and make a crown and place it on his head* (ZEC. 6:11). Consequently, even though Zekharyah had unambiguously indicated that all of his prophecies had referred to Zerubbabel, later generations, unwilling to acknowledge that prophecies could fail, concluded that the messiah promised by Zekharyah was not Zerubbabel but a descendant *still* unborn.

Despite setbacks in Greece in 490 and 480 BCE, the Persian empire that had been the Jews' overlords since 538 BCE prospered. Under Xerxes it numbered over twenty-seven provinces, which the author of *Esther* retro-actively raised to 127. Jews were free to move at will, and a sizeable com-munity migrated to the Great King's capital at Susa. Those whose parents had returned to Jerusalem had little cause for complaint. They were able to worship in Yahweh's Temple. They were taxed no more severely than the Great King's other subject peoples. They had a degree of self-government under Jewish satraps, of whom Nehemyah was probably the best known. The only serious imperfection was that, despite Yahweh's solemn promise to David, Zerubbabel had died uncrowned and Darius's successors had steadfastly refused to permit the installation of a Jewish king in Jerusalem.

It was almost certainly for the purpose of winning the favour of Artaxerxes III, in the hope that he would authorise the restoration of a Jewish king (a somewhat forlorn hope), that a member of Susa's Jewish community wrote the purely fictitious *Book of Esther. Esther's* unequivocal purpose was to demonstrate that the Jews were the Great King's friends (just as *Mark* was later written to prove that the Christians were Vespasian's friends). Not only did the author of *Esther* claim that a Jew named Mardukay had saved King Xerxes from assassination and done him other valuable services; he also pretended that Xerxes had made a Jewish woman named Ishtar ('Esther' is an alternative transcription of the same Hebrew letters) his queen.

Esther's claim to be valid history can be refuted on the basis of internal inconsistency. Mardukay was allegedly carried off from Jerusalem at the time that Nabu-akh-adon-assur carried off king *Yakhonyah* to Babylon (EST. 2:6). Since Yakhonyah cannot reasonably be equated with Tsedekyahuw, carried off in 586 BCE, he can only have been Yahuwikhin, whom Nabu-akh-adon-assur deposed and transported to Babylon in 597 BCE.[2]

---

2. *4 Kings* 24:6 named Yahuwikhin as Yahuwikim's son, and Tsedekyahuw as Yahuwikhin's uncle. *2 Chronicles* 36:8 named Yahuwikhin as Yahuwikim's son, and Tsedekyahuw as Yahuwi-khin's brother. *1 Chronicles* 3:16 called Yahuwikim's son Yakhonyah, and gave Yakhonyah both a brother and an uncle named Tsedekyahuw.

In the Hebrew *Esther* (the Greek differs), Mardukay saved Xerxes's life in the seventh year of his reign, 479 BCE (EST. 2:16-23). If Mardukay was newborn in 597 BCE, then he must have been 118 years old in the seventh year of Xerxes. That may be within the bounds of possibility. However, Ishtar was Mardukay's first cousin, his uncle's daughter. It is somewhat difficult to imagine the cousin of a 118-year-old man being deemed a suitable bedfellow for the Great King of Persia.

The chronology is no more reasonable if Ishtar's royal husband, Akhsuwruws, is identified as Kyaxares of Media rather than Xerxes. (The author of *Tobit* (14:15) used a Greek transliteration of Akhsuwruws to mean Kyaxares.) In the seventh year of Kyaxares, Yahuwikhin was not yet king. And no author who expected to be believed would have credited Kyaxares with ruling over 127 provinces. As for Akhsuwruws being Artaxerxes, as the Septuagint made him: that equation would necessitate Mardukay being 138 years old.

In the Greek additions to *Esther*, included in RC bibles but rejected by Jews and Protestants, the internal inconsistencies were more pronounced. The additions contained an editor's note dating them to the reign of Ptolemaios and Kleopatra, apparently Ptolemaios XI and Kleopatra VI, who reigned from 80 BCE. The additions had Mardukay save Xerxes from assassination in the second year of his reign (11:2), with the consequence that Catholic bibles show Mardukay saving Xerxes twice.

Mardukay and Ishtar bore the names of Babylonian gods, while the queen whom Ishtar/Esther replaced was Vishtu, another goddess; and this suggests that the book had its origin in a tale told of the gods. Certainly Ishtar and Vishtu were not historical queens of Persia. While Xerxes may have had concubines of those names, his queen's name, according to Herodotos (HIST. 7:61), was Amestris. As for *Esther*'s assertion that the Great King chose Ishtar queen because, of the unspecified number of beauteous virgins who auditioned in his bed, she gave the best performance (EST. 2:2-3, 12-17), that aspect of the Esther myth is for some reason ignored in Judaism's annual *Purim* festival. *Esther* eventually found its way into the Judaeo-Christian bible, but it made no contribution to Jewish independence.

The Persian overlordship came to an end with the victory of Alexander, only to be replaced by a Ptolemaic overlordship and then a Seleukid one. Unwilling to believe that Yahweh had abandoned them, the Jews blamed their misfortune on the planetary gods, *Serafiym* ('Watchers'), whom Yahweh had appointed to administer punishment to his Chosen Nation. Clearly the serafs had been overzealous, and were allowing foreign domination to continue far longer than Yahweh had intended. For this they would one day answer to Yahweh.

As years, decades, even centuries rolled by without any end to Jewish subjugation by one overlord or another, the belief that the serafs were merely overzealous punishers became harder and harder to maintain. Gradually their crime evolved into outright rebellion against Yahweh, and by the time the Essene *Book of Enoch* was composed, the Jewish bad angels had emulated the Persian bad angels by challenging the power of the King of gods, and had been forcibly thrown out of the skies.

And through all of this time the Jews seized upon the messiah concept and made it the central feature of their hopes for freedom. The occupations were seen as temporary. In his own good time Yahweh would order the serafs to stop supporting the foreign overlords. He would then overthrow the foreigners in the only conceivable way, by sending a warlord who would repeat the victories of Yahuwshua and David. That warlord would be the descendant of David, *Mashyah*, by this time firmly believed to have been prophesied in the Towrah. David's descendant would put an end to the occupation and establish the permanent monarchy prophesied by Jacob. Such was the belief and the hope.

Then came the Maccabees. Jewish independence was proclaimed in 166 BCE, and recognised in 143 BCE. Zekharyah's prophecy that a theocrat would rule as a *priest upon his throne*, actually written of Zerubbabel, was seen to be fulfilled when High Priest Shimeown Hasmon was recognised as ruler of Judah by the Seleukids. The apocalyptic portions of *Daniel* were written, backdating to a nonexistent spokesman of Babylonian times a prophecy of the Hasmonean monarchy. The Davidic king, the messiah, was all but forgotten. No more prophecies of his coming were written, and the old ones were ignored. How could Yahweh send a messiah to free Judah when it was already free? Why would he send a king when the Jews already had a perfectly good king? Besides, *Daniel* had prophesied that the Hasmonean monarchy was to last forever (7:27).

And then along came Rome. Once again the messiah became a daily expectation. The Sanhedrin, the council of seventy priests and rabbis instituted by the Maccabees in the belief that they were restoring a body first appointed by Moses (NUM. 11:16), studied *Daniel* and found in it what they took to be a prophecy of the date of the messiah's birth. Fourth Daniel had mentioned a period of seventy weeks during which the Jews were to *pay compensation for their disobedience* (9:24), from the time that the order was given to rebuild Jerusalem until the advent of *Mashyah Nagiydh*, 'Messiah the Prince' (9:25).

As *Jubilees* makes clear, the word 'week' was habitually used at this time to mean a period of seven years. Seventy weeks therefore meant 490 years. Since it was believed that *Daniel* had been written during the reign of Kyros, the 490 years presumably should have been counted from Kyros's first order to rebuild the Temple in 538 BCE. That would have ended the sixty-nine weeks until the messiah's first appearance in 55 BCE, and the seventy weeks until his triumph in 48 BCE. If any messianic claimant appeared in either of those years, his name has not survived.

The 483 and 490 years could, however, be counted from almost any date that a messianic candidate found convenient. Certainly any of the following would have been acceptable:

597 Nabu-akh-adon-assur's first capture of Jerusalem;
586 Nabu-akh-adon-assur's sack of Jerusalem;
538 Kyros's abortive order to rebuild the Temple;
521 Darius's order to rebuild the Temple;
516 the completion of the Temple;
459 the sending of Ezra to refurnish the Temple;
446 the sending of Nehemyah, who rebuilt the walls of Jerusalem;
434 the completion of the walls of Jerusalem.

The earliest claimant to messiahship seems to have been the leader of the Essene sect, the Righteous Rabbi. While he first materialised around 140 BCE, it may be that he counted 483 years from 586 BCE and had himself proclaimed King of the Jews in 103 BCE. Such an action would explain why the Hasmonean King Alexander Yanay hanged him in that year. According to the Talmud, the hanging occurred on the eve of Passover (SANH. 43a), but as there is little doubt that the Talmud authors confused the execution of the Righteous Rabbi in 103 BCE with the execution of Jesus the Nazirite 133 years later, that detail may have belonged only to the latter event.

By counting 483 years from 521/520 BCE, the Sanhedrin reached the date 38/37 BCE, the year of the effective succession of King Herod. The possibility that Herod was the messiah was seriously discussed by that august body, but dismissed on the ground that the messiah's task was to save the Jews, not contribute to their enslavement as Herod was doing.[3] Since Fourth Daniel had mentioned the rebuilding of the city walls in his prophecy (9:25), an alternative calculation was made that dated the messiah's coronation to 36 CE. Since he was bound to be crowned at the age of forty, that put his birth in the year 4 BCE. Among the persons who accepted the validity of the Sanhedrin's dating was one who may well have been born in 4 BCE, the aforesaid Jesus.

By 30 CE pious Jews were confident that the messiah was already on earth, ready to raise the standard of rebellion against Rome at any moment.

---

3. Hugh Schonfield, The Pentecost Revolution, pp. 30-31, quoting the Slavic interpolations from Josephus's Jewish War.

Every few years a man came along who, usually but not always on the basis of some kind of prophecy-fulfilment, believed that *he* was the messiah. One who had good reason to think so, since he fulfilled two prophecies and was in an excellent position to head a revolution, was King Herod Agrippa I. One who is not known to have fulfilled any prophecies, although he was *reputed* to have been born in Bethlehem, was John the Immerser. And one who certainly fulfilled no prophecies, since he was a Galilean carpenter's son whose ancestors had been gentiles, was Jesus the Nazirite.

At the same time that the prophesied King of the Jews was being transformed from David into David's unborn descendant, Yahweh was likewise undergoing a transformation, from the volcano-god that the Jews had worshipped in Anatolia, into the universal sky-god of whom they had first learned from the Israelites.

Just as Zeus had been worshipped as a bull, a wolf, an oak tree and various other animate and inanimate objects by different groups of Greeks, so Yahweh had originally been as many different kinds of gods as there were tribes and clans in the Jewish confederacy. To the Elohist he had been near-anthropomorphic: *'You can't see my face. . . . I'll cover you with my hand . . . and you'll see my backside'* (EXOD. 33:20-23). To one psalmist he was the personified sea: *Deep calls to deep at the noise of your waterspouts. All your waves and billows are gone over me* (PS. 42:7). To another psalmist he was a hawk-god like the Egyptian Thoth: *He will cover you with his feathers, and keep you safe under his wings* (PS. 91:4). To sheikhs and kings from Abraham to Solomon he had been a phallus: *Yaakob erected a stone phallus on which he poured an offering of wine and oil* (GEN. 35:14). But mainly he was a volcano:

J   Mount Siynay was completely wrapped in smoke, because Yahweh had descended on it in the form of fire. The smoke from it rose like the smoke of a furnace, and the whole mountain shook violently. . . . 'Don't let the priests or the people come up to Yahweh, or he'll erupt over them.'   (EXOD. 19:18, 24)

E   At Khoreb . . . the gods' mountain . . . . The people saw and heard the thunder and lightning and the mountain smoking.   (EXOD. 17:6; 18:5; 20:18)

E   Yahweh had a tantrum. Yahweh's fire burned among them, wasting all in the outer fringes of the camp.   (NUM. 11:1)

D   'What creature has heard the thunder of erupting gods roaring from the middle of the lava, as we have, and survived?'   (DEUT. 5:26)

P   The magnificence of Yahweh was like a devouring fire on top of the mountain.
(EXOD. 24:17)

R   You heard his orders from the middle of the flames.   (DEUT. 4:36)

The volcano-god Yahweh massacred a randomly-chosen segment of his own worshippers because *the nation grumbled, arousing Yahweh's temper* (NUM. 11:1), just as Enlil had drowned the human race because '*The uproar of mankind is intolerable, and sleep is no longer possible on account of the babble.*' That comparison between two capricious, temperamental, homicidal gods tells a good deal about why the Jewish priests in post-exilic days saw an urgent need to change their chief god's image. But right down to the time of the Babylonian Captivity Yahweh remained primarily a volcano:

> I called upon Yahweh, and cried out to my Allah.
> He heard my voice out of his Temple. . . .
> Then the land shook and trembled. . . .
> There went up a smoke out of his nostrils,
> And out of his mouth a fire that devoured.
> Coals were kindled by it. . . .
> Yahweh thundered in the skies,
> And Ilion gave his voice:
> Hail and coals of fire. . . .
> The land's foundations were exposed, O Yahweh,
> At the blast of the breath of your nostrils.
> (PS. 18:6-15)

Yahweh's origin as a multiplicity of incompatible gods, combined with the title the Yahwist had given him, *Yahweh Elohiym*, 'Yahweh the gods,' led to his being viewed as the local god of several widely scattered Jewish shrines. Jews living at Khebrown regularly offered sacrifices to Yahweh of Khebrown, but also made pilgrimages to the capital in order to sacrifice to Yahweh of Jerusalem. Survivors of Sargon's conquest who sacrificed to *the gods* in Galilee and Samaria, travelled to Judah to sacrifice to Yahweh. The Deuteronomist, ambivalent about non-Jewish gods, had no doubts about the unity of Yahweh. It was to drive home that the Yahweh of Khebrown and the Yahweh of Shiloh and the Yahweh of Jerusalem were the same Yahweh, and that *the gods* was also Yahweh, that he wrote, *Listen, Yisrael: Yahweh is our gods, Yahweh alone* (DEUT. 6:4). So effective was D's unification of Yahweh that a generation later the Priestly author was able to ban all sacrifices outside of Jerusalem, thereby forcing all Jews to bring their offerings to the Temple priests (LEV. 17:3-9) without the masses refusing to obey out of fear of the neglected local Yahweh.

It was not so much Yahweh's volcanic or oceanic or hawk-like or phallic qualities that eventually led the priestly caste to attempt to purge him from their mythology altogether, as his indelible association with the atrocities of David and Yahuwshua. It had, for example, been *in compliance with the orders that Yahweh had given Yahuwshuakh* (JOSH. 8:27) that the Jews of old had murdered the entire population of Jericho, *both man and woman, young and old* (JOSH. 6:21). And it was because *Yahweh hardened Pharaoh's heart so that he would not let the Yisraelites go* (EXOD. 10:20) that Yahweh had created his excuse for murdering *all of the firstborn in the land of Egypt, from the firstborn of Pharaoh to the firstborn of the prisoner in the dungeon* (EXOD. 12:29).

Nor did Yahweh limit his mass murders to infidels, *gowyim*. When a Jew married a Midianite woman, Yahweh's response to that single act of race pollution was to send a plague that killed 24,000 Jews. The racist god had only terminated his murder of innocent hostages when *Fiynkhas speared them both through* (NUM. 25:7-8). And when the Israelites grumbled against Moses' tyrannical rule, Yahweh had hurled down a thunderbolt, *wasting all in the outer fringes of the camp* (NUM. 11:1).

Yahweh was a mass-murderer who slaughtered thousands of individuals for the crimes, real or imagined, of a single offender. But he was not above capriciously unleashing his malevolent, unstable temper against individuals for reasons that only he could comprehend. For example, when the Chest of the Treaty was about to fall over and David's aide-de-camp, Khuzah, reached out to protect it, *Yahweh's tantrum flared against Khuzah, and the gods snuffed him for his mistake, and he died beside the gods' Chest* (2 SAM. 6:6-7).

Similarly, when Balaam of the talking ass agreed to accompany the Mowabites, in obedience to a command from Yahweh the gods, *his going ignited the gods' temper*, and Yahweh sent a messenger to execute Balaam for his obedience (NUM. 22:19-22). It was the mixing of a J story in which Yahweh wanted Balaam dead for going, with an E story in which he gave him permission to go, that caused the problem. But to persons who maintain that the current Judaeo-Christian bible is Revealed Truth, it is no less an embarrassment. A similar capricious whim caused Yahweh to come within an inch of murdering Moses for the crime of not knowing that he should have circumcised his son (EXOD. 4:24-26).

All gods were capricious and vindictive. Artemis murdered Aktaion, having him torn apart by dogs, for the crime of accidentally seeing her naked. Only Yahweh, however, imposed such monstrous and disproportionate 'punishment' on children. When forty-two children laughed at Eliyshakh's bald head, the spokesman called on Yahweh to avenge the insult, and Yahweh dutifully sent two bears that tore the children to shreds (4 KGS. 2:23-24).

Yahweh murdered children for behaving like children. He murdered the many for the crimes of the few. And (again, unlike any other god before or since) he murdered thousands for the crime of obeying his own orders: Yahweh ordered David to conduct a census and, when David obeyed, Yahweh sent an epidemic that killed 70,000 in punishment for the crime of conducting a census (2 SAM. 24:1-16). Again, the problem stemmed from the riffling together of stories by a pro-census chronicler and an anti-census chronicler; but again the amalgam was an embarrassment to believers, then and now.

Moses, who had never heard of Yahweh, was accused by the Priestly author of murdering 90,000 Midianites. In the version of the story told in *Numbers* (31:16-18), which already existed in Seleukid times, that atrocity was associated with Yahweh: '*You saw them cause the Yisraelites to insult Yahweh. . . . So massacre every* (male child and non-virgin female).'

Yahweh endorsed slavery. He permitted Jews to sell their daughters as concubine-slaves (EXOD. 21:7). He endorsed human sacrifice, and declared that *no human who has been solemnly vowed is to be redeemed. He's to be sacrificed without fail* (LEV. 27:29). He demanded the death penalty for being a priestess of any god but himself (EXOD. 22:18); for heresy (EXOD. 22:20); for insulting his name (LEV. 24:16); for failure to possess an intact hymen at the time of marriage (DEUT. 22:20-21); for working on Saturday (EXOD. 31:14-15); for adultery (LEV. 20:10); for cursing one's parents (LEV. 20:9); for gay sexual recreation (LEV. 20:13); for zoophilia (EXOD. 22:19); and for fortune-telling (LEV. 20:27). He was also the kind of sadist who derived pleasure from inflicting pain (DEUT. 28:63).

The chronicler who accused King Amatsyahuw of summarily executing 10,000 prisoners-of-war, also declared that Amatsyahuw *did the things Yahweh saw as righteous* (2 CHR. 25:12; 25:2). And, while *Judges* (11:30-39) did not specifically state that Yahweh approved, it was to fulfil a vow to Yahweh that Yefthah had sacrificed his daughter rather than break the extinct volcano's commandment that *You're not to swear in Yahweh your gods' name that which is false* (DEUT. 5:11).

Yahweh had committed atrocities worthy of Yahuwshua or Hitler. But more than that, in a society that was still monistic, he was responsible for all evil: *Can there be evil in a town, except that Yahweh has done it?* (AMOS 3:6). *I create good fortune, and I create evil. I, Yahweh, do all of these things* (ISA. 45:7). *Who has only to speak to make things happen? Doesn't his lordship ordain (everything)? Don't good and evil come from the mouth of Ilion? Let's consider and examine our behaviour, and return to Yahweh* (LAM. 3:37-38, 40). Yahweh's record was indefensible, and the day was coming, the priests knew, when anyone associated with such a god would go down with him.

In view of Yahweh's record, it was no surprise that the priestly caste concluded that he had to go. The history of the Israelite god Allah was much more respectable, and much less likely to cause the masses someday to turn against a priesthood that endorsed such a god.

As the first step toward severing all connection with Yahweh, the priests declared his name *taboo*, too sacred (*taboo* means 'sacred') to be spoken under any circumstances.[4] This was not a particularly radical proposition. The belief that a god or a person could be harmed by speaking his name had been around for centuries, perhaps for millennia. Names were regarded as such an integral part of the organism named that the ancients believed, quite literally, that if a way could be found to remove the *snap* from a *snapdragon*, the end result would be a dragon.

Since the Towrah contained the name *Yahweh* on almost every page, and the priestly caste would have undermined its own power if public readings had ceased, the priests invented a system of substitution. Whenever a document written in the vowelless Hebrew alphabet contained the name *YHWH*, the reader was required instead to pronounce the word *Adown*, meaning 'His Lordship' (Hebrew nominative: *Adownay*; Greek nominative: *Adonis*). While the word *Adown* carried no implications of divinity (and in modern Hebrew means *Mister*), it quickly came to be recognised—and used—as a substitute for the tribal god's unspeakable name. By the time vowel points came to be added to written Hebrew seven centuries later, the taboo had been in effect for so long that the correct pronunciation of *YHWH* had been long forgotten. Consequently, when editions of the sacred writings were produced that contained vowel points, the name *YHWH* was pointed, not with the vowels that would have been needed to speak the unspeakable name *Yahweh* (or perhaps *Yahuweh*), but with the vowels needed for the permitted substitute *Adownay*. It was this combination of the consonants of *Yahweh* and the vowels of *Adownay*, transcribed into German, that gave rise to the mongrel word *Jehovah*, used by no Jews and only unlearned Christians. When the Christian masochist Jerome translated the Jewish scriptures into Latin around 400 CE, he was sufficiently intimidated by the Jewish taboo to change *Yahweh* to *Dominus*, Latin for *Adownay*, and

---

4. The imposition of taboo status on words can occur for a variety of reasons. In recent years the word *Nigger*, the literal meaning of which is 'black,' has been replaced by *Black*, apparently because it has acquired the connotation of 'slave' is unacceptable to a free people. And following the French conquest of England in 1066 CE, those English words that pertained to bodily functions (including eating) came to be viewed as *vulgar*, meaning pertaining to the *vulgi*, the illiterate masses, and were replaced by French or Latin equivalents. Thus the English words *pig*, *cow* and *sheep*, when referring to food, were supplanted by the French *pork*, *beef* and *mutton*; English *cunt* by Latin *vagina*; English *fuck* (O.E. *fachen*) by Latin *intercourse*; and other now-taboo English words by substitutes from the language of the conquerors. Many languages besides English developed 'dirty word' concepts for analogous reasons; but some, including Hebrew, did not.

this in turn led to the eventual production of English bibles in which Yahweh was never mentioned, but was replaced by a character called 'the LORD.'

As always when practical considerations necessitated a modification of current mythology (papal reaction to Martin Luther and Hans Küng comes to mind), there were conservatives to whom the proposed changes were anathema. The spokesman known only as 'My Messenger' (*Malakhiy*) bitterly opposed the Levite priesthood's suppression of the name of his god, and protested: '. . . *where is my honour? . . . where is my reverence?' says Yahweh, commander of armies, 'to you, O Priests, who despise my name. . . . you have corrupted Levi's treaty,' says Yahweh, commander of armies . . . .* Unless the priestly caste restored Yahweh's name to its former dignity, Malakhiy threatened: *'I'll derive no pleasure from you,' says Yahweh, commander of armies,* and *'My name will be exalted among the infidels,' says Yahweh, commander of armies* (MAL. 1:6; 1:10-11; 2:8).

Even though Malakhiy's threats were ignored and the purging of Yahweh from the Jewish vocabulary continued, and even though a passage attributed to Zekharyah, who had lived more than two centuries before Malakhiy, declared that Zekharyah was to be the last spokesman (ZEC. 13:3), *Malachi* was nonetheless later incorporated into the Judaeo-Christian bible.

Psalmists likewise contributed to the changing of Yahweh's image. A lament that bewailed Israel's subject status in a gentile empire asked 'Yahweh the gods, commander of armies' (*Yahweh elohiym tsabaowth*) to send *Ben Adam* to restore Jewish hegemony, and called Yahweh, *the friend of Yisrael, who inhabits the stars* (PS. 80:4; 80:17; 80:1), thereby far removing him from his former location in the bowels of a decidedly unfriendly volcano.

Ultimately it was the priestly caste's own pious superstition that defeated their purpose. While they had no qualms about removing Yahweh's name from the spoken vocabulary, they dared not delete *YHWH*, or even such other items as obvious scribal errors, from the sacred writings. A form of the name survived, although not necessarily with the original pronunciation. Yahweh is the god of the Jews to this day, even though Jews still deem it a blasphemous breach of taboo to pronounce his name.

Yahweh was not the only Jewish god to change his image under the influence of foreign infiltration and Jewish reaction. While the lord of the volcano was shedding his ancient name and becoming the lord of the clear blue skies, an even more startling change was taking place in Yahweh's great Enemy. Just as the primeval Mother who had given birth to the universe through her lava-spewing Anatolian vulva had changed sex and become the god Yahweh, so the goddess who had tempted Eve changed her sex and became the rebel messenger Khazazel, thereafter known as the Satan ('the enemy').

It was the evolution of monotheism that triggered a need for the Satan. Obviously there was much imperfection in Yahweh's world, and just as obviously he, as a perfectionist, could not have been responsible. The Babylonian Captivity had exposed the Jews to the Zoroastrian pantheon, with its good gods headed by Ahura Mazda ('God of Light') and its bad gods headed by Ahura Manah or Ahriman ('God of Darkness'). This led to the belief that the prolonged overlordship that outlasted the Captivity was the fault of the bad gods, rebel messengers who had refused to obey Yahweh's orders.

Alternative versions of the serafs' original disobedience were postulated, the most popular being that they were the *sons of the gods* who had sired the giants by illegally recreating with mortal women. Such rebels had to have a leader, and since the concept of a divine antagonist, a Jewish Ahriman, had been assimilated before there was any speculation as to the antagonist's identity, he was simply styled the Enemy (*ha-satan*). The first reference to the Enemy as a male in Jewish mythology was made by Zekharyah (ZEC. 3:2) in 520 BCE.

The Satan's identity presented a problem. The logical choice was Ashtaroth, but her femininity was a disqualification. Just as a male-dominated world had refused to tolerate a female ruler of the skies, so it refused to grant such a responsible position as Monarch of Evil to a woman. The Satan became a male. And since Yahweh's prime antagonist had long been the fertility goddess identified with the planet Venus, so the Jewish Venus, Khazazel (Jewish planetary gods were all male), became the Satan. Satan's planetary origin was clearly recognised by the mythologians who gave him the alternative name of Lucifer ('Bringer of Light'), the Roman name for Venus as Morning Star.

With the transformation of the Satan into a male, the way was opened for the reinterpretation of the Enemy's tempting of Eve in Eden as a heterosexual seduction. A myth that failed to find a place in the Judaeo-Christian bible, although it had a wide circulation in Hasmonean and Roman times, told of how two fallen angels,[5] one assuming the shape of a woman, taught sexual recreation to Adam and Eve.[6] That, however, was a later fantasy that only came into existence when adherents of the buddhistic philosophy that spawned the Essenes had succeeded in convincing themselves that the disobedience of Adam and Eve had been sexual recreation *per se*. The earliest version of the reinterpretation made Eve's crime adultery, and Adam's presumably that he failed to kill the Satan's bastard as soon as it was born. If a line attributed to Jesus the Nazirite, a renegade Essene, by his most

---

5. Once Judaism had become monotheistic, *c.* 250 BCE, the concept of a heavenly messenger (*melekh*), formerly a minor god, corresponded closely to the modern concept of angel.

6. R. Graves and R. Patai, *Hebrew Myths*, 15a. This story probably represents a late interpretation of the sculpture of a male and female kherub copulating, which was an integral part of the Holiest of Holies in the second Temple (See also Patai, *The Hebrew Goddess*, p. 59).

imaginative biographer can be taken seriously, the Nazirite clearly believed that Cain was the Satan's son (JOHN 8:44).

A little later, in order to make Adam's and Eve's crimes identical, the Satan's seduction of Eve was counterbalanced by a tale of Lilith's seduction of Adam.

The Satan evolved slowly. He was male by 520 BCE. By analogy with Ahriman he became leader of the rebel messenger-gods (later angels) shortly thereafter. But only after the conquest of Alexander of Macedon did he become, by analogy with the Greek underworld god, Hades (and the Norse underworld god, Hell), ruler of the underworld realm of the dead.

The Satan's physical body, with its bifurcated hoofs, tail, horns, and generally goat-like countenance, was borrowed, after 330 BCE, from the pre-Greek goat-god, Pan. Pan was the only god known to the Greeks, apart from resurrected saviours such as Persephone and Dionysos, ever reputed to have died. It was ironic that, just as Pan was dying to the Greeks, he was being reborn in Jewish mythology as a combination Ahriman, Hades and transsexual Ashtaroth. Only one aspect of the Satan's physical appearance betrayed his female origin. Although Christians later enlarged it to titanic proportions in accordance with their masochistic dogma that the sharing of joy was diabolical, the Satan's penis was originally depicted as no bigger than a clitoris.

The Satan's physical body was borrowed from non-Jewish sources. His pernicious character was not. From the beginning he was viewed as malevolent, malicious, vindictive, vicious, sadistic, pathologically addicted to being worshipped despite the absence of any qualities that would entitle him even to be admired, capricious, given to entrapping the innocent for the sole purpose of luring them into the pre-Christian equivalent of damnation, a liar (*diabolos* eventually came to mean 'liar'), and the antithesis of everything that was just, moral and decent. It was because they recognised that those were precisely the qualities of Yahweh that the priestly caste had attempted to oust the lava-spewer from their pantheon. The creators of the Satan had attempted to give Yahweh an opposite. Instead they gave him an identical twin. Apparently they failed to ask themselves: With a god like Yahweh, who needs a devil?

The years between David and Jesus saw great changes in Jewish mythology. They also saw comparable changes in the Jewish self-image and, in consequence, Jewish attitudes toward *gowyim*, a word that meant no more than 'other tribes' when first coined. By the death of Ezra, however, around 400 BCE, *gowyim* had come to mean 'dirty unchosen subhuman infidel scum.'[7]

---

7. To some Jews, including Israel's most fanatic Prime Minister, it still means that, just as to some Christians, Muslims, Hindus etc., anyone outside their little sect is predestined to damnation (or equivalent).

David had no prejudice against Mowabites, Ammonites, Edomites or Philistines. They just happened to occupy land that David wanted to rule. The Yahwist justified David's bloody conquests with his 'Chosen Nation' fantasy and his myth of Levit's daughters, thereby planting the seeds of Jewish xenophobia (Yahuwshua and his horde were simply murderers by instinct. They had no belief that non-Jews *deserved* to die).

Nothing fuels prejudice as effectively as war. When the Davidic empire collapsed at the death of Solomon, the kings of Judah and Israel spent the next several centuries trying to win it back. However, as the Mowabites and other former Jewish serfs did not wish to be reconquered, the consequence was virtually permanent war. The Jews consequently formed a hatred of the Mowabites as intense and irrational as the American hatred of the Japanese as depicted in American war movies of 1942.

By 621 BCE Jewish xenophobia had reached such a fever pitch that the Deuteronomist was able to write: *No Khamownite or Mowabite is to be admitted into Yahweh's community. Not even their tenth-generation descendant is to be admitted into Yahweh's community, forever. . . . You're not to seek their welfare or their prosperity as long as you live, forever* (DEUT. 23:3, 6).

In the fifth century BCE the High Priest Ezra ordered all Jews who had non-Jewish wives and children to expel them from the Jewish community (EZRA 10:10-12). A generation after that a chronicler accused King David of appalling atrocities against Ammonite prisoners in the belief that David should have so behaved (1 CHR. 20:3). And toward the end of the fourth century the Jews saw their Persian oppressors defeated by Alexander, and Alexander's short-lived empire disintegrate, only to have their desperate hopes of independence crushed by Ptolemaios I and Antiokhos I. Xenophobia became total.

Then, as has happened many times in history, out of war, xenophobia and unreasoned hatred came a breath of sanity, in the form of the *Book of Ruth*.[8]

Ruth was written around 200 BCE by an anonymous Jew at a time when, although he did not say so directly, the author apparently believed that the Jews and the Mowabites should be working together against the common Seleukid enemy. Its heroine was a woman of the hated Mowabite tribe. The story was set in the time of the Judges. A Jewish man and his wife and two sons migrated to Mowab to escape a famine. While there, one of the sons married a local girl, a dirty infidel bitch named Ruth (*Ruwth*). The man and his sons died, leaving Ruth and her mother-in-law, Naomi, as widows with no means of support. Naomi recognised that her only chance

---

8. The following paragraphs parallel chapter 13, 'Lost in Non-Translation,' in Isaac Asimov's *The Tragedy of the Moon* (NY, 1973).

of survival lay in returning to Judah. However, knowing how a Mowabite woman would be treated by the Jews, she urged Ruth to remain in Mowab. Ruth loved Naomi, and answered, 'Where you go, I go' (RUTH 1:16).

Jewish law required that, when a man died childless, his nearest male relative marry the man's widow in order to keep his name from dying. The nearest relative of Ruth's husband was a racist who was as likely to marry a Mowabite woman as a Ku Klux Klansman was likely to marry a black woman. The next-closest relative, however, was Bowaz, who won admiration from some quarters and contempt from others by fulfilling his obligation under the levirate law to marry his kinsman's foreign widow and produce a son who would be the legal offspring of Ruth's first husband, obligated to preserve his name by ancestor-worship.

The climax of the book was that Ruth indeed bore Bowaz's son, and Naomi's friends told her, 'The child will renew your life and cherish you in your old age; for your daughter-in-law who loves you, who has proven better to you than seven sons, has borne him' (4:15). In a culture in which sons were considered a blessing and daughters a burden, such praise for a hated shiksa was unprecedented. But in case his beautiful parable about the humanity of gentiles should fall on deaf ears, the author of Ruth added a clincher: Ruth and Bowaz turned out to be the great-grandparents of King David.

Few Jewish sacred writings escaped interpolation, and Ruth was no exception. Even though the story centred on Bowaz's willing acceptance of his obligation to sire a son who would bear the patronym of a dead kinsman (whereas Tamar had been obliged to trick Yahuwdah into fulfilling the same obligation), an interpolator added a genealogy borrowed from 1 Chronicles (2:5-15), that traced David's descent from Yahuwdah's son Parets through Bowaz, rather than through Makhlown, for whom Bowaz was a mere biological surrogate (RUTH 4:18-22). The original author's point was that, had Bowaz not married a Mowabite woman in fulfilment of the law, David would never have been born. If the Towrah could require a Jew to marry a Mowabitess, then surely the Jewish hatred of Mowabites was monstrous. To think otherwise was to label the Towrah imperfect, and that could not be.

Ruth was not a total loss. Because it allegedly traced the ancestry of David, it was eventually incorporated into the Judaeo-Christian bible. Perhaps its message that trans-Jordanians are humans will one day get through to fanatics who believe that a military victory in 1967 was engineered by a god. But it failed to promote the Jewish-Mowabite friendship that was its author's objective. Within a couple of generations of the composition of Ruth, the Jews had completed the extermination of the Mowabites implicitly sanctioned by Deuteronomy. And by the time of Jesus the Nazirite, xenophobia was more firmly entrenched than ever. The only difference was that the new Mowabites were the Samaritans.

Ptolemaic and Seleukid overlordship exposed the Jews to many new myths, Egyptian, Persian and Greek. Besides Hades and Pan, these included conflicting concepts of a Judgement and an afterlife. Thanks to the Yahwist's Adam and Eve fable, the Jews had regarded death as Yahweh's final, terrible punishment that returned all mortals to the nothingness whence they came. Now they learned of the Egyptian Judgement, in which dead shades were tried before Osiris and those found wanting were consumed by the crocodile-god while the just were granted a bodyless immortality. They learned of Zarathustra's Purgatory (which Jesus the Nazirite later converted into the Christian Hell by making the torture permanent), where the wicked were tortured with flamethrowers until their souls were fully purified. And they learned of the Greek Tartaros, a cold, damp underworld in which the shades of all who died were doomed to spend eternity.

Tartaros, the Jews learned, was not entirely egalitarian, despite the lack of a Judgement as such. While the wicked were not snuffed out as in Egypt, or purged by torture as in Persia, neither were they permitted to join the Heroes in the Isles of the Blessed where at least the sun still shone. And for particularly notable offenders such as Tantalos, who had distributed the body of a sacred king for consumption by non-initiates, there were punishments worse than boredom. Tantalos was obliged to stand in water up to his chin, ever tired but unable to lower his head lest he drown.[9]

Tartaros was worse for some than for others; but it was the ultimate unpleasant destination for all human shades. The author of the *Odyssey* expressed the Greeks' attitude toward life-after-death when he had the incomparable warrior Akhilleus declare that he would rather be a poor farmer's slave on earth than the greatest prince in Tartaros. While the Greeks and Jews accepted Homer's evaluation, the seventeenth-century Christian poet John Milton did not. In *Paradise Lost* (1:263), Milton put into the mouth of his hero Satan the line: *'Better to reign in Hell than serve in Heaven.'*

Exposure to the myths of the occupying powers led to the formation of Jewish sects that adopted some of the foreign beliefs, but otherwise remained strictly orthodox in their acceptance of every teaching attributed to Moses and the spokesmen. Possibly out of fear that they would be labelled heretics, the new sects tended to be sticklers for the letter of the law, even refusing to administer medication to the sick on the Seventh where such medication could safely be delayed until the evening. The earliest such sect was the *Khasidiym*, 'the pious.'

The Khasidites appear to have come into existence early in the third century BCE, and to have lasted almost a century before splitting into two

---

9. In a later version, Tantalos was ever thirsty but unable to drink because, every time he lowered his head, the water receded.

opposing factions. Khasidism was in effect Jewish Zoroastrianism. The Khasidites equated the Zoroastrian God of Light, Ahura Mazda, with the Jewish Yahweh-Elohiym, and the Zoroastrian Prince of Darkness, Ahriman, with Yahweh's formerly female antagonist, the Satan.

Around 200 BCE, a large proportion of the Khasidite rank and file found their leaders moving in directions that they were unwilling to follow. Zoroastrianism had penetrated Judaism, and the result had been the Khasidites. Also, the genesis of the Khasidites had triggered the formation of an anti-Khasidite, or more accurately anti-Zoroastrian, party dedicated to the preservation of Jewish orthodoxy against the Persian heresy. These were the 'Descendants of Zadok,' *Tsadowkiym*, Sadducees. Now Buddhism, with its communism, celibacy and other masochism, and rejection of family, began to influence the Khasidite leadership. The majority of Khasidites, rejecting Buddhist masochism, separated from Khasidism, thereafter calling themselves the Separatists, *Parushiym*, Pharisees.

The remnant of the original Khasidites, who became more and more buddhistic without becoming any less Zoroastrian, appear to have undergone a sixty-year dark age, or period of obscurity. Then around 140 BCE, having adopted a buddhistic hierarchy headed by a Rabbi (teacher) who had all the status and authority of a spokesman, they reemerged with a new name: the Essenes, 'saints.' By the beginning of the first century BCE there were no more Khasidites, just Pharisees, Essenes and Sadducees. In modern terms, the Pharisees can be equated with liberals, the Sadducees with conservatives, and the Essenes with communists.

The Pharisees accepted the concept of an afterlife. They rejected the Egyptian modification of a Judgement as superfluous, since in the afterlife all Jews would be raised and all gentiles exterminated. To adherents of the comparatively recent dogma, invented to end wars that were destroying all participants, that all mythologies contain part of the Truth and can lead to Salvation, this may sound worse than xenophobic; but it was a logical extension of the mythology invented by the Yahwist. Since the Jews were already Yahweh's Chosen Nation, and Yahweh had evolved (in Jewish minds) into the One True God, naturally the Jews alone would be saved without the necessity of any further Judgement. The fifteenth-century Christian king of England who burned a man to death for declaring that a conscientious Muslim or Jew could go to Heaven, obviously had a similar belief; and the Roman Catholic church teaches that there is no salvation for ex-Catholics to this day.

The Pharisees did not accept the Greek idea of the afterlife as a permanent bodyless existence in a place that was at best imperfect. The Pharisee *sheowl*, underworld, became a place where the soul, the personified breath, of Jew and gentile alike, resided after death to await the coming of the messiah.

On that day the Jews would be bodily raised to a deathless existence in a new Jerusalem ruled by David's anointed descendant. The gentiles would be consumed in a fire that was the equivalent of the soul-eating crocodile-god of Egypt.

There would, however, be a time lapse between the messiah's first appearance on earth and the Resurrection. The messiah's first task would be what it had always been, to drive out the Romans (formerly the Hasmoneans, formerly the Seleukids, formerly the Ptolemies, formerly the Persians, formerly the Babylonians). He would then rule a Jewish kingdom in a predominantly gentile world as an absolute theocrat (analogous to Imam Khomeini or the medieval Popes) for precisely one thousand years. At the end of that time the world would end, *sheowl* would open, and all Jews past and present would begin a deathless life in a gentile-free new Eden won for them by the second Adam. Belief in a messianic millennium followed by the end of the world was not limited to the Pharisees.

Quite hostile to the Pharisees were the Sadducees. These had no belief in an afterlife, and first became a political power when King Hyrkanos I converted to their cause around 110 BCE. Although incompatible, the two sects each contributed significantly to the Judaeo-Christian bible. Eastern Orthodox bibles now contain eight books by Sadducees (*Proverbs, Job, 1 Esdras, Song of Solomon, Wisdom of Solomon, Ecclesiastes, Sirach* and *1 Maccabees*), and five by Pharisees (*Daniel, Baruch, 2 Esdras, Tobit* and *2 Maccabees*). So evenly were the sects balanced that in 67 BCE a civil war between Hyrkanos II, a Pharisee, and his brother Aristoboulos II, a Sadducee, could only be resolved by Roman intervention. Pompeius Magnus, petitioned for support by both parties, chose to end the squabbles in Judah by the same means that an earlier generation of Romans had used to end the squabbles in Greece in 140 BCE: annexation.

With the coming of the Romans, the Sadducees collaborated with the occupying power to a degree that made Jeremyah look like Hereward the Wake. Sadducees dominated the Sanhedrin, but were held in little esteem by the Pharisee-supporting Jewish masses. It is certain that all passages in the Christian gospels that showed Jesus vituperating the Pharisees, whose beliefs he shared, were originally written of the Sadducees.

The sect that contributed most to the professed beliefs and observable practices of Christianity was the Essene. The Essenes accepted totally Siddhartha Gautama's teaching that sex was evil, and became celibate masochists. Unwilling to risk contamination by living among a society that recreated regularly with no sense of guilt, the new sect carried the Pharisees' idea of saintly separation to its logical conclusion and moved to an isolated spot on the shore of the Dead Sea called Qumran, where they formed a unisexual, communistic community that believed all copulators and property owners to be destined for Gehenna, the Pharisee/Essene Purgatory.[10]

The Essene founder called himself the Righteous Rabbi, a title close enough to Jeremyah's *Yahweh's Righteousness* to indicate that he saw himself as the messiah of Jeremyah's prophecy. His followers accepted him as such, and did not abandon that belief even after his execution in 103 BCE. Rather than acknowledge that their messiah was totally and permanently *dead*, the Essenes maintained for the 170 more years that they remained in existence that their Righteous Rabbi would fulfil his messianic function of deposing the Hasmoneans (or, after 63 BCE, driving out the Romans) and making himself king of Judah, at the time of his 'Second Coming.'

The Righteous Rabbi's name seems to have been Yeshu (Greek: Iesous; Latin: Jesus), the Aramaic equivalent of Yahuwshua. The Talmud's declaration that, *On the eve of Pesakh, Yeshu ha-notsriy was hanged* by Alexander Yanay, can only be a hybrid of the Nazirite's execution by Pilatus and the Essene's execution by Yanay, and it seems incredible that the two events could have been confused unless the two messiahs shared a common name (SANH. 43a).

Further evidence that the Righteous Rabbi was named Jesus can be found in one of the letters written by Paul of Tarsus to the Nazirites at Corinth. Paul, a nominal disciple of the Nazirite messiah, warned the Corinthians against proselytisers who preached a different Jesus from the Jesus Paul preached (2 COR. 11:4). So far as is known, at the time that Paul wrote only three sects were touting their respective dead leaders as Messiah and promoting each one's Second Coming. They were the Nazirites, whose messiah was Jesus bar Joseph; the Immersers, whose messiah was John[11]; and the Essenes, whose Righteous Rabbi must have been the Jesus against whom Paul warned.

It was the Essenes who first turned Sheowl (the underworld) into Gehenna (Purgatory, later Hell). The original Gehenna was a cemetery, sacrificial baby-burning furnace and garbage dump in the Valley of Hinnom (*gey Hinnom*) just outside Jerusalem.[12] Pseudo-Isayah had written of the carcasses of Yahweh's enemies lying unburied in Gehenna that: *Their worm will not die, nor will their fire be extinguished. They are to remain an abhorrence to all flesh* (ISA. 66:24). Jesus, quoting pseudo-Isayah's words, agreed that they referred to the inhabitants of Gehenna (MARK 9:47), but followed

---

10. Detailed evidence for the Buddhistic and Zoroastrian origins of the Essenes, and the Essene origin of Christian moral philosophy, can be found in Martin Larson's *The Essene-Christian Faith*.

11. While Paul was preaching Jesus at Ephesus, Apollos was simultaneously preaching John the Immerser as Messiah (ACTS 18:24 to 19:3; 1 COR. 1:12).

12. 4 KGS. 23:10; 2 CHR. 28:3; 33:6; JER. 7:31-32; 19:2; 19:6; 32:35; 1 ENO. 27:2; 48:9; 90:26.

the Essene *Book of Enoch* in seeing those inhabitants as tortured souls rather than inanimate bodies, and Gehenna as a metaphysical Sheowl with flame-throwers rather than a physical dumping ground.

Essene moral and ethical teaching, which later became Christian teaching, was self-contradictory. On the one hand it introduced to the western world an enlightened code of interpersonal behaviour similar to that taught to the Persians by Zarathustra in the early seventh century BCE, and to the Chinese by Confucius in the late sixth century BCE. The Righteous Rabbi taught his followers a form of the Zoroastrian dictum: *Do not do to another that which is hateful to yourself.* Essene scrolls found at Qumran, written two hundred years before the earliest of the Christian gospels, contained all of the admonitions to altruistic love for one's fellow sectarians that the anonymous author of the gospel known as *Matthew* put into the mouth of Jesus in the fictitious Sermon on the Mount. Since the Essene pantheon of good and bad angels, as delineated in *Enoch* and *Jubilees* and still accepted by Christians, was taken almost verbatim from the *Zend Avesta* of Zarathustra, it is a reasonable assumption that the Essenes' duplication of Zoroastrian ethical philosophy was likewise no coincidence.

On the other hand, the teachings that the Essenes derived from Siddhartha Gautama ('Buddha'), whose disciples had penetrated as far as Egypt, were masochistic and anti-human, and equated sexual recreation with the promulgations of the goddess-turned-devil. The Essenes rejected Zarathustra's classification of celibacy as a cardinal vice, and accepted Gautama's delusion that deliberate joy-deprivation was a virtue.

Gautama was not the first man to glorify sexual abstinence. Almost from the time of the Big Discovery, virginity had been acclaimed as admirable—for women. Since a woman was only entitled to breed with her legal owner, it followed that a goddess who had never been assigned a husband must be a virgin. And since anything pertaining to a god was regarded as good by definition (and in modern mythology, still is), virginity likewise became a trait to admire.

Celibacy for men was a quite different proposition. The earliest mythology to preach such a creed, in the second millennium BCE, was Brahmanism. As with all new taboos at the time of their invention, the Brahmanas' argument in favour of celibacy stemmed from sheer expedience.

The Brahmanas, the conquering priestly caste who had subjugated India, allowed themselves four wives. Subordinate castes were allowed, respectively, three, two and one wife per man. Untouchables, the outcaste masses whose parents had broken the Brahmanas' mating laws, were permitted no wives at all. As the proportion of outcastes in the Indian population grew in succeeding generations (the offspring of an outcaste woman was automatically an outcaste, regardless of the status of her impregnator), the possibility of a peasants' revolt grew into a real and present danger. The Brahmanas therefore decreed that celibacy was the supreme virtue (except for themselves, of course), and that outcastes who lived blameless celibate lives, or in other words did not try to take the Brahmanas' women by violent revolution, would be reincarnated in their next lives as members of copulating castes. Brahmanism was, in fact, very much an early form of the modern chainletter hoax, with the men at the bottom of the social hierarchy surrendering all available women to those higher up in the hope of being themselves at the top of the copulation pyramid in a future life.

A similar tactic of promising his womanless rank and file pie in the sky when they died, so that he and his lieutenants could appropriate all desirable women for their harems, was used by Mohammed. Mohammed promised his followers seven heavens in which:

> They are to cohabit with demure virgins . . . as beauteous as corals and rubies . . . full-breasted maidens for playmates . . . in the gardens of delight. . . . They're to lie face to face on jewelled couches, and be serviced by immortal youths . . . young boys, their personal property, as comely as virgin pearls. . . . We created the houris and made them virgins, carnal playmates for those on the right hand. . . . We are going to wed them to dark-eyed houris.[13]

Each Muslim man, in exchange for a lifetime of mindless obedience, was to be rewarded after death with an unspecified number of pretty boys to bugger, plus eight heavenly houris, each more phallus-raising than the others and each endowed with the capacity to grow a new hymen after each bout of sexual recreation. The male chauvinist Muslim could thus satisfy his virginity fetish by deflowering them over and over again, for eternity. When one compares Mohammed's gardens of delight with the Christian heaven of harps and celibacy, it becomes apparent why significant numbers of Christian men turn Muslim while conversions the other way are almost nonexistent.

It was Gautama who first spread the perversion of self-inflicted celibacy beyond India. Gautama, a renegade Brahmana who was either impotent or more subtly ill, taught that *all* sexual intercourse, even when strictly pro-creational and performed in the missionary position as a duty to the Party while thinking of the Motherland, was evil beyond forgiveness, as was the owning of even the tiniest piece of private property. The highest virtue, to Gautama, was the renunciation of wives, parents, siblings, children, home and occupation to become a wandering parasite. Gautama's teachings were accepted *in toto* by the Essenes, who remained celibate communists for the

---

13. *The Koran*, 55:56; 55:58; 78:33; 56:12; 52:16-17, 24; 56:35-38; 52:20. Mohammed's houris appear to have been based on Norse mythology's valkyries.

whole of their two-century existence.

Jesus the Nazirite, a renegade Essene who abandoned the Righteous Rabbi and founded his own neo-Essene sub-sect when he became convinced that *he* was the messiah, was particularly vehement in his denunciation of family ties and private property.[14] He organised a sect of fanatic communists whom he called 'The Poor' (Ebionites). The Ebionites survived until the fifth century CE as the only true practitioners of Jesus' teachings. They reemerged in the sixteenth century as the Anabaptists, and more recently as the Hutterites, Mennonites and Amish, sects that still practise the uncompromising communism that Jesus considered necessary for 'salvation.'[15] Whether Jesus practised Gautama's other innovation, celibacy, is a question that will be considered in a later chapter.

The ultimate rationalisation of self-inflicted joy-deprivation was penned in the third century CE by a Christian whose thinking was pure Essene. Clement of Alexandria, a believer in the Essene concept of demon-possession, wrote:

> But the reason why the demons delight in entering into men's bodies is this. . . . Being spirits, and having desires after meats and drinks and sexual pleasures . . . and lacking organs fitted for their enjoyment, they enter into the bodies of men in order that, getting organs to minister to them, they may obtain . . . sexual pleasure by means of men's members. Hence, in order to put the demons to flight, the most useful help is abstinence and fasting and suffering of affliction. For . . . it is manifest that they are put to flight by suffering.[16]

Even a Pope who offered such a rationalisation of masochism today would be recognised as a very sick man. The Christian churches now play down Clement's role in the formulation of their mythology, but they have never repudiated it. To this day, Christian priests and nuns practise lifelong sexual masochism (or pretend to), lest they unwittingly provide pleasure for a demon that might be tempted to inhabit their bodies.

In a society conditioned to regard masochism as a virtue, it is perhaps no surprise that the equation of orgasm-deprivation with god-pleasing is seldom questioned; but the acceptance of such a teaching at a time when Gautama's philosophy was new to non-Asiatics, in a society in which no man needed to be womanless, could only have occurred in an atmosphere

---

14. See especially *Luke* 14:26 and *Mark* 10:25.

15. The Ebionites never ceased to be Jews, and regarded the Christian gospels as infidel documents. The later communistic Jesus sects, on the other hand, viewed themselves as Christians, not bound by Jewish laws and customs. That difference is probably more significant than the similarities.

16. *Clementine Homilies* 9:10.

of intense anti-fertility-god fanaticism. As self-contradictory as it was, celibacy was accepted by the Essenes as an extension of the subjugation of women (and goddesses) as the privately-owned breeding stock of the male ruling classes.

Free sexual recreation with as many fellow-worshippers as one could accommodate had been a predominant feature of the Morning-Star-god(dess)'s planting festivals since the time of the Big Discovery. Now that Venus (Khazazel) had become the Satan, and since recreation had been practised as an act of worship to her/him, it came to be viewed with suspicion. The combination of buddhistic teaching/preaching and the imminence of the end of the world (prior to the designated messiah's execution in 103 BCE) tipped the scale in favour of rejecting the Satan's delightful invention. As a consequence the *orgia*, the sacred celebration of a fertility god's rites, came to be viewed as profane. The English word *orgy* now connotes something indecent, even though the Greek *orgia* is still sometimes used to mean a secret religious rite.

During the Righteous Rabbi's lifetime all Essenes lived in isolated communes, or perhaps in the single commune at Qumran, as buddhistic celibate monks. Following their leader's execution and his failure to manifest a Second Coming within a reasonable time, the sect formed a secular wing whose members were allowed, even encouraged, to live among sinners (*essene* meant 'saint'), lead a normal life, and breed more Essenes. They were not, however, to engage in recreational copulation. Copulation was a necessary evil that could be performed · only within marriage, and only for the purpose of procreation. It was not to be *enjoyed*. The modern Christian god who created fifty joys only to declare forty-nine of them illegal was essentially the creation of the Essenes.

The celibate Essenes remained at Qumran in obedience to Second Isayah's admonition: *Prepare in the desert a pathway for the expected one* (ISA. 40:3), until they were routed by the Romans in the first Jewish War, 66-70 CE. Like all organisms that failed to breed, they eventually became extinct. As unresisting noncombatants it is unlikely that they were slaughtered by the Romans, but the last inhabitants of Qumran would certainly have been the last Essenes.

The secular Essenes either became or were absorbed by the Nazirites, a neo-Essene commune of men and women established in Jerusalem by Jesus' brother Jacob at about the time of Jesus' death. Jesus' leading disciples, including Peter and the sons of Zebedyah, joined the Nazirites and accepted the leadership of Jacob. Other disciples apparently rejected Jacob's organisation on the ground that Jacob had rejected his brother's messianic claims during Jesus' lifetime. They remained Ebionites, differing from the Nazirites only in name and leadership. The Nazirites also became extinct in the fifth century CE, leaving as the self-proclaimed followers of Jesus only the Christians, adherents of a Greek mystery religion founded by Paul of Tarsus that had no more connection with Jesus than the John Birch Society has with John Birch.

Although agreed on almost everything else, and united in their scorn for the this-world-only beliefs of the Sadducees, the Pharisees and Essenes differed strongly in their attitude toward sexual recreation. Since Yahweh had created humankind male and female, the Pharisees reasoned, then the recreation between them that produced children must have been part of his Plan. As such it could not have been, as the Essenes maintained, the disobedience for which Adam and Eve were deprived of immortality; nor could its avoidance be deemed virtuous. It was to refute the Essene glorification of behaviour as unnatural and perverted as sexual abstinence that the Pharisees proclaimed, and later wrote in the Talmud: *Anyone who causes himself anguish by abstinence from something he desires is to be deemed a sinner* (NAZIR 19a). The Christian monk Jovinian, who died *c.* 405 CE, agreed with the Pharisees, declaring that such masochism as celibacy and fasting could not possibly be pleasing to a god who was not a sadist.

The Jewish historian Flavius Josephus, who described the Pharisees, Sadducees and Essenes in his *Jewish Antiquities*, named one additional sect, the Zealots. He also described the Iskariots ('Assassins'),[17] but declared them to be not a separate sect but merely a radical wing of the Zealots. That equation was supported by the later writer, Hippolytos: *They were called Zealots by some, Sicarii by others.*[18]

The Zealots were founded in 6 CE by Judas (*Yahuwdah*) of Galilee in reaction to the deposition of the Herodian Ethnarch, Arkhelaos, and the consequent imposition of direct Roman rule and Roman taxation. It was perhaps no surprise that Judas should have led the opposition to direct Roman rule, since it had been Judas's father Khezekyah who had led the armed opposition to Roman suzerainty in 48 BCE, when direct Roman rule had been first imposed by Julius Caesar. Josephus called Khezekyah a bandit,[19] but that had not been the view of his contemporaries. Judas and his daggermen, disdaining to wait any longer for an overdue messiah, set out to rid Judaea of the Romans by terror, intimidation and assassination.

Like his father, who had been caught and executed by the procurator's

---

17. Latin: *sica*=dagger; *sicarius*=daggerman, assassin. *Sicarius*, transliterated into Aramaic, became *iskariot*.

18. *Philosophumena* 9:26.

19. *Jewish Antiquities* 14:167; 17:271. Even though Khezekyah's anti-Roman campaign coincided with one of the years *Daniel* could have been interpreted as prophesying the appearance of the messiah, and two of Khezekyah's descendants, Menakhem and bar Kokhba, claimed the messianic title, there is no evidence that Khezekyah ever did so.

son (later king) Herod, Judas was equally quickly dispatched on a Roman cross. His sect, however, survived, under the leadership of his sons and grandsons, until 74 CE. That Jesus the Nazirite's treasurer, Judas the Iskariot, son of Simon, was the grandson of Judas of Galilee, is not impossible, but no evidence survives to support such a speculation. The original Judas's sons, Jacob and Simon (who *may* have been the Simon the Zealot who was Jesus' disciple), rebelled again in 46 CE and were caught and crucified.[20]

When the first Jewish War broke out in 66 CE, Judas's grandson Menakhem led the Zealots at the beginning, but was assassinated for being as much of a tyrant as the tyrants that the revolution was trying to overthrow. Jerusalem was sacked and the Temple burned by Titus in 70 CE, but the Iskariots, led by Judas's grandson Eleazar, held out at Masada for four more years. The sect of Zealots or Iskariots came to an end when Eleazar, faced with certain defeat and aware that terrorists could not expect the same mercy as the inhabitants of Jerusalem, ordered the murder and suicide of every man, woman and child left in Masada fortress.[21] But Judas's family survived to produce bar Kokhba.

Josephus made no mention of the Christians, whom he would have viewed as gentiles, or the Nazirites and Ebionites, whom he would have equated with the Essenes, among the schools of Jewish philosophy; nor did he mention the Immersers, also neo-Essenes. Belief in a messiah was common to all Jews, and the identification of an individual who had been hanged, crucified or beheaded as the messiah did not strike Josephus as in itself the mark of a separate philosophy. Had the adherents of a particular messiah equated their dead leader with Yahweh, or even labelled him a lesser god, that would certainly have constituted a unique creed that could not have failed to attract Josephus's notice; but in the late nineties CE, when *Mark* and perhaps *Matthew* had been written but *Luke* and *John* had not, no such creed existed. Both the Jewish Nazirites, whose leaders had been Jesus' brother Jacob and his disciple Peter, and the gentile Christians, whose leaders had been Paul and Stephen, viewed their executed messiah as simply the prophesied King of the Jews, the successor and equal of King David. The pagan cult of a resurrected Jewish god did not arise until 130 CE, by which time Josephus was dead.

While all Jewish sects demanded that unmarried women remain virginal, only the Essenes expected unmarried men to do so. Since not every man could afford a *shiksa* slavegirl, the most common method of satisfying the body's need for regular orgasm in the past had been to patronise the temple nuns, priestesses whose ever-open legs were in effect altars to Ashtaroth.

---

20. *Ibid.* 20:102.
21. Josephus, *Jewish War* 7:399.

Jewish customers of the nuns had rationalised away the holy women's sacramental function by viewing them as common prostitutes. The compulsory offering that patrons of the temple were required to make to the goddess, the Jews regarded as a harlot's fee for services rendered.

Temple nuns were no more prostitutes than participants in modern Jesus-eating rituals are cannibals. Historians who describe the nuns as 'sacred prostitutes' are, perhaps unintentionally, comparing another culture's religion unfavourably with their own. The nun's transubstantiation in the sacrament of Holy Fornication into the very body of the goddess was as real to the worshippers of the various fertility goddesses as the transubstantiation of bread and wine into the body and blood of a dead Jew is real to the aforementioned Jesus-eaters. The worshipper inserted his phallus into an *asherah* that was the substance of the goddess while retaining the accidents of the nun.

Similarly, since the nun was the bride of the saviour-god who was the Mother's son and lover, at the moment a fornication was consummated the male worshipper was transubstantiated, for her, into the invisible Bridegroom. The nun was thus a perpetual virgin whose copulations were always with her bridegroom the god, even though to nonbelievers such as the Jews she appeared to be spreading her legs for all comers.

Temple fornication differed qualitatively from the secular prostitution that inevitably followed once women learned that men could be persuaded to pay for recreation that was as enjoyable to the seller as to the buyer. Perhaps the best analogy would be to compare a devout Jesus-eater with a boy eating an identical piece of bread with peanut butter. Nonetheless, in societies that had long since developed an adultery concept, the idea of a respectable privately-owned woman selling herself to strangers became a cause for disquiet. It mattered not that the fornication was a sacred duty, and in some cultures required of all women. In Babylon, for example, Herodotos reported that: *Every woman who is a native of the country must once in her life go and sit in the temple of Aphrodite and there give herself to a strange man* (HIST. 1:199).

While it was recognised as necessary that a nun, temporary or permanent, do her duty to the goddess, it came to be realised that there was no reason why an upper-class woman, forced to copulate with a lower-class man, should thereafter be recognised by him as a woman he had humbled. The custom consequently developed of hiding the nun's face behind a veil. It was by wearing the trademark of a temple nun that Tamar was able to seduce Yahuwdah and bear him the ancestor of David: *When Yahuwdah saw her, he thought she was a nun, because she had covered her face* (GEN. 38:15).

Since the veil was a symbol of the nun's respectability, evidence that she copulated for piety rather than profit, at least one society, the Assyrian, forbade secular prostitutes from likewise concealing their faces: *A common harlot shall not veil herself; her head shall be uncovered.*[22] The veil that allowed a woman to sell sexual recreation without being recognised was eventually abandoned by most societies, but it continues to feature in Christian bride-bestowing rituals,[23] and some Muslim countries require women to wear it for life.

In most parts of the world fertility nuns eventually degenerated from surrogate brides whose recreational needs were fulfilled by casual worshippers, into metaphysical brides conditioned to believe in a divine husband while actually practising the perversion of sexual abstinence. Rome's priestesses of Vesta were required to be literally virgins, while the world's largest salvation mythology imposes a similar condition on its priestess 'brides of the god' to this day. Considering Christianity's Zoroastrian roots, this is quite an irony. Zarathustra wrote: *This is the worst deed that men and tyrants do, namely, when they deprive maids, that have been barren a long time, of marrying and bringing forth children.*[24]

But in the fertile crescent in the centuries between David and Jesus, the temple nun retained her original function. The Redactor's initial attempt (LEV. 20:5) to ban fornication as false-god worship had probably met little success. But with the evolution of Ashtaroth into the Satan, the vocally orthodox began condemning fornication, sacramental nun-tupping, as a breach of the first Commandment to worship no god but Yahweh. Paul of Tarsus, whose belief in the Nazirite messiah did not make him any less a Pharisee, was particularly hostile to the practice (1 COR. 5:1-13); while another Pharisee, equating behaviour that was deemed virtuous at a fertility festival with everyday practice, bewailed: *The son had intercourse with the mother, and the father with the daughter, and all of them committed adultery with their compatriots' wives.*[25]

The inevitable consequence of the institution of a fornication taboo was that the gentile monopoly on mercenary recreation had to end. If Jews were to be persuaded not to offer cash and phallus to a goddess, then it was necessary that they be permitted to recreate under conditions that

---

22. Quoted in Tannahill, *Sex in History*, p. 81. Tannahill has been included in the bibliography mainly for her entertainment value. Her book is so riddled with false facts and indefensible guesses as to be virtually worthless. In quoting the line above, she imagined that prostitutes were the only Assyrian women who did *not* wear veils.

23. Christian bride-bestowing rituals clearly confirm the status of women as property, by having the presiding theocrat ask, 'Who gives this woman to this man?' The 'giver' is not always the woman's original owner, her father; but it is always a man.

24. *Zend Avesta*, Ashi Yast 10:59.

25. *Psalms of Solomon* 8. A slightly different translation can be found in Platt, *Forgotten Books of Eden*, p. 111.

were not sinful. Thus arose the Magdalenes,[26] Jewish prostitutes who were looked down on by the ruling classes but were tolerated because they provided a sin-free outlet for men who might otherwise fornicate.[27]

By 30 CE the fornication taboo was entrenched. The homosexuality taboo was entrenched. The nakedness taboo was entrenched. The glorification of celibacy was entrenched, with Essenes being admired even by non-Essenes. Monotheism was entrenched; despite their unrelated origins, Yahweh of Judaea and Allah of Galilee were accepted throughout the Jewish world as the same god. The Romans had been in power for a century. The Messiah was expected at any moment. The Essene monks were still living in their isolated commune at Qumran awaiting his (second) coming. Other Jews, familiar with the Sanhedrin's calculation based on *Daniel*, believed that the messiah was already thirty-four years old and living in Bethlehem.

The Zealots were murdering Jews in the Temple for paying taxes to Rome. The land abounded with mystics, spokesmen and would-be messiahs, of whom the most notable was John the Immerser. Into such a society stepped or was thrust an illiterate Galilean carpenter and demagogue who was not born in Bethlehem and was not descended from King David, but who nonetheless came to believe that he was the messiah: Joseph's son Jesus.

---

26. The Aramaic word *Magdalene* commonly meant prostitute. The Mary Magdalene of the Christian gospels is therefore traditionally regarded by Christians as having been a recreational lady, even though this was nowhere explicitly stated. Mary's surname is sometimes interpreted as referring to a native of Magdala, a village not far from Jesus' hometown of Capernaum.

27. The much later belief that prostitution was *sinful* led to the passing of anti-prostitution laws even in countries where such laws clearly violate constitutional prohibitions of any *law pertaining to the establishment of a religion.*

Fourteen

Requiem for a Dead Jew

That the scribes and Pharisees are presented in the Gospels as Jesus' chief opponents, makes it difficult for even the shrewdest reader to realize how deep a deception has been practised upon him.

Robert Graves, *The Nazarene Gospel Restored*.

In or about 5 BCE in a seaport town in Galilee, a Jewish carpenter named Yowsef tupped his twelve- or thirteen-year-old bride Miriam.[1] Nine months later, also in a seaport town in Galilee, she bore him a son whom Yowsef named after the conqueror Yahuwshua. A year or so later Miriam bore Yowsef's second son, Yaakov, the man who became Head Nazirite and possibly Head Essene, bearing his predecessor's title, *The Righteous*, and who was also the author of the *Letter of James*. Miriam and Yowsef had three further sons who lived: Yowsef, Yahuwdah and Shimeown; and at least two daughters (MARK 6:3; LUKE 4:22).

By the time the various names had been translated from primitive to late Hebrew, to Aramaic, to Greek, to Latin, to German, to English, Miriam had become Mariamne, Maria and Mary; Yaakov had become Iakob, Jacob

---

1. The earliest gospel, *Mark*, which contained no nativity myths, gave Jesus' mother the name Maria (MARK 6:3). Since the author of *Mark* cannot be accused of choosing the name to fit the myth, we can accept as probable that Miriam/Mary was indeed her name, even though the author of *John* left her nameless and gave the name Maria to her sister (JOHN 19:25).

and (in English bibles) James; and Yahuwshua had become successively Yeshu, Joshua, Iesous, and finally Jesus.

There is no reason to doubt that Jesus was Joseph's natural son. Accusations that he was illegitimate were first made seventy years after Jesus' death, when his equation in Greek eyes with the resurrected saviour-god Dionysos led an interpolator to insert a virgin-birth myth into the gospel now known as *Matthew*. Since a Christian gospel was thus made to concede, in effect, that Jesus had not been sired by his mother's husband, a Jewish writer accepted that (false) concession at face value and explained it by the most logical means. In fact Jesus died believing that Joseph was his father; Joseph died believing that he was Jesus' father; and Mary died believing that Joseph was Jesus' father. The pretence that such was not the case was first made in the reign of Trajan, when all three principals were safely dead and unable to sue for libel.[2]

The fable of the magi's visit to Jerusalem and Bethlehem was consistent with at least one previous instance of alleged magi behaviour. Seven hundred years earlier magi were said to have followed a new star to the birthplace of Zarathustra, whom they then presented with expensive gifts. And before that new stars had heralded the births of Abraham and Krishna.

The magi, Persian astrologers, would almost certainly have associated the conjunction of Jupiter and Saturn that occurred three times in 7 BCE with a preeminent birth. That they associated it with a Jewish birth is highly improbable, although they would have been familiar with the Jews' messianic expectations.

Had they travelled to Herod's court seeking a newborn King of the Jews, Herod may indeed have sent them to Bethlehem where Miykhah was thought to have prophesied that the messiah must originate (MIC. 5:2). Perhaps the magi continued their hypothetical journey to Bethlehem, where perhaps they found a newborn boy among the local aristocracy and saluted

---

2. Michael Arnheim, in *Is Christianity True?*, argues that villagers' description of Jesus in *Mark* as Mary's son rather than Joseph's son, patronymics being more normal, implies unknown paternity. There is, however, an alternative explanation. Mark was the only gospel author who may conceivably have interviewed living Nazirites. Those Nazirites would have remembered Mary as a woman who had lived among them in a place of honour for more than thirty years, whereas they had never met Joseph, who either died or disappeared before Jesus' execution. Referring to Jesus as Mary's son would have been a logical practice—especially if Joseph had divorced his wife and her resentment of him forced members of the sect to avoid mentioning his name at all cost. Since allegations of illegitimacy by the Nazirites' enemies were first made at about the same time as the virgin-birth interpolation in *Matthew*, it seems more reasonable that the former was triggered by the latter, than that it had any historical validity. In *John* (1:45), in a passage copied (as I argue in the next chapter) from a source written thirty years earlier than *Mark* by Jesus' closest companion, Jesus is called the son of Joseph.

him as King of the Jews. If they did, then the fate of the child whom they so greeted is not known. It was certainly not Jesus, who was born more than a hundred kilometres away in Galilee. As for a star being small enough to identify Jesus' house by hovering over it (MAT. 2:9-11), few today would take such a claim seriously.

The pretence that Jesus was born in Bethlehem originated with Matthew.[3] Believing that Miykhah's retroactive prophecy, that the king of Israel (David) would be born in Bethlehem, referred to the messiah, and that Jesus was the messiah, Matthew assumed that Jesus *must* have fulfilled the prophecy. He accordingly wrote: *Iesous was born in Bethlehem in Ioudaia in the days of Herodes the king* (MAT. 2:1). To get Jesus from Bethlehem to Galilee, where he was known to have originated, Matthew had him taken out of Bethlehem as a baby and, after a short stay in Egypt, taken to 'Nazareth' in Galilee when his father feared to return to his Judaean homeland (MAT. 2:22-23). The earlier writer, Mark, not having Matthew's addiction to prophecy-fulfilment at any price, made no mention of Bethlehem. He declared instead that *Iesous came from the dispersion* (nazareth) *of Galilaia* (MARK 1:9).

Matthew wrote of Jesus' father that, following his return from Egypt with the baby Jesus: *He migrated to . . . a town called Nazareth, in order to fulfil what was spoken by the prophets: 'He's to be called a Nazirite* (nazoraios)' (MAT. 2:23). Clearly Matthew did not believe that Joseph and Mary had lived in 'Nazareth' before Jesus' birth. Rather, they had been natives of Bethlehem.

Luke, on the other hand, wrote that, in compliance with the terms of the taxation decree of Augustus Caesar when Judaea was brought under direct Roman rule in 6 CE, Joseph and his pregnant wife *departed from Nazareth town in Galilaia, to Ioudaia, to David's town, which is called Bethlehem, since he belonged to the clan and family of David* (LUKE 2:4).

Since Matthew and Luke were agreed that Jesus was born in Bethlehem and taken to 'Nazareth' in Galilee as a child, their disagreement as to whether Joseph and Mary were native Judaeans who migrated to Galilee after Jesus' birth, or native Galileans who happened to be visiting Judaea at the time of Jesus' birth, may seem minor. If neither author had any reason to invent a Bethlehem birthplace, then their mutual corroboration could be deemed significant. But in fact each was aware of Miykhah's prophecy and was prepared to invent any rationalisation that would make his Galilean messiah fulfil it. Trying to explain how an itinerant preacher from Galilee could have been born in Bethlehem, Matthew and Luke both racked their

---

3. The designations *Mark, Matthew, Luke* and *John* will be used throughout to mean the anonymous authors of the gospels known by those names. For the historical persons wrongly alleged to have been the authors, Greek forms will be used: *Markos, Maththaios, Loukos, Ioannes.*

imaginations for an explanation that they could believe, and they came up with contradictory fantasies. They were not liars in the usual sense of the word. Each believed that, since the messiah *had* to be born in Bethlehem, therefore Jesus *was* born in Bethlehem. And each figured out an imaginative set of circumstances that *could have* taken him from Bethlehem to Galilee, and promptly believed that those circumstances had occurred. The truth was that Joseph and Mary were Galileans, the great-grandchildren of gentiles who had lived in Galilee when there were no Jews there, who never visited Bethlehem in their lives.

Luke's attempt to uphold the Bethlehem birthplace led him to invent a fable that was not even credible. Augustus Caesar did, in 6 CE, order a census in Judaea in order to impose Roman taxation on what had hitherto been a dependent monarchy. It seems unlikely that that census included Galilee. In Judaea, the Herodian Ethnarch Arkhelaos had been replaced by a Roman procurator. But in Galilee Herod Antipas was allowed to remain Tetrarch until 39 CE; and not until 44 CE did Galilee come under the jurisdiction of the procurator of Judaea. The man who led the rebellion against the first census was known as Judas the Galilean, and it seems unlikely that he would have been so designated unless his guerilla activities were conducted outside Galilee, in Judaea. In all likelihood the census of 6/7 CE did not even affect Joseph and Mary, as they were residents of a province still being taxed by Antipas, not by Rome.

Nonetheless, there was a census, and the probability that it did not include Galilee is peripheral. But that a journey to register in an ancestral village could have played no part, and did play no part, is self-evident. Though historians have levelled many accusations against Augustus Caesar, none has ever accused him of being stupid. Had any Jew registered as a taxpayer in one province and then travelled to his permanent residence in another province, the whole purpose of the census would have been defeated. Since Joseph lived in Galilee, it would have been the Galilean tax collectors with whom he needed to register if Caesar were to benefit. The imposition of such an absurd condition, which was certainly not imposed on any other Roman province, would in any case have been mentioned by the Roman historians, certainly by Josephus. It was recorded by Luke alone. Certainly Luke needed some way to get Mary to Bethlehem in order for Jesus to be born there; but the only conceivable explanation for his coming up with such an incredible flight of fancy is that he had heard a version of the Hindu myth that had Nanda make a journey to Mathura to pay his taxes.

The final argument against a Bethlehem birthplace concerns Jesus' age. Since Jesus was the son of Galileans whose only reason for visiting Bethlehem was to comply with the terms of the census, then either Jesus was born at the time of the census, 6/7 CE, or he was not born in Bethlehem.

Jesus was executed in 30 CE. In order to have been born in Bethlehem, he would have needed to be not older than twenty-four years at the time of his death. Yet according to the fourth gospel (JOHN 8:57), his age was estimated by observers as *not yet fifty*; and Josephus, in a now-lost passage, described Jesus as *old-looking*. It seems most unlikely that a man who looked to be over forty could in fact have been in his early twenties. Also, Luke put Jesus' age at the beginning of his public life at *about thirty*, thereby dating his birth at least four or five years earlier than the census.

Mark's declaration that Jesus came from the dispersion (*nazareth*), meaning the worldwide community of Jews outside Judaea (equivalent to *diaspora*), was misinterpreted by Matthew and Luke to mean that he came from a city called Nazareth. Matthew compounded his error by having Joseph and Mary settle in Nazareth to fulfil a prophecy that the messiah was *to be called a nazirite* (Greek: *nazoraios*; Hebrew: *naziyr*; MAT. 2:23). In fact the term *nazirite*, or *nazoraios*, had nothing to do with any city of Nazareth, since no such place existed until the fifth century CE when one was built by a Christian Emperor to whom the nonexistence of Jesus' alleged hometown was an embarrassment. (Although the site of Nazareth was occupied in the first century, there is no evidence of any village *named* Nazareth earlier than the fifth century. Since no Jew would have given a town in Galilee a name tantamount to 'Elsewhere,' that an existing village was renamed at the order of the Emperor is a logical deduction.) Rather, *nazirite* was a concept that had been in common usage for centuries before Jesus was born.

The basis of Matthew's quotation is difficult to determine, for nowhere in Jewish orthodox or Essene sacred writings was there any prophecy that the messiah should be a nazirite. The most probable explanation is that Matthew was distorting a passage in *Isaiah*. Isayah, in the days when *messiah* would have been an impossible concept because the Davidic monarchy still stood, prophesied that the captive Israelites would be rescued by a sprig (*netser*) from the root of Yishay (ISA. 11:1).

Jeremyah and Zekharyah, the inventor and first elaborator of the *messiah* concept, picked up Isayah's reference to a sprig or sprout from Yishay's family tree, but they called their respective messiahs, not *netser* but *tsemakh*, which meant the same thing. However, *netser* was phonetically almost identical with *naziyr*, nazirite, and *tsemakh* was not. Clearly it did not occur to Jeremyah or Zekharyah that *netser* was intended as a double entendre, that Isayah was prophesying that the messiah was to be a nazirite, or they would have used the same word. To Matthew, however, even the wildest interpretation of a scriptural passage was acceptable if it could make Jesus fulfil another prophecy. He read in *Mark* that Jesus came from the *nazareth*, and he read in *Isaiah* that the rescuer of the Israelites was to be a *netser*, and he turned those unrelated passages into a fulfilled prophecy.

An alternative explanation is that Matthew took a line that specifically referred to Samson (JUDG. 13:5) and applied it to Jesus. In view of the peculiar way Matthew's mind worked, that is by no means impossible.

Jesus was known throughout his public life as *the Nazirite*, a title that was even affixed to his cross. But Jesus was not a nazirite, which was, more or less, a temporary monk who had vowed to observe certain forms of self-deprivation for a specified period. Occasionally, however, a child's parents would take a nazirite vow on the child's behalf that was binding for life. Samson, for example, was committed to be a nazirite from birth (JUDG. 13:5), and a similar vow was taken by the mother of Samuel (1 SAM. 1:11). Also, Jesus' brother Jacob was a nazirite for life, the vows having been made by his parents before he was born.[4] The rules of nazirite living were finally codified by the Priestly author with his usual thoroughness around 600 BCE.

A nazirite was required, for the duration of his vow, to separate himself from secular society and devote his life to Yahweh. He was not permitted to cut his hair or consume any wine or strong drink. P made no stipulation concerning sexual deprivation, but almost certainly as Jewish society became Essene-infested the nazirite vow would have been seen as worthless if it did not match the sacred masochism of the Essenes. At the termination of his retreat the nazirite was required to shave off the hair that he had allowed to grow and burn it on the altar (NUM. 6:2-21).

The origin of the nazirite vow is revealed in that last clause. Herakles and a hundred other Mycenaean heroes had shaved their heads to avoid being recognised by an avenging ghost, and burned the locks as part of the ritual purification undertaken by all who had committed homicide. The custom had continued among the Jews long after its association with man-killing had been forgotten, and by the age of the messianic prophets the nazirite life had come to be regarded as the norm for anybody with a claim to be particularly close to Yahweh.

Jesus may have taken nazirite vows at the beginning of his career. Three months of temperence would not have been more than a newly-converted fanatic could bear. On the other hand, if Jesus was indeed the drunken whoremonger that the gospels hint, then the title of *nazirite* might well have been attached to him satirically as a mark of scorn. Since Jesus had undeniably been styled *the Nazirite*, and he was known to have drunk wine and consorted with prostitutes, the great rationaliser, Matthew, explained away Jesus' designation, *nazoraios*, by the philologically impossible alternative of making it refer to a nonexistent city called Nazareth. While all four canonical gospels agreed that Jesus was from *the nazareth of Galilee*, only Matthew and

---

4. Eusebius, *Ecclesiastical History* 2:23.

Luke, misinterpreting *Mark*, imagined *nazareth* to be the name of a city.

Jesus' actual birthplace and residence as an adult was *Kafer Nahum*, Capernaum, on the west coast of Lake Galilee. Matthew got him there by writing: *And leaving Nazareth, he went to live in Kafar Nahoum* (MAT. 4:13). Mark located Jesus' first essay into preaching in the synagogue at Capernaum (MARK 1:21). It was at Capernaum that Jesus' mother and brothers came to the seashore looking for him (MARK 3:31; MAT. 17:24). The *Gospel of the Hebrews* declared that Jesus' immersion (*baptisma*) occurred when John the Immerser happened to be in the neighbourhood, while two canonical gospels located that immersion in the Jordan river (MARK 1:9; MAT. 3:13). Capernaum was six kilometres from the Jordan. Nazareth, when it was finally built, was twenty-three kilometres from the Jordan, with mountain ranges in between. It was at Capernaum that Jesus was assessed for Antipas's taxes (MAT. 17:24-27). And when Jesus, in one of his many temper tantrums, condemned to Hades (i.e., burial) the towns that had rejected him, he gave top billing to Capernaum, declaring it to have been exalted to the skies (presumably because *he* had been born there) (MAT. 11:23); but he made no mention of any *Nazareth*, even though Luke identified Nazareth (actually it was Capernaum) as the place where an enraged mob had tried to lynch him (LUKE 4:29).

Jesus grew up in Capernaum and succeeded to his father's business (MARK 6:3; MAT. 13:55). According to Luke (4:16) he learned to read. A passage in *John*, however, while superficially supporting Luke's claim, in fact implies the opposite: *The Ioudaians were amazed, and asked, 'How does this one know how to read, never having learned?'* (JOHN 7:15). Later Talmud authors, by no means Jesus' admirers, not only accepted that Jesus was literate, but also that he was learned in canon law, and some commentators even made him a pupil of the Pharisee rabbi Hillel. The Talmud was, however, compiled at a very late date and accepted uncritically many Christian claims about Jesus that were clearly false, including his status as a learned rabbi. Since literacy in a Galilean carpenter would have been extremely rare, it seems a safe assumption that Jesus was illiterate.

No Christian gospel author offered any details of Jesus' physical appearance. While that omission cannot be taken as evidence in itself that Jesus was less than handsome, a story told by Luke sheds some light on the matter. At the synagogue in 'Nazareth' Jesus declared himself to be the fulfilment of a prophecy of Isayah. He then added, '*You're sure to recite this proverb to me, "Doctor, heal yourself"*' (LUKE 4:23). Why, one wonders, would Jesus expect his audience to react in such a manner? What was there about him that needed healing? While the canonical gospels offered no answer, later Christian writers did.

In his diatribe *Against Celsus*, the second-century Christian apologist

Origen quoted his pagan adversary's words: *Surely a god would never have such a body as yours, that is so contemptible, being subject to such numerous and considerable imperfections* (ch. 59). Origen, who offered laughable rationalisations of all of Celsus's other anti-Christian arguments, made no attempt whatsoever to dispute that Jesus' body was so stricken with 'imperfections' as to be 'contemptible.' Instead he argued that Celsus *cannot deny that if our liberator was born as we say he was* (by divine impregnation of a virgin), *that then his body had in some sense a stamp of divinity upon it.*

Origen's non-rebuttal of Celsus's description shows that, a little after 200 CE, even Christians of the Jesus-is-God school accepted Celsus's description of Jesus, found originally in a now-expurgated passage of Josephus, as accurate. Tertullian, writing in 207 CE, conceded that Jesus was misshapen: *His body was not even of honest human shape.* Clement of Alexandria described him as *ugly of countenance.* Cyril of Alexandria attributed to him a *very ugly countenance*; while Andrew of Crete declared that he had *eyebrows which meet.* Also, both *Acts* (8:32-33) and *John* (12:38) equated Jesus with Second Isayah's suffering slave (ISA. 53:1-12). And Second Isayah said of his hero: *Having neither proper shape nor beauty, lacking good looks that would have attracted him to us . . . . We regarded him as someone contaminated, plagued and afflicted by the gods.* It seems unlikely that two writers would have independently equated Jesus with such an unfortunate creature unless the physical description also matched that of Jesus.

The synoptic authors included a scene in each of their gospels in which *the appearance of his face changed* (LUKE 9:29), so that *his face shone like the sun* (MAT. 17:2), and *his garments became luminescent* (MARK 9:3). While subject to other interpretations, those passages can also be viewed as an admission by the writers that a messiah as ugly as Jesus must have had an alternative, beautiful body that he saved for special occasions. According to a medieval writer, Josephus described Jesus as an old-looking man, balding, stooped, with joined eyebrows, and approximately 135 cm (4ft 6in.) tall.[5]

Jesus' sexual orientation has been the subject of considerable speculation. Jews' obligation to marry young and breed more Jews was spelled out in the Talmud: *Elohiym utters a curse against those who remain celibate after they are twenty years of age. Those who marry at sixteen please him, and those who do so at fourteen even more* (KIDD. 29b). Yet despite the tremendous social

---

5. Or perhaps 160 cm, if Josephus was using the 53 cm special cubit, rather than the 46 cm regular cubit (quoted by Don Cupitt, *Who Was Jesus?*, chap. 1.) The suggestion that the body painted (as is now established) on the Turin shroud was a contact image of Jesus is somewhat absurd, since the image on the shroud is of a man 180 cm tall. Had Jesus been so tall he would certainly have been described as a 'giant.' The earliest acknowledgement that Jesus was misshapen was written within 35 years of his death by Paul of Tarsus (PHIL. 2:5-9).

pressure to marry, Jesus appears to have reached the age of at least thirty without ever acquiring a wife. For an ordinary Essene, planning on leaving the secular wing to join the Qumran monks, such behaviour would have been understandable. But in the first place Jesus remained a secular carpenter long after he would have departed for the monastery had such been his intention; and in the second place, his belief in his messiahship also necessarily involved the belief that he must found a dynasty.

The most commonly postulated explanation for Jesus' unmarried state, endorsed by a bishop of Oxford, is that he was homosexual. The rationale for such a position is that he allegedly travelled with twelve men, that he referred to himself as a bridegroom and his disciples as sons of the bridal chamber (LUKE 5:34), that among the twelve was one, *the disciple whom Iesous loved* (JOHN 21:20), whom he encouraged to lean on his breast at supper, and that in *Matthew* 26:50 Jesus addressed Judas as *hetaire*, a word that commonly denoted a hired catamite. In fact the homosexual thesis does not survive examination.

Jesus lived at a time when, thanks to the Priestly author, homosexuality ranked as a grade-A capital sin. While Jesus' claim, recorded in *Gospel of the Hebrews*, that in a society that recognised hundreds of victimless sins he had never sinned, need not be taken seriously, the suggestion that he indulged in a capital crime that he could not have kept hidden is untenable. No Jew would have followed a spokesman who was a known sinner. Since Jesus was constantly surrounded by his chief disciples, it follows that he could not have been homosexual without their knowledge. And since no man of more orthodox leanings would have remained with men whom he viewed as perverted and doomed to Gehenna, it follows that if Jesus was homosexual then so were all of his lieutenants.

It is here that the impossibility of keeping such a situation secret is most apparent. Jesus toured Galilee with his salvation show for several weeks, playing to capacity houses and winning a province-wide reputation as a spokesman. The slightest suspicion of deviant behaviour would have ruined him. The claim that a community of homosexuals could have remained undetected on the road in a totally intolerant society is unreasonable.

That Jesus was a practising heterosexual is more probable. Certainly he was in no position to commit adultery or fornication even if he had wanted to do so. But there was no Levitical law or cultural taboo to prevent him from accepting the services of the Jewish prostitutes who featured prominently among his camp followers. He would have been aware that he could not sin without being forced into an early retirement; but tupping a Magdalene, a common commercial prostitute, was not a sin and did not become a sin until long after Jesus' death.

There is no doubt that Jesus *preached* celibacy. As an Essene, he was bound to do so. But so did Rasputin. Had a lifetime of celibacy been possible, Jesus may have accepted it as readily as any other fanatic. Since, for a messiah destined to found a royal dynasty, it was not, he would have seen no virtue in delaying recreation to which he was predestined. His Essene upbringing no doubt caused him to view recreational tupping as an imperfection at best; but as he did not abstain from the imperfection of immoderate eating and drinking (MAT. 11:19), it would have been a trifle inconsistent for him to have abstained from the even more satisfying imperfection of copulating, especially as the Magdalenes in his company would not have charged him. That he rejected at least part of the Essene Rule is evident from his attitude toward handwashing (MAT. 15:20). In the absence of evidence that Jesus lacked normal needs, it must be assumed that such perquisites of his big-frog-in-a-little-puddle status as came his way he accepted with thanks.

Jesus was clearly something of a misfit. Long before forming his delusion that he was the messiah, he had reneged on his obligation to marry and perpetuate his father's name. Like all secular Essenes, he idealised marriage, declaring it mystical and non-repeatable (MARK 10:11-12). Yet he evidently saw that ideal as out of reach for himself. One does not need to be Sigmund Freud to speculate that Jesus' parents must have divorced while he was quite young, and that the experience left him embittered and unwilling to risk a similar broken marriage himself. The combination of his fear of marriage, his unfortunate physique, and perhaps jealousy of his younger brother Jacob who may have already been Head Essene in Jerusalem, may have created in Jesus the *I'll show the bastards* attitude that led him into the unlikely career that caused his early death.

On most day-to-day issues, however, Jesus thought and behaved as a typical man of his time, a typical Jew and a typical Essene. He believed no superstition invented by the Christians (whom he would have repudiated) after his death; but he believed every superstition that every other first-century Essene believed. He believed, for example, that the fraudulent *Daniel* was genuine prophecy (MARK 13:14). He believed that the Satan had seduced Eve and sired Cain (JOHN 8:44). He believed that the Satan's followers consisted of fallen angels and evil spirits, the latter being the souls of the giants whom the fallen angels had sired upon mortal women. He believed that those evil spirits could *possess* living human beings (just as the Homeric Greeks believed that the gods could participate in the Trojan war by *possessing* the bodies of prominent warriors).[6] And he practised the art of exorcism, now known to be a form of hypnotism used to cure the delusions of sufferers of religious hysteria.

He believed in reincarnation, including the Brahmana propaganda that

---

6. Paris by Aphrodite; Diomedes by Athena; Hektor by Ares.

low caste or birth defects could be inflicted as punishment for sins committed in a past life. When his disciples asked him if a man had been born blind because he had sinned, Jesus answered that he had not, but added the stipulation that his answer was applicable only to the specific case that had prompted the question (JOHN 9:1-3). He did not denounce the question as illogical, and even implied that some birth defects were indeed imposed as punishment for past sins.

Jesus was accused by Matthew of believing that Jonah had lived for three days inside a whale (MAT. 12:40), just as Herakles had lived for three days inside a whale, and the Mesopotamian sun-god Oannes was nightly swallowed by a whale and regurgitated in the morning. However, as that belief was put into Jesus' mouth in the context of a retroactive prophecy of his own death, an event that Jesus believed *could not* happen, the entire scene can be dismissed as Matthew's invention.[7] Beyond imagining that he was the prophesied King of the Jews, Jesus was no more committed to fanciful beliefs than any other product of his culture; but neither was he any less so.

Jesus' career, before he took it into his head to play Jerusalem, was modelled very much on that of John the Immerser, whom he encountered when John was preaching and immersing along the Jordan river in 29 CE. John had already acquired a reputation as a spokesman and possible messiah, and when he came reasonably close to Capernaum Mary urged her children to accept John's sacramental immersion for the forgiveness of their sins.

Mary's belief that sins could be washed away by immersion was decidedly Essene. The belief that forgiveness of all sins could be obtained by submitting to an initiation ritual had originated among the devotees of the Persian saviour-god Mithra, and had reached the Essenes via the same route that Zoroastrian doctrines had reached the Essenes. That John the Immerser was an Essene cannot be doubted. Mark acknowledged that John preached forgiveness of sins by immersion, that his converts practised confession, a peculiarly Essene ritual, and that John actually quoted the line from *Isaiah* that had caused the Essene monks to isolate themselves in the desert at Qumran (MARK 1:3-5). The original sin-forgiveness initiation of the Mithra-worshippers involved anointing the initiate's forehead. John substituted immersion either because anointing carried implications of royalty or because immersion was more spectacular. To a touring showman, the latter consideration would not have been insignificant. In the fourth century CE, some Christian congregations abolished immersion (*baptisma*) and substituted anointing (*khris-*

---

7. The passage in which Jesus quoted *Daniel* was also in a context that reveals it to have been the gospel author's invention, since it referred to the presence of Zealots in Yahweh's Temple in 66/67 CE. The gospels in fact contain no evidence that Jesus believed in the genuineness of either *Daniel* or *Jonah*. However, as an Essene Jesus certainly believed in *Daniel*, and as a Jew he almost certainly believed in *Jonah*.

theis). The more conservative Western-rite churches practise *christening* to this day, but misname it *baptism*, while denominations deemed radical have revived *baptism* but as often as not call it *christening*.

Jesus was reluctant to accept John's immersion: He asked them, 'How have I been disobedient, that I need to be immersed (forgiven) by him? Unless perhaps these very words constitute one of ignorance?' (Gospel of the Hebrews). That admission by Jesus that he might have sinned unwittingly (a standard Jewish belief) was later deemed incompatible with the Johannine concept of Jesus-the-god, with the consequence that the gospel in which it was recorded was excluded from the Christian canon. Yet the statement was entirely consistent with Jesus' own beliefs about himself, and of the dozens of quotations put into Jesus' mouth by his various biographers it is one of perhaps four or five that can be accepted as genuine.

Jesus did submit to John's immersion. As embarrassing as that submission was to Jesus' biographers, it was too well known for them to pretend that it had never happened. For in being immersed by John, Jesus was unequivocally acknowledging that John was his superior, empowered to forgive his sins. Beyond question he had not yet formed the conceit that he was the messiah, or he would never have allowed himself to be forgiven his sins by a mere spokesman.

Jesus seems to have experienced at the time of his immersion the kind of emotional upheaval suffered by the converts of such latter-day evangelists as Billy Graham, Leon Trotsky and Adolf Hitler. He became a preacher and immerser like John, and, also like John, gathered himself a cadre of full-time disciples.

Two of Jesus' disciples were reported to have earlier been John's disciples (JOHN 1:37), and this is not unlikely. Jesus did not begin his own career until John had been imprisoned by Herod Antipas (MARK 1:14). Men accustomed to following a journeyman-preacher would have been in the market for a new master once John was gone. However, the allegation in *John* that the Immerser encouraged his own disciples to join Jesus is untrue. John the Immerser and Jesus the Nazirite were rival messiahs, and remained so to their followers long after both were dead and buried and eaten by worms. John at no time recognised Jesus as his equal, let alone his superior.

All four canonical gospels declared that Jesus selected twelve of his disciples to be his chief lieutenants and called them ENVOYS (*apostoloi*). Scholarly opinion is that he did nothing of the sort. The Nazirite commune in Jerusalem, like all Essene communes, was administered by a Twelve after Jesus' death, and it seems probable that this was what led Jesus' biographers to assume that there had been a Twelve during Jesus' lifetime.[8] The authors

---

8. A.F. Loisy, *The Birth of the Christian Religion*, p. 373, n. 50.

of the gospels seem to have learned the names of seven of Jesus' genuine disciples, and to have invented the rest. Even though Matthew and Luke had *Mark* from which to copy, their lists of apostles were not identical with *Mark*'s or with each other's:

Mark 3:16-19	Matthew 10:2-4	Luke 6:13-16	John
Simon/Petros	Simon/Petros	Simon/Petros	Simon/Petros
Andreas/Netser	Andreas/Netser	Andreas/Netser	Andreas/Netser
Iakobos bar Zebedaios	Iakobos bar Zebedaios	Iakobos bar Zebediaos	Iakobos bar Zedebaios
Ioannes bar Zebedaios	Ioannes bar Zebedaios	Ioannes bar Zebedaios	Ioannes bar Zebedaios
Philippos	Philippos	Philippos	Philippos
Thomas	Thomas	Thomas	Thomas the (Jesus') twin
Ioudas the Iskariot	Ioudas the Iskariot	Ioudas the Iskariot	Ioudas bar Simon, the Iskariot
bar Tholomaios	bar Tholomaios	bar Tholomaios	
Maththaios		Maththaios	
(Lewis bar Halphaios)	Maththaios the tax collector	(Lewis the tax collector)	
Iakobos bar Halphaios	Iakobos bar Halphaios	Iakobos bar Halphaios	
Thaddaios	Lebbaios Thaddaios	Ioudas bar Iakobos	Ioudas
Simon the Kananite (Zealot)	Simon the Kananite (Zealot)	Simon *Zelotes* (Zealot)	Nathanael of Kana (Kananite?)

Of the fifteen names listed, only the first four and the three Zealots were probably historical disciples. The rest were invented by the synoptic authors to give continuity to the Twelve by backdating them to the time of Jesus. The hostile *Toldot Yeshu*, composed in the second century CE, knew of no Twelve, and instead credited Jesus with five disciples: *Mattathyah* ('when'); *Nakay* ('innocent'); *Netser* ('sprig'); *Buwniy* ('son'); and *Howdah* ('thanksgiving'). Of the five, only Mattathyah duplicated any name on the Christian lists, although Netser can tentatively be identified with Andreas. Andreas was a Greek name, but could have been born by a Jew with a Greek mother. The historicity of Peter (*Petros*) is not in dispute; and the tradition that his brother was also a disciple cannot reasonably be denied. Since *Andreas* was a reasonable approximation of the meaning of *Netser*, it may also be that Mark gave a historical disciple a Greek equivalent of his Jewish name.

It is tempting to equate Buwniy with bar Tholomaios or Thaddaios and, since an independent tradition could hardly have come up with three correspondences out of five by coincidence, to accept Maththaios as corroborated and therefore historical. But it must be remembered that the *Toldot Yeshu* was composed at a time when one of the Christian gospels had already acquired the name *Matthew*, so the inclusion of Mattathyah in the Jewish list was a logical move. In fact all five names were chosen for their pun value, so that the worthiness of Jesus-followers for capital punishment could be etymologically demonstrated. The five disciples, along with other information from the *Toldot Yeshu*, were later incorporated into the Talmud (SANH. 43a).

Of the canonical gospels, only *John* did not list a Twelve as such, probably because John's oldest source had not mentioned any Twelve (although his later source, *Luke*, did so). Since Mark and Luke named Lewis (Heb.: *Levi*) as a disciple but did not include him in the Twelve, there was no dispute as to the total. Mark had Lewis recruited while at a tax collector's office, and tax collectors as Lewis's houseguests. He did not, however, identify either Lewis or Maththaios as tax collectors, and he did not in any way imply that Lewis and Maththaios were the same person.

The author of *Matthew*, in making an otherwise verbatim copy of *Mark*'s recruitment scene at the tax collector's office, changed the recruit's name from Lewis to Maththaios and nowhere in his gospel mentioned any Lewis. Luke likewise copied Mark's recruitment scene, and he also made a change. Where Mark had written *Lewis of Halphaios*, Luke wrote *a tax collector named Lewis*, assuming that Lewis associated with tax collectors because he was one of them. Matthew made the same assumption, and included in his Twelve *Maththaios the tax collector*. Since the author of *Matthew* clearly equated the Lewis of *Mark*'s recruitment scene with the Maththaios of the same author's Twelve, official Christianity not surprisingly does likewise. But neither *Mark* nor *Luke* supports such an equation. And *John*, based partly on an account of Jesus' last days written by a close associate of the dead Jew, mentioned neither Maththaios nor Lewis.

Mark included in his Twelve a man with the nickname *Thaddaios*, an epithet roughly equivalent to the American idiom, 'son of a bitch.' Probably Matthew did likewise, and it was an interpolator who changed 'son of a bitch' to 'love-child,' *Lebbaios* (both nicknames imply illegitimacy). A second interpolator, intent on harmonising the two versions found in different manuscripts, gave the apostle in question the designation, *Lebbaios, known as Thaddaios*, and that was the version adopted by the 1611 *Authorized Version* but rejected by most later bibles.

Luke, even more ready than Matthew to change anything in his source that he did not like, threw out the offensive nickname and substituted a second Judas (*Ioudas*), son of an unidentified Jacob (*Iakobos*). The *Authorized Version* called him *brother of James*, in the hope of identifying him with the Judas, brother of Jacob, who wrote the *Letter of Jude*; but later bibles have corrected *brother of James* to son of James. John, using *Luke* as a source, also included Judas.

The synoptics listed an apostle named bar Tholomaios, while John mentioned a Nathanael. It has been speculated that, since *bar Tholomaios* was not a given name but a patronym, he may have been *Nathanael bar Ptolemaios*, a Jew with a Greek father. Perhaps. Certainly Nathanael does not appear to be fictitious. Probably John misinterpreted the Aramaic word *Kananaya*, Zealot, as meaning a native of Kana, and described Nathanael as such. By retaining Judas the Iskariot while substituting Nathanael the Zealot for Simon the Zealot, John wound up with two Zealots, the same number as the synoptics.

Discrepancies such as the above are no more than a historian is bound to expect in books written from forty to one hundred years after Jesus' death. In chronicles already acknowledged to be the fallible propaganda of writers not above lying to make a point, they would by no means totally destroy the writers' credibility. But in biographies that Christian mythologians tout as Revealed Truth, it is far from insignificant that the authors are revealed to have been men who neither were Jesus' disciples nor obtained firsthand information from Jesus' disciples. Nobody who had spent half a year on the road with as small a touring company as that led by Jesus could have confused the names of the alleged twelve principal supporting players.

It can be no coincidence that at least two and probably three of Jesus' disciples were Zealots. Whether Simon and Judas were father and son, as *John* (13:26) seems to imply, or whether either was descended from Judas of Galilee, we cannot know. But we can be quite sure that Jesus would not have appointed as his lieutenants members of an organisation already in revolt against Rome unless revolution was his purpose also.

Jesus began his career as a journeyman preacher, or *Galilean itinerant* as the Judaeans derogatorily called such men, in the synagogue at Capernaum. There he preached such an unfortunate sermon that he narrowly escaped being lynched (LUKE 4:28-29). His family, convinced that he had gone out of his mind, managed to persuade the mob to release him in their custody: *But when his family heard, they came to take him into custody, for they declared, 'He's gone mad'* (MARK 3:21). The consequence was that Jesus repudiated all family ties, and never again had anything to do with his mother or his brothers (MARK 3:31-35; LUKE 14:26).

Luke later pretended that Jesus' mother and brothers were among his disciples immediately following his execution (ACTS 1:14; but *cf.* JOHN 7:5), while John pretended that Jesus had maintained a close relationship with his mother until his death (JOHN 19:25-27; but *cf.* JOHN 2:4). In fact it was only after Jesus' death that the breach with his family was annulled, and the commune of Essenes led by his brother Jacob accepted Jesus as their dead messiah in place of the Righteous Rabbi, about whom there had never been a resurrection myth.

Jesus toured Galilee with his salvation show for less than a year. No rabble-rouser who whipped his audiences into frenzied expectation of an imminent declaration of independence could have survived longer. Nonetheless, details in *John* are consistent with two possible execution dates: 30 CE, a year after John the Immerser; and 33 CE, four years after the death of John; and scholars who favour the later date maintain that Jesus' faith healing career lasted three years. In fact Herod Antipas, fearful of being deposed by Rome if he appeared to be soft on revolutionary preachers, arrested and executed John the Immerser within weeks of his opening performance. As soon as he learned that a new reputed messiah (opposition king) had arisen to take John's place, he plotted Jesus' death (LUKE 13:31). That Jesus could have escaped Antipas's assassins for more than a few weeks at the outside seems most unlikely.

Word of Jesus' preaching reached Jerusalem, along with reports of miracles similar to those claimed by nineteenth-century humbugs such as Mary Baker Eddy and twentieth-century humbugs who peddle their salvation swindles on television. Few such miracles—persuading a deaf man that he could hear by screaming in his ear—found their way into the Christian gospels. Gospel miracles tended to be the retroactive kind, borrowed from the mythology already existing concerning Eliyah and Eliyshakh and added to Jesus' legend long after his death.

For example, Jesus was credited with healing lepers as Eliyshakh had allegedly done (4 KGS. 5:6-14; LUKE 17:12-14), even though in Jesus' day lepers were forbidden by law from wandering near populated centres and were in fact confined to isolated colonies. Only by deliberately visiting a leper colony could Jesus have even seen a leper. In view of the superstitious horror with which Hansen's disease was viewed, we can be very sure that Jesus stayed well away from such places.

There is no reason, however, to doubt that, like modern faith healers, Jesus was confronted by psychosomatic illnesses and effected his share of cures. Indeed, Mark's admission that in his own country Jesus was unable to effect any cures (MARK 6:5) is good evidence that cures really were achieved elsewhere. Eighty percent of all illnesses will heal spontaneously with no treatment whatsoever. Investigations of modern faith healers have established that their success rate is precisely eighty percent (for a *divine intervention* quotient of zero), and there is no reason to suppose that the law of averages failed to work equally well for Jesus.[9]

Whether, like television healers, Jesus achieved his greatest successes with stooges, we cannot know. A reasonable assumption is that Jesus believed himself to be a genuine healer and would not have resorted to trickery; but the same cannot be said with certainty of all of his disciples. If, for example, the Zealots Simon and Judas believed that a revolution would have a better chance of success under the leadership of an accepted messiah, they may well have engineered a few discreet miracles to build up a belief in Jesus' divine mission. Indeed, in view of the outrageous nature of Jesus' pretensions, they may have concocted some stooged miracles to convince *him* of his messianic identity. It is by no means unlikely that Jesus' role in a plot stage-managed by Zealots was analogous to that of Christopher Sly in the induction of *The Taming of the Shrew*.

If Jesus was not manipulated by the Zealots, then no plausible answer is available to the question: How could a man who had grown up believing that the messiah must be born in Bethlehem and descended from King David, have come to believe that neither of those conditions was necessary? But Jesus did become convinced that he was the messiah. On a Sunday morning, the eighth day of the month of Nisan (6 April) in the year 30 CE, he rode into Jerusalem to start the revolution. He was arrested and executed five days later after a minor skirmish that in a later age would have been named the Ten Minute War.

In that passage lies the proof of Jesus' historicity. He took upon himself the task of overthrowing the Roman empire, and failed so miserably that Roman historians did not deign him a single mention. The only historian who acknowledged Jesus' revolution was Josephus, whose account was so unflattering that it was totally expurgated from Greek manuscripts. A passage survived in a Slavonic translation, but it was so altered as to be worthless. The extant version actually contains the statement that Jesus was the messiah,

---

9. Chiropractic has a success rate of eighty percent. Psychiatry has a success rate far lower than eighty percent. Readers can draw their own conclusions. For evidence of the fraudulence of homeopathy, naturopathy, osteopathy and chiropractic, see Martin Gardner, *Fads and Fallacies in the Name of Science*, NY, 1957, chapter 16, 'Medical Cults.' For a discussion of the usefulness of psychiatry, see Thomas Szasz, *The Therapeutic State*, Buffalo, 1984.

The willingness of the time-healed to attribute their recovery to *post hoc ergo propter hoc* causes was exemplified by the Emperor Julian in a passage regarding the pre-Trojan War demigod Asklepios (*Against the Galileans* 235D): 'When I have been sick Asklepios has often cured me by prescribing remedies; and of this Zeus is witness.'

a belief that Josephus most certainly did not hold. Like Moses, Jesus must have existed because nobody would have invented him. Mythologians do not invent folk heroes who fail; and Jesus failed, not gloriously like Leonidas, Spartacus or bar Kokhba, but so insignificantly that, had it not been for Paul of Tarsus, his name most likely would not have survived.

Jesus entered Jerusalem riding on a donkey. Zekharyah had decreed that the prophesied King of the Jews (by whom he meant Zerubbabel) must arrive in such a manner (ZEC. 9:9).[10] The Jewish masses knew this and Jesus knew it. He could not have proclaimed himself King of the Jews and Commander in Chief of the War of Independence more effectively if he had been preceded by a ten-metre neon sign that flashed MASHYAH in five colours. The crowd did not mistake Jesus' message. They lined the streets and cried out, '*Liberate us, Descendant of David*' (MAT. 21:9).[11]

In Jerusalem Jesus faced the toughest audience of his career. The illiterate masses had screamed '*Descendant of David*' without questioning the correctness of that epithet. The Sadducees and Pharisees were more skeptical: *But others asked, 'Since when is the Messiah (Khristos)[12] to come out of Galilaia? Don't the Writings say that the Messiah is to come from the sperm of David, and from Bethlehem, the village where David used to be?'* (JOHN 7:41-42).

Jesus had been willing to allow the rabble to believe that he was Davidic. He could not use such a tactic with the educated classes. He acknowledged that he was not descended from David, and argued that the messiah did not need to be. He quoted a psalm attributed to David that had come to be regarded as referring to the messiah: *Yahweh said to my master, 'Sit at my right hand until I subdue your enemies under your feet'* (PS. 110:1). He then asked, '*Since David called him master, how can he be his descendant?*' (MARK 12:35-37; MAT. 22:41-45; LUKE 20:41-44).

That unqualified admission by Jesus that he was not Davidic was not recognised as such by the compilers of the Christian canon; otherwise it would have been expurgated as other passages that flatly contradicted evolved Christian mythology were expurgated. The handful of anti-Christian passages that escaped the censors' notice provide the only clues to what the historical Jesus really did and said. How Jesus answered the challenge that the messiah

---

10. Matthew, with his usual paranoia for prophecy-fulfilment, made Jesus ride on two donkeys simultaneously in the belief that such was required of the prophecy. Had Matthew been able to read Hebrew he would have realised that Zekharyah's poem followed the usual Hebrew verse pattern of saying the same thing twice in different words (e.g., PS. 27:1; 35:1; 49:1; 58:1). Matthew read *Zechariah* in Greek and misinterpreted it accordingly.

11. *Hosanna to huio David. Hosanna*, the imperative of the Hebrew verb to free or rescue, is roughly equivalent to '*Help!*'

12. *Khristos (Christos, Christ)* = the christened (anointed) one. It was the Greek equivalent of *Mashyah*, 'Yahweh's Anointed.'

had to be born in Bethlehem, no gospel author reported. But clearly he did not claim that he *was* born in Bethlehem, or the authors who recorded his handling of the Davidic issue would have said so.

It can be accepted as historical that Jesus' claims to messiahship were strongly challenged by the Sadducees. Although the Sanhedrin, composed mainly of Sadducees, was in no way comparable with the Vichy government of 1940-1944, it nonetheless occupied an enviable advisory position in the Roman hierarchy—or had under procurators less brutal and anti-Semitic than Lucius Pontius Pilatus. The last thing that the Sanhedrin wanted was a messianic uprising that could not fail to erode what little influence on Roman policy it still possessed: *'If we leave him alone, everyone's going to have credulity in him, and the Romans will capture both our territory and our people'* (JOHN 11:48).

The Sadducees' initial policy was to discredit Jesus with the masses. A messiah in whom nobody believed was no threat. They made an issue of his non-Davidic ancestry and his Galilean origin. Jesus' argument that these were no disqualifications was scorned by the educated classes, but *the huge crowd blissfully swallowed this* (MARK 12:37). If Mark is to be believed, then Jesus' admission that he did not fulfil the two most important prophecies did not destroy the belief of the masses that he was the fulfilment of the prophecies! A modern parallel can be seen in those Christian mythologians who unhypnotise themselves long enough to recognise that their bible is full of lies but, despite their mythology's total dependence on the bible's veracity, cannot bring themselves to recognise that without the bible's alleged revelations, all basis for Christian belief has ceased to exist.

Hoping to elicit a foolish answer, the Sadducees questioned Jesus on the belief in an afterlife that he shared with the Pharisees and other Essenes. It is unlikely that he gave the answer delineated in the synoptic gospels (MARK 12:18-27; MAT. 22:23-33; LUKE 20:27-38), but apparently his doctrine was sufficiently thought out to enable him to sound learned. It is possible that he had learned arguments to rebut the Sadducees as a secular Essene; but the reasoning of *Mark* 12:26-27 sounds more typical of the Pharisees than of the less sophisticated Essenes. Jesus may have quoted an answer that he had picked up from listening to Pharisees.

The Sadducees tried a tougher approach, asking, *'Does the Towrah permit paying taxes to Kaisaros* (Caesar)?' (MARK 12:14). That it was the Sadducees who asked this question, and not the Pharisees as the gospels claimed, it is not difficult to deduce. The Pharisees had no political supremacy to protect, and no other reason for opposing a man who taught their own doctrines. The similarity of Jesus' totally-Essene teachings and those of the Pharisees can be verified on almost any page of the Talmud, a Pharisaical composition. After the Zealots, the Pharisees were Jesus' strongest supporters.

The Sadducees asked, *'Is it lawful to pay taxes to Caesar?'* A negative answer would have been deemed treason, thereby enabling the Sadducees to solve their problem and at the same time increase their credibility in Roman eyes by denouncing Jesus to the procurator, Pilatus. An affirmative answer would have discredited Jesus with the masses permanently, for no Jew could have believed that the messiah would uphold the taxing authority of the occupation that Yahweh had sent him to overthrow.

Mark wrote that Jesus gave an answer which the crowd could recognise as an unambiguous *No*, but which Vespasian, for whose benefit Mark was writing, could not have interpreted as such (12:17). Perhaps he did. The story implies a degree of sophistication in Jesus that is inconsistent with the overall picture one gleans from the few reliable portions of the sources. It may be that such a question was asked of Jesus, but that his clever reply was supplied retroactively. It is more likely that he abused his questioners and refused to reply, as he was reported to have done on other occasions when confronted by questions beyond the competence of an illiterate Galilean carpenter (MAT. 21:27; LUKE 11:29).

Mark wrote: *They conspired to arrest him, but they were afraid of the mob* (MARK 12:12). In fact the Sadducees had no such desire. Had they really sought Jesus' death they would not have had the slightest difficulty in convicting him of hundreds of separate instances of three capital crimes: seducing the people from orthodox mythology; violating the sabbath; and false prophecy.[13] But as much as they needed credibility with the Romans, they needed credibility with the masses even more. They would not have dared associate themselves with the execution of a reputed spokesman—particularly when it was unnecessary, since the spokesman was absolutely certain to be arrested and executed by the Romans for the treason of claiming a kingly title not granted to him by Caesar.

In forcing Jesus to choose between denying his messiahship and committing treason against Rome, the Sadducees had no doubt that he would choose treason. But they in all likelihood also assumed that he possessed sufficient sanity then to recognise his danger and flee the city. There lay the Sadducees' real aim: they wanted the rabble-rouser out of Jerusalem before he could upset an already precarious *status quo*. What they did not anticipate was the auto-reinforced fanaticism that to this day convinces messiahs, ayatollahs, and self-styled moral majorities that are neither moral nor a majority, that they have been appointed to a divine mission and that anyone who opposes their whims will answer to a tribal god even sicker than themselves. That the Sadducees' policy of preventing Jesus' revolution was sound is evident from the disastrous consequences of the rebellions of 66-70 CE and 132-135 CE. The execution of one would-be messiah in 30 CE, before he could

---

13. H.E. Goldin, *The Case of the Nazarene Reopened*, pp. 422 ff.

become sufficiently organised to be dangerous, postponed the disaster and ensured the survival of the Jewish state for a further forty years.

In all fairness to the Sadducees, to whom even collaboration had limits, it must be pointed out that a Davidic, Bethlehem-born messiah would have been received quite differently. King Herod Agrippa I, for example, won the unanimous support of all Jewish parties and other Semitic leaders for a revolution that was only aborted by his sudden fatal illness during the reign of the Emperor Claudius. Although Josephus did not say so, there is good reason to speculate that Agrippa, who was born in Bethlehem and had been to Egypt, believed himself the messiah and formed his anti-Roman coalition by winning his allies to that belief. Unlike Jesus, Herod acknowledged his *hubris* before his death, and perhaps for that reason no new cult arose to await Agrippa's second coming.

Jesus lost no time after entering Jerusalem in proclaiming the revolution:

> Don't imagine that I've come to bring the land peace. I've come to bring, not peace, but rather a sword. For I've come to set a man warring against his father, a daughter against her mother, and a bride against her mother-in-law. Members of a man's own family are going to become his enemies.
> (MAT. 10:34-36)

> I've come to set the land on fire, and I wish it were already lit. . . . From now on a household of five is going to be divided, three against two.
> (LUKE 12:49-52)

> Anyone who doesn't have a sword is to sell his cloak and buy one.
> (LUKE 22:36)

> There are some standing here who are not going to experience death until they have seen Allah's theocracy established by force.   (MARK 9:1)

Jesus' reference to the Saints' enemies being members of their own households, although quoted from *Micah* 7:6, accurately reflected his own attitude toward the family that had tried to incarcerate him as a lunatic. It is significant that the second-century *Gospel of John*, which was not a biography of the Jewish messiah Jesus but a theogony of the Greek god Jesus, expunged all statements by Jesus that revealed his actual beliefs concerning his identity and his revolutionary mission. Gods do not proclaim Wars of Independence—and lose.

Jesus was arrested for treason by the Roman procurator Pontius Pilatus within hours of Pilatus's arrival in Jerusalem from his administrative capital of Caesaria. He was not taken without a fight. His disciples knew why they had come to Jerusalem, and had taken appropriate action:

They answered, 'Sire,[14] look. Here are two swords.' And he told them, 'It'll be enough.' (LUKE 22:38)

But one of those standing by drew his sword and struck the High Priest's slave and amputated his ear. (MARK 14:47; MAT. 26:51)

And those around him, seeing what was about to happen, asked, 'Sire, are we to strike with the sword?' And one of them struck the High Priest's slave and amputated his right ear. (LUKE 22:49-50)

So Simon Petros, who had a sword, drew it and struck the High Priest's slave and amputated his right ear. (JOHN 18:10)

Although Luke's version went on to add the fairy tale that Jesus magically healed the servant's severed ear, its intimation that Jesus' lieutenants were all armed seems to reflect the true circumstances of the arrest, particularly since Mark later mentioned a man *among the imprisoned revolutionaries who had committed homicide in the uprising* (MARK 15:7). Although the author of *John* made the ear-slicing swordsman Peter, that Peter was not arrested and outlived Jesus by several years is clear evidence that he was not present.

All gospels declared that Jesus was betrayed by Judas the Assassin; but those gospels were composed after 70 CE when Christianity was trying to win acceptance from the Roman Emperors by dissociating itself from the Jews who had fomented the recent revolution. High on the list of Rome's enemies were the Pharisees, the revolution's original leaders until they were murdered by the Zealots for being too moderate.[15] Mark, copied by Matthew and Luke, retroactively made the Pharisees Jesus' enemies also.

The prime instigators of the revolution, however, had been the Zealots; and the last holdouts, who defended Masada for four years after the fall of Jerusalem, had been the sect's ultra-terrorist wing, the *sicarii*, Iskariots.[16] The Romans viewed the Zealots, particularly the Iskariots, in much the same light that a later imperial power viewed the Mau Mau. It could not be concealed that two or three of Jesus' lieutenants had been Zealots, one of them an Iskariot. The logical way to dissociate Jesus from the Zealot cause was to pretend that Judas had *really* been Jesus' enemy and had ultimately betrayed him. That one of Jesus' lieutenants sold him out is improbable.

---

14. *Kyrios*, signifying the Hebrew word *adownay*. 'Lord' is a misleading translation on account of its recently-acquired connotations of divinity. *Kyrios/adownay* was a combination of 'Your lordship,' 'Master,' 'Excellency,' 'Boss,' 'Leader,' '*Caudillo*' and '*mein Führer.*' 'Sire' is the most accurate translation in the second person, and 'His Lordship' in the third person.

15. Josephus, *Jewish War* 2:563; 2:651-653; 4:314-318.

16. *Ibid.* 7:253; 7:399.

That a member of the one organisation bound to back Jesus' revolution to the hilt did so is beyond belief.

Jesus was given a brief trial before the procurator, Pilatus. Pilatus was the anti-Semitic appointee of Tiberius's anti-Semitic deputy-Emperor, Sejanus. Philo, in his *Embassy to Gaius*, described Pilatus as:

> naturally inflexible, a blend of self-will and relentlessness. . . . He feared that (the Jews) would also expose the rest of his conduct as Procurator by stating in full the briberies, the insults, the outrages and wanton injuries, the executions without trial constantly repeated, the ceaseless and supremely grievous cruelty. So with all his vindictiveness and furious temper . . . .   (38:300-303)

Philo's assessment of Pilatus was fully borne out by Josephus, whose descriptions of Pilatus's atrocities leave little doubt that his impeachment in 36 CE was long overdue.[17] Fortunately for Pilatus, Tiberius died while he was en route to Rome to stand trial; so it is entirely possible that he was never brought to justice. And this was the man whom Mark credited with a sense of justice and a reluctance to execute one rebellious Jew.

Jesus was not tried by the Sanhedrin. The gospel accounts of his trial for blasphemy before that body were all concocted by men who knew nothing whatsoever about Jewish law. Mark accused Jesus of many acts for which he could have been condemned to death under Jewish law (MARK 2:5-7; 2:27-28; 7:15; 10:2-9; 13:26-27); yet he declared the Sanhedrin to be so inept as to bring against him only accusations that reflected on his sanity but were not legally actionable (MARK 14:58). And Matthew accused the High Priest, Yowsef Kaiafa, of the incredible blasphemy of asking Jesus: *'Tell us if you're the Messiah, the descendant of the god?'* (MAT. 26:63). While the declaration that a properly enthroned king was Yahweh's son was reasonably acceptable, that a pretender could claim such a title as his own was so impossible that Kaiafa would have needed to commit a capital offence himself to ask such a question.[18]

Mark went on to declare that, when Jesus gave an affirmative answer that did not breach the blasphemy law, although it did qualify him for death by stoning on two other charges, Kaiafa demanded and received a conviction for blasphemy on the basis of Jesus' own confession (MARK 14:63-64). In fact accused persons were not only not required to testify against themselves; they were not permitted to do so. To use Jesus' own words against him, a new trial before new judges would have had to be called, with Kaiafa and the other judges from the first trial acting solely as witnesses.

---

17. *Ibid.* 2:8; *Antiq.* 18:61-62, 88-89. See also *Luke* 13:1.
18. H.E. Goldin, *loc. cit.*

Mark's final inaccuracy in his description of a trial that never happened was his attributing to Kaiafa the role of President of the Sanhedrin. In fact the office was held at the time by Gamaliel.

Jesus was tried by Pilatus, convicted and executed. Pilatus massacred hundreds of Jews without trial or justification; but in executing a claimant to a title that had always meant the leader of an anti-Roman revolution (and meant precisely that to Jesus), he acted as any procurator must have done in similar circumstances. The Sadducees of the Sanhedrin, although they deemed Jesus expendable and viewed one execution as infinitely preferable to the thousands of Jewish deaths that would occur if Jesus were left unhindered (JOHN 11:50), had nothing to do with his fate. Jesus committed the Roman crime of rebelling against Caesar, was tried and condemned by the Roman procurator, and was executed by a method used only by Romans and only for rebels and slaves. Had he been convicted by Jews of the Jewish offence of blasphemy, which he did not commit, or *mesiyth* (seducing Jews to foreign religious practices), which he may have committed, or profaning the sabbath and false prophecy, which he did commit, he would have been executed by the Jewish method of stoning. Among the many ironies of Christianity, not the least is that the leadership of the present cult of Jesus-the-god is centred in the city that was solely and totally responsible for the historical Jesus' execution.

Jesus was stripped naked and affixed to a T-bar by nails. The recent discovery of an anklebone with a nail still in it confirms that this was the normal method of crucifixion. Jesus was affixed by nails just as the five thousand survivors of Spartacus's last battle whom Pompeius crucified were affixed by nails. The nails were driven through the wrists, for the hands would never have withstood the weight of the human body without ripping.

Crucified persons died of asphyxiation. To speed the process the Roman guards, who were required to remain at their posts until death was established, customarily broke the prisoners' shins. Since Mark, Matthew and Luke reported no variation from normal procedures, it is probable that this was done to Jesus, particularly since Jesus was dead in a matter of hours. However, the synoptic authors' silence on a minor point cannot be taken as conclusive.

John alone declared that Jesus' legs were not broken (JOHN 19:33), and John alone declared that a Roman soldier threw a spear into Jesus' side (JOHN 19:34). However, as each of John's additions caused Jesus to fulfil another prophecy (19:36-37), too much credence should not be attached to them. While an extremely weak man could have died in the short time prior to leg-breaking, Jesus' conviction that he was Messiah and that Yahweh would shortly send forty legions of winged messengers to rescue him would have kept him alive until the loss of the support of his legs made breathing impossible.

At that point two things would have happened. Crucified men always emptied their bowels prior to dying; only a man who had not eaten for several days could have avoided doing so. And crucified men always died with erections, an inevitable consequence of hanging. The Romans were aware of both effects of their execution method, and regarded them as part of the degradation that was intended to discourage others from committing similar crimes.

Probably in the moments following the breaking of his shins, but perhaps, as the gospels hint, when he found himself passing out from the effects of a drugged drink (MARK 15:36), Jesus finally realised that he was going to die, and that he therefore could not be the messiah. He is reported to have screamed the opening line of Psalm 22: 'Allah, Allah, why are you abandoning me?' (MARK 15:34), before passing into a coma and quickly dying.[19]

There is good reason to accept Jesus' exit line as genuine. It is utterly incompatible with the Johannine doctrine of Jesus the god ('Self! Self! Why are you abandoning me, Self? Are you there, Self? Self? Self?') It was equally incompatible with Mark's own belief in a resurrected king who had known all along that he must suffer a temporary death. A messiah who had many times prophesied that he would be dead for only two days could not have imagined in the last moments of his life that Allah was abandoning him. The line that Jesus actually screamed at his death was recorded by Mark, copied by Matthew, and not later expurgated by Johannine Christians, because neither the historical novelists nor the censors recognised that it contradicted their respective dogmas.

Jesus' addressing his dying screams to El rather than Yahweh or Adownay is easily explained. Jesus was a Jew, and as such believed that every word in the Towrah and the Prophets was literal truth. But he was also an Essene, and as such believed that celibacy and communism were virtues, in defiance of the beliefs of other Jews. And he was a Galilean, from the northern province that had once been the kingdom of the Israelites. And like all Galileans he worshipped, not the Judaean god Yahweh, but the Israelite god El/Allah/Elohiym, a deity with a most peculiar history.

Long before the Big Discovery, the inhabitants of an area stretching from the Persian Gulf to Troy had worshipped a goddess named Allah

---

19. Mark, whose native language was Greek, recorded Jesus' last words in both that language (Ho Theos mou, ho Theos mou, eis ti egkatelipes me?) and Hebrew (Eloi, Eloi, lama sabakhthanei?). What Mark did not realise was that, while the Greek meant 'Why are you abandoning me?' the Hebrew meant 'Why are you offering me as a sacrifice?' Clearly, in an attempt to add a spurious authenticity by quoting Jesus' words in his own language, Mark asked a Jew to translate 'Why are you abandoning me?' into Hebrew, and was given a mistranslation by an Aramaic-speaker whose own Hebrew was shaky. The alternative possibility is that the Hebrew represents Jesus' actual words and the Greek is the mistranslation; but as Mark would have had no way of ascertaining Jesus' actual words, this seems unlikely.

or *Eloh* (the Hebrew *aleph-lamedh-he* can be transcribed either way). Following the male revolution, the feminine ending *-ah* was dropped, to produce the male god *El*, after whom *Ilion* (Troy) was named. Some Semites, however, retained the name *Allah* unchanged, even after Allah had become male, just as some Babylonians retained the name *Sin* when they masculinised their moon-goddess.

When one god proved insufficient to protect the Israelites in Moses' day, *Allah* was pluralised to *Allahiym*, more commonly transcribed *Elohiym*, by adding the male-plural suffix *-iym* after the feminine-singular suffix *-ah*, producing the androgynous unified committee, 'the gods and goddesses.'

Jesus, as a typical Galilean, did not actually reject Yahweh as a foreign god. He regarded *Yahweh* and *El* as alternative names for the same deity. But he could no more have directed his prayers to *Yahweh*, under that name or its customary substitute, than a modern Christian could direct his prayers to *Allah*, or a Muslim to *God*.

Jesus died on the stake. Theories that he passed out from drugged vinegar and later regained consciousness in his tomb attach an unwarranted credibility to the gospel authors' claims that Jesus was seen alive after his execution. In fact the tales of Jesus' posthumous personal appearances were concocted long after his death in order to prop up a faltering resurrection myth that had originated on the basis of nothing more than the disappearance of his body from its tomb. Jesus died, and in so doing proved to the thousands who had hitherto believed in him that he was not the messiah.

Jesus' crucifixion occurred on a Friday. He died late in the afternoon, by which time there was no possibility of giving his body the washing, anointing and other ritual that was a spokesman's due, before the onset of the sabbath when such duties could not be performed. Joseph of Harimathaia, a pious Jew who was not Jesus' disciple,[20] was unwilling that a spokesman be given the unceremonious dirty burial that the proximity of the sabbath would have otherwise necessitated. He therefore offered Jesus' disciples his own tomb in which to lay the unwashed corpse for the duration of the sabbath. There was no suggestion that Joseph's tomb was to be Jesus' final burial place.

At sundown on Saturday, unwilling to allow the body of a holy man to remain unwashed one minute longer than necessary, Joseph returned to the tomb. He had his servants perform the necessary purification ritual, and buried the body at a site of his own choosing.

---

20. Since there does not appear to have ever been a place called Harimathaia, Joseph's existence has been disputed. However, regardless of his name or place of origin, the existence of some person to fill this role appears to be necessary. That Joseph was not Jesus' disciple is evident from the admission by Matthew (27:57) that Joseph was rich. Jesus' followers, like all Essenes, were required to liquidate their holdings and give the proceeds to the communal treasury, administered by Judas the Iskariot.

On Sunday morning, three of Jesus' female disciples arrived at Joseph's tomb with the necessary spices for anointing a body, unaware that the task had already been accomplished (MARK 16:1). Finding the tomb empty, they informed Peter and the unidentified *disciple whom Iesous loved* (JOHN 20:2). The Beloved Disciple immediately jumped to the conclusion that Yahweh had transported the body to Heaven for a final briefing before sending his reconditioned messiah back to start the revolution. When word of Jesus' 'resurrection' reached Joseph of Harimathaia (if it did reach him), Joseph chose to suppress the truth, either because he favoured the newly-generated messianic fervour that the story triggered, or because he regarded the latest piece of lunacy being preached by hillbilly Galileans as too good a joke to spoil. By the time the story got out of control and Jesus had become a resurrected saviour-god like Dionysos, Joseph was as dead as Jesus.

Jesus died, totally and permanently, and remained dead. Nonetheless the Nazirites, the Essene commune in Jerusalem led by his brother Jacob the Righteous, taught and maintained that he was alive and in the skies and would one day return to drive out the Romans. A comparable belief came into existence in the mythology of the Welsh, who maintained until the late twelfth century CE that their sixth-century hero, King Arthur, was alive and in Avalon and would one day return to drive out the English. So far neither one has done so.

Jesus' teaching presents a problem. Like Sokrates he wrote nothing, probably because writing was not one of his accomplishments. Like Sokrates, he was posthumously credited with many speeches that may or may not have paraphrased what he really said. But Sokrates was quoted by Plato, who had been his disciple. While Plato may have lied, he could not have misquoted his teacher out of sheer ignorance. Jesus, on the other hand, was quoted by four men who had never met him, three of whom had not been born at the time of his death.

The synoptic gospels were written forty, sixty-five and seventy years after Jesus' death for the specific purpose of proving that he was the messiah. John's gospel was written one hundred years after Jesus had become indistinguishable from Yorick, for the purpose of repudiating the buddhistic doctrines of the synoptics and proving that Jesus was the new Persephone. Obviously any philosophy put into Jesus' mouth by such questionable sources must be viewed with the greatest of caution.

Jesus was credited by his biographers with teaching doctrines that can be traced to two main sources, both Essene, and several minor sources, also Essene. From the *Book of Enoch*, an Essene adaptation of the metaphysical elements of the mythology of Zarathustra, Jesus or his retroactive speechwriter took the fires of Gehenna into which sinners were thrown for purification. And from the *Covenant of the Community* (also known as the *Manual of*

Discipline and the *Community Rule*), prepared by the Righteous Rabbi for the edification of the first Essenes, he took the doctrine with which his name is most frequently associated:

ESSENE JESUS 140 BCE	NAZIRITE JESUS 29 CE
You are to love each man his compatriot like himself.	You're to *agape* your compatriot as yourself. (MARK 12:31)
You are to grasp the hand of the poor, the needy and the outsider.	When you did it for one of the lowest-ranking of these kinsmen of mine, you did it for me. (MAT. 25:40)
	If you forgive humans their transgressions, your father in the sky will also forgive you. (MAT. 6:14)
You are to seek each man the welfare of his fellows.	Whoever has two tunics is to share with him who has none, while whoever has food is to do the same. (LUKE 3:11)
	Don't judge, so that you won't be judged. (MAT. 7:1)
You are neither to take vengeance nor bear any grudge.	How many times must I forgive him if my kinsman keeps injuring me? As many as seven times? . . . up to seventy-seven times. (MAT. 18:21-22)
You are not to shed the blood of an infidel for the sake of profit.	Love your enemies and pray for those who persecute you. (MAT. 5:44)

The *Covenant* was not, however, the only source of Jesus' ethical teachings. The *Testaments of the Twelve Patriarchs*, the *Damascus Covenant* (also known as the 'Zadokite' *Document* and the *Damascus Rule*) and *Tobit*, the first two Essene and the last Pharisaical, were quoted by the gospel authors as the words of Jesus, while further sayings attributed to Jesus were identical with Essene beliefs as described by Josephus in his *Jewish War*:

JOSEPHUS

When adherents arrive from elsewhere, all local resources are put at their disposal as if they were their own. . . . When they travel they carry no baggage at all. . . . In every town one of the order is appointed especially to look after strangers and issue clothing and provisions.

Every word they speak is more binding than an oath. Swearing they reject as something worse than perjury; for they say a man is already condemned if he cannot be believed without invoking a god.

They are communists to perfection, and none of them will be found to be better off than the rest. Their rule is that novices admitted to the sect must surrender their property to the order. . . . Each man's possessions go into the pool and . . . their entire property belongs to them all. . . . Everyone gives what he has to anybody in need. . . . Even without giving anything in return they are free to share the possessions of anyone they choose.

Men convicted of major offences are expelled from the order and the outcast often comes to a miserable end; for bound as he is by oaths and customs he cannot share the diet of nonmembers, so is forced to eat grass till his starved body wastes away and he dies.
(WAR 2:8 ff)

MATTHEW

Take no gold or silver or copper in your belts, nor a bag for the journey, nor two tunics. Take no sandals or staff. . . . Whatever town or village you enter, enquire who in it is a worthy (*an Essene*) and stay there.   (10:9-11)

I'm warning you not to take an oath at all, neither by the sky . . . nor by the land . . . nor by Jerusalem. . . . Nor are you to swear by your head. . . . Let what you say be simply 'Yes' for yes and 'No' for no.   (5:33-37)

MARK

Iesous instructed him, 'Sell whatever you have and give it to the Ebionites ("*The Poor*," Iesous' name for his sect) . . . and become an acolyte.'   (10:21)

ACTS

The mass of believers were united heart and psyche, and not one claimed any of his possessions as his own. Everything they had became communal property. . . . All who owned land or houses sold them and brought the proceeds.
(4:32-35)

A certain Hananias sold a property, and with his woman's connivance he withheld part of the proceeds. . . . Petros asked, 'Hananias, how did the Enemy fill your heart to withhold some of the proceeds?' When Hananias heard those words, he collapsed and died (*as did his wife*).
(5:1-10)

TESTAMENT OF DAN

Unless you keep yourself from the spirit of lying and anger, and love truth and long-suffering, you are going to perish. (2:1-2)

MATTHEW

Whoever is enraged against his kinsman without cause is liable. . . . Whoever calls his kinsman 'scoundrel' is liable. (5:22)

TESTAMENT OF BENJAMIN

He who has a pure mind in love does not look at a woman with a view to sexcrime. (8:2)

Anyone who stares lustfully at a woman is already committing adultery with her in his heart.[21] (5:27-28)

TESTAMENT OF JOSEPH

I was hungry and Yahweh himself fed me. I was alone and my gods comforted me. I was sick and Yahweh visited me; slandered and he pleaded my cause; bitterly spoken against and he rescued me. (1:1-3)

I was hungry and you fed me. I was thirsty and you gave me a drink. I was a foreigner and you welcomed me . . . naked and you gave me clothing . . . sick and you visited me. (25:35-36)

PRAYER OF NABONIDOS

I was smitten with a malignant inflammation for seven years. . . . But I petitioned the gods and an exorcist, a Jewish man, one of the exiles, forgave my sins.

MARK

They came, bringing him a paralytic carried by four. And when Iesous saw their credulity, he told the paralytic, 'Son, your disobediences are forgiven.' (2:3-5)

DAMASCUS COVENANT

He (the Head Essene) will loose all the chains that bind them. (13:10)

. . . preaching an immersion . . . for annulment of disobediences. (1:4)

(attacks divorce and remarriage as adultery) (4:19-21)

(attacks divorce and remarriage as adultery) (10:11-12)

It is worth noting the difference between Jesus' so-called Golden Rule and Confucius's original, more logical dictum, now damned with faint praise as the Silver Rule:

---

21. The Greek author of *Matthew* used the word for 'adultery' rather than 'sexcrime' because he failed to realise that the celibate Essenes made no distinction between the two, and regarded even marital intercourse as adultery.

CONFUCIUS

Tzu Kung said: 'What I do not wish others to do to me, that also I wish not to do to them.'   (ANALECTS 5:11)

When Chung Kung asked the meaning of Virtue the Master said: 'When abroad behave as if interviewing an honoured guest; in directing the people act as if officiating at a great sacrifice; do not do to others what you would not like yourself; then your public life will arouse no ill-will nor your private life any resentment.' (ANALECTS 12:2)[22]

LUKE

What you would have humans do to you, do the same to them.   (6:31)

TOBIT

What is hateful to yourself, don't do to your compatriot.   (4:15)

RABBI HILLEL

Do not do to your compatriot that which is hateful to yourself. That is the entire Towrah. All else is mere commentary.
          (Talmud, SHABAT 31a)

MATTHEW

So whatever things you want humans to do to you, you also do the same to them. For that is the Towrah and the Prophets.   (7:12)

There is an almost universal belief in the West that Jesus' inversion of the Confucian/Zoroastrian rule improved it. In fact the inversion changed perhaps the most perfect summation of true morality ever propounded into an impossibility. A person who does not want to be assaulted, killed or robbed, can without difficulty avoid assaulting, robbing or killing anyone else. But what of the person who wants a billionaire to give him a million dollars? He *cannot* give the billionaire a million dollars, for the logical reason that he does not have a million dollars. Neither can he perform the inverse if he desires the United Nations to name him President of Earth. Far from improving the *true* Golden Rule, Jesus (or the author of the Q source copied by Matthew and Luke) destroyed it.

The foregoing fully explains why Josephus did not need to add Nazirites or Ebionites to his catalogue of Jewish philosophies. Whether a New Covenant commune called itself Essenes ('saints'), Ebionites ('the poor') or Nazirites

---

22. *The Analects of Confucius*, tr. William Edward Soothill, NY, 1968 (originally published in 1910). The 'Silver Rule' also appears in the Hindu *Mahabharata*, the Zoroastrian *Dadistan-i Dinik*, and the Buddhist *Panchatantra* and *Udana Varga*.

('the separated') was of little consequence; the names were interchangeable. Josephus chose *Essenes* because that was the name commonly applied to all such communes by nonmembers. In modern Jesus mythology, *saint* has come to mean a demigod believed to have intervened positively in human affairs; but originally all members of a Christian *ekklesia* were saints by definition, and were automatically styled *Saint X-Y-Z* at death.

Jesus was a secular Essene who, like John the Immerser, lost his belief in the Righteous Rabbi's Second Coming and came to believe that *he* was the messiah. If Jesus' brother Jacob was already Head Essene at the time of Jesus' breach with his family, that would adequately explain Jesus' action in turning against his parent commune and setting himself up as an opposition spokesman. Only on one issue was Jesus reported by his biographers to have repudiated Essene teaching. When the Pharisees, whose doctrines generally paralleled those of the Essenes, rebuked Jesus because his Galilean disciples failed to wash their hands before eating, Jesus answered that, *'Eating with unwashed hands doesn't pollute the human'* (MAT. 15:20). Yet Josephus reported of the Essenes that, *Although emptying the bowels is quite natural, they are taught to wash after it, as if it polluted them* (WAR 2:8:120).

Jesus' breach with Essene doctrine was minimal, just enough to assert his independence of any higher (mortal) authority. Ninety years after Jesus' death, the gentile sect founded by Paul of Tarsus had put a considerable distance between itself and its Essene nursery. Pseudo-Paul in *1 Timothy* 4:1-3 attacked as *hypocritical lies* the Essene/Nazirite doctrines of celibacy and abstinence from meats. By 120 CE (when *Timothy* was written) Christianity was clearly anti-Nazirite; but by that date it was also anti-Pharisee and, indeed, anti-Semitic.

It is usually Jesus' ethical material that is preached in churches and on street corners (with no acknowledgement that he was not its author), as if that were the only thing he taught. The Zoroastrian mythology from the *Book of Enoch*, to which the gospel authors devoted equal space, is seldom quoted by Christian apologists, perhaps in the belief that if they ignore it it will go away:

BOOK OF ENOCH	JESUS
Their spirits are going to be thrown into a blazing furnace. They are going to be wretched in their immense agony, and into darkness and chains and burning flames . . . you will have no peace. . . . We have been tortured and destroyed and not hoped to see life from day to day. (98:3; 103:7-10)	Being tortured in the underworld . . . he called out . . . 'Dip the tip of his finger in water and cool my tongue, for I'm in agony from the flames.' (LUKE 16:23-24)
	. . . be tossed into Gehenna, where their worm never dies and the fire is never extinguished. For everyone is going to be pickled with fire. (MARK 9:47-49)

Jesus' sabre-toothed worm that devoured the damned was reminiscent of the eagle that daily ate Prometheus's regrowing liver. The worm itself was not Jesus' invention. Four hundred years earlier, the last interpolator of *Isaiah* had written: *Their worm will not die; nor will their fire be extinguished* (ISA. 66:24). Like Jesus, pseudo-Isayah had been referring to the inhabitants of Gehenna. Nor was it Jesus who transformed Gehenna from an open cemetery outside Jerusalem into a torture chamber for dead souls. The authors of *Enoch* did that before his birth, adapting the physical Gehenna to the mythology of Zarathustra to produce an Essene/Pharisee purgatory, identical with the Christian Hell except for the lack of permanence. Prior to Jesus, the Essenes had pictured Gehenna as a monstrous torture chamber that sinners needed to endure as the only method of cleansing them of their sins and making them fit for the afterlife of the saints. It was not, as modern masochists claim, the suffering through which a sinner was purified, but rather exposure to the sacred power of Fire. Zarathustra did not quite deify Fire, but he saw it as an aspect of the divinity of Ahura Mazda. Nothing else could purify like Fire, because nothing else was as pure as Fire.

It was the element of permanence that transformed Gehenna from the Essene purgatory into the Christian Hell, and it is difficult to escape the conclusion that it was King Jesus in whose fevered mind that transformation first took place. If the flamethrowers of Gehenna are viewed as a self-centred wish-fulfilment that Zarathustra and the Essenes were willing to inflict on outsiders to drive home that 'They won't doubt me again,' one can perhaps understand such thinking without applauding it. It is rather more difficult to understand the kind of malignant hatred that could cause a man to wish such torture to last for eternity. And Jesus did not reserve the new improved Gehenna for the Herods and Tiberiuses of the world. He made clear that the rich (MARK 10:25), the learned (MAT. 23:29-33; LUKE 11:46), and those who refused to accept his messianic pretensions until he could offer some proof (MARK 6:11; MAT. 12:39), all had places in Gehenna prepared for them before they were born.

Jesus was not an innovator. But he did develop and elaborate the doctrines assimilated from his Essene teachers into a dichotomous philosophy that, viewed as a whole, was new in degree if not in substance. By examining the two elements of Jesus' teaching that seem to reflect his personal ideals, it is possible to reach some tentative conclusions about the kind of man he was and what motivated him:

Philosophy 'M'	Philosophy 'S'

Fortunate are you when they revile and persecute you . . . for your reward in the sky is going to be enormous.
(MAT. 5:11-12)

Fear him who, after killing, has the power to toss into Gehenna.   (LUKE 12:5)

If your right eye scandalises you, gouge it out.   (MAT. 5:29)

He'll say, 'Go away from me, you accursed, into the eternal fire.'
(MAT. 25:41)

Don't resist an evildoer. If someone punches you on the right cheek, allow him to punch the left as well.   (MAT. 5:39)

As for you, Kafar Nahoum, you're going down to Hades.   (LUKE 10:15)

Don't accumulate treasure.   (MAT. 6:19)

Anyone who does not despise his father and mother and wife and children and brothers and sisters cannot be my disciple.   (LUKE 14:26)

Don't be anxious about your psyche.
(MAT. 6:25)

Whoever has no credulity is prejudged.
(JOHN 3:18)

There are eunuchs who have made themselves eunuchs for the sake of the kingdom in the sky. Whoever is able to comprehend, let him comprehend.   (MAT. 19:12)

All those in the grave will come out . . . those who have been disobedient to a resurrection of punishment.
(JOHN 5:28-29)

Fortunate are those who mourn, for they are going to be comforted.   (MAT. 5:4)

It's easier for a camel to pass through the Needle's Eye than for a capitalist (property owner) to enter Allah's theocracy.   (MARK 10:25)

Taken as a whole, Jesus' preaching can be paraphrased:

Jews, I am your king. You say, 'Yes, Sire. Prove it and we'll follow you.' But I refuse to prove it. And if you don't believe me and follow without proof, my omnibenevolent father in the sky will skin and gut you, put you on a spit, barbecue you with flamethrowers, and feed you to a worm that never dies. And you will suffer forever.

It is perhaps anachronistic to refer to doctrines propounded centuries before the birth of Sacher-Masoch or de Sade as masochism and sadism. But there can be no denying that Jesus urged his followers to accept and delight in treatment that any rational person would be bound to find intolerable, and to torture themselves with guilt for mentally paying an attractive woman the compliment of desiring to recreate with her. And for those who rejected his Essene glorification of masochism, Jesus threatened countless trillions of years of unrelieved agony in a torture chamber that can only be described as a sadist's dream. Few Christian mythologians dispute that the quoted teachings 'seem' sadomasochistic; but most argue that Jesus' more repugnant doctrines were intended as metaphors, not to be taken literally. Such was not the case.

To this day, a member of any of several dozen neo-Christian cults is required to *despise his father and mother and wife and children and brothers and sisters*, so long as they remain outside the cult. The Essenes thought likewise, and Jesus was a typical Essene. The rationale behind the Essenes' repudiation of all family ties, even within the community, was explained by Philo: *For he who is either fast bound by the love lures of a wife, or under the stress of nature makes his children his first care . . . has passed from freedom to slavery.*[23] Jesus' wholehearted endorsement of the hate-unconverted-kinsmen doctrine was directly related to his nonbelieving family's conviction that he was insane; but the doctrine itself was Essene orthodoxy.

Jesus' advocacy of self-castration as a great virtue was likewise intended to be taken literally. Coming as he did from a sect that *has no women and has renounced all sexual desire,*[24] Jesus had been conditioned from birth to glorify celibacy even if the necessity of founding a royal dynasty relieved him of the obligation to practise it. It was a logical extension of such an attitude, that ending sexual desire surgically was a desirable procedure.

Three hundred years after Jesus' death the Christian church had adopted the pretence that Jesus had been speaking metaphorically, and that by *eunuch* he had simply meant a practitioner of celibacy. The RC church uses the same misinterpretation to justify its maintenance of a celibate priesthood. In fact, since the Essenes' pro-celibacy position was common knowledge and was widely admired, had Jesus wished to praise celibacy he could have done so openly. That he needed to be circumspect, ending his sermon with, '*Whoever is able to comprehend, let him comprehend,*' is a clear indication that he was treading on dangerous ground, perhaps even committing *mesiyth*. Self-castration by priests of fertility goddesses was so widely practised in the Roman empire's Asian provinces, including Greek cities in Judaea such as Caesaria, that a hundred years after Jesus' death the Emperor Hadrian felt obliged to issue an edict declaring it illegal. Jesus was risking Jewish wrath by advocating a practice that, regardless of its intrinsic repugnance, was bound to be rejected by the majority on the ground that the infidels did it. The true meaning of Jesus' doctrine was still recognised as late as

---

23. *Hypothetica* 2:18.
24. Pliny, *Natural History* 5:15:73.

200 CE, when the Christian mythologian Origen castrated himself in obedience to Jesus' order.

Jesus' hatred of the rich may have been related to his status as the son of a poor carpenter; and the reluctance of the rich to sell their possessions and give him the proceeds in order to join his sect (MARK 10:21-22) likewise would not have endeared them to him. But Jesus' prime reason for condemning all rich persons to Gehenna was that Essenes regarded the owning of any private property as an unforgivable sin (ENOCH 93-97).

Consider, for example, Jesus' declaration: *It's easier for a camel to pass through the Needle's Eye than for a capitalist to enter Allah's theocracy.* The Needle's Eye was a narrow, triangular mountain pass not far from Jerusalem. Goats and goatherds could negotiate it without difficulty. Getting a camel through presented a problem. A camel needed to bend its knees, lower its head, and crawl through on its belly. In other words, it needed to adopt the posture assumed by god-worshippers at prayer. But even that was not sufficient. It also needed to be divested of its cargo. A camel could indeed pass through the Needle's Eye, but only if it first disposed of all of its property. A rich man could become a loyal subject of King Jesus by the same means.[25]

Jesus' preaching was saturated with sadomasochism. It is necessary to stress that point to counter the self-hypnosis that causes Jesus-worshippers to believe that any teaching attributed to their posthumously-deified god must be enlightened. Certainly much of the teaching that Jesus copied from the Righteous Rabbi, particularly from the *Covenant of the Community,* was enlightened—but not all, and not even most. Jesus himself was a fanatic. If he cannot be criticised for believing repugnant doctrines that an Essene was bound to believe, he also cannot be acquitted of embracing those doctrines with the manic enthusiasm symptomatic of religious hysteria. Albert Schweitzer suggested that the only reason Jesus could not be deemed insane was that delusions such as his were not rare in the society in which he lived.

Only on one count can Jesus be condemned without qualification. Assuming that his preaching has been reported with reasonable accuracy in the Christian gospels, we are obliged to regard him as the sole creator of the most repulsive superstition ever to come out of a disturbed mind: the everlasting torture of the Christian Hell.

But did Jesus in fact preach the sadomasochistic philosophy attributed to him? The answer is a definite maybe. Had the gospel known as *Mark* been written by a Nazirite, a member of the Essene commune infiltrated

---

25. If *Needle's Eye* was intended to mean a sewing needle, which a camel could not pass through under any circumstances, the point remains the same. A rich man could not possibly enter King Jesus' theocracy, but a *formerly* rich man could do so.

by Jesus' disciples after his death and converted to a belief in Jesus' messiahship, or had it been written by an Ebionite, then we could not doubt that Mark had obtained his information from a reliable source. But Mark was a Paulinist, otherwise called a Christian, a member of a gentile community that followed the teachings of Paul of Tarsus rather than those of Jesus. Paul had never met Jesus, and any resemblance between the two men's teachings was purely coincidental. The only way Mark could have obtained accurate information would have been for him to have visited the genuine Jesus commune, led by Jesus' cousin Shimeown bar Klofas, in the Decapolis where Shimeown had led it at the outbreak of the first Jewish War. If that is in fact what Mark did, then the enormous discrepancy between the story of Jesus' career that Mark heard from the Nazirites, and the story that he wrote, makes one wonder why he bothered.

On the other hand, it was Mark who recorded that Jesus' mother and brothers tried to constrain him as a madman. It was also Mark who reported that in Jesus' hometown he was unable to work any miracles, due to the absence of his patients' disposition to believe, without which no hypnotist can be successful.[26] The probability of Mark, whose discernible purpose was to praise Jesus, inventing such negative anecdotes was vanishingly small. And if Mark's informants were sufficiently well-informed to know of Jesus' estrangement from his family, they were surely also in a position to give their Greek interrogator an accurate account of what Jesus preached. On balance, it is more reasonable to conclude that Jesus was raised as a secular Essene and preached purely Essene doctrines, than that Mark, looking for sermons to put into Jesus' mouth, chose a collection of sources that just happened to be all Essene.

But the conclusion that Jesus indeed preached the philosophy attributed to him remains tentative. According to the gospel authors, Jesus preached a god that so hated the human race that it allowed only one person out of every billion to escape the torture chamber that it had created for its recreation. If that is indeed what Jesus preached, then far from being an enlightened philosopher of comparable stature with Confucius, Hillel and Wilberforce, he must be recognised as a very sick man. And if Jesus did not preach the everlasting torture doctrine attributed to him, then the books by the anonymous authors arbitrarily designated Mark, Matthew, Luke and John contain the most obscene libel of a good man ever penned.

---

26. The word *hypnotist* is used to mean a practitioner of suggestion therapy, regardless of whether he calls himself a hypnotist, faith healer or something else. Scholarly opinion is that patients whose psychosomatic symptoms are alleviated by such techniques are *not* in any altered state of consciousness. See Robert Baker, *They Call It Hypnosis*, Buffalo, 1990.

Fifteen

The Making of a God

Faith is that quality which enables us to believe what we
know to be untrue.

The Omnibus Boners.

Octavian Augustus Caesar was barely cold in his grave when the Roman
Senate by a unanimous vote formally pronounced him a god. The Emperor
Claudius was deified so quickly that the Senate only learned afterwards
that the new god's divinity did not meet with his successor Nero's approval.
The god Claudius was reduced to mortal status at the demand of Nero,
and only reinstated in Olympos after the accession of Vespasian.

No such immediate promotion to the ranks of the immortals followed
the death of Jesus. He was not nominated for godship until 130 CE, and
was not officially voted god of the Christians until the convening of the
Council of Nicaea in 325 CE. He was de-deified and re-deified twice in
the decades that followed, and pumpkinified permanently in 380 CE. But
from his death in 30 CE until the publication a century later of the unknown
Greek author's *Gospel of John*, he had to be content with the role of a
resurrected but mortal King of the Jews.

Hugh Schonfield in *The Passover Plot* dated the origin of the resurrection
myth to the Sunday following Jesus' execution. On that day Peter and the
unidentified *disciple whom Iesous loved* visited the tomb in which their dead
leader had been laid, and found it empty. The Beloved Disciple reached
the tomb first, but, being a Levite priest who could not afford to be defiled

by the proximity of a corpse, refused to enter until Peter had assured him that Jesus' body was indeed gone (JOHN 20:2-9).

The Beloved Disciple, not considering for a moment that the body might have left the tomb the same way it had come in, promptly declared his belief that Jesus had been bodily raised into the skies by Yahweh and would shortly return to start the revolution. The Beloved Disciple's imaginative fantasy spread rapidly among Jesus' former followers with the result that, while the Jewish masses whose hopes had been cruelly dashed—dead men do not lead revolutions—recognised Jesus' death as the ultimate, incontrovertible proof that he had not been the messiah, the incredibly naive Galileans saw his 'resurrection' as proof of the opposite.

According to the earliest tradition, recorded by Mark (16:7) and Matthew (28:16) but contradicted by Luke (LUKE 24:29; ACTS 1:12), Jesus' disciples initially returned to Galilee after his death; but within a matter of weeks Peter and the sons of Zebedyah (Greek genitive: Zebedaios) were reported to be back in Jerusalem preaching Jesus as a crucified messiah (ACTS 3:1).

According to Luke, the number of believers in the resurrected Jesus rose overnight from 120 to 3000 as a consequence of Peter's preaching (ACTS 1:15; 2:41). Yet Luke also acknowledged that when Peter attempted to preach in the Temple he was quickly arrested (ACTS 4:1-3); and it was not long afterwards that the public preaching which Luke anachronously associated with Stephen led to the persecution of all last-times and new-covenant sects (ACTS 11:9).

The only way Peter could have preached the messiahship of Jesus to a receptive multitude without incurring reprisals from the Sadducean hierarchy would have been to restrict his preaching to a commune that had already separated itself from the mainstream of Jewish life; and that was what he did. Instead of following Jesus' fatal example of preaching an anti-Roman king publicly, Peter and the disciples who had neither been killed trying to prevent Jesus' arrest, crucified with him, defected after their leader's disillusioning death, nor remained Ebionites, independent of the Nazirites, joined an Essene commune in Jerusalem led by Jesus' brother Jacob and, with Jacob's consent, converted it to a belief in Jesus.

It is highly unlikely that the most prominent disciples' decision to go to Jacob the Righteous was the consequence of any agreement reached prior to the crucifixion. The *Gospel of Thomas* declared that before his death Jesus had instructed his disciples to accept Jacob as their leader; but in view of Jesus' pathological hatred of his family, that retroactive commissioning of Jacob must be deemed as improbable as the alternative claim in *Matthew* that he conferred the leadership on Peter. It may be that the disciples' first decision on returning to Jerusalem was to inform Jacob of Jesus' apparent assumption into the kingdom in the sky, and that the sect's change of messiah occurred as an unanticipated consequence of Jacob's acceptance of their tale.

The earliest date for which there is direct testimony that Peter was a lieutenant in a commune led by Jacob was about 40 CE, ten years after Jesus' death (GAL. 1:18-19); but probably the infiltration occurred in the first year after that event. That Jacob was head of the Jesus commune in Jerusalem in the lifetime of Paul of Tarsus is evident from *Acts* 21:18 and *Galatians* 2:9-13. That he was also Head Essene, recognised as the successor of the Righteous Rabbi, may be inferred from his bearing the same title.

Why Jacob, who had hitherto regarded his older brother as a pitiful madman, came to accept Jesus' messiahship on the basis of evidence as flimsy as an empty tomb, is difficult to grasp. Perhaps, having been conditioned from birth to believe in the Second Coming of a dead man (the Righteous Rabbi), the alleged evidence of an alleged messiah's alleged resurrection was more than he could resist. But Jacob did accept Jesus as messiah, and was eventually executed for false prophecy when he asserted to the Sanhedrin that, despite the prophecies that the messiah must be Davidic, his non-Davidic brother was nonetheless Messiah.

Probably only after transferring its allegiance to Jesus did the Jerusalem commune and its satellite colonies come to be known as Nazirites. Certainly it bore that name in 58 CE when Paul was arrested and accused of being a ringleader of the Nazirite heresy (*Nazoraios haireseos*) (ACTS 24:5). Prior to its Jesus connection, Jacob's commune probably called itself the Saints, the title Josephus and others rendered in Greek as *Essenoi*.

Word of mouth proved adequate to keep the resurrection myth alive for a limited time only. When it became apparent that Jesus' second coming was no more imminent than the Righteous Rabbi's, an unknown Nazirite propped up the myth by committing it to writing. What he wrote was a christology, a book designed to prove that Jesus had fulfilled every known messianic prophecy and a few others that could only be interpreted as messianic by a free exercise of the imagination, and only by quoting them out of context. This was the Q gospel (German *quelle*=source), the document now lost that was the source of all of the material duplicated in *Matthew* and *Luke* but not recorded in *Mark*. In all likelihood it was Q who first added the embellishment that Jesus appeared and talked to his closest disciples after his execution.

The Q gospel, being lost, obviously cannot be dated; but it is reasonable to assume that it did not exist when Paul of Tarsus wrote his series of letters to various Christian communities between 50 and 62 CE, or he would have utilised it. In fact Paul's letters contained no information about Jesus beyond the allegation that he had risen from the dead.

Paul was the man most responsible for the spread of Jesus-mythology from Judaea, where it remained monotheistic, to the pagan world where, in the second century CE, God, Jesus and Mary became simply new names for Zeus, Dionysos and Semele. Paul, although a Jew and a Pharisee, transformed Jesusism from a Jewish heresy into a gentile mythology unrelated to Judaism, by accepting converts to his innovative sect without requiring that they be circumcised or obliged to adhere to the levitical laws attributed to Moses.

It was early in Paul's career, while he was preaching at Antioch as Barnabos's subordinate, that the term Christians (Khristianoi, 'Anointers') first came into existence. Then as now, it meant a follower of the mythology of Paul, not an adherent of the Jewish sect founded by Jesus, reorganised by Peter, and led by Jacob. While it would have been logical for a sectarian who called his dead leader Khristos to be himself designated Khristianos, the name was in fact coined by the new sect's detractors and was quite pejorative.

To a Greek, khristheis, anointing, meant the process of massaging with olive oil, usually performed by catamites, that took place in public bathhouses. A khristos was a customer, and a khristianos a body-servicer, in a massage parlour. While it is doubtful that the name Christian sprang from any belief that Christians were especially addicted to bathhouse practices (although their Essene rejection of man-woman recreation might have raised such suspicion), it was certainly invented as a joke. Had khristianismos been translated into other languages rather than being rendered in modified Greek, one is tempted to wonder how long a mythology known as Anointianity might have survived.

Within thirty years of Jesus' death, thanks (?) largely to Paul, Christian communities had been established in Syria, Anatolia, Greece and Rome. Many of those established by Paul and his followers as gentile Christian sects were later converted by followers of Jacob and Peter to Naziritism, that is to orthodox Judaism (to the degree that Essenes were orthodox) with Jesus in the role of an earthly king temporarily recalled to Heaven.

Only those Pauline communities established among practising pagans, rather than among gentiles who already attended synagogue, survived to become an independent mythology that was in no sense Jewish. And where Judaism had only been intolerant of other mythologies in Judaea, in front of Yahweh's face, Christianity was from the start fanatically intolerant of all other mythologies in all places. Not surprisingly, it quickly drew the unfavourable attention of the Roman authorities.[1]

There has never been a paramount power more tolerant of religious diversity than Rome. In an empire as widespread and with as many gods

---

1. Roman magistrates . . . began to see—quite correctly—that Christian intolerance was a threat to the empire such as Jewish nationalism had never been—a threat that was in fact made good when the church took over the empire. (A.P. Davies, The First Christian, Mentor edition, p. 105.)

as the Roman, any policy other than total freedom of belief would have been impractical. Into the capital of such an empire came a sect that ridiculed every god but its own, committed wanton sacrilege against Rome's most revered deities, vandalised shrines and temples, and threatened all who could be made to listen with eternal torture in Jesus' Hell if they continued to worship gods who differed from Yahweh only in name. Just as the equally tolerant British empire was forced to make an exception in the case of India's Thugs, so the Roman empire drew the line at tolerating the Christians. The Emperor (who happened to be Nero), with massive public support, took steps to destroy the Christians before the Christians could destroy the empire.

Josephus, who wrote about thirty years after Nero's death, recorded that half of the biographies of Nero extant at that time treated the Emperor favourably.[2] Thanks to the Christian book-burners, none survives today; and the assertion that Nero himself started the great fire of Rome and blamed it on the Christians is accepted as historical fact. Almost certainly it is nothing of the sort. Many years after Nero's death and vilification the most common belief was that the Christians were indeed guilty as charged.

Tacitus, who was fifteen years old when Nero died, wrote of the Christians accused of burning Rome:

> The confessions of those who were seized revealed a great multitude of their accomplices, and they were all convicted, not so much for the crime of setting fire to the city as for their hatred of the human race.[3]

That Tacitus was not alone in viewing the Christians unfavourably is confirmed by the Christian bible. On Paul's arrival in Rome he called upon the Jewish community. The Jewish leaders, knowing that Paul was a Jew as well as a Christian, consented to hear about Anointianity:

> We do think we should hear from you. For what is known to us about this heresy is that it's being castigated everywhere.   (ACTS 28:22)

Paul's timing was bad. Once the Christians had been convicted of burning Rome, being a Christian became a capital offence. Paul's appeal against a death sentence imposed in Caesaria was rejected by Nero, and he was executed. Unfortunately, he had already written the letters that, as much as Jesus' own sadomasochism, gave Christianity the anti-human orientation that it has retained to this day.

---

2. *Antiquities* 20:154-155.
3. *Annals of Imperial Rome* 15:44.

Paul's influence on the culture of a distant age was far greater than that of Jesus. Jesus' twisted teachings were so extreme that modern Christians, while paying lip service to every word attributed to their executed god, in fact do not castrate themselves, do not invite assailants to strike them further, do not hate their parents, siblings and spouses, do not amputate their phalluses for having an erotic dream or fantasy about a privately-owned woman, and do not (obviously, since they *are* gentiles) equate gentiles with dogs, as Jesus did (MARK 7:27). It is the more subtle masochism that derives from Paul that continues to cripple one-fifth of the human race; while until recently Paul's endorsement of slavery, autocratic tyranny and the subjugation of women were accepted without question.

It was Paul, for example, who by his example created the belief that labelling oneself a sinner, no matter how unjustly, was to be deemed a virtuous act. Jesus allegedly told a parable about a tax collector who confessed himself a sinner and asked Yahweh's mercy; but it must be remembered that in Jesus' eyes tax collectors *were* sinners, since they worked for the wrong King of the Jews. Paul, however, declared that *no one is righteous* (ROM. 3:10), and that libel of at least fifty and perhaps ninety percent of the human race contributed significantly to the universal guilt complex without which priests could not survive.

Paul's hint to the Galatians that they should undergo phallus amputations in order to avoid debate on circumcision (GAL. 5:12), is best viewed as an attempt at levity. (That it paralleled a teaching of Jesus was pure coincidence.) But it was his fanatical preaching against fornication, and the later generalisation of that word from the sacramental nun-tupping that Paul meant to all non-marital recreation, that caused the survival of the recreation taboo for post-pubertal women in an age when modern birth control methods have eliminated all of the practical considerations that brought the taboo into existence. Teenage sexual recreation continues to be viewed as immoral mainly because Paul is believed, incorrectly, to have preached against it.

Paul gave theocratic tyrannies a powerful weapon in his letter to the Romans (13:1): *There is no authority except through a god, and that which exists has been ordained by a god.* On the basis of Paul's letter, all attempts by oppressed masses to demand basic human rights were for centuries denounced as rebellion against God. Similarly Paul's admonition, *Slaves, obey those who are physically your masters as you would the messiah* (EPH. 6:5), was regularly read in southern American churches as a reminder that slavery, too, was ordained by the chief Christian god. Paul was also the inventor of the obscenity that even Popes have condemned, predestination (ROM. 8:29-30).

The longest surviving Pauline injustice, however, has been his confirmation of the status of women as men's private property:[4]

Women, submit yourselves to your men as to his lordship. For the man is his woman's head. Just as the community is subject to the messiah, so are women to their men in all things.   (EPH. 5:22-24)

Women in the community are to remain silent. They are required to be obedient, as even the Towrah commands.   (1 COR. 14:34)

The man was not created for the woman, but the woman for the man.
                                                                (1 COR. 11:9)

Paul's misogyny has begun to be rejected in the secular world, but in Christian churches women's demands for full membership in the human race continue to be ignored. And even in the secular world laws granting women equality with men have remained unratified because female victims of Paul's mind-warping have campaigned against them.

Paul died thirty years after Jesus, long before Jesus' deification by the Greek author of *John*. Since the doctrinal dispute between Paul and the Jerusalem commune led by Jacob and Peter is well documented,[5] and since Paul himself admitted that he had never heard Jesus or any of his disciples preach (GAL. 1:11-12), Paul's letters obviously cannot be taken as indicative of the doctrines of the genuine Jesus commune. However, where Paul's letters expressed beliefs that were not in conflict with those of Jesus' disciples but are incompatible with current Christian doctrine, we can be certain that the evolved doctrine was unknown in Paul's lifetime to any subject of King Jesus, Jewish or Paulinist. The Christian concept of Jesus thirty years after his death is revealed in Paul's comments on who and what he believed Jesus to be:

Physically our master, Iesous Messiah, was descended from David's sperm; but his consecrated breath was powerfully demonstrated to be a god's son by his resurrection.   (ROM. 1:3-4)

Messiah (i.e., King) Iesous, who did not have a god's shape, on the contrary considered becoming equal with a god stealing. He degraded himself, taking the shape of a slave. That's why the god has elevated him.   (PHIL. 2:5-9)

---

4. *The Bible . . . has made it possible for a great many holy men of the past to speak of women in terms that (I) would hesitate to use in referring to mad dogs.* (Isaac Asimov, *The Solar System and Back*, Discus edition, p. 224.)

5. ACTS 15; GAL. 1:16 to 2:16; JAM. 2:14-18.

You are all God's sons through credulity in Messiah (King) Iesous.
(GAL. 3:26)

Though there are many gods and many masters, to us on the other hand there is a single god, the father from whom everything exists, and a single master, Iesous Messiah, through whom everything exists.   (1 COR. 8:6)

If there is no resurrection of corpses, neither has Messiah been raised. And if Messiah has not been raised . . . we have misrepresented the god. For we have testified that the god raised the Messiah. But if corpses are not to be raised, neither has Messiah been raised.   (1 COR. 15:15-16)

Death has reigned from Adam to Moyses. Through the crime of one, many have died. By the compassion of the one human, Iesous Messiah, the god's compassion has abounded to the many.   (ROM. 5:14-15)

You welcomed me as a messenger of God, as (you did) Messiah Iesous.
(GAL. 4:14)

We preach a crucified Messiah, a scandal to Ioudaians and nonsense to infidels.
(1 COR. 1:24)

The foregoing passages leave little doubt that Paul viewed Jesus as unique, the anointed King who alone could mediate with Yahweh on behalf of other men. But they also leave no doubt that he saw Jesus' uniqueness as one of degree, not of substance. Paul's Jesus was not the Jesus of history; but neither was he the Jesus of the modern Christians. Paul saw Jesus as strictly Yahweh's creation, and his titles, including God's son, as signs of Yahweh's favour.

In declaring the concept of a crucified messiah a sacrilege, or insult, to the Jews, Paul was conceding that to most Jews a future War of Independence led by a man already dead was a self-contradiction, and the suggestion that Yahweh's anointed King could die an affront to Yahweh's foresight. And to the Greeks of the Roman empire, it was the idea of a man returning from the dead that was nonsense. Had Paul or Peter ever preached that a god had returned from the dead, that would not have struck any Greek as foolish. Belief that the virgin-born saviour-god Adonis had risen from the dead on the third day had been part of Hellenism for at least five centuries.

Paul did not call Jesus a god. Paul's translators did. Editors of recent Protestant bibles, perhaps from embarrassment that the Authorized Version of 1611 contained no mention of Jesus-the-god in the letters of Paul or pseudo-Paul (the second-century author of Timothy and Titus), have concocted translations that support modern Christian mythology by inserting into the Pauline letters beliefs that neither author held:

MISTRANSLATION: PAUL	CORRECT TRANSLATION
according to the grace of our God and Lord, Jesus Christ. (2 THES. 1:12)	according to the compassion of our god and of his Lordship Iesous Messiah.

MISTRANSLATION: PSEUDO-PAUL	CORRECT TRANSLATION
of our great God and Saviour Jesus Christ. (TITUS 2:13)	of the great god, and of our liberator, Messiah Iesous.

It could be argued that, while the mistranslation of *Thessalonians* is indefensible, the Greek of *Titus* could mean literally either of the above. However, as the Christianised translation directly contradicts pseudo-Paul's declaration that: *There is one god, and one mediator between God and men: the man Iesous the messiah* (1 TIM. 2:5), there can be no doubt that the monotheistic translation is the correct one. Pseudo-Paul would not call Jesus a god in one letter, and a purely human mediator with God in another.

Some of Paul's metaphors do appear at first glance to support the Jesus-is-God doctrine that came into existence long after Paul's death. That Paul had no such intention can be ascertained by comparing his statements about Jesus with passages in which he and the Towrah authors applied identical terminology to persons whom they clearly did not intend to categorise as Yahweh-incarnate:

(God) was pleased to have all his fullness dwell in (Jesus). (COL. 1:19)	You may be filled with all the fullness of the god. (EPH. 3:19)
It is in him that the fullness of the godly wisdom bodily resides. (COL. 2:9)	The gods created human in his own shape. (GEN. 1:27)
He is the depiction of the unseen god, the firstborn of all creation. (COL. 1:15)	Yahweh says, 'Yisrael is my son, my firstborn.' (EXOD. 4:22)

Obviously, if Paul could picture the fullness of Yahweh living in every member of the Christian community at Ephesus, then his application of the same metaphor to Jesus could not have meant that one so filled was the incarnation of Yahweh.

Paul did, however, contribute to Jesus' eventual deification by calling him *kyrios*, the Greek equivalent to *adownay*, 'His Lordship.' The application of such a title to Jesus would not have caused confusion had *adownay*, Hellenised to *Adonis*, not also been the name of a Syrian resurrected saviour-god with whom the Greek author of the second-century *Gospel of John* was familiar. In the eastern parts of the Roman empire Adownay/Adonis was known as the saviour-god who, for love of the fertility goddess Venus/Aphrodite, annually died and rose from the dead at the full moon following the vernal equinox—in other words, at Passover, when Jesus had also died and allegedly 'risen.'

Paul also called Jesus *soteros*, 'liberator,' a word that Paul saw as a readily understood gentile equivalent of the difficult Jewish concept, *mashyah*. To Paul and his immediate followers, *soteros* meant no more than the one who would liberate Judaea from the Romans. The same title was borne by several Roman Emperors including Hadrian, and also by Alexander's successor in Egypt, Ptolemaios I. Since Jesus had become a resurrected king, and possessed the same titles as a god resurrected the same day, it is less of a surprise that he was eventually equated with the Syrian saviour-god than that the equation was not made much sooner. In fact nobody called Jesus a god until Paul had been dead for sixty years.

The mythology of *Letter to the Hebrews*, written probably at Alexandria between the execution of Paul in 64 CE and the fall of the Temple in 70 CE, although essentially Pauline, was more advanced in its christology than that of Paul. To the author of *Hebrews*, Jesus' appointment as messiah raised him to a level previously restricted to Yahweh's winged messengers (*angeloi*):

> To which of the messengers did he ever say, 'You are my son; today I have become your father'? Or again, 'I will be a father to him, and he will be a son to me'. . ∴. Or again, 'All of God's messengers are to pay him homage.' . . . For it seemed appropriate to him . . . in raising many sons to high honour, to perfect by sufferings the one entrusted with their liberation.
>
> (HEB. 1:5-6; 2:10)

Hebrews's author saw the lines, 'You are my son . . . ,' actually written of King David (PS. 2:7), and 'I will be a father to him . . . ,' written of King Solomon (2 SAM. 7:14), as messianic and therefore applicable to Jesus. He made Jesus, alone of all men, outrank the angels. But he also, as his reference to Yahweh's *many sons* made clear, saw Jesus' special sonship as unique only in degree. In crediting Jesus with being *entrusted with their liberation*, he assigned to Jesus the role previously played by such saviour-gods as Adonis and Dionysos; but he stopped short of equating Jesus with the gods whose function he had usurped. The author of *Hebrews*, who some scholars think may have been Apollos, shared Paul's view that Jesus was just an anointed king, not a god.

The first-century Christians, whose views obviously coincided with those of their teacher, Paul, did not regard Jesus as a god. Nor did the Nazirites, as the surviving letter of *their* teacher, Peter, reveals. The Judaeo-Christian bible contains two letters attributed to Peter, but only *1 Peter* could be genuine. Its recommendation of Silvanos's reliability, presumably in accurately writing Peter's Aramaic dictation in Greek, would make little sense if the letter were pseudepigraphic. Peter, a Galilean fisherman, cannot reasonably be credited with the capacity to speak Greek, and he was certainly illiterate: *When they observed the audacity of Petros and Ioannes, whom they recognised as illiterate idiots, they were amazed* (ACTS 4:13).

The virtual acknowledgement in Peter's letter that the author lacked the ability to verify that his words had been recorded accurately, attests strongly to the letter's authenticity. About forty years after Peter's death it had become fashionable to pretend that the disciples were not only literate but also skilled in foreign languages (ACTS 2:4-8).[6]

The letter known as *2 Peter* was certainly a second-century forgery. Not only did it refer to the man whom Peter detested as an arch-heretic as *our beloved kinsman Paulos* (3:15); it designated Paul's letters as *graphas* (3:16), literally 'writings' but in the letter's context 'sacred writings,' a status they did not acquire until long after Peter's death. Pseudo-Peter, even though he wrote at a time when *John* had already turned Jesus into a god, adhered to the pre-Johannine orthodoxy that Jesus was merely king: '. . . *credulity in the righteousness of our god, and the liberator Iesous Messiah*' (1:1).

Peter (the genuine Peter) ended his letter: *The also-chosen in Babylon greets you* (1 PET. 5:13), a reasonable indication that he was writing from Babylon. Sometime after Peter's death an Essene apocalyptist used the name *Babylon* as a pseudonym for Rome, and this led a Manichaean around 200 CE to write an *Acts of Peter and Paul* in which Peter travelled to Rome and was crucified there. The compilers of the Christian canon recognised the Manichaean *Acts* as late and historically valueless, and excluded it from the Christian bible. But the tale that Peter had been crucified in Rome in the manner described by the Manichaean novelist, and had been Rome's Christian *episkopos*, supervisor, nonetheless became part of Christian mythology. No other document located Peter in Rome, and almost certainly he never visited the Empire's capital in his life.

The equation of Rome with Babylon was first made in 69 CE. The original author of *Apocalypse* called Rome *Babylon* (ch. 17-18) in order to prevent any Roman into whose hands the document might fall from recognising Rome as the object of the author's invective. So that Jews would correctly interpret the equation of the earlier Captivity with the present occupation, the apocalyptist included considerable specific descriptions of

---

6. The A.V. has the disciples 'speak with other tongues,' and a misinterpretation of those words has led some modern fringe sects to spout gibberish.

Rome: *seven hills on which the woman sits*. Such clarification would not have been necessary if the designation of Rome as Babylon was already established practice. Since the use of such a pseudonym was innovative in 69 CE, Peter could not have casually called Rome *Babylon* and expected to be understood twenty years earlier.

The suggestion has also been made that by *Babylon* Peter meant Jerusalem, the rationale being that, in Essene eyes, Jerusalem was occupied by a heretical Jewish majority that daily polluted the Temple by celebrating festivals on dates determined by the 'false' lunar calendar rather than the 'true' solar calendar that the Essenes had instituted. But the simplest explanation of Peter's designation of his current abode as Babylon is that, since Babylon was still standing and was by no means an improbable destination for a missionary who had certainly travelled to Antioch (GAL. 2:11), Peter was indeed writing from Babylon.

Peter's letter contained no attack on Paul's reform doctrines, as it must have done had it been written after the rupture of the shaky truce between the Pauline and orthodox branches of Jesus-mythology which occurred before Paul's death, so it can be dated earlier than 60 CE. Peter's view of Jesus was an impossible ideal, but like his enemy Paul he agreed that Jesus was no god:

He committed no disobedience; nor was duplicity found in his mouth.
(1 PET. 2:22)

God . . . raised him from a corpse and gave him magnificence. (1 PET. 1:21)

Iesous Messiah has departed to the sky and is on the right hand of God.
(1 PET. 3:21-22)

The god and father of our master Iesous Messiah is eulogised.   (1 PET. 1:3)

The god has appointed Iesous both master and Messiah.
(ACTS 2:36, quoting Peter)

Iesous the Nazirite was a man whom the god endorsed through power and wonders and omens, which the god worked through him.   (ACTS 2:22)

The god elevated him to his right hand as archon and liberator (*soteros*).   (ACTS 5:31)

Peter's speech in which he called Jesus *soteros* was composed as part of a scene in which Gamaliel anachronously referred to a rebellion that had not yet happened. Obviously, no such scene occurred. Nonetheless, it is by no means improbable that Peter at some time described Jesus with an Aramaic word roughly equivalent to *soteros*, although without risen-god implications. Luke's action in having Peter call Jesus by such a title, moved Jesus one step further along the road to eventual deification.

The *Letter of James* was probably written by Jesus' brother, Jacob the Righteous, in 48 CE. It was in that year that Jacob first learned from John Markos, a Nazirite who had accompanied Paul and shared Paul's ability to speak Greek, that Paul had been preaching heretical doctrines (in Greek) in Cyprus (ACTS 12:25; 13:13; 15:37-39). Jacob's letter, written for the specific purpose of repudiating Paul, made no comment on Jesus' status other than to call him *kyrios*. That Jacob was an Essene is evident from his advocacy of the Essene ritual of confession (JAM. 4:16; *cf.* MARK 1:5), and from his reference to the *Covenant of the Community* as scripture:

COVENANT OF THE COMMUNITY	JAMES
He has appointed for man two spirits . . . truth and falsehood. . . . Let no man address his companion with . . . envy prompted by the spirit of wickedness. (3, 5)	Do you think that the scripture is invalid that says, 'The spirit that resides in you prompts to envy'? (4:5)

Jacob, a typical Essene in his strict observance of the Levitical Law, strongly resented Paul's claim, reported to him by Markos, that salvation depended entirely on what a man believed rather than on what he did as a consequence of those beliefs. He wrote a stinging attack on Paul's mythology that was so self-evidently valid (and still is), that without exception the communities receiving Jacob's letter abandoned Christianity (Paulism) and became Nazirites (circumcised Jews) (2 TIM. 1:15):

PAUL	JACOB
We, being natural Ioudaians and not degenerate infidels, realising that a human is not deemed righteous by deeds of the Towrah but by credulity in Messiah Iesous, have credulity in Messiah Iesous, so that we might be deemed righteous by credulity in Messiah and not by (performing) deeds of the Towrah. For nobody is to be deemed righteous by deeds of the Towrah. (GAL. 2:15-16)	Can credulity liberate him? If a brother or a sister is naked and destitute of daily food, and one of you says to him, 'Depart in peace; be warmed and filled'; but you give him none of the things his body needs, what good is that? Even so, credulity unaccompanied by deeds is dead, being alone. Rather, one may say, 'You have credulity and I have deeds. Show me your credulity without your deeds, and I'll show you my credulity through my deeds.' (JAM. 2:14-18)

The contrast between the teaching of Jesus' brother, whose commune Jesus' most prominent disciples did not hesitate to join after their leader's death, and that of the man who attached Jesus' name to his gentile mythology as the result of an imagined revelation,[7] could not be greater. Jacob's letter was a logical continuation of the *seek each man the welfare of his fellows* doctrine spelled out by the Righteous Rabbi almost two centuries earlier. Paul's allegation that gullibility was the only virtue, although consistent with King Jesus' paranoid damnation of all who refused to accept an illiterate malformed runt from Galilee as Yahweh's anointed King of the Jews, was essentially a repudiation of Jesus' prescription: *For the tree is known by its fruit* (MARK 12:33). That Jacob's teaching, not Paul's, paralleled that of Jesus can also be verified from *Matthew* 25:34-40:

> Then the king will say . . . 'I was hungry and you fed me, thirsty and you gave me a drink. . . . I'm telling you, when you did it for one of the lowest-ranking of these kinsmen of mine, you did it for me.'

Jacob was executed by the High Priest Hanan in 62 CE. Under Roman law, his execution was as illegal as it was unjust, since the procurator, who alone could authorise Hanan to convene a Sanhedrin, had suddenly died and no replacement had yet arrived. Both the procurator-designate, Albinus, and King Herod Agrippa II, sent orders to Hanan not to proceed with the execution; but Hanan, who resented the Nazirite commune's establishment of an opposition Sanhedrin (LUKE 10:1), had already seen it carried out. Thus died a truly righteous man. Christianity retroactively claimed Jacob as the first Christian bishop of Jerusalem. But Jacob was neither a bishop nor a Christian. Until well into the second century CE, *episkopos* meant *supervisor*, not *bishop*. And the Nazirites were not Christians. They were Jews who saw Jesus as the fulfilment of the orthodox Jewish concept of *mashyah*. In the fifth century they were hunted into extinction—by the Christians.

Agrippa promptly removed Hanan from the high priesthood, but whether for executing a just man or for defying Roman law is uncertain. Agrippa was, after all, a Roman appointee who could not afford to give the impression of being less than subservient. Not too long afterwards Agrippa deemed it politic to turn a blind eye when his partner in recreation, his sister Berenike, moved out of his bed and into that of the Emperor Vespasian.

In 64 CE the Christians in Rome tried to burn down the city. Nero,

---

7. The author of *Acts* (9:3-9) and an interpolator in *Acts* (22:6-11) give incompatible accounts of Paul's conversion that, if based on fact, indicate that he suffered a chronic hallucination. However, since Paul's own account (GAL. 1:15-17) describes a mere revelation, as well as an earlier 'call,' both common forms of self-delusion to this day, the *Acts* accounts are best viewed as fiction composed after Paul's death. (See Appendix B.)

as much an *eye for an eye* man as any Jew, responded by tying Christians to stakes, covering them with oil and setting them afire. Unfortunately for Nero's public image, the average Roman was less vengeful than his Emperor, and the consequence was a pro-Christian backlash: *Despite their guilt as Christians, and the ruthless punishment it deserved, the victims were pitied. For it was felt that they were being sacrificed to one man's brutality rather than to the national interest.*[8]

Had Nero restricted capital punishment to the incendiaries, reaction might have been different; but he executed everyone found guilty of being Christian. Among the executed innocents was one who, while he must be held morally culpable for two thousand years of crimes against humanity, was no arsonist: Paul of Tarsus.

In 66 CE a rebellion broke out in Judaea that quickly grew into an all-out Jewish War of Independence. Vespasian's son Titus, in the process of winning the war, burned down the Temple—unintentionally, according to Josephus. But as Josephus had personal reasons for flattering the Flavians (whose name he adopted), his version of the burning need not be accepted as definitive.

It was the Jewish War, and the death of Nero and accession of Vespasian, that led to the writing of the earliest Christian gospel. Nero had been anti-Christian. Now, for obvious reasons, Vespasian was anti-Jewish. The Christians saw Vespasian's accession as a golden opportunity; for if the new Emperor could be convinced that Christianity was not merely a sect of the religion that had rebelled against the empire, but a mystery cult analogous to the Mithraism to which Vespasian as a soldier was favourably inclined, the Emperor might be persuaded to view Jesus mythology in a whole new light.

Mark, as the anonymous Greek author of the earliest surviving gospel has erroneously been designated, wrote his *evangelion* shortly after the destruction of the Temple that occurred in 70 CE. This is revealed by the retroactive prophecy that he put into the mouth of Jesus concerning the Temple's fate: *Under no circumstances is there going to be one stone left on another that isn't torn down* (MARK 13:2). Mark's 'prophecy' was far too precise to have been written before the event that it described; the prophecy of the Temple's destruction made in 63 CE by a deranged fanatic named Jesus (by a double coincidence) was much vaguer. Mark wrote after 70 CE, but almost certainly within two or three years of that date.

Mark's purpose in writing was to persuade the new Emperor to end the persecutions of Christians begun by Nero, and grant Christianity equal rights with Rome's hundred other mythologies. To that end, Mark set out to prove that the Christians were not anti-Roman like the rebellious Jews,

---

8. Tacitus, *Annals* 15:55.

but were in fact the friends of the Romans and the enemies of the Jews. His task was simplified, indeed made possible, by the decision of Jesus' cousin Shimeown, who had succeeded Jacob the Righteous as Head Nazirite, to lead his followers out of Jerusalem and into the Decapolis at the first sign of impending war. The presence in Jerusalem of the Nazirites, a Jesus commune, led by Jesus' relatives, that was unquestionably Jewish, would have made the dissociation of Christianity from Judaism impossible. To achieve his objective Mark had to falsify much history.

The prime instigators of the war had been the Zealots. Mark made the Zealot terrorist who had been Jesus' treasurer his betrayer. That Judas's betrayal was a late invention is attested by a Pauline letter's interpolator's unawareness of such an event. Paul's letters to the Corinthians were written c. 55 CE, and the interpolations inserted some time after that. The interpolator wrote that the risen Jesus was seen *by the Twelve*. That one of the (nonexistent) *Twelve* had defected or hanged himself before Jesus' alleged resurrection, as stated in *Matthew* (27:5), was a theory that the interpolator had not heard (1 COR. 15:5).

The author of *Acts* (1:18) was similarly unaware of any suicide, for he had Judas die from an accidentally sustained chest wound. And even eighty years after the composition of *Mark*, Docetic Christians who followed Gnostic rather than synoptic traditions continued to regard Judas as an apostle in good standing: *But we, his Lordship's twelve disciples* (after the crucifixion) *were weeping and were in sorrow.*[9] Clearly there was a school of Christianity that as late as 150 CE had never heard of Judas's betrayal.

Mark made no mention of Judas's death. Matthew and Luke, on the other hand, wrote incompatible accounts that coincided only on one point: They agreed that Judas did not long outlive Jesus' arrest. If their information on that point was accurate, it raises the question: Why did Mark suppress Judas's deserved fate for his monstrous crime? The most logical answer would seem to be that the details of Judas's actual death were incompatible with the actions Mark attributed to him, that in fact Judas either died trying to protect his leader, or was crucified with him. That would also explain why Matthew and Luke, seeing the desirability of reporting Judas's death but unable to give the true account, resorted to their respective imaginations (as they had done with Jesus' alleged Bethlehem birth) and came up with accounts that were mutually exclusive.

The evidence is contradictory. If Judas died at about the same time as Jesus, why did later writers think he was still alive much later? Alternatively, if he did not die in 30 CE, why did Matthew and Luke concoct the tale

---

9. *Gospel of Peter*, Akhim fragment 1:59. A slightly different translation can be found in Platt, *Lost Books of the Bible*, p. 286.

that he did? Answers to that must remain conjectural. But that Judas was not in any way responsible for Jesus' arrest is a conclusion that cannot reasonably be denied.

Vespasian's other chief enemies, the sect that had actually been goaded by the Zealots into starting the war, were the Pharisees. Even though Jesus' teaching was identical with that of the Pharisees, and the Sadducees regarded him as an upstart Pharisee, Mark included in his gospel passages in which Jesus called the Pharisees hypocrites and warned against their doctrines (MARK 7:6; 8:15), passages based on Jesus' actual attacks on the Sadducees.

The true relationship between Jesus and the Pharisees was revealed by Luke, who recorded that Jesus once fled from Herod Antipas after being warned by some Pharisees that Antipas planned to assassinate him (LUKE 13:31-33). Luke also acknowledged that some Pharisees joined the Nazirites after Jesus' death (ACTS 15:5), a most unlikely occurrence if the Pharisees had indeed been the target of Jesus' Galilean invective. Mark knew of Jesus' confrontations with a particular Jewish sect, but found it politically expedient to pretend that that sect had been the Pharisees. In fact the only Pharisees who did view Jesus unfavourably were the high-priestly families, who saw him not as an Essene (and therefore an ally) but as a dangerous Zealot.

Evidence that the original recipients of Jesus' invective were the Sadducees, who indeed rejected Jesus' Essene/Pharisaical doctrines as heretical, survives in the line, *The lawteachers and the Pharisees sit in Moyses' chair* (MAT. 23:2). By *Moyses' chair*, Jesus meant the Sanhedrin, the Maccabee-instituted Council of Seventy that he believed had been established by Moses (NUM. 11:16). While a minority of Pharisees sat in the Sanhedrin, including the high-priestly families who were *ex officio* members, the body as a whole was dominated by Jesus' real enemies, the Sadducees.

Mark's greatest falsification, however, was his rewriting of Jesus' trial and execution, reversing the roles actually played by Jews and Romans. For example, he exonerated the Roman procurator, Lucius Pontius Pilatus, who had dealt with Jesus as with any rebel, of all responsibility for the execution that he alone could have ordered. Instead Pilatus was credited with trying to save Jesus' life, an action about as probable as the Grand Inquisitor trying to save the life of a confessed devil-worshipper. A modern analogy would be for a black bossboy to haul a slave before Simon Legree and accuse him of being a rebel against Ol' Massa; for Legree to ask the slave, 'Are you really the Niggers' rightful king?' and the slave to reply, 'Did you figure that out all by yourself or did someone have to tell you?' and for Legree then to respond, 'I find no fault in this man.'

It was the Jews, so Mark pretended, who rejected Pilatus's offer to spare Jesus and demanded instead that he pardon another rebel, Jesus bar Abbas, who like Jesus bar Joseph was one of *the imprisoned revolutionaries who had committed homicide in the uprising* (MARK 15:7).[10] The significance of Mark's admission that Jesus' arrest coincided with an insurrection in which men were killed appears to have escaped the notice of Christian mythologians who uphold Mark's anti-Jewish libel

In fact the releasing of a prisoner on the occasion of a local religious festival was never a Roman custom, and had Pilatus freed a prisoner who had killed a Roman or ally in an insurrection, his own execution would have swiftly followed. To convince Vespasian that Jesus had been legalistically lynched as an enemy of the Jews, rather than executed as an enemy of Rome, Mark transferred the culpability for the death of the Christians' figurehead from Caesar's representative in Judaea, who alone was responsible, to the innocent Jews. Thirty years later Matthew would compound Mark's anti-Semitism by having the Jews declare: *'His blood be on us and on our descendants'* (MAT. 27:25). From that monstrous fiction would follow two thousand years of pogroms, culminating in Auschwitz, Dachau and Belsen.

It was Mark who transformed Jesus from a faith healer, who exorcised psychosomatic demons, into a miracle-worker of the calibre of Eliyah and Eliyshakh by the simple expedient of copying Eliyah's and Eliyshakh's alleged miracles and attributing them to Jesus. *Every* miracle described in the Christian gospels was nothing more than an adaptation of a myth already existing in the Jewish sacred writings.[11]

For example, Eliyah had made a small amount of food last for several days. Mark topped that by having Jesus feed a crowd of thousands with enough bread and fish for a handful—twice! (MARK 6:38-44; 8:5-9). To justify the separate incidents, he had twelve baskets of fragments left over on one occasion and seven on the other, and included an anecdote that drew attention to the sacred numbers, twelve and seven, representing the masculinised zodiac and the seven planets (8:19-21).[12] It is possible that Jesus' later biographers found Mark's duplication of miracles an embarrassment, since Luke copied one bagels-and-fish fable from Mark and ignored the other. However, since everything in Mark between the two bagels-and-

---

10. Robert Eisler theorises that Jesus bar Abbas, whose patronym identifies him as a son of the President of the Sanhedrin, was arrested for being at the site of Jesus' uprising at an inopportune moment. He may have been there by coincidence, or he may have been there to try to dissuade the rebels from their hopeless intent. When the mistake was arrested by the leaders of the Sanhedrin, bar Abbas was released *for the festival*, that is, in time to celebrate Passover. Bar Abbas, real name Yeshu bar Gamaliel, became High Priest in 63 CE. (*The Messiah Jesus and John the Baptist*, pp. 473 ff.)

11. Compare 3 KGS. 17:17-22 with MARK 5:22-24, 35-42; 3 KGS. 17:16 with MARK 8: 5-9; 3 KGS. 19:4-8 with MARK 1:12-13; 4 KGS. 4:42-44 with JOHN 6:9-13; 4 KGS. 5:6-14 with LUKE 17:12-14; 4 KGS. 2:21-22 with JOHN 2:7–9; and 4 KGS. 2:8 with MARK 6:48.

12. Josephus, *Jewish War* 5:5:5; ZECH. 4: 10; Zoroastrian *Menok i Xrat*.

fish stories is missing from *Luke*, a better explanation is that Luke finished copying the first tale, rerolled the scroll, and later resumed copying from the second such tale in the belief that that was where he had left off.

Mark introduced into his pseudo-Jewish mythology certain elements of pagan worship that, despite centuries of foreign overlordship, had not previously penetrated Judaism. For example, he had Jesus describe himself as a shepherd and his followers as sheep (MARK 14:27), as Zarathustra had done over six hundred years earlier. He emulated Zarathustra's biographers in describing his Hero's death as a sacrifice for many (14:24). He gave Jesus a last supper with twelve followers, identical in every way with the last supper of the Persian god Mithra, down to the cannibalisation of the god's body in the form of bread and wine (14:22-26).

The Spartan King Kleomenes had held a similar last supper with twelve followers four hundred years before Jesus.[13] Kleomenes, however, had been consciously imitating his god as an act of worship. Mark apparently attributed such a ritual to Jesus in the hope of making Christianity observably similar to Mithraism, a religion to which most of Vespasian's soldiers adhered and which the Emperor held in high regard. Much later an interpolator inserted Mark's last-supper myth into Paul's letter to the Corinthians (1 COR. 11:23-25). That Paul could not have written such a scene is self-evident. Mark, a Greek, could have accused Jesus of such a pagan act. Paul, a Jew, could not. Mark also had Jesus, during the forty-day fast copied from the myth of Eliyah (3 KGS. 19:4-8), tempted by the Satan (MARK 1:13), just as Zarathustra had been tempted by the Satan's Persian prototype, Ahriman; and Gautama was tempted by Mara,[14] the original Night Mara (nightmare), whose vampire fangs drained men's lifeblood while she rode them to orgasm during sleep.

Mark recorded probably the Judaeo-Christian bible's only genuine account of an unlikely prophecy that came true. In 63 CE, three years before the insurrection that evolved into total war, a man named Jesus bar Hanan began howling: '*Alas for Jerusalem. Alas for the city and the nation and the Sacred Dwelling.*' He was questioned by the procurator, Albinus, but was released when he was found to be of unsound mind. He continued his daily ravings until Yahweh's Temple was in fact levelled by Titus in 70 CE.[15] Mark reported the prophecy of the Temple's destruction, made it much more specific than it had actually been, and attributed it to a different Jesus who, at the time the prophecy was actually made, had been dead for thirty years (MARK 13:3).

---

13. Plutarch, *Parallel Lives*, 'Agis and Kleomenes' 37:2-3.
14. *Zend Avesta*, Vendidad, Fargard 19:6:20; M. Lurker, *Dictionary of Gods and Goddesses*, pp. 128, 221.
15. Josephus, *Jewish War* 6:5:3.

Mark put into Jesus' mouth perhaps the most repulsive mythology in the entire Judaeo-Christian bible; yet it was a logical extension of a concept that had been invented in a primitive form by the Elohist and perfected by Paul: predestination.

Eight hundred years earlier the Elohist had written: *I (Yahweh) show compassion to whom I choose, and mercy to whom I choose* (EXOD. 33:19). That admission that Yahweh was arbitrary, choosing who was to live and who to die by the toss of a coin, is damaging to Yahweh's image even when viewed in the context of the Elohist's mythology. But it must be remembered that the Elohist wrote at a time when Zarathustra and Jesus had not yet invented Heaven and Hell. To the Elohist, the extinction of death was the end of existence. If Yahweh chose to end some people's lives earlier than others, that was his privilege. Eventually all must cease to exist in any case.

To the Pharisee Paul of Tarsus, death was not the end of existence. Not only did he believe in separate afterlives for *Us* and *Them*; he also imagined that Moses, who he thought had written *Exodus*, had believed the same thing. Consequently, where the Elohist had accused Yahweh of arbitrarily shortening men's lives, Paul read the passage as indicating that Yahweh arbitrarily consigned men to Heaven or Hell. Thus it did not occur to Paul that he was crediting Yahweh with a hitherto unparalleled atrocity when he wrote:

> Whom he foreknew, he predestined; and whom he predestined, he called; and whom he called, he also justified; and whom he justified, he also glorified. . . . What are we to say then? Can the god be unrighteous? May it not happen! You will say to me then, 'Why does he find fault? For who can withstand his whim?' Human, who are you to contradict the god? . . . Doesn't the potter have power over the clay, to make from the same lump one vessel in honour and another in dishonour?   (ROM. 8:29-30; 9:14-15, 19-21)

Paul's mythology, that Yahweh created humans for the specific purpose of having someone to torture with his flamethrowers, was obscene. Mark made it more so:

> The Twelve asked him about the fables. And he told them, 'To you, permission has been given to understand the mystery of Allah's theocracy. But to those who are outside, all things are to be told in fables, so that in seeing they may not perceive, and in hearing they may not understand, in case they convert and obtain forgiveness.'   (MARK 4:10-12)

The Jesus who deliberately spoke in riddles in case he accidentally caused the salvation of persons whom his sadistic father had predestined to damnation, has been given very little coverage in the Christian press.

Mark wrote what was on the surface a simple fairy tale about exorcism and pigs, but was in fact a promise to the Jews of the fate that awaited their Roman overlords, written in symbolism that the Roman censors would fail to understand. Jesus asked a man possessed by *Enoch*'s evil spirits his name, and was answered, '*My name is Legion.*' Jesus sent the man's inhabitants out of him and into a herd of pigs, which then ran off a cliff and drowned in the sea (MARK 5:8-13).

Since the fall of the city a few months earlier, Jerusalem had been occupied by the Roman Tenth Legion, whose emblem was a pig. Mark's reference to *about two thousand* pigs, the size of the occupying Legion, combined with his blatant designation of the evil beings as *Legion*, left no doubt in Jewish minds that the pigs in the fable represented the army of occupation. Mark's fable in effect promised that the messiah, when he returned, would drive the Romans into the sea as he had earlier driven their four-legged surrogates.

Such a story could only have originated with Mark, as it could not have been composed prior to the assignment of the Tenth Legion to Judaea. And prior to the outbreak of war in 66 CE, Jerusalem had been occupied, not by a Legion but by a garrison of two hundred auxiliaries. In Jesus' time the nearest Legion had been stationed in Syria.

Mark recorded a promise by Jesus to his followers that even at the time of writing was observably unfulfilled and unfulfillable:

There's no one who has abandoned home or brothers or sisters or mother or father or children or lands for my sake and the sake of the evangelion, who will not receive one hundred times as many homes and brothers and sisters and mothers and children and lands in this time, and eternal life in the coming aeons.   (MARK 10:29-30)

It was a recurrent theme in Jesus' preaching that his followers should abandon their unbelieving families as he had done. As an incentive, he not only offered them worldly possessions that he proved unable to deliver; he also bestowed on them the power of telekinesis:

Whoever says to this mountain, 'Be torn up and tossed into the sea,' and is uncritical in his heart and credulous that what he asks will happen, it will be done for him.   (MARK 11:23)

In the nineteen hundred years since Mark's Hero promised that journeys past a mountain could be simplified by ordering the mountain to move out of the way, no Christian who has attempted such a feat has succeeded in moving a single pebble.

Mark reported that, when a man addressed Jesus as 'Righteous Rabbi,' Jesus responded, 'Why do you call me righteous? No one is righteous except the god alone' (MARK 10:17-18; MAT. 19:16-17; LUKE 18:18-19). Jesus' declaration that, not being God, he was not and could not be righteous, was incompatible with anything that a Christian author would have invented after his death, and for that reason may be accepted as historical. And Jesus' unambiguous denial that he was 'the god,' besides demolishing the modern Christian dogma of Jesus' divinity, also shows that Mark had never heard of such a theory or he would not have so casually recorded Jesus' words without commenting on them.

Almost certainly it was not the description righteous that Jesus was repudiating, particularly as the Hebrews gospel recorded his claim never to have sinned, but the title Righteous Rabbi. To have accepted such a title would have amounted to an admission that he was no more than the equal of the original Righteous Rabbi—and perhaps no more than the equal of his younger brother Jacob, the (possibly) current Head Essene. By denying that he or anyone else could rightfully be styled Righteous Rabbi, Jesus was furthering his claim to be unique, not merely the successor of founders of sects who had usurped unmerited titles.

The authenticity of Mark's story was lent some support by Matthew. Matthew reported that Jesus denied the right of any person (obviously including the Head Essene) to be called rabbi, on the ground that the messiah was the only rabbi (MAT. 23:8).

Mark made a further reference to the War of 66-70 CE in his 'Little Apocalypse' (13:5-27). He wrote:

> When you hear of wars and rumours of wars, don't be alarmed. While this is bound to happen, it will not be the end yet. . . . But when you see the desolation-inducing sacrilege standing where it does not belong, then those in Ioudaia are to flee to the mountains. . . . Oy vay to women carrying in the belly and breast-feeding in those days.

The term desolation-inducing sacrilege had been coined by Fourth Daniel, and referred to the pollution of the Temple by Antiokhos IV in 168 BCE (DAN. 9:27; 12:11; 1 MACC. 1:20-21). Antiokhos's act had led to a war that, although ultimately successful (from the Jewish viewpoint), had taken many Jewish lives. In 66 CE the Temple was again polluted, this time by the presence of Zealot warmongers who would start a War of Independence without waiting for the return of the Nazirite messiah to lead it. It was at that point that Shimeown bar Klofas, Jesus' cousin, led the Nazirites out of Jerusalem to the safety of the Decapolis. Mark's Little Apocalypse retroactively turned that exodus into the consequence of a prophecy by Jesus.

Mark recorded as fact a tale that had originated as a parable. Jesus told a fable of a fig tree that had borne no fruit for three years. The owner of the tree declared that he would cultivate it for one more year, then if it still proved nonproductive he would cut it down.

The story had originated with Q, whose original version has been preserved by Luke (LUKE 13:6-9). In the few years between Q and *Mark* it had become somewhat elaborated. Mark wrote that Jesus saw a fig tree and, being hungry, desired to eat its fruit. Learning that figs were out of season, Jesus cursed the tree, causing it to wither and die (MARK 11:12-14, 20-21). Confronted by two versions of the same story, one in *Mark* and one in Q, Luke recorded the original while Matthew (21:19) copied *Mark*.

Like all books of its day, *Mark* was written on rolled parchment, with the beginning of the gospel nearest the axle. As a consequence, the end of the scroll, being the most susceptible to wear, dampness and other damage, has not survived. Later gospels, written when Christianity was better organised, did not suffer the same fate. The last surviving verse of the original author's work is *Mark* 16:8. The twelve verses with which *Mark* now ends in most bibles were composed in the second century to replace Mark's own lost conclusion, and were based on material borrowed from *Matthew* and *Luke*. Evidence of the spuriousness of the concluding verses can be verified in the surviving manuscripts, which are reasonably near-identical only up to 16:8. Thereafter endings differ. Eusebius around 300 CE declared that the interpolated ending was missing from almost all manuscripts known to him.

Toward the end of the reign of Vespasian's son Domitian (81-96 CE) were published the *Letter of Jude* and the final Nazirite version of an earlier Essene *Apocalypse*. *Jude*, apart from its reference to *tou kyriou hemon Iesou Khristou*, contained nothing to identify its author as a Christian or a Nazirite rather than an orthodox Essene. It is within the bounds of possibility that by *Iesous Khristos* he meant the Righteous Rabbi; but in view of the widespread use of the term *Khristianos* to denote a follower of the crucified Jesus, this seems unlikely. Whether new or old, he was an Essene, since his direct quotation from *Enoch* (JUDE 14), and paraphrasing of the *Assumption of Moses* (JUDE 9) leave no doubt that he belonged to a sect that regarded those Essene books as sacred.

Identification of *Ioudas*, as the author identified himself, has proven difficult. He called himself the brother of Jacob (JUDE 1) and, in an attempt to maintain the pretence that the Christian bible was written by persons close to Jesus, this has led English-language bible translators to render *Luke*'s questionable apostle, *Ioudan Iakobou*, as 'the brother of James' rather than 'the son of James.' That *Jude* was written by a disciple of whom Mark and Matthew had no knowledge is somewhat improbable.

The hypothesis that the author of *Jude* was Jesus' brother likewise cannot be taken seriously. Had such been the case it would be incomprehensible that he called himself *brother of Iakobos* rather than *brother of his lordship*, the title commonly applied to Jacob. Also, the likelihood of Jesus having *two* brothers who had not only learned to read but were also competent in Greek must be extremely low. Jesus' brother Judas (*Yahuwdah*) certainly became a Nazirite, but that he wrote *Jude* is most unlikely.

Hugh Schonfield's identification of the letter's author as the grandson of Jesus' brother Yahuwdah makes the most sense. However, references to Jesus' grand-nephews by the earliest Christian mythologians and chroniclers named them as Jacob and Zakharyah, not Jacob and Judas. And Domitian's action in freeing Jacob and Zakharyah after arresting them, on the ground that they were too ignorant to be dangerous, also argues against one of them being sufficiently learned to have written *Jude*. However, since Judas's identification of himself as the brother of Jacob clearly implied that Jacob was a person of some standing in the Nazirite (or other Essene) community, the possibility that he was Jesus' relative cannot be ruled out.

The *Apocalypse*, in its original form, was written in barbaric Koine Greek by a man whose native language was Aramaic. Its composition can be precisely dated to the time of the siege of Jerusalem. The author was aware of the death of Nero, which occurred in 68 CE (APO. 13:3-5), but unaware of the burning of the Temple, which he confidently prophesied could never happen (APO. 11:1-2), but which in fact occurred in 70 CE. The author can be identified as an Essene by his reference to the war in the sky in which the planet Mars (*Mikhael*) and his angels expelled the planet Venus (*ho Satanas*) and his angels (APO. 12:7-9). That Zoroastrian myth, found in *Enoch*, was never part of orthodox Jewish mythology.

Apocalypse was essentially an invective against Rome, built around a never-fulfilled prophecy that the imperial capital would be totally annihilated for daring to besiege Jerusalem (17:3 to 18:21; esp. 17:9; 18:8). Further invective was directed against the two Emperors responsible for the siege. The apocalyptist called them *beasts*, and declared that one had been *fatally killed, but its fatal wound had healed* (13:3), while the second, whom he significantly described in the present tense, bore the number 666 (13:18).

The first beast can easily be identified as Nero, in whose reign the war started and who first sent Vespasian to Jerusalem *to wage war against the Essenes and to defeat them* (13:7). Nero committed suicide, but was nonetheless rumoured for many years to have cheated death and to be planning a comeback.

The beast whose number was 666, who *is exercising all the authority of the first beast* (13:12), sometimes identified as Domitian in the belief that the author was a Christian and that his target must have been a persecutor of Christians, was in fact Vespasian. Vespasian was responsible for the assault upon Jerusalem, and was the reigning Emperor at the time of writing.[16]

The anti-Roman Essene author was nothing if not confident. Writing at a time when Jerusalem had already been under siege for more than two years, he prophesied that the Romans were *going to trample over the consecrated town for forty-two months* (11:2). In predicting that the war would end in about a year, he was perfectly correct. Unfortunately for his credibility, he failed to predict that the Romans would win. He also miscalculated by 150 kilometres the location of the last battle. He placed it at Mount Megiddo (*har Magedon*, or *Armageddon*), north of Jerusalem (16:16). In fact it took place at Masada, to the south.

Following the defeat of the Roman army at *har Magedon*, Rome itself was to be burned to the ground (ch. 17-18). After that would come the extermination of all who did not have Yahweh's phylactery sealed (strapped) to their foreheads (9:4). However, while the wearing of a phylactery, a leather pouch containing selections from the Towrah, might have been a reliable external indication of who were the Saints, it was not in itself the criterion for who was to be saved. Yahweh's exterminators were to wipe out the entire population of planet Earth *except the 144,000 who had been ransomed from the land, celibates who had never degraded themselves with women, for they had remained unpolluted* (14:3-4). The 144,000 were to consist of 12,000 from each of the tribes of Israel. For some reason, however, the 'twelve tribes' included Joseph and Menasheh, but not Efrayim or Dan (7:4-8).

The Essene author left no doubt of his sect's unequivocal hatred of the human race when he consigned to the eternal flamethrowers *all* gentiles, *all* women, *all* orthodox Jews, and even all secular Essenes, for the unforgivable sin of abandoning celibacy. To a celibate Essene monk, salvation was restricted to 144,000 celibate Essene monks. Not until *Apocalypse* was expanded and edited by a Nazirite at a time when the alleged virtue of celibacy was being downplayed, were copulators, including circumcised converts to Nazirite Judaism, admitted into Yahweh's elect: *a huge crowd which no one was able to number* (because numbers higher than 'ten thousand times ten thousand' could not be recorded in existing numerations) *from every infideldom and tribe and nation and language* (7:9). Obviously, that crowd would not include any uncircumcised *Khristianoi*.

The Nazirite redaction of *Apocalypse* was made toward the end of the

---

16. It is not necessary to show a sample calculation to prove that 666 could be Vespasian. Both historians and mythologians have demonstrated that, by regarding such words as *Caesar* and *Imperator* as optional, by including or excluding dates or other information that might have been on the public inscription that the author used to make his calculation, and by feeling free to make the calculation in Greek, Latin, Hebrew or Aramaic, it is possible to make Vespasian, or Nero, or Domitian, or for that matter George Washington, Joseph Stalin or Pope Borgia, add to 666, or 616, or any other number one cares to choose.

reign of Domitian (81-96 CE) by a man named Ioannes, who was neither the anonymous author of the gospel to which the name *John* has been arbitrarily attached, the anonymous author of the letters similarly designated *John*, nor the Beloved Disciple who was long dead before the composition of *John* and whose name remains unknown. Even though the Essene original author and the Nazirite redactor both wrote in Koine, and much of *Apocalypse* is compatible with the mythology of both, a reasonably accurate separation of the two is possible, and can be found at the end of this chapter.

The Nazirite redactor, who composed the letters to seven Nazirite communities with which the edited work begins, endorsed his predecessor's attacks on Rome; but he also added a new target: the Christians, and their founder, Paul. He wrote:

> I'm aware of the rantings of those who call themselves Ioudaians and are not, but are a synagogue of the Enemy.   (APOC. 2:9)

> I do have a few things against you, however, since you have some there who adhere to the teaching of Balaam, who taught . . . to eat food dedicated to godlets and to practise nun-tupping.   (2:14)

> I do have this against you, that you tolerate the woman Iezabel who calls herself a prophetess but beguiles my slaves to practise nun-tupping and to eat food dedicated to godlets.   (2:20)

> I am aware of your deeds, and that you have the reputation of being alive when you are (really) dead.   (3:1)

By *those who call themselves Ioudians and are not*, the Nazirite author meant the uncircumcised Christians. The *teaching of Balaam* represented the Nazirite view of the teaching of Paul. The identity of *the woman Iezabel* remains a mystery. Even though the redactor was writing at a time when celibacy was out of favour, and Paul was known to have been a staunch supporter of celibacy and to have practised it (possibly because he suffered from psychosomatic impotence),[17] it is most unlikely that he would have called Paul a woman. And he could not have been referring to the goddess Mary, mother of the god Jesus, because neither had been invented yet. Perhaps in the late first century Christianity's chief spokesperson was the woman

---

17. Paul certainly had a medical problem. He wrote that he had three times prayed for the removal of *a thorn in the flesh, the Satan's messenger, sent to prick me* (2 COR. 12:7). Mythologians have claimed that this was a tendency to satyriasis, making it hard for Paul to remain celibate. The evidence of *Galatians* 4:13-15 indicates that it was in fact advancing blindness, although some scholars believe it was epilepsy.

named Priscilla of Acts 18:24-26. Some scholars think she, rather than her student Apollos, wrote *Letter to the Hebrews.*

The *Gospel of the Hebrews*, parts of which survive in quotations by later writers, was composed around the year 100 CE. Its author wrote in Hebrew, probably at Alexandria, and claimed to be the historically dubious apostle Maththaios. For that reason *Hebrews* is sometimes called *Hebrew Matthew.* The author of the canonical gospel known as *Matthew*, on the other hand, wrote in Greek at about the same time and did *not* claim to be the apostle Maththaios.

Early in the second century CE the Christian writer Papias expressed the belief that Maththaios had written, in Hebrew, a collection of the maxims of Jesus. Almost certainly he was referring to *Hebrews*, although it is not impossible that he had in mind the Q gospel. He declared that Maththaios's Hebrew tract had been widely translated. When *Hebrews* was discovered and found to contain an admission by Jesus that he might have sinned, that passage was deemed adequate evidence in the eyes of second-century Christians that it was a pseudepigraphic forgery. *Hebrews* was excluded from the Christian canon and an alternative *Matthew* was sought.

An anonymous Greek-language gospel then in existence appeared to conform to Papias's general description, even though it was not a translation of a gospel originally composed in Hebrew, and contained no hint that its author had been Maththaios. It was this Greek gospel that, in order to uphold Papias's claim that the nonexistent Maththaios had written a gospel, was given the name *Matthew* and retains the name *Matthew* to this day. While many of the sayings attributed to Jesus in *Matthew* were indeed Greek translations of Hebrew verse (7:1; 7:6-8; 11:17; 23:34-35; 23:37-38), the gospel as a whole was composed by a man who could not read Hebrew.

Hebrews contributed to the evolution of Christianity's only unique god. As early as 140 BCE the Essenes had regarded man's good and evil tendencies as springing from the influence of antithetical instincts or spirits (life forces)[18] placed in him by Yahweh:

---

18. In Hebrew (*nefesh*), Greek (*pneuma*) and Latin (*spiritus*), a word that meant literally *breath* was also used to mean the extra-corporeal 'life' that turned a mere carcass into a living being. I have translated JOHN's *pneuma tes aletheias* as 'spirit of truth'; but it could as accurately be rendered 'breath of truth' or, idiomatically, 'living truth.' I have retained 'holy spirit' for *pneuma to hagion*, but it could be rendered as 'sacred life' or even 'God's breath' without distorting the author's meaning. Unquestionably the Greek gospel authors (but *not* the Jew Jesus) thought of the *pneuma* (*nefesh*) as a thinking being; but originally the 'spirit' or 'soul' meant nothing more than the breath that distinguished the living from the dead. For more on this point see 'The Subtlest Difference' in Isaac Asimov's *The Road to Infinity*, NY, 1979.

Yahweh has created man to govern the land, and has assigned for him two spirits in which to walk until the time of his visitation: the spirits of truth and falsehood.

He is to be cleansed from all his sins by the spirit of holiness that unites him to the gods' truth.

He is going to pour the spirit of truth onto him like purifying waters to cleanse him of all unorthodoxy and falsehood.

Let no man address his companion with . . . envy prompted by the spirit of wickedness.

(COVENANT OF THE COMMUNITY 3, 4, 5)

That the various *spirits* mentioned in the *Covenant* were not *persons*, living beings, is readily apparent. That Jesus, like any Essene, used the terms *spirit of truth* and *spirit of holiness* as metaphors for a pious state of mind, similarly need not be doubted. Mark reported that Jesus once said: *Anyone who slanders contrary to the holy spirit will never be forgiven. He is guilty of eternal disobedience* (MARK 3:29). If *spirit of truth* is substituted for *holy spirit* in Jesus' declaration, not only does it make sense out of nonsense; it also reveals that he was quoting from the *Covenant* stipulation that only unintentional sins can be purged by penance. Sins committed wilfully, contrary to the spirit of truth and holiness, carried automatic excommunication from the commune and, as a consequence, inevitable death.

Gospel of the Hebrews, accepting *Mark*'s personification of the just man's *truthful spirit* into a living being, gave Mark's creation an identity. 'Maththaios' put into Jesus' mouth the words, '*Even now my mother the holy spirit took me by one of my hairs and carried me to Tabor Mountain.*' Luke, uncertain whether to treat Mark's *holy spirit* as a being or a metaphor, compromised and gave it a physical existence but not necessarily an identity (ACTS 2:1-4).

John furthered *Hebrews*' designation of the holy spirit as a goddess by having Jesus say, '*Unless a man is born of water and the spirit, he cannot enter the theocracy*' (JOHN 3:3). Jesus and his predecessor had immersed their followers in the cleansing waters of the Jordan river, so that the disciple having his sins forgiven was in a sense reborn sinless from the Jordan's womb. *John*, the only gospel to use the terms *spirit of truth* and *holy spirit* interchangeably (14:17; 14:26; 15:26), imagined that Jesus saw immersion as a double rebirth, with the purified body emerging from the womb of the river, and the purified soul emerging from the womb of his mother the holy spirit.

In following *Hebrews* and making the holy spirit female, the author of *John* was apparently unaware of the existence of an interpolated version of *Matthew* in which the holy spirit had been masculinised and made to emulate Zeus by impregnating the virgin Mary/Semele. Sometime later, toward the end of the third century CE, another interpolator inserted into *Luke* a passage in which the circumstances of Mary's impregnation were made to conform to the myth currently found in *Matthew*, with a male holy spirit again supplying the sperm. Thus in modern bibles, since they include the interpolations but exclude *Hebrews*, the masculinised holy spirit outnumbers the original feminine version by two books to one.

Too little of *Hebrews* survives to allow for any assessment of its author's sources. *Matthew*'s sources, however, are more easily discernible. The author's three main sources were *Mark*, from which he took, among other things, Jesus' pretended hostility to the Pharisees and Judas's role as Jesus' betrayer; Q, from which he obtained the parables not found in *Mark*; and a genealogy composed after Jesus' death to prove that, despite his own admission to the contrary, he really was descended from King David.

Matthew began his gospel with: *The scroll of the ancestry of Iesous Messiah, descendant of David, descendant of Abraham* (MAT. 1:1), thereby establishing from the start that Jesus was the prophesied Davidic king. *Matthew*'s original wording has been preserved only in an early Syriac codex, in which the genealogy concluded: *And Iakob fathered Ioseph, the husband of Mariam, and he fathered Iesous, the reputed Messiah.*

All surviving Greek manuscripts contain the revised genealogy: *Iakob fathered Ioseph, the husband of Mariam, of whom was born Iesous, the reputed Messiah* (MAT. 1:16). That amendment was made in order to harmonise the genealogy with the virgin-birth fable that the interpolator inserted immediately after it. As with most interpolations, the insertion created an inconsistency, since it made the genealogy fail to live up to its opening sentence.

Q had written an annunciation scene. Just as a winged messenger had been sent by Yahweh to Abraham to inform him that Sarah would bear his son (GEN. 18:10), and later to Samson's mother with a similar announcement (JUDG. 13:3), so Q requisitioned a messenger to announce to Joseph and Mary that they were to be the parents of the messiah. Both Matthew and Luke incorporated Q's tale into their gospels (MAT. 1:20-21; LUKE 1:26-33). Luke's original wording survives, since the interpolator merely inserted additional verses (LUKE 1:34-35) but otherwise left the original annunciation scene complete and unchanged. Matthew's annunciation scene, being incompatible with virgin birth, was altered to harmonise with the interpolation. *Matthew*'s original wording has also been preserved in the Sinaitic Syriac codex:

INTERPOLATED VERSION	ORIGINAL VERSION
She's going to bear a son, and you're to name him Iesous. (MAT. 1:21)	She's going to bear you a son, and you're to name him Iesous.

In its present form, *Luke* contains a passage in which Mary asked Gabriel/Hermes/Mercury how she could bear a son when she was currently a virgin, and was given an answer that echoed *Matthew*'s virgin-birth myth (LUKE 1:34-35). Since Mary was already espoused to Joseph such a question would have been absurd. That the passage was not originally part of Luke's gospel, and that the disclaimer of Joseph's paternity in *Luke* 3:23 was likewise interpolated later, is evident from Luke's consistent references to Joseph and Mary as Jesus' parents, and to their other children as Jesus' brothers (LUKE 2:48; 3:23; 4:22; 8:19).

Luke also wrote several passages in which strangers' glorification of Jesus, and Jesus' references to Yahweh as his father, caused Joseph and Mary to be astonished (LUKE 2:19, 33, 48-51). Luke could not have written such passages if he had previously written that Joseph and Mary were well aware that Jesus was the offspring of divine parentage. Matthew likewise could not have been so inconsistent as to make Jesus simultaneously the physical son of Yahweh from birth (MAT. 1:18-25), and the adopted son of Yahweh from the time of his immersion by John (MAT. 3:17).[19]

Matthew in its original form (containing the genealogy but not the virgin-birth myth) could not have been composed much before 100 CE; otherwise Luke would have been aware of its existence and borrowed its genealogy rather than promoting an incompatible genealogy of his own. Yet, since the accusation of bastardy against Jesus was first raised as early as 100 CE,[19] and that accusation was based on interpolated-*Matthew*'s claim that Jesus was virgin-born, it is evident that *Matthew* must have been interpolated within about a decade of its original composition. As unlikely as such a prompt interpolation may seem, the alternative, that the original author contradicted himself in successive paragraphs so blatantly that he could not have been unaware of the inconsistency, is even more unlikely.

The reason an interpolator of *Matthew* composed a fable that denied Jesus' Davidic descent as the son of Joseph, was that he erroneously believed that Isayah had prophesied that the messiah was to be the son of a virgin. In fact Isayah had prophesied nothing of the sort. The interpolator, a Greek who could not read Hebrew, read in a Greek mistranslation of *Isaiah*: *A virgin is going to become pregnant and bear a son who is to be named Emmanouel.* He quoted the prophecy (MAT. 1:23), and made Jesus fulfil it. In fact

---

19. These points will be elaborated a little later.

Isayah had actually written: *A young woman* (khalmah) *is going to become pregnant and bear a son who is to be named 'Allah is on our Side'* (Emanuw-El) (ISA. 7:14). When *Isaiah* had been translated into Greek, the Hebrew word *khalmah*, which did not mean *virgin*, was mistranslated as *parthenos*, which did mean *virgin*. Had Isayah meant Emanuwel's mother to be a virgin he would not have called her a *khalmah*, commonly used to denote a young married woman, but *bethuwlah*, the Hebrew word for *virgin* (*cf.* GEN. 24:16; DEUT. 22:23).

Had the interpolator of *Matthew* been able to read Hebrew, the fable that Jesus was the son of a virgin would never have been concocted. Indeed, had he bothered to read the *Emanuwel* prophecy in its proper context, he would have realised that Emanuwel's birth was one of several omens (including a man giving milk!)[20] that Isayah had allegedly shown King Akhaz as evidence that Yahweh would aid him against the kings of Syria and Israel (ISA. 7). Emanuwel, in fact, appears to have been Isayah's son (ISA. 7:16; 8:3-8), and certainly Isayah made clear that his 'prophecy' of Emanuwel's birth had been fulfilled at the time of writing. Only a man desperate to find prophecies for Jesus to fulfil could have seen the *Emanuwel* passage as messianic; and only a man self-hypnotised to a fanatic degree could have imagined that the woman's son *who is to be named Emmanouel* was Jesus, who was never called *Emmanouel* in his life.

The interpolator of *Matthew* was chronically addicted to imaginative prophecy fulfilment—and so was the gospel's original author. Since the mental functioning (or dysfunctioning) of the two authors was so similar, and since *Matthew* was interpolated unreasonably soon after its composition, the possibility exists that the interpolator *was* the original author. Matthew may have completed his gospel in its original form, discovered the *Emanuwel* passage in Greek *Isaiah*, and then clumsily inserted a virgin-birth fable into his own finished work without adequately altering earlier passages that were incompatible with the new addition. But that is speculation. What is certain is that the virgin-birth fable was squeezed into a gospel that did not originally contain it.

Matthew located another 'prophecy,' actually a reference to the Exodus of Moses' day: *Out of Egypt I am calling my son* (HOS. 11:1; MAT. 2:15). Jesus had never been to Egypt, so Matthew invented a story that took him there. Following Jesus' birth, an unspecified number of maguses, Zoroastrian astrologer-priests from Persia, informed King Herod that they had seen a

---

20. ISA. 7:21. In an age of universal credulity, such a claim would not have struck the reader as absurd. Eight centuries later the usually-critical Tacitus could write in his *Annals*: *A woman gave birth to a snake* (14:12); . . . *two-headed offspring of men and beasts* (15:47); *Half-bestial children were born, and a pig with hawk's claws* (12:63).

new star that heralded the prophesied King of the Jews. Herod was not the kind of man to tolerate a rival king, so he ordered the massacre of all children born in Bethlehem, the prophesied messiah's predestined birthplace, within the previous two years. In so doing he fulfilled a prophecy of Jeremyah: *A voice was heard in Rhama, Rakhel weeping for her descendants, refusing to be comforted, for they no longer existed* (MAT. 2:18). In fact Jeremyah's 'prophecy,' as the context made clear, referred to the Babylonian Captivity (JER. 31:15).

To protect Jesus from Herod's order, Joseph and Mary took him to Egypt where he remained until Herod's death (whereas in Luke's nativity myth he was taken directly from Bethlehem to Galilee). That the Herod involved was the dynasty's founder who died in 4 BCE was made clear by Matthew's declaration that he was succeeded by his son Arkhelaos (MAT. 2:22).

Josephus detested Herod the Great, and catalogued every atrocity that Rome's Idumaean puppet ever perpetrated. Yet nowhere in Josephus's pages (nor in the less-than-flattering biography of Herod written by Nicholas of Damascus) was there recorded any mention of this most repulsive crime of all, for a very good reason: Herod's massacre did not happen. A disciple of John the Immerser had borrowed the infant-massacre tale from older Jewish mythology and applied it to Herod in order to add an element of the miraculous to the birth of John.[21] Matthew changed Herod's intended victim from John to Jesus for the sole purpose of propping up his pretence that Jesus had come *out of Egypt*. The number of would-be messiahs to come out of Egypt was high enough to suggest that Matthew was not the first to view Hosea's Exodus passage as messianic; but the only messianic claimant known to have fulfilled a second prophecy was Herod Agrippa I. The spuriousness of Jesus' trip to Egypt did not prevent a later mythologian from inventing a sailor who took him there: Saint Christ-carrier (*Khristophoreas, Christopher*).

As a Greek, Matthew was probably aware of the myth that the virgin-mother Isis had hidden her saviour-god son Horus from the rage of the sun-god Set until the waning of Set's power, that is, for the duration of the summer. The hiding of Jesus until the waning of Herod's power was an obvious parallel. The story of a Hero's escape from a massacre of children had first been told in connection with the birth of the Hindu god Krishna. In Judaism the earliest intended victim was Abraham, whom the jealous King Nimrod of Babylon had tried to destroy when he learned of Abraham's birth through the sudden appearance of a new star (just as the magi learned of Zarathustra's birth through the appearance of a new star). The Yahwist added a similar massacre of infants to his fable of the birth of Moses.

---

21. H. Schonfield, *The Lost Book of the Nativity of John*.

The identity of the mythical Star of Bethlehem continues to be discussed by mythologians as if such a phenonemon actually occurred. It is by no means improbable that sightings of spectacular astronomical events about a century earlier (the conjunction of Jupiter and Saturn three times in 7 BCE; Halley's comet in 12 BCE) were known to Matthew. Retroactively associating such phenomena with the birth of Jesus was so logical as to be inevitable, especially at a time when the date of Jesus' execution and his approximate age on that occasion were no longer readily verifiable. Attempting to date Jesus' birth by identifying a phenomenon that was associated with that birth retroactively is self-evidently absurd. There was no Star of Bethlehem.

It was Matthew who first set out to persuade the followers of the dead messiah John the Immerser to transfer their allegiance to the equally dead messiah Jesus the Nazirite. He showed that Jesus and John had had the same enemies (as indeed they had) by making John vilify the Pharisees as Jesus had allegedly done (MAT. 3:7).

Mark had reported that, in rebuttal of the objection that Eliyah was to return before the coming of the messiah (MAL. 4:5), Jesus declared that Eliyah had already returned (MARK 9:13). Matthew added his interpretation that the reincarnated Eliyah was John the Immerser (MAT. 17:13). Matthew also repeated Mark's pretence that John had said, 'One is coming after me who outranks me, one whose sandals I am not fit to carry' (MAT. 3:11; MARK 1:7), and repeated Mark's implication that John was referring to Jesus.

Matthew did stop short of having John identify Jesus as Messiah. At a time when persons who had heard John preach might conceivably still be alive, such a claim would have been too dangerous. Luke likewise contributed to the amalgamation of the two messiahs' sects by turning Jesus and John into cousins (LUKE 1:36). But it was left to the author of the fourth gospel to have the Immerser unequivocally deny that he was the messiah and to confer the title 'son of God,' which meant the same thing (PS. 2:7), on Jesús (JOHN 1:20; 1:34), even though, in a passage copied from his most reliable source (see page 352), John elsewhere acknowledged that the Immerser had identified *himself* as Messiah: 'Every claim Ioannes made really applied to this one' (JOHN 10:41)..

Matthew tried to explain away the embarrassing circumstance of Jesus' immersion by John, by having John say to Jesus, 'It's I who need to be immersed by you' (MAT. 3:14). The fourth gospel solved the problem arising from the sinless man's acceptance of sin-forgiveness from a subordinate by the simple expedient of omitting Jesus' immersion altogether. And since the fourth gospel's Jesus was a god and therefore not the mortal messiah whom Eliyah had to precede, *John* directly contradicted *Matthew* by having the Immerser deny that he was Eliyah (JOHN 1:21).

Jesus had been immersed by John. Since that unpalatable fact could not be denied (in 70 CE; John denied it sixty years later), Mark (1:11) had made the most of a bad situation by turning Jesus' immersion into the occasion of Jesus' adoption as the son of Yahweh, that is, as messiah. Mark wrote that, when Jesus was immersed, a voice from the sky called: 'You are my son. Today I have become your father.' Matthew (3:17) repeated that wording, as did Luke (3:22). Since the thesis that Jesus became Yahweh's son by adoption at his immersion was incompatible with interpolated-Matthew's virgin-birth myth, post-Nicene Christians expurgated the line, 'Today I have become your father', from the synoptic gospels, and substituted, 'in whom I am well pleased.'

That 'Today I have become your father' was the wording of Matthew until at least 160 CE is attested by Justin Martyr in his Dialogue with Trypho (103); while evidence that Luke contained that wording until after 400 CE can be found in Augustine's Reply to Faustus the Manichaean (23:2). Since the common source from which Matthew and Luke took the incident was Mark, obviously its wording must have also been, 'Today I have become your father.'

Mark had stated that Jesus gave the apostle Simon the surname Petros (MARK 3:16), a Greek translation of the Aramaic word Kefa ('Rock'), which John Hellenised to Kephas (JOHN 1:42). A very late interpolator added to Matthew a reason for the appellation: 'You are ROCK, and on this rock I'm going to found my community, and the gates of the underworld (death, extinction) will not overcome it. I'm giving you the keys of the kingdom in the sky' (MAT. 16:18-19).

Those words are often quoted as 'proof' that Jesus founded a church that was to be permanent and ruled over by the designated successors of the apostle Peter, a church that could only have been the Roman Catholic. In fact, quite apart from Jesus' inability to guarantee anybody anything (as his unfulfillable prophecies demonstrate), the words were never spoken by him. The interpolator invented the scene for a purely political purpose. According to the Codex Strasburg, the name Kefa was actually acquired by Peter because he received his alleged 'call' while standing on a kefa on which Ezekiel had once made a prophecy.

In the interpolator's day, as today, the office of Head Christian carried considerable prestige and power. Since the death of the last of Jesus' relatives, his grand-nephews Jacob and Zakharyah, the Nazirites had been led by persons not of his family, and that had already enabled the Christians to denounce the Nazirites as heretics. But there was no universally recognised Head Christian, and not until 384 CE would the bishop of Rome, Siricius, create the papacy by claiming that he alone was 'pope,' and the popes of Jerusalem, Constantinople, Antioch and Alexandria were his subordinates. Whether

Siricius based his claim on the *Matthew* interpolation, or the interpolation was made to justify Siricius's action (the pretence already existed that Peter had been bishop of Rome), is not known. Either way, the interpolator's purpose was to identify the bishop of Rome as the true Head Christian. Apart from the other popes' claims to equality was the embarrassing fact that Jesus' true heir had been his brother Jacob,[22] supervisor of the Jerusalem commune, so the only bishop with any real claim to primacy was the pope of Jerusalem. If it could be established by a spurious quotation that Jesus had named someone other than his brother Jacob as his heir, and that that heir had in turn named *his* heir, then the primacy claimed by Jerusalem could be transferred anywhere the spurious heirs wished.

The interpolator wrote his *keys of the kingdom* fable for the purpose of proving that not Jacob's successor but Peter's successor was the true Head Christian. And since a Manichaean novelist had already sent Peter to Rome as *episkopos*, Peter's successor was thereby identified as the current bishop of Rome.

Whether the interpolator wrote before or after Pope Siricius first claimed primacy over all Christians in 384 CE, his purpose of making the Roman pope Head Christian succeeded. For the past sixteen hundred years the pretence has been maintained that a man who was never head Nazirite (his subservience to Jacob is fully attested in *Galatians* 2:12 and *Acts* 21:18), and who regarded the *Christians* as pseudo-Jewish infidels, was designated Head Christian by Jesus; that he was supervisor of a city he never visited in his life; that he was succeeded by two men, Linus and Anacletus, who did not exist and whose names were invented in the second century; that all three were bishops at a time when *episkopos* meant nothing more than 'supervisor'; and that Head Christians ranging from guileless simpletons to prototype Napoleons all held office by virtue of a commission granted to Peter by the demigod Jesus at a time when the historical Jesus was dead and buried.

Besides its most famous creation, the keys of the heavens, *Matthew* also contains the Sermon on the Mount. The contents of that sermon were taken from Q, as is evidenced by component parts being found distributed throughout *Luke*; but it was Matthew who turned an account of several weeks of preaching into a single sermon. The best-known element of that alleged sermon was the *Pater Hemon*, the *Our Father*:

> Our father in the sky whose name is taboo,
> May your theocracy be established.
> May your whims be gratified

---

22. Eusebius, *Ecc. History* 3:11.

On the land as in the sky.
Provide us with tomorrow's bread today,
And absolve us from the injuries we commit,
As we absolve those who injure us.
Do not encourage us to be defiant,
But rather liberate us from the intolerable
(*i.e., from the Roman occupation*).   (MAT. 6:9-13)

That Jesus indeed preached the *Our Father* is by no means unlikely. The prayer was totally Jewish, similar to Jewish prayers recorded elsewhere, and in two places incompatible with Christian doctrine.

A prayer in the Talmud reads: *Blessed be the gods every day for the daily bread that he provides us.* Jesus' wording was: *Provide us with tomorrow's bread today.* And where the Sadducee author of *Ecclesiastes* had written: *Absolve your compatriot of the injury he has done you, and the injuries you do will be similarly absolved* (ECCL. 28:2); Jesus' version was: *Absolve us from the injuries we commit, as we absolve those who injure us.*

Neither of those sentiments was peculiar to any one mythology. However, in addressing his prayer to *Our father in the sky whose name is taboo* (sacred), Jesus was speaking strictly as an orthodox Jew. Only to Jews is Yahweh's name too sacred ever to be spoken; Christians have no such belief. And in asking Yahweh: *May your theocracy be established*, Jesus was petitioning for the establishment in Jerusalem of the promised messianic monarchy of which he was to be King. That prayer was never granted, and now that Jesus is dead it never can be.

It is unlikely that Matthew ended the *Pater Hemon* with: *For the theocracy and the army and the magnificence are eternally yours*,[23] found in a small number of manuscripts and included (in a slightly different translation) in the *Authorized Version*, since those words are missing from all manuscripts of *Luke*, which likewise copied the prayer from Q (MAT. 6:9-13; LUKE 11:2-3).

Matthew made a slight alteration to a story he found in *Mark*. According to Mark, Jesus taught: '*Anyone who discards his wife and marries another, commits adultery with her. And if she abandons her husband and marries another, she commits adultery*' (MARK 10:11-12). That teaching was pure Essene and, as a comparison with the *Damascus Covenant* (13:10) reveals, allowed for no exceptions. It was not that the Essenes saw marriage as sacramental, nonreversible in the same way that immersion was nonreversible. Rather, even among secular Essenes celibacy was so glorified that the lawgivers were not willing to allow anybody to repudiate it twice. Remarriage (not divorce)

---

23. The *Jerusalem Bible*, the *New American Bible*, the *James Moffat Bible* and the *New World Translation* all omit this sentence from MAT. 6:13, in recognition that it was an interpolation.

was banned, not to discourage divorce, but to force divorced persons to become celibate.

Matthew, unwilling to believe that Jesus had intended the ban on divorce and remarriage to be absolute, inserted the loophole: *'Anyone who discards his wife* except for sexcrime *and marries another, commits adultery'* (MAT. 19:9). Just what kind of sexcrime Matthew included in *porneia* ('whoring') is uncertain. No doubt he was familiar with Paul's teaching that men who sacramentally copulated with nuns in a goddess's temple were breaching Yahweh's first Commandment. But that he used *porneia* to include not only nun-tupping (its original meaning) but also adultery and premarital recreation (where the husband had not knowingly wed a non-virgin) is not improbable. The Roman Catholic and Anglican mythologies, in imposing the total ban on divorce and remarriage decreed in *Mark*, are correctly recognising that *Mark*'s account of Jesus' teaching is more authentic; but they are also tacitly acknowledging that words attributed to Jesus in *Matthew* were never spoken by him.

Matthew's gospel was much longer than Mark's, containing as it did most of *Mark*, most of *Q*, and much that was original. Not surprisingly, Matthew was unable to avoid completely the kind of inconsistency that was the main risk in using contradictory sources. He included, for example, both a genealogy that showed Jesus to be Davidic, and Jesus' own acknowledgement that he was not Davidic. He included *Mark*'s last supper that equated Jesus with Mithra, and also a repudiation of the Mithraic custom of calling priests 'Father' and the chief priest 'Father of Fathers' (MAT. 23:10).

Matthew ended his gospel with the resurrected Jesus instructing his disciples: *'Go and make disciples of all the infidels, teaching them every order that I've given you'* (MAT. 28:19a, 20), thereby transferring to Jesus a gentile-proselytising policy that was in fact originated by Paul. Yet earlier in his gospel Matthew had revealed Jesus' typical Jewish xenophobia in the more accurate quote: *'Don't go anywhere among the infidels, and don't enter any Samaritan town. Go instead to the lost sheep of the house of Israel'* (MAT. 10:5-6).

Matthew did not include in Jesus' fictitious instructions to his followers to preach to gentiles, the words: *immersing them in the name of the father and of the son and of the consecrated breath* (MAT. 28:19b). That piece of Nicene mythology was interpolated into *Matthew* no earlier than the generation immediately preceding the Council of Nicaea in 325 CE. Eusebius, who wrote in the early fourth century CE, quoted from some manuscripts of *Matthew* that contained 28:19b and some that did not. Since there was no conceivable way that a copyist could have accidentally omitted the trinitarian formula, that it was not part of the original version of *Matthew* is the necessary conclusion. No extant manuscript of *Matthew* lacks 28:19b;

but no extant manuscript dates from as early as the time of Eusebius. Clearly the formula was interpolated into *Matthew* (and a similar passage into *1 John*) at a time when the absence from the Judaeo-Christian bible of any mention of the divine triad invented by Theophilos of Antioch around 180 CE and unified into a tripartite being by Athanasius was deemed an embarrassment to the trinitarian minority.

Matthew was followed within five or ten years by two further biographies of Jesus, one Jewish (not Nazirite) and the other Christian (also, obviously, not Nazirite). The former was the *Toldot Yeshu*, or *Genealogy of Jesus*. It told of a virgin named Miriam, espoused to a man named Yohannan, who was virtually raped by a carpenter, one Yowsef ben Pandera, who entered her bed after dark in the guise of her husband. Miriam's bastard child, *Yeshu ha-notsriy* (Jesus the Nazirite), became a pupil of the greatest rabbi of his day, but while in Egypt misused his learning and became a sorcerer. Current Jewish thinking on the taboo on pronouncing the name *Yahweh* was evidenced in Yeshu ha-notsriy's learning the ineffable name and pronouncing it to work his evil. Yeshu was hunted by the agent of all that is good, Yahuwdah (Judas), captured through Yahuwdah's efforts (Yahuwdah had also been taught the unspeakable name, and pronounced it against Yeshu), and hanged on a tree. He was buried in a cabbage patch, thereby freeing the world from his evil.

The *Toldot Yeshu* was based totally on interpolated-*Matthew*, and was the inevitable Jewish response to *Matthew*'s absurd pretence that Jesus had not been the son of Joseph. Shimeown ben Azzay, around 100 CE, had been the first person known to have called Jesus a bastard, obviously in response to the newly invented virgin-birth myth; but how soon after ben Azzay's declaration the *Toldot Yeshu* was composed is uncertain. The story of Mary's seduction by Pandera was in circulation around 150 CE, when it was cited by Celsus[24]; and the *Toldot Yeshu* was quoted by Tertullian in 198 CE. Almost certainly its author did not intend his work to be taken seriously, but was rather ridiculing *Matthew* by writing a parody. Nothing else could explain his making Jesus *huios pantherou* (son of a panther), a transparent pun on *huios parthenou* (son of a virgin).

The *Toldot Yeshu* was composed as a joke. Nonetheless it was taken seriously, by both Jews and Christians. Just as the Jewish author of *Toldot Yeshu* had accepted uncritically that Jesus was not Joseph's son, that he had been to Egypt, that he was a learned rabbi, and that his death had been caused by Judas, and just as the Pharisees who wrote the Talmud accepted that same information on the dubious authority of the *Toldot Yeshu*, so Christians accepted uncritically the reality of the pun that Jesus was

---

24. Origen, *Contra Celsum*.

descended from Panther.

Epiphanius in about 375 CE concocted a genealogy that made *Panther* the surname of Jacob, the man named in *Matthew* as the father of Joseph.[25] John of Damascus 350 years later named Levi *Panther* as the grandfather of Yoakhim, the alleged father of Mary.[26] And two different Talmud authors referred to Jesus as *ben Pandera*.[27] How anybody could have failed to see the joke is difficult to understand. (However, since the pun was in Greek it may have deceived Aramaic speakers.) Even Jesus' title, *ha-notsriy*, was a pun (in Aramaic) on *Nazirite* and *carpenter*.

The Christian gospel written soon after *Matthew*, during the reign of Trajan (98-117 CE), was *Luke-Acts*. Luke's introductory dedication to one Theophilos ('God-Lover') was a stylistic conceit borrowed from Josephus's *Antiquities*, published in 94 CE, just as the introduction to *Acts*, likewise addressed to Theophilos, and referring to the author's *previous treatise*, was an imitation of Josephus's later work, *Against Apion*. That *Luke* and *Acts* were composed as a single work has long been acknowledged. *Acts'* repetition of *Luke*'s list of apostles could be explained by assuming that the author of *Acts* used *Luke* as a source. But Luke's rejection of Mark's ending, in which Jesus' disciples returned to Galilee after their leader's death, would have been pointless unless Luke was already planning to write a sequel in which the disciples did *not* return to Galilee but, under Peter's leadership, established a Jesus commune in Jerusalem.

Since *Acts* incorporated four segments of a first-person narrative written by someone who had accompanied Paul from Troas to Rome, and a doctor named Loukos had been one of Paul's companions, the need of the early Christian hierarchy to attach a name to their sacred writings led them to imagine that Loukos had written the entire two books. In fact there is no possibility whatsoever that a man who had worked closely with Paul could have put into the mouth of Peter the words: '*From the earliest days the god chose that through my mouth the infidels were to hear the words of the evangelion and be credulous*' (ACTS 15:7). Paul was adamant that, at the time those words were allegedly spoken, Peter's mission was to Jews only; gentiles were Paul's responsibility. Loukos could not have failed to know that. While it is within the realm of possibility that doctor Loukos wrote the 'we' passages that Luke incorporated into *Acts*, that he wrote the gospel that bears his name, or the rest of *Acts*, is not.

Luke's main sources were *Mark*, Q, *Jubilees*, and the works of Flavius Josephus.

---

25. *Adversus Haereses* 77:7.
26. *De Fid. Orthod.* 4:14.
27. SHAB. 104b; SANH. 67a.

Luke was essentially a novelist, and as such wanted to tell a complete story. Since nothing was (or is) known of Jesus prior to his immersion by John, Luke invented a birth fable borrowed from the now-lost *Nativity of John the Immerser*, supplemented by passages from *Jubilees* and Josephus. *Luke* cannot now be compared with *Nativity* or *Q*, but the ultimate source of his annunciation scene is evident:

JUDGES	LUKE
A *messenger of Yahweh appeared to the woman and said. . . . 'You're going to conceive and bear a son . . . a nazirite . . . and he's going to begin delivering Yisrael out of the hands of the Philistines.'* (13:3-5)	The messenger Gabriel was sent from the god. . . . 'You're going to see yourself pregnant to bear a son. He's going to be a potentate . . . for his Lordship the god is going to give him the throne of his ancestor David.' (1:26-32)

1 SAMUEL	LUKE
And the child Samuwel advanced in age, in favour with Yahweh and humans. (2:26)	And Iesous advanced in wisdom and age, in favour with god and humans. (2:52)

Luke borrowed the songs of praise known as the *Magnificat* (LUKE 1:46-55) and the *Benedictus* (LUKE 1:58-79) from the *Nativity of John*. As the context makes clear, Luke followed his source in attributing the former to Elizabeth and the latter to Zakharyah. This is confirmed by surviving manuscripts of *Luke* in which the *Magnificat* retains its original attribution. At an early date, however, interpolators transferred the *Magnificat* to Mary. Both songs closely resemble *Nativity*'s immediate source, songs that the author of *Jubilees* put into the mouths of Rebekah and Isaac (JUB. 25:15-23; 31:15-20). But the ultimate source was much older:

1 SAMUEL	LUKE
My heart rejoices in Yahweh; I exult from your liberation. None is as sacrosanct as Yahweh. Cease your exceedingly proud boasting. The bows of potentates are broken, And those that stumbled are girded with strength. The satiated have hired themselves out for bread, And the hungry have been filled. (2:1-10)	My psyche glorifies his Lordship. My breath exults in the god, my liberator. . . . His name is sacrosanct He has scattered the proud. . . . He has deposed dynasties from their thrones, And elevated the low-born. He has filled the hungry with good fare, And sent the capitalists away empty-handed (1:46-55)

Following Jesus' birth, Luke was faced with a further thirty years for which he likewise had no information. To fill the gap he borrowed a highly boastful and highly dubious incident from Josephus's account of his own life:

JOSEPHUS	LUKE
While I was still a mere boy, about 14 years old, I won universal applause for my love of letters; insomuch that the chief priests and learned men of Jerusalem used constantly to come to me for precise information on some particulars of our statutes. (LIFE)	When he was twelve . . . they found him sitting in the Temple among the law-teachers, listening to them and asking them questions. And all those hearing him were amazed at his comprehension and by his answers. (2:42-47)

Luke's borrowing from Josephus did not end with stories of Jesus' alleged childhood. In repeating a parable told by Q, Luke added to the basic tale, also picked up by *Matthew* (25:14-30), superficial details taken from Josephus's account (WAR 2:1-7) of the accession of Arkhelaos. Luke's *certain nobleman who travelled to a distant country to receive the rule of a kingdom,* even though *his citizens detested him, and sent an embassy after him to say, 'We don't want this man to be king over us,'* was a carbon copy of Arkhelaos, who was indeed granted the Jewish ethnarchy by Augustus Caesar despite petitions from the Jewish population that Arkhelaos not be made king (LUKE 19:12-27).

Like Matthew, Luke included both Jesus' acknowledgement that he was not Davidic, and a genealogy composed to prove that he *was* Davidic. However, not being aware of the existence of *Matthew* and therefore unable to borrow its genealogy, Luke inserted into his gospel a genealogy that gave Jesus a different paternal grandfather from the man named in *Matthew*, traced his descent from a different son of David, and consisted of forty-three generations from David to Jesus, compared with Matthew's twenty-eight:

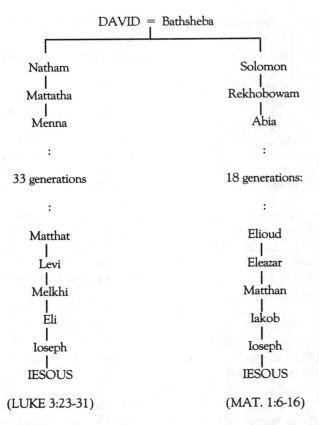

DAVID = Bathsheba

Natham	Solomon
Mattatha	Rekhobowam
Menna	Abia
⋮	⋮
33 generations	18 generations:
⋮	⋮
Matthat	Elioud
Levi	Eleazar
Melkhi	Matthan
Eli	Iakob
Ioseph	Ioseph
IESOUS	IESOUS
(LUKE 3:23-31)	(MAT. 1:6-16)

Luke's genealogy, being completely fictitious from Nathan (*Natham*) to Joseph, is the more difficult to refute. Matthew, on the other hand, traced Jesus' descent through five hundred years of kings of Judah, from Solomon to Yoshyahuw, and in so doing made King Azaryahuw the son of Yahuwram who was actually his great-great-grandfather. Matthew arbitrarily divided his genealogy into groups of fourteen generations, fourteen being the numerical value of the name *DWD* (David) in the genealogy's original language, Hebrew. Since there were in fact seventeen generations from David to the Babylonian Captivity, Matthew achieved his magic number by the expedient of omitting Azaryahuw's father Amatsyahuw, his grandfather Yahuwash, and his great-grandfather Azkhazyahuw. From Yoshyahuw's great-grandson Zerubbabel to Joseph, Matthew's genealogy was also fictitious.

The existence of incompatible genealogies within eighty years of Jesus' death was not an unforseeable circumstance. Anyone who has examined the Harleian genealogical manuscripts prepared by the English census-takers during the sixteenth-century Visitations will be aware that brothers did not always name the same grandfather. Some made honest mistakes, while others inserted into their pedigrees ancestors whom for political or economic reasons they deemed desirable. Henry Tudor, attempting to justify his spurious claim to the English crown, produced a genealogy that showed his descent from Cadwallador, last king of Britain before the English conquest. Jesus' repudiation of Davidic descent was known to few Christians, most of whom assumed that to be Messiah he must have been Davidic. It was no more difficult for two Christians, working independently, each to connect the historical Jesus to the historical David, than for the Redactor to trace the ancestors of the nonexistent Noah to the nonexistent Adam.

The incompatibility of *Matthew*'s and *Luke*'s genealogies became, not surprisingly, a source of embarrassment to Christians once the claim was made that both historical novels were 'inspired' and of equal authority with the Towrah. Around 200 CE Julius Africanus concocted an imaginative rationalisation that Eusebius later canonised into *tradition*. According to the Christian apologists, Joseph's two alleged fathers, Jacob and Eli, were half-brothers. Jacob was the son of Estha by her first husband, Matthan, of the line of Solomon. Eli was Estha's son by her second husband, Melkhi, of the line of Nathan. When Eli died childless, his brother Jacob, in fulfilment of the levirate law, impregnated Eli's widow in order to produce a son who would be the biological son of Jacob but the legal son of Eli.[28] In fact the obligation to impregnate Eli's widow under levirate law would have fallen upon the heir male of Eli's father, Eli's father's brother's son. A half-brother by the same father would have qualified. A half-brother by the same mother would not.

A further main weakness of Africanus's rationalisation was that Luke would not have attempted to show that Jesus was *the progeny of (David's) genitals* (ACTS 2:30) by showing the descent of Joseph's *adoptive* father. This was finally conceded by Catholic mythologians in 1502, with the consequence that it was replaced by an equally absurd rationalisation, now hardened into Catholic dogma, that *Matthew*'s genealogy was that of Joseph, while *Luke*'s was that of Mary. Not only does such a thesis amount to an acknowledgement that Luke (who called Joseph the son of Eli, and Mary an Aaronic Levite) was lying; the postulation that Jesus' claim to be David's heir could be established through female descent was incompatible with Jewish thinking.

Despite its absurdity, Africanus's rationalisation was accepted as valid, and the following genealogy became part of early Christian mythology:

---

28. Eusebius, *Ecc. Hist.* 1:7.

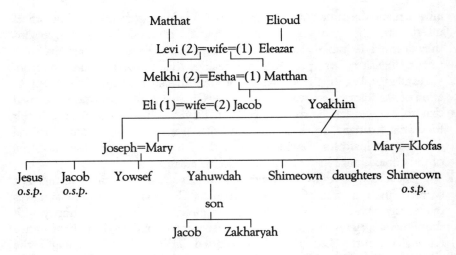

The rationalised genealogy did not explain away all of the gospels' incompatibilities. For example, in making Joseph's wife the daughter of his uncle Yoakhim, the rationalisers were ignoring Luke's claim that she was Aaronic (LUKE 1:5; 1:36). And in order to accept the synoptics' claim that Jesus' mother was named Mary and John's declaration that his mother's sister was named Mary (JOHN 19:25), it was necessary to credit Yoakhim with two daughters of the same name, an extremely unlikely occurrence.

Nonetheless, according to Eusebius the rationalisation was accepted (retroactively?) by Jesus' grandnephews, who in all likelihood really did believe that they were Davidic. They in any case acknowledged their royal descent when Domitian arrested them for the purpose of putting into effect a plan first conceived by Vespasian of exterminating the entire Davidic family.[29] Domitian changed his mind and released them when he concluded that they were too simple to be dangerous.

Domitian's failure to execute the extremely competent Shimeown bar Klofas is more difficult to fathom. Perhaps he took pity on the Head Nazirite because of his advanced age and because the surviving Davidic heirs would soon enough solve his problem by dying childless. Such compassion would have been inconsistent with surviving portraits of Domitian's character; but then few historians regard it as coincidence that the Emperors of whom only unfavourable biographies survive tended to be those who took the severest measures to protect the empire from the malevolence of the

---

29. Vespasian believed that exterminating the family from which the prophesied King of the Jews was to come would eliminate the messianic belief that had triggered so much rebellion. Since Jews continue to expect a messiah, long after the Davidic family's extinction, clearly he was wrong.

Christians. Following the deaths of Shimeown (whom Trajan *did* execute in 105 or 107 CE), Jacob and Zakharyah, leadership of the Nazirites passed to persons not of Jesus' family, and this enabled the Christians finally to dismiss the Nazirites as heretics and claim that *they* were the true heirs of Jesus' teachings.

Luke was the author of the tall tale that had Joseph and Mary travel from Galilee to Bethlehem in order to comply with the terms of Augustus Caesar's census. Augustus's first Judaean census, imposed while Quirinius was legatus of Syria as Luke correctly stated, occurred as a consequence of the deposition of Arkhelaos in 6 CE and the transfer of Judaea from Herodian to direct Roman rule. Jesus' conception, therefore, by Luke's chronology, occurred in 6 CE. But Matthew at about the same time was writing that Jesus was taken to Egypt to escape the malevolence of Arkhelaos's father Herod, who died in 4 BCE.

If Matthew's nativity tale is accepted, then the tale that Jesus was born in Bethlehem must be rejected on the ground that at the time of Joseph's taxation journey to Bethlehem, Jesus was ten years old. And if Luke's fanciful fantasy is accepted, then Matthew's story of Herod's massacre must be rejected on the ground that anything Herod did occurred ten years before Jesus' birth. If, however, the conclusion that either Matthew or Luke was lying is rejected, then Jesus was born ten years before he was conceived—a miracle indeed.

Christian apologists, in a desperate attempt to harmonise the incompatible birth fables of *Matthew* and *Luke*, have proposed that Quirinius's appointment as legatus in 6 CE was not his first, and that he conducted not only the Judaean census of that year but also an earlier Galilean-Judaean census during the life of Herod the Great (as if Rome would compile taxation data on a province being taxed by Herod). Unless the harmonisers are prepared to assert that Quirinius's hypothetical earlier legateship (and therefore Jesus' birth) occurred earlier than 10 BCE, this rationalisation can be proven wrong. Titius is known to have been legatus until 9 BCE, possibly for longer than a year; Sentius Saturninus from 9 to 6 BCE; and Quintilius Varus from 6 BCE until after the death of Herod. Further, Josephus stated unequivocally (ANTIQ. 17:355) that the census taken when Arkhelaos was replaced by the first procurator was the first, as indeed it must have been. The imposition of a Roman taxation before Judaea came under direct Roman rule would have been impossible. The first Judaean census occurred in 6/7 CE, and the first Galilean census either in 44 CE, when the death of Herod Agrippa placed Galilee under the Judaean procurator, or in conjunction with the Judaean census of 48/49 CE.

It was, however, in *Acts* that Luke committed his greatest blunder. In an attempt to convince the Pharisees, who by 100 CE were indeed the enemies of the Jesus communities, that their hostility was unjustified, Luke concocted the tale that the great rabbi Gamaliel ben Hillel, a Pharisee, had defended the early Nazirites from orthodox Jewish persecution. Luke had Gamaliel describe the rebellion of Theudas, who led an abortive uprising in 46 CE, and then declare that *after* Theudas came Judas of Galilee, who was in fact crucified in 6 CE.

If that had been the only error, it could be argued that Gamaliel made the mistake and that Luke quoted him correctly. But Luke attributed Gamaliel's speech to the days immediately following Jesus' execution, more than a decade earlier than the rebellion Gamaliel supposedly described (ACTS 5:34-39). In fact Gamaliel's speech, like his alleged defence of the followers of King Jesus, was a product of Luke's imagination. Gamaliel might have defended Jesus' preaching, but not the claim of a Galilean that he was the messiah ('*Look and you'll see that no prophet is to arise out of Galilaia*' JOHN 7:52), and certainly not the claim that a dead man was the messiah. Indeed, had Jesus ever been tried and convicted by the Sanhedrin, as all gospels falsely claimed, Gamaliel as President of that body would have been the judge who sentenced him. The source of Luke's error is readily discernible. Josephus described Judas's rebellion, in a flashback, immediately following his account of Theudas (ANTIQ. 20:97-103). Luke's assumption that the events occurred in the order they appeared in Josephus is further proof that he was using Josephus as a source.

Luke did not limit his borrowing to sources that were essentially Jewish. Like his predecessors he was not averse to utilising any mythology that happened to be convenient. Just as *Matthew* had appropriated to Jesus the gift-bearing magi who followed a new star to the birthplace of Zarathustra, so Luke requisitioned the poor shepherds who, at an early date (Mithra was cited in a Hittite document of the fourteenth century BCE), had been the first persons to visit the newborn Mithra in his stable (LUKE 2:8-18), and before that had visited the newborn Krishna in *his* stable. To explain how Jesus came to emulate Mithra in being born in such an unlikely place, mentioned by Luke only (whereas *Matthew* 2:11 has Jesus born in a house), Luke declared that there was no room at the inn.

Luke, as a Paulinist and a gentile, not surprisingly furthered the pretence that Paul's revolutionary practice of preaching to gentiles had also been the practice of Jesus' personal appointees. In describing Jesus' instructions to his lieutenants to preach Jesus as Messiah, Luke followed *Mark* (6:7-10) in not specifying to whom the envoys were to preach (LUKE 9:1-4). He suppressed the passage in Q (which Matthew must have derived from that source, since he would not have invented a scene that contradicted his own fiction) in which Jesus specifically forbade his followers from preaching to Samaritans or gentiles (MAT. 10:5-6). Instead, he recorded that Philippos, one of the Twelve, *went down to the town of Samaria and preached the Messiah to them* (ACTS 8:5).

Since *Philippos* was a Greek rather than a Jewish name, it is not unlikely that the first preaching of Jesus' alleged resurrection in Samaria was by a Philippos; but Philippos would have been a Paulinist, not a Nazirite, and not a disciple of the xenophobic Jewish nationalist, Jesus.

Jesus' xenophobic nationalism, a nationalism that his true successors, the Nazirites, were continuing, was a source of severe discomfort to Luke, whose own status as a loyal subject of King Jesus was severely compromised by Jesus' equation of gentiles with dogs (MARK 7:27). Luke therefore invented a parable which he put into Jesus' mouth in which Jesus praised a Samaritan as more worthy of brotherly love than a member of the Levite caste or a Temple priest (LUKE 10:29-37).

Literally, the word *Samarites* meant a resident of Samaria. But such was the Jewish hatred for Samaritans, whose religion was so similar to that of the Judaeans and Galileans as to qualify them as *heretics* rather than *infidels*, that to a Jew, *Samarites* had much the same connotations as *nigger, kike, scab, spic, gook, fag, chink* or *wog*. Had Jesus ever told a parable favourable to a Samaritan he would in all likelihood have been lynched. But there was no possibility of that. Jesus' hatred of Samaritans was as strong as any other Jew's. The parable of the Samaritan's kindness to a sworn enemy was Luke's invention, and differed markedly from anything Jesus ever preached.

Luke alone makes Jesus say of his executioners, '*Father, forgive them, for they don't realise what they're doing*' (LUKE 23:34).[30] Christian pretence to the contrary notwithstanding, such a line would have been quite inconsistent with the character of Jesus that one gleans from the sources. Jesus was more plausibly reported to have said on another occasion, '*Even though scandals are inevitable, oy vay to the human through whom the scandal comes*' (MAT. 18:7). It is difficult to imagine the author of that vindictive sophistry asking his god to forgive his executioners. In fact as brainwashed a Christian apologist as Eusebius conceded that the line was actually spoken by Jesus' brother Jacob on the occasion of his execution by High Priest Hanan in 62 CE.[31]

Luke put into Jesus' mouth a parable that, for sheer obscenity, rivalled *Mark*'s allegation that Jesus spoke in riddles to avoid saving the predestined damned. Luke told of a steward who, on being given notice of termination, called in all of his employer's debtors and arbitrarily reduced their debts. There was no suggestion that he was acting in his employer's interests, offering the debtors discounts in exchange for prompt payment. He gave away his

---

30. This passage is an interpolation in *Luke*, missing from ancient manuscripts.
31. *Ecc. Hist.* 2:23:16.

employer's future income for the sole purpose of winning the personal gratitude of the debtors in the hope that one of them would hire him after his current employment expired.

Jesus, according to Luke, approved of the steward's swindle, for he declared at the end of the parable: 'Use swindled money to buy companions, so that when it runs out they'll accept you into their residences' (LUKE 16:1-9). The moral of the parable was clearly: 'Cheat those who are no longer useful to you, and use the stolen money to bribe those who are in a position to do you good.' Did Jesus actually preach such a parable? one wonders. If so, perhaps Luke forgot to mention that the employer was a Samaritan.

Luke copied Mark's Little Apocalypse (MARK 13:5-27; LUKE 21:10-28), but added the detail that the Nazirites' flight to the mountains was to take place 'when you see Jerusalem surrounded by armies' (LUKE 21:20). But whereas Mark had prophesied that, within a few months of the Saints' exodus, Then they'll see Ben Adam advancing on clouds with a mighty army (MARK 13:26), Luke, who knew that thirty more years had elapsed and Jesus' return at the head of forty legions of winged messengers did not seem imminent, had Jesus prophesy that: 'Jerusalem is going to be downtrodden by infidels until the period of the infidels is concluded' (LUKE 21:24).

Luke was the first writer to record any details of Jesus' alleged personal appearances after his execution. Two disciples, Klofas and Shimeown (whom later Christian writers identified as Jesus' uncle and cousin), were walking near Jerusalem when they were joined by Jesus. They talked with him for some considerable time but did not recognise him. Finally he gave them bread and, by that symbolic act, revealed his identity (LUKE 24:13-31).

The holes in such a story are obvious. The disciples had been Jesus' constant companions for weeks. They had last seen him three days earlier. Yet they were supposed to have conversed with Jesus and not recognised him. Such nonrecognition by close associates would have been impossible. If Klofas and Shimeown did discuss mythology with a stranger a day or two after Jesus' execution, it was not until many years later that one of them got the idea into his head that the stranger had been Jesus.

Luke's final rewriting of history occurred in the highly fictionalised Acts. It would take unwarranted space to give a detailed comparison of Luke's version of Paul's travels with Paul's own account as revealed in his letters. The reader can check the many incompatibilities for himself.[32] But after tracing Paul's career up to his arrival in Rome as a prisoner, Luke deliberately suppressed Paul's condemnation and execution by Nero.[33] Just as Mark had made Jesus' executioner, Pilatus, his defender, rather than admit that Jesus

---

32. Compare Acts 9:19-28 with Galatians 1:15-19.
33. Eusebius, Ecc. Hist. 2:25:5.

had been executed as an enemy of Rome, so Luke thought it inexpedient to admit that Paul had been executed for the same cause.

All three synoptic gospels put a time limit on Jesus' second coming. However, by the time *Mark* was written forty years had passed and still he had not returned. While the Christians could accept their messiah's tardiness up to that point, they found it impossible to believe that he had revealed his identity to a generation that would never see the restored theocratic monarchy. Mark accordingly recorded a prophecy that in all likelihood Jesus actually made, that he would be crowned king of an independent Judaea within the lifetime of the persons listening to him preach. Matthew and Luke, who each wrote at a time when it was still believed that the prophecy could be fulfilled, copied it from *Mark*. John, who wrote after Jesus' time limit had expired, not surprisingly left it out. In fact Jesus had expected the prophecy to be fulfilled within a matter of months at the outside, without any intervening death and 'second coming.'

MARK	MATTHEW	LUKE
There are some standing here who are not going to experience death until they have seen Allah's theocracy established by force. (9:1)	There are some standing here who are not going to experience death until they have seen Ben Adam established in his theocracy. (16:28)	*There are some standing here who are not going to experience death until they have seen Allah's theocracy.* (9:27)

Mark's reference to the establishment of the theocracy by *dynamis* (power, might, force) fully refutes the Christian pretence that the Jewish Jesus meant something other than his Jewish audiences imagined him to mean. Allowing that his hearers included small children, some of whom might conceivably have lived for a further ninety years, we can calculate that Jesus promised to end Roman overlordship and have himself crowned king of an independent Judaea no later than 120 CE. He seems to have been delayed.[34]

Jesus' unfulfillable prophecy proved an embarrassment to Christians almost from the moment his self-imposed time limit expired. In an attempt to make the impossible possible, desperate Christians in medieval times invented the *wandering Jew*, a man who heard Jesus' prophecy and reviled him with it as he was dying on the stake. Jesus in consequence cursed the man to remain alive until his second coming. Although widely believed

---

34. The Jehovah's Witnesses, after unsuccessfully prophesying that Jesus' second coming would occur in 1844, and then 1874, refused to acknowledge failure when their third attempt, 1914, also failed. To this day the Witnesses maintain that the second coming *did* happen in 1914, but that Jesus has been keeping a low profile for eight decades.

for a long time, and therefore a great comfort to Christians who were thus enabled to believe that the prophecy *could* be fulfilled, the tale of the wandering Jew was one myth that official Christianity was wise enough not to canonise.

Early in the reign of Hadrian, and certainly before the composition of *John*, pseudo-Paul wrote the so-called pastoral letters, *Timothy* and *Titus*. Pseudo-Paul spelled out the obligations of an *episkopos* and a *diakonos* in such terms as to leave no doubt that the letters were composed at a time when the former had come to mean 'bishop' (in the modern sense) rather than 'supervisor,' and the latter 'deacon' rather than 'administrator.' That the letters are late, and therefore spurious (since the author claimed to be the long-dead Paul), is demonstrated by the Christian heretic Marcion's never having heard of them. To Marcion, (excommunicated in 144 CE), the only valid scriptures were Paul's genuine letters and an edited version of *Luke*.

Pseudo-Paul did demonstrate, however, in the lines, *All those who are in Asia have abandoned me* (2 TIM. 1:15), and *Only Loukos is with me* (2 TIM. 4:11), that he was aware of the Anatolian and Levantine communities' abandonment of Pauline Christianity and conversion to the Jesus-Judaism of the Nazirites. That knowledge gives the letters a certain amount of reliability, since it reveals their author to have been a Paulinist well acquainted with his founder's work. The letters can therefore be taken as evidence that, as late as 120 CE, even the Christians had not yet heard the theory that Jesus was God: *There is one god, and one mediator between god and humans, a human, Messiah Iesous* (1 TIM. 2:5).

It was the *Gospel of John*, written at about the time of bar Kokhba's rebellion of 132-135 CE, that transformed Christianity from a monotheistic sect of pseudo-Jews into a pagan polytheistic mythology with two paramount gods, Yahweh and Jesus. It did not, however, make Jesus part of a divine trinity. The masculinised triple-goddess would not be inserted into Christianity for a further two centuries after the publication of *John*.

John was in no sense a continuation of the synoptic tradition. Rather, it made Jesus the figurehead of a purely pagan mythology that even Paul would have repudiated. Yet it came into existence as a direct consequence of the division of Jesusism into Nazirites and Ebionites (Jews) on the one side, and Christians (gentiles) on the other, begun by Paul and made permanent by the destruction of Jerusalem.

Christianity, or non-Jewish Jesusism, was originally sanctioned by Jacob and Peter when they gave Paul permission to establish among the gentiles communities that worshipped Yahweh and acknowledged Jesus as king, but did not conform to the laws attributed to Moses (ACTS 15). What the Nazirite leadership had not anticipated was that Paul would see his commission to the *uncircumcision* as including practising pagans rather than those gentiles who already attended synagogue.

The first rift between Paul and the leaders in Jerusalem occurred in about 48 CE, when Jacob learned from John Markos (who did *not* write the first gospel) that Paul was sanctioning breaches of Jewish orthodoxy. Three years later an accommodation was reached whereby Paul agreed to impose on his pagan converts only those Jewish taboos that Jacob deemed essential (nun-tupping, sacrificing to opposition gods, eating meat not fully drained of blood), but not the entire Towrah (ACTS 15:19-20).

The shaky alliance between Jacob's Nazirites and Paul's Christians was still holding in 58 CE when Paul came to Jerusalem for the last time and Jacob advised him to take a nazirite vow in order to demonstrate his orthodoxy to the Zealots who planned to murder him (ACTS 21:18-26; 23:12). Paul was nonetheless arrested shortly thereafter, and kept prisoner at Caesaria for two years when he persistently ignored procurator Felix's hints that he could be released in exchange for a suitable bribe.

In 60 CE, when incoming procurator Festus indicated that he was willing to hand Paul over to the Sanhedrin for trial, Paul declared himself a Roman citizen and demanded trial before Nero (ACTS 25:9-11). Luke, playing down the Jewish antipathy toward Christianity at a time when the first Jewish War was all but forgotten and it had actually become expedient for Christianity to claim to be Judaic (since Judaism was legal), had King Herod Agrippa II declare that Paul might have been freed had he not appealed to Nero (ACTS 26:32). In fact, such was the Sanhedrin's attitude toward all last-times sects, not only those that committed the intolerable insolence of claiming to be Jews when they were not, that, as Paul well knew, had Paul allowed himself to fall into their hands his chances of survival would have been approximately equal to those of a snowflake on the sunny side of Mercury.

That Paul was not born a Roman citizen is certain. Most likely he was granted denization papers about 48 CE by Sergius Paulus, proconsul of Cyprus, whom Paul converted to Christianity and whose name he thereafter adopted (ACTS 13:6-12). Paul's prudence in concealing his Roman status for a decade was confirmed by the consequences of his enforced revelation. Jacob had barely tolerated Paul to begin with. At the news that Paul had accepted citizenship from the hated occupying power, Jacob in effect ex-communicated him. Envoys were sent from Jerusalem to convert all of Paul's Christian communities to Nazirite Judaism. All cooperation between the Nazirites and Paul's gentile followers ceased, and the way was open for a Christian (John Markos was a Nazirite) to write the *Gospel of Mark* (as it was later called), which all but repudiated Jesus' Jewishness.

It was the fall of Jerusalem in 70 CE that led the two Jesus sects, while both were still monotheistic, into establishing separate headquarters and separate leaderships, neither of which acknowledged the legitimacy of the other. Nazirite Judaism, the religion of Jesus' brother and his former disciples, survived a second and permanent expulsion from Jerusalem after bar Kokhba's defeat in 135 CE, as did the Ebionites, the sect actually founded by Jesus and continued in Galilee by those disciples who did not move to Jerusalem and become Nazirites. Some centuries later the masochist Jerome, translator of the Vulgate, wrote of them that, wanting to be both Jew and Christian, they were neither Jew nor Christian.[35]

Christianity, the mythology founded by Paul, similarly split in two. The original Pauline creed established itself at Alexandria where it accepted all synoptic myths, including the virgin-birth interpolation, but otherwise remained essentially unchanged from original Paulinism until its last champion, Arius, was declared a heretic in 325 CE by the same Council that formally pronounced Jesus a god.

The post-Pauline sub-sect that evolved into modern Christianity became centred in Rome where, after the death of Paul's immediate followers, contact with polytheistic creeds, particularly virgin-born-resurrected-on-the-third-day-saviour-god mystery cults, led its adherents to speculate that perhaps Jesus, too, had been a saviour-god. There was ample evidence, to a Greek, for such a view, in the gospel accounts of Jesus' virgin-birth and resurrection, and in the terminology by which Jesus had been designated by Paul. Finally the first Christian in the modern sense, a Greek who was also a mystery-cult initiate, wrote the book in which Jesus was transformed from anointed king to god-incarnate. That book was *John*.

John was not the first Christian scripture written to repudiate earlier Christian scripture. *James* had been written to repudiate the teaching (and by implication the letters) of Paul, as P had been written to repudiate J/E. But *John* was the first Christian gospel written to repudiate earlier Christian gospels, of which *Luke* was John's specific source.

All three synoptics, but particularly *Luke-Acts*, had spelled out in unambiguous terms Jesus' adherence to buddhistic Essenism. Among Jesus' moral absolutes were the necessity of abolishing private property and instituting pure communism (ACTS 4:32-35); the glorification of celibacy (LUKE 20:35), even to the point of advocating self-castration (MAT. 19:12); the subhuman status of soulless gentiles (LUKE 7:4-5; MAT. 10:5); and perhaps the most repugnant of all Essene doctrines (still practised by Moonies and similar cults), the repudiation of all family ties and the hatred of (indifference to) kinsmen who remained outside the sect (LUKE 14:26; Philo, HYP. 2:18). In addition, the synoptics had shown Jesus preaching a worldwide theocracy with its capital in Jerusalem, to be established within a time limit that had already expired.

With the exception of the messianic theocracy and the pre-damned

---

35. *Commentaries on Isaiah* bk. 18.

status of gentiles, those doctrines were anathema to the majority of Jews. To Greeks and Romans who had never been conditioned to think of chronic masochists as *Saints*, the repugnance of synoptic Christianity was overwhelming. It was for the purpose of suppressing the synoptics and offering a new version of Christianity that would endorse marriage,[36] the family, and private property, and remove the last vestiges of Jesus' Jewishness, including his status as a theocratic king, that the author of *John* invented the religion of Jesus-the-god. Whether the eventual inclusion of his assault upon the synoptics, in a *bible* in which they were also incorporated, would have made him cry or laugh, we can only guess.

John was in a very real sense the successor of Paul. Their mythologies were dissimilar. Paul was, after all, a monotheist. But it had been Paul who established the precedent of abolishing Jewish laws and beliefs for Christians, and John carried Paul's policies to their logical conclusion. Perhaps the most apt delineation of their comparative roles would be to say that Paul was the first reform rabbi, whereas John was the first Catholic priest.

As with the synoptics, the real name of the author of *John* is unknown. Certain similarities between the gospel, letters and apocalypse that now bear that name led the early Christians to imagine that they had been the work of a single author; and since the redactor of *Apocalypse* had called himself *Ioannes*, that name was attached to the unsigned works also. In fact, while the author of *Apocalypse* had been a Jew whose Greek (Koine) left a lot to be desired, the author of *John* was a native Greek whose handling of that language was skilled and erudite.

The gospel author's excellence in Greek is best illustrated by the scene in which, without quite making Peter Head Christian as an interpolator of *Matthew* would eventually do, he did make Peter Jesus' special envoy. In the English translation, Jesus asked Peter three times, 'Do you love me?' and Peter answered three times, 'I love you' (JOHN 21:15-17). In fact, as the scene was written, Jesus' first two questions were, 'Do you agape me?' and Peter's reply was, 'I philos you.' The distinction between the two Greek verbs was that *agape* meant the kind of compassionate regard that one usually feels for close relatives, whereas *philos* denoted the passionate love felt by an artist for his art, a miser for money, a gambler for his compulsion, an autocrat for power, and a masochistic saint for his sadistic god. Jesus' third question was, 'Do you philos me?' By switching to the verb Peter had twice used, Jesus indicated his acceptance of Peter's assurance that he indeed

---

36. By attending a marriage at Kana, and coming to the host's rescue when the wine ran out, Jesus thereby endorsed the validity of marriage—and that was John's purpose in inventing such a scene (JOHN 2:1-11). Since John's Jesus was a god, John had him turn water into wine, as the god Bacchus did in the annual festival of Martinalia.

possessed the fanatic devotion to his leader that would justify his appointment as a prototype Head Christian.

Only a highly educated man whose native language was Greek could have utilised the subtle distinction between *agape* and *philos* to such advantage. Matthew had used both verbs, but far less skilfully, and had actually put into Jesus' mouth the demand that his followers *agape* Yahweh (MAT. 22:37), but *philos* Yahweh's anointed king (10:37). It was precisely because Ioannes was *not* skilled in Greek that he had written in Koine, the pidgin Greek used only by persons unable to master formal Greek. Since *Apocalypse* was written in Koine, the claim that its author, Ioannes, also wrote *John*, is absurd.

The climax to the *agape/philos* scene was a prophecy put into Jesus' mouth that Peter would die by execution (JOHN 21:18-19). The inclusion of such a prophecy leaves little doubt that by 130 CE a tradition already existed that Peter had been executed. However, since the wording of the prophecy implied that Peter had died with his clothes on, it severely undermines the conceit that he was crucified.

The similarity of the 'John' documents, as they are now known, that led to their being attributed to a single author, lay in their common references to Yahweh and Jesus as *the Father and the Son*, in such a way as to imply that the Father and the Son constituted a duality (JOHN 14:9; 1 JOHN 1:3; 2 JOHN 9); in their use of the term *spirit of truth* (JOHN 15:26; 1 JOHN 4:6); and in their calling Jesus the *Logos* of God (JOHN 1:14; 1 JOHN 1:1; APO. 19:13).

The idea that a man could be the *Logos*, the incarnation of the First Cause, originated in Persia where identical terminology was applied to Zarathustra.[37] It meant essentially that Zarathustra (or Jesus) spoke for Ahura Mazda (or Yahweh) as his True Priest. That the author of *Apocalypse* could introduce such a concept into Judaism is further evidence that he was an Essene, a member of a sect that had already introduced so much that was Zoroastrian into the *Book of Enoch*. For the gospel author then to utilise the term was no big step.

Neither the Naziritised *Apocalypse*, edited and expanded by a man named Ioannes, nor the 'John' letters, written by an otherwise unidentified author who called himself *ho Presbyteros* ('the Senior'), designated Jesus a god. The *Gospel of John*, on the other hand, had Jesus claim equality with Yahweh on several occasions (JOHN 8:58; 10:30; 14:9; 20:28). While Mark had originated the slander that the Jews had procured Jesus' death on a charge of blasphemy (MARK 14:64), it was John who particularised that blasphemy into a claim to be Yahweh's mirror-image: '*Anyone who has seen me has seen the father*' (JOHN 14:9); '*I and the father constitute a unity*' (JOHN 10:30).

---

37. *Zend Avesta*, Mihir Yast 32:137.

In fact if Jesus had been alive to do anything about it, it would have been John who was executed for blasphemy. As paranoid as Jesus was, he was a committed monotheist who under no circumstances could have uttered the claims to godship put into his mouth by John. Nor could he have done so and survived. In a society as intolerant as that in which Jesus grew up, any man who uttered the incredible blasphemy, *'Before Abraham existed, I Yahweh'* (JOHN 8:58), would never have lived to stand trial. He would have been torn apart on the spot.

John's allegations of Jesus' claim to godship directly contradicted the portrait of Jesus painted by Mark, Matthew, Luke, Paul, Peter, Jacob, Judas, pseudo-Paul and pseudo-Peter, none of whom reported any speech or action by Jesus or any disciple that could possibly be interpreted as indicating a belief that Jesus was Yahweh. Had Jesus made the claim that he had once played checkers with Noah or Adam, his biographers might conceivably have deemed such a revelation too insignificant for inclusion in their gospels. But those biographers would have had strange priorities indeed to have dismissed as not worth recording a claim by their messiah to be the incarnation of Yahweh. The reason that no claim by Jesus to be any kind of god was mentioned by any biblical author but John was that no such claim was ever made. The god Jesus was John's invention and John's alone.

The author of *John* is sometimes identified with *the disciple whom Iesous loved* (JOHN 21:20), even though the Beloved Disciple would have had to be at least 120 years of age when *John* was written. In fact John made no claim to be the Beloved Disciple. What he did claim was that he copied some of his gospel from a document written by the Beloved Disciple, and to that claim he added his opinion, *'We are certain that his testimony is accurate'* (JOHN 21:24). Since the *we* referred to John and the *his* to the Beloved Disciple, the claim that they were the same person is untenable.

The Beloved Disciple, as John knew, was long dead, and John explained away a prophecy that he would not die until Jesus' second coming with the words: *'However, Iesous did not say to him that he was not going to die, but rather, "If it's my whim that he remain until I'm established, what's that to you?"'* (JOHN 21:23). John's gospel would indeed have some claim to represent original Christianity if its author had been Jesus' disciple; but such was not the case. By the time *John* was written, Jesus' last disciple had been dead for fifty years.

Most current versions of *John* contain the fable that Jesus intervened to prevent the execution of a convicted adulteress. The *Authorized Version* placed the story at *John* 7:53 to 8:11, even though some old manuscripts did not contain it at all, while others included it in *Luke* between the A.V. chapters 21 and 22. The suspicion has arisen that the story is an interpolation that was not originally part of either *John* or *Luke*. Perhaps it was not. But it must be recognised that the story was more consistent with something the early Christian hierarchy would have tried to suppress than with something they would have invented.

Since the story was written in Koine it could not have been part of John. The best assumption is that it was originally part of *Luke*, and that Christian censors deleted it rather than have Jesus condone adultery. It was eventually restored, but to the wrong gospel. The anecdote's punchline, 'Go, and from now on don't disobey (the Towrah),' may have been added to make the tale more palatable at the time of its restoration to orthodox texts. Certainly the incident was spurious; the Sanhedrin had abolished the death penalty for adultery before Jesus' birth (SANH. 41a).

Mark had written a tale in which, at the home of Simon the leper, an unidentified woman anointed Jesus' head with expensive ointment. Being rebuked for allowing such a wasteful use of a product that could have been sold to aid *the Poor*, Jesus responded, '*The Poor you're always going to have with you, and can benefit them whenever it's your whim, but me you won't always have*' (MARK 14:3-7).

John retold the story with a few changes (JOHN 12:1-9). For example, while John retained the Bethany location, he changed Jesus' host from Simon the leper to one Lazaros. No doubt John was more aware of Judaean realities than Mark, and realised that a leper could not have occupied a house in Bethany or any other Judaean village.

John identified the woman who anointed Jesus as Lazaros's sister Mary. In John's verson, however, Mary did not anoint King Jesus' head. Luke had changed *Mark*'s scene so that the unidentified woman became a *sinful woman*, who anointed Jesus' feet and dried them with her hair (LUKE 7:38). John had Mary do likewise, thereby indicating that he must have been using *Luke* as a source.

According to Mark, objections to such ostentatious waste had been widespread. John made the objector Judas the Iskariot. To lessen the validity of Judas's objections, John credited the daggerman with larcenous rather than altruistic motives. He did not, however, delete Jesus' affirmation that there must always be *poor*. Presumably John accepted poverty, along with disease and suffering, as an integral part of Yahweh's incomprehensible Plan. Since Jesus' words, '*You won't always have me (with you),*' are best interpreted as referring to his presence in Simon/Lazaros's house, and are therefore not inconsistent with his beliefs about his identity and his mission, the possibility cannot be ignored that they were actually spoken by him. In that case Jesus, too, must have believed that poverty was a good thing, instituted by Yahweh his Allah. And if *the poor (ptokhois)* was simply a Greek translation of *ebioniym*, meaning Jesus' commune, then his prophecy that there would always be *ptokhois* failed when the Ebionites became extinct

1500 years ago.

John repeated a story told by Luke. Peter and others had been fishing all night and caught nothing. On Jesus' instructions they cast their nets again, whereupon the enormous catch proved almost more than the boats would hold. In Luke's version the nets had been torn by their huge load (LUKE 5:6). John saw torn nets as a reflection on Jesus' power and specifically declared that, *Even though there were so many, the net did not rip* (JOHN 21:11). Luke had used the tale as the means by which Peter was first recruited as a disciple. In John's theogony, the fish story was placed after Jesus' 'resurrection.'

John borrowed another story from *Luke*, that of the death of Lazaros, but followed *Mark*'s precedent of turning a parable into a miracle. In *Luke*'s version, a beggar named Lazaros had died and gone to *Abraham's bosom*, while the rich man at whose door Lazaros had sought crumbs had gone to *hades*. The rich man, tormented by Jesus' flamethrowers, asked Abraham to send Lazaros back to earth as a warning to his five brothers. Abraham replied that anyone who would not learn from Moses (i.e., the Towrah) would be no more impressed by someone returning from the dead (LUKE 16:20-31).

In John's retelling, the parable's hero, Lazaros, became Jesus' host in the feet-washing scene, and was *actually* raised from the dead (JOHN 11:1-44). John may have been familiar with the Greek myth in which Asklepios raised the dead, thereby causing Zeus to rekill Asklepios's resurrected patient as well as Asklepios himself. John made the parallel of having the chief priests react to Jesus' alleged miracle by plotting the death of both Jesus and Lazaros (JOHN 11:53; 12:10). In accusing the Jewish priests, who had been waiting six centuries for a messiah in whose reality they did not doubt, of rejecting a claimant who could raise the dead, and even plotting to kill a man resurrected through the agency of their god (who alone, they believed, could raise the dead), John was not merely insulting his readers' intelligence. In expecting them to believe such a tale, he was expressing an opinion of their sanity. A modern analogy would be for a man claiming to be Jesus to walk into St Patrick's cathedral during a funeral and validate his claim by resurrecting the corpse, and for the church hierarchy which has been preaching a Second Coming for almost two thousand years to order the murder of both the claimant and the ex-corpse.

The story that Jesus, after his resurrection, appeared magically in a locked room and showed his wounds to his twin brother, Thomas, was authored by John. It represented a considerable advance on the questionable incident reported by Luke, and was undoubtedly composed to still the skepticism that the earlier story could not have failed to arouse. John left no doubt that the man seen alive after the crucifixion was indeed Jesus. Unfortunately for his credibility, however, he had Thomas examine nail-holes in Jesus' *hands*, rather than his wrists. Clearly, John had never seen a crucifixion at close range.

In giving Jesus a twin brother, John was following a common Greek tradition. The divine offspring of a god and a mortal woman invariably had a mortal twin (Herakles and Iphikles; Kastor and Polydeukes), and it seemed to John as a Greek that Jesus ought also to have a twin. John hedged his bets, however, by referring to Thomas as *ho legomenos didymos*, 'the (his) reputed twin' (JOHN 11:16; 20:24; 21:2). That John was the first gospel author to give Jesus a twin was hardly surprising, since he was also the first gospel author to make Jesus a god. Thomas's twinship was later endorsed by the *Gospel of Thomas*, whose Gnostic author wrote: *These are the proverbs secretly spoken by Iesous during his life, which his twin Ioudas Thomas wrote down. . . .*

John promoted Jesus from king to Emperor by having Thomas address him as 'My *master and my god*,' the salutation demanded by the Emperor Domitian of all who came into his presence.[38] Evidently John wished to convey that his new god had proven his right to titles that Emperors had merely usurped. It was John's portrayal of Jesus in this scene as the True Emperor that led Christian iconographers to depict Jesus, and later the goddess Mary, as wearing the Emperor's halo.

John changed the date of Jesus' execution. According to all three synoptics the crucifixion had occurred in a year in which Passover fell on a Friday. John, on the other hand, dated the crucifixion to a year in which Passover was a Saturday. Since the crucifixion occurred during the procuratorship of Pontius Pilatus, we can pinpoint it between 26 and 36 CE. Hugh Schonfield, in *The Passover Plot*, argues that, since the date of Passover in any given year was based on naked-eye observations of the new moon rather than precise calculations of the true new moon, and overcast conditions could have caused a discrepancy of several days, that a Friday or Saturday Passover could have been observed in any year of the designated decade. In Schonfield's view, the logical time for a rabble-rouser such as John the Immerser to appear was during the unsettled conditions that always accompanied the Roman census, held every fourteen years. The only census during Pilatus's procuratorship occurred in 34/35 CE. Schonfield therefore dates John's execution to the autumn of 35 CE, and Jesus' to the spring of 36 CE.

There are weaknesses in Schonfield's argument. *Luke* dates the advent of John the Immerser in *year fifteen of the hegemony of Tiberious Kaisaros* (LUKE 3:1), 28/29 CE, and it is inconceivable that a man who so angered Herod Antipas could have remained at large for more than a few weeks.

---

38. Suetonius, *The Twelve Caesars*, Domitian 13.

Also, since the Jews had long been dominated by cultures quite capable of calculating new moons mathematically, it is not reasonable to suppose that they had never learned to do likewise. By assuming that John was executed within a year of his first appearance, and Jesus within a year of John, we come up with a crucifixion date consistent with the assumption that the Jews could and did calculate the date of Passover correctly.

The synoptics' declaration that Jesus was executed on Passover was incorrect. Between 29 and 36 CE there was no year in which Passover fell on a Friday. Also, the synoptics had Jews behaving on the day of Jesus' death in ways that contravened the strict observance of Passover, and in so doing provided further proof that Mark, Matthew and Luke could not have been Jews or they would have noticed the inconsistency in their sources and rectified it. John, in dating the crucifixion to the day before Passover, was consistent with the Jewish calendar. Passover fell on a Saturday in 30 CE and again in 33 CE.

John cannot be credited with rectifying the synoptics' error on the basis of his better knowledge of Jewish customs. It is highly unlikely that he recognised the impossibility of the synoptics' dating. Yet he seems to have been right. Talmud entries, which were based not on *John* but on a parody of *Matthew*, also put the execution of *Yeshu ha-notsriy* for sorcery on the eve of Passover, and it would be quite a coincidence if that were in fact the execution date of the Righteous Rabbi. John's purpose in preferring a source that put the execution on the eve of Passover, rather than on Passover as his alternative source, *Luke*, declared, may have been political.

In 130 CE the Emperor Hadrian issued an edict prohibiting any subject of the empire from mutilating his phallus. Hadrian's target was not the Jews but the priests of Kybele and other goddesses who were castrating themselves in increasing numbers. A side effect of Hadrian's edict, however, was that it prohibited circumcision, and to the Jews that prohibition was a violation of their mythology. Although full-scale war, led by bar Kokhba, did not break out for a further two years, at any time from 130 CE on the Jewish resistance to Hadrian's edict would have made Christianity's Jewish connection as much a negative factor as it had been in Vespasian's day. By moving Jesus' execution, in effect, one day forward, John avoided the necessity of drawing attention to Jesus' Jewish orthodoxy, as making Jesus' last meal with his disciples the Passover celebration would have done.

In the synoptics, Jesus' last supper had been the Passover. In *John* it was not. Yet in John's description of the last supper he incorporated features not recorded in the synoptics that were in fact peculiar to the Passover meal (JOHN 13:25-29). While John's failure to recognise that Passover procedures could have played no part in a meal eaten twenty-four hours earlier than the onset of Passover indicates that he was not a Jew, his awareness of such procedures at all indicates that he was not lacking a Jewish source. Also, his exclusion of the ritual cannibalisation of the sacred king in the form of bread and wine from the last supper, even though he had included such a eucharistic meal at an earlier point in his gospel (6:54-57),[39] indicates that he possessed a source sufficiently valid, or at least sufficiently Jewish, to know that no such pagan ritual could possibly have been practised by the Jew Jesus. While other explanations are available, the one that best fits the facts is that John really did have access to better information than that available to Mark, Matthew or Luke, and the source of that information was exactly what John claimed it to be.

John did, as he claimed, have the Beloved Disciple's memoir of his relationship with Jesus. Certainly his omission of any mention of Jesus' birth supports his claim to have been using a source written at a time when neither Q's annunciation scene nor *Matthew*'s virgin-birth fable had yet been invented.

Probably the Beloved Disciple's memoir contained only an account of Jesus' last days, since no other part of *John* is remotely plausible. But it did contain an account of Jesus' last meal. It told of how Jesus dipped a crust and handed it to Judas the Iskariot before sending him out to buy Passover supplies and give alms to the poor (JOHN 13:26-29). Reasoning that the Beloved Disciple had not then known that Judas was a traitor, John amended the scene to accord with the fiction he found in *Luke*. Since the Beloved Disciple had mentioned nothing of a bread-and-wine as body-and-blood ritual, for the obvious reason that there had not been one, John did not mention it either.

Further evidence that John possessed an account of Jesus' last days more authentic than that used by the synoptics is to be found in his account of the sign placed over Jesus' stake. The synoptics had mentioned the sign: *The King of the Ioudaians* (MARK 15:26); *The King of the Ioudaians, This* (LUKE 23:38); *This is Iesous, the King of the Ioudaians* (MAT. 27:37). John made the sign read, *Iesous the Nazirite the King of the Ioudaians*, and added that the Jewish hierarchy asked Pilatus to change it to, *This one said, 'I'm King of the Ioudaians,'* and that Pilatus refused (JOHN 19:21-22).

Matthew had written a scene in which Pilatus washed his hands and declared, *'I am innocent of this one's blood'* (MAT. 27:24), in imitation of Daniel's line, *'I am innocent of this woman's blood,'* found in the Greek additions

39. John put into Jesus' mouth a long speech offering his body and blood as food and drink (6:32-58), so different from the eucharistic scene he found in *Luke* (22:17-20), that it is better viewed as stemming from John's mystery-cult experience than 'copied from *Luke*,' and is accordingly not listed as such in the chart at the end of this chapter. Similarly, *John* 21:15-17 is not attributed to a synoptic source, since the analogous passage in *Matthew* (16:19) is an interpolation inserted long after the composition of *John*.

to *Daniel* (13:46) and echoed in *Deuteronomy* (21:6-8). Since the scene was unlikely to have been unknown to John, his motive in having Pilatus refuse the Jews' request could hardly have paralleled Matthew's or he would have used Matthew's more effective ploy for the purpose. In fact John's scene can be accepted as authentic for the good reason that it was consistent with the anti-Semitic procurator's true motivation, but rather less consistent with the motivation that John, following the tradition started by Mark and continued by Luke, attributed to him.

To Lucius Pontius Pilatus, procurator of Judaea and murderer of countless Jews, a *King of the Jews* was Rome's enemy. It did not matter in the slightest whether Jesus' claim to the title was valid under Jewish law or invalid. Pilatus was determined to make an example of Jesus, to show the rebellious masses whom he despised that any *King of the Jews* not appointed by Tiberius could expect similar treatment. The Sanhedrin, in asking Pilatus to change the sign, wished to create the impression that Jesus was being executed for making a false claim, and that a genuine messiah could not possibly be crucified. That, of course, was precisely why Pilatus refused. To have complied would have destroyed the execution's value as an object lesson to all future messiahs and their followers.

The Beloved Disciple, who had close connections with the Sanhedrin, being a relative of the High Priest (JOHN 18:15), knew that the request had been made and refused, although he had not been present at Jesus' summary trial. Even so, it is not unlikely that he wrote an account of the trial based on eyewitness reports. The author of *John*, however, faced with incompatible accounts, preferred *Luke*'s, not so much because he thought it more likely to be correct (or cared), but because it was again politically expedient that Jesus not be revealed as a rebel against Rome.

The identity of the Beloved Disciple remains a mystery. Since he was the author of Christianity's core dogma, that Jesus rose from the dead, and deserves the recognition to which that dubious achievement entitles him, this is unfortunate. We know who he was not: He was not the redactor of *Apocalypse*, whose name was Ioannes and who lived on the island of Patmos. He was not the author of the fourth gospel. He was not Ioannes bar Zebedaios. But who *was* he? It may be that the Beloved Disciple's name does not appear anywhere in any of the Christian gospels, and therefore will never be known. But there is some evidence that he may have been Nathanael the Zealot.[40]

The fourth gospel contains five references to the Beloved Disciple, three

---

40. Frank Yerby, in his novel, *Judas My Brother*, identified the Beloved Disciple as Nathanael. However, since he presented no evidence for such an equation, I did not at the time of reading take Yerby's claim seriously.

of them by the B.D. himself (13:23; 20:2; 21:20), and two by the gospel author (19:26; 21:7), and two references to Nathanael, one by the B.D. (1:45-49) and one by the gospel author (21:2). They do not overlap in any way, and that suggests that the gospel author was unaware that the two were, or may have been, the same man.

To validate marriage, John had Jesus attend a wedding at a town named Kana, and perform a miracle there (JOHN 2:1-11; 4:46). He declared that Jesus' disciples were present, but did not specifically name Nathanael as being among them. Later, however, he described Nathanael as *from Galilaian Kana* (21:2). What seems probable is that the gospel author had a source, possibly a portion of the Beloved Disciple's memoir that he did not incorporate into his gospel, in which Nathanael was described as a *kananaion*, a Hellenised Aramaic word meaning Zealot (*cf.* MARK 3:18), and the gospel author misinterpreted this as meaning 'from Kana.'

Nathanael was a Zealot. The Beloved Disciple was a relative of the High Priest and himself a priest. The argument that a member of the ruling hierarchy was unlikely to belong to an organisation trying to overthrow the *status quo* presents a problem; but to say that a chief priest *could not* have been a Zealot, and therefore the Beloved Disciple could not have been Nathanael, is to confuse an unlikely event with an impossible one. And since the Beloved Disciple *did* follow a master whose lieutenants included other Zealots, that he was himself a Zealot is far from impossible.

It is most unlikely that the Beloved Disciple's memoir contained no clue to his identity. It is even more unlikely that the gospel author would have deleted any passage involving a disciple whose name appeared nowhere else. The clue to the Beloved Disciple's identity must therefore lie in those portions of his memoir preserved in the fourth gospel.

The anecdote in *John* in which Jesus asked Peter, *'Do you love me more than these?'* and Peter answered, *'Sire, you know that I cherish you,'* implied that Peter had a special status in Jesus' affections. Yet Peter was clearly not the Beloved Disciple, because the scene at Jesus' empty tomb had Mary the prostitute run *to Simon Petros and to the other disciple, the one Iesous cherished* (JOHN 20:2).

Of the other disciples named in the fourth gospel, Philippos, Andreas and the sons of Zebedyah were mere names, mentioned in passing, as was the second Judas; Judas the Iskariot was described as a *diabolos* (JOHN 6:70-71); Lazaros was not a historical person; Joseph of Harimathaia was the person who removed Jesus' body from its tomb, and therefore could not have been amazed at its disappearance; Thomas was identified as Jesus' *reputed twin* and therefore included in the statement that, *his brothers had no credulity in him* (JOHN 7:5). And for any disciple to win Jesus' special affection, he would have needed unquestioning credulity in Jesus' messianic pretensions.

By process of elimination, we are already left with only Nathanael. But the case for Nathanael would be weak indeed if it were nothing more than that. Better evidence can be found in a comparison of *John* and *Matthew*.

Only two disciples were portrayed in the Christian gospels as the recipients of Jesus' flattery: Peter in the synoptics and Nathanael in *John*. And the scenes are so similar as to suggest a common origin, with only the name changed:

JOHN	MATTHEW
(1:42) Iesous looked at him and said, 'So you're Simon bar Ioannes? You're going to be called Kephas,' which translated means Petros ('Rock').	(16:15) So he asked them, 'But who do you say I am?' And Petros answered, 'You're the Messiah, the descendant of the god.'
(1:43, 45) The following day he found Philippos. . . . Philippos found Nathanael. . . .	(16:17) And Iesous answered him, 'You're lucky, Simon, son of a Greek woman *(bar Iona)*, for flesh and blood has not revealed this to you, but my father in the sky.
(1:47) Iesous saw Nathanael coming toward him and said of him, 'Indeed, I see an Israelite in whom is no guile.'	
(1:49) Nathanael answered him, 'Rabbi, you are the descendant of the god. You are the King of Israel.'	**PSEUDO-MATTHEW** **(4th Century)**
	(16:18) I'm telling you this also: You are ROCK (PETROS), and on this Petros I'm going to found my community.'

Since *Messiah* meant 'Anointed by Yahweh,' in other words, 'King of Israel,' the statement of credulity that the synoptic authors attributed to Peter was identical with the words that, according to the Beloved Disciple, were actually spoken by Nathanael. Such a declaration of blind faith would indeed have won Jesus' unqualified love. And any man who could describe another as *an Israelite in whom is no guile* was lacking objectivity, to say the least.

The truth appears to be that, of all Jesus' disciples, Nathanael alone accepted his messianic claims from their first meeting, and that acceptance caused Jesus to hold him in such high regard that Nathanael could, without unduly distorting the facts, refer to himself as *the disciple whom Iesous loved*. By the time the first gospel was composed, forty years after Jesus' death, jealousy of Nathanael may have caused his name to be suppressed—especially if, as *John* 1:47 hints, he was mentally retarded. Consequently, the author of *Mark* never learned his name and did not include him among the mythical 'twelve apostles.'

Since Peter was the second-ranking member of the Nazirite commune, after Jacob the Righteous, it comes as no surprise that Nathanael's unique status was retroactively transferred to Peter in gospels based on the testimony of men who had known Peter but had never known Nathanael or Jesus. While it is far from certain that Nathanael was the Beloved Disciple, it seems highly probable that he was.

Once it was supported by a gospel, the doctrine of Jesus-the-god won a following among gentiles. To Jews, not surprisingly, the tale that Yahweh/ Zeus had lusted after the virgin Mary/Semele and sired upon her the saviour god Jesus/Dionysos was an obscene blasphemy (just as, to the rational, the tale that an extinct volcano placed arbitrary restrictions on who could share joy is an obscene blasphemy). All Christians (not Nazirites, to whom all gospels were infidel documents) were saddled with interpolated-*Matthew*'s virgin-birth fable, but the majority rejected *John*'s transformation of Jesus into a god. In order to win followers the Johannine minority added a few embellishments.

The Roman world was full of saviour-gods, of whom the most popular was Mithra. Mithra, however, restricted salvation to military-class males. The god Jesus offered admittance into Heaven to women and slaves. That single concession should have eliminated Mithraism as a serious competitor within a generation. In fact Mithra remained Jesus' main rival for three centuries, and the Christians found it necessary to borrow much from the older god. So thoroughly did the Jesus myth come to duplicate the Mithra myth that Tertullian could find no better rationalisation of the similarities than *the zeal of the devil rivalling the things of God*.[41]

For example, Mithra, like all sun-gods, celebrated his birthday on the sun's resurrection day after the winter solstice, the day that the duration of daylight had measurably begun to lengthen, December 25. December 25 became Jesus' birthday. Mithra's name day, Sunday, was observed by his worshippers as a day of rest. Christianity, which had dropped the Jewish sabbath-observance in emulation of Jesus' pretended nonobservance, declared the first day of the week the Christian *Seventh* (*shabat*) when Constantine, a Mithra-worshipper, became officially Christian.[42]

The Mithraic Holy Father wore a red cap and garment and a ring, and carried a shepherd's staff. The Head Christian adopted the same title and outfitted himself in the same manner. Christian priests, like Mithraic priests, became 'Father,' despite Jesus' specific proscription of the acceptance of such a title (MAT. 23:9). That Jesus had been repudiating, not the Mithraists with whom he was unfamiliar, but the Sanhedrin, whose President was styled *Father*, is hardly relevant.

---

41. *De Baptismo* 5.
42. Eusebius, *Life of Constantine* 4:18.

Mithra's bishops wore a *mithra*, or mitre, as their badge of office. Christian bishops also adopted mitres. Mithraists commemorated the sun-god's ascension by eating a *mizd*, a sun-shaped bun embossed with the sword (cross) of Mithra. The hot cross bun and the *mass* were likewise adapted to Christianity. The Roman Catholic *mizd*/mass wafer continues to retain its sun-shape, although its Episcopal counterpart does not.

All Roman Emperors from Julius Caesar to Gratian had been *pontifex maximus*, high priest of the Roman gods. When Theodosius refused the title as incompatible with his status as a Christian, the Christian bishop of Rome picked it up. Magi, priests of Zarathustra, wore robes that featured the sword of Mithra. Identical robes are worn by Christian priests to this day. German worshippers of the virgin-born resurrected-saviour-god Atthis commemorated his metamorphosis into a fir tree by including such a tree in the god's rebirth festival. The Atthis tree became a Christmas tree. The Druidic winter solstice festival of Yuletide included a representation of the goddess's blood and the god's sperm in the form of red holly berries and white mistletoe berries. Holly and mistletoe became Christmas symbols. And because German worshippers of Frig ate the vulva-shaped fish that was her sacramental body on the goddess's name day, Friday, Friday likewise became fish-eating-day to a hundred generations of Christians. Hindus prayed to Kali, utilising a *rosary upanishad* in which alternating red and white beads represented the goddess's virgin and mother states, just as the Egyptian *Book of the Dead* prescribed the use of beads on a string as a memory aid in reciting repetitive prayers. Rosary beads are now used for a similar purpose by Catholic Christians.

Greeks and Romans were accustomed to the benevolence of hundreds of gods, each of whom had jurisdiction over perhaps a single river or household fitting. Christianity left the minor gods their prerogatives but gave them a new designation: *saints*; and converted their festivals into saints' days. In Ireland, for example, the Celtic goddess Brigid became *Saint Briget*, whose worship continues to this day.

Women preferred to pray to goddesses, woman-to-woman. Christianity gave them Mary, not as an admitted goddess but as a nonetheless immortal mediator in Heaven who could intercede with her son the god on behalf of other women. Saviour-gods and fertility-goddesses held their resurrection festivals at the full moon following the vernal equinox. Christianity celebrated its resurrection feast on the same date. One of the best-known fertility-goddesses was Easter, also spelled *Ishtar*, *Astarte* and *Ashtaroth*. In parts of the world Christians refused to alienate the goddess by removing her name from the festival, with the consequence that the name *Easter* was retained even after her festival had been rededicated to a male god.

The world had long worshipped a triple-goddess. *John's* creation of a dual-god, Yahweh and Jesus, the Father and the Son, had disturbed a lot of worshippers on account of its uniqueness. It was inevitable that, following the masculinisation of the androgynous *holy spirit*, he would eventually be added to the unfamiliar duality to create the more familiar trinity. When this happened the west had a triple-god to match India's Brahma/Vishnu/Siva. However, since this development did not occur until two centuries after the completion of the Christian bible, and the absence from that bible of any mention of Yahweh and Jesus having a third partner was an embarrassment, trinitarian passages were interpolated into *Matthew* and *1 John*. That the line, *immersing them in the name of the father and of the son and of the consecrated breath* (MAT. 28:19b), was not originally part of *Matthew* is attested by Eusebius. That the *presbyteros* did not write, '*the father, the logos and the consecrated breath; and those three are a unity,*' is evident from the absence of those words from the oldest manuscripts.[43]

Since Christianity leaned over backwards to accommodate every superstition that had ever existed, there is some cause to wonder why it did not spread further and faster in the two centuries between the writing of *John* and the convening of the Council of Nicaea. One reason was the series of persecutions by ten Emperors that saw between two thousand and three thousand Christians executed in 250 years. Another reason must surely have been Christianity's retention of the Essenes' masochistic rejection of sexual recreation as a sharing of joy.

One example of Christianity's anti-sexualism can be seen in the expansion of the concepts *adultery* and *fornication*, which by 325 CE had come to include between them all acts of recreation other than those between husband and wife. But the full extent of Christianity's pathological hatred of humankind's most fulfilling and totally joyful activity was exemplified by such Christian theologians and 'saints' as Augustine of Hippo, who declared that, '*We are born between shit and piss*'; Jerome, who saw women as *a tool of Satan and a pathway to Hell*; Marcion, who denied that his celibate god was the creator of *the disgusting paraphernalia of reproduction*; Tertullian, who called women *a temple built over a sewer*, and eventually informed his wife that '*There will be no more resumption of voluptuous disgrace between us*'; and Ambrose who, along with Augustine, contributed to the world the pious belief that someone as clean as Jesus could not have come out of something as dirty as a female recreational orifice, but instead magically appeared outside Mary's body without the necessity of utilising her birth canal.[44] To this day the Catholic church maintains, on the basis of Ambrose and Augustine's

---

43. The *Jerusalem Bible*, the *New American Bible*, the *James Moffat Bible* and the *New World Translation* all omit this passage as spurious.

44. G.L. Simons, *Sex and Superstition*, pp. 99, 103, 107, 108.

fantasy, that Mary remained an *intacta* virgin even after Jesus' birth.

From the belief that joy-rejection was virtuous, early Christianity graduated to the belief that all masochism was virtuous, and masochism practised for the purpose of taking one's mind off the pleasures of sexual recreation guaranteed the masochist an honoured place in Heaven. For example, Jerome lived *in the desert amid scorpions and wild beasts* until '*my skin was dry and my frame gaunt from fasting and penance, my body . . . that of a corpse,*' trying to suppress the *cravings of desire and the fire of lust* that '*burned in my flesh.*'

A monk committed suicide by leaping into a furnace after sharing a joyful experience with a consenting woman. John of Lycopolis boasted that he had not seen a woman in forty-eight years (although he made no mention of avoiding the company of ewes). Ammonius covered his body with burns from a hot iron. Christine of St Trond had herself wheeled, racked and hung beside a corpse. Margaret Marie Alacoque licked up her patients' vomit with her tongue, deriving much pleasure thereby. John of the Cross licked out the sores of lepers. Rose drank a bowl of blood drawn from a diseased patient. Mary Magdalene dei Pazzi, after an erotic hallucination, rolled on thorns and whipped herself. Simeon wore an iron belt that ulcerated his flesh.[45]

All of the foregoing were canonised, not despite their pathological masochism, but because of it. That every one of those *saints*, if he lived today, would be institutionalised as incurably insane cannot reasonably be disputed. That Popes and others responsible for their canonisation must have been similarly disturbed is a reasonable inference. While some of the examples cited occurred as recently as the seventeenth century, they nonetheless typified the Christian concept of saintliness that existed from the first century.

Since the ultimate Christian virtue was to be persecuted or martyred for one's mythology, and the surest way to achieve that objective was to treat others as the Christians themselves wished to be treated, not surprisingly many achieved their objective. Perhaps as many as two-thirds of the roughly 2500 Christians executed by Roman Emperors were virtual suicides. Others, however, were not, and even a single instance of a virtuous man being executed for being Christian must have deterred many potential Christians from committing the capital offence of joining the proscribed sect.

Christians were persecuted by the Emperors Nero, Domitian, Trajan, Hadrian, Marcus Aurelius, Septimius Severus, Valerian, Maximian, Diocletian and Galerius. That list included three of the noblest men ever to hold the imperium: Trajan, Hadrian and Aurelius. Of the others, Severus and Diocletian were the kind of men who would not knowingly have persecuted the innocent.

---

45. *Ibid.*, pp. 117-120.

A good percentage of the Christians executed, as mentioned, deliberately sought martyrdom as a morally acceptable form of suicide. Suicide had long been regarded as reprehensible in some societies. The Greek Hero Aias (Ajax), for example, was refused military burial at Troy on the ground that a suicide was unworthy of such an honour. But Christianity flourished, not in classical Greece, but in the world of Imperial Rome. And to the Romans suicide was an honourable death. Not surprisingly, therefore, Christians whose earthly lives were less than satisfying, promised eternal bliss in a hereafter in the sky, were singularly attracted to the shortcut. A similar syndrome survives to this day: in 1956, an Australian member of the Rosicrucians killed himself for the specific purpose of entering his next incarnation. Whether the mass suicide in Jonestown, Guyana, in 1978, was analogous is debatable.

No social movement can survive if its members keep killing themselves. The Christian hierarchy recognised this and quickly declared suicide a heinous sin, using as their justification the verses in the third-century-BCE *Job* (2:9-10) in which the poem's hero rejected the opportunity to escape his misfortunes by such a method. Suicide by martyrdom, however, was not only exempted from the general prohibition; it was declared utterly desirable. A Christian killed for strict adherence to the teachings of his mythology was promised immediate admission to the heavenly kingdom without the necessity of fulfilling any other conditions. Consequently, innumerable swallowers of this teaching made a point of vandalising temples and boasting of their guilt for the specific purpose of being caught and executed. Cyprian, bishop of Carthage and the first Christian priest to be executed, refused to plead *not guilty* to just such a charge, and was proudly hailed by his biographer as having indeed committed the temple desecration of which he was accused.

The last persecution of Christians by a pagan Emperor was ordered by Diocletian in 303 CE. For the previous eighteen years of his reign Diocletian had granted Christianity the same toleration accorded the empire's dozen other resurrected-saviour mythologies.[46] But in 303 the Christians set fire to the Imperial Palace in an attempt to frame Diocletian's deputy, Galerius, a devotee of the deified Jesus' chief rival, Mithra. The plot failed and, realising that his toleration had been misplaced, Diocletian outlawed the sect in an attempt to stamp out an antisocial menace once and for all. He executed perhaps two hundred Christians in the remaining two years before his

---

46. A.P. Davies, in *The First Christian* (pp. 116-117), identifies cults of Atthis, Osiris, Tammuz and Adonis as flourishing in the Empire; and Augustus worshipped the risen Persephone at Eleusis. Tacitus put down 'the notoriously depraved Christians' and similar religions in the words, 'All degraded and shameful practices collect and flourish in the capital' (*Annals* xv:44).

abdication, while as many as an additional 1500 or more were executed by his successor Galerius in accordance with Diocletian's edict.

Galerius was followed by Constantine (*Constantinius*), another Mithraist, who nonetheless ended the proscription and declared Christianity legal. Some years later Constantine himself became a Christian, for reasons explained by his nephew Julian: Constantine at various times murdered his son, his second wife, and several other close relatives. Refused purification by the Mithraic Holy Father, who informed him that such crimes were unforgivable, Constantine turned to the Christians. He was told that *all* sins could be washed away by the Christian immersion initiation and, since Jesus differed from Mithra only in name, he promptly converted.

He did not, however, accept immediate immersion. Since the rite could be performed once only, and no alternative method of sin-removal yet existed, Constantine kept a priest at his side for the remainder of his life with instructions to immerse him the moment it became evident that he was about to die. He was thus enabled to sin with impunity for many more years, knowing that he could still obtain a no-questions-asked ticket to the pie in the sky when he died. Much later, when the Christian hierarchy recognised that the one-forgiveness-only rule was keeping people from being immersed until they were near death, the alternative ritual of forgiveness-through-confession was added to their mythology's mythology.

In 325 CE Constantine moved to end the dichotomy within Christianity. Aware that approximately two-thirds of all Christians, led by Arius, presbyter of Alexandria, were monotheists who revered Jesus as Yahweh's anointed king, while the remaining third, whose chief spokesman was Athanasius, bishop of Alexandria, were polytheistic worshippers of the newly-invented triple-god, Constantine ordered the leaders of the Christian hierarchy to attend a Council at the city of Nicaea that would make a definitive pronouncement on the status of Jesus. The Council's decision, Constantine declared, would be imposed on all Christians with all the force the most powerful man in the world could bring to bear.

The Council of Nicaea, like almost all fourth-century Councils, Athanasian and Arian, was rigged. The trinitarian minority staged a *coup d'ekklesia* that formally pronounced Jesus a god (as the Senate had twice pronounced Claudius a god) at a time when the monotheist majority had not yet reached Nicaea. Constantine enforced Jesus' godship and purged the hierarchy of all monotheists. The belief in Jesus as a purely human Christened King, which had been Christian orthodoxy for almost three hundred years, was thereafter designated the Arian heresy. The consequence of the *coup* of 325 CE, combined with the Athanasian status of the Emperor Theodosius who finally made Christianity compulsory (all Christian Emperors in between having been Arians), is that Christians to this day worship as a god a man who never claimed to be a god, whose disciples never claimed that he was a god, and whose first three biographers made no claim that he was a god.

Despite Constantine's enforcement of the Nicene creed, Jesus' alleged godship and the holy spirit's alleged godship continued to be debated for fifty years. Ten years after Nicaea, a Council at Tyre repudiated the three-headed god and demoted Jesus to Anointed King. In the next three years, Councils at Jerusalem, Constantinople and Alexandria confirmed the Jesus-as-created-mortal Arian (and Nazirite/Ebionite) creed. Then in 341, 347 and 351, Councils at Antioch, Sardica and Sirmium restored King Jesus to his Nicene divinity. The Council of Rimini in 360 again de-deified him, much to the satisfaction of Constantine's son and successor, Constantius, an Arian. Jesus' final deification took place at the Council of Constantinople in 380 CE, under the patronage of the Emperor Theodosius, an Athanasian.

Some centuries later, when the claim was put forward that Councils were 'inspired' by the triple-god's third head and therefore could not err, the Arian resolutions of early Councils were rationalised away by retroactively pronouncing the Councils of 325 and 380 the First and Second Ecumenical Councils and granting them infallible status, and retroactively repudiating those Councils that had rejected the three-headed god and labelling them schismatic. That Rimini was attended by more bishops than either of the so-called Ecumenical Councils, and appears to have been the only fourth-century Council that was not stacked by one or other of the parties, could not save it from being anathematised. Apparently the holy spirit only *inspired* those Councils that voted for the ultimate winner.[47]

Constantine's nephew Julian, while he was Emperor (360-363), tried to revive the old gods. He had seen the atrocities committed by his uncle and cousin in the belief that they could do anything they wished and still obtain forgiveness by immersion, and it had given him a perspective of Christianity that, if not objective, was at least accurate. He wrote a tract against his relatives' mythology, borrowing heavily from the earlier rebuttals penned by Celsus and Porphyrios. Julian's tract survives in part in the pathetic attempted rebuttal by Cyril, while some of Celsus's work is preserved in Origen's *Contra Celsum*. No part of Porphyrios's writing is extant; yet thirty Christian scholars had written tracts that attempted to refute Porphyrios's arguments. Not only did later Christian censors consign Porphyrios to the flames; all thirty rebuttals were also discreetly eliminated in a tacit acknowledgement that Porphyrios could not in fact be rebutted. Similar realisation that the ridiculous has no defence against ridicule caused the defunct Soviet Union to ban *Animal Farm*.

Julian was no more able to halt the onrush of Christianity in a mere three years in the fourth century than Queen Mary I of England was able

---

47. J. Hefele, A *History of the Christian Councils*, vols. 1 and 2.

to halt the onrush of Protestantism in five years in the sixteenth. Toward the end of the reign of Theodosius (378-395), the Emperor, under pressure from the fanatically intolerant 'Saint' Ambrose, outlawed all mythologies but his own. Like Constantine, Theodosius had initially been tolerant of all religions. For example, when a mob of rampaging Christians burned down a temple of the old gods and a synagogue, Theodosius had ordered them to make restitution; but when Ambrose threatened him with excommunication if he dared grant human rights to non-Christians, he withdrew the order.[48] A similar situation occurred in England in 1688, when King James II's action in granting human status to Catholics caused the Protestant majority to turn on him and force him to flee for his life.

Theodosius's ban on diversity succeeded, and within a few generations the four-thousand-year-old worship of gods named Zeus and Jove disappeared forever. The menshevik coup at Nicaea had made that possible, by transforming Christianity from a monotheistic mythology that could not have conquered a polytheistic world, into a polytheistic mythology that could and did.[49]

Human beings cannot be forced to change their mythologies. More than one thousand years of Muslim rule in India could not reduce Hinduism to minority status. Had Theodosius attempted to impose monotheism, with or without King Jesus, on his polytheistic empire, he would surely have failed. In fact Theodosius imposed nothing more than new names for old gods. Women continued to worship Diana, Kybele, Isis, Hera, Ishtar, and the empire's hundred other goddesses; but now they called her Mary. (That Mary was identical with older goddesses can hardly be doubted by anyone who compares depictions of the sorrowing mother Kybele and the mutilated Atthis with Michaelangelo's *Pieta*; or statues of Isis and the baby Horus with Christian renderings of Mary and Jesus.)

Worshippers of Priapos, Adonis, Mithra, Dionysos, Osiris, Atthis, Tammuz and various other saviour-gods, continued in the mythology that they had always followed; but now they called their god *Jesus*. Men accustomed to going straight to the top and directing their prayers and offerings to Zeus or Jove continued to do so; but now, to create the belief that all Kings of Heaven were identical with Yahweh, they simply called him/them God.

Sailors who had never crossed a fishpond without asking the aid of Poseidon offered the same prayers to the same god; but now they called him *Saint Christopher*. Believers in an abode of the dead continued to accept that admittance could only be granted by the ferryman Kharon; but Kharon's

---

48. Edward Gibbon, *Decline and Fall of the Roman Empire*, chap. 27.

49. 'Anyone who can worship a trinity and insist that his religion is a monotheism can believe anything—just give him time to rationalize it.' (Robert Heinlein, *Job: A Comedy of Justice.*)

new name was *Saint Peter*. Pantheists who could not conceive of Zeus without his messenger Hermes continued in their belief; but now Hermes was to be called *Gabriel*. Soldiers who sought inspiration from the war-god Ares continued to do so; but now his name was *Mikhael*.

No imperial decree could have ended polytheism, and no imperial decree did end it. Polytheism is as widespread today as it was five thousand years ago. Only the name has changed. Now it is called *Christianity*.

Sources and Authors of the Christian Testament

Corinthians

A = first letter
B = second letter
C = third letter
D = fourth letter
I = interpolation

B. 1 Cor. 1:01-8:13	I. 1 Cor. 13:01-13:13	A. 2 Cor. 6:14-7:01
A. 1 Cor. 9:01-10:22	B. 1 Cor. 14:01-15:02	D. 2 Cor. 7:02-9:15
B. 1 Cor. 10:23-11:21	I. 1 Cor. 15:03-15:11	C. 2 Cor. 10:01-13:14
I. 1 Cor. 11:22-11:29	B. 1 Cor. 15:12-16:24	
B. 1 Cor. 11:30-12:31	D. 2 Cor. 1:01-6:13	

John letters

A = original author
I = interpolation
P = the presbyteros

A. 1 Jn. 1:01-5:08a	A. 1 Jn. 5:09-5:21	P. 3 Jn. 1:01-1:14
I. 1 Jn. 5:08b	P. 2 Jn. 1:01-1:13	

Apocalypse

E = Essene author
N = Nazirite redactor

N. 1:01-3:22	E. 7:15-12:17a	N. 16:06b	E. 19:11-20:03a
E. 4:01-7:08	N. 12:17b	E. 16:06c-19:10a	N. 20:03b-22:21
N. 7:09	E. 13:01-14:12a	N. 19:10b	
E. 7:10-7:12	N. 14:12b	E. 19:10c	
N. 7:13-7:14	E. 14:13-16:06a	N. 19:10d	

Mark

A = no known source
I = interpolation
M = modification of a parable told by Q

A. 1:01-1:11a	I. 7:16	A. 9:47-10:34a	M. 11:20-11:21
I. 1:11b	A. 7:17-7:19a	I. 10:34b	A. 11:22-11:25
A. 1:12-3:32a	I. 7:19b	A. 10:35-10:46a	I. 11:26
I. 3:32b	A. 7:20-9:43	I. 10:46b	A. 11:27-15:27
A. 3:32c-6:11a	I. 9:44	A. 10:46c-11:11	I. 15:28
I. 6:11b	A. 9:45	M. 11:12-11:14	A. 15:29-16:08
A. 6:12-7:15	I. 9:46	A. 11:15-11:19	I. 16:09-16:20

Matthew

A = copied from *Mark*
B = no known source
Q = from Q gospel
I = interpolation

B. 1:01-1:16a	A. 3:01-3:06	B. 4:13-4:16	I. 6:13b
I. 1:16b	Q. 3:07-3:10	A. 4:17-4:24a	A. 6:14-6:15
B. 1:16c-1:17	A. 3:11	I. 4:24b	Q. 6:16-7:02a
Q. 1:18a	Q. 3:12	A. 4:24c-4:25	A. 7:02b
I. 1:18b-1:20a	A. 3:13	B. 5:01a	Q. 7:03-7:27
Q. 1:20b	B. 3:14-3:15	Q. 5:01b-5:12	A. 7:28-7:29
I. 1:20c	A. 3:16-3:17a	A. 5:13-5:15	B. 8:01
Q. 1:21	I. 3:17b	B. 5:16	A. 8:02-8:04
I. 1:22-1:23	A. 4:01	Q. 5:17-5:28	Q. 8:05-8:10
Q. 1:24	Q. 4:02a	A. 5:29-5:32a	B. 8:11-8:12
I. 1:25a	A. 4:02b	B. 5:32b	Q. 8:13
Q. 1:25b	Q. 4:02c-4:11a	A. 5:32c	A. 8:14-8:16
B. 2:01-2:23	A. 4:11b-4:12	Q. 5:33-6:13a	B. 8:17

A. 8:18
Q. 8:19-8:22
A. 8:23-9:09a
B. 9:09b
A. 9:09c-9:12
B. 9:13a
A. 9:13b-9:27a
B. 9:27b
A. 9:27c-9:31
Q. 9:32-9:33
A. 9:34-9:36
Q. 9:37
A. 10:01-10:03a
B. 10:03b
A. 10:03c
I. 10:03d
A. 10:03e-10:05a
Q. 10:05b-10:08a
B. 10:08b
A. 10:09-10:10a
Q. 10:10b-10:13
A. 10:14
Q. 10:15-10:16
A. 10:17-10:22
Q. 10:23-10:25a
B. 10:25b-10:26a
A. 10:26b
Q. 10:27-10:39
A. 10:40
B. 10:41
A. 10:42-11:01
Q. 11:02-11:13
B. 11:14-11:15
Q. 11:16-11:27
B. 11:28-11:30
A. 12:01-12:04
B. 12:05-12:07
A. 12:08-12:10
B. 12:11-12:12
A. 12:13-12:14
B. 12:15-12:21
Q. 12:22-12:24a
A. 12:24b-12:26
Q. 12:27-12:28
A. 12:29
Q. 12:30
A. 12:31

Q. 12:32a
A. 12:32b
Q. 12:33
B. 12:34-12:37
Q. 12:38-12:45
A. 12:46-13:15
Q. 13:16-13:17
A. 13:18-13:23
B. 13:24-13:30
A. 13:31-13:32
Q. 13:33
A. 13:34
B. 13:35-13:52
A. 13:53-14:27
B. 14:28-14:31
A. 14:32-15:11
B. 15:12-15:13
Q. 15:14
A. 15:15-15:22
B. 15:23-15:24
A. 15:25-15:28
Q. 15:29-15:31
A. 15:32-16:02a
I. 16:02b-16:03
Q. 16:04a
A. 16:04b-16:10
B. 16:11-16:12
A. 16:13-16:16
B. 16:17
I. 16:18-16:19
A. 16:20-16:22a
B. 16:22b
A. 16:23-16:27a
B. 16:27b
A. 16:28-17:12
B. 17:13
A. 17:14-17:19
Q. 17:20a
A. 17:20b
I. 17:21
A. 17:22-17:23
B. 17:24-17:27
A. 18:01-18:03
B. 18:04
A. 18:05-18:06
Q. 18:07
A. 18:08-18:09

B. 18:10
I. 18:11
Q. 18:12-18:15
B. 18:16-18:35
A. 19:01-19:09a
B. 19:09b
A. 19:09c
B. 19:10-19:12
A. 19:13-19:28a
Q. 19:28b
A. 19:29-19:30
B. 20:01-20:15
A. 20:16-20:20a
B. 20:20b
A. 20:20c
B. 20:20d
A. 20:20e-20:21a
B. 20:21b
A. 20:21c-20:30a
B. 20:30b
A. 20:30c-21:02a
B. 21:02b
A. 21:02c
B. 21:02d
A. 21:02e-21:03
B. 21:04-21:05
A. 21:06-21:07a
B. 21:07b
A. 21:07c-21:10a
B. 21:10b-21:11
A. 21:12-21:13
B. 21:14-21:16
A. 21:17-21:27
B. 21:28-21:32
A. 21:33-21:42
B. 21:43
I. 21:44
A. 21:45-21:46
Q. 22:01-22:09
B. 22:10-22:14
A. 22:15-22:39
B. 22:40
A. 22:41-23:01
B. 23:02-23:03
Q. 23:04
B. 23:05
A. 23:06-23:07a

B. 23:07b-23:10
A. 23:11
Q. 23:12-23:13
I. 23:14
Q. 23:15-23:39
A. 24:01-24:11
B. 24:12
A. 24:13-24:25
Q. 24:26-24:28
A. 24:29-24:36
Q. 24:37-24:41
A. 24:42
Q. 24:43-24:51
B. 25:01-25:13
Q. 25:14-25:30
B. 25:31-25:46
A. 26:01-26:15a
B. 26:15b
A. 26:16-26:24
B. 26:25
A. 26:26-26:49
B. 26:50a
A. 26:50b-26:51
B. 26:52-26:54
A. 26:55-27:02
B. 27:03-27:10
A. 27:11-27:18
B. 27:19
A. 27:20-27:23
B. 27:24-27:25
A. 27:26-27:42
B. 27:43
A. 27:44-27:49a
I. 27:49b
A. 27:50-27:51a
B. 27:51b-27:53
A. 27:54a
B. 27:54b
A. 27:54c-27:56a
B. 27:56b
A. 27:57a
B. 27:57b
A. 27:58-27:61
B. 27:62-27:66
A. 28:01
B. 28:02-28:05a
A. 28:05b-28:08a

B. 28:08b-28:15   B. 28:18-28:19a   I. 28:19b   B. 28:20
A. 28:16-28:17

Luke

A = copied from *Mark*
C = no known source
Q = from Q gospel
N = *Nativity of John*
J = parallels Josephus
I = interpolation

J. 1:01-1:04	I. 3:23b	Q. 7:18-7:28	Q. 11:02c
N. 1:05-1:25	C. 3:23c-3:38	C. 7:29-7:30	I. 11:02d
C. 1:26a	A. 4:01-4:02a	Q. 7:31-7:35	Q. 11:03-11:04
Q. 1:26b	Q. 4:02b-4:13	A. 7:36a	C. 11:05-11:08
A. 1:26c	A. 4:14-4:15a	C. 7:36b	Q. 11:09-11:14
Q. 1:27-1:33	C. 4:15b-4:21	A. 7:36c	A. 11:15-11:18
I. 1:34-1:35	A. 4:22	C. 7:36d	Q. 11:19-11:20
C. 1:36-1:37	C. 4:23	A. 7:36e-7:37a	A. 11:21-11:22
Q. 1:38	A. 4:24	C. 7:37b	Q. 11:23-11:26
C. 1:39-1:45	C. 4:25-4:30	A. 7:37c	C. 11:27-11:28
I. 1:46a	A. 4:31-5:02a	C. 7:37d	Q. 11:29-11:32
N. 1:46b-1:55	C. 5:02b-5:09	A. 7:37e	A. 11:33
C. 1:56	A. 5:10a	C. 7:38-7:43	Q. 11:34-11:35
N. 1:57-1:80	C. 5:10b	A. 7:44-7:46a	C. 11:36-11:37
C. 2:01-2:41	A. 5:10c-5:17a	C. 7:46b-8:03	A. 11:38a
J. 2:42	C. 5:17b	A. 8:04-9:42	C. 11:38b
C. 2:43-2:45	A. 5:17c-5:21a	C. 9:43a	A. 11:38c
J. 2:46-2:47	C. 5:21b	A. 9:43b-9:50	Q. 11:39-11:43a
C. 2:48-3:02a	A. 5:21c-5:27a	C. 9:51-9:55a	A. 11:43b
A. 3:02b	C. 5:27b	I. 9:55b	Q. 11:44-11:52
C. 3:02c	A. 5:27c-5:28	C. 9:56	C. 11:53-12:01a
A. 3:02d-3:04	C. 5:29a	Q. 9:57-9:62	A. 12:01b
C. 3:05-3:06	A. 5:29b-5:38	C. 10:01	C. 12:01c
Q. 3:07-3:09	C. 5:39	Q. 10:02-10:15	A. 12:02
C. 3:10-3:16a	A. 6:01-6:15	A. 10:16	Q. 12:03-12:10a
A. 3:16b	C. 6:16a	C. 10:17-10:20	A. 12:10b-12:12
Q. 3:17	A. 6:16b	Q. 10:21-10:24	C. 12:13-12:21
C. 3:18-3:20	Q. 6:17-6:38a	A. 10:25-10:28	Q. 12:22-12:34
A. 3:21-3:22a	A. 6:38b	C. 10:29-10:42	C. 12:35-12:38
I. 3:22b	Q. 6:39-7:10	Q. 11:01-11:02a	Q. 12:39-12:40
C. 3:23a	C. 7:11-7:17	I. 11:02b	C. 12:41

Q. 12:42-12:46	Q. 17:05-17:06a	C. 21:24	A. 23:34b-23:39a
C. 12:47-12:48	A. 17:06b	A. 21:25-21:33	C. 23:39b-23:43
Q. 12:49-12:59	C. 17:06c	C. 21:34-21:38	A. 23:44
C. 13:01-13:05	A. 17:06d	A. 22:01-22:02	C. 23:45a
Q. 13:06-13:09	C. 17:07-17:21	C. 22:03a	A. 23:45b-23:46a
C. 13:10-13:17	Q. 17:22-17:24	A. 22:03b-22:19a	C. 23:46b
A. 13:18-13:19	A. 17:25	I. 22:19b-22:20	A. 23:46c-23:47a
Q. 13:20-13:21	Q. 17:26-17:35	A. 22:21-22:27	C. 23:47b-23:48
C. 13:22	I. 17:36	Q. 22:28-22:30	A. 23:49-23:50
A. 13:23	Q. 17:37	C. 22:31-22:32	C. 23:51a
Q. 13:24-13:27	C. 18:01-18:14a	A. 22:33-22:34	A. 23:51b-24:03a
C. 13:28-13:29	Q. 18:14b	C. 22:35-22:38	I. 24:03b
A. 13:30	A. 18:15-18:43a	A. 22:39-22:42	A. 24:04a
C. 13:31-13:33	C. 18:43b-19:12a	I. 22:43-22:44	C. 24:04b
Q. 13:34-13:35	J. 19:12b	A. 22:45-22:47	A. 24:04c
C. 14:01-14:10	Q. 19:13	C. 22:48-22:49	C. 24:04d-24:05a
Q. 14:11	J. 19:14-19:15a	A. 22:50	A. 24:05b
C. 14:12-14:15	Q. 19:15b-19:26	C. 22:51	C. 24:05c
Q. 14:16-14:27	C. 19:27	A. 22:52-23:01	I. 24:06a
C. 14:28-14:33	A. 19:28-19:38a	C. 23:02	C. 24:06b-24:11
A. 14:34-15:03	C. 19:38b	A. 23:03	I. 24:12
Q. 15:04-15:07	A. 19:38c	C. 23:04-23:16	C. 24:13-24:36a
C. 15:08-16:12	C. 19:39-19:44a	I. 23:17	I. 24:36b
Q. 16:13	A. 19:44b	A. 23:18	C. 24:37-24:39
C. 16:14-16:15	C. 19:44c	I. 23:19	I. 24:40
Q. 16:16-16:17	A. 19:45-20:16a	C. 23:20	C. 24:41-24:51a
A. 16:18	C. 20:16b	A. 23:21-23:22a	I. 24:51b
C. 16:19-16:31	A. 20:17	C. 23:22b	A. 24:52a
Q. 17:01	C. 20:18	A. 23:23-23:26	C. 24:52b
A. 17:02	A. 20:19-21:19	C. 23:27-23:31	A. 24:52c
Q. 17:03	C. 21:20	A. 23:32-23:33	C. 24:53
C. 17:04	A. 21:21-21:23	I. 23:34a	

Acts

C = author of *Luke*
W = 'we' passages
J = parallels Josephus
I = interpolation

J. 1:01-1:02a	C. 5:38-8:36	C. 9:06b-15:33	C. 17:01-20:04
I. 1:02b-1:03a	I. 8:37	I. 15:34	W. 20:05-20:15
C. 1:03b-5:35	C. 8:38-9:05a	C. 15:35-16:08	C. 20:16-20:38
J. 5:36-5:37	I. 9:05b-9:06a	W. 16:09-16:40	W. 21:01-21:18

C. 21:19-21:36 I. 23:09b C. 24:08b-26:32 I. 28:29
I. 21:37-22:22 C. 23:10-24:06a W. 27:01-28:16 C. 28:30-28:31
C. 22:23-23:09a I. 24:06b-24:08a C. 28:17-28:28

John

A = also in *Mark* and *Matthew*, but not *Luke*
B = only in *Matthew*
C = copied from *Luke*
D = no known source
E = Beloved Disciple
I = interpolation
M = modification of a parable in *Luke*

D. 1:01-1:22	E. 6:67c-6:69	D. 11:57b	C. 13:20b-13:22
C. 1:23	C. 6:70-6:71	E. 11:57c	E. 13:23
D. 1:24-1:25	D. 7:01	D. 12:01a	D. 13:24-13:25
C. 1:26-1:27	E. 7:02-7:09	A. 12:01b	A. 13:26a
D. 1:28-1:29	D. 7:10-7:11	D. 12:01c-12:03a	E. 13:26b
C. 1:30-1:33	E. 7:12	C. 12:03b	C. 13:27a
D. 1:34-1:39	D. 7:13-7:20	D. 12:03c-12:04	E. 13:27b
E. 1:40-1:51	E. 7:21-7:24	A. 12:05	D. 13:28-13:29a
D. 2:01-2:12	D. 7:25-7:29	D. 12:06	E. 13:29b-13:30
C. 2:13-2:16	E. 7:30-7:31	A. 12:07-12:08	D. 13:31-13:35
D. 2:17	D. 7:32-7:39	D. 12:09-12:11	E. 13:36
A. 2:18-2:19	E. 7:40-7:44	E. 12:12-12:16	C. 13:37-13:38
D. 2:20-2:22	D. 7:45-7:51	D. 12:17-12:18	D. 14:01-18:10a
E. 2:23-2:25	E. 7:52	E. 12:19	C. 18:10b
D. 3:01-4:43	I. 7:53-8:11	D. 12:20-12:36	D. 18:10c-18:14
A. 4:44	D. 8:12-9:41	E. 12:37-12:42a	E. 18:15-18:16
D. 4:45-5:03a	E. 10:01-10:06	D. 12:42b	C. 18:17
I. 5:03b-5:04	D. 10:07-10:18	E. 12:42c-12:43	E. 18:18
D. 5:05-6:04	E. 10:19-10:21	C. 12:44	C. 18:19-18:20
C. 6:05-6:13	D. 10:22-10:39	D. 12:45-12:50	D. 18:21-18:24
D. 6:14-6:15	E. 10:40-10:42	E. 13:01	C. 18:25-18:26a
A. 6:16-6:21	D. 11:01-11:25a	C. 13:02a	D. 18:26b
D. 6:22-6:41	I. 11:25b	D. 13:02b	C. 18:26c-18:27
E. 6:42a	D. 11:25c-11:42	C. 13:02c	D. 18:28-18:32
D. 6:42b-6:58	M. 11:43-11:44	D. 13:03-13:10a	C. 18:33
E. 6:59-6:62	D. 11:45	I. 13:10b	D. 18:34-18:37a
D. 6:63	E. 11:46-11:50	D. 13:10c-13:16a	C. 18:37b
E. 6:64-6:67a	D. 11:51-11:54	C. 13:16b	D. 18:37c-18:38a
D. 6:67b	E. 11:55-11:57a	D. 13:17-13:20a	C. 18:38b

A. 18:39
C. 18:40
E. 19:01-19:03
D. 19:04-19:05
C. 19:06
D. 19:07-19:09a
A. 19:09b
D. 19:10-19:11
C. 19:12a
D. 19:12b
C. 19:12c

D. 19:13-19:15
C. 19:16a
E. 19:16b-19:24
D. 19:25-19:27
E. 19:28-19:32
D. 19:33-19:37
E. 19:38a
B. 19:38b
D. 19:38c
E. 19:38d
D. 19:39a

E. 19:39b-20:10
A. 20:11a
D. 20:11b
C. 20:11c-20:12
D. 20:13
C. 20:14
D. 20:15-20:17a
A. 20:17b
D. 20:17c
C. 20:18
D. 20:19

C. 20:20a
D. 20:20b-20:29
E. 20:30-20:31
C. 21:01-21:02a
D. 21:02b
C. 21:02c-21:11a
D. 21:11b-21:19
E. 21:20a
D. 21:20b
E. 21:21-21:22
D. 21:23-21:25

Appendix A

The Koran

$$\frac{dx}{dt} = -.0000078t^2x \qquad (x_0 = 10^9)$$

where $x=$world population of Christians and Jews and $t=$elapsed years since the publication of this book.

The Koran was dictated by Mohammed over a period of several years commencing c. 610 CE. It cannot be refuted on the basis of internal inconsistency for the obvious reason that, unlike the Judaeo-Christian bible, which was composed by dozens of men who many times disagreed with one another, it was authored by one individual. Mohammed's delusions were every bit as incredible as those of the bible authors, but they were consistent delusions. Mohammed apparently possessed a good memory, and for that reason was able to dictate the same lies at the end of his career as at the beginning.

Like Jesus, Mohammed influenced his hearers in either of two ways: Some believed him and accepted him at his own evaluation, while others regarded him as a self-deluded madman. That the latter attitude was sufficiently widespread to suggest that it may have had a factual basis can be inferred from the number of times he deemed it necessary to issue a denial in the *Koran: You are not mad* (68:2); *Why was this Koran not revealed to some mighty man from the two towns?* (43:31); *Give no heed to this Koran. Interrupt its reading with booing and laughter* (41:26); *Are we to renounce the gods for the sake of a mad poet?* (37:36); *Has he invented a lie about Allah, or is he mad?* (34:8); *Surely you are bewitched* (26:153); *The man you follow is surely bewitched* (25:8; 17:47); *When you do not recite to them a revelation they say, 'Have you not yet invented one?'* (7:203); *He is but a cunning enchanter* (38:4); *Their compatriot is no madman* (7:184).[1]

Although Mohammed's preaching was internally consistent (did not contradict itself),[2] it was not always externally consistent. Like any man who lived in a prescientific age, Mohammed expressed beliefs now known to be incompatible with the discoveries of geography and astrophysics. He also expressed belief in many of the myths of the Judaeo-Christian bible: *He created man from potter's clay and the jinn from smokeless fire* (55:14-15); *He created seven heavens one above the other, placing in them the moon for a light and the sun for a lantern* (71:15-16); *I seek refuge . . . from the mischief of conjuring witches* (113:1, 4); *Let them reflect on . . . the heaven, how it was raised on high; the mountains, how they were set down; the earth, how it was levelled flat* (88:17-20); *All this is written in earlier scriptures; the scriptures of Abraham and Moses* (87:18-19); *He (the Immerser) shall be called John; a name no man has borne before him* (19:7); *'How shall I bear a child,' (Mary) answered, 'when I am a virgin, untouched by man?'. . . . 'That is no difficult thing for Him'* (19:20-21); *'We carried in the ark with Noah. . . .'* (19:58); *We will call them to account in company with all the devils and set them on their knees around the fire of Hell* (19:68); *His master's wife sought to seduce (Joseph)* (12:23); *He raised it (the sky) high and fashioned it, giving darkness to its night and brightness to its day* (79:27-29); *Do not act like him who was swallowed by the whale* (68:48); *Allah . . . in six days created the heavens and the earth* (10:3); *We built the heaven with Our might, giving it a vast expanse, and stretched the earth beneath it* (51:47-48); *We spread out the earth and set upon it immovable mountains* (50:7); *Jesus worked his miracles* (43:63); *Noah . . . dwelt amongst them for nine hundred and fifty years* (29:14); *(Adam and Eve) both ate of its fruit, so that they beheld their nakedness and began to cover themselves with leaves* (20:121); *Remember the words of Lot, who said to his people: 'Will you persist in these indecent acts which no other nation has committed before you? You lust after men instead of women. Truly, you are a degenerate people'* (7:80-81); *He set firm mountains upon the earth lest it should move away with you* (16:15); *You have heard of those of you that broke the Sabbath.*

---

1. All quotations are from the Penguin Classics edition of *The Koran*, fourth revised edition, 1974 (revised again, 1990). I considered *Quran: The Final Scripture (Authorized English Version)*, translated by R. Khalifa, Tucson, 1981, but found it to be so innocuous, suppressing unpleasant passages by misleading interpretations, as to be valueless for my purpose.

2. There were minor exceptions, mainly either to allow Mohammed himself to violate the mating laws he had imposed on his followers, or to repudiate the concessions he had earlier made to feminist principles (see note 3).

We said to them: 'You shall be changed into detested apes' (2:65); *Whoever is the enemy of . . . Gabriel or Michael, shall make Allah Himself his enemy* (2:98); *Allah has appointed Saul to be your king. But . . . he is not rich at all* (2:247); *David, to whom We gave the Psalms* (4:163); *It is Allah who has created seven heavens, and earths as many* (65:12); *Jesus . . . healed the blind man and the leper, and by My leave restored the dead to life* (5:110); *He holds the sky from falling down* (22:65).

As the foregoing passages reveal, Mohammed (and by implication, the god who inspired him) believed that the earth is flat, immobile, held in place by mountains, and covered by seven solid domes called *skies* or *heavens* to which the sun and the self-illuminating moon are attached. He also believed that the Barbary apes were descended from human ancestors.

Mohammed was a sexist to whom women were an inferior species: *Has your Lord blessed you with sons and Himself adopted daughters from among the angels? A monstrous blasphemy is that which you utter* (17:40); *Men have a status above women* (2:228); *Call in two witnesses from among you, but if two men cannot be found, then one man and two women* (2:282); *Men have authority over women because Allah has made the one superior to the other. . . . Good women are obedient. . . . As for those from whom you fear disobedience . . . beat them* (4:34).

Not only did Mohammed's male chauvinist god deem men superior to women; he declared it a blasphemy to suggest otherwise.[3]

Mohammed preached predestination: *Allah misleads whom He will and guides whom He pleases* (74:31); *Who can guide those whom Allah has led astray? There shall be none to help them* (30:29); *We have predestined for Hell many jinn and many men* (7:179); *None can guide the people whom Allah leads astray* (7:186); *But he whom Allah guides none can lead astray* (39:37); *Allah misleads many and enlightens many* (2:26); *Would you guide those whom Allah has caused to err? He whom Allah has led astray cannot be guided* (4:88); *Allah misleads whom He will, and guides to the right path whom He pleases* (6:39).

He endorsed slavery: *Who restrain their carnal desires (save with their wives and slave-girls, for these are lawful to them) . . . shall be laden with honours* (70:29-35); *Do your slaves share with you on equal terms the riches which We have given you?* (30:28); *You shall not force your slave-girls into prostitution in order that you may make money, if they wish to preserve their chastity* (24:33); *You are also forbidden to take in marriage married women, except captives whom you own as slaves* (4:24); *A believing slave is better than an idolator, although*

---

3. To win converts from the worship of the Arabian goddesses, Allat (Venus), Al-Uza (Mercury) and Kore (the moon), also a Trinity, Mohammed initially accepted them as Allah's daughters. As indicated above (17:40), he later repudiated that acceptance. And his earlier declaration that both men and women would be admitted into the Muslim Heaven would seem incompatible with his later Gardens of Delight (see page 248).

she may please you. . . . A believing slave is better than an idolator, although he may please you (2:221).

Like the Deuteronomist, Mohammed banned murder. And also like the Deuteronomist, he limited the concept to the capricious killing of a fellow believer: *Do not kill except for a just cause* (25:68); *He that kills a believer by design shall burn in Hell for ever* (4:93).

Like the Towrah (DEUT. 20:16) and the gospels (JOHN 3:18), Mohammed's *Koran* made clear that belonging to the wrong superstition was a capital offense: *For the unbelievers We have prepared fetters and chains, and a blazing Fire* (76:4); *The unbelievers among the People of the Book and the pagans shall burn for ever in the fire of Hell* (98:6); *They (the Jews) are the heirs of Hell* (58:17); *Allah has laid His curse upon the unbelievers and prepared for them a blazing Fire* (33:64); *Those that deny Our revelations We will burn in Hell-fire* (4:56); *He that chooses a religion other than Islam, it will not be accepted from him and in the world to come he will be one of the lost* (3:85).

The foregoing citation of Mohammed's contrary-to-fact beliefs and unevolved concept of justice may be insufficient to satisfy a convinced Muslim that his mythology is no more valid than Judaism or Christianity (a scholar competent in Arabic will have to accomplish that, as large portions of the *Koran* can be traced to sources that predated Mohammed, all of them in Arabic); but it is surely sufficient to prevent a chronic god-addict, deprived of his former mind-crippling superstition and suffering withdrawal symptoms, from substituting one opiate for another. Anyone so tempted, in the belief that any god is better than no god, should keep in mind the observation of science fiction author Philip K. Dick:

I hope, for His sake, that God does not exist—because if He does He has an awful lot to answer for.

Appendix B

The Judaeo-Christian Bible Fully Translated

Where the text cites passages from *The Judaeo-Christian Bible Fully Translated* that reveal an original meaning suppressed from existing translations (but not passages that emphasise a meaning downplayed but still not hidden in other bibles), the *Fully Translated* rendering is given below.

GENESIS

(1:1) At commencement the gods (elohiym) *made the skies* (ha-shemiym) *and the land* (ha-arets).* **(P)**

(1:2) The land was shapeless Tehow (goddess of the sea), *and on* Tehowm's (alternative spelling) *face was darkness. The breath* (ruwkh) *of the gods* merakhefeth *(brooded/incubated) on the waters'* (i.e., Tehow's) *face.*

(1:14) The gods said, 'Let lights be attached to the solid dome of the skies to divide the day from the night, and let them serve for atheth *(signs, i.e., horoscopes) and seasons and days and years.*

GENESIS

(2:4b) On the day that Yahweh the gods *(Yahweh elohiym)* made *the land* and *the skies . . . .* **(J)**

(1:6) The gods said, 'Let there be a solid dome *(rakiyakh)* in the middle of the waters, and let it divide the waters from the waters *(i.e., bisect the goddess).*

(1:8) The gods called the solid dome Skies *(shemiym)*. And the nighttime and the daytime constituted the second day. [Jewish days began at sunset.]

(1:16) The gods made two powerful lights, the greater light to rule the day and the lesser light to rule the night, as well as the stars.

(1:17) The gods attached them to the dome of the skies to give light upon the land.

(14:13) But one who escaped came to Avrum the easterner (khibriy).

(14:18) Molokhiy-Tsedek ('King Storm god'), an allied king, brought bread and wine, for he was a priest of El Khelyown *(the god Ilion).*

(14:19) And he blessed him with this blessing: 'Avrum has been blessed by the god Ilion, the creator of the skies and the land.'

(35:14) So Yaakob erected a mitsbah *(phallus-image) at the place where he had talked to him, stone* mitsbath *(plural) on which he poured an offering of wine and oil (to the phallus-god).*

(26:8) Abiymolokh, king of the Philistines/ Palestines, looked out of a window and saw Yitskhakh metsakhek *(recreating sexually) with his woman Rebekah.*

(38:15) When Yahuwdah saw her, he thought she was a zownah, *because she had covered her face.*

(7:11) In the 600th year of Noakh's life, on the 17th day of the 2nd month, all the waters of the subterranean ocean gushed up, and the sluice gates of the skies were opened.

(1:27) The gods-and-goddesses (allah-iym) conjured the human (ha-adam) in their own shape. In the shape of the gods they conjured them. Prong (zokar, but probably originally zobar) and tunnel (nukivah) they conjured them.

(The first god sacramentally eaten in the form of bread and wine was the Egyptian Osiris, c. 3000 BCE.)

(24:2) Abraham instructed his senior household slave, his chief of staff, 'Put your hand under my crotch [in order to swear an oath to a phallus-god],

(24:3) while I have you invoke a curse before Yahweh, the gods of the skies and the gods of the land.'

PSALMS

(104:26) There goes Leviathan, whom you made to *sakhek* (recreate) with.

(38:21) He asked the men of the area, 'Where's the kedeshah who was soliciting on the road near Kheynayim?' But they answered, 'No kedeshah works this beat.'

[J used the words *zownah* (prostitute) and *kedeshah* (nun) to describe Tamar in this scene, to show that he made no distinction between sacred copulatory worship and commercial prostitution.]

EXODUS

(2:18) They returned to their father (Moses' father-in-law) Reuwel. **(J)**

EXODUS

(3:1) Mosheh was tending the flock of his father-in-law Yithrow. **(E)**

(4:10) Mosheh said to Yahweh, 'Your lordship, neither before nor since you spoke to your slave am I a man of languages (aish daberiym). They come uneasily from my mouth, for I have difficulty translating (khebad lashown).

(6:12) Why should Pharaoh listen to me, a man who speaks *(only)* the language of the uncircumcised *(kharal sefathiym)*? **(P)**

(4:14) Yahweh's temper flared against Mosheh, and he asked, 'What about your kinsman Aharon the Levite? I know he can translate (khiy-daber yedaber).

(6:30) But Mosheh answered, 'I speak the language of the uncircumcised *(kharal sefathiym)*. Why should Pharaoh listen to me?' **(R)**

(4:16) He's to speak to the nation as your spokesman.' **(J)**

(13:1) Yahweh ordered Mosheh,

(34:19) All that first issues from the belly belongs to me. **(J)**

(13:2) 'Kedesh ('make sacred,' i.e., sacrifice) to me all of the firstborn, the first issue of every belly. It belongs to me.' **(R)**

(34:20) You may buy back all the firstborn of your sons. **(R)**

LEVITICUS

(27:29) No human who has been solemnly vowed is to be redeemed. He's to be sacrificed *(yafadah mowth)* without fail. **(R)**

(As the *Leviticus* passage makes clear, a human vowed or consecrated to Yahweh was to be sacrificed.)

NUMBERS

(24:21) He (Balaam) also looked at the Kayinites and spouted this poem: 'Your house was strong, Kayin (Cain).

GENESIS

(4:8) Kayin said to his brother Habel. . . .

(24:22) But your nest (kan) *is now burning, / And you are captives of Assyria.'*

1 SAMUEL

(20:41) They (David and Yahuwnathan) *kissed each other and wept with each other until David* hegediyl *(reached the peak or climaxed, i.e., orgasmed).*

DEUTERONOMY

(34:6) He buried (Moses) *. . . but to this day no one has ever found his grave.*

NEHEMIAH

(9:26) They killed your spokesmen . . . .

ZECHARIAH

(4:10) They are going to see in the hands of Zerubbabel the candlestick with the seven (branches) that are Yahweh's eyes that roam back and forth over the whole land (i.e., the seven ancient 'planets').

DEUTERONOMY

(23:17) No Yisraelite woman is to become a kedeshah *(nun who copulates with male worshippers of a fertility god), and no Yisraelite man is to become a* kedesh *(monk who copulates with male worshippers of a fertility god).*

JEREMIAH

(2:30) Your own sword has devoured your spokesmen.

3 KINGS

(19:14) The descendants of Yisrael have . . . killed your spokesmen with the sword.

DANIEL

(4:11) The tree reached the skies, so that it could be seen from the edge of the world.

JOB

(22:14) He walks on the kowg *('circle,' i.e., dome) of the skies.*

MATTHEW

(1:18a) While his mother Mariam was betrothed to Ioseph,
(1:20b) a messenger of his Lordship appeared to him in a dream and said,
(1:21) 'She's going to bear you a son, and you're to name him Iesous.'
(1:24) So Ioseph took possession of his woman (i.e., tupped her),
(1:25b) until she had borne a son. **(Q)**

MATTHEW

(1:18b) but before they had yet coupled, she was found to have one in the belly by the consecrated breath.
(1:22) All that took place in order to accomplish what his Lordship promised through the prophet when he said, 'A virgin is going to become pregnant.'
(1:25a) But he did not tup her until she had borne a son). **(Interpolator)**

LUKE

(1:30) *The messenger told her, 'You're going to find yourself pregnant in the belly. You're going to bear a son, and you're to call his name Iesous.* **(Q)**

ISAIAH

(7:14) *A young woman* (khalmah) *will become pregnant and bear a son.*

LUKE

(1:34-35) But Mariam asked the messenger, 'How can that be, since no man has tupped me?' And the messenger answered her, 'A consecrated breath is going to *epeleusetai* (mount) you, and a force from the summit is going to *episkiasei* (encompass) you. The consecrated one thus born is going to be reputed to be a god's son. **(Interpolator)**

ACTS

(9:3-9) *What happened as his journey neared Damascus was that a light from the sky suddenly flashed around him. He collapsed to the ground, and he heard a voice asking him, 'Saulos, Saulos, why are you persecuting me?' . . . . The men who were travelling with him stood dumbfounded, for they had heard the sound but had seen nothing. . . . And for three days he was unable to see, and he neither ate nor drank.* **(Original author)**

ACTS

(22:6-11) What happened as I was nearing Damascus on my journey, was that about noon a powerful light suddenly shone around me out of the sky. I collapsed to the ground, and I heard a voice asking me, 'Saulos, Saulos, why are you persecuting me?' . . . Those who were with me saw the light, but they didn't hear the sound of anyone speaking to me. . . . And since I could not see because of the magnificence of that light, I went into Damascus led by the hand. **(Interpolator)**

GALATIANS

(1:15-17) *But when the one who had set me apart straight from my mother's hollow belly and summoned me through his compassion, was pleased to reveal his son to me so that I could preach him among the gentiles, I neither conferred at once with flesh and blood nor travelled to Jerusalem.* **(Paul)**

Bibliographical Note

The gods can either take away evil from the world and
will not, or being willing to do so they cannot, or they
neither can nor will, or lastly they are both willing and
able. If they have the will to remove evil and cannot, then
they are not omnipotent. If they can but will not, then
they are not benevolent. If they are neither willing nor able,
then they are neither omnipotent nor benevolent. Lastly,
if they are both able and willing to annihilate evil, how
does it exist?

Epikuros, 341-270 BCE

Most of *Mythology's Last Gods* is based on my own analysis of the Judaeo-
Christian bible. Not surprisingly, few of the conclusions reached are new
or unusual. Nonetheless, it seemed necessary that *Mythology's Last Gods* be
written, partly to throw open to scholarly discussion such findings as are
new, but mainly to bring together sufficient evidence of the fictional status
of the bible to satisfy any objective reader that gods who have revealed
their existence (I make no comment on any other kind of god) are indeed
products of the human imagination. It was my purpose to make it unnecessary
to read more than one book simply to obtain sufficient facts to prove the
point, and this I have done.

Obviously, however, it will always be necessary for a reader whose
field of expertise is something other than biblical history to verify that my
facts are indeed facts and that my methodology accords with acceptable
procedures. Accordingly I have listed in my bibliography primarily books
that satisfy this purpose; books that discuss the same issues raised in

Mythology's Last Gods, provided they do so in accordance with the methodology of history, not the methodology of god-mythology (which can be used to prove that the Judaeo-Christian bible, the *Iliad*, *Gulliver's Travels* and *Alice in Wonderland* are all nonfiction); and general collections of the main source documents in translation.

For readers insufficiently acquainted with primitive religion, a good place to start would be Frazer's *Golden Bough* and Plutarch's *Isis and Osiris*. On the composition of the Towrah, Ellis's *The Yahwist* is unsurpassed. Artur Weiser's *Introduction to the Old Testament*, although less thorough than *The Yahwist*, covers the work of the Elohist and the Priestly author in more detail than was possible here. Friedman's *Who Wrote the Bible?* is also recommended.

Torrey's *Second Isaiah*, although written at a time when it was generally believed that *Isaiah* had only two main authors, is nonetheless worth a close reading as an illustration of the method of dating so-called prophecies. Rowley's *Darius the Mede* provides detailed proofs where the present work simply summarises *Daniel*'s more obvious inconsistencies.

That every Christian dogma and legend existed centuries before the birth of Jesus can be confirmed by the works of Larson in particular, as well as Conybeare, Cupitt, Dawson, Glover, Grant, Griffiths, Legge, Ross, and the Robertsons. For the social background into which Jesus was born, the works of Flavius Josephus and Philo should be consulted. The life of the historical Jesus and his posthumous metamorphosis into a Greek god are dealt with effectively in the works of Hugh Schonfield. Schonfield's *Passover Plot* contributed little to the present reconstruction of Jesus' life, since it credits Jesus with sophistication and mental equilibrium that he appears to have in fact lacked, but it should not be ignored. Schonfield's main fault lies in his blind spot that enables him to recognise the falseness of Christianity but not the equally transparent falseness of Judaism. Other listed works on Jesus' life say more than could be squeezed into two chapters.

In compiling a bibliography that would present both sides of the central issue, I tried very hard to locate a book based on sound historical method that reached opposite conclusions. Unfortunately none exists. I have therefore not listed the English publications of 1977, *The Myth of God Incarnate* and *The Truth of God Incarnate*, which argue the relative merits of rational mythology versus intuitive mythology, since both are worthless. Equally worthless is James Robinson's *A New Quest of the Historical Jesus*, 125 pages of Faculty-of-Mythology doubletalk that has no connection whatsoever with the book's title or with historical reality. I mention it only to avoid the accusation that I have ignored the case for Christianity's authenticity. That Robinson and his ilk ignore the real issues and aim their arguments at the reader's emotions is good evidence that there *is* no case for Christianity's authenticity.

Of the myriad novels written about Jesus, the only one that paints an accurate picture of the period and portrays Jesus as he really was, and in my view will help the reader understand what really happened, is Frank Yerby's *Judas My Brother*. While Yerby's novel contains historical inaccuracies, they are minor inaccuracies. Anthony Burgess, in *The Kingdom of the Wicked*, tries to demythologise biblical fantasies, but his ignorance of the valid source documents and his undiscriminating acceptance of biblical fiction renders his novel worthless. Robert Graves's *King Jesus* presents a theory that no biblical historian takes seriously. My forthcoming *Uncle Yeshu, Messiah* gets the facts right, but I do not claim to be a fiction writer of Yerby's calibre. All other Jesus novels are worthless, but particularly worthless is Taylor Caldwell's fairy tale, *I Judas*.

Biblical quotations are my own translations. Where possible, they are from the finished volumes of my *The Judaeo-Christian Bible Fully Translated*. In translating passages attributed to Jesus (or another Jew) I have, where necessary, first converted a significant word into the Hebrew that he would have used in quoting Jewish scriptures, and then given the precise meaning of the Hebrew, rather than translating directly from Greek to English. Thus *huios anthropou* became 'Ben Adam,' not 'son of man'; *didaskale agathe* became 'righteous rabbi,' not 'good master'; *grammateis* became 'lawteachers,' not 'scribes'; and *basileian tou Theou* became 'Allah's theocracy,' not 'God's kingdom.'

Translated bibles reflect the beliefs of the translators as much as those of the Hebrew or Greek authors. Within that limitation, *The Jerusalem Bible* can be recommended for its refusal to change *Yahweh* to 'the LORD,' and the *New American Bible* for some scholarly footnotes. Hugh Schonfield's *The Authentic New Testament* has the obvious advantage of being translated by a man not emotionally committed to doctrinally acceptable interpretations of ambiguous passages. *The New International Version* is generally sound in conveying the intended meaning of the original in comprehensible English, and *The Good News Bible* also does this satisfactorily. Both, however, contain subjective mistranslations. No bible currently available identifies more than the most doctrinally-harmless interpolations, even when a significant passage's spuriousness is attested by unimpeachable early Christian sources. The 1611 *Authorized Version*, with its *thou* and *shalt* and *begat* and other words that were standard English in 1611 but do not exist in twentieth-century English, was a vernacular translation when it was made, but is now a foreign-language translation. Its retention is favoured only by mythologians who realise that a truly accurate translation of the Judaeo-Christian bible could destroy god-mythology unassisted.

Transcriptions of Greek and Hebrew words are based on *The R.S.V. Interlinear Greek-English New Testament*, and *The Holy Scriptures of the Old*

Testament, Hebrew and English.

Several books that came to my attention only after *Mythology's Last Gods* had been completed have been added to the bibliography for the purpose of making the reader aware of their existence. Both Friedman and Larue offer breakdowns of the Pentateuch authorship that differ slightly from my own. Ongoing debate on such minor details should not cloud the reader's mind to the unanimity among competent scholars on all of the major conclusions.

Bibliography

Printed Primary Sources

Ante-Nicene Library, The, 22 vol., Edinburgh, 1867 etc.

Breasted, J.H. (ed.), *Ancient Records of Egypt*, 5 vol., NY, 1906.

Brown, L. (ed.), *The Wisdom of Israel*, London, 1955.

Budge, E. A. (ed.), *The Book of the Dead*, NY, 1953.

Cartlidge, D.R. and D.L. Dungan (eds.), *Documents for the Study of the Gospels*, Cleveland, 1980.

Champdor, A. (ed.), *The Book of the Dead*, tr. F. Bowers, NY, 1966.

Charles, R.H. (ed.), *The Apocrypha and Pseudepigrapha of the Old Testament in English*, 2 vol., Oxford, 1913. *The Assumption of Moses*, London, 1897. *The Book of Henoch*, Oxford, 1912. *The Book of Jubilees*, London, 1902.

Doria, C. and H. Lenowitz (eds.), *Origins: Creation Texts from the Ancient Mediterranean*, NY, 1976.

Dupont-Sommer, A., *The Essene Writings from Qumran*, Gloucester, MA, 1973.

Epstein, I. (ed.), *The Babylonian Talmud*, 18 vol., London, 1948 etc.

Erman, A. (ed.), *The Ancient Egyptians: A Sourcebook of Their Writings*, NY, 1965.

Eusebius, *The Ecclesiastical History*, 2 vol., tr. H. Lawler, Loeb Classical Library, Cambridge, MA.

Gaster, T. (ed.), *The Dead Sea Scriptures*, NY, 1976.

Gordon, C. (ed.), *Ugaritic Literature: A Comprehensive Translation of the Poetic and Prose Texts*, Rome, 1949.

Gray, J. (ed.), *The Legacy of Canaan: The Ras Shamra Texts and Their Relevance to the Old Testament*, Leiden, 1965.

Grayson, A., and D. Redford (eds.), *Papyrus and Tablet*, Englewood Cliffs, NJ, 1973.

Hennecke, E., and W. Schneemelcher (eds.), *The New Testament Apocrypha*, 2 vol., Philadelphia, 1963-5.

Holy Scriptures of the Old Testament, Hebrew and English, London, 1977.

Homer, *The Iliad*, Loeb Classical Library, Cambridge, MA. *The Odyssey*, Loeb Classical Library, Cambridge, MA.

James, M.R. (ed.), *The Apocryphal New Testament*, London, 1953.

Josephus, *The Works of Josephus*, 9 vol., Loeb Classical Library, Cambridge, MA.

Julian, *The Works of the Emperor Julian*, 3 vol., Loeb Classical Library, Cambridge, MA.

Mendelsohn, I. (ed.), *Religions of the Ancient Near East: Sumero-Akkadian Religious Texts and Ugaritic Epics*, NY, 1955.

Milik, T.T. (ed.), *The Books of Enoch*, Oxford, 1976.

Mondadori, A. (ed.), *Eros in Antiquity*, Milano and NY, 1978.

Montgomery, J.A., *Aramaic Incantation Texts from Nippur*, Philadelphia, 1913.

Miller, F. (ed.), *The Sacred Books of the East*, vols. 4, 23, 31, *The Zend Avesta*, tr. J. Darmesteter, Oxford, 1880.

Philo, *The Embassy to Gaius*, in *Works*, vol. 10, Loeb Classical Library, Cambridge, MA. *Every Good Man is Free*, in *Works*, vol. 9, Loeb Classical Library, Cambridge, MA. *Hypothetica*, in *Works*, vol. 9, Loeb Classical Library, Cambridge, MA.

Platt, R.H. (ed.), *The Forgotten Books of Eden*, NY, 1980. *The Lost Books of the Bible*, NY, 1979.

Pliny, *Natural History*, vol. 2, Loeb Classical Library, Cambridge, MA.

Plutarch, *Isis and Osiris*, Loeb Classical Library, Cambridge, MA.

Pritchard, J.B. (ed.), *Ancient Near Eastern Texts Relating to the Old Testament*, Princeton, 1955.

Quasten, J. and J. Plumpe (eds.), *Ancient Christian Writers*, 40 vol., NY, 1946, etc.

R.S.V. *Interlinear Greek-English New Testament*, Grand Rapids, 1970.

Rahlfs, A. (ed.), *Septuaginta*, Stuttgart, 1935.

Roberts, A. and J. Donaldson (eds), *The Ante-Nicene Fathers*, 10 vol., Buffalo, 1885 etc.

Robinson, J.M. (ed.), *The Nag Hammadi Library in English*, Leiden, 1977.

Sanders, N.K (ed.), *The Epic of Gilgamesh*, London, 1960.

Schaff, P. (ed.), *Nicene and Post-Nicene Fathers*, 20 vol., Buffalo, 1886 etc.

Schonfield, H., *The Authentic New Testament*, London, 1958. *The Song of Songs*, NY, 1959. *Toldot Yeshu*, London, 1937.

Schopp, L. (ed.), *The Fathers of the Church*, 67 vol., Washington, 1962 etc.

Simpson, W.K. et al. (eds.), *The Literature of Ancient Egypt: An Anthology of Stories, Instructions, and Poetry*, New Haven, 1972.

Vermes, G. (ed.), *The Dead Sea Scrolls in English*, London, 1962.

Secondary Works

Akerley, B.E., *The X-Rated Bible*, Austin, 1985.

Ablrektson, B., *History of the Gods*, Lund, 1967.

Albright, W.F., *Yahweh and the Gods of Canaan*, London, 1968.

Allegro, J.M., *The Dead Sea Scrolls and the Christian Myth*, Buffalo, 1984. *The Dead Sea Scrolls and the Origins of Christianity*, NY, 1957. *Lost Gods*, London, 1977.

Allen, G., *Evolution of the Idea of God*, NY, 1897.

Arnheim, M., *Is Christianity True?*, Buffalo, 1984.

Augstein., R., *Jesus: Son of Man*, tr. H. Young, NY, 1972.

Bachofen, J.J., *Myth, Religion and Mother Right*, tr. R. Manheim, Princeton, 1967.

Baigent, M., et al., *The Messianic Legacy*, London, 1986.

Ball, W.P. and G.W. Foote, *The Bible Handbook*, Austin, 1986.

Barthel, M., *What the Bible Really Says*, tr. M. Howson, NY, 1982.

Beek, M.A., *Concise History of Israel*, NY, 1957.

Bloom, H., *The Book of J*, tr. D. Rosenberg, NY, 1990.

Bohannan, P. end d. Middleton (eds.), *Marriage, Family and Residence*, NY, 1968.

Bowker, J., *Jesus and the Pharisees*, NY, 1973.

Brandon, S.G., *Certain Legends of the Ancient Near East*, London, 1963. *The Fall of Jerusalem and the Christian Church*, London, 1974. *Jesus and the Zealots*, London, 1967. *Religion in Ancient History*, NY, 1969. *The Trial of Jesus of Nazareth*, London, 1971.

Brown, R.E., *The Birth of the Messiah*, NY, 1977.

Budge, E.A., *Osiris and the Egyptian Resurrection*, NY, 1961.

Burke, J.A., *The X-Rated Book: Sex and Obscenity in the Bible*, Houston, 1985.

Burrows, H., *More Light on the Dead Sea Scrolls*, London, 1958.

Carus, P., *The History of the Devil and the Idea of Evil*, NY, 1968.

Chadwick, H. and J.E. Oulton, *Alexandrian Christianity*, London, 1954.

Cohen, E.D., *The Mind of the Bible-Believer*, Buffalo, 1985.

Cohn, H., *The Trial and Death of Jesus*, NY, 1971.

Conybeare, F.C., *The Origins of Christianity*, NY, 1958.

Coote, R. and D. Ord, *The Bible's First History*, Minneapolis, 1988.

Cross, F.M., *Canaanite Myth and Hebrew Epic: Essays in the History of the Religion of Israel*, Cambridge, MA, 1973.

Cupitt, D., *The Christ Debate*, London, 1979. *The Sea of Faith*, London, 1984. *Who Was Jesus?*, London, 1977.

Davies, A.P., *The First Christian*, NY, 1957. *The Meaning of the Dead Sea Scrolls*, NY, 1956.

Dawson, M.M., *The Ethical Religion of Zoroaster*, NY, 1956.

De Wulf, L.M., *Faces of Venus: Prostitution Through the Ages*, NY, 1980.

Dimont, M., *Jesus, God and History*, NY, 1962.

Doane, T.W., *Bible Myths and Their Parallels in Other Religions*, NY, 1971.

Dodd, C.H., *Historical Tradition in the Fourth Gospel*, Cambridge, 1963.

Drohan, F.B., *Jesus Who? The Greatest Story Never Told*, NY, 1985.

Dumezil, G., *Archaic Roman Religions*, 2 vol., Chicago, 1970.

Eisenman, R.H., *Maccabees, Zadokites, Christians and Qumran*, Leiden, 1986.

Eisler, R., *The Messiah Jesus and John the Baptist*, NY, 1931.

Eissfeldt, O., *The Old Testament: An Introduction, Including the Apocrypha and Pseudepigrapha, and also the Works of Similar Type from Qumran*, tr. P.R. Ackroyd, NY, 1965.

Elliott, J.K., *Questioning Christian Origins*, London, 1982.

Ellis, P., *The Yahwist, the Bible's First Theologian*, Notre Dame, IN, 1968.

Engels, F., *The Origin of the Family, Private Property and the State*, ed. & tr. E. Leacock, NY, 1972.

Falk, H., *Jesus the Pharisee, A New Look at the Jewishness of Jesus*, Ramsey, NJ, 1985.

Ferguson, J., *The Religions of the Roman Empire*, London, 1970.

Fox, G.M., *The Vanishing Gods*, NY, 1984.

Frankfort, H., *The Problem of Similarity in Ancient Near Eastern Religions*, Oxford, 1951.

Frazer, J.G., *The Golden Bough*, NY, 1959.

Freeman, J., *Manners and Customs of the Bible*, NY, 1959.

Friedman, R.E., *Who Wrote the Bible?*, NY, 1987.

Freud, S., *Moses and Monotheism*, tr. K. Jones, NY, 1955.

Fuller, C.J., *Servants of the Goddess*, Cambridge, 1984.

Furneaux, R., *The Roman Siege of Jerusalem*, London, 1973.

Gaster, T.H., *Myth, Legend and Custom in the Old Testament*, NY, 1969.

Gibbon, E., *History of Christianity*, NY, 1883.

Gimbutas, M., *The Goddesses and Gods of Old Europe*, Berkeley, 1982.

Glover, T.R., *The Conflict of Religions in the Early Roman Empire*, London, 1909.

Godfrey, L. (ed.), *Scientists Confront Creationism*, NY, 1983.

Goldin, H., *The Case of the Nazarene Reopened*, NY, 1948.

Goldsmith, D. (ed.), *Scientists Confront Velikovsky*, NY, 1977.

Goldstein M., *Jesus and the Jewish Tradition*, NY, 1950.

Goodenough, E.R., *Jewish Symbols in the Greco-Roman Period*, 12 vol., NY, 1953.

Goodsell, W., *A History of Marriage and the Family*, NY, 1974.

Gordon, C., *The Common Background of Greek and Hebrew Civilization*, NY, 1965.

Graham, L.M., *Deceptions and Myths of the Bible*, NY, 1979.

Grant, F.C., *The Earliest Gospel*, NY, 1943. *Roman Hellenism and the New Testament*, NY, 1962.

Grant, M., *Jesus, An Historian's Review of the Gospels*, NY, 1977.

Graves, R., *The Greek Myths*, London, 1955. *The White Goddess*, London, 1952.

Graves, R. and R. Patai, *Hebrew Myths*, NY, 1964.

Graves, R. and J. Podro, *The Nazarene Gospel Restored*, London, 1953.

Greeley, A.M., *The Mary Myth: On the Femininity of God*, NY, 1977.

Griffiths, J.G., *The Conflict of Horus and Seth, from Egyptian and Classical Sources: A Study of Ancient Mythology*, Liverpool, 1960.

Grosser, P.E. and E.G. Halperin, *The Causes and Effects of Anti-Semitism*, NY, 1978.

Guthrie, W.K., *Orpheus and Greek Religion*, London, 1935.

Halsberghe, G.H., *The Cult of Sol Invictus*, Leiden, 1972.

Harris, R., *The Twelve Apostles*, NY, 1984.

Hartland, E.S., *Primitive Paternity*, London, 1910. *Ritual and Beliefs*, London, 1914.

Hefele, J., *A History of the Christian Councils, vols 1 and 2*, NY, 1972.

Heidel, A., *The Babylonian Genesis: The Story of the Creation*, Chicago, 1951. *The Gilgamesh Epic and the Old Testament Parallels*, Chicago, 1949.

Helfer, J.S., *On Method in the History of Religions*, Middletown, CT, 1968.

Helms, R., *Gospel Fictions*, Buffalo, 1989.

Hersh, H., *The Sacred Books of the Jews*, NY, 1968.

Hinnells, J.R., *Persian Mythology*, London, 1973.

Hoffmann, R.J., (ed.), *The Origins of Christianity*, Buffalo, 1985. *Jesus Outside the Gospels*, Buffalo, 1984.

Hoffmann, R.J. and G.A. Larue, (eds.), *Jesus in Myth and History*, Buffalo, 1985.

Hooke, S.H., *Babylonian and Assyrian Religion*, NY, 1953. *Middle Eastern Mythology*, London, 1963.

Howlett, D., *The Critical Way in Religion*, Buffalo, 1984. *The Essenes and Christianity*, NY, 1957.

Hurvitz, A., *A Linguistic Study of the Relationship Between the Priestly Source and the Book of Ezekiel*, Paris, 1982.

Ingersoll, R.G., *Some Mistakes of Moses*, Buffalo, 1986.

Jackson, J.G., *Christianity Before Christ*, Austin, 1985.

Jacobsen, T., *The Sumerian King List*, Chicago, 1939.

James, E.O., *Christian Myth and Ritual*, London, 1933. *The Concept of Deity*, London, 1950. *The Cult of the Mother Goddess*, London, 1959.

Jastrow, M., *Aspects of Religious Belief and Practice in Babylonia and Assyria*, NY, 1971.

Jenks, A.W., *The Elohist and North Israelite Traditions*, Decatur, GA, 1977.

Johnson, A.R., *The One and the Many in the Israelite Conception of God*, Cardiff, 1942.

Johnson, M.D., *The Purpose of the Biblical Genealogies*, 1969.

Kavanaugh, J., *The Birth of God*, NY, 1969.

Kee, A., *Constantine Versus Christ*, London, 1982.

Kelly, H.A., *The Devil, Demonology and Witchcraft: The Development of Christian Beliefs in Evil Spirits*, NY, 1974.

Kenyon, K.M., *The Bible and Recent Archaeology*, London, 1978.

Kerenyi, C., *The Gods of the Greeks*, tr. N. Cameron, London, 1951.

Khal, J., *The Misery of Christianity*, London, 1971.

King, L.W., *Babylonian Religion and Mythology*, London, 1899.

Knight, M., *Christianity: The Debit Account*, London, 1975.

Knox, W.L., *Sources of the Synoptic Gospels*, 2 vol., Cambridge, 1953, 1957.

Küng, H., *Eternal Life?*, tr. E. Quinn, Garden City, NY, 1984.

Kurtz, P., *The Transcendental Temptation*, Buffalo, 1986.

Larson, M.A., *The Essene-Christian Faith*, NY, 1980. *The Story of Christian Origins*, Talequah, OK, 1977. *The Religion of the Occident*, London, 1959.

Larue, G.A., *Ancient Myth and Modern Man*, Englewood Cliffs, NJ, 1975. *Ancient Myth and Modern Life*, Long Beach, CA, 1988. *Old Testament Life and Literature*, Boston, 1968. *Sex and the Bible*, Buffalo, 1983. *The Supernatural, the Occult and the Bible*, Buffalo, 1990.

Legge, F., *Forerunners and Rivals of Christianity*, NY, 1950.

Lewis, J., *The Ten Commandments*, NY, 1946.

Loisy, A.F., *The Birth of the Christian Religion* and *The Origins of the New Testament*, in 1 vol., tr. L.P. Jacks, NY, 1962.

Lurker, M., *Dictionary of Gods and Goddesses, Devils and Demons*, NY, 1987.

McCabe, J., *The Bankruptcy of Religion*, London, 1917. *The Growth of Religion*, London, 1918. *A Rationalist Encyclopaedia*, London, 1948. *The Religion of Woman*, London, 1905. *The Social Record of Christianity*, London, 1935. *The Twilight of the Gods*, London, 1923.

Macchioro, V., *From Orpheus to Paul: A History of Orphism*, NY, 1930.

Maccoby, H., *Revolution in Judaea*, London, 1980.

Maisch, H., *Incest*, tr. C. Bearne, NY, 1972.

Martin, M., *The Case Against Christianity*, Philadelphia, 1991.

Matthiae, P., *Ebla: An Empire Rediscovered*, NY, 1981.

Mattill, A.J., *Jesus and the Last Things: The Story of Jesus the Suffering Servant*, Gordo, AL, 1989.

Mead, G.R., *Did Jesus Live 100 B.C.?*, NY, 1968.

Momigliano, A. (ed.), *The Conflict Between Paganism and Christianity in the Fourth Century*, London, 1970.

Morenz, S., *Egyptian Religion*, Ithaca, NY, 1973.

Morgenstern, J., *The Ark, the Ephod, and the "Tent of Meeting,"* Cincinnati, 1945.

Motylewski, L.F., *The Essene Plan*, NY, 1976.

Moule, C.F., *The Birth of the New Testament*, London, 1962.

Mylonas, G.E., *Eleusis and the Eleusinian Mysteries*, Princeton, 1961.

Neumann, E., *The Great Mother*, NY, 1955.

Neusner, J., *Judaism in the Beginning of Christianity*, London, 1984.

Nickell, J., *Inquest on the Shroud of Turin*, Buffalo, 1987.

Nickelsburg, G., *Resurrection, Immortality and Eternal Life in Inter-Testamental Judaism*, Cambridge, MA, 1972.

Ochs, C., *Behind the Sex of God*, Boston, 1977.

Oesterley, W.,.*Persian Angelology and Demonology*, London, 1936.

Ohlsen, W., (ed.), *Perspectives on Old Testament Literature*, NY, 1978.

Otto, W. F., *Dionysos: Myth and Cult*, Bloomington, IN, 1965.

Pagels, E., *The Gnostic Gospels*, London, 1980.

Paine, T., *The Age of Reason*, Buffalo, 1985.

Patai, R., *The Hebrew Goddess*, NY, 1978.

Persuitte, D., *Joseph Smith and the Origins of the Book of Mormon*, Jefferson, NC, 1985.

Pettinato, G., *The Archives of Ebla*, NY, 1981.

Phipps, W.E., *The Sexuality of Jesus*, NY, 1973. *Was Jesus Married?*, NY, 1970.

Potter, C.F., *The Lost Years of Jesus Revealed*, NY, 1962.

Ranke-Heinemann, U., *Eunuchs for the Kingdom of Heaven*, NY, 1990.

Reed, W.L., *The Asherah in the Old Testament*, Fort Worth, 1949.

Reuther, R.R. (ed.), *Religion and Sexism*, NY, 1974.

Rhoads, D.M., *Israel in Revolution 6-74 C.E.*, Philadelphia, 1976.

Ringgren, H., *Religions of the Ancient Near East*, Philadelphia, 1973.

Roberts, J.J., *The Earliest Semitic Pantheon*, London, 1972.

Robertson, A.H., *Jesus: Myth or History?*, London, 1946. *The Origins of Christianity*, London, 1953.

Robertson, J.M., *Christianity and Mythology*, London, 1936. *Pagan Christs*, London, 1911.

Ross, P., *Jesus the Pagan*, NY, 1978.

Rowley, H.H., *Darius the Mede and the Four World Empires in the Book of Daniel*, Cardiff, 1935.

Russell, D.S., *The Method and Message of Jewish Apocalyptic 200 B.C.-A.D. 100*, Philadelphia, 1964.

Russell, J.B., *The Devil: Perceptions of Evil from Antiquity to Primitive Christianity*, Ithaca, NY, 1977.

Sanders, E.P., *Jesus and Judaism*, London, 1985.

Sannella, L., *The Female Pentecost*, Port Washington, NY, 1976.

Schonfield, H., *The Bible Was Right*, London, 1959. *For Christ's Sake*, London, 1975. *The Essene Odyssey*, Longmead, 1984. *The Lost Book of the Nativity of John*, Edinburgh, 1929. *The Passover Plot*, NY, 1966. *The Pentecost Revolution*, London, 1974. *Secrets of the Dead Sea Scrolls*, NY, 1957. *Those Incredible Christians*, NY, 1968.

Schurer, E., *A History of the Jewish People in the Time of Jesus Christ*, tr. J. MacPherson, vol. 2, Edinburgh, 1890.

Schweitzer, A., *The Mystery of the Kingdom of God*, Buffalo, 1986. *The Quest of the Historical Jesus*, London, 1910.

Scott, G.R., *Phallic Worship*, London, 1941.

Seznec, J., *The Survival of the Pagan Gods*, Princeton, 1953.

Simons, G.L., *Sex and Superstition*, London, 1973.

Smallwood, E.M., *The Jews Under Roman Rule*, Leiden, 1976.

Smith, G.H., *Atheism: The Case Against God*, Buffalo, 1980.

Smith, H.W., *Man and His Gods*, Boston, 1953.

Smith, M., *Jesus the Magician*, London, 1978. *The Secret Gospel*, NY, 1973.

Smith, M. and R.J. Hoffmann (eds.), *What the Bible Really Says*, Buffalo, 1989.

Stiebing, W.H., *Out of the Desert?*, Buffalo, 1989.

Stein, G. (ed.), *The Encyclopedia of Unbelief*, 2 vol., Buffalo, 1985.

Stone, M., *When God Was a Woman*, NY, 1976.

Story, R., *The Space-Gods Revealed: A Close Look at the Theories of Erich von Däniken*, NY, 1976.

Tannahill, R., *Sex in History*, NY, 1980.

Taves, E.H., *Trouble Enough: Joseph Smith and the Book of Mormon*, Buffalo, 1985.

Tennant, F.R., *The Sources of the Doctrines of the Fall and Original Sin*, NY, 1968.

Theile, E.R., *The Mysterious Numbers of the Hebrew Kings*, Chicago, 1951.

Thiering, B. and E. Castle (eds.), *Some Trust in Chariots*, NY, 1972.

Thompson, J., *The Bible and Archaeology*, Grand Rapids, MI, 1972.

Thorsten, G., *God Herself: The Feminine Roots of Astrology*, NY, 1981.

Torrey, C.C., *The Second Isaiah*, NY, 1928.

Vermaseren, H.J., *Mithras, The Secret God*, London, 1963.

Vermes, G., *The Dead Sea Scrolls: Qumran in Perspective*, Philadelphia, 1981. *Jesus and the World of Judaism*, London, 1983. *Jesus the Jew*, London, 1977.

Weiser, A., *Introduction to the Old Testament*, tr. D. Barton, London, 1961.

Wells, G.A., *The Historical Evidence for Jesus*, Buffalo, 1982. *The Jesus of the Early Christians*, London, 1971.

Westermarck, E., *A Short History of Marriage*, NY, 1972.

Widengren, G., *The Great Vohu Manah and the Apostle of God: Studies in Iranian and Manichaean Religions*, Uppsala, 1945.

Wilken, R.L., *The Christians as the Romans Saw Them*, New Haven, 1984.

Wilson, I., *Jesus: The Evidence*, London, 1984.

Winter, P., *On the Trial of Jesus*, Berlin, 1971.

Wynne-Tyson, E., *Mithras: The Fellow in the Cap*, London, 1958.

Yerby, F., *Judas My Brother* (a novel), NY, 1968, notes pp. 505-542.

Yoder, J.H., *The Politics of Jesus*, Grand Rapids, MI, 1972.

Zaehner, R.C., *Concordant Discord: The Interdependence of Faiths*, Oxford, 1970.

Index

A new scientific truth does not triumph by convincing its opponents and making them see the light, but rather because its opponents eventually die, and a new generation grows up that is familiar with it.

Max Planck

Aias (Ajax), 360.
Aigeos, 136.
Aiolians, 63-64, 83-84, 100.
Aiolos, 84.
Akhab, 197-199.
Akhaians, 63-64, 83-84, 100, 181.
Akhaz, king of Judah, 200, 323.
Akhazyahuw, king of Israel, 198.
Akhazyahuw, king of Judah, 334.
Akhet-Aton, *see* Amarna.
Akhilleus (Achilles), 73, 81, 120, 142, 243.
Akhiymaats, 221.
Akhiymolokh, 221.
Akhiytuwb, 221.
Akhsuwruws (Xerxes), 230.
Akkad *see* Babylon.
Akrisios, 128.
Aktaion, 235.
Albinus, 306, 311.
alcohol as god's blood, *see* bread.
Alexander VI, Pope, 87, 317.
Alexander the Great, 81, 165, 206-207, 209, 230, 240-241, 302.
Alexander Yanay, 232, 246.
Alice in Wonderland, 16, 382.
Alkmene, 60, 184, 192.
Allah (god) *see* Elohiym.
Allah (goddess), 280-281.
Allah's Erection, 97, 150.
Allat and Al-Uzza (Venus and Mercury), 373.
Allegro, John M., 49.
almond as sacramental vulva, 48.
amanita muscaria, 49.
Amarna (Tell Amarna), 102.
Amaryah, 221.
Amazons, 41.
Amatsyahuw, king of Judah, 196-197, 236, 334.
Ambrose, 'saint,' 358, 363.
ambrosia, 73, 77.
Amen (Amun), 37, 81, 98, 101.
Amenhotep III, 89, 101.
Amenhotep IV, *see* Ikhenaton.
Amestris, 230.
Amin, Idi, 177.
Amish, 249.

Ammonites (Khamownites), 85, 109, 195-196, 241.
Ammonius, 'saint,' 359.
Amnown, 82.
Amos, book of, author of, 208, 211.
Amphitryon, 60, 84.
Anabaptists, 249.
Anacletus, mythical Pope, 327.
Analects, 286.
Anaxibeia, 84.
ancestor worship, 95, 139, 162, 242.
Andreas, brother of Peter, 268-269, 354.
Andrew of Crete, 263.
angels (*angeloi*, 'messengers'), 20, 130, 133, 138, 142, 169, 193-194, 199, 230-231, 239-240, 247, 265, 302, 316, 321, 340, 373.
Animal Farm, 362.
animal sacrifice, 40, 42, 78, 159, 161, 234, 343, 377.
animal worship, 33, 76, 142, 160, 179-180, 205, 233.
Ankhesenpaaton, 89.
annunciation of birth of Hero, 321, 332, 352.
Anointers (*Khristianoi*), 296, 317.
Anointianity (*Khristianismos*), 296-297.
anointing, 228, 245, 266-267, 273, 296, 300, 348.
Antigone, 149.
Antigonos, 210.
Antiokhos I, 209. 241.
Antiokhos IV Epiphanes, 190, 205-206, 209, 314.
Antiokhos VII, 209.
Antipas, *see* Herod.
Antipatros, 210.
anti-Semitism, 274, 278, 287, 310, 353.
Antonius, Marcus, 82, 211.
Anu, 135.
Anuket, *see* Nuah.
Apam Napat, 142.
Aphrodite, 32-33, 35, 39, 62, 66, 74, 120, 253, 265, 302.
Apis, 160.
Apocalypse (Revelation), 15, 303, 315-318, 345-346, 353, 364-365.

I